Come back to Portofino

THROUGH ITALY WITH THE 6TH SOUTH AFRICAN ARMOURED DIVISION

JAMES BOURHILL

30° South Publishers

Published in 2011 by 30° South Publishers (Pty) Ltd.
3 Ajax Place, 120 Caroline Street, Brixton
Johannesburg 2092, South Africa
www.30degreessouth.co.za
info@30degreessouth.co.za

Design and layout by 30° South Publishers (Pty) Ltd.

Maps by Genevieve Edwards

Printed and bound by Pinetown Printers, Durban

ISBN 978-1-920143-56-5

For my children
Stuart, Victoria and Rebecca
and for future generations

CONTENTS

Author's note

It has been said that history is not the 'the past', neither is it the surviving past. It is a reconstruction of certain parts of the past from surviving evidence, which in some way have relevance for the present circumstances of the historian who reconstructed them.[1] Further justification for telling the stories of a few selected individuals who took part in this great endeavour is provided by John Tosh: "The stories they [historians] tell and the human subjects they write about, are merely subjective preference, drawn from an infinity of possible strategies."[2]

If my father were alive, he would be amused and a little uncomfortable at featuring in a history of the Second World War. Like many veterans, he underplayed his personal war effort. However, the one achievement of which he was extremely proud was having written down the name of every town, village and hamlet in which he stopped during the Italian campaign of the 6th South African Armoured Division, together with the relevant dates. He made 82 stops in total, through Egypt and Italy, for periods ranging from one night to four months. Nowhere in the literature or the archives have I come across a more useful, complete and accessible record of the movements of a single formation or unit during the campaign. If history is simply an empty space waiting to be filled in by the historian, then each position occupied by A Troop of the 1/6th Field Regiment and the days spent there constitute the empty spaces which I have been able to partially fill. Using my father's notes as a framework, other details fell into place.

I have also made use of the 350 or so letters which John Hodgson wrote to his family over a three-year period, drawing on them more than any other source document. Although it was not originally my intention to rely on any single source to such an extent, it would have been a travesty not to bring them to light. What is most remarkable is that they have been kept untouched for 65 years. These chronicles of everyday life on campaign make an important contribution to the historical record. It is pure providence that brought me into contact with John Hodgson and it seems that providence has played a role in every aspect of researching, writing and publishing this book.

---

2 J. Tosh, *The pursuit of history*, pp. 202–204.

Mention must be made of the helpfulness of the staff at the military archives and also of the many people who have given me access to their personal archives, diaries, memoirs, letters, artifacts and books.

Most of all, I am grateful to 30° South Publishers for putting their faith in me—so emphatically. Our team included Genevieve Edwards who created the unique maps and Lisa Witepski who dealt patiently with my constant changes while she was editing.

On some of my travels in search of the 6th South African Armoured Division, I was privileged to have the company of family and friends—they know who they are—which made for some memorable times on the road and in Chianti. I owe special thanks to Fran Harrison for typing up the Hodgson letters, and to Mauro Fogacci whose local knowledge proved invaluable.

Naturally, my mother Iris was a source of much information. She personifies 'the greatest generation'. Her own father served with the Black Watch and was killed during the break-out from Tobruk on 21 November 1944.

Lastly, my wife Jackie deserves a mention in dispatches for her devotion to duty and for taking this sentimental journey with me.

The Germans were in the habit of demolishing buildings to block the narrow roads. The rubble was then mined and booby-trapped. The speed of the advance was routinely determined by the rate at which the engineers could sweep for mines—at times crawling on their bellies. *Photo: Comune di Castiglione dei Pepoli*

Regiments and formations: abbreviations

Designations and abbreviations were determined by the military staff at the time. Regiments and formations occasionally received new designations.

6 SA Armd Div	6th South African Armoured Division
Arty	**Artillery**
1/6 Fd Rgt	1/6th Field Regiment, CFA, SAA
4/22 Fd Rgt	4/22nd Field Regiment, SAA
7/23 Med Rgt	7/23rd Medium Regiment, SAA
1/12 Lt AA Rgt	1/12th Light Anti-Aircraft Regiment, SAAF
1/11 A/T Rgt	1/11th Anti-Tank Regiment, SAA
Armoured Reconnaissance	
NMR/SAAF	Natal Mounted Rifles/South African Air Force Regiment
Support Group	
RDLI	Royal Durban Light Infantry
11 SA Amd Bde	**11 South African Armoured Brigade**
PR (PAO)	Pretoria Regiment (Princess Alice's Own)
PAG	Prince Alfred's Guard
SSB	Special Service Battalion
ILH/KimR	Imperial Light Horse/Kimberley Regiment
FFR or FF Rif	4/13th Frontier Force Rifles
12 SA Mtd Bde	**12 South African Motorized Brigade**
FC/CTH	First City/Cape Town Highlanders
RNC	Royal Natal Carbineers
WR/DLR	Witwatersrand Rifles/Regiment De la Rey

13 SA Mtd Bde	**13 South African Motorized Brigade**
ILH/KimR	Imperial Light Horse/Kimberley Regiment
NMR/SAAF	Natal Mounted Rifles/South African Air Force Regiment
RDLI	Royal Durban Light Infantry
15 Fd Rgt	15th Field Regiment, SAA
BPS	Regiment Botha/Regiment President Steyn

Reserves

DSR	Duke of Edinburgh's Own Rifles
TSR	Transvaal Scottish
RLI	Rand Light Infantry

Officers watching an artillery concentration. Concentrations could be made by a division or a regiment. A 'Mike' target is a regimental target and an 'Uncle' target is a divisional target. A 'stonk', originally called 'the hate' is a routine fire-control procedure—not pre-planned. It is believed that the origin of the word 'stonk' is from 'standard concentration' where fire from two or more batteries is brought down on a square about 1,200 x 600 yards' square. A 'murder' is a concentration brought down onto a predetermined spot with no ranging shots necessary. Both terms were coined in the Second World War. *Photo: DODAR*

Glossary of terms and abbreviations

Compiled with the kind assistance of Colonel William Marshall, SANDF

AES	Army Education Service
AP	armour piercing or anti-personnel
APM	assistant provost marshal
APO	army post office
A. Tk or AT	anti-tank
A. Tps	army troops
AA	anti-aircraft
ACF	Active Citizen Force
ADMS	Assistant Director Medical Services
ADQT	Assistant Director Quartermaster Technical
ADS	advanced dressing station
Adm	administrating or administrative
Adv	advance or advanced
AFHQ	Allied Force Headquarters
AFV	armoured fighting vehicle
Amb	ambulance
Armd or Amd	armoured
AMG	Allied Military Government
AMGOT	Allied Military Government of Occupied Territories
Att	attached
AWL or AWOL	absent without leave
Bde	brigade
Bdr	bombardier
Bn	battalion
Brig	brigadier
Brig-Gen	brigadier-general
Bty	battery
Ca	*casa* (house: Italian)
CB	counter-battery
CC	Cape Corps

CCP	casualty clearing post
CCS	casualty clearing station
CIC	Counter Intelligence Corps (American)
C-in-C	Commander-in-Chief
CMF	Central Mediterranean Forces
CO	commanding officer
Coy	company
CSM	company sergeant-major
Col	colonel
Colm	column
Comd	command, commander or commanding
Comd HQ	command headquarters
Conv Depot	convalescent depot
Cpl	corporal
CRA	Commander Royal Artillery (divisional artillery commander)
CWGC	Commonwealth War Graves Commission
Det	detachment
DI	dangerously ill
Div	division or divisional
Div (Bde) Wkshop	Divisional (Brigade) workshop
Div Docs	divisional documents
DODAR	Department of Defence Archives Repository
DR or DonR	dispatch rider
ENSA	Entertainments National Services Association
Eyetie, Itie, Iti	Italian person (slang)
FDL	foremost defended locality or forward defence location
FDS	field dressing station
FFI	free from infection
FGCM	field general court martial
FOO	forward observation officer
Fd Amb	field ambulance (South African Medical Corps)
Fd Pk Coy	field park company (South African Engineer Corps)
Fd Sqn (Tp)	field squadron (troop)

Fd	field
FSS	field security section
FUP	forming-up position
Fwd	forward
GCM	general court martial
GHQ	general headquarters
GOC	General Officer Commanding
GRO	general routine order
GS	general service or general staff
GSO	general staff officer or general service oath
GSW	gunshot wound
Gen	general
Gen Hosp	general hospital
Gnr	gunner
Gp	group
GRU	Graves Registration Unit
HE	high explosive
HQ	headquarters
Hosp	hospital
Hr	hour
Hy	heavy
IO	intelligence officer
i/c	in charge of
Inf	infantry
Inf Bde (Bn)	infantry brigade (battalion)
K/D	khaki dress
LAD	light aid detachment
LMG	light machine gun
LO	liaison officer
L/Bdr	lance-bombardier
L/Cpl	lance-corporal
Lieut	lieutenant
Lt	light
Lt-Col	lieutenant-colonel
Lt-Gen	lieutenant-general

LRDG	Long Range Desert Group
MAC	motor ambulance convoy
MDC	military disciplinary code
MDS	main dressing station
Mech	mechanized
Med	medium
MG	machine gun
MT	mechanical transport or motor transport
Mtd or Motd	motorized
NAAFI	Navy Army and Air Force Institute
NCO	non-commissioned officer
NEAS	Non-European Army Services
NMC	Native Military Corps
O. i/c.	officer in charge
OC	officer commanding
OP	observation post
OPA	oservation post assistant
O/Rs	other ranks
Offr	officer
PIAT	projectile infantry anti-tank
PO	post office
PW or POW	prisoner of war
Pk	park
Pl	platoon
Pnr	pioneer
Posn	position
Pr or pdr	pounder (as in 25-pdr)
Pro or Provo	provost
Pt	point
Pte	private
PTSD	post-traumatic stress disorder
QM	quartermaster
RAP	regimental aid post
RSM	regimental sergeant-major

Rd	road
Rec	recovery
Rec Sec	recovery section
Recce	reconnaissance or reconnoitre
Ref	reference
Regt or rgt	regiment
Res	reserve
Rfn	rifleman
SAA	South African Artillery
SAAC	South African Armoured Corps
SACS	South African Corps of Signals
SAEC	South African Engineer Corps
SAAF	South African African Force
SAMC	South African Medical Corps
SAMNS	South African Military Nursing Service
SAPA	South African Press Association
SATC	South African Tank Corps
Sec	section
Sergt or Sgt	sergeant
Shelrep	shelling report
SI	seriously ill
Sig	signal
Sigmn	signalman
Sigs	signals
SP or SPG	self-propelled gun
Tac R	tactical reconnaissance
Tks	tanks
Tpr	trooper
Tpt	transport
TSMG	Thompson submachine gun
UDF	Union Defence Force
UDFI	Union Defence Force Institutes
WAAS	Women's Auxiliary Army Service
WET	war establishment tables
WD	War Department

PART I

SETTING THE SCENE

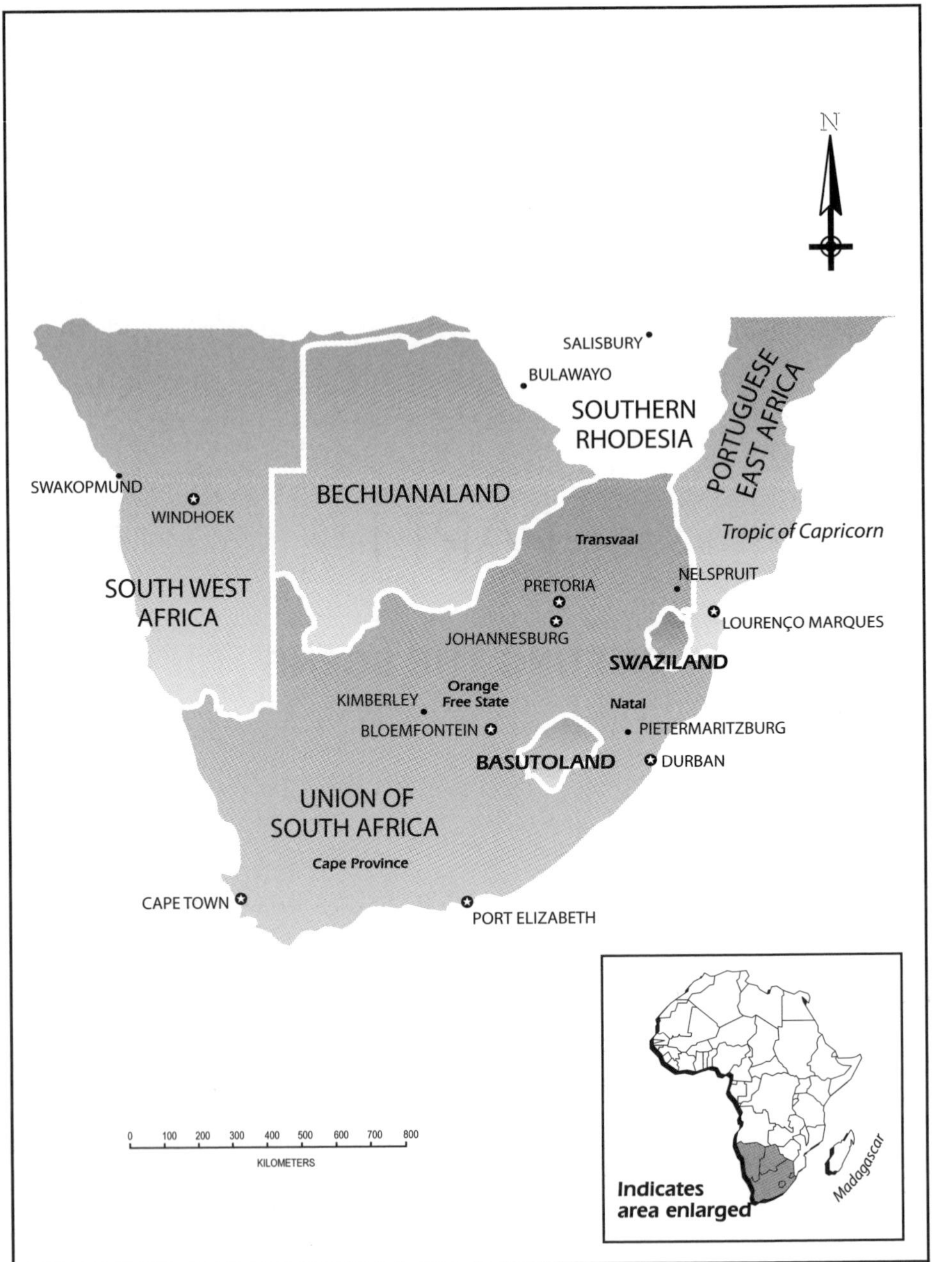

SOUTHERN AFRICA

Chapter One

Life in the Union: 1940 - 1943

"Soon we shall be passing from the old year to the new. It has been a black year in human history, but thank God, the tide is at last turning. For us in the unprepared state of our defences, it has been a year of preparation. Those preparations are now approaching the stage when we must seek fulfillment of our aim. The time for action will come in the new year."
—General Jan Smuts in a message to the troops in East Africa before Christmas 1940[3]

NEW YEAR'S EVE AT THE OLD JOHANNIAN CLUB in 1940 was unlike any other. Because 31 December fell on a Sunday, the dance started at midnight with the singing of *Auld Lang Syne*, by what was described in the St John's College magazine as "an orderly and tidy throng in a room not yet warm". It was obvious, however, that some had already begun celebrating.

Because space for dancing was limited, each person was given a red or blue button to wear, and took turns to dance according to the colour of their button.

The new Glenn Miller hit, *In the Mood*, was at the top of the charts. The girls were adept at the latest dances from Britain and America, like the Lambeth Walk and the jitterbug, and the prettiest among them hardly sat down for dancing.

The evening ended with a titanic squash match between two well-known club members, played in full evening dress with bare feet. Then, it was off to see the sunrise at Sylvia Pass and finally, breakfast. It was a memorable New Year—a good show.

Only two weeks prior to this, on 16 December 1940, the 1st South African Division had its first taste of battle at El Wak, Italian Somaliland, with the loss of only two lives. As their fathers had done before them in 1914, young men at first clamoured to join up. Bungalows and bell tents were filled to capacity from Kimberley to Kafferskraal, where the South African Armoured Car Regiment was based. A military base and POW camp was set up at Zonderwater near

---

3 E. Goetzsche, *The NMR history*, p. 187.

Cullinan. Staff officers completed countless courses at Roberts Heights. The infantry trained in the traditional pursuits of squad drill, bayonet drill and marksmanship, interspersed with bouts of boredom and 'bull'. Route marches, like the 32-mile slog from Barberton to Nelspruit, were particularly memorable.

The traditional training ground of the Natal Mounted Rifles was in the hills around Ladysmith where their forefathers had been besieged during the Anglo–Boer War. The regiment also had the misfortune of spending time in Piet Retief, which has been described as a hellhole consisting of flea-infested straw huts with mud walls, situated about two miles from the town. A night out in Piet Retief was as much fun as a "blackout in the Congo", whereas in Pietermaritzburg, every night was "either a dance, a party, a wild orgy of drink or the flicks".[4] Trooper John Hodgson's letters provide a glimpse into the day-to-day life at Hay Paddock military camp:

> I am sorry I did not tell you all about our camp life here but I was under the impression that I told you in one of my previous letters. Anyway here it is. We get up in the mornings any time between seven and half past. As soon as we are dressed we go and have breakfast, when we have finished that it is just on eight, at 8-0am we have roll call, after which we wash, shave and clean up our tents. At 9-0am we have to go for a route march if you don't play in the squadron's soccer or rugby teams. As I am in the soccer team I play soccer instead.
>
> After this we while away the time until lunch (this is when I write my letters). After lunch we go on leave. Sometimes we go directly after lunch and sometimes about 2-30pm but never later. When we go on leave we usually first of all go and have a bath at the Imperial Hotel which is the posh place of Maritzburg. This is always on the house. After this we go to the Soldiers' Club and play games until it is time for dinner which we also have there. After dinner we go to the pictures or to see people we know or sometimes we come back to camp and go to bed. We spend our weekends at Hilton. On Saturday we are going to see the Michaelhouse match at Hilton. The food here is really very good indeed and they don't let us go short of much in that line. We don't get joints or anything like that, but what we do get is very nice and well cooked. Yesterday we went and saw the trials for the Natal Schools' Rugby Team, and Hilton got five into the side, and Michaelhouse only got one. On Tuesday we are going up to Hilton as the Carbineers are playing a rugby match against them. We are not playing only watching.[5]

By the middle of 1941, the 1st Division was in the thick of it in North Africa. On 23 November 1941 the 5th South African Infantry Brigade was overrun at

[4] D.M. Baker, *War, wine and valour*, p. 481.

[5] J.B. Hodgson–M.V. Hodgson, 10/6/1943.

Sidi Rizeigh, and then came the harrowing retreat known as the Gazzala Gallop. Of the 5th South African Infantry Brigade's 5,700 men, only 2,306 found their way back to the Union of South Africa.

Men and material also had to be replaced. An advertisement for war bonds appeared in the *Cape Times* of 1 September 1942 with the slogan 'Buy the tanks and earn the thanks of the Springboks', and lists the cost of various ordnance:

Tank	£17,000
Bren gun	£70
Parachute	£40
Rifle	£8
Tommy gun	£10
1,000 rounds of rifle ammunition	£7

The people attending the New Year's Eve dance at the Old Johannian clubhouse in Linksfield at the end of 1941 numbered less than the 300 of the previous year. More than 500 of the 800 members were now on active service and the club was struggling to survive. The school magazine, *The Johannian*, was dominated by news of old boys who were home on leave, the latest casualties and decorations, as well as sporting triumphs achieved by old boys at the Gezira Country Club in Cairo. On the front line in the desert, the New Year was marked by men firing every weapon available in the general direction of the enemy until their officers managed to put a stop to it.

The real news from 'Up North' was not good, despite the best efforts of the local press to 'accentuate the positive'. The headlines in the *Cape Times* of 5 June 1942 stated "Rommel foiled again" and "Springboks full of confidence". The headline on 8 June 1942 proclaimed 'Crucial tank battle now raging—Rommel without one major success'.

Only two weeks later, General Klopper surrendered Fortress Tobruk with 25,000 Allied soldiers taken prisoner, including 10,722 men of the 4th and 6th South African Brigades. It was a serious blow to the national psyche. Throughout the Commonwealth, people became addicted to the news bulletins on the BBC. Churchill's radio oratory was perhaps more highly valued in South Africa than it was in Britain. It was the popular music which was most appreciated. British comedy radio, like *It's That Man Again* made light of wartime conditions and was one of the best morale boosters. "There would be news of those missing or killed in battle and there would be great sorrow if it was a local man reported killed,"[6] one listener recalls. Extended families moved in together to stretch their meagre resources. Wastage was frowned upon, and using old clothing was considered 'good form'. People were encouraged to make do, to mend and to keep a 'rag bag'. Meat, butter, cheese, coffee and canned goods were rationed. Fruit and vegetables (often from one's own garden) were the staple diet. Typical meals included macaroni and cheese or meatloaf made with more breadcrumbs and grated carrot than meat. The Hodgson family kept ducks and chickens in fowlhouses at the bottom of the garden of their Craighall Park home.

Because petrol and tyres were rationed, the extended family spent a lot of time at home with only each other and the radio for company. When there was a piano in the room, people gathered around for a singalong. Some of the favourites included the inane *Run Rabbit Run*, *I'll Be Loving You Always*, *Isle of Capri*, *White Cliffs of Dover*, and the universally loved *Lili Marlene*. In a letter to his mother, written while at the Soldiers' Club in Pietermaritzburg, Hodgson reminisced about one such evening:

> There is a chap playing *Deep in the Heart of Texas* on the piano down here and it reminds me of the time we danced to it in the diningroom while I was on leave and let us hope it will not be very long before we are doing it again.[7]

Patriotic or propaganda songs like *Hang out the Washing on the Siegfried Line* apparently did not catch on. It was the songs with a sexual connotation like *They're Either too Young or too Old* which were the most popular. Hope of fidelity was also a common theme, hence *Don't Sit Under the Apple Tree with Anyone Else but Me* and *Somebody Else is Taking my Place*.[8]

There was dancing every Saturday night at the Old Edwardians Club and the Orange Grove Hotel. The orchestra played the dance tunes of Glenn Miller and Tommy Dorsey; the young at heart did the Conga and the Boomps-a-Daisy. The more sedate danced to Victor Sylvestor, George Formby and Gracie Fields.

In the coastal towns, the social life flourished in spite of nightly blackouts. Peggy Timmons was South Africa's answer to Vera Lynn, singing mainly in Durban movie theatres. Dancing was a way of life—almost a duty for the young

6 Kalk Bay Historical Society, Bulletin No. 6, March 2002, p. 132.

7 J.B. Hodgson–M.V. Hodgson, 25/6/1943.

8 P. Fussell, *Wartime*, pp. 182–186.

women when there were so many soldiers and sailors needing a partner. For a schoolgirl living at False Bay in the Cape, the height of sophistication was to stop at Spotties on the main road at Retreat after attending a concert or 'bioscope' up the line.[9] On the other side of South Africa's political divide, supporters of the Ossewa Brandwag held 'Boere dances' at the Werda Club in Johannesburg. The venue was out of bounds for soldiers as a result of a fracas which had occurred there, and tensions started to simmer between the two factions. Pitched battles were fought, such as the one in Harrison, Loveday and President streets which occurred on 31 January 1941 when soldiers broke up a 'cultural concert' in the City Hall. The battle continued the following night. On both occasions, serious injuries were inflicted on the soldiers and a Corporal Gillham was clubbed to death on the Saturday night. The ensuing commission of inquiry found that the police had used excessive force in a brutal baton charge. Soldiers who were itching to exact revenge on the Ossewa Brandwag were restricted from carrying sidearms when on leave, lest they be used with fatal effect.

The Ossewa Brandwag was formed in 1938 on the centenary of the Great Trek, with membership reaching 300,000 to 400,000 during the war years. Its funding came from robberies and hold-ups. In one of his speeches, the leader of the Ossewa Brandwag, J.F. Janse van Rensburg, stated, "a German victory is an obvious condition for an Afrikaner republic to come into existence. Liberation can only happen as a result of a German victory."[10] Manie Maritz, a prominent member, came from a family with strong political beliefs which he called "pro-Boer, rather than pro-German". He went to Grey College in Bloemfontein. As a measure of anti-Jewish feelings at the school, Maritz mentions that he drew up a petition at the College to have the Jewish pupils expelled. The petition bore 240 signatures. According to him, Ossewa Brandwag members, especially teachers and railway workers, took the General Service Oath (or 'Red Oath', so called because of the red tabs worn by those who had taken the oath) and joined the army not out of choice, but because "they had a sword over their heads".[11])

There was friction between soldiers and civilians in various parts of the country. During the early stages of the war, soldiers travelling alone through *platteland* towns were subjected to taunts of, "Go home, the English are finished"

---

9 Kalk Bay Historical Association, Bulletin No. 6, March 2002, p. 112.

10 J. Crwys-Willians, *Mood of a nation, a country at war 1939–1945*, p. 117.

11 *Ibid.*

and "Heil Hitler". Oudtshoorn and George were two of the flashpoints while the Potchefstroom University College was a hotbed of anti-Smuts sentiment. A number of clashes occurred at the local bioscope, where each screening was opened with the singing of *God Save the King*, prompting the students to walk out. Serious damage was caused to the property and persons of the students on the evening of 7 August 1940. The Afrikaanse Nationale Studentebond adopted the Vierkleur as its emblem and to the *stormjaers* of the Ossewa Brandwag, the red tabs on the shoulders of Smuts's 'Khaki Ruiters' were like a red rag to a bull. Soldiers were advised not to walk the streets of Potchefstroom on their own. Even within the camp, a volunteer was in danger of being assaulted in the dark of night.

The artillery school was located near the showgrounds of Potchefstroom in the western Transvaal, where the Regiment De la Rey was raised and reserves of the regiment were mobilized when the war broke out. For its first three months, the regiment was accommodated in the asbestos buildings of the Premier Mines camp. Over the next three years, it moved back and forth between Piet Retief and Barberton with a sojourn at Saldanah Bay. At one stage, it found itself at Andulusia near Warrenton, guarding German civilians at an internment camp. One of the guards was Lionel Wulfsohn, the younger son of a travelling *smous* who had built up a small business empire in Rustenburg. Lionel had joined the peacetime army reserve in 1938 and was therefore automatically called up when war was declared. Commenting on an anti-Semitic remark made by one of the inmates, he remembers that "they were very cocky in 1941 when things were going well for Germany".[12]

Permanent Force (Regular Army) officers were notorious for avoiding active service. Many resigned rather than take up arms in a conflict to which they were ideologically opposed; others stayed on as instructors but did not take the General Service Oath. There were those, however, like Major-General Evered Poole and many of his senior officers, who were extremely able.

The red tabs worn by those who had taken the General Service Oath were strips of orange scarlet, prominently displayed on the shoulder to signify that the wearer was a volunteer, and became synonymous with South Africans on active service. As with other South African institutions, there were great divisions among SABC staff when it came to prosecuting the war. Percy Baneshik, who

12 L.M. Wulfsohn, personal information, interview, 28/4/2008.

was news editor during the war, noticed that the anti-war faction grew in step with the initial Nazi successes. The pro-war faction triumphed in the end with the sacking of the most virulent Nazi supporters and their internment at Koffiefontein. Radio Zeesen broadcast a nightly barrage of Nazi propaganda into South Africa—and the public was riveted by it.[13] A favourite topic on Radio Zeesen was the destruction of Allied shipping and aircraft. The station reported that during the Battle of Britain in August 1940, the Luftwaffe shot down 1,800 British planes for the loss of 395 German planes. "In spite of being overwhelmingly outnumbered, the Germans still gained a brilliant victory." The Ministry of Information felt the need to counter this with propaganda of its own. In *Gems of the week* and *Pearls of propaganda*, the counterpropaganda press rubbished German news reports; their claims sometimes embellished by exaggeration.

During the early part of the war, when South Africa's involvement was questioned by a segment of the population, the Bureau of Information found it necessary to explain 'Why South Africa Fights' in a series of broadcast 'talks'. Leading academics, politicians and prominent citizens broadcast discussions with such unsubtle titles as *South Africa in danger*, *German imperialism unmasked*, *Our land and the North*, *We fight for a free family life*, *The Nazi new order—a fraud*, *Bombers over Africa*, *A free press or political parrots* and *Native Africa at the crossroads*, to name but a few.

Farmers volunteered in their droves. Captain Blamey of the Natal Mounted Rifles estimated that 90 per cent of the men in three rifle companies were farmers. All the company commanders were farmers who had left their wives in charge: apparently, their farms prospered. The war years, especially 1941 and 1942, were drought years and these conditions enticed many black farmers to leave the land and take the King's Shilling. In tribal areas, where the headman was often paid for the number of volunteers he could raise, the tribesmen had little choice. Indians and coloureds (persons of mixed race) also joined, hoping that their show of patriotism would entitle them to better treatment.

While the men were away, there was no shortage of work for women in industry and commerce. Some volunteered for the Women's Auxiliary Army Services, Women's Auxiliary Air Force or Women's Auxiliary Naval Service. They undertook mainly administrative duties but also served on coastal

[13] J. Crwys-Willians, *Mood of a nation*, pp. 106–11; The chief announcer was Erich Holm, a former teacher from Natal (now KwaZulu-Natal) of German extraction.

batteries and searchlight units, and some were trained as pilots. The South African Women's Auxiliary Services was made up of volunteers who worked to make troops of all units and nationalities more comfortable, especially when convoys were on the move. They put together comfort packages and provided entertainment. It was the first of the women's organizations to be founded and numbered 65,000 women.

At the outbreak of the war, there were 15 trained nurses in the South African Defence Force. Eventually, 3,700 served in the South African Military Nursing Service outside South Africa and at home, where they staffed 26 auxiliary military hospitals. Not all were qualified nursing sisters; many were in the Red Cross Voluntary Aid Detachment.

Mobilization was a fiasco in the early days. Existing training camps were unprepared for the influx of recruits and conditions were inadequate. Equipment was obsolete; in some cases comically so. The Minister of Defence, Oswald Pirow, was ridiculed for purchasing a number of the First World War-era 'Bush Carts'. The Union Defence Force possessed not a single tank, and the South African Air Force answer to the Stuka and the Messerschmitt was the Hartebeest and the Junkers airliner, converted for use as a bomber.

However, the situation regarding war materials improved drastically during 1941 and 1942. By this time South Africa was self-sufficient and had become an essential supplier of ammunition, armoured cars, boots, steel helmets and mortars. The 6-pounder replaced the South African-made 3.7-inch howitzer and ineffectual 2-pounder anti-tank guns. The excellent 25-pounders were made in Canada and Australia, but later in the war South Africa supplied the shells for these and for the 2-pounder anti-tank guns.

Despite the shortage of modern aircraft, or perhaps because of it, South Africa became a centre for training pilots, in conjunction with the Royal Air Force. This Joint Air Training Scheme produced 190 pilots and 80 observers for the Royal Air Force and South African Air Force every month.

The naval forces were employed in patrolling coastal waters, mine sweeping, hunting U-boats and rescuing survivors from the 118 ships which were sunk due to enemy action within 1,000 nautical miles of the South African coast. U-boat activity was at its height in 1942, when 85 ships were sunk. Posters bearing the warning 'Don't talk about ships and shipping' were displayed in all coastal towns, because of the very real danger that information would fall into the hands of enemy agents.

Now that the reality of war had sunk in, it became more difficult to find recruits. The cause had to be actively marketed, and newspaper advertisements, radio programmes, posters, pamphlets, parades and newsreels in the cinemas all emphasized the urgent need for recruits.

Recruitment offices were established in most major towns at police stations, railway stations and army bases. Artisans and men with key skills were kept at home: 13,891 of 21,836 people employed by 430 engineering firms and 195 power supply enterprises were considered key personnel. The *Rand Daily Mail* of 29 June 1942 ran the headline '7,000 recruits needed immediately', and a large advertisement urged 'Avenge Tobruk—every woman recruit releases a man for the 7,000 needed to fight for South Africa Now'.

This message was even carried down the Durban racecourse by a squadron of armoured cars after the Durban July Handicap. Major-General Daniel Hermanus Pienaar lent his considerable influence to the recruitment drive. Shortly after the battle of El Alamein, he broadcast a message "... to you from all of us serving in the north, and especially from those of us who are serving in the 1st Division". He warned that although a resounding victory had been won at El Alamein, and many might consider the war already won, there was no room for complacency:

> I therefore call on every able-bodied man in South Africa who is capable of carrying arms to come forward and join the services now. Recruits are particularly needed for our armoured formations which include infantry, artillery, tank personnel, signallers and workshops personnel. Your fellow countrymen in the north have faced the music for a long time. Now it is your time to come forward and help them in order to be ready to go forward to meet the enemy during the next phases in which the South African troops will take part.[14]

With uncanny foresight, Pienaar went on to stress that even in modern warfare, the days of guns and bayonets were not past: "... no armoured formation can fight without adequate infantry and artillery support".[15] (The much-loved Pienaar was killed on 17 December 1942 when the aircraft carrying him home crashed into Lake Victoria just after taking off from Kisumu. A court of inquiry found that the 51-year-old pilot made an error of judgement brought on by fatigue, killing all 12 people on board. As the general was an old artilleryman,

14 J. Crwys-Willians, *Mood of a nation*, p. 291.

15 *Ibid.*

the Guard of Honour at Pienaar's funeral was made up of gunners from the artillery school at Potchefstroom.) At the battle of El Alamein, South Africa helped turn the tide of the war—and incurred 734 casualties in the process. Starting on 13 October 1942, the battle lasted 12 days. Apart from the troops' romp through East Africa during the Abyssinian campaign of 1940/41, Alamein was South Africa's first real taste of victory. The words of Winston Churchill at this juncture were entirely relevant to South Africa's contribution: "This is not the end. It is not even the beginning of the end. But it is, perhaps, the end of the beginning." The 1st South African Division was pulled out of the line and shipped home shortly after the battle of El Alamein. Leaving Suez on 1 January 1943, the *Nieu Amsterdam* was greeted in Durban ten days later by Perla Siedle-Gibson (the Lady in White) with the song *When the Lights Come on Again*.

Finally, there was a new year with something to celebrate—at least for those whose sons and husbands were coming home. Trains throughout the country were swamped by soldiers returning home on 'ex-north' leave. A large proportion of them would not be making themselves available to fight again. Airmen, engineers and signallers stayed on to fight through Tripoli, Tunisia and Sicily, but it would be 15 months before a South African brigade again went into action.

Chapter Two

The 'Div'

"Though we knew that non-Div men were also doing essential work, we could not help having an extra special fondness and admiration for the Div."[16]

WHEN THE 1ST SOUTH AFRICA DIVISION was pulled out of the line after the Battle of El Alamein, the plan was for South Africa to re-form two divisions that would be sent back for further operations in North Africa. However, manpower shortages made this impossible.

In a speech to the 1st Division at Quassasin, Egypt on 22 November 1942, Field Marshal Jan Christian Smuts had hinted about the force of the future.

> Now just a word about the future, officers and men. As I said, the first phase has closed and another phase lies before us. There is a pause. You have been withdrawn from the front, you are here for rest and you are here for a great change. And the question today is how to utilize that pause. You know the idea is to transform the First and Second Divisions, into tank divisions. All the preparations, the movements of armaments for that purpose are being carried out. No decision has been reached as to what to do with you in the meantime, but my own idea is to send the whole of the First Division to the Union on leave. [prolonged cheers][17]

Amid much controversy, the 1st South African Division was disbanded and re-formed as the 6th South African Armoured Division. The demise of the proud South African Tank Corps, in particular, caused much bitterness. The division was officially formed on 1 February 1943 at a conference at Defence Headquarters in Pretoria. The first divisional parade was held at Sonderwater on 13 February. The next day, at a wings parade at Waterkloof, General Poole wore the new divisional flash (yellow superimposed on a larger blue triangle)

---

16 S. de Wet, *Shifty in Italy*, p. 56.

17 R.W. Tungay, *The fighting Third*, p. 364.

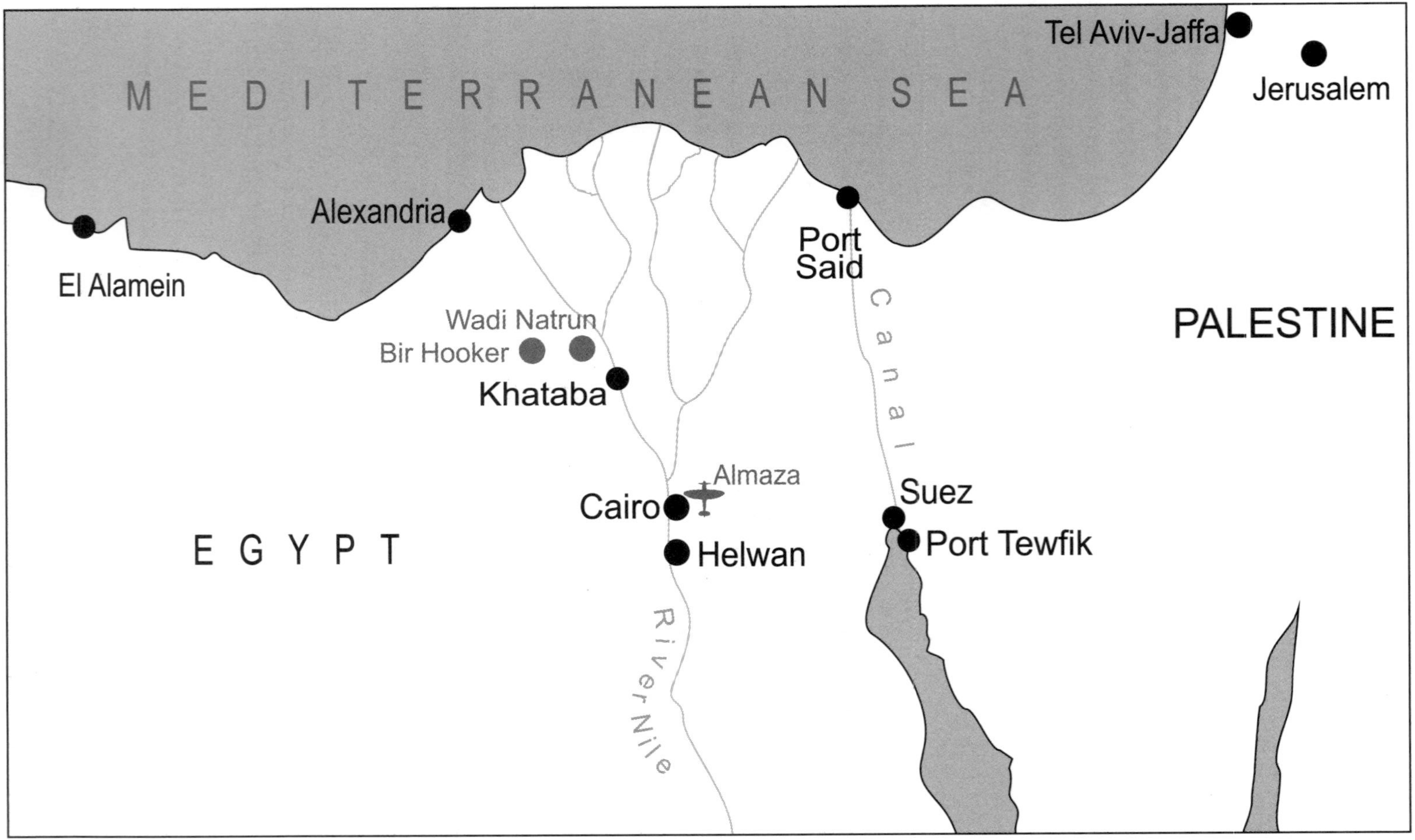
MEDITERRANEAN SEA
Tel Aviv-Jaffa
Jerusalem
PALESTINE
El Alamein
Alexandria
Port Said
Canal
Wadi Natrun
Bir Hooker
Khataba
Almaza
Cairo
Helwan
Suez
Port Tewfik
EGYPT
River Nile

to signify carrying out his first official duty as General Officer Commading. The divisional emblem was a sable head which had been selected as a tribute to the Rhodesians who were an integral part of the force.

In terms of men, machinery and composition, the 6th South African Armoured Division was vastly different to the amateur armies that had taken the field in East and North Africa. In terms of firepower, it was four times greater than the 1st South African Division had been at its strongest.

The division was a mixed bag made up of desert war veterans as well as new recruits, sometimes referred to as 'Tobruk Avengers', who had answered Daniel Pienaar's call to arms. There were also those who had been in uniform since the start of the war but had not left the Union. Of these, some were volunteers, as keen as mustard, who had been kept out of active duty because of age; others were career soldiers who had spent the war thus far in a training role. Although he had attended Hilton College, which is historically linked with the Royal Natal Carbineers, John Hodgson was a Transvaaler. He attested at Voortrekkerhoogte. Like many boys, he wanted to be a pilot but because there were no vacancies, he signed on for the armoured cars and began his training at Kafferskraal. When the Royal Natal Carbineers (then an armoured car regiment) asked for recruits to be posted up north immediately following embarkation leave, John Hodgson and his friends jumped at the opportunity. He was happy with his choice:

> As you can see I am in 'B' Squadron, and George is in the same one but David Alexander is in 'D'. Everyone says that we have got the best crowd of officers as they have had the most experience, although all our officers are ex-north men. Lt. Col. Comrie is our O.C. and he seems a very decent man. He gave us a talk on Tuesday in which he said that our regiment is the oldest and has the highest traditions in South Africa. He also said that out of all South Africa our regiment was chosen to be the independent armoured car regiment attached to the Imperial army … The whole crowd are very sociable here and we have made some very good friends. With us there are quite a few old 'Desert Rats,' Transvaal Scottish and Old Natal Carbineers.[18]

However, Hodgson's parents were concerned to learn that the regiment was being converted to infantry. He tried to reassure his mother:

> I suppose Mrs. Mennie has told you that we have been transferred out of armoured cars into infantry. There is absolutely nothing to worry about as everyone here in the

[18] J.B. Hodgson–W.A Hodgson, 3/6/1943.

> regiment who has already been up north says it is much better in the infantry and they are all very pleased with the change. We won't do any fighting in trenches or things like that as we are attached to the 6th Armoured Division and after the tanks have gone through a town we come up and consolidate the position. So don't start getting worried because it is absolutely unnecessary.

Hodgson was justifiably proud of his regiment and its heroes: "You know Quentin Smythe, the South African VC. He has just come back to this regiment after completing an officers' course; but it is not definite whether he will be coming up with us when we go."

The Natal Carbineers had its roots in the Natal Midlands and was headquartered in Pietermaritzburg. The regiment's record includes the Langalibalele Rebellion, the Battle of Isandhlwana (where two of its officers and 19 other ranks were killed) and the siege of Ladysmith. Its name was changed to the Royal Natal Carbineers in 1935. The regiment's cap badge depicts crossed carbines bearing the motto *Pro Patria*.

Apart from the usual medical tests, the main qualification for inclusion in the 6th South African Armoured Division was the signing of the General Service Oath or Red Oath, which had been introduced on 29 March 1940. By signing the oath, the volunteer agreed to serve anywhere in the world. While it was optional for those already serving, one could no longer join without taking the oath.[19] Conflict existed between the volunteers and certain permanent force members who refused to take it. However, many felt the same way as W.L. Fielding, author of *With the 6th Div*, who in 1946 became the first to publish a book on the Italian campaign, that "there was no compulsion, no force about it. Except the compulsion of the inner man himself. A something which said 'I cannot be left out of this thing ... I would never forgive myself ... I must go'".[20]

Hodgson explained to his younger sister:

> The old oath is the one where soldiers have only signed on to serve anywhere in Africa but the new oath is for anywhere in the world. The latter only came into force in March before then you could sign either but after then you had to sign the new one. George and I both signed the new oath and all those who do sign it, get 'v' after their number to distinguish them from the others.

---

19 J. Crwys-Willians, *Mood of a nation*, p. 61.

20 W.L. Fielding, *With the 6th Div*, p. 6.

Glen Easton, on the other hand, hesitated to take the oath. Aged 35 years and seven months, he was older than the average volunteer. Fair-haired and good-looking, Easton was married to Ellen Petit and owned a farm, Devonia, at Syferbult in the Western Transvaal. The couple had two sons, aged seven and four. Easton attested on 30 June, answering the call to 'Avenge Tobruk' after its fall on 20/21 June 1942. In his endeavours to see action, he spent time in Potchefstroom and Pietermaritzburg, serving in the South African Tank Corps, the Pretoria Regiment and the Transvaal Scottish before ending up the Royal Natal Carbineers.

Like most others, Trooper Easton was not keen to fight the Japanese in the jungles of Burma. Having arrived in Egypt only in December 1942, he was not due for home leave with the rest of the 1st Division. In a letter dated 1 March 1943, he wrote to his wife of his primary concerns:

> As I told you in my last letter, I have not signed the new oath yet as I am really not prepared to go to the Far East although I should really like to volunteer for Europe. In any case, I am not doing anything at present. Whatever happens, I don't think that there is a chance of seeing the Union before Europe is finished with. I see that you harrowed the beans twice this year on account of grass in the lands. Didn't the harrow thin them out too much?

While South West Africa contributed its fair share of men, the men of Southern Rhodesia had volunteered with particular alacrity when the war broke out. Of the 9,187 white men in the forces, 6,520 served outside the colony. They were to suffer 228 casualties and earn nine decorations in the Italian Campaign. White Rhodesian casualties in all services were to total 913 men and three women killed in action or died during service.

Rhodesia's total white population at the time numbered between 70,000 and 75,000. The Rhodesian Armoured Car Regiment was absorbed into the Pretoria Regiment, Prince Alfred's Guard and Special Service Battalion. A particularly large group of Rhodesians joined the First City/Cape Town Highlanders. In total, 1,400 Rhodesians went to Italy with the 6th South African Armoured Division.

Some units contained separate Rhodesian squadrons, batteries or companies, complete with their own officers, and an attempt was made to keep them as exclusively Rhodesian as possible. These units were 3/17 (Rhodesia) Battery, 1/6th Field Regiment, 1/22nd (Rhodesia) A/Tank Battery, 1/11th A/Tank

Regiment, B Squadron Prince Alfred's Guard, C Squadron Special Service Battalion, A Squadron Pretoria Regiment and B Company First City/Cape Town Highlanders.

Rhodesians posted to the Special Service Battalion during the reorganization of the 6th South African Armoured Division initially objected because of the regiment's humble origins. The Special Service Battalion was formed during the depression in 1933 in response to high unemployment, which had given rise to the 'poor white problem'. However, although the first recruits were of poor farming stock, the officer corps—partly British army—was always first class. At the outset the regiment had received standard infantry training but during the Second World War, it became a tank regiment. The commanding officer during the Italian Campaign, Lieutenant-Colonel E.G. 'Papa' Brits, became known for his strong leadership and caustic comments.

Regiments were amalgamated to increase their strength. Each of the artillery regiments in the division was amalgamated, but some infantry and tank regiments maintained their individual identity. Others changed their function, as with the Royal Natal Carbineers' conversion to infantry, which saw Trooper Hodgson become Private Hodgson. He informed his mother: "The organization of the regiment has been changed a lot; as you can see by my address we are no longer in squadrons but companies, which is the proper thing for the infantry."

The 'order of battle' refers to the composition or line-up of a fighting force. It is defined by the renowned military theorist, Karl von Clauswitz, as "that division and combination of the different arms into separate parts of the whole army, and that form of disposition of those parts which is to be the rule throughout the whole campaign or war."[21]

In the case of the 6th South African Armoured Division, the order of battle was to change and, at the end of the campaign, was very different to that originally envisaged.

In June 1943, when the division was based in Egypt, its strength was recorded as approximately 12,000 Europeans and 7,000 Cape Corps. Reinforcements continued to arrive throughout the year. The Royal Natal Carbineers shipped out from the transit camp at Hay Paddock in Pietermaritzburg in September 1943 on the *Stratheden*, five months after the main contingent. The Royal Durban Light Infantry conducted its own recruitment campaign in the Durban

21 K. von Clausewitz, *On war*, p. 245.

area. Initially, it was not going to be given a 'second innings', however, after an unintentional three months of embarkation leave, the regiment sailed on 27 November 1943 to join the rest of the division.

It is clear that the amalgamations did not please everyone. Baker, a member of the division, wrote of "the ridiculous process of amalgamating, merging and joining regiments to the original Natal Mounted Rifles that had been mobilized in 1940".[22] Throughout 1943, regiments in Egypt and at home continued to amalgamate, sometimes reluctantly. For example, the Natal Mounted Rifles refused to marry its Durban rival, the Royal Durban Light Infantry, but was prepared to join with the South African Air Force Armoured Car Batallion. The Natal Mounted Rifles retained its motto, 'Rough but Ready', and its badge depicting a top boot and spur.

The Royal Durban Light Infantry operated in armoured trains in the Anglo–Boer War, and in Italy it was at first a heavy support weapon group. Like the Natal Carbineers, this regiment also became 'Royal' in 1935. Its motto was *Primus in Africa*. Fielding describes the role of the Royal Durban Light Infantry as to provide aid where most needed. "Little bits and pieces of its family being sent from place to place on the battlefield ... The father of this clan, Lieutenant-Colonel Metcalf, had lots of journeys to make, shepherding his widespread sections."[23] Weapons used by the battalion included long-range Vickers machine guns and heavy mortars.

Two kilted regiments, the First City Highlanders from Grahamstown and the Cape Town Highlanders, were amalgamated on 4 October 1943 to form the First City/Cape Town Highlanders. During the Basuto War, volunteers of the First City Highlanders had faced the charging Basuto alongside the Prince Alfred's Guard from Port Elizabeth. The First City tartan was that of Graham of Montrose. The Cape Town Highlanders had linkages with the Gordon Highlanders and wore the Gordon tartan. They had served in North Africa and only 52 per cent of the men took the new oath. The hackle worn by the amalgamated regiments (1943–1945) was green and gold.

Fielding commented favourably on the amalgamation of the Witwatersrand Rifles and the Regiment De la Rey: "... the human background of this married unit is the Free State farmer and the Rand miner and businessman." The new

---

22 D.M. Baker, *War, wine and valour*, p. 440.

23 W.L. Fielding, *With the 6th Div*, p. 128.

regiment acquired the nickname 'Royal *Boere*'. The regimental headquarters of the Regiment De la Rey, whose motto was *Ons Waarsku* or 'We Warn', was in Rustenburg and more than half its members refused to take the new oath.[24] Monick writes that the amalgamation process had a positive result for the two regiments. Nevertheless, A Company was predominantly Witwatersrand Rifles, B Company predominantly De la Rey and C Company a mixture of both.[25] Even after amalgamation, the regiment was under strength by 347 European other ranks. Since 'bigamy' was out of the question, the shortfall had to be made up by other means.

Another unlikely couple was the Johannesburg-based Imperial Light Horse and the Kimberley Regiment which combined to form the Imperial Light Horse/Kimberley Regiment. Both had their beginnings in the Anglo–Boer War. One of the *bittereinders* (Boers who fought to the 'bitter end') of that war, Deneys Reitz, was in fact made an honorary colonel of the Imperial Light Horse.[26] In a memo to General van Ryneveld, General Poole stated that the Kimberley Regiment with its 295 European other ranks would only agree to marriage with the Imperial Light Horse provided that they embarked with an equal number of other ranks, and no less. Dubbed *Iykona Lo Horse*, the Imperial Light Horse/Kimberley Regiment was a proud regiment. The shoulder title was worn only by those who had been in action within the battalion and had to be kept highly polished. At a regimental parade on 9 July 1944, the officer commanding, Colonel Reeves-Moore, outlined the conditions for wearing the Imperial Light Horse/Kimberley Regiment shoulder title and threatened dire consequences for those who did not jealously safeguard the privilege:[27]

> I am anxious that the following conditions and reservations in regard to the wearing of the ILH/KimR shoulder titles shall be strictly and rigidly observed and enforced and I rely on every officer, NCO and man of the Regiment to count it his duty to ensure that the privilege and honour of wearing these is in no way abused or misconstrued.

---

24 S. Monick, *A bugle calls*, pp .309–333.

25 S. Monick, *A bugle calls*, p. 333.

26 H. Klein, *Light Horse cavalcade*, p. 171.

27 Department of Defence Archives Repository (DODAR), War Diaries WD, Box 635, File B8 60, Imperial Light Horse/Kimberley Regiment, 1–31 July 1944.

1. The title shall be issued for wearing to every man who serves with the Bn in fwd ops and will remain in his possession.
2. SACS, SAMC and TSC personnel serving with the Bn fwd, shall be entitled to wear them.
3. Reserves who have NOT served fwd with the Bn, will not be entitled to wear them.

According to Captain Power, a staff officer in the 11th Armoured Brigade, the procedure of marrying battalions was generally not successful, although the Imperial Light Horse/Kimberley Regiment proved an exception:

> The FC/CTH were always an unhappy unit. The ILH/KimR were alright because Lt-Col Reeves Moore was completely ruthless and scrapped all KimR traditions, and practically all their officers. He made his Bn to all intents and purposes the ILH.

Many junior officers and non-commissioned officers found themselves without a place in the newly amalgamated regiments. Some were prepared to relinquish their rank. Douglas Baker had been an infantry lance-corporal but when the Natal Mounted Rifles converted to armour, he was asked to surrender his stripe. Others preferred to transfer to the infantry rather than be demoted. Corporal Lionel Wulfsohn was initially in a Vickers platoon in the Regiment De la Rey but on amalgamation with the Witwatersrand Rifles, there were too many non-comissioned officers, so he transferred to a rifle platoon.

Those who reverted at their own request were given the option of having their original rank reinstated later on in the war. They would be regarded as having served uninterruptedly in the rank they held before reversion. There was a catch, however: although they would be reinstated at their former rank and rate of pay, no assurance could be given that they would continue to serve in their current corps. In fact, such was the need for infantry that they could be called upon to serve in any corps, in any capacity. Applications for reinstatement had to be submitted between 20 October and 11 November 1944.

To ensure maximum efficiency, the artillery was controlled by divisional headquarters while the infantry was organized into motorized brigades (motorized brigades function as infantry within the context of an armoured division). Clausewitz explains that a brigade typically numbered between 2,500 and 5,000 men, this being the number which can be directly commanded by one man, with all men remaining within hearing range of his voice.

Initially there was only one infantry brigade, the 12th South African Motorized Brigade. This consisted of the First City/Cape Town Highlanders, the Royal Natal Carbineers and the Witwatersrand Rifles/Regiment De la Rey.

Immediately after the Battle of Monte Cassino, the 24th Guards Brigade, an elite British formation, came under command and remained with the division until February 1945. Although some said that the Guards were attached to the division to 'stiffen' them, Orpen put forward the opinion that the nature of the Italian terrain required that the tanks be supported by an extra infantry battalion.[28] The Guards Brigade had its own support personnel while its infantry consisted of 1st Battalion Scots Guards, 3rd Battalion Coldstream Guards and 5th Battalion Grenadier Guards.

The Pretoria Regiment came to have a particularly close association with the Guards Brigade during its time in Italy. It had served in Madagascar during the first years of the war. Only about 50 per cent of the regiment had taken the new General Service Oath when it converted to armour at Sonderwater.[29]

After the Gothic Line battles, on 8 October 1944 Brigadier Clive (officer commanding the Guards Brigade) "informed Lieutenant-Colonel Johnstone of the Pretoria Regiment that approval had been granted for the incorporation of the Household Colours of the Brigade into the Pretoria Regiment's badge 'to perpetuate their happy association which he hoped would continue for generations'."[30] The badge, an impala facing left and standing on a representation of the Magaliesberg mountains, was superimposed onto the Guards emblem, wings of red and blue.

When it became known that the Guards Brigade would be passing out of command in February 1945, the division underwent a reshuffle and the 13th South African Motorized Brigade was formed. This comprised some experienced regiments as well as some newly arrived from the Union, including the Imperial Light Horse/Kimberley Regiment, Natal Mounted Rifles/South African Air Force, the Royal Durban Light Infantry, the 15th Field Regiment, SAA and Regiment Botha/Regiment President Steyn.

The division included only one brigade which was 'armoured' in the true sense of the word, and that was the 11th South African Armoured Brigade.

---

28 N. Orpen, *Victory in Italy*, p. 123.

29 H.J. Martin & N. Orpen, *Military and industrial organization 1939–45*, p. 224.

30 N. Orpen, *Victory in Italy*, p. 218.

This comprised the three tank regiments—Pretoria Regiment (Princess Alice's Own), Prince Alfred's Guard and the Special Service Battalion—working in cooperation with infantry.

Just as the Pretoria Regiment had a special relationship with the Guards Brigade, the Special Service Battalion worked closely with the Imperial Light Horse/Kimberley Regiment, which was under command of the 11th South African Armoured Brigade and had been specially trained for this role.

After the rest period at Siena in August 1944, the Frontier Force Rifles was brought in to alleviate the shortage of supporting infantry. Affectionately known as 'The Rif', this was a highly regarded infantry unit from India. The commanding officer, Lieutenant-Colonel Armstrong, was British, as were many other officers. The regiment was under-equipped, especially in terms of transport and certain support personnel, such as signallers, had to be supplied by the 6th South African Armoured Division. The Frontier Force Rifles bore its full share of the fighting between September 1944 and February 1945, when it went to rest at Lucca. During its first action, the regiment numbered 19 officers and 920 other ranks. The men were not issued green battledress until October. In their first few actions, they wore khaki uniforms which left them feeling extremely conspicuous against the backdrop of Italy's green hills. The men eventually dyed their uniforms with a mixture of elderberries, blackberries and tealeaves. The Natal Mounted Rifles/South African Air Force Regiment (usually referred to as the NMR rather than NMR/SAAF), which provided armoured reconnaissance, operated independently of the brigades, as did the Royal Durban Light Infantry. The latter functioned as a support unit but reverted to infantry during the final phase of the campaign.

The anti-tank and anti-aircraft artillery found themselves out of a job in Italy. Because of the virtual absence of enemy aircraft, 1/12 Light Anti-Aircraft Regiment, South African Air Force eventually converted to infantry. Meanwhile, 1/11th Anti-Tank Regiment, South African Artillery was never used in the role for which it was trained.

The 4/22nd Field Regiment was equipped with self-propelled guns which were initially armed with 105mm guns and were called 'Priests'. In November 1944, the armament was replaced with 25-pounders and renamed 'Sextons'. The 25-pounder guns of the 1/6th Field Regiment were towed behind gun tractors or 'quads', as were the 5.5-inch guns of 7/23 Medium Regiment. The 1/6th Field Regiment was an amalgamation of the 1st Field Regiment, Cape

Field Artillery and the 6th Field Regiment. It consisted of three batteries, which in turn were made up of two troops of four guns each; 24 guns in total. As previously mentioned, the artillery came under divisional control.

Stephen Bourhill left St John's at the age of seventeen. As a concession to his mother, he waited until his 18th birthday before joining up, working for his uncle on a farm near Clocolan in the Free State in the interim. The uncle, the former Captain H.W. Stockdale DSO, DFC and bar, had learned enough during the Great War to decide that his nephew should join the artillery. However, although the artillery provided a more comfortable existence, it was by no means completely safe. The South African Artillery had been in the thick of the action in North Africa and the 25-pounders had been overrun at Sidi Rizeigh. Full-time components of the division included engineers, signals, field ambulance, 'Q' Services, workshops, military police and divisional and brigade headquarters. Apart from the 24th Guards Brigade and the Frontier Force Rifles, various other units—mainly non-South African—flowed in and out of the division as dictated by the tides of war. One of the more permanent attachments was the 166 (Newfoundland) Field Regiment. When the 6th South African Armoured Division came under the command of the American 5th Army in August 1944, there were at times a wide variety of American units under divisional command. These included, among others, a regiment of American negro infantry and an infantry dog scout platoon.

South African surveyors and sappers (non-divisional personnel) had been active in Italy since the Salerno landings. The sappers suffered their share of casualties in the five years of war: in total, 108 were killed in action, 52 died of wounds, 30 went missing, 18 died as POWs and 303 died on active service. The survey companies compiled maps and interpreted aerial photographs.

In addition to the South African Engineer Corps' more conventional tasks, such as building roads, railways, airfields and bridges, clearing minefields and bomb disposal, it was also responsible for water supplies and laying pipelines.

The aim of the 80th Engineer Base Works was to eliminate the need to ship the engineer stores required by the armies, by providing as many supplies—including nails, steel, cement and oxygen gas for welding and high flying—as possible. To this end, South African engineers took over Italian factories and workshops, occasionally employing the owners and staff on a contract basis under their supervision. In many cases, the factories had been damaged during battle and had to be repaired before they were operational. Items that were manufactured by the 80th Engineer Base Works ranged from components for Bailey bridges to buttons and brass eyelets, from gun barrels to wooden crosses. The Non-European Army Services included both coloured and black troops. Many served in Italy and some are buried there, but only the Cape Corps played a role in the 6th South African Armoured Division. Unhappiness and frustration was rank among the non-European units, both in Egypt and at home, partly due to unsympathetic officers and partly because of long periods of absence. It appears that the biggest grievance among the coloured community was that its members were not engaged in a fighting capacity. There had been some rioting and mutinous behavior, more prevalent in the Cape Corps than the Native Military Corps. In addition, according to authors H.J. Martin and N. Orpen, "there had been an increase in cases of crime by individuals, including attempted rape, insolence, a growing disregard for discipline and a rapid falling off of morale".[31] The South African Air Force and South African Engineer Corps had employed black troops in Italy before the arrival of the 6th South African Armoured Division. Major problems were encountered as they were faced with all the unfamiliar temptations and emotional stresses generated in Europe at war. For this reason, the 6th South African Armoured Division decided in 1943 that the Native Military Corps would be not be engaged outside the country. It was replaced by the Cape Corps which had absorbed the Indian and Malay Corps.[32]

The (approximately) 5,000 men of the Cape Corps were scattered throughout the division. Most were attached to 'Q' Services but there were also many in fighting regiments. Some of the Cape Corps had been gunners in the 21st and 22nd Field Regiments South African Artillery, but had been replaced by whites when they went overseas. Initially, a 'dilution policy' was introduced whereby there were two Cape Corps members in each field gun or anti-tank detachment and four ammunition bearers per battery, but in a document marked 'Most Secret', General Poole, who was considered liberal for his time, stated his reasons for needing 277 more white artillerymen:

---

[31] H.J. Martin & N. Orpen, *Military and industrial organization 1939–45*, p. 246.

[32] *Ibid*, pp. 224–252.

I request modification of the dilution policy in respect of C.C.'s serving in gun detachments.

a. On active service, the European gunners have to live and eat together with C.C.s for months on end. This is very much resented by the Europeans.
b. Training is more complicated by having mixed gun dets. The problem is not only social but also mental. The C.C. is naturally slower and requires a great deal more trg. It is therefore not possible to train them together.
c. In the event of casualties, the two C.C's, although normally used as ammunition numbers will have to man the gun as either loaders or layers. This will decrease accuracy and efficiency.
d. To summarise the above, the inclusion of C.C.s in dets does just NOT work in practice. The same difficulty was experienced in 1 SA Div, which fact can be corroborated by Brig. C.L. du Toit, who was for a very long time the C.R.A. of that Div. What happens in practice is that the Europeans man the guns shorthanded. This is an unsatisfactory state of affairs for the Div and I consider the change essential.[33]

Each Cape Corps member was rated 'A', 'B', 'C' or 'D' according to his 'character classification'. The meaning of these classifications is not clear but, for example, in the First City/Cape Town Highlanders there were 229 Cape Corps troops, of whom 155 were given an 'A' classification. The Royal Natal Carbineers and Witwatersrand Rifles/Regiment De la Rey, on the other hand, gave no 'A' classifications, preferring to give mostly 'B' ratings.[34]

Partly due to a surplus of junior officers and non-commissioned officers, nearly 3,000 South Africans applied to be transferred to the British army, Royal Navy or Royal Air Force. Many served in 'glamour' regiments like the Black Watch, the Gordon Highlanders and the Royal Scots Fusiliers. Reasons cited for joining these regiments included their affiliations with South African regiments such as the Transvaal Scottish, Cape Town Highlanders and Prince Alfred's Guard. Indeed, a battalion of the Royal Scots Fusiliers had been commanded by Deneys Reitz during the First World War.

Selby Webster was one of approximately 400 men who went over to the UK forces, and one of six of the South Africans in his draught to the Black Watch. Webster was the third South African to take over 6 Platoon, the other two having

33 DODAR, Divisional Documents (Div Docs), Box 196, File AQ 23/1 (V1) WE Tables Secret, Dilution Policy-C.C.'s, 28 May 1943.

34 J. Keene, *South Africa in World War II*, p. 161; DODAR, Div Docs, Box 183, File AQ 16/26, 6th South African Armoured Division, C.C. Character Classifications.

been killed. He appealed to the Union Defence Force for help, as the British army was desperately short of junior officers. A number of Rhodesians, initially part of the 6th South African Armoured Division, transferred to the Rhodesian unit of the elite Long Range Desert Group. A team of 30 South African dispatch riders or 'Don Rs', as they were called, was attached to the Polish army. These members of the South African Corps of Signals were responsible for carrying messages across the mountain range to the forces on the Adriatic.[35]

Even when on 'foreign service', General Service volunteers wore their distinctive red tabs. The public relations unit wrote an article about a number of red tab wearers whom they had encountered in Italy. However, in addition to the glamorous postings, there were some very ordinary people doing ordinary jobs. The common thread was that they were intensely conscious of their South African identity and getting back to the Union was their constant hope.

The 6th South African Armoured Division had its own provost or military police, but there were many other MPs who were not attached to the division. The detention barracks, for example, were staffed by the South African Corps of Military Police and catered for men of all units, including the South African Air Force.

Likewise, the entertainment units of ENSA, the Entertainments National Services Association—including the Amuseliers, Modernairs, Wot Nots and Sundowners—reached out to Division, non-Division and non-South African units alike, playing a key role in sustaining the morale of all nationalities in the Mediterranean Theatre. The African Stars, the concert unit of the 3rd Cape Corps, apparently did wonders for the morale of the Non European Army Services. While some of the offerings of some units were of a low standard, the Crazy Gang had an outstandingly popular show which was considered clean and wholesome. Many bands conducted special broadcasts for the forces and played at dances and functions, especially in hospitals. Some of these entertainment units sustained casualties through illness and accident.[36]

From the perspective of the South African people, however, it was the fighting units of the 6th South African Armoured Division that made up the cast of characters. These were actors who played the leading roles on the Italian stage.

---

35 *Rand Daily Mail*, 31/7/1944, 30 Crack Springbok Dispatch Riders with Polish Army.

36 DODAR, Div Docs, Box 140, Monthly summary of non-Div Activities, February and March 1945.

Route through Italy taken by the 6th South African Armoured Division (1944 -1945)

Chapter Three

The Italian Theatre: 1943 - 1944

> *... It is easy to forget the days of blood and toil, when time and again overwhelming disaster seemed imminent and as a nation, we were stricken near to death.*[37]

ITALY WAS A POOR COUNTRY. In 1940, the per-capita GDP was less than one quarter that of Britain. The south was, moreover, much worse off than the north. The poverty and squalour in Naples would have shocked a South African, even before it was ravaged by war. Italy has sided with Germany but ordinary people were hungry, and the universal cry was "May they [the Allies] come soon."[38] The Marchesa Iris Origo and her husband lived on the estate La Foce 100 miles north of Rome, in the path of the approaching South Africans. On 30 May 1943, almost a year before the liberation of Rome, Iris Origo lamented:

> Food in Rome is becoming scarcer: fruit and vegetables are practically unprocurable. A chicken costs 300 lire. The milk ration is two 200 grams per day (less than a cupful). Flour, ham etc can still be bought on the black market, but at a price far beyond the reach of the average purse. Yesterday, a friend who has six small children sold 12 silver spoons and bought a ham. At the same time, small restaurants continually spring up, provide excellent meals (mostly consumed by fascist officials) at exorbitant prices—and then, after a few weeks, are closed by the police, only to open again elsewhere. It is generally expected that the harvest fields will be destroyed by the Allies with incendiary bombs.

For those in their twenties who knew no leader besides Mussolini, it was a disconcerting time. Bombing, curfews, rationing, black markets, apprehension and uncertainty became a way of life. Even the aristocracy complained that they were living a peasant's life—a life which had returned to the medieval pattern.

---

[37] J.F. MacDonald. *Lion with tusk guardant*, p. 3.

[38] I. Origo, *War in Val d'Orcia*, p. 83.

Perhaps no industry in Italy was as hard-hit by war as the electrical power industry south of the Po valley. It was singled out for destruction by retreating enemy, Allied bombers and partisan saboteurs alike.

With the requisitioning of supplies, including food and equipment (even cars) from the farms, Iris Origo noted that it was impossible to attach importance to material possessions, saying "all that one clings to is a few vital affections". As the supply of rations for the German troops was erratic (possibly due to the bombed railways), the soldiers raided farms for sheep, pigs and geese. The population feared the implementation of a scorched earth policy by the Germans. Nevertheless, many Italian peasants continued to live in their houses and work their lands amid the fighting. They would even pay social calls on their neighbours and discuss the damage that had been done to their houses. Young girls could be seen riding their bicycles in areas where a soldier would not dare stick his head out of his foxhole.[39]

Nevertheless, the Val d'Orcia was a relative safe haven for the refugees from port cities like Grosseto and Livorno. The Gestapo hunted for Jews, escaped prisoners of war and partisans. All Italian men between the ages of 16 and 55 were ordered to report for forced labour or face execution on the spot. Jews were declared enemy aliens, their property was confiscated and they were deported to concentration camps. Iris Origo found that this horrified all the Italians she met.

On the evening of 25 July 1943, it was announced that Mussolini had resigned and was to be replaced by Marshal Badoglio. Mussolini was held in captivity until he was sprung from his Apennine cell by German commandos.

In a cable to Churchill, Sir H.R. Alexander GCB CSI, DSO, MC, ADC, proclaimed: "By 10am this morning, August 17 1943, the last German has been flung out of Sicily and the whole island is in our hands." The campaign had lasted just 38 days but the cost was high: 2,237 American and 2,721 British dead.

Sir Alexander, known to all as General Alex, was the very model of a professional soldier: blue-blooded with a red-banded cap, swagger stick and thick moustache. He took charge of the Italian campaign during the Salerno landings. The American 5th Army, meanwhile, was commanded by Major-General Mark W. Clark who, at the age of 47, was one of the youngest and most competent three-star generals in the US Army. Unfortunately, he was also

---

39 M. Parker, *Monte Cassino*, p. 264.

extremely arrogant, and an anglophobe.[40] Prior to the arrival of the 6th South African Armoured Division, General Oliver Leese had taken over command of the British 8th Army from General Montgomery.

Following a clandestine mission to Rome by two American officers, the unconditional surrender of the Italian government was announced on 8 September 1943. The next day, the Americans landed at Salerno and lost approximately 1,200 men. The German deaths numbered 630, "a modest butcher's bill for an army that in September alone would suffer 126,000 casualties in Russia".[41]

After the Italian government capitulated, the gates of POW camps in Italy were thrown open and thousands of Allied prisoners, many of them South Africans who had been captured in North Africa, walked out into the Italian countryside. For most, freedom was short-lived as the Germans quickly took over the camps. Nevertheless, there are countless stories told of escaped POWs who were hidden by Italian peasants while being hunted down by the Germans and fascist sympathizers. Some joined partisan bands; others made their way south to meet up with the advancing Allies; and still others became integrated within Italian communities. The attitude of many escapees is reflected in this anonymous statement:

> Months went by and one day we learned that Allied troops were in the valley, therefore we ex-POWs held a meeting in the wood to decide what to do next. Several men reached the same conclusion: "I'm safe here, I could work on the farm. I did my stint for my country, I don't want to be put back in a unit and be killed next week. I'm staying."[42]

As the locals speculated on when and where the next strike would take place, a civil war raged between the fascists on the one hand and the partisans on the other. The civilian population was caught in the middle, with life's necessities becoming more scarce and rumours abounding.

On 14 October 1943, Italy declared war on her erstwhile ally. However, some Italian soldiers maintained their former allegiance. Initially, four Italian fascist divisions served with the 23 German divisions. This figure would eventually

40 R. Atkinson, *The day of battle*, p. 183.

41 R. Atkinson, *The day of battle*, pp. 216–236.

42 G. Rosignoli, *The Allied forces in Italy 1943–45*, p. 64.

grow to around 60 divisions. In spite of the peace agreement, the bombing of Italy continued. One of the greatest fears expressed by Iris Origo in her diary was that the homes of Italians would become a battleground:

> Moreover we shall then learn as Poland and Czecho-Slovakia have learned, what it is to be occupied by a hostile and vindictive Germany; we shall become a battlefield, despised on both sides as traitors, destroyed by both combatants. No, there is nothing left for us but passive endurance, until the final defeat of Germany.

The hope was that the Germans would abandon the whole of southern Italy and that the Apennines would become the first line of defence. The population watched with apprehension as German troops took over villages like Chiusi, where a tank corps was deployed—an ominous sign that the war would not bypass them.

It was now 'total war'. Naples, in particular, experienced the wrath of the Germans; possibly because of the feeling of betrayal that developed when Italy switched sides, but also in retaliation for the uprising of civilians on the eve of the German departure. The city, already damaged by Allied bombing, was the victim of cultural atrocities when German troops burned libraries and sank every ship in the harbour. Deadly time bombs were left to greet the Allies and the implementation of a scorched earth policy left devastating hunger in its wake.[43]

The thieves of Naples rivalled even those of Cairo as the city's citizens did everything they could to survive. Trade on the black market was rampant. One Allied report, released in spring, estimated that 65 per cent of Neapolitan per-capita income derived from dealing in stolen Allied supplies. It was pointless to stop and search the city's inhabitants because virtually every Italian wore clothing made from army blankets, wore army socks, or at least had a packet of American cigarettes. It was estimated that out of a nubile female population of 150,000, about one third was engaged in prostitution.[44]

On its arrival in Italy, the 6th South African Armoured Division was warned that there were individual and organized gangs of thieves operating in their area and that their 'skill and cunning' made their detection almost impossible. Vehicles, in particular, had to be guarded at all times. Any

---

43 R. Atkinson, *Day of battle*, pp. 241–247.

44 M. Parker, *Monte Cassino*, pp. 217–219.

offenders caught were to be handed over to the Carabinieri. A friend of Iris Origo wrote: "There is a patrimony common to all humanity, made up of decency, sensibility and civilized behaviour, which is every day diminishing and will soon be bankrupt ..."[45]

Some Italians benefited from the arrival of the Allies by taking on jobs like laundry or receiving handouts. According to one Italian civilian, the Americans were the most generous, followed by the New Zealanders, and then the Indians. The British were admired because of their discipline and military correctness but they gave little away materially, because they had so little to give.[46]

New Year's Eve in Rome at the end of 1943 was a very quiet affair. Food shortages and lack of heating allowed little cheer, and thanks to the curfew imposed by the German occupiers, the Roman population was obediently indoors by 9 o'clock. Denied the opportunity to dance with local girls, German soldiers spent the night carousing in the bars. Midnight was marked by the obligatory firing of guns into the air.[47]

One of the worst atrocities of the war in Italy occurred on 23 March 1944 in reprisal for a bomb blast in Rome, which killed 32 German officers and men. Hitler was incensed and wanted to blow up an entire quarter of Rome. If that was not possible, 50 Italians should be killed for each 'martyr'. In the end, ten 'hostages' were shot for each soldier killed. A total of 335 civilians was shot, five at a time, inside the Ardeatine Caves which were sealed a few days later.

The battle of Monte Cassino can be seen as either two, three or four separate battles which took place between January and May 1944. By the time the 6th South African Armoured Division arrived on the front line, there had been three ill-fated attempts by the Americans, Indians and New Zealanders to break through the Gustav Line. They had spent a winter in the mountains of Italy and had learned that it is futile to fight a war under such conditions. Twenty inches of rain fell during the last three months of 1943, and the advance of the 5th Army front slowed to less than a mile per day. During the first battle of Monte Cassino, on 21 and 22 January 1944, an attempt was made to cross the Garigliano River. The US 36th Division lost an estimated 1,430 men. This was a high tally even by American standards and a Congressional Investigation was

45 I. Origo, *War in Val d'Orcia*, p. 62.

46 M. Parker, *Monte Cassino*, p. 265.

47 R. Wallace, *The Italian Campaign*, pp. 39–40.

carried out after the war to assess whether Mark Clark was to blame for this suicidal attack. Clark was exonerated.

The 6th South African Armoured Division came into the line on 4 May 1944 and took part in the final phase, which saw the Polish forces finally wrest the ruins of the Benedictine monastery from the hands of German paratroopers on 15 May. The small contingent contributed to the total line-up of 1,600 guns, 2,000 tanks and 3,000 aircraft which were assembled along a 20-mile front.

With contingents from more than 20 different countries, the Allied army in Italy was the most cosmopolitan ever to have taken the field.

To alleviate the hold-up at Monte Cassino, the Allies made a landing at Anzio on the west coast, just south of Rome, on 22 January 1944. This combined American and British effort, which was criticized by General Clark and Winston Churchill for being insufficiently aggressive, was however the closest approximation of First World War trench warfare in recent experience.

The Germans, intent on eliminating the abscess in their flank at any cost, threw in all available resources, including some very heavy artillery which shelled the air strip, the hospital and everything else on the beachhead.

The final breakthrough at Anzio occurred after the fall of Cassino at the end of May and the two fronts met up just south of Rome on 2 June. The so-called soft underbelly of Europe was proving to be more of a hard spine (or tough old gut) and many questions were being asked about the wisdom of continuing. The occupation of Italy and the administration by the Allied Military Government was being called a strategic folly as it placed an economic burden on the Allies instead of the Germans. At the same time, it apparently did nothing to win the hearts and minds of the people. When the Allies arrived in Rome, the first question the locals asked of them was "Why did it take you so long?"[48]

[48] R. Atkinson, *Day of battle*, pp. 575–576.

PART II

CHRONICLE OF OPERATIONS, EVENTS AND EXPERIENCES

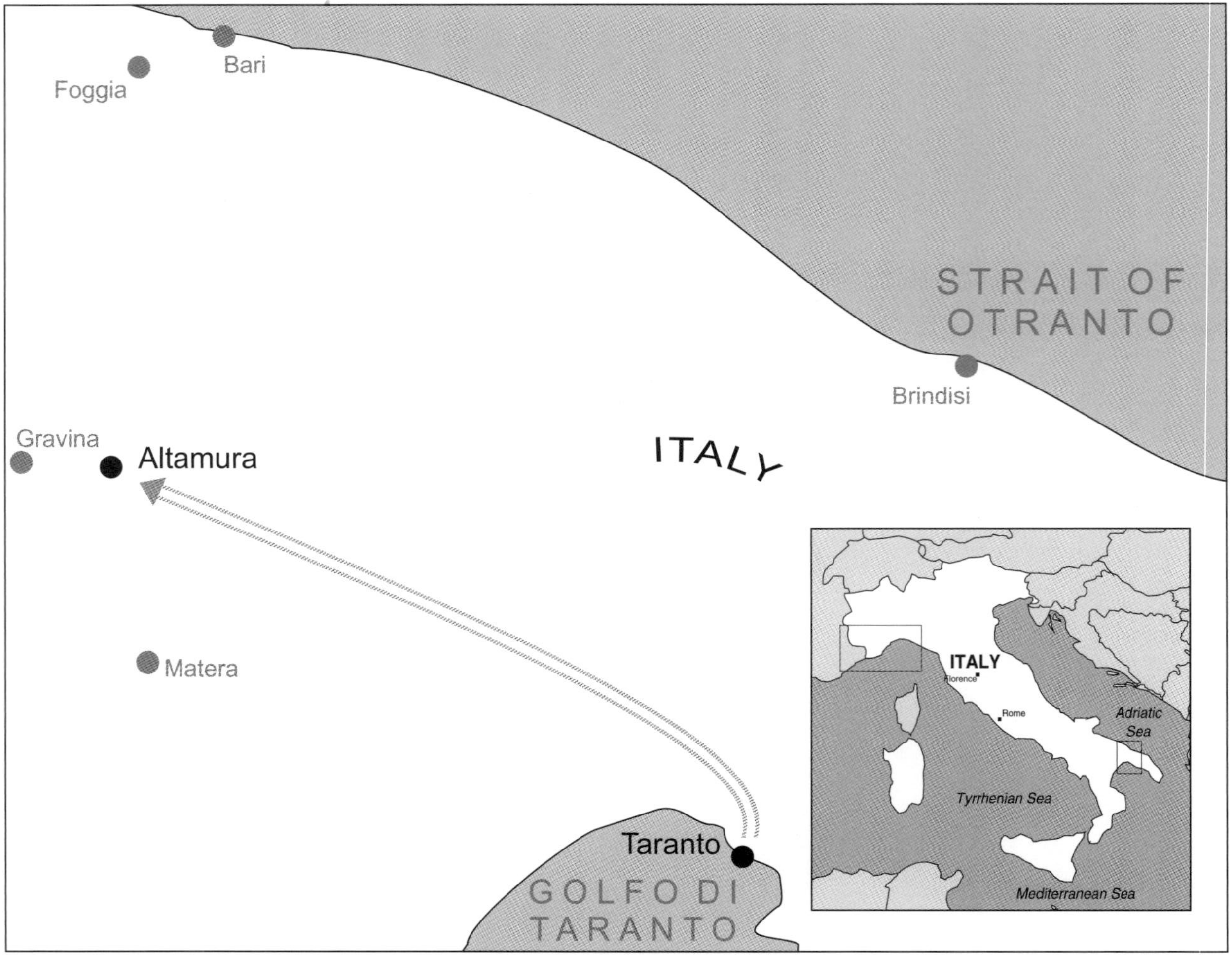
Foggia
Bari
STRAIT OF
OTRANTO
Brindisi
Gravina
Altamura
ITALY
Matera
Taranto
GOLFO DI
TARANTO
ITALY
Florence
Rome
Adriatic
Sea
Tyrrhenian Sea
Mediterranean Sea

Chapter Four

Clouds and dust

"Much lies ahead of us. Much is expected of us. We go forward to a theatre of war, either in or extended beyond this great continent, in defence of our homeland and the vital interests connected with it. The great name of South Africa has been committed to our care. Let no man fail in his duty."

—Personal message from the Divisional Commander to all units of the 6th South African Armoured Division, 3 February 1943

Pietermaritzburg

Sensing that there would soon be tears, John Hodgson cut short the farewell to his parents as they stood on the platform at Park station. He had made the overnight journey to Natal many times when he was a schoolboy at Hilton College and he knew that the mood would lighten after passing through Germiston. As usual, his closest friend, George Mennie, was with him. The other three in the compartment were 'ex-north blokes', distant acquaintances who were surprisingly friendly.

Padkos (lit. 'road food') was shared out in accordance with an unwritten code, although soldiers travelling long distances on ex-north or embarkation leave received meal tickets and bedding. Each travel document carried a warning not to damage the carriages and not to talk about service matters, but veterans of the desert war could not resist giving a few 'tips' to the uninitiated. Conversation flowed throughout the night. There would be time to catch up on sleep in the morning, when the young men sprawled among their kitbags on the platform at Pietermaritzburg station as they waited for transport to Hay Paddock.

Hodgson spent many a weekend pass stooging around his old stomping grounds, watching the unbeaten Carbineers rugby team in action or, best of all, being seen at the traditional Hilton/Michaelhouse match. Sporting red tabs on his shoulders, a bloke could create quite a stir among the girls from St Anne's. To round off the weekend, there was nothing better than a lazy Sunday lunch at the Hilton Road Hotel. But Durban was, as ever, the most popular destination for a spot of leave. The place to meet was the Athlone Gardens Hotel where the dancing would start in the afternoon and continue into the night. Another favourite haunt was the Caister Hotel which was good for breakfast and a game of squash, or one could play deck quoits at the Rugby Hotel.

There were non-stop film shows at the Metro and the 20th Century. Currently on circuit was *Keeper of the Flame* with Katherine Hepburn and Spencer Tracy, followed by *Rage in Heaven* starring Ingrid Bergman. In the way of live theatre, *No No Nanette* enjoyed a long run and eventually made its way to Italian stages. Balmy days and nights were spent listening to records, wandering around town, and swimming in the sea. Despite a campaign to discourage civilians from travelling by rail, the trains from Durban to Pietermaritzburg were always crowded, and after a full weekend the men slept head to toe on the bunks.

Across the country, men were on the move. An incident occurring in March 1943 dispelled any notion that all was well within the Union. A leave party of 350 Cape Corps soldiers belonging to the 6th South African Armoured Division, travelling in third class and said to be under the influence of liquor and *dagga* (marijuana), jumped off the train at Laingsburg station and looted the goods shed. There were approximately 170 white soldiers on the train, travelling in second class. According to the officer in command, Lieutenant A. Christiansen, they were subjected to threats that "after this war we'll fuck your women because we'll be the bosses". Bottles and stones were thrown and three men were seriously wounded by the shots fired when the reserve was called out; one of whom subsequently died.[49]

In the world of the Union Defence Force, all tracks led to Pietermaritzburg where three new military establishments—Oribi Military Hospital and Camp, the Durban Road Prisoner of War Camp, and the Hay Paddock Transit Camp—had sprung up in the veld on the outskirts of town.

Oribi was an infantry camp during the early days of the war, and it was from here that the Royal Natal Carbineers departed for East Africa. It became a hospital in 1940, predominantly serving the Imperial troops railed up from Durban. Hospital patients wore blue tunics, blue trousers, white shirts and red ties on their excursions into town, which invariably brought forth offers

---

49 Department of Defence Military Archives Repository (DODAR), Chief of the General Staff (CGS), Box 47, Laingsburg Riot Inquiry, Report and Findings of the Court, 22/7/1943.

of a meal or an outing. The POW camp held mainly Italians, although some Germans captured in North Africa were imprisoned here while en route to Canada and other countries. From among the POWs there emerged an excellent military band as well as some master chefs who were employed at the Oribi Camp.[50]

Hay Paddock was established on a 72-hectare site on the southeastern fringe of the town near Scottsville, in what is today the suburb of Hayfields. The camp was within walking distance of the town; however, conditions left a lot to be desired. The problems were highlighted in a letter written by Mrs M. Cochrane, MPC to the Honorable F.C. Sturrock, the Acting Minister of Defence:

> It has been brought to my notice by officers and men stationed at Hay Paddock, P.M.Burg, of the bad conditions prevailing in that camp. I understand that it has been built on the side of a hill, the men are under canvas. In dry weather they are blinded by dust and in wet weather they are up to their knees in mud. These men are waiting to embark up north and across the seas, but some of them have been here for months on end and have been home on embarkation leave as many as three times, and still they do not proceed out of 'Maritzburg.[51]

Trooper John Hodgson came from a caring and affluent family who sent him regular parcels and encouraged him to phone home regularly, reverse charges. The jersey, sleeping bag and balaclava cap sent by his mother ensured that he was better equipped than most to withstand the extreme and varied weather conditions which could freeze the taps in the washhouse in winter. His three army issue blankets could be used as a mattress or kept in reserve. Although Hodgson's letters portray a remarkable ability to look on the bright side, they did corroborate Mrs Cochrane's report:

> Yesterday and today have been very windy and extremely dusty. Last night our tent was hit by what you could practically call a hurricane. Half of our tent doesn't hook down so the wind just swept right through and smothered everything in dust, and all we could do was to get right down under the blankets to prevent ourselves being choked by the dust; so you can imagine what a mess we were in this morning. We were very lucky that our tent was not swept away, because we would have really

50 J. Laband. & R. Haswell (eds), *Pietermaritzburg, 1838–1988: A new portrait of an African city*, pp. 110–113.

51 DODAR, Chief of the General Staff, Box 283, Tentage Camp at Hay Paddock, M. Cochrane, F.C. Sturrock, 12/10/1943.

> been in the soup then; three tents were swept away and the occupants are still searching for their belongings. Except for the dusty wind the climate is very pleasant and extremely warm.

The camp accommodated 25,000 men at peak times during 1943, although the average occupancy was 15,000 and the facilities were meant for 20,000. Petty theft was rife at Hay Paddock (alternatively named 'Clay Paddock' and 'Flea Paddock); however, by all accounts the food was good, the routine none too strenuous, and Pietermaritzburg had a lot to offer in the way of entertainment. The hospitality of the townspeople extended to taking in laundry despite the existence of an inexpensive laundry service in the camp. Ten different venues catered for servicemen and -women, and were run by service organizations such as TocH, the YMCA and the SAWAS. One could get a cheap meal at the Soldiers' Club, housed in a handsome old building at 168 Longmarket Street, or take in a Perks pie and a film show. Every Tuesday night there was a uniformed dance in the city hall from seven o'clock to ten-thirty. Hotels and bars were well patronized. Soldiers on picket duty patrolled the streets, helping the Military Police ensure that there was no fighting or drunkenness. Even accounting for the ever-cheerful tone of Hodgson's letters to his mother, it appears that life was not half bad:

> Monday 7th June 1943
> Up to now we have been having a wonderful time, although we are beginning to get a bit bored. We have roll call at eight in the morning and nothing of any importance happens during the morning and then we get leave from lunch time until eight the next morning. The food we get is very good indeed. We get a colossal amount of butter and jam & all we eat is bread, butter and jam. We spread the butter as thick as we like and we have bread with our butter and jam. It is nothing for George and I to put away a pound of butter and a lb tin of jam.

> Thursday 15th July 1943
> At the moment I am on stores guard and when we were here on guard last night we had a lovely feast. We looked around the kitchen and we managed to get hold of a lovely leg of lamb which was most probably meant for the officers. Also half a dozen eggs which we fried, also a loaf of bread and a chunk of butter which we made lovely hot buttered toast and to cap it all we had plenty of hot coffee. I was appointed cook and I think I made a good job of it as nothing was left, and we didn't finish eating until well after eleven o'clock.

> Tuesday 20th July 1943
> We have been having such a lazy time here for the last seven weeks so we have at last

decided to get back into training again. Each morning we get up at 6-0am and go off for a cross-country run. It is bitterly cold and with plenty of frost on the ground. Also the sun doesn't rise until after we get back. When we do get back we have a cold shower which is as cold as one could imagine. After this we go and have a breakfast of hot porridge and bread and coffee and do we get stuck into it! After this we feel on top of the world and we are already getting into good training.

The Soldiers' Club was a sanctuary where one could relax in the writing room or join in the singalongs at the piano in the lounge. One could go dancing at the Welcome Club, or there was live theatre and film shows at the Grand where soldiers got a special concession.

It was boom time for the cinema. In 1941, the 20th Century joined the Excelsior and the Kings, opening in Longmarket Street as the city's largest and most modern cinema. Each feature film was preceded by an *African Mirror* newsreel. Hodgson's letters to his mother are not only a commentary on contemporary film, but also reveal his enviable social life:

Friday 25th June 1943
At the moment it is quarter to eight on Friday evening, and I am in the writing room of the Soldiers' Club. George has gone up to Nottingham Road for the day and is coming back at about 3 in the morning ... This afternoon David and I went to see a film called 'Laddie' which was very enjoyable indeed. We had dinner this evening at the Soldiers' Club as usual and now we are amusing ourselves here.

Tuesday 29th June 1943
Last night George and I saw a film called 'Alibi' starring Margaret Lockwood. It was very clever and well acted, and we both thoroughly enjoyed it. Tomorrow night we are going to the Technical College Hall to see a boxing tournament in which the majority taking part are Carbineers.

Thursday 1st July 1943
Last night we went to the Grand Theatre to see 'Holiday Inn' with Fred Astaire and Bing Crosby. I thought it was very good and we all thoroughly enjoyed it. The music and dancing in it was really grand. The theme being 'White Christmas' which is really a lovely tune.

Participating in sport was sometimes an excuse to get out of a route march or other duties. Soccer was played between units stationed in Pietermaritzburg and hockey matches were played against the fun-loving nurses from Grey's Hospital. Hodgson was lucky enough to find female company in a place where demand far outstripped supply:

Tuesday 15th June 1943
The other night at the 'Victoria League Club' (It is a place similar to the 'Soldiers' Club') we met two young married women. One of them used to come up to dancing at school in 1941. Well we told them how difficult we found it to get around; the result was that we are going to a dance at the city hall with them tonight and they are going to introduce us to quite a few people and some young girls, so things seem to be looking up.

Thursday 17th June 1943
On Tuesday night, as I told you, we were going to a dance at the city hall. Well we went along and we had a really good time. On top of it all we met two very nice girls, who are both nurses at Grey's Hospital here in Maritzburg. One went to Roedean and the other went to St Anne's, and they both left school last year. The one from Roedean, her name is Cynthia Erskin, and the one from St Anne's is Jill Logan. They get quite a bit of time off from the hospital and we saw them again last night. If we have someone to go out with the time here will brighten up considerably and will pass much quicker. Also we will be able to have partners to take to the dances instead of missing them.

Friday 23rd July 1943
We haven't seen the two nurses from Grey's Hospital for over four weeks now as it was so much trouble to get hold of them as they had such awkward hours for duty and also your pay goes too quickly when you start going out with girls so we just left them alone.

At times, Pietermaritzburg lived up to it's reputation of being a 'Sleepy Hollow' and some men preferred to remain in camp, playing soccer, cards or chess. Hodgson passed time by completing Bren gun and musketry training courses, and scored 84 out of 100 on the rifle range. The monotony was broken by a surprise visit from his father accompanied by a Mr Grinaker, who took him and his friends to town for a meal and a couple of 'spots':

It has been very dusty down here for the last two days and last night we nearly got blown out of our tent. All our belongings and kit, etc., were practically buried in dust and all our clothes are in a filthy state. We were lucky that we did not lose our tent as well, as happened to three lots of chaps who had their tents swept away, and they are still looking for their kit. Except for the dusty wind, the weather is very pleasant indeed; it is extremely warm for this time of the year … I have been to town a couple of times with Peter and Bert. They seem to be finding it very nice down here but are beginning to get bored already. We have been to see a couple of films but apart from that all is going along just the same.

Among the many Old Hiltonians serving with the Carbineers was David Alexander—another of the 'famous class of '42'. Although his war was cut short by a shell fragment, he would later make his name by opening up the Sani Pass (up the Drakensberg to Lesotho). On their weekend passes, Alexander and Hodgson meandered around the Natal Midlands. It helped to have connections:

> We spent most of the weekend with Colonel Alexander, that is David Alexander's father. We got out of camp early on Saturday morning and we met David's father in town. He took us all to the Imperial Hotel for lunch, after which he took David, George and me up to Hilton to watch the 1st XV play against Michaelhouse. It was really a wonderful match and Hilton won again with 24 points to 12. After this we came back to Maritzburg and had a bath; this was followed by a good meal at the Creamery Hotel. Then we went to see a play acted at the Technical College Hall by St Anne's; as David's sister was in it, we went backstage afterwards and spoke to the girls we knew. On Sunday we spent the day at the Hilton Road Hotel which was very nice ... I am not going out on leave today as I am on guard tonight but as our squadron is only on duty every sixth day, it is not at all bad.

Signs of the war were common in Pietermaritzburg. Off-duty soldiers were a frequent sight, while the comings and goings from the station along Commercial Road and Church Street and regular march-pasts of men and equipment were other reminders. In mid-1943, the Royal Natal Carbineers held a parade through the town's streets, and the *African Mirror* was there to film the event. On one such occasion, the Caledonian Pipe Band was at the head of the long procession and the town council treated all the troops to beer and sandwiches afterwards.

Hodgson was very disappointed that his was not one of the names drawn to go home at the beginning of September, but only five of about 35 men received home leave. He speculated that his chances would be good for the weekend of 18 September, not knowing that within a week, he would be on his way to Suez to join the 6th South African Armoured Division, which had been stationed in Egypt since April. Fortunately, his embarkation leave had been memorable:

> I will take the chance now of thanking you & Dad most sincerely for the absolutely wonderful time I had while I was at home. You don't know how much I appreciated it all and I am sure I will never forget these last few weeks. I didn't thank you on the station as I thought someone would have started to cry if I spoke to you too much which would have made leaving more difficult.

> You are not to be silly and start worrying about me as it is quite unnecessary as I will take very good care of myself. All we can do is hope that everything gets straightened up soon and then it won't be long before I will be home again. Besides it won't be very long in any case.

Sunday 18 April 1943: Durban

When the 6th South African Armoured Division boarded the train in Pietermaritzburg, there was the usual contingent of SAWAS in their tobacco-brown uniforms, serving tea and sandwiches on the platform. "You'll be s-o-r-r-y," taunted some onlookers, who had gone before as part of the 1st Division. However, nothing could dampen the enthusiasm of the troops spilling out of the carriages in their crisp khakis and sun helmets.

The Natal Mounted Rifles, which sailed with the main body of the 6th South African Division, had moved to the coast on 7 April after refitting at Hay Paddock. Douglas Baker was a member of the regiment, having joined at the age of 16 after attending Durban High School. Baker served throughout the East and North African campaigns. He spent his last night in the Union carousing in Durban, his hometown. Drunken British sailors would pick a fight at the drop of a hat and Baker got into an altercation, despite carrying wounds from Alamein.

There was no shore leave once the troop train arrived in Durban, but the mood was buoyant as equipment was hoisted on board and the men crammed below decks. The *Ile de France* carried only 7,500 men. They comprised the nucleus of the 6th South African Armoured Division which was still greatly under strength. The Royal Natal Carbineers, Royal Durban Light Infantry and other regiments would be trickling in by sea and plane throughout the rest of the year. In fact, replacements were still making the journey well into 1945, sometimes by air.[52] Even before the *Ile de France* arrived in the Middle East, the division had a skeleton staff working out of Cairo. Some, like Glen Easton, had only arrived in Egypt in December 1942 and so did not return to the Union on the *Niew Amsterdam* with the 1st Division. Instead he remained in Egypt attending church parades while awaiting the arrival of the 6th South African Armoured Division. There were also non-divisional troops, engineers and others, who had been left behind in the Middle East, much to their resentment.

---

52 The Royal Natal Carbineers sailed on the *Stratheden* in September 1943.

Monday 19 April 1943 – Friday 30 April 1943: *Ile de France*

The rank and file had no idea where they were heading as the convoy set sail on 19 April; some speculated that it might be England. All who could, surged up to the deck at the first sign of movement, almost causing the ship to list.

Unaware that he was witnessing a legend in the making, W.L. Fielding recorded that "on the opposite bluff, an elderly woman stood singing hymns". This was the 'Lady in White', Perla Siedle-Gibson, dressed in her trademark wide-brimmed hat and billowing white dress, holding a megaphone. Gibson was most frequently asked to sing *When the Lights Go on Again*, *White Cliffs of Dover*, *Annie Laurie* and *Avé Maria*. Men of all nations requested *We'll Meet Again*. Americans were not keen on hymns besides the Marine Corps Hymn, *To the Shores of Tripoli*, which she took the trouble to learn; South Africans requested *Sarie Marais*; the Australians *Waltzing Matilda*; and the British just wanted her to keep on singing, no matter what. She never missed singing to a convoy, even on the day she received news that her son had been killed:

> As she sang, she held her audience enthralled. A deeper feeling gripped all of us soldiers, a strange contracting of the throat. A chorus started, wavered, fell away into poignant silence. Gradually the troopship drew away, and at the end of the jetty, that white-clad figure started 'Auld Lang Syne'. As the gap grew, only snatches of the words came to us, and we swear she was still singing. We may forget many things of this war, but never the songs of Durban's 'Lady in White'.[53]

It was a powerful moment in the lives of those on board, as well as for the crowd on the wharf. It is said that when the *Llangibby* sailed in 1940, "every man and woman, though still waving their handkerchiefs stood silent—awe-struck".[54]

Now the men were singing, "Wish me luck as you wave me goodbye, cheerio here I go on my way." Tears were choked back as the convoy forged through Maydon Channel and past the Bluff. British and foreign ships in the docks saluted with a series of blasts and the final farewells were transmitted by mirrors flashing from one end of Durban to the other. As he sailed, Hodgson made a promise to himself and to his mother:

---

53 *Sunday Times*, s.n., Soldiers will not forget Durban's Lady in White.

54 D.M. Baker, *War, wine and valour*, p. 483.

> I will never forget the day when we left Durban. We sailed at three o'clock in the afternoon. There was quite a crowd to see us off as I told you about. When we got out into the bay it brought a lump into one's throat to look at all the houses on the Berea. Then we crossed the bar and the city slowly faded in the distance. The day which we all now await is when we shall see exactly the same thing in the distance but this time it will get clearer and clearer and then into the docks and home—forever. No more dashing off to school or to camp—next time I come home it will be to stay.

The U-boat threat was mostly under control by now, although there had been some attacks on the east coast. The troopships were accompanied by an escort of destroyers and were themselves well armed, each carrying over 300 anti-aircraft guns as well as a 4- or 6-inch gun astern. There was life-boat drill every morning and a blackout every evening, when even smoking on deck was prohibited. Most preferred being in the open air despite the frequent squalls; only the officers and non-commissioned officers had cabins but even these were crammed with up to 26 men, depending on rank.

The wire bunks were so cramped that it was impossible to roll over. Below decks, there were narrow tables and benches with hammocks overhead. Only seawater was available for washing and flushing. The overriding memory of those who sailed on troopships is that of seasickness and the smell: vomit sloshed about everywhere, to be mopped up by the unfortunate men on fatigue. This was no pleasure cruise.

However, there was some entertainment on board. A highlight was the 'crossing of the equator' ceremony during which certificates were handed out. Chess, contract bridge and other card games kept the boredom at bay.

The crew was kept very busy on their zigzag course, keeping a sharp lookout, but for the passengers much of the time was spent queuing for meals.

Hodgson, who endured the carnage of Monte Cassino and lived for months in a dugout in the winter line, said later of the troopship: "It was by far the worst experience of my life." Yet his letters home made it sound like heaven. His natural optimism may have been enhanced by receiving four meals a day (at seven o'clock in the morning, noon, four o'clock and seven o'clock in the evening), a change in diet and the novelty of sleeping in a hammock.

Although Hodgson sailed five months after the main body of the division, on the *Stratheden* rather than the *Ile de France*, his detailed account provides a rare insight into life on board a troopship:

This letter is started on Monday the 20th of September and as far as I can gather it is about the middle of the voyage but of course I may be hopelessly out. I will not finish this letter today but I will keep adding to it as things happen and I will post it as soon as I can after reaching our destination.

When we got onto the boat we were all given tickets allotting us to our different parts of the boat. As you can easily imagine we are terribly crowded. We are right down in the hold of the ship and it is consequently very hot but it is extremely well ventilated. The conditions under which we sleep are very queer but comfortable. All the mess decks as they are called are laid out with rows and rows of tables, above the tables are rows and rows of hooks for our hammocks. Thus we sleep in our hammocks just above the table I eat at.

So far I have only slept down on our mess deck twice, all the other times I have slept up on deck. You have no idea how grand it is sleeping up there. We go to bed about nine o'clock each night and I often lie there for hours gazing at the stars with the cool sea breeze blowing over the deck. Each morning I get up at six and it is then that the cool breeze is best. The block-out conditions make things a bit awkward at times but we are all used to it by now.

The food we are getting is excellent; for breakfast we always have porridge but this is without milk or sugar but this difficulty is easily overcome as we put condensed milk on it (this we get at the canteen). Sometimes this is followed by eggs and bacon or sausages or fish (usually haddock). At lunch time we usually get roast beef or roast pork (the latter is excellent) with two vegetables (usually potatoes and peas.) This is followed by rice pudding or stewed fruit but as there is no sugar in these, condensed milk again comes to the rescue. High tea at 4-0pm we usually get cold storage apples, excellent new-made white bread and butter and tea. Supper is very varied; we have had minced bully beef, brawn and usually thick vegetable soup. At breakfast we get bread (new-made, white) and butter; there is enough of this left over for lunch and the same at high-tea there is enough left over for supper. We eat off crockery supplied by the ship. We are also supplied with the following to eat with our meals: a jar of mustard pickles, a bottle of vinegar, salt, pepper, mustard and jam. About every other day we get a bottle of lime juice or tomango. As you can see we are looked after very well.

For washing purposes there are always hot and cold salt showers and baths. For a short time each morning and evening there is fresh water at the wash basins.

As you can well imagine the voyage gets a bit boring at times having to do all the same things but up to now I have occupied myself quite well. There is a library on board here and so far I have read three very good novels. I think I will give up reading those small books as they are not very good reading and if I read some good novels instead, it will do me more good. I have played an enormous amount of bridge and I am getting really hot stuff at it. Just to show you how much I have been playing it; yesterday (Sunday) between breakfast and supper I played for eight hours.

I am getting very good at sewing these days as I can do all my own darning etc. quite successfully. This afternoon I am going to sew the sleeve onto my overalls which got torn off while coming aboard and I expect some good results. The other day I put a patch on someone's trousers for him and my success astounded me.

A couple of days ago and again today we passed through a school of whales and it was quite fascinating watching them spouting water into the air.

I have been doing quite a bit of sunbathing and I have taken on an excellent colour. I have done it carefully so I haven't peeled at all.

The biggest surprise I have got so far this voyage is that up to now I have not been sea-sick at all. Just outside Durban we had some rough weather but it affected me only a very little and since then I haven't worried about it at all. In fact I am enjoying every minute of the voyage. At the moment we don't get much exercise but we will make up for that when we arrive at our destination.

Yesterday I was on guard but it was quite pleasant because even when there was nothing much to do there was always the sea to look at, which seems to have an everlasting fascination and one can gaze at it for hours. For the first part of my beat there was a band playing, of one of the regiments on board. It is actually a very good one and it played all our old favourites.

There is one thing that has struck me as quite odd although I suppose it is quite natural. One does not have that lovely smell of the sea right out here that we used to like so much at the seaside. Now and again one can smell it very faintly but that is about all.

We have got a very good canteen on board; here we can get all the things we want and the prices are extremely low. You know those pants I got while I was up for the weekend, well it is possible to get similar ones here for 6/6. Springbok cigarettes only cost 1/3 here while in the Union 2/-.

The day we arrived down in Durban to leave there was quite a number of people to see us off and I had the good fortune to come across three people whom I had met. They were all there to see friends off. It was very nice seeing those few people that I knew before getting aboard. Before we left there were masses of people but they were not allowed on the actual docks.

It is getting excessively hot these days and we just perspire morning, noon and night. The sea is wonderfully calm and there is not even a ripple upon it as there is no wind at all.

Of late there have been quite a number of concerts and community singing which has helped to pass the time away. In fact life on board is going along with a real swing and I will feel quite sorry when the voyage is over.

The officer has just come in and told us that we have a chance of posting letters so I will close. I will be very cross if you worry about me as I promise to look after myself (there isn't very much else I can do) and everything is done to make life pleasant; it is just like having a glorious holiday at the expense of the government.

Approaching the Red Sea, the men could see the interior of the Sudan, which one veteran described as a "haze of brown horribleness—blazing hot".[55]

[55] D.P.G. Putterill, personal information, interview, 8/3/2009.

Hodgson felt the same way: "The journey was very pleasant until we reached the Red Sea where it was absolutely unbearable. Even while we were eating the sweat used to run into our food and our clothes were always wet through."[56] General Poole was waiting in a motor launch at Port Tewfik to meet the ships on 30 April. The men had to clamber down narrow, inclining rope ladders to reach the barges waiting to take them to the quay, carrying their packs on their backs. They received a meal from the NAAFI as they formed up on the docks, and regimental pen-pushers recorded 'Disembarked Suez' on each of their DD 293 personnel cards, which would accompany them for the duration of their service. Finally, the thousands of men were shepherded into cattle trucks which served as troop trains. En route, they passed through Cairo which looked like the "the slum parts of Jo'burg" and crossed over the Nile River which, to Hodgson, looked "terribly dirty, something like the Vaal but larger". The pyramids could be seen in the distance, and looked "just like what one sees in the pictures, very plain and simple looking but [with] a certain uncommon grandeur about them"[57]

The journey was not without mishap: some men were injured getting on and off the moving trains. At every station where the trains stopped, the men would be met with cries of "cheap, very cheap, George" from Egyptian vendors trying to flog dirty postcards and worthless 'gold' watches. Others sold bottles of Johnny Walker Red Label whisky, from which the original contents had been drained and replaced with tea or urine. This they accomplished without damaging the seal by carefully opening the cellophane wrapping at the bottom and drilling a minute hole in the glass. After the liquid had been replaced, the hole was plugged with a transparent stopper and the wrapping stuck with glue. Feelings of antagonism were vented by kicking Egyptian peasants up the backside and some Egyptians would lift their *galabiyas* (long gowns) to show their privates.[58]

> I have arrived here safe and sound after a journey that was as pleasant as we could expect. Until we reached the Red Sea it was very pleasant, but after entering it, it was so extremely hot that one could not enjoy it in the least … After disembarking

[56] J.B. Hodgson–M.V. Hodgson, 5/10/1943.

[57] J.B. Hodgson–M.V Hodgson, 5/10/1943; J.B. Hodgson–D.M. Hodgson, 7/10/1943.

[58] J.B. Hodgson, personal information, interview, 28/11/2008; D.P.G Putterill, personal information, interview, 8/3/2009; J. Bosman, *Providence was my guide*, p. 29.

> we had quite an amusing experience, although it was not at all pleasant. At eight o'clock in the evening we were herded into cattle trucks (25 per truck) where we spent the night. The trucks are not sprung at all and we were bumped and thrown about continually during the night. We had very little room, so all we could do was level our kit all over the floor and curl up on it and sleep the best we could. The next morning it was extremely hot but we arrived here about lunch time.[59]

Saturday 1 May 1943 – Wednesday 1 December 1943: Khatatba

After a short stretch across the desert, the men arrived at the lush Nile delta where the scenery and farming methods had not changed since biblical times. The train finally halted at a station called El Khatatba, two hours or 45 miles northwest of Cairo on the road to Alexandria. In spite of its delta location, close to the Rosetta Nile, the regiment's camp is described as being in a truly bleak part of the desert. By all accounts, it was far worse than the South African base camp at Helwan. It was moderately cool inside the tents, which were of good quality; however because they were not properly pegged down they would flap in the wind, becoming filled with sand during dust storms. It was difficult to see or even breathe. Even the ever-positive Hodgson could not hide his dismay at this situation, all reference to which the censor removed:

> We have at last arrived at our destination in the Middle-East. Our camp is right out in the desert. As you can well imagine all we can see for miles and miles is just sand. It is terrible when the wind is blowing but at other times it is quite pleasant; in fact it is exactly like being camped on a very dry beach. The heat up to now has been oppressive at times but on the whole it is not as hot as I expected but even then it is much hotter than we ever have at home … I am writing on a book on my knee because it is the cleanest place I can find, because there is a wind blowing and the dust is just pouring into the tent, which is quite unavoidable. You can easily imagine that it is impossible to keep the sand out of things. Flies here are quite a pest, but there is also another pest which will seem quite funny to you down there—they are ladybirds; they are even commoner than flies yet not quite so annoying but they crawl over you and give one quite a nip, like an ant.
>
> Last night we went along and saw a whole lot of old Hiltonians who are in the artillery, who are up with the Sixth Division, of which we are now a part. We are going over to see Peter and Bert this evening but it is about five miles away as they are situated in another part of the camp. It just shows you how large this camp is.

The division was to undergo training in Egypt for almost a year. The continuous courses covered the use of enemy weapons, wireless operating,

---

59 J.B. Hodgson–W.A. Hodgson, 3/10/1943.

signalling, gas-mask training, mine laying and lifting, the disarming of booby-traps and a lecture on what to expect in the event of being wounded. The infantry completed assault courses, engineers became proficient in the building of Bailey bridges, and the artillery calibrated their guns using survey tools and trigonometry. Those who were converting to armour were given driving and maintenance courses. Training also included 'practical digging', as the roads were very poor and tracked vehicles were not permitted to drive on them.

On 14 June a multi-national parade was held in Cairo. South Africa was represented by "two companies of strapping six-footers from the Regiment De la Rey, a squadron of tanks and a squadron of armoured cars".[60] It was to be the last time that the regiment paraded before its amalgamation with the Witwatersrand Rifles. Another diversion was provided by the South African general election of 25 June. The Progressive Party regularly announced meetings in the *Bullsheet*. After some in-the-field voter education, white and coloured personnel were allowed to vote. Smuts won, but Malan's National Party received three-quarters of the Afrikaner vote. Everyone in camp was kept up to date with momentous happenings worldwide by the so-called 'Egyptian mail', which was brought around each morning by Egyptians.

The messing conditions were very primitive and often situated a long walk away from camp. Food was dished up straight from the big bins in which it arrived. The building which passed for a mess was constructed from mud and contained no furniture. Men preferred to eat on the sand outside unless there was dust blowing, in which case they ate inside squatting on the floor.

The ration of Chandlers beer was a treat but, as the saying went, "a quart per week per man per-haps". Another big treat was the odd occasion when doughnuts were served with tea. There were, however, fairly well-equipped NAAFI canteens where one could buy luxuries such as lime juice and tinned fruit, and still have some pay left over. A mobile canteen had been presented by the Rand Club, and when it visited his line, it made Hodgson feel that Johannesburg was near.

Water was scarce and taps were turned on only once a day; water bottles were filled and hung in the breeze to cool down. After a shower (also a long walk away), Hodgson and his 12 tent mates would sit outside the tent and have 'sundowners' of coolish water mixed with lime juice from the canteen.

---

60 N. Orpen, *Victory in Italy*, p. 8.

It was entirely possible to get lost among the thousands of tents, especially after a night of carousing. By October, the division had been at Khatatba for six months. Most men had had enough, although newcomers like the Royal Natal Carbineers were still finding it quite exciting to be preparing for war. For the new arrivals, the day began at six o'clock in the morning with a routine of parades and physical training. The day ended with sport between four and five o'clock, after which came a much-needed cold shower. A far as Hodgson was concerned, this was the good life:

> It is a grand life up here and I am loving it. It is going to be strenuous but it will build us up into big strong fellows in no time. It is really grand to sit down in the cool of the evening feeling on top of the world with a good day's work behind you. The cleaning of our rifles and the rest of our equipment takes up the little spare time we have so we are very seldom idle. Our new rifles are absolutely superb weapons and I have taken to mine like a friend, and take a great deal of care over it.
>
> On Monday we spent the whole day on the rifle range. I have never experienced a day of such extremes in all my life. We arrived out there just after eight; it is situated right out in the desert, miles from anywhere. All morning it was excessively hot and we just roasted as there was no shade anywhere. After lunch the wind sprang up and it soon developed into a minor gale, and as there was no shelter at all we just got smothered with sand. Then just after we had started for camp it began to rain; one of the few occasions when it does rain in the desert. The water fell in a solid sheet and in no time we were absolutely soaked from head to foot. The rain did not last for long. It was really grand marching on in the damp air; it was lovely and cool after the heat of the day. When we got back I had a cold shower and a change into clean clothes and I was feeling on top of the world.

Douglas Baker was sent on a technical course in Cairo where he stayed in the Abassia Barracks, which stank of tobacco and hash left by generations of soldiers. The evenings were free and apart from drinking and brawling in "Pole Nord, La Americaine and ... sundry illicit drinking dens". He also enjoyed the cinema. Currently showing to packed audiences at the Cairo Metro was *Gay Desparado* and *Random Harvest*.

Although the work pressure was harder than at school, Hodgson was delighted to be sent on a six-week wireless course at Helwan to become "qualified in something other than just a plain rifleman":

> At the moment I am not with the rest of the regiment as three of us were chosen from each squadron to go and attend a special wireless course and I was one of those from our squadron. The camp we are in at the moment is a hotel compared

> with the one where we were stationed. We are kept very busy here as we start at 7.30 in the morning and we work through until 1.15 with half-an-hour's break for tea; then after lunch we continue until five. It is just like school actually as it is nearly all lectures at the moment, but soon we will spend all our time on wirelesses. We are doing a large amount of Morse and I am getting on very well, as I can do four words a minute after four days. We have to be able to do at least eight and if you can do twelve or fifteen you pass out with honours so I am aiming to get as high as that.

The compulsory church parades were hated by almost everyone but the sport and entertainment had a positive effect on morale. The Union Defence Force entertainment unit, which was based in Helwan, performed on a collapsible stage. It featured some well-known names, like Gordon Mulholland, but nothing to match Bob Hope and the big bands that entertained the American troops. Noel Coward, a film star riding high on the success of his 1942 naval drama, *In Which We Serve*, was touring the Union and also performed in Egypt. Gerald Bright and his ensemble, better known as 'Geraldo and his Dance Orchestra' or 'Geraldo and his Sweet Music', was one of the most accessible entertainment groups of the time. Hodgson was a huge fan: "Geraldo and his orchestra have just arrived in Cairo and I intend going to see him play as soon as the show opens as it will be great fun to say that I have seen him play to all my friends, as he is one of the jazz-band favourites. If you remember most of our best records are played by him."

Sports fields were dotted among the tents, separating the regimental lines. Men played football, hockey and rugby on the sometimes hard, sometimes sandy, always uneven ground. Football was quite popular as it was the only convenient game to play on soft sand. Hockey was the sport of choice for men of average build. Rugby was best left to the professionals. In the Natal Mounted Rifles, "the regimental personnel were mainly farmers; most were heavily built, older [than Douglas Baker aged 18] and frequently bald and toothless".[61] Even the football could get rough and an injury would result in a court of inquiry, as when Trooper A. Brown of the Natal Mounted Rifles injured his knee on 5 May 1943. The mandatory court of inquiry was held three weeks later. After calling a number of witnesses including the referee and the medical officer, the president of the court of inquiry, Lieutenant Frank, found that there had

61 D.M. Baker, *War, wine and valour*, p. 99.

been no misconduct. International matches took place at the Alamein Club in Cairo, and convoys of trucks took men to see South Africans establish their dominance over New Zealand in rugby:

> On Sunday last I went into Cairo for the afternoon to watch South Africa play rugby against New Zealand. We left camp here just on twelve on Sunday morning. We arrived at the rugby ground a little after one and managed to get some good seats. There was a large crowd estimated at ten thousand, of which there was not nearly a hundred civilians. The first game of the afternoon was between the two second teams. This game was a bit scraggy but fairly entertaining. Then the two first teams came on. They lined up on the field and Anthony Eden came out and was introduced to each one in turn. The game began and we were to see some very good and exciting rugby. At half time the New Zealand team was leading by five points to three and it looked as if South Africa was going to have a very tough time before they won. After the rest the South Africans were really on their toes and it was not long before they had their opponents on the run and at the end of the game they had nearly run them to a standstill. The final score was twenty-two to five—a smashing victory for South Africa.[62]

Desperate to find ways of keeping the men occupied, the division organized an 'art, stage and hobbies' competition in which men were encouraged to exhibit their artworks and creative skills. The Cape Corps put on a talent show and concert at the Empire Theatre, and classical music evenings brought some culture and finesse to North Africa. At the end of the year, Hodgson wrote home about a show to be performed by members of the Royal Natal Carbineers: "The regiment is putting on a play on the 29th of this month, entitled: *Journey's End*. I am not in it but I am going along to see it as I hear it will be very good. They are putting it on twice, for the whole camp to see it." *Journey's End* is a protest story about the trenches in the First World War and real explosions were used for effect. Half a year later in Italy, a real-life tragedy would unfold, uncannily connected to the play. For Douglas Baker, life in the desert was epitomized by dust and extreme heat in summer (reaching up to 55°C), cold in winter, flies, boredom, brackish water, flash floods, bully beef and biscuits, ticks, fleas, crabs and masturbation. But, as the training intensified, there was little time left for tedium or household chores. Hodgson describes the routine:

62 J.B. Hodgson–M.V. Hodgson, 9/11/1943.

> From now on we are going to get on with our training. We start at six in the morning and we don't finish until quarter past five in the evening. As you can see it does not give us much spare time and because by the time we have had supper and a wash and got our things fixed up for the next day, we will be feeling very much like bed.

By October the weather had cooled down and was relatively pleasant although the heat could, on occasion, return with a vengeance. Daylight saving came into effect at the end of October and clocks were set back one hour. By the end of November, there was a pronounced nip in the air and the men were grateful for their winter battledress and two extra blankets. Base camp routine consisted of washing and mending clothes, hygiene fatigues, kitchen fatigues, and hauling water and supplies. Route marches in the desert were an unwelcome pastime.

Thieving became a problem as Egyptian civilians took to loitering around the camp. Legend has it that they could steal a tent while people were sleeping in it. Men slept with their rifles under their blankets or tied to their legs. Theft was also prevented by passing a chain through the trigger guards of the men's rifles, "making a bundle that is almost impossible to carry away". Weapons had to be kept under direct supervision even during the day. There was a ready market for arms and ammunition and any person not serving in the armed forces was considered to be an arms thief.[63] Nevertheless, the prospect of cheap labour was too good to pass up:

> We are not troubled by having to do our own washing as the bunch of us have managed to get hold of a native to come to our tent each day and do it for us. He is one of the officer's batmen but he comes to us in our spare time and on the whole he is extremely cheap. Considering the hard conditions he has to wash under, he is the cheapest one we have come across so far.[64]

Sentries were instructed to challenge "Halt; who goes there?" three times. If there was no response, the sentry should loudly work the rifle bolt to insert a round in the chamber. If there was still no response, a shot should be fired above head height; and if still no response was forthcoming, another shot should be fired below knee height.

63 DODAR, Div Docs, Box 181, Standing Orders, Camp standing orders, UDF Adm HQ MEF.

64 J.B. Hodgson–M.V. Hodgson, 10/10/1943.

One night when returning to the Royal Natal Carbineers lines, Private Donald Ogilvie failed to observe the challenge and was shot through the right thigh by a sentry from 7/23rd Medium Regiment. According to witnesses at the court of inquiry, the Royal Natal Carbineers men had been drinking and "skylarking".

'Tent orderlies' were appointed as a further measure to prevent thieving. The men took it in turns to perform this duty. The tent orderly would be excused from all parades and training for the day and, besides seeing to it that nothing was stolen, would usually take it upon himself to tidy up the tent and do chores for his tent mates. Some would water the floor of the tent to keep the dust down. Ahmed Fawzy was an Egyptian who had a contract for the removal of swill. He also acted as a tailor, shoemaker and barber. On 9 July 1943, he wrote to the major-general of Khatatba camp asking to be allowed to sell fruits, ice cream and lemonade, acknowledging that these would first have to be examined by a medical officer. "With great respect to your Excellency, I beg to draw your attention that I lost and am still losing my money in this camp … I know I am dealing with the most venerable people and I am quite willing to accept your orders whilst such as my requests are diminutive."[65]

'Gypo-guts' was a common affliction as likely to be brought on by drinking the water as anything else, while a diet of bully beef and biscuits caused constipation. Water buffalo, which occurred commonly in the lands of the delta, often ended up in the pot to make a change from bully beef, although there was no disguising its taste. With no cows in the delta, buffalo milk was used even to make ice cream.

All dishes included desert grit as an ingredient. In a letter to his wife Ellen, Glen Easton wrote: "Have had awful heartburn since we came here. I wonder if it is the food! As you know, I have never been troubled by it before."

Hodgson, who did not complain much, told his sister: "The food here has not been too good so far but I don't suppose they have got properly organized as yet. We get boiled eggs for breakfast as a rule. They are Egyptian eggs and they are honestly not as big as a bantam egg; also they seem to collect a lot of water inside … The bread we get is white but it is very soggy." Hodgson lost four pounds in two months and consequently weighed 163 pounds. The effect of tinned rations on the digestive system is evident from Hodgson's

65 DODAR, Div Docs, Box 177, File AQ 3/26 Contracts.

correspondence: "I received the medicine that Lays sent up to me by Air Mail, last Saturday. The laxative arrived in good condition but the other stuff which I presume was camphor ice had suffered fairly badly from the heat, but don't worry about that as someone managed to get some for me from Cairo."

Rumours were rife, and sometimes even had substance. On 5 November, the division was informed that it would move to Palestine, but the move was cancelled one week later and training and preparation continued.

Hodgson was lucky enough to be away from Khatatba on a wireless course during November and his letters contradict the perception that Helwan was hell on earth for the soldiers:

> We have moved to a lovely little camp on the banks of the Nile in the midst of an old orchard … The camp does not consist of bungalows but of nice semi-marquees which are sunk right into the ground to protect them against the wind, as all the sides are built up of concrete. The showers and mess are both very near and not half a mile away as has been the case in the last couple of camps I have been to. To add to all these luxuries we have got mattresses and mosquito nets; the latter are necessary as the mosks [mosquitoes] are a pest here. The nets are also very useful during the day as we can put them over us when resting and thus keep all the flies off us, as they are a real nuisance during the heat of the day … after we had got settled in on Saturday we went off into Cairo for the evening. We got there just after dark which was earlier than we expected as we had the good fortune to get a lift on a lorry. Well, we went and had a grand supper at a very nice American bar; it was the first bit of good food that we had had for the last three weeks. First of all I had a large soup plate of really good spaghetti and tomato sauce with cream cheese on the top. This we followed with grilled steak, three eggs and chips, then ice cream and coffee. After we had finished we went and played snooker for three hours then went back to camp to a very comfortable bed.
>
> I took my time about getting up on Sunday. Just before lunch we went back to Cairo and went to the really posh joint there called Graffi's where we had a seven-course dinner which took us just over two hours. It beats any place in the Union I think and it was really good. It was a very nice place and we could sit and see fashionable people, who are very few and far between in that city. After lunch we walked round and had a good look at the place. Later in the afternoon we went to the skating at the roller-skating rink. We spent about an hour and a half down there which we all thoroughly enjoyed and it passed the time away well. It is not nearly as good as the ice rink is though but they have not got one up here.

There was a general feeling among the troops that they were over-trained. They worried that the war would be over before they could enter it. On 29 September 1943, Field Marshal Smuts addressed a big parade and made his famous promise: "*Julle sal daar wees*. You will be there." The daily newssheet gave a blow-by-blow account of Smuts's visit:

> ... Droves of war correspondents, broadcasters and photographers had gathered around the saluting base ready to snap into action ... As Oom Jannie got out of the Jeep, the parade noted with pleasure that he was wearing a tank beret. After a general salute, Oom Jannie addressed us, commencing in Afrikaans but switching to English and back again to Afrikaans frequently during his talk.

The famous passage which made such an impression is quoted verbatim in *el Bullsheet* No. 142 of 8 October 1943:

> Officers and men, dismiss from your minds the idea that the war is just about over and there is nothing left for you to do. You, the Sixth South African Armoured Division, will have to fight as South Africans have never fought before in their history before we see the end of this war. You will be there when the great final battles of the war are settled. The fortress of Europe will have to be attacked and demolished, and you will be there with your tanks in an effort greater than you have ever made before.

On conclusion of the speech, came the command: "Sixth South African Armoured Division: ATTENTION." The march-past took place in columns of 18 from the right, artillery leading, with the music provided by the bands of four regiments including the Imperial Light Horse/Kimberley Regiment, First City/Cape Town Highlanders, Special Service Battalion band and Cape Corps. Afterwards, Smuts, Sir Pierre van Reyneveld and General Poole climbed onto a Sherman tank for a photo opportunity. It was one of the seminal days in the history of the division.

Thursday 2 December 1943 – Saturday 1 January 1944: Almaza

Almaza was a Royal Artillery base, conveniently located north of Helwan, close to Cairo on the edge of the open desert. It had served as a civil airport prior to the war, and it was from this humble point that 28 Squadron South African Air Force ran the shuttle service at the end of the war. By 1944, the squadron was equipped with 30 Dakotas and 14 Ansons, and in that year transported 87,029 passengers and more than 36.6 million pounds of freight. Over-congestion was a problem at all transit camps and aerodromes. However, before hosting the shuttle service, in December 1943, Almaza was the site for a gunnery course attended by the 1/6th Field Regiment. Dubbed 'Cape Town' and 'Durban', training exercises saw all units, formations, vehicles and armaments put to the test day and night, churning up the barren earth into swirling fogs of fine dust. Training exercises inevitably resulted in some casualties and on 6 December, Sergeant P.A. Woodward (South African Medical Corps) and Private W. Worrall (First City/Cape Town Highlanders) were killed by a shell which fell short.

Training for gas warfare was still considered necessary. Stephen Bourhill found this a bit of a lark, and was especially amused by the Permanent Force instructor's pronunciation of the words "pungent odour". However, Hodgson took the training more seriously: "The gas masks we had were absolutely perfect and no gas got in, though the stuff burnt our skin terribly. It seemed just as if we had been covered with mustard, and it was all burning like it does when you put it in your mouth. Nevertheless after half-an-hour it had all worn off, much to our relief."

The tedium of the moonscape was relieved only at the *wadis,* where a little scrub could be found. This desert terrain meant that there was no opportunity to train on the narrow roads or mountainous landscape typical of Europe. The commanders of the division therefore had no option but to learn from others' past experience. While the division was training at Khatatba, a delegation was sent to Algeria to observe the British armoured divisions which had been involved in operations in the mountainous terrain of North Africa. The visiting South Africans learned about the importance of movement control (especially on a single road), the employment of an armoured reconnaissance unit, and the movement of the large divisional main headquarters in big bounds.

After completing his wireless course, Hodgson had the opportunity of operating on 'the net', an important part of tank warfare:

> The last couple of days have been the best as we have spent the majority of our time tearing about the countryside in armoured cars keeping in touch with each other all the time. We had two in each car besides the driver, and when I was not operating, I found it great fun to sit up in the top turret and watch all the people as we went through all the small villages. We would often sound the siren as we went through and it was a scream to see the look of surprise on their faces.

Standing orders dictated that all native dwellings, encampments and villages were out of bounds to all ranks. Nevertheless, some men were inclined to go looking for alcohol and 'Gippo bint'. On 20 December 1943, Trooper J.W. Davidson allegedly took an armoured car from the motor pool, picked up his friend Trooper A.L. Whittle and went for a joyride to a watering hole called Halfway House. After getting very drunk they drove to Bir Victoria near Wadi Natrun. The armoured car bumped into a hut and the men got out, roughed up a security guard and, according to one witness, demanded 'bints'. The evidence relates that a bottle of Zibib brandy was acquired, after which the events become blurred. The military and civil police were called but by the time they arrived, Trooper Davidson was dead, his skull crushed by the back wheel of the armoured car. It is not clear when or how this happened, although an autopsy was carried out and Trooper Whittle was acquitted of culpable homicide. Guy Fawkes was usually spectacular on the front line, but in 1943 it was something of a non-event, both in the Union and in Egypt. Christmas was more of an occasion, but frugal nevertheless:

> Christmas is past and we are back at work again. Over the holidays we had a good break from work as we did not do anything on Friday, Saturday or Sunday. Generally speaking all went off very pleasantly and we had the best time that we could expect which was enjoyable. All Friday we just had a general loaf and cleaned up. In the evening we all got a double issue of beer, so our section joined round in a friendly circle and we had a very chatty evening which was prompted by food we cooked on our petrol stove. On Christmas morning I was up early just after six; as I went to early communion. After breakfast I just lazed about; mainly lying on my bed in the sun reading. I did a bit of washing but that has become quite a pleasant way of passing the time, so I did not mind in the least. Lunch was put off until three o'clock when we had our Christmas dinner. This was a very jolly affair in which the officers all got dolled up and served up our food. We had the following for dinner—turkey, chicken, pork, rice, sweet potato and Christmas pudding. It was all very enjoyable but as you can imagine none of the portions was very big, and I really missed the usual second helping of turkey. The rest of the day—there was not much left of it mind you—we spent resting. In the evening we all got round in a family circle again and chatted. Much of the talk was of home and all those in the Union. There was a bit more beer to go round and we all drank to the health of those at home, the same as we had done on the previous evening. On Boxing Day I was again up early as I went to communion before breakfast; the rest of the day was spent sitting round and dozing in the sun.[66]

For those in camp, New Year's Eve came and went with none of the fun and games which had become a tradition on the front line:

66 J.B. Hodgson–M.V. Hodgson, 28/12/1943.

> At the moment I can imagine you all over in Pretoria at the Newbury's. How I wish I was there spending the weekend with you. As you can see it is New Year's Day—I am lying on my bed writing this by candlelight. There are only three of us here tonight, as George and the rest of them have been in Cairo for the day and have not returned as yet. They went in to watch the Springboks play rugby against the Kiwis (New Zealand). Today has been a quiet day as there were no parades; the three of us stayed behind as we were chosen to play in a Regimental Soccer Tournament—we could have gone in but we preferred to stay. We played our match this morning and were unfortunately beaten. The weather has been beastly all day, as there has been a terrific dust storm. So after lunch we came back to our tent and sealed it up as best we could and got into our pyjamas and went to bed as it was the best place. At teatime we made some lovely hot tea on our stove, which was very enjoyable. On New Year's Eve it was also very quiet, there were only four of us in the tent as the others were on guard. To celebrate the end of the old year we did the best we could by having a good meal. Each of the others produced a large tin of fruit and I put in a tin of milk—we made a very enjoyable dish. We went to bed early as there was nothing much doing.[67]

Little did Hodgson know, but the following year would present an opportunity to let loose on New Year.

Sunday 2 January 1944 – Friday 21 January 1944: Khatatba

Exercises called 'Grahamstown', 'Standerton' and 'Tussle' took place early in the new year in bitterly cold and windy weather—and under a blanket of secrecy. Some units had been involved in manoeuvres since the middle of December, living in the open. The objective of the exercise was to break through a narrow, strongly defended gap. The umpires were British and among the defenders were Imperial units "who had won fame in the Western Desert and Libyan campaigns".[68] It was early to bed and early to rise, even in base camp, for the duration of the training. Infantrymen lived in two-man tents; it rained on more than one occasion and everything got wet through. However, the men still managed to enjoy a few of the comforts of base camp, such as early morning coffee made on a petrol stove, and infantry training in the desert during winter, as described by Hodgson, seems almost enjoyable:

> This last week we had another bout of strenuous work and we have got back to our usual standard of fitness. With this cold weather one really does appreciate his bed.

[67] J.B. Hodgson–M.V. & W.A. Hodgson, 1/1/1944.

[68] *el Bullsheet*, Special Edition, 1/2/1944, p. 3.

> You at home hate getting out of bed on a cold morning so you can just imagine how we hate getting up when we are woken at four in the morning, it being pitch dark, a bitter wind blowing and not a tent or anything about us, as we are out in the open; that is when it is difficult to get up. Also when we are up it is still cold and then we go off and practise some dawn tactics or something like that, but it is alright when it is all over, and we sure do have a good appetite for breakfast at about eight o'clock.

It was a group of very fit but filthy men who marched back into base camp. There had been no showering or shaving for the duration of the training; in any case, winter dust storms sometimes made it futile to shower as one would be filthy before getting back to the tent. Fortunately, 'civilization' was only a short distance from camp, despite the exploitation, squalour and disease.

Cairo was a fleshpot; a melting pot of nationalities, all in uniform. Hodgson was shocked on his first visit there and vowed to his mother that he would never ever return. However, he had found that the dinner had been good and the taxis, although decrepit, were dirt cheap. Despite having been stung by the unethical business practices of the Egyptians, he tried to find something positive to tell his sister:

> Last Saturday I went into Cairo for the day but on the whole I did not enjoy it; mind you, I think we definitely went the wrong way about it, as we did not get a guide to show us all the places of interest but if we go in again we will make certain of doing the thing correctly. In my opinion and I think most will agree with me, that it is not a patch on Johannesburg, although it is very much larger. The streets are narrow (most of them), dirty and twisted. The majority of the buildings are not very large, and there are very few that are at all imposing. The place is absolutely crowded out with people in uniform and Gippos (that is the nickname for the Egyptians). On the whole I think they are a very slovenly and dirty race. The lower classes go round in something that resembles a nightshirt, and I could swear that these do not see the laundry very often. If you stand still for one minute in the streets to have a look around and get your bearings, a whole mob of these Gippos descends upon you with their wares and tries to get you to buy something. Also they are very cheeky and extremely rude at times. Mind you, this does not apply to all of them, mainly the lower class only; on the other hand the higher classes are quite courteous and clean in comparison.

When in Cairo, officers stayed at the Continental, the Carlton or the Shepheard Hotel on the Nile, with its expansive veranda and wicker chairs. Other exclusive establishments were the Union Defence Force Officers' Club and the Gezira Club where it was even possible to enjoy a game of golf. A good meal was always expensive, as were most other things, except a taxi. In the numerous curio shops, one of the popular items was a leather watch cover to prevent sand and dust from getting into the works. One had to be wide awake to avoid being overcharged.[69]

An escape from the seedy streets could be found in one of the many cinemas. A major hit of 1943 was *For Whom the Bell Tolls* with Ingrid Bergman and Gary Cooper. One cinema, the Femina, in Emad el Dine Street, played non-stop newsreel programmes during the day, free to the forces. Clearly, Hodgson's first cinema experience in Cairo was disappointing:

> We had a look round and at last we found the best place to go to, called the Miama. The film was called, *The Boy from Stalingrad*. Well, we went to this show. The inside of this place was not too good. It was a little smaller than the Plaza but the inside was something like the Parysia but the seats were a little harder. The place on the whole was fairly clean. The first half of the film was fairly good but then came the big film; somehow we managed to sit the first half hour out but in the end we had to get up and walk out. I think it is about the first film that I have walked out of; but in the circumstances I think it was practically impossible to stay.

At Khatatba, there were three open-air cinemas named after their familiar counterparts in Johannesburg. Different films were shown every night; very often, these were war films, regular tearjerkers which would crack the brittle emotions of young soldiers. When the lights came on, they would be careful to avoid eye contact so that nobody could see their tears. At Helwan, there were two outdoor cinemas, the Pall Mall and the Coliseum, where a plastered brick wall served as a screen and audience members arranged themselves on a hillside on the sand. Some of the films had not yet been released in the Union; while at Helwan, Hodgson saw *Du Barry was a Lady*, *Dr Jekyll and Mr Hyde*, *Ziegfield Girl*, *Time Out for Rhythm*, *Bitter Sweet*, *Sunny* and *You'll Never Get Rich* with Rita Hayworth and Fred Astaire. He watched some of the films twice.

Enlisted men on leave were directed to the third floor of Smuts House at 43 Sharia Cherif Pasha. Here there were hot baths, hot and cold running water in all the bedrooms, lounges, a library and a music room—"an excellent place to stay". Bed, bath and morning tea cost 10pt; breakfast, 8pt; lunch 10pt and

[69] A.E. Blamey, *A company commander remembers*, p.170; D.P.G. Putterill, personal information, interview, 8/3/2009; The Shepheard Hotel named after Samuel Shepheard and built in 1841 is often mistakenly spelled 'Shepherds'.

dinner 12pt. In the likely event there was no room, you might be booked into the YMCA or one of the many "good clean hotels",[70] courtesy of the Union Defence Force Institute. Some soldiers were accommodated in houseboats on the Nile. There were also some good, clean (military) clubs such as the SA Women's Services Club and the Empire Club. The Springbok Club was on the first floor of the Metro Goldwyn (Metro Cinema) building. It was well situated and its reading room, which was well stocked with reading matter and free writing materials, was a haven of peace and quiet.

Gezira Island is in the middle of the Nile River, connected with a number of bridges to central Cairo. On the island was the newly opened Alamein Club with its large grounds, sporting and recreational facilities, as well as a restaurant open to all soldiers. Set among beautiful lawns, dotted with trees, there was a swimming pool, golf course, tennis courts, squash courts, sports fields and a roller-skating rink. The club also offered 13 full-size snooker tables.

Entertainment offered at Smuts House, the Victory Club and a club called Music for All included a daily music concert, lectures and plays.

Those wishing to tour the area could consult the *New Guide to Cairo* which listed places of historical interest like the pyramids and the Blue Mosque, as well as museums and other attractions such as the Zoo Gardens and the Bazaar Area. Although some serious types hired guides to take them to the historical sites, few would have found this information useful as the favourite pastime was carousing in the brightly lit bars, clubs and cafés which were to be found on almost every street corner. All were licensed to sell liquor up until ten o'clock at night—and closing time could easily precipitate a bar brawl. Cabarets were patronized by civilians and soldiers of all nationalities. The Bardia was a large, elegant music hall with a long bar counter. Entertainment on offer included a jukebox, live music and the usual belly dancing. The routine was the same at La Americaine and the Royal. Food was cheap, but the drinks were not. The 'hostesses' would flirt with the soldiers while ordering 'Champagne' (which was, in fact, simply coloured water) at £5 per bottle. At the end of their leave, men would invariably arrive back in camp totally fleeced.

In the streets, urchins would offer the services of their 'sister' or 'mother' and escort clients to a house or brothel. Such an experience could involve a single

---

70 An Egyptian pound was made up of 100 piastres which amounted to 2½ piastres (or six pennies) more than the South African pound; Cairo information for Union Defence Force Personnel. p. 2, *A new guide to Cairo*, Lehnert & Landrock.

prostitute servicing a long line of hard-up men of all nationalities and races. Alternatively, one could make a selection from a range of services. Gordon Mulholland, a well-known entertainer, recorded that sex with a 17-year-old prostitute in Cairo cost 2/6 and included a little cake of soap and a condom.[71]

A pamphlet containing 'do's and don'ts while on leave' strongly advised men not to risk VD, but if they had done so, they were urged to visit the clinic AT ONCE. "Don't delay," it read, "safety is allied to speed." Regardless, the men were subjected to 'short arm inspection' on a regular basis in order to be proclaimed FFI (Free From Infection) ... or not.

For the final week of his course, Hodgson was fortunate enough to be based at Heliopolis, five or six miles from the city centre (three miles from the airport). The 'village' was just outside the army camp and was easily accessible, with train fare into Cairo costing 2½ pence. Heliopolis was largely populated by French people. It boasted pretty gardens and hotels and offered most amenities, including the famous Heliopolis Club. The Commonwealth War Cemetery was opened here in 1941 for burials from the many hospitals in the area. As winter began to bite and the camp routine became tedious, Hodgson's optimism turned to melancholy:

> I received a lovely balaclava cap with today's post which Mum knitted for me; it is a lovely one, and it fits me perfectly. Also it keeps me so warm that I hate taking it off ... The hot weather is definitely over now; in fact the winter has set in with a vengeance. Now and again we get a warm spell but even then one has to stay in the sun all the time to feel really warm ... I can just imagine how beautiful all the flowers are in the garden at this time of year. What with all the rain you have been having all the suburbs must look very nice ... At the moment I am sitting in the tent on my folded blankets writing on one of our water tins. It makes quite a good desk and it is fairly comfortable. Some of the others have gone to see a film—I have not the faintest idea what is showing. I very seldom go as I prefer to sit in the tent and read and write. There are a couple of others here in the tent who are either reading or writing. I don't suppose it will be very long before we are in bed even though it is only just after six at the moment; but as we are always up before six it is nice to get to bed early.

Saturday 22 January 1944 – Sunday 19 March 1944: Helwan

Today, Helwân, or Hulwân, is the last stop on the Cairo Metro after the Helwan university, ten miles south of Gisa and 20 miles from the city centre.

---

71 J. Crwys-Williams, *Mood of a nation*, p. 192.

During the war, it was the site of a large base camp, officially called No.1 R&T (Reserve and Transit) Depot. It was situated on ground allocated by the Egyptian government. The camp was originally intended for 5,000 men accommodated in 20 blocks, each housing 250 soldiers. Other facilities included an administration block incorporating the camp reception station. The military referred to the civilian settlement as 'Helwan Village'.

Hodgson described the change in scenery between Khatatba and Helwan:

> At our old camp it was all sand and not one bit of vegetation anywhere, but one very startling thing that I noted was, when we travelled towards the delta of the Nile … all of a sudden you come over the hill and it is all green in front of you. It is not a very nice green, in fact it is a very dirty type, but there is a definite line of distinction between the green and the sand; it is remarkable how the sand will run right up to the first row of trees without a blade of grass in it, and from then on there will be hardly any sand. Also travelling to Cairo by rail; all the way except near Cairo, it is very well vegetated and even cultivated land, yet on the other side it is just sand as far as one can see … A very pretty sight that I have seen since we have been at this camp is the remarkably brightly coloured sunsets. They are really wonderful to look at, and to add to this is the sight of the pyramids in the foreground. There are three of them situated to the west of our camp.

In January the division as a whole moved from Khatatba to Helwan. The move took place in two phases which were detailed in a nine-page order. The first phase involved a march of ten miles in the direction of Alexandria over a period of three days, at a speed of two and a half miles per hour. The march would start at 0330 hours on 18 January, 0130 hours on 19 January and 0100 hours on 20 January. In Phase II, troops were to be moved by continuous transport service beginning at 0700 hours on 20 January. Full marching order was worn plus greatcoats, and one blanket was to be carried.

At this late stage, reinforcements from the South African Air Force Regiment arrived at Helwan on 22 January to be amalgamated with the Natal Mounted Rifles. New equipment continued to arrive. Helwan was not too overcrowded yet and Hodgson was not complaining after Khatatba:

> This place here is like coming to a hotel after being used to the place where we have been camped. Here we all live in bungalows but there are no beds or anything like that but you have no idea how nice it is to be sheltered from the wind and have a nice concrete floor to sleep on. There is plenty of room in the bungalow as there are only a few of us in it. The food is also very much better; the mess is also very nice and well equipped in that there are tables and benches; also the food is well cooked

> and well served up and we get as much margarine and jam as we like for every meal. The mess is a terrific distance from our bungalow as it takes us nearly ten minutes to walk there.

The dislike of divisional parades was surpassed only by that of church parades, which took a chunk out of a Sunday's relaxation. A parade was held on 1 February, the first birthday of the division. Hodgson was one of the 'lucky' ones chosen for the march past:

> Thirty of us have been chosen to represent the regiment in the march past at a retreat ceremony on Tuesday. I happen to be one of the 30. (It is said the smartest have been chosen, but myself, I doubt it.) All of us have been excused from normal parades, and instead we go to a short rehearsal for the march past—that is why the last week has been such an easy one. This is supposed to be a very posh affair, and the salute is being taken by the Commander-in-Chief of the Middle East.

Among the pack of photographers present was a representative from the BBC, and a recording of the event was broadcast from Daventry. Hodgson was in the front row and speculated that parts of the parade would appear on *African Mirror* in due course. Field Marshal Smuts and General Sir Bernard Paget, commander-in-chief of the Middle East, sent messages of congratulations on the occasion. After vowing to fight until the unconditional surrender of the enemy, who "are tough and skilful fighters" and "have their backs to the wall of disastrous defeat", General Paget concluded:

> You have all volunteered to fight for the cause anywhere in the world. And that is a splendid sprit, on which I congratulate you, for it will make you as invincible a team on the battlefield as you are on the rugger field … To my mind, the redeeming feature of the war, is the spirit of comradeship it creates, a spirit which is often so lacking in time of peace. And perhaps the most remarkable example of comradeship in the history of the world is that between your country and mine. Less than 50 years ago, we were bitter enemies, fighting a bloody war against each other, and now we are fighting as one in the common cause. And no man has done more to achieve that remarkable comradeship, than your great leader, Field Marshal Smuts who personifies all that is best in the British Commonwealth of Nations. In our comradeship, I include Non-European troops who are doing their full share in helping to win this war, and I welcome their sense of service in so doing … I wish you all good fortune and Godspeed in your great endeavours both in war and in peace.[72]

[72] *el Bullsheet*, Special Edition, 1/2/1944, p. 1.

Once again, there was talk of this highly trained division assuming a peacekeeping role in Palestine. An advance party was sent to the area on 7 February, but returned to Egypt within a week. Some thought that this must have been a deception plan or a training exercise, while others had visions of remaining in North Africa as garrison troops for the duration of the war.

Soldiers had made short trips to Cairo throughout the previous year; now many had chance to visit Alexandria and Palestine, for in the middle of February they were given a seven-day pass. Bourhill and his companions went to Tel Aviv in the 'Promised Land'. Hodgson also put in for Palestine, but only one man in his platoon made the cut so he went to Alexandria with his tent mates instead. Always looking on the bright side, Hodgson rationalized that Alexandria was "one of the noted places on the African continent".

More than one Jewish soldier travelling to Palestine felt the same sense of awe experienced by his ancestors as they emerged from the Sinai desert and beheld the green fields and mountains. Tel Aviv was a brand-new metropolis with modern buildings, wide boulevards and spacious continental cafés, and it was sparkling clean.

Like Cairo and Alexandria, Tel Aviv's usual population of 162,000 was supplemented by the military personnel of many nationalities. The neighbouring city of Jaffa had a population of 110,000 but much of it was out of bounds to Allied personnel.

Most soldiers had never before toured a foreign city, so the Union Defence Force made an effort to give them support and guidance. A list of dos and don'ts was distributed, together with a map of the city, from the Town Major's office. A party of 7,000 South African soldiers toured Palestine in a single visit during 1943. Jews and non-Jews alike were overwhelmed by the hospitality they received as they travelled across the country, a land overflowing with milk and honey (relatively speaking). Those with a farming background were impressed by the agriculture and the way of life found on the *kibbutzim*. Some spent nights in private homes in the settlements or 'colonies'. Day trips could be made to Jerusalem (40 miles), Gaza (52 miles), Nazareth (86 miles) and the Dead Sea (65 miles).

Soldiers enjoyed subsidized prices at restaurants, clubs and cinemas, except at the Orion. Among the dos and don'ts was the instruction: "Don't expect your girlfriend to be charged military prices". Prices for barbers, laundries, taxis, drinks and cigarettes were fixed by the army of occupation.

In terms of accommodation, options included TocH, War Comforts Hostel, St Andrew's House and Hibbert House, as well 66 hotels. Some of the Jewish residents also opened their homes.

Three different brands of beer were available (Gold Star, Eagle and Pioneer), but draught was cheapest. A packet of cigarettes cost about the same as a bottle of beer and the selection included Players, Craven 'A', Gold Flake, Capstan, State Express and Woodbines.[73]

Contrary to popular belief, soldiers did not simply run amok in foreign fleshpots. Military discipline prevailed. The military police ensured that uniforms were smart, officers were saluted and arms and ammunition were handed in to the armoury. Compared to the freedom of Cairo and Alexandria, the Palestine leave option was more like an organized tour, with certain days at liberty. Palestine provided an opportunity for the Jewish soldiers to be among their own people and absorb their heritage. The other soldiers, like any other young people on holiday, were mostly there for the beer, which was disappointingly unlike the South African Castle and Lion.

On the seventh day of the 1944 trip, the men travelled back across the desert, over the Suez Canal by way of a pontoon bridge and into bondage at their base camp on the Nile. Once the 6th South African Armoured Division had departed for Italy, members of the reserve regiments still in the Middle East had an opportunity to go on leave. The author of the Reserve Artillery Regiment war diary wrote on 6 April 1944:

> The Jewish Padre has exerted his influence and 'skinned' the Egyptian Railway of one of their 'De Lux' trains to take the chosen few to Palestine for the Passover. Twelve of our more religious Jewish personnel have elected to undergo this long and tiring train journey and will be away until the 12th inst.

Alexandria, the cosmopolitan, mystic city of vice, porn and intrigue, was most appealing for a spot of leave. The city was cleaner than Cairo, but not much. Tatty blocks of flats and hotels were built right up to the edge of the promenade and the sea came up to the promenade wall. The harbour area had been bombed and buildings did not have to receive a direct hit in order to collapse.

---

73 TocH is a Christian service club open to all ranks dating from the First World War. The name is derived from the army phonetic spelling for Talbot House; 'Do's and don'ts– while on leave'.

In his memoirs, *Providence was my guide*, J. Bosman described Alexandria as an "incongruous juxtaposition of modern and ancient", typified by high-rise buildings and mud huts, western ladies and veiled eastern women. The foreign contingent was mainly French and Greek. Flamboyant trees lined the streets, not unlike Durban or the Lowveld, although these specimens bloomed in May, June and July rather than December.[74]

A popular watering hole for officers in Alexandria was the Cecil Hotel where the cuisine and other appointments were excellent. Enlisted men could stay in the Victory or any of the many private hotels. Sister Street (Rue de la Soeur) was the red light area of Alex where, among the many nightclubs, were the Thief of Baghdad and the Minorah Club. Along the crescent shaped beachfront of Stanley Bay were scores of hotels, pensions, nightclubs, cocktail lounges and restaurants. Hodgson gave a comprehensive account of an ordinary soldier's leave experience:

> We left by train for Alexandria on the morning of Thursday 24th. The journey down was quite a pleasant one, although it was on the long side; we arrived at our destination just on three. The journey back yesterday was worse as the train did a lot of messing about. Actually we had close on nine days leave because while we were in Alex our time of departure was extended from Wednesday evening to Friday midday, which was a very nice break. When we got there we first of all procured accommodation; we got a good big room with five beds in it (there were five of us.) It was a very nice place and the charges were fairly low for Alex. By the time we had got settled in it was just about dark, so we had dinner, and what a dinner it was, and when I think back I feel quite ashamed of all that I ate. This was the beginning of our eating which became our most important occupation as we used to have four or five meals a day. It was really grand to get away from all the routine, and we took full advantage of it. Our beds seldom saw us before midnight but on the other hand we only left them before ten in the morning on two occasions.
>
> It was good sleeping between clean sheets again and having hot baths; this was the first time that I have had a hot bath since leaving Durban. We used to take our time about getting up, then we would go out and have a shave (it's not right to shave yourself on leave). Most days we used to go along to the Alexandria Sporting Club and play tennis or squash. Here we would hire rackets and balls so we had plenty of exercise like that. It was really good getting back on the field of sport and we had some very good tennis. The courts were very good, all equipped with ball boys (I tell you, we really did our leave in style). This usually took us till two or three and after a hot shower we would return to town and have lunch; we never used to worry about the time, we just did things as we pleased. If we were walking past a decent

74 A.E. Blamey, *A company commander remembers*, p. 181.

restaurant and we felt hungry we would go in and have a meal, and as soon as we were hungry again we would go and have another meal. Some of the restaurants were very nice and in most cases the food was good. We had plenty of strawberries and cream as they were in season. As well as mealtimes there are always two shows every night at 6:30 and 9:30; there are some good cinemas but all a bit old-fashioned but quite comfortable. A great deal of the room is taken up with boxes. They are all much the same as The Standard. We saw about half a dozen films that were really good. Last Tuesday night we went to the opera which was showing, produced by a London Company, including Cyril Richard and Madge Elliot. It was entitled, *The Merry Widow*; it was very good and there was some lovely music in it; also the cast was good. We went along to the beach a couple of times, this is only small; it is called Stanley Bay, which is a very pretty place, and very pleasant, also the water looked very nice and clean. I did not swim but two of our party did, the water was too cold for my liking. The breakers are very, very small as the rise and fall of the tide is negligible (only a couple of inches).

We saw King Farouk's Palace which is quite nice, but I was not very impressed by it. There were five in our party: there was George, Frank Ledingham, Michael Wood and Ben Harley plus yours truly. As I have said our hotel was a very clean and pleasant place, besides being well run. It was fairly centrally situated and the sea was just round the corner. It was good to have someone bring you early morning tea, clean your shoes and wash and iron your clothes.

Last Saturday to celebrate my birthday, we had a very posh dinner and then went to a late show. On the whole we had a very merry evening, and I thoroughly enjoyed myself. There are most probably quite a few things that I have forgotten to tell you about but I will write again soon and tell you the rest as I cannot put it all in one letter. I will say that I thoroughly enjoyed my leave, and it was a very good break and I am itching to get down to some hard work again.

The division had been informed that a move was imminent but the destination was not disclosed. The men had recently been equipped with new vehicles of all types and on 18 March, 24 new guns arrived for 1/6th Field Regiment. They were painted green—an indication that there wouldn't be any more time in the desert.

A cold, dusty wind blew during these last days in the desert. In an atmosphere of excitement, the men began to pack for departure.

Monday 20 March 1944 – Wednesday 22 March 1944: Port Said

The previous month's leave seemed a distant memory as days blended into weeks and perceptions of time became distorted. Hodgson made one last foray into Cairo before leaving Helwan with Frank Ledingham as his travel companion:

> Tomorrow I am going into Cairo; we leave here at eleven in the morning and we come back at six in the evening. I am going with Frank Ledingham—only four from the company are allowed to go and we were both lucky in the draw. We are going to watch a United Services Boxing Tournament which ought to be very enjoyable and I will tell you all about it in my next letter. It will be a very nice break as I have not had a single break from camp for close on ten weeks—the time does fly.

Having been immunized against typhoid and a plethora of other diseases, the men were transported by truck to Giza and from there by train to Port Said; others took the train from the cement factory siding at Helwan.

The 7/23rd Medium Regiment recorded its first death of a European soldier the day before leaving Helwan. Gunner E. Carcenac passed away suddenly from meningitis. The disease had infected many men, who had required hospitalization. Other members of the division were diagnosed with cerebral malaria, apparently contracted in Helwan, on reaching Altamura in Italy.

Embarkation officers and staff had been hard at work for some days already when the men arrived. Tanks, guns and trucks had already been hoisted aboard with giant cranes. For security purposes, all distinguishing insignia, including the divisional flash and red tabs, were removed from the serge battledress. Badges were removed from berets and caps.

The hawkers in 'Bum Boats' on the water and the street sellers were not fooled, however. They advertised "tangerines, tangerines" to men of other nationalities, but on seeing a South African, they'd call out "*naartjie, naartjie*". It was the men's brown boots, the presence of the Cape Corps and the use of Afrikaans which gave away their nationality. Some of the men's baggage was emblazoned with the words, 'Union Defence Force'. One soldier wrote that "security was bad enough to convince us that this was an elaborate hoax, to convince the enemy that this was any division but the South African division".[75] Nevertheless, only the top brass and intelligence personnel knew that their destination was Italy.

The South African public was even more in the dark and it was only on 15 May that the *Cape Times* carried the story of 'How the 6th South African Armoured Division landed in Italy'. In the evocative style of the day, the report read:

75 E. Axelson, *A year in Italy*, p. 8.

> Soon bronzed and hardened soldiers of outstanding physique were moving up the gangways shouldering rifles, automatic weapons and bulging kitbags. In the grey light of early morning, the ships carrying the Division ... formed up in a big convoy which dipped westwards through a choppy white-capped sea.[76]

In reply to a question asked by his sister's friend Sue, Hodgson wrote the final word on his North African experience:

> You ask me how I like Egypt—well that is a difficult question to answer, because one's opinions of the place differed with moods, but I can safely say that once the war is over I will never return of my own free will! The statement about masses of flies is only too true, but this only applies in summer. It is also full of dirty, smelly and desperate Gippos. I think the war against Gippos is the hardest war, up here in Egypt.

Thursday 23 March 1944 – Monday 27 March 1944: *Derbyshire*

The convoy carrying the first batch of soldiers to follow the advance party sailed on 23 March. Other convoys followed: one, carrying the 7/23rd Medium Regiment, Royal Durban Light Infantry, Natal Mounted Rifles, Witwatersrand Rifles/Regiment De la Rey and the 11th South African Armoured Brigade, sailed on 15 April and sighted the Italian mainland on 19 April—exactly one year after leaving Durban. This convoy included the ships *Winchester Castle*, *Derbyshire*, *Sobieski*, *Circassia*, *Alcantara*, *Ascania*, *Tegelberg*, *Princess Catherine* and *Estonia*; four of which had sailed from Alexandria where elements of the First City/Cape Town Highlanders had embarked, joining later with the main convoy.

Hodgson's voyage with the advance party was a bit rough:

> The trip over was accomplished without mishap, although we struck a couple of storms and many were seasick; I was lucky enough to survive. When we landed we were greeted with very unpleasant weather as we disembarked in sleet; once since then we had a cold spell with more sleet, but the rest of the time the weather has been perfect; luckily the rain is over, but we have had a couple of pleasant showers.[77]

Only at the end of April did the Reserve Group of the 6th South African Armoured Division entrain at 'Cement Siding', Helwan. On arriving at Port Said, they were accommodated in tents and enjoyed 'swimming parades' in

76 V. Alhadeff, *South Africa in two world wars: a newspaper history*, p. 106.

77 J.B. Hodgson–W.A. Hodgson, 13/5/1944.

the morning and evening. The group which assembled included some nurses from 102nd General Hospital. This later convoy comprised eleven passenger ships and six destroyers. A Catalina flying boat and two fighters flying overhead were a welcome sight.

British troopships of the era were often named after English shires such as Lancashire, Oxfordshire and Gloucestershire. The HMS *Derbyshire (2)* was launched in 1935 as a passenger ship for Bibby Brothers & Co, Liverpool (Bibby Line). She was requisitioned by the Admiralty in 1932 and converted into an armed merchant cruiser and later, into a troopship. She had a length of 842 feet and was armed with two six-inch guns, two three-inch anti-aircraft guns, and machine guns. With this armament, she undertook convoy escort duty. HMS *Derbyshire* served as a Landing Ship Infantry during the invasion of Sicily and also carried troops to Anzio on 22 January 1944. In August 1944 she took part in Operation Anvil in the south of France. After the war, she was deployed to repatriate troops. It was a little too chilly for the soldiers en route to Italy to sleep on deck. As before, routine consisted of blackouts and lifeboat drill. Lifebelts were carried at all times, even during meals. "In the distance, destroyers foamed about the horizon … In the air, long-range bombers patrolled,"[78] Fielding writes.

The passage was too short for boredom to set in. The men attended lectures on what to expect in Italy; prayer services and practice shoots were held, although there was no disturbance from submarines or from the air. However, on 2 May, members of the Reserve Group on board the Polish ship SS *Sobieski* heard three violent explosions. These caused some consternation, but no damage. "The theory advanced by experienced seamen was that submarines, believed to be chasing the convoy, had fired torpedoes from a considerable range, and they had sunk deep in the water when they exploded, violently shaking the ship, without damaging the plates."[79]

Meanwhile, a later convoy had a number of 'blue warnings': the first was a mine which it fired upon, the second was a submarine scare, and the third warning was issued because of the nearby presence of enemy aircraft, although none subsequently appeared.

---

78 W.L. Fielding, *With the 6th Div*, p. 40; *The Star*, 15/5/1944, Sixth South African Armoured Division now in Italy.

79 DODAR, WD, Box 630, Reserve Artillery Regiment South African Artillery, 6th South African Armoured Division Reserve Gp, 2/5/1944.

The demographics of the Royal Natal Carbineers is revealed in this textual snapshot of members of 7 Section, 7 Platoon, B Company, Royal Natal Carbineers, on the eve of battle:

> In your last letter you asked me to tell you about our tent. Well, I will tell you all about the chaps in our section. The seven in this tent are in it and two in another tent, making nine of us in all. First of all there is our Corporal: Corporal C.G. Mitchell, he has been with the Carbineers and has served up here for two years. He is considered as the best corporal in the regiment. We all call him Claud or by his nickname: Gideon. Then our Lance-Corporal Ellis-Shaw, he has also served his time up here before with the Carbs, he is a good chap like the Corporal. Then come the privates: there is John McClaren from Johannesburg, he is nearly 20, we have been together since we joined up. By the way our corporal is 23 and our Lance-Corporal is 22. Then Lawrence McNicholas, known as 'Mac', he is just over 17. Then there is George, known as 'Fat Sam'. Then Michael Wood from St John's. He was at Waterkloof with me. Benjamin Harley from St John's and Northern Transvaal, known as 'Ben'. The last two are about 18 and a half. Then comes Frank Ledingham from Port Elizabeth, we were together at the Kraal [Kafferskraal]. He is 18. Then last but not least comes yours truly commonly known as 'Smiler' as I am always smiling. All of us get parcels regularly but I think that George and I are a bit luckier than they are.[80]

Tuesday 28 March 1944 – Wednesday 29 March 1944: Taranto

It was early spring when the South Africans arrived in Taranto. The days were fresh and sunny but the nights were cold. Lionel Wulfsohn found Taranto to be "disappointing, but more pleasant than the desert … the grass and olive groves were a pleasant change". Gunner Peter Johnston kept a diary from the day he landed in Italy with the Reserve Artillery Group and noted that the green fields and red poppies were "amazing after the desert".

Douglas Baker's first impressions were that "Taranto is rather decayed … the people have an air of defeat about them and poverty is rife. Mentally, physically and morally they seem to have degenerated." He did notice that there were "some pretty children and a few beautiful girls". Others found the shoreline to be colourful with substantial buildings. Once the censorship restrictions were lifted, Hodgson wrote to his father: "It is very pleasant coming here after the desert and the contrast is that of two extremes."

The town was full of soldiers and sailors. Officers in transit were forced to sleep on the floor of dilapidated hotels. At Bari, the other major port at the foot

[80] J.B. Hodgson–M.V. & W.A. Hodgson, 1/1/1944.

of Italy, there was a South African hospital and some decent hotels. In Cairo, all Allied troops had been known to the locals as 'George', but when they landed in Taranto, they were met with the constant call for "Cigarette Johnny!" It did not take long for some drivers to stick notices on their windscreens saying '*niente biscotti, niente sigarette*' (no biscuits, no cigarettes). The shops sold little besides wine, scent and art. It came as a surprise to Hodgson that there was not a lack of food among the civilians: "There are lots of things that are unobtainable but there is a plentiful supply of agricultural produce, all those who beg in the streets beg for cigarettes, even the little children as young as four or three, and what's more they smoke them."

From Taranto, it was a journey of 50 to 60 miles along narrow roads through rolling fields of wheat and wild flowers to the concentration area around Gravina and Altamura. The road climbed a little from the sea, and the snow-clad peaks came into view once in open country. Hodgson's first impressions of Italy are profound:

> I will tell you a bit about the country, what I have seen of it to date; but I will only be able to tell you a very little because to tell you all would take a full pad but I will tell you bit by bit. The country to look at is very pleasant indeed; my personal opinion is that it is a storybook country; I say this because it looks exactly like the pictures you see in books—lovely rich green fields, much deeper green than I have seen before. It is all a little greener than the lucerne fields that you see at home. Most of the ground is under cultivation. I should say every single square yard of it except for the higher mountain slopes—with the result that the country looks like a massive patchwork quilt of different shades of rich green with patches of dark and light brown interspersed (ploughed fields). The mountains are really very pretty—on the films you often see through a window and right in the distance are beautiful snow-capped mountains. As it is spring now there is only snow on the higher parts of the mountains, although we have encountered sleet on two occasions; these two times are the only two cold spells we have experienced; the rest of the time the weather has been absolutely perfect. We have had two or three thunder storms—the first being on the boat coming over—it was really marvellous to hear thunder again. We never heard it in the desert so the last time I heard it was early last year in the Union … As I have said, it is spring and in places where there are enormous fruit orchards, the blossoms are very pretty. In the most southern portion it is nearly all grape vines and looks very much like the Cape except for the houses.

Thursday 30 March 1944 – Tuesday 2 May 1944: Altamura

A few miles west of the town in the direction of Gravina, south of the Foggia plain, was the big base camp of Altamura. Alternately muddy and dusty, at this time of year it was cold and depressing. For a while it was also the divisional headquarters. Altamura had previously been the site of the Campo di Concentramento No. 65, where South Africans and other POWs had lived two years previously in ankle-deep mud, struggling to survive on a typical daily ration of 80 grams of macaroni, a ladle of dandelion soup, 200 grams of bread and a tiny cube of cheese each day. As the new occupants cleaned up, they came across drawings and poems on the walls of the bungalows. In one of the workshops, a homesick South African POW had painted a wall mural of an ox-wagon with a background of aloes and mountains. Another showed Table Mountain in vivid green.

The sight of vast armadas of bombers taking off from one of the many airfields around Foggia and circling overhead did something to lift the spirits of the newly arrived troops.

The routine of guard duties, fatigues, church parades and training continued during the men's stay at Altamura. There were lectures on mines and mules, and tank crews went on map reading exercises.

There was little in the way of sightseeing apart from a beautifully decorated cathedral, but there was booze aplenty and some live music from time to time. The theatre in Altamura was situated in Piazza Mercadante where ENSA concerts and film shows could be seen. All restaurants were out of bounds, except those controlled by the Allied forces themselves, as were all brothels.

Major I. Moore, Brigade Major of 12th South African Motorized Brigade, was part of the advance party which arrived in Italy to set up base camp at Campo 65. According to him, there were no reception arrangements, virtually no facilities apart from the perimeter fence, no kitchens and no cooking fuel. In a 1948 interview, Moore blamed the poor organizing on the Union Defence Force Administration Headquarters and stated that base administration arrangements were shocking throughout the war. Hundreds of Italians had to be turned out of their homes so that the houses could be used as billets. This was done with the help of the local mayor as the Union Defence Force had provided no training in this area.

The camp at Altamura was totally overcrowded. Showers were rotated between units; for example, 1/6th Field Regiment was allowed to shower on Mondays, Wednesdays and Fridays.

Likewise, the local NAAFI, was unable to cope with the numbers and could only be used on alternate days.

While the main body of the division landed at Taranto, the various advance parties also landed at Bari and Naples. Hodgson had been chosen by lottery to go to Italy with an advance party about five weeks ahead of his regiment. He had been playing cards in his tent one evening when Lieutenant Arthur Newey entered and asked for a volunteer to accompany him on an observer mission to Cassino. He was to be hosted by the Scots Guards and it was their tradition for officers to be accompanied by a batman. When no volunteer was forthcoming, the matter was decided by drawing cards. Hodgson drew the Ace of Spades. The two were provided with a Jeep. Hodgson had never driven before, and it was a harrowing trip on the congested roads.

On arriving at Cassino that night, the Scots Guards supplied Newey and Hodgson with tennis shoes (to muffle any noise) and took them to their forward positions. Hodgson's reaction to the hectic activity, ammo dumps and smoke screens was one of bewilderment.

Despite censorship and secrecy, it took only a little imagination to be able to inform loved ones of the men's whereabouts. For example, Hodgson was able to convey the message by commenting on the lack of dust storms and the Canadian beer:

> The weather is quite pleasant these days, although it is still a bit chilly on occasions. The dust storms and all the rest are 'non est' any more.
>
> You will notice there is a marked absence of news in this letter. I am sorry but it is quite unavoidable as there is very little news, and what little there is would most probably be cut out by the censor. You know what it is, things here and there that one cannot mention, but I will be able to tell you it all in good time when we are allowed to—not that it is of any great importance.
>
> I am still very fit and happy as we are kept busy which makes the days much more enjoyable and one looks forward to his quart of Canadian beer each week. It's good stuff!

On Easter Sunday, 9 April 1944, Hodgson wrote: "It is hard to realize that today it is Easter. Nothing changes in the army for any day except Christmas and New Year's Day. On Friday I did not realize that it was Good Friday until late in the morning. This morning I went to communion which is the first time for quite a while."

Before the men had a chance to explore their new exotic surroundings at Altamura, they were issued a general order which included dire warnings about the dangers of venereal disease:

> In Italy, the VD sickness rate has been greater than the casualty rate. Italian women are causing as much damage as German men. At least four out of every five women here who will go with a soldier, are infected with gonorrhoea or syphilis or both. Many of them are suffering from a very virulent form of gonorrhoea.
>
> Uncured syphilis means insanity, heart disease, palsy, blindness, defective children, infected wives and results in inability to earn a living and enjoy life. Uncured gonorrhoea leads to damage and deformity to sex organs and to sterility. All men are reminded that in the interests of the Division, of their wives and children, and of themselves, they MUST avoid infection. The risk of infection when going with any woman who offers herself in this country is nearly 100%.[81]

The rain went away but the ground was still muddy at the end of April, when the artillerymen put finishing touches to their equipment and loaded ammunition into the limber. Frank Watson of the 1/6th Field Regiment Rhodesian Battery voiced the frustrations of all in his diary entry of 28 April 1944:

> We are all wondering when and where we are going into action, some say it will be very soon, I am inclined to believe it. I hope so in a way, because the bullshit about guards etc is getting beyond human endurance and imagination.[82]

Watson's feelings are understandable. In addition to the dress regulations being strictly enforced, and a clamp-down on 'unsoldierly bearing', the following order was issued:

> Since the arrival of the Division in this theatre, there has been a noticeable slackness on the part of ORs in saluting officers ... this may be due to an impression which appears to have been gained that in an operational area saluting is dispensed with. This impression is erroneous ... all officers will in future take particulars of any personnel failing to pay correct compliments and in glaring instances, will immediately place the offender under open arrest.[83]

The Royal Durban Light Infantry, which was becoming accustomed to changes, converted one of its companies to 4.2-inch mortars. Those who had been to the battle area gave lectures to an enraptured audience, one of which was titled 'Know your enemy'. The excitement was mounting. Hodgson was

---

81 DODAR, WD, Box 624, 1/6th Field Regiment, D.R.O 87/44, 22/4/1944.

82 J. Crwys-Williams, *Mood of a nation*, p. 359.

83 DODAR, WD, Box 624, 1/6th Field Regiment, D.R.O. 87/44, 22/4/1944.

by now back from his observer mission to Cassino and finding life in base camp intolerable:

> There is very, very little news up here these days, and apart from fairly heavy training—mainly getting fit, etc. there is nothing very much to report. I am still happy and enjoying the army life as much as it can be enjoyed, but as I remarked in my letter to Mum, that I am not contented as I want to get home and get on with some work and help you, instead of all this messing about.

As newcomers to this theatre, the South African troops received detailed instructions on how to behave. An order dated 22 April 1944 prescribed the base camp routine, starting with reveille at 0700 hours, roll call and sick parade at 0730 hours and last post at 2200 hours. Mealtimes, including morning tea, were only 30 minutes' long. Customized clothing was still an issue at this early stage, before supply problems and the ravages of winter made a mockery of such orders. Soldiers were warned not to modify their shirts in any way. No summer clothing was to be worn before 25 April.

Personnel were warned that inferior wine which had proved injurious to health was being sold at exorbitant prices. Worse still, some alcohol was 'poisoned' with wood alcohol and contaminated with lead. Several deaths had occurred and men were warned to be particularly careful in the Foggia area. Alcohol could be obtained in camp but only in an authorized mess or canteen area. The regular ENSA shows provided alternative entertainment for the clean-living Hodgson:

> About a week ago I saw *Sunny* again; it was really wonderful and I enjoyed it just as much the second time. It was put on by ENSA for us—they put one on every night, but I have only been that once ... At the moment I am very fit and full of beans. I had a touch of a cold a couple of days ago but I have got rid of that already.

The divisional artillery and 12 South African Motorized Brigade (with Imperial Light Horse/Kimberley Regiment under command) finally moved to the front. The remainder of the division would follow two weeks later, taking in the sights of Salerno and Mount Vesuvius en route. At Bari the tanks were loaded onto flatbed railway trucks and the journey continued through the beautiful scenery and many tunnels. From Caserta, the tanks were transported by road to the concentration area in Campania, around Limatola and Sant'Agata de' Goti.

Built in 1925, the luxury ocean liner *Île de France* was celebrated for its stylish interior. After being seized by the British in 1940, it was converted into a troopship. The stern is still recognizable although there are no *chaises longues* to be seen. *Photo: Author's collection*

Happy campers at Khatatba. Gnr J.V. Carmichael is back row right; he was killed on 10 June 1944. *Photo: Author's collection*

Polling day, 25 June 1943. *Photo: Author's collection*

'A' and 'B' subs of 'A' Tp 1/6th Field Regiment firing over open sights during desert manoeuvres. *Photo: Author's collection*

Training on tanks of various types. Crew members were trained as specialists in their own field but could do the jobs of others; everyone did maintenance work. In a Sherman, the gunner would be familiar with Vickers, Browning, Bren, 6-pounder, 75mm and 105mm. *Photo: DODAR*

'Brass Hats' pay a visit to the gun positions during training. Lt Harry Barker, second left, was killed in action on 12 June 1944. *Photo: Author's collection*

Long walk back to the lines after a parade at Khatatba. *Photo: Author's collection*

Christmas-time at Almaza: all spruced up to go on pass into Cairo. Note high-rise buildings in the background. Gnr S.F. Bourhill stands second from right. The rag-doll accompanied this group of friends through Italy. *Photo: Author's collection*

The original caption read: "Last day in Tel Aviv. Much beer on empty tummies produces smiles like these." *Photo: Author's collection*

Promenade in Tel Aviv; Old Jaffa in the distance. *Photo: Author's collection*

Tour group in Jerusalem. *Photo: Author's collection*

Section '7' of '7' Platoon, 'B' Company, 1st Royal Natal Carbineers. This photograph was taken in a *wadi* near Helwan during the final phase of their training. Of this group only John Hodgson would finish the war unscathed. Back row from left: Mennie, Hodgson, Wood, Cpl Mitchell, McClaren; front from left: Maj Gallimore, Lt Back, L/Cpl Airey, Ledingham, Harvey, Sgt Lee. *Photo: J.B. Hodgson collection*

At Port Said, embarkation officers and staff hoist aboard trucks bound for Italy. *Photo: DODAR*

First impressions of Italy: crisp spring air and looming mountains. *Photo: Author's collection*

The start of the 'North Passage' where the road from Acquafondata crests the hill and begins the descent to Vallerotonda and the Rapido River. *Photo: Author's collection*

Gun pit of 'C' Sub, 'A' Troop 1/6th Field Regiment at Acquafondata (Cassino). *Photo: Author's collection*

The big barrage at Monte Cassino on the night of 11 May 1944. *Photo: Author's collection*

Wine ration at Acquafondata; original caption read: "Cassino vino." *Photo: Author's collection*

At Sant'Agata, south of Cassino, Stephen Bourhill wrote to his mother: 'The water runs over smooth white stones and is about 1ft deep. We laze away the afternoon on the sand bank and sip vino bianco. High-wooded mountains on either side and a blue, blue sky on top! Only in Italy could this be so.' *Photo: Author's collection*

Bumper-to-bumper traffic on 'Highway 6' to Rome. It is still named Route 6 today and is virtually the same width. *Photo: Author's collection*

The most unusual battlefield grave of Tpr G.T. Ferriera (Natal Mounted Rifles), 17 miles north of Rome. *Photo: Tienie du Plessis*

6-pounder anti-tank gun in action at Bagnoregio with tracer bullets overhead. During the advance, 1/11th Anti-Tank Regiment worked up front with the infantry in a field artillery role. *Photo: J.B. Hodgson collection*

1/6th Field Regiment command post staff; Lt Harry Barker at left. *Photo: Author's collection*

Harry Barker's battlefield grave in a small vineyard near Bagnoregio. *Photo: Author's collection*

Originally captioned 'Front line!' Civilians continue to work the land as the war passes through. *Photo: Author's collection*

Typical overnight position in an olive grove. *Photo: Author's collection*

'Dust means death'. A well-garnished Sherman enters a typical Tuscan village. *Photo: DODAR*

Around Belvedere, close to where seven carbineers were scythed down, a German Spandau is inspected by Cpl van Jaarsveld of Wynberg and Rfn H. O'Connor of Johannesburg. *Photo: DODAR*

Idyllic *outspan* in a Tuscan vineyard; vehicles are well camouflaged too. *Photo: SANMMH*

Tank troop harboured in a farmyard while ploughing carries on in the age-old way. *Photo: DODAR*

First City/Cape Town Highlanders buried at Chiusi. From left: *illegible*, Pte J. McNaught-Davis; Pte L.G. Nash, unknown SA soldier, L/Cpl F.J. Ritchie, Pte G.H. Gush. *Photo: SANMMH*

'Sampie' de Wet, a member of the SAWAS, wrote of her journey from Rome to Florence: 'All along the way, thrown off to the sides of the road were the corpses of "shot-up" and burned out transport, mostly German, as ours had been removed for their spare parts. There were tanks, troop-carriers, staff cars, and other unrecognizable vehicles ... sometimes, there were Italians chiselling away at them, removing bits and pieces.' *Photo: Wikipedia*

A mountaineering feat performed by Sherman tanks near Radda in Chianti. *Photo: DODAR*

The 6th Division moved through Radda, Panzano and Greve, in the heart of the Chianti region. Views over the terraced vineyards have hardly changed but when this photograph was taken there were shells flying overhead in both directions.
Photo: SANMMH

Original caption simply says: "Jerry gun." *Photo: Author's collection*

PRIVATE LAURENCE GREGORY McNICHOLAS, of an infantry regiment of the Sixth Division, who was killed in action in Italy on July 21. He was the only surviving son of Mr. and Mrs. W. P. McNicholas, of Kensington. His brother, Lieut. Walter McNicholas, H.A.C., died of wounds in Italy on June 12. Laurence was educated at the Marist Bros. College, and joined the army at the age of 16, shortly after matriculating. He was 17 at the time of his death. A Requiem Mass will be said at St. Anne's Church, Belgravia, on August 5, at 8 a.m.

Military churning up quaint country lanes. *Photo: SANMMH*

Infantrymen riding into battle on the back of tanks pass through Mercatale, no doubt feeling very exposed and vulnerable. *Photo: J.B. Hodgson collection*

Notices such as this were often placed in the newspapers by the families of the fallen. Once or twice a month, newspapers published a roll of honour for all branches of the service, beginning with: 'The Department of Defence regrets to announce the following South African casualties ...' *Scan: J.B. Hodgson*

Dodge 3-tonner passing through a ruined village (probably Mercatale). Most of the walls are still standing which indicates shelling and not bombing. Holes in the slopes of the roofs facing the retreating enemy indicate it was given a 'stonking' by the Germans after they left. *Photo: SANMMH*

Artillery observers in a forward observation post; note how they sit to one side of the window to avoid becoming targets themselves. *Photo: SANMMH*

Well-dressed local ladies serve tea and sandwiches to soldiers on leave in Siena. *Photo: SANMMH*

Training and maintenance continued during periods of rest and reorganization. *Photo: DODAR*

Chapter Five

Rubble and roses

"Today the bad times are behind us and tomorrow we can see victory ahead … we are going to destroy the German armies in Italy. The fighting will be hard, bitter, and perhaps long, but you are warriors and soldiers of the highest order, who for more than a year have known only victory. You have courage, determination and skill. You will be supported by overwhelming air forces, and in guns and tanks we far outnumber the Germans. No armies have ever entered battle before with a more just and righteous cause. So with God's help and blessing, we take the field—confident in victory."

—H.R. Alexander, General, Commander-in-Chief, Allied Armies in Italy, May 1944

Wednesday 3 May 1944: Isernia

Spring was well on its way; flowers were peeping through and the trees were budding. The nights still had a bite but the days were comfortable. An air of excitement prevailed. It was a time for the last-minute preparation of equipment, for pondering the beauty of the surrounding mountains—and the future. Having travelled the 120 miles from Altamura, through the wheat fields of the Foggia plain, the 1/6th Field Regiment was finally told that it would be taking over from a Canadian regiment in the line.

With only a short distance to travel from the assembly point, the gunners had a sleep-in and enjoyed a last hot shower courtesy of a mobile British bath unit. They then began pulling the guns up the steep track to Acquafondata with the help of two Canadian bulldozers.

The signs of war were now visible. By 1900 hours, when the guns were finally in position, a heavy mist set in and with it came a feeling of unease. The mediums moved up from their concentration area at Baiano, and established their headquarters at Isernia.

On 2 May, the Royal Natal Carbineers gathered at a point near the top of the Inferno Track which led down to the Rapido River. David Alexander, of 7 Platoon, B Company, Royal Natal Carbineers, wrote of his initiation to war:

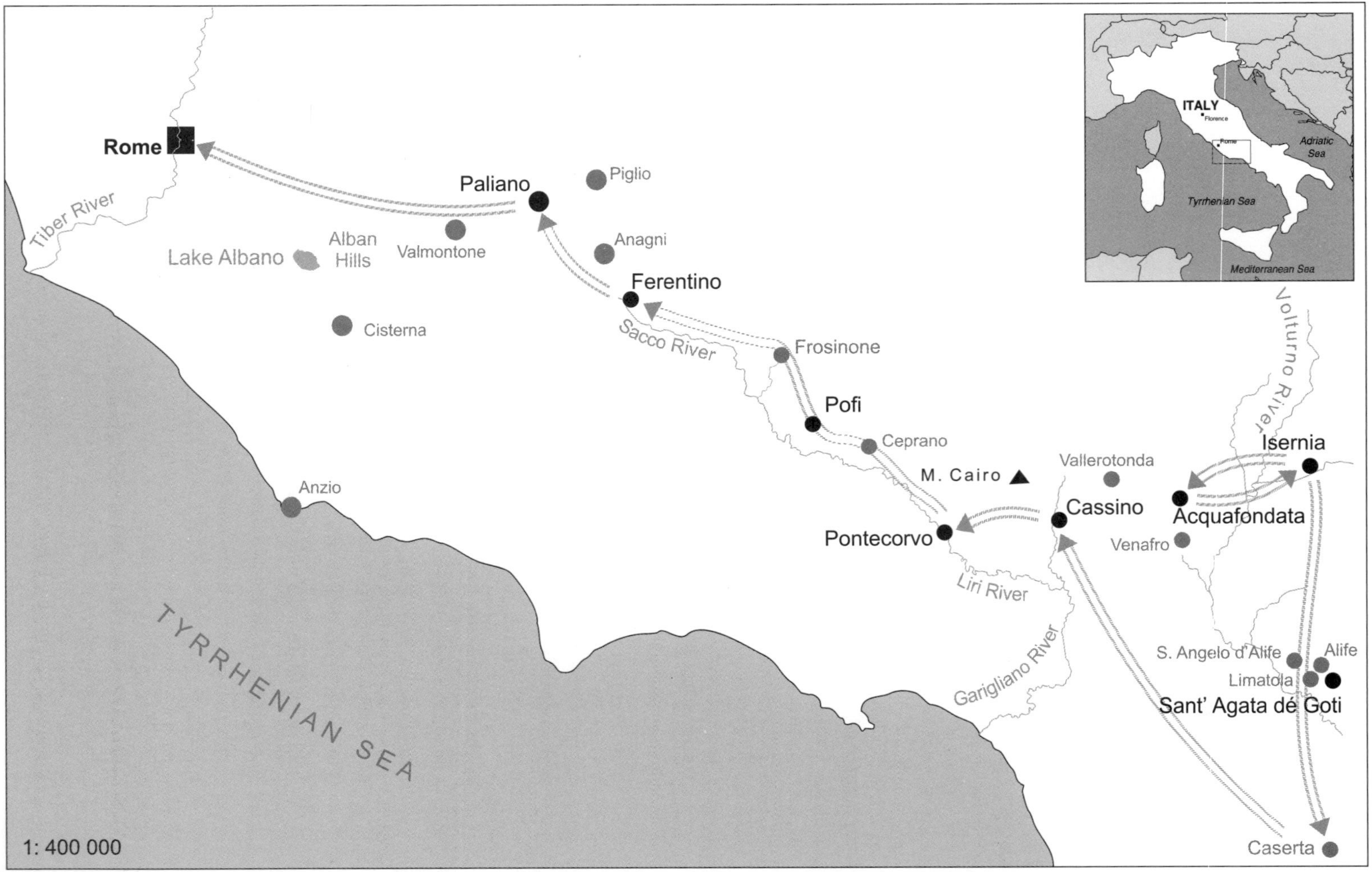
ITALY
Florence
Rome
Adriatic Sea
Tyrrhenian Sea
Mediterranean Sea
Rome
Tiber River
Paliano
Piglio
Valmontone
Anagni
Lake Albano
Alban Hills
Ferentino
Cisterna
Sacco River
Frosinone
Pofi
Ceprano
Isernia
Volturno River
Vallerotonda
M. Cairo
Cassino
Acquafondata
Venafro
Pontecorvo
Anzio
Liri River
Garigliano River
S. Angelo d'Alife
Alife
Limatola
Sant' Agata de Goti
TYRRHENIAN SEA
Caserta
1: 400 000

> I was 18 and very concerned about showing my fear. I avoided talking in case the tremor in my voice betrayed my feelings. From the distant, gentle, almost inaudible murmur of gunfire we heard at our preparatory base in the small village of Gravina, we were now in the midst of the thunder. At Hove Dump, close by, a 5.5 gun fired without warning and my heart leapt.[84]

The Inferno Track was in full view of the enemy and could only be travelled at night. At the end of the road was the depot, known as Jeephead. From here, the Carbineers walked in felt-covered boots to the positions along the Rapido River now being vacated by the Canadians. Mules, also felt-shod, carried their equipment. Shells crashed into the road that had led them to their current positions.

Many were facing a baptism of fire but David Alexander was alone in expressing his true feelings that night: "Certainly, there was a degree of fear and elation, but it was not the cold, bowel-weakening fear of waiting for a beating outside the prefect's room … on that moonlit night under fire, there was no guarantee of being hurt. You might be one of the lucky ones."[85]

Thursday 4 May 1944 – Sunday 21 May 1944: Acquafondata

While the rest of the division continued training at Altamura, the 12th South African Motorized Brigade, together with the artillery, was given its first taste of action at Cassino. The 25-pounders were positioned in a valley a few miles from Acquafondata, toward Vallerotonda. It was possible to see Monte Cassino and the surrounds from the wind-swept ridge in front of their camp. Meanwhile, the medium 5.5s were based in another valley, closer to the village, which means that civilians lived in close proximity to the guns. The South African sector also encompassed the village of Venafro on the plains to the rear, where the Moroccan-style French cemetery is situated.

Acquafondata was the supply base from where the infantry moved into their positions. Supplies were transported at night down treacherous tracks to Jeephead, from where they were carried in on foot. The town of Cassino was the biggest centre on the road between Naples and Rome, about 75 miles south of the capital. The Battle of Monte Cassino had been raging for months

84 G.B. Hobbs, *From Sicily to the Alps*, p. 87; According to 7/23rd Medium Regiment war diary, the 5.5s fired their first shot on 5 May, scoring a direct hit on an enemy observation post.

85 G.B. Hobbs, *From Sicily to the Alps*, p. 88.

before the 6th South African Armoured Division arrived on the scene, and all 22,000 citizens had either fled the town or died. In early January the front line had run right through Acquafondata and the town was destroyed. The French colonials had passed through here during their approach to the Gustav Line and the local population had been traumatized. Bourhill wrote to his mother the day after his arrival at Cassino (which, apart from the aircraft overhead, was not unlike a scene from the First World War). His letter was rambling and emotional, containing cryptic clues which left her in no doubt that her son had now arrived in harm's way: "Remember, there is nothing to wonder or worry at … never will be as far as I'm concerned … It's because my spirit is so near to yours, day and night. I feel so at peace with the world and near to you. I guess it is easier for me, being at the business end of things, so to speak."

The task of the infantry (the 12th South African Motorized Brigade together with the Royal Durban Light Infantry) was to hold the line at all costs and keep an eye on the enemy. This involved night patrolling, mainly to capture prisoners. One South African wrote: "Plenty of action … never seen so many dead soldiers, never-ending stream of ambulances filled with the dead and dying." There was a stench of death in the Rapido Valley where the infantry lived in scattered farm buildings in shallow trenches behind sangars. The Royal Natal Carbineers, in particular, were under the enemy's nose—booby-traps and mines littered the place. It was the dead mules that caused the worst stench in this sector.[86]

The weather was warming up. There was shelling from one side or the other every day. On Sunday 7 May, Frank Watson wrote: "For a long time to our left, the noise has been like continuous thunder. This morning has been more peaceful but it was the calm before the storm because soon after two, Jerries began ranging with airburst on a nearby crest.

Then the fun started. Our mediums opened up, but it did not stop Jerry, and the crest under heavy fire was switched over to the front of us."[87] According to Eric Axelson, the historical recording officer, the brigade's main action at Cassino occurred when a fighting patrol of the First City/Cape Town Highlanders killed six Germans.

---

86 S. Monick, *A bugle calls*, p. 340; J. Kros, *War in Italy*, p. 38; W.L. Fielding, *With the 6th Div*, p. 56.

87 J. Crwys-Williams, *Mood of a nation*, p. 361; E. Axelson, *A year in Italy*, p. 12.

Although there was never a dull moment during this deployment, what with the intermittent mortaring and shelling in both directions, it was at night that the front came alive. The events of the night of 10/11 May as experienced by the First City/Cape Town Highlanders can be appreciated by this extract from the regimental war diary:

1955	Jeephead shelled
2005	R Coy mortared
2230	CO returns and has conference with coy comds at Bn HQ re forthcoming ops
2325	C Coy mortared—R/T com out with pls
0030	Lt Jackson and 1 O/R killed while on recce patrol
0307	Jeephead shelled

It was only on 10 May that the men of the 6th South African Armoured Division were allowed to reveal their whereabouts to their families. Hodgson wrote a light-hearted letter to his sister before going out on a patrol where the Carbineers would incur their first casualties:

> "How is my little ray of sunshine this morning?"—One of the many expressions that remind me of home. At the moment I am a long way from home—even further than you think— this will no doubt surprise and puzzle you, but the answer is a simple one—I am in Italy at the moment, hence the slight change of address. You are the first person to know this because this is the first day we have been allowed to mention it in our letters. If you get a chance this evening you can phone up Dad and tell him as I am sure he would like to know; I will be writing to him in a couple of days but today I can only manage a letter to you. There is no need whatsoever to get worried or anything like that because I am quite safe and perfectly happy.[88]

The men of the Royal Natal Carbineers' Section 7, 7 Platoon, B Company were returning from their first mission on the night of 10 May when they set off one of their own booby-traps. Lance-Corporal Bruce Airey of Uitenhage was killed and two others were wounded right beside Hodgson. At 23, Bruce Airey was a father figure and had played a major role in the lives of his men for almost a year. The Royal Natal Carbineers' area then came under heavy attack, and the men called for the support of the Royal Durban Light Infantry which

[88] J.B. Hodgson–D.M. Hodgson, 10/5/1944.

fired 6,000 rounds from its machine guns. A few nights later, another patrol of the Royal Natal Carbineers met a similar fate. Lieutenant Michael Corbett, who was to become Chief Justice of South Africa in 1989, was leading a night patrol to investigate enemy positions and capture a prisoner. The hillside was thick with trip-wires. An 'S' mine killed three men and fatally injured a fourth. The young lieutenant was unhurt and summoned a stretcher party to carry away the remains of his men.[89] All are buried in the Commonwealth cemetery at the foot of Monte Cassino.

The Witwatersrand Rifles/Regiment De la Rey was in a holding position in the hills, but still within range of artillery and mortars, as the war diary of A Company shows:

> Wed 10 May
> A grim day this! At 10.55 hrs this morning, three shells fell in the company area, shrapnel killed Rifleman van Aswegen outright and wounded Lance-Corporal Cunningham R.E. in the back so severely that he died 40 minutes after ... They were buried in a common grave just below the road. The Padre, Captain Cloete, performed the poignant ceremony.
>
> Thurs 11 May
> An outstanding day this indeed! At an order group held in the morning, it was officially disclosed that tonight at 23.00 hrs ... the Allied Armies would launch their spring offensive.[90]

On the night of 11 May, South African artillery contributed to the massive bombardment in support of the Polish attack on the monastery. Spectators of all kinds, military and civilian (including a multitude of war correspondents), found a vantage point from which to view the fireworks display which started at 2300 hours and continued through the night in a series of concentrations. The fire-plan scheduled a single gun to fire 620 rounds in five hours and forty minutes, or one round every thirty seconds.

Some said that the sound of the guns was louder than thunder. "In the mountains it became almost impossible [to hold a conversation] because of the lingering peals and echoes."[91] According to the historian Axelson, the hills

89 G.B. Hobbs, *From Sicily to the Alps*, p. 84. Three months later, Corbett was injured in a road accident which ended his campaign.

90 S. Monick, *A bugle calls*, pp. 342–343.

91 J. Kros, *War in Italy*, p. 52.

in fact muffled the noise and the Cassino barrage was not as loud as that at Alamein. The enemy-held slopes were in blackness, but lit up with red flashes where they were hit by shells. A larger orange puff would materialize when a gun position or ammo dump went up. Streams of tracers lit up the corridors through which the infantry would advance. As the Battle of Monte Cassino reached its crescendo, the artillery barrage died down.

That evening the gunners "got one beer and there was some mail".[92]

The next day, Frank Watson wrote: "As the large shells passed over us on their way to the enemy lines it was like an express train in a tunnel. It was amazing, almost incredible to those of us for whom all of this was a new experience."[93] Watson did not record that one gun detachment had a narrow escape when a 170mm shell drilled a hole through the wall of one of the gun pits, missing the gun by inches and coming to rest 100 yards up the opposite slope. Axelson recorded that two men at brigade headquarters were killed and four wounded in a bombing raid by British aircraft on 12 May.

According to the war diary of 1/6th Field Regiment, it was very quiet on 14 May, quite an anti-climax after the barrage of the night 11 May. It was several days before the enlisted men received any news of the attack's progress. At the time, the gunners were not aware that they were firing at the wrong mountain in a diversionary shoot to confuse the enemy. In fact, it was many years before the men understood their actual role in the battle.

Only now that the battle of Monte Cassino was well under way did the South African public read in the press that their boys had landed in Italy. A report in the *Cape Times* of Monday 15 April described in great detail the embarkation process in Egypt, the uneventful voyage and the move inland. The same newspaper, in the edition of Friday 19 May, reported that the monastery had finally been captured by Polish forces on Ascension Day, 18 May, but there was no mention of the South African contribution. It was only on Wednesday 24 May that the *Cape Times* ran the headline: 'SA Sixth Division in Action'. The folks at home were now well aware that the division was in Italy and that they had seen action. For the first and last time, Hodgson told his parents something of his experiences in action:

92 J. Crwys-Williams, *Mood of a nation*, p. 362.

93 *Ibid.*

> As you have most probably heard, we have been in action since near the beginning of the month, which is why the rest is so welcome. On the whole all went off as well as could be expected and I hope you are not worried as I am quite safe and know how to look after myself and I can assure you no Jerry will get near me. We are all very happy and full of beans; that includes George who seems to be thriving on it. At the present rate of progress the war will be over before we know what's happening. There was only one regrettable incident during the stay and that was when Bruce Airey, our Lance-Corporal, who was a close friend of mine, was killed by a grenade, otherwise there were no regrets. We lived in a shell-gutted house during the day, where we were very comfortable—we went out to dug-in positions at night; we did not sleep at all by night only during the day, but we got used to this. The rations came up to us every night and I must say we were fed excellently, all tinned grub and fresh bread; we never went hungry. The time we were in the line we never saw the sun at all and have consequently lost all our sunburn, but we will soon get it back as we are living now. We occupied the front positions and we could not have been much more than 200 yards from Jerry's forward defences—the undergrowth was very thick so we never saw them. They occupied another house opposite us, about 370 yards away, and one morning one of our kitty-bombers returning from their lines at very low altitude was shot at by one of their Spandaus (LMG)—but the pilot thought the firing came from our house so he turned and dropped a couple of bombs near us and strafed the house. Otherwise we were not bothered from the air, although we saw some Jerry planes in the distance. As for the artillery, we had an overwhelming superiority—if a Jerry mortar or machine gun opened up on us it was quite customary for a battery and on occasions a regiment of artillery to be turned on it—the Jerry artie was practically non-existent except for one night—the night of the push; the rest of the time it appeared that he only had a couple of guns working on our sector.
>
> I suppose you heard roughly when the division landed in Italy, but I got here about five weeks before the rest as I was on the advance guard. Actually I was the second chap in the regiment to set foot on Italian soil, not counting the five officers who came with us. We had a wonderful time here as there were only a few of us; but I will tell you all about this in my next letter.

There were heavy downpours of rain as the battle reached its climax on 17 May, creating thick, sticky mud and causing concern that the offensive would be held up as it had been at Anzio. Fortunately, the long-awaited breakthrough occurred on both fronts. The situation was summed up in the war diary of the 1/6th Field Regiment: "Monastery Hill reported captured by the Poles. The once proud Fortress Cassino is now more a heap of rubble." Among this rubble, 860 Polish dead and 900 unburied German dead were found.

On 21 May, the 1/6th Field Regiment began handing over to the 6th New Zealand Field Regiment. Refitting then took place at Fragneto before the men set off for the divisional assembly area east of Caserta, between Sant'Agata and Limatola. The First City/Cape Town Highlanders handed over to the 6th New Zealand Infantry and arrived at the concentration area on the night of 23 May. The demand was first for baths, and then sleep.

Monday 22 May 1944 – Tuesday 23 May 1944: Isernia

Gunner Peter Johnston was a little older than the average soldier, having worked on the mines for a few years after leaving Potchefstroom Boys' High School. He arrived in Taranto with the Reserve Artillery Regiment and began keeping a diary. In one of his first entries he described his unit as a "lousy mob" and was thankful to go on a two-week signalling course at the nearby village of Torritta. Gunner Black of the 1/6th Field Reserve Battery was knocked down by a truck on the tar road outside his camp on 23 May, while the Reserve Group was stationed at Taranto. He died later that night in the 102nd General Hospital at Bari. A burial party went to Bari to officiate. Reserves were still landing at Taranto on 24 May. Among them was the Natal Mounted Rifles Reserve Squadron. Three days after their arrival in the theatre of war, three members were killed in a motor accident. They were Major W.F.B. Baseley, Lieutenant S.S.S. Bruce and Trooper J.H. Steyn. All are buried at Bari war cemetery. Hodgson would write home about anything and everything *but* his immediate circumstances when the action was most hectic and there was greater danger. On Thursday 11 May 1944, the opening of the final battle for Cassino, he decided to tell his mother about the towns and countryside to the south of Cassino:

> Now to tell you a bit about Italy: my personal opinion is, it is a very pleasant country to look at and from the point of view of a country dweller, he could wish for nothing better, but the towns are lousy. Considering that it is spring now I don't think I have ever seen a place that is so green. All the fields are a lovely emerald green. There is no veld, as all the land is cultivated; every square inch of it, except for the higher slopes which have orchards, above which are the wooded slopes, above which are the snow-capped peaks. The whole place looks like an enormous patchwork quilt, mainly of different shades of very rich green, interspersed with shades of brown [ploughed fields]. In places there are enormous fruit orchards which look wonderful, all in bloom. In the southerly parts, it is much like the Cape—vineyards. The towns are the filthiest places I have ever seen. The buildings are good and strong but there is no upkeep whatsoever and all the people are naturally dirty. Since we have been here, we have had sleet twice and the rest of the time the weather has been marvellous. I'll tell you some more in each letter, as I can carry on for weeks. I am perfectly happy and fit, and there is no cause for any worry.

Isernia is a sizeable town northeast of Cassino, a convenient staging area for the Gustav Line in the British sector. Since 7 May, it had served as the headquarters of the 7/23rd Medium Regiment.

The mobile shower unit was still stationed there and was much in demand. It was a well-organized affair comprising a tent measuring about 50 yards square, with 12 showers and slatted floors. The men would hand in their clothes and personal belongings at the entrance. These would be put into a bag displaying the soldier's number and handed back on the other side. American soldiers would be given a clean uniform after their showers, but South Africans were lucky if they were given clean underwear. Although there were still some cold winds and the nights were chilly, winter clothing was withdrawn during the middle of May. The British bath unit which had served the 12th South African Motorized Brigade during it deployment at Cassino remained unofficially attached to the South Africans for the remainder of the campaign. It was run by "two little cockneys who got on well with the 12 Brigade men".[94]

From Isernia, it was a 68-mile journey south to the concentration area well behind the lines in the Volturno River valley, known by some as Champagne Alley. Most units had arrived there by 1400 hours on 24 May and by 1800 hours, all units of the division were officially back under their parent command. Resistance at Anzio had started to crumble by 24 May, and by the next day, there was only one 5th Army front. It was only now, a full month after his observer mission to the front line at Monte Cassino, that Hodgson told his family something of that first experience of Italy:

> I will tell you a thing that will surprise you. While Dad was celebrating his birthday, I was in the ground workings of Cassino. One of our officers went there to have a look around and I went with him. I drove him up there in a Jeep which took us a day and a half. This trip of ours took from the 15th–23rd of April and we were right up in the front line of Cassino about 50 yards from Jerry. It is good to say that I was in Cassino—there is only one other chap who can say that in the regiment. On the way up there and back we passed through Naples, but I was not particularly struck by the place, although it has been messed about a lot by the war, one can see that it must have been a great place in the Italian way—mind you, I did not see any of the renowned places there, except for Mount Vesuvius erupting; this was quite an awe-inspiring sight. We landed at Taranto and I saw the result of our repeated air attacks on the place. In places the whole area was flattened.

---

[94] DODAR, UWH, Box 142, interview with Major I. Moore, former Brigade Major of 12th South African Motorized Brigade, undated.

Wednesday 24 May 1944 – Monday 29 May 1944: Sant'Agata

The division was concentrated in Campania, around Limatola and Sant'Agata de' Goti, between Caserta and Foggia to the east. Caserta was a place to be avoided by the ordinary soldier because it was swarming with 'brass hats'. Today it is home to a Commonwealth war cemetery. The wide Volturno River and its smaller tributaries crisscross the valley. The American 88th Infantry Division had been based nearby at Piedimonte d'Alife for training before Cassino and Anzio. A South African base camp was set up in the area (fed by Piedimonte d'Alife, Alife and Sant'Angelo d'Alife) and operated for the remainder of the war as a station for replacements, reserves and invalids in transit.

Bourhill was camped at Sant'Agata de' Goti, an untidy old town in the hills on the southern side of the valley from where small streams flow down to the Volturno.

> We have been having the most perfect weather yet, if this sort of thing continues I'll start criticizing the Union and I'll never do that, not as far as weather goes anyway ... I've just had an uphill walk from the river, after standing nude and washing clothes in midstream. Every now and again, in I duck to cool off. The water is crystal clear and too warm to be really bracing ... On beat last night for three hours with a whimpering dog for company was awful and I used to quite enjoy pounding a beat in the desert at night.
>
> I suppose the big news really is that our regiment has been in action lately and we have fired several hundred shells against the Hun in anger. I hope its OK to say that we were in the barrage that started the new offensive on the front. It was a night to remember alright! All in all I definitely prefer the front line to base camp life. If the censor doesn't like the above paragraph I'm afraid there is going to be a big hole in this letter and you will be none the wiser to boot. It was nothing very important if it happens to have been erased ... Anyway except for broken sleep the life was fine. Grub good, decent hours, and a healthy life.
>
> At present we are camped under large green cherry trees and Alec and my 'bivvy' is parked bang up against a field of wheat waist high! The poplar-lined river is some way away, down steep banks through wheat lands, cherry orchards and leafy lanes. The water runs over smooth white stones and is about 1 foot deep. We laze away the afternoon on the sand bank and sip 'Vino Bianco'. High wooded mountains on either side and a blue blue sky on top! Only in Italy could this be so. Our last position was the best yet. I'll tell you of the walk down to the stream there. First down a 1 in 6 slope then vivid red poppies, just like the Armistice Day ones, with a head 4 inches across and pitch-black centre, not just one poppy here and there but a whole land full. Then up the other side full of crimson and mauve flowers. Then into a lane—like on the postcards from England—but white with May flowers in a solid bank the whole way down to the river ... From the wetting in the stream and the tingling feeling after it, lie on your back and look at the snow-splotched hills

until you feel hungry and then back to the position and to supper and sit on a petrol tin and listen to Tommy Dorsey or Vic Sylvester dance tunes which remind you of home, while the twilight fades slowly slowly away. Then a pill, mosquito cream, put up the nets and into a friendly blanket [and] sleep 11 hours, and up just in time for breakfast. What a life! But I suppose it will have to be broken into again by that nuisance no. 1—Jerry! I hope you understand that I am enjoying life.

Hodgson was just as enthusiastic about life and revelled in his improved circumstances. At this stage he was still relatively forthcoming about his personal experiences—but to his sister, he says little about the death and destruction of Monte Cassino:

At the moment we are having a lovely rest in a most beautiful spot. Lawrence McNicholas and I have got our two-man tent pitched on a ledge fairly high up on a hill. It is a lovely green ledge overshadowed by a large olive tree. We are above most of the company and as we occupy all the ledge we have a very secluded little possie. On the ledge we have our own fireplace and we have got everything very well organized. We make tea, Nescafé, Milo or anything we like at any time so we are living like lords. I received four parcels from Mum the other day so I am well off for grub and we are having some good meals. We have also made our tent very comfortable and have plenty of magazines to read which Mac received in a parcel. As I have said we are on the side of a hill in lovely country—at the bottom of the hill is a large river where we swim—it is about 50 yards wide and too deep to stand in, so we can have a lovely swim. All we take down is a cake of soap between us and have a good wash. This is only our second day here but so far we have been down twice.

No doubt you have heard about us having been in action and the division arriving in Italy a little while ago—actually I came on the advance guard and arrived here about five weeks before the rest came. There were only a few of us over here then and we had a royal time. We went into action near the beginning of the month as you will have seen in the papers. Actually on the whole it was not at all bad, but I must say we were all pleased when it was all over. There were some very funny and amusing incidents, but I am sorry to say that there was also one regrettable one; and that was when Bruce Airey, our Lance-Corporal, who was a close friend of mine was killed by a hand grenade and two others were wounded.

We are really enjoying the sunshine and rest because during the time we were in there we never saw the sun. We used to live in a shell-gutted house by day and then crawl out to dug-in positions at night. We had to keep awake all night but we got as much sleep as we required during the day. We got quite used to this after a bit and now it is quite strange to sleep at night, but one thing that I found was I could not get as much rest by sleeping in the daytime as by night.

Just in time to join the chase, Johnston transferred from the Reserve Artillery Regiment to the 7/23rd Medium Regiment as the driver of an observation post tank. He spent the day camouflaging and painting his newly acquired tank at San Vittore. The Natal Mounted Rifles, who had missed out on the Battle of Cassino, had moved up. Baker found himself feeling gloomy, despite the abundance of flowers:

> Saturday 27th May '44, Nr Cassino: Arose late and had fresh meat and porridge for breakfast. Tank tracks had to be tightened and it was an all-day sweat job. I bathed in the river down in the valley about ten. Stewed some cherries and gave Bokkies (gunner) fire orders for practice. Refuelled tank and after dinner went for a stroll alone through the poppy-strewn valley. Am once again in the depths of despair and morbidity.

It rained a little at the end of May, but it was a relief for the men to be able to lower their guard, despite the appearance of enemy bombers. The only excitement occurred when a camouflage net covering a 5.5-inch gun caught alight, damaging a Mack truck. The cause of the fire remained unknown. People rested and wrote overdue letters home. The Boomerangs, a Union Defence Force entertainment unit, performed at Limatola, using a flat-bed trailer as a stage. Stragglers kept arriving at the concentration area around Sant'Agata, where the division was spread out over many kilometres, during the last week of May. The men were joined by the 24th Guards Brigade, which had fought in North Africa as well as Anzio and Salerno, and which became an honorary South African unit for the next nine months.

Division headquarters was one of the first formations to move forward. It set off as one block on 27 May but by nightfall, it had split into the Main and Rear Divisions, the former travelling four miles ahead. The secondary roads used by the divisions gave rise to clouds of fine white dust.

Elements of 1/6th Field Regiment followed as part of an advance party going ahead to the next position at Cox's Corner. This was located less than ten miles south of Cassino, where Highway 6 skirts around Monte Trocchio on the approach to the Rapido valley. The view from here was dominated by Monte Cairo, a feature which dwarfs Monte Cassino.

Although he had been in action at Acquafondata, this was the first time Watson saw the ground which had been at the epicentre of the Cassino battles:

> 28 May: I am writing this near Cassino, just off the famous Highway 6. In front, looming majestically against the sky is Mount Cairo, which overlooked the Allied positions ... The journey here—the Division dispersal area—was beautiful ...

> we are quite near the position—as the crow flies—that we were in over a week ago, having travelled 100 miles to get here. We are camped in an old vineyard full of shell holes and bomb craters, with poppies bravely trying to add some colour to this war-scarred area.[95]

On 28 May, commanding officers updated their men on the present situation and their future roles. The division was apparently "overjoyed to be told that they would be involved in the general advance on Rome".[96] Final equipment checks were made. Three thousand camouflage nets were issued, ready garnished for the country which lay ahead. Leaving Sant'Agata on 28 May, the 7/23rd Medium Regiment spent the night six miles east of Cassino. A number of teller mines were found in their harbour area and engineers were called in to lift them.

By the next day, tanks were moving forward on Highway 6. Johnston was still cleaning weapons and taking care of details on 30 May. After joining the convoy at 1700 hours on 31 May, he waited in his tank until 2100 hours before moving forward. Some units took even longer to make a start. Hodgson, for instance, was still living the good life in Champagne Alley on 29 May:

> We are still having a marvellous rest, and taking full advantage of the facilities that this place offers. I have been down for a swim every day and I am thoroughly enjoying it. I have never known your parcels to arrive at a more suitable time, with the result that we have had everything we could wish for. At the moment I am sitting in the front of our truck writing upon a book resting on the steering wheel. Fairly nearby there is a wireless going, playing some good music—talking about a wireless, your very good offer of me getting one up here, I think we will have to let it go by the board, for the present time at any rate, but I will remember the other one when I get home, which I hope will not be long. It will not be long before all the fruit will be ripe, so we are eagerly awaiting the time. Everywhere around us are orchards and vineyards so we will not have to look far. The cherries are already ripe and we have had quite a few; they have really got a fine taste picking them straight off the trees. It is all very peaceful and the war seems to be very far away. As you can well imagine all our spirits are very high and I am very happy, also very well.

It appears that their feelings of euphoria were brought on by the great victory and the fact that the men had survived their first action, rather than the splendour of their surroundings. Although the cherries were ripe, the poppies

---

95 J. Crwys-Williams, *Mood of a nation*, p. 364.

96 E. Goetzsche, *The official Natal Mounted Rifles history*, p. 279.

were in bloom and the temperature was warmer than in the mountains from whence they had come, not much else was impressive: the Volturno River is as wide as the Vaal and much the same colour; and while Alife is home to striking Roman walls and narrow streets, Limatola is devoid of charm.

While the Allies were on a high, the German occupiers in Rome were gripped by panic and commandeered any type of transport to get out of the city. Fascist Blackshirts begged to be taken along. The wounded hobbled out on crutches, soldiers taking whatever loot they could with them. At Val d'Orcia, north of Rome, Iris Origo was aware that Cassino had fallen and that events were moving fast. She saw Allied aircraft bombing columns of German transports and wrote "our own personal crisis is just beginning".[97]

Tuesday 30 May 1944 – Wednesday 31 May 1944: Cassino

The 6th South African and 6th British divisions were to pass through the Canadian Corps and proceed up Highway 6, toward Rome. Despite the best efforts of the military police, the roads could not cope with the volumes. It was every company, squadron or battery for themselves as they waited to find a space on the road. Queues made up of thousands of vehicles stretched for miles. Units were split up and some got lost. By now, there were elements of the 1/6th Field Regiment already in Ponte Corvo. John Smallwood features prominently in the history of the North African and Italian campaigns of the Imperial Light Horse. He was ultimately appointed captain and was awarded the US Army Silver Star. He was also an articulate man, as his diary shows:

> 31 May: Yesterday, we had just completed one leg of the nightmare journey ... through the narrow side roads alongside the modern Highway 6 on the road to Rome. Tanks, guns, half-tracks and ambulances were mixed up with three-ton lorries, carriers and more tanks. An endless column, nose to tail, either waiting with engines running in the overpowering heat and dust or tearing through narrow lanes trying to catch the vehicle in front. Trees and bushes are smashed and twisted. Houses are either completely collapsed or have huge rents in them. Civilians in ragged clothes stand in small groups staring pathetically at the never-ending stream ... Enemy equipment is everywhere. Broken trucks, burned out tanks, guns upside down are scattered about. Great broken cobwebs of barbed wire and telephone lines are tangled in the hedgerows and above all hangs a thick, nauseating blanket of dust and the stench of the dead.[98]

97 I. Origo, *War in Val d'Orcia*, p. 187.

98 H. Klein, *Light Horse cavalcade,* p. 141.

Since few of the men of the 11th South African Armoured Brigade had been involved in the Battle of Cassino, this constituted the first close-up view of a European battlefield for many. Baker's diary bears out the sights and smells of the Liri valley:

> Wednesday, 31st May '44—Liri Valley: Saw some beautiful country, the shattered Monastery, destroyed bridges, pottered around and smelt the nauseating stink of dead bodies again. Ponte Corvo and every village were absolutely shattered and smashed flat. Saw dozens of Churchills and Shermans bashed out on the Hitler line. Went over a Churchill. Carried out maintenance—heard some dope and went to bed to die.

Thursday 1 June 1944: Pontecorvo

While the 1/6th Field Regiment and others were already in Pontecorvo and beyond, by 1 June the Royal Natal Carbineers had still not left the concentration area. It was obviously preparing for the coming battles, however:

> We are still having a wonderful rest and I can assure you I am thoroughly enjoying life at the moment. For the last eight or nine days I have been having a swim once and sometimes twice every day. The water could not be better and the river is so big one can have a very enjoyable swim as one cannot stand in most parts. During the day we have nothing in particular to do except keep our weapons in a good condition. This afternoon I spent about four hours giving my 'Tommy' [sub-machine gun] a good overhaul. I am no longer an unskilled labourer (ie rifleman). I operate a 2-inch mortar and my 'Tommy' gun. The former is really a good bit of work and is a formidable weapon—so you see I am kept quite busy these days.[99]

Nobody passed through Pontecorvo without remarking on its utter destruction. Traffic jams were worsened by the presence of rubble, mines, booby-traps and blown bridges, so that vehicles of every type—from trucks to quads to tanks—queued, bumper-to-bumper. The 6th South African Armoured Division was under command of the Canadian Corps at this time. It was directed up the Canadian axis of advance, while the 12th South African Motorized Brigade headquarters harboured in the fields to the west of the town. Following in the footsteps of the Canadian division, it fell to the South Africans to bury any dead Canadians and to take care of the necessary paperwork. On 3 June, the body of Private Henry Francis Litfin of the Royal Canadian Regiment was found and

[99] J.B. Hodgson–D.M. Hodgson, 1/6/1944.

buried at Pontecorvo. He had been lying in the rubble for four days; the exact spot was marked on a tracing of the 1:50,000 map of Italy and he was later reinterred at the Cassino war cemetery. North of Pontecorvo the men crossed the Liri and Melfa rivers. Baker made use of the opportunity to wash off the dust:

> Thursday, 1st June '44—Nr Cassino: Had a real humid snorter of a day. Went down to Melfa River to bathe. Len and I fired my Tommy gun. Slept in the afternoon and read. Had bad meat and dehydrated vegetables for dinner. Swam in the Liri in the afternoon. Went to bed in clothes and were pulled out to move up two miles to Ceccano which took us all night; no sleep ... many vehicles and tanks crashed off the roadside. Cecil Ritson's [tank] into the river.

When Private Willem Booysen, a 48-year-old Cape Corps soldier from Malmesbury, went for a swim in the Volturno River near his camp on 4 June, he was washed away in the strong current. Onlookers ran along the riverbank, through the thick undergrowth and saw him disappear under the water a number of times. His body was never found and his name appears on the memorial in the Cassino cemetery.

Friday 2 June 1944: Pofi

Pofi is a small village just off Highway 6. Major W.F.B. Baseley was killed here in a battle accident, before contact had been made with the enemy, when the Natal Mounted Rifles passed through on 27 May.

The South Africans were in a pursuit role for the first time. On 2 June, the Witwatersrand Rifles/Regiment De la Rey assumed the lead with the Natal Mounted Rifles providing a reconnaissance screen. The First City/Cape Town Highlanders advanced on the left, but the objective assigned to them was attacked by the French before they could reach it. Contact was finally made near Ferentino where the infantry went in with fixed bayonets. Two trucks belonging to the 1/6th Field Regiment were waved on by the Military Police by error and were hit by Spandau fire. They caught alight and soon 25-pounder ammunition "was going up in all directions, to the consternation of the infantry who were definitely not amused".[100]

Congestion on the roads meant that units could not always travel together, but rather moved forward when allotted a space. During the first two days of June, Johnston's tank crew functioned as a unit on its own:

[100] N. Orpen, *Gunners of the Cape*, p. 224

> Bypassed Cassino, through Pontecorvo. Slept a few hours on our own then battled all day to find Regt—found them in the evening, supper and refuelled. Left at 04.30 for Ceprano. Filter trouble and missed turning, so through Pofi. Found Regt by suppertime. Refuelled, stroll with Eric, parked on railway line.

Apparently the intended route had been signposted but there were no division road signs beyond Pontecorvo because a tank had crashed through a bridge and the route had to be changed. The Canadian provosts were blamed for the chaos and relations became quite strained. Many of the units got completely lost; for example, half of the Rear Division headquarters overshot its destination and ended up on the Melfa River. According to Major H. Rushmere, Brigade Major of 11th South African Armoured Brigade, no movement table had been formulated for the brigade. Vehicles were merely fed onto the road at a rate of 25 vehicles every 15 minutes. Meals were erratic while the division was in pursuit mode with mobile kitchens caught up in the traffic. Men made do with what they carried in their trucks, pooling their resources:

> You for one have been super about writing of late. Two long letters and a letter-card and the Farming in SA and a tin (large sized) of mebos with peaches on the top and those lovely cookies on the bottom and this time besides being a pleasure they were very useful.[101] We went a very long time without food and there in my cubby hole in the quad reposed a full tin of eats! But those cookies were too perfect; one bite and it was gone—not even necessary to swallow, cause they just melted. At intervals I dished out mebos and we did much better than other subs. When the food came up at last I really wasn't very hungry—it's wonderful what sweet goods can do to keep one going.[102]

The abundance of fruit (especially cherries) and vegetables in the countryside provided some variation in the men's diet. Drinking water was seldom a problem. Hodgson was having his first taste of living off the land:

> The cherries form a large part of our diet, as these days we are mainly fed with Bully Beef and biscuits, so these make a good break. One good thing about this country is, we are never short of water; wherever we go we find wells and the water therein is really wonderfully clean and cool. It also has a very nice taste as it all comes from these springs in the wells and never gets anywhere near metal pipes, etc.

---

101 *Mebos* is defined by Encarta as "sweetened dried apricots—a confection that has been made from apricots that have been pickled, sugared and dried" (mid-19th century Afrikaans).

102 S. Bourhill–E. Bourhill, 12/6/1944.

Frosinone is one of the bigger towns which the division passed through on Highway 6. Situated on top of a hill overlooking Ferentino, the roads through the town are narrow and crooked, giving the drivers a taste of what was to come. It was here that the French colonials went on a spree of raping and pillaging.

Saturday 3 June 1944: Ferentino

The Royal Natal Carbineers had caught up and was now leading the way, expecting to 'bump' the 26th Panzer Division at any moment. The roadsides were littered with abandoned and destroyed equipment. Highway 6 started to enter into the foothills, having passed through the flatness of the Liri plain.

The Natal Mounted Rifles suffered two casualties during operations—Corporals Hunter and Milligan are buried at Beach Head Cemetery at Anzio, which was the most convenient place for reinterment. On 3 June, the 6th South African Armoured Division received their first operation order which read: "6th South African Armoured Division will secure PIGLIO G2858 and PALIANO D2156."

These are the geographic coordinates of the Modified British System which was used by the Allied armies in Europe. The coordinates represent points in a box or square with sides one-kilometre long; a grid reference with six digits is accurate to within 100 metres. When referring to a specific location or a target, the grid reference is usually given. The war diaries and location statements (locstats) usually indicate the exact positions occupied by their own or enemy units. Gun positions were surveyed in and identified with an eight-digit reference, which were therefore accurate to within ten square metres.

An appendix was attached to this operational order which indicated a total ignorance of the disposition of enemy forces at that time. It stated: "If the enemy does not know who is on our front, how can we?" It concluded: "German forces in Italy are now NOT capable of making a strong stand south of the Po. Isolated units may fight but morale is low and supplies are not arriving."[103]

The predicament in which the German army and Italian civilians found themselves was not an enviable one. Iris Origo wrote on 3 June:

> Violent fighting on the Alban hills [near Anzio]. Now it can only be a matter of days. Bombing and machine-gunning on the roads is now continuous. All day the

[103] DODAR, WD, Box 630, 7/23rd Medium Regiment, 28/5/1944; DODAR, WD, Box 598, Recording Officer, The 6th South African Armoured Division in Italy, provisional outline.

> planes fly over us, the big bombing formations of 24 or 36 planes for the large-scale attacks on trains or military objectives, and, far more dreaded by us, the small swift-flying groups of six or seven fighters, swooping down in an instant, machine-gunning any vehicle on the road and bombing lorries or bridges. They are at work from dawn until dusk, and now that there is a moon, go on attacking all night.

The main thrust of the division was against Piglio, nine miles north of Anagni, which in turn is nine miles south of Paliano. The task fell to the Guards Brigade and the 12th South African Motorized Brigade, which were supported by tanks. The 1st Scots Guards captured a complete German infantry section before being halted by demolitions.

After a tiring day of traffic problems, which had started at 0300 hours, the 7/23rd Medium Regiment established itself three miles west of Frosinone, with both batteries in the immediate vicinity. The regiment was in action as a complete unit for the first time and was immediately engaged in a number of regimental concentrations.

Johnston's diary is full of references to breakdowns and mechanical trouble, but not much detail is given about his first battles:

> 3 June: Ferentino, and into action at Agnone [Anagni]. Fred nearly rode over Venter.
> 4 June: Moved up six miles and units in action again …

Sunday 4 June 1944 – Monday 5 June 1944: Paliano

The leading tanks reached Gloria, two and a half miles south of Paliano. A blown bridge 1,000 yards ahead halted the advance. The leading troop of tanks from Prince Alfred's Guard took hull-down positions, from where they had a good view of the village. A patrol of Natal Mounted Rifles, a Stuart and a Sherman, moved up to the forward slope. Inside, the crew brewed tea. Three hours later, an 88 opened up on them. The Sherman burned out and the Stuart lost a track. Two men were killed and two wounded. These were the first battle casualties to be experienced by the divisional armour.

The gunners of the 1/6th Field Regiment caught sight of the enemy for the first time on Highway 6. To Bourhill, they resembled grey rodents as they went scurrying over the hill in the direction of Paliano. The guns dropped into action and for the first time in Italy they fired over open sights at a range of 1,000 yards. The Royal Natal Carbineers secured the high ground to the southwest of the village and had a frustrating time watching the enemy tanks, vehicles and guns streaming away in retreat. They met light resistance and dug in for the night. A counter-attack was made against them, which they drove off and the enemy then pulled out of Paliano. The First City/Cape Town Highlanders followed up and declared the town clear of the enemy at 0800 hours on 5 June.

This was the first of many hilltop villages to be taken by the South Africans in Italy. It was the last hill before Rome, and the plains now opened up before them. The retreating Germans had left inferior *Volksdeutch* troops as a rearguard, and many deserted without putting up a fight.

After a night of almost continuous fire on German lines retreating to the northwest, the mediums were ordered to move forward to gain increased range. By 0845 hours they were in a new position, about four miles farther along Highway 6. Most of their fire was directed at fleeing enemy vehicles and infantry beyond Paliano, Piglio and Acuto, which villages the 12th Motorized Brigade was busy clearing. Before long, the enemy was out of range, and with the French troops on the left flank moving up quickly, it became impossible to find targets within range and safety. In the afternoon the order came from the Commander Royal Artillery: "No firing until further notice." The efficacy of the gunners' shelling was evident in the wrecked vehicles and buildings of the pitiful town of Valmontone, which they passed through later that day.

On 5 June, a flying column comprising tanks of the Natal Mounted Rifles and a company of the Witwatersrand Rifles/Regiment De la Rey was ordered to proceed up Highway 6 into Rome. A spot of rain provided a welcome relief from the heat. However, traffic congestion was as bad as usual, and unfriendly Americans prevented the column from carrying out its mission. The Americans had walked from Anzio, a distance of 30 miles, and were exhausted. Nothing was heard from the flying column as the division moved from its concentration area near Anagni, then through Valmontone.

Hereafter, an American general halted the convoy. He expressed first surprise and then indignation at finding a strange formation advancing up a road that had been designated his exclusive axis by the 5th Army. General Poole argued the division's case, but to no avail. The column was pulled off the road and its advance briefly halted. Allied vehicles, travelling three abreast in places, presented a wonderful target; fortunately, though, only one enemy aircraft appeared, dropping anti-personnel bombs which inflicted casualties on a nearby British formation.

Thus it was the Americans who liberated Rome and at 0130 hours on Monday 5 June, both the Stars and Stripes and the Union Jack were flying in the Piazza Venezia. At 0730 hours Mark Clark landed in a Piper Cub in a wheat field outside the city and from there he went by Jeep through the streets to the Capitoline, where he gave a press conference. The following morning, 6 June, at 0600 hours, Clark was woken in his suite at the Excelsior Hotel to be told that the Normandy landings had taken place.[104]

Tuesday 6 June 1944: Rome

Of this epic day, Lieutenant Smallwood wrote: "We entered the southern outskirts of Rome at first light and for two hours slowly moved through the centre of the city, across the Tiber and on to the northern suburbs. The crowds of cheering people were going mad. The war was over for them but we were in steel helmets watching out for snipers …"[105] Well-dressed and well-groomed, the Roman women were a striking contrast to the southern peasants the South Africans had previously encountered.

The 1/6th Field Regiment was up with the reconnaissance tanks which passed through Rome at 0730 hours. In a letter written on 12 June, Bourhill describes his journey through what some referred to as "The Infernal City":

> I believe that we are now allowed to say that we have been thru Rome. The S. Africans were lucky to have been able to go that route thru the outskirts of the city, because many other columns by-passed it. I think we only went thru the posh suburbs on the fringe and thru a bit of the modern shopping centre. The people were very pleased to see us. I reckon in a month they'll be sick of the sight of us! However, they most likely liked us a lot more than Jerry, as millions of people with flags and roses (the little bright red ones) clapped and cheered for us for miles thru the streets. The women have been improving a great deal as we go north and Rome's girls are perfect. I've seen some of the most beautiful girls I've ever seen in the villages too. I sat on the top of the quad and was smothered in roses. At first I put them in my tin hat and then took that off and stuck them in my hair. I thought that I was getting a lot of attention but I looked over my shoulder and there were two Cape Corps boys doing even better. Tin hats and roses! Hell, the roses were still in my hair and we were pumping H E into the blokes for all we were worth. Two-faced bloody show this. Here I sit and dream of home and write about beauty and girls and roses and I've been interrupted four times already to go and pour shells into

[104] R. Atkinson, *Day of battle*, p. 574.

[105] H. Klein, *Light Horse cavalcade,* p. 141.

> the cunning Hun! What a life! We went in fits and starts thru Rome, some places crawling along, when lovely things had the chance to get fags off me for a very quick shy kiss! But these folks are so emotional that I guess that by now all that pent-up feeling in them has flooded out and they are fully realizing that they are free. For a long time we parked alongside the Tiber in full view of St Peters and some Roman ruins or other, the Colosseum or the Citadel or something like that. But as I said, with the roses still fresh we'd dropped into action, and since then till today we've been chasing him like a mad thing. It's been like this for some time now.

There was a terrible traffic jam but 1/6th Field Regiment was granted road priority behind the Natal Mounted Rifles. There was no pausing to sightsee. The column wound its way past the Piazza del Popolo, across the ancient Ponte Milvio over the Tiber on the northern outskirts of the city, then up the Via Flaminia through Castelnuovo where they were deluged with more roses. They encountered pockets of resistance and smouldering remains of vehicles and had their first experience of Nebelwerfer fire, suffering a number of casualties. "The artillery were peeved at not being able to chase through the night,"[106] and pulled up on the outskirts of Civita Castellana late on the night of 6 June.

Although the South Africans were denied the privilege of being the first into Rome and had hurried through the outskirts, the enormity of the occasion did not escape them. It was a pleasant surprise to see that the city was undamaged and some of the girls were "really beautiful". The shops were open and "... when we stopped for a moment we hopped out and bought some bread and sweets; they did not ration us as I think they were a bit scared of the look of our guns".[107] Hodgson also found the day's events awe-inspiring:

> Of late we have been having a very interesting time. The height of all this was attained when I saw Rome. Mind you, it was a very short look at the city as we passed through in a bit of a hurry. I must say, the place (the little I saw of it) struck me as being a wonderful city. After seeing all the Italian towns, I thought I was going to be disappointed with Rome but I am glad to say I was not. The buildings all look very fine—the majority in the city are all very large (not in height but length and breadth), very sturdily built and all in a very historic style; the streets are very broad and the pavements are all lined by trees. There are many statues and monuments

---

106 N. Orpen, *Victory in Italy*, p. 55; E. Axelson, *A year in Italy*, p. 14; E. Goetzsche, *The official Natal Mounted Rifles history*, p. 282; The exact position where the 7/23rd Medium Regiment was in action at 1815 hrs on 6 June is F734898, close to the village of Sacrofano.

107 J.B. Hodgson–D.M. Hodgson, 8/6/1944.

Bill Maudlin cartoon illustrating the symbiotic relationship between armour and infantry, captioned: "We'll go away an' stop bothering you boys now. Jerry's got our range".

as you can well imagine. It really gave me a thrill when I passed through, to see and hear the genuine pleasure of the people to see us. They were really happy and they spared nothing in showing it. By the time we emerged from the place our truck was a mass of beautiful fresh flowers—these were the first fresh flowers I had handled and smelt since leaving the Union. They were really beautiful—we were also given bottles of wine and baskets and baskets full of cherries. It was quite a job to worm our way through; it actually took us about an hour and a half to get through. All the people seemed in a very good condition—even food was not too scarce, as we were able to buy quite a bit of bread. This was the first place in Italy where I have seen anyone decently dressed or any pretty girls—there were some really posh pieces around. Mind you, this is accounted for mainly by the fact that the south is all agricultural and is practically totally inhabited by farmers and the poorer classes. Just after passing through the city we looked back and we could see St Peter's Cathedral in the distance. Even from where we were (about ten miles distant) it looked a wonderful building (we used field glasses).

Chapter Six

Iron and earth

"Ek het julle gese: 'julle sal daar wees'—en nou is julle daar!" [I told you: you will be there—and now you are there!]
—General Jan Smuts in a speech to the 6th South African Armoured Division near Orvieto on 24 June 1944[108]

Wednesday 7 June 1944: Civita Castellana

The advance had been too swift for the flanking formations and it was necessary to hold up for a short while. The 12th South African Motorized Brigade was in the lead and made a stop about 15 miles north of Rome near one of the countless Italian towns named Castelnuovo. It was an opportunity to wash in the cool streams; the weather was perfect, cloudless skies, "delightful temperatures".[109]

After receiving the order 'Prepare to advance', a message came through to 7/23rd Medium Regiment that 2,000 Germans and a number of tanks were coming in from the left flank. The guns were immediately ordered into action in such a position that they could engage the enemy over open sights. Lookouts were posted and Bren guns were laid out on fixed lines.

As it happened, the 2,000 Germans turned out to be a mere patrol which withdrew as soon as the armour was brought up. The scare made enough of an impression on Johnston for him to mention it in his diary on 7 June, although he was not entirely convinced: "Civita Castellana just after lunch where everybody panicked, 13 tanks and 2,000 Germans behind us on left flank."

In their role as armoured reconnaissance, the Natal Mounted Rifles started taking casualties immediately north of Rome. On a secondary road to Fiano Romano, the Witwatersrand Rifles/Regiment De la Rey, supported by the tanks

---

108 A.B. Theunissen, Major-General W.H. Evered Poole, CB, CBE, DSO: 1902–1969 personal retrospects. *Military History Journal.*

109 W.L. Fielding, *With the 6th Div*, p. 90.

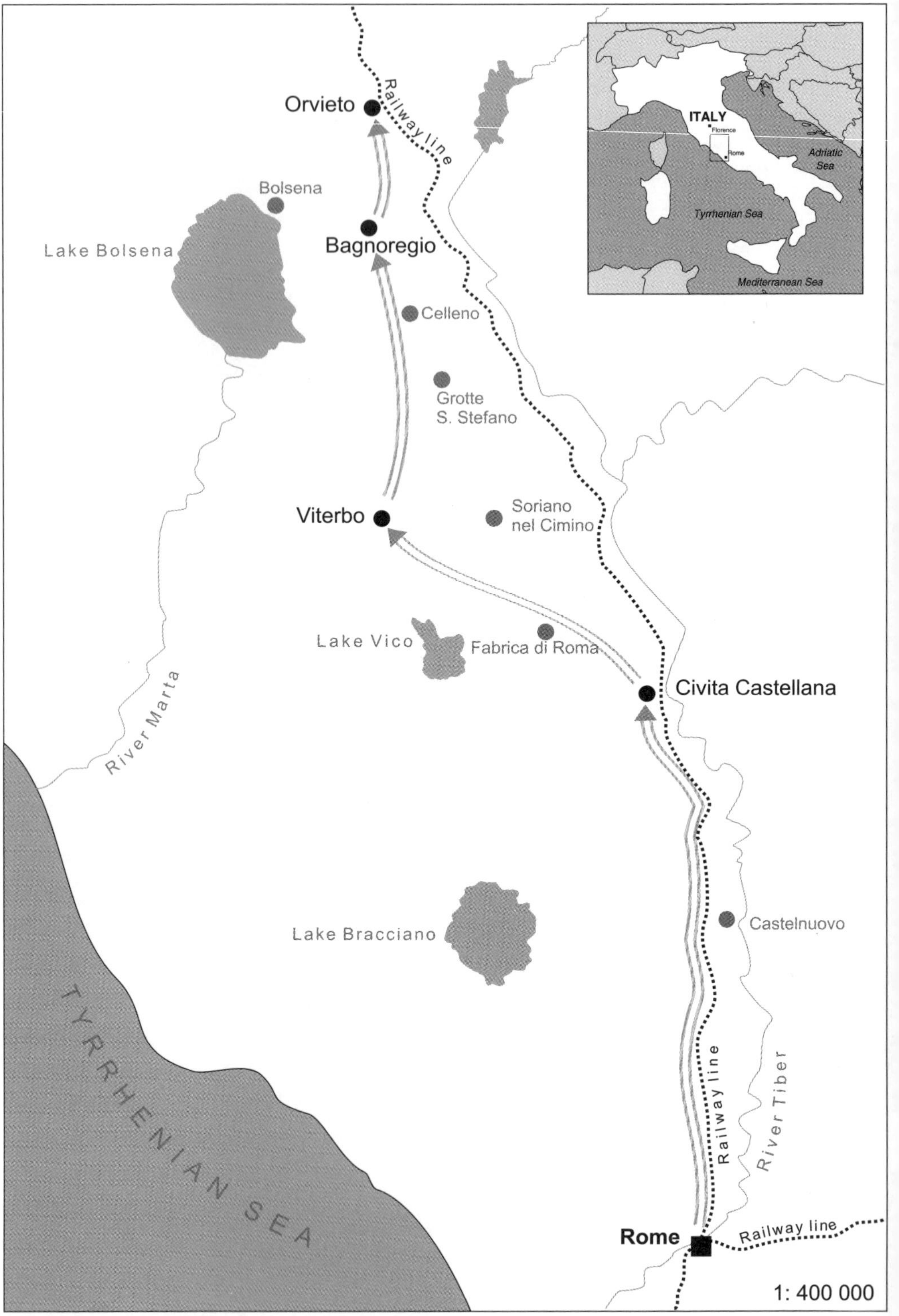

ITALY
Florence
Rome
Adriatic Sea
Tyrrhenian Sea
Mediterranean Sea
Orvieto
Railway line
Bolsena
Lake Bolsena
Bagnoregio
Celleno
Grotte S. Stefano
Viterbo
Soriano nel Cimino
Lake Vico
Fabrica di Roma
Civita Castellana
River Marta
Lake Bracciano
Castelnuovo
TYRRHENIAN SEA
Railway line
River Tiber
Rome
Railway line
1: 400 000

of the Natal Mounted Rifles, came under fire from 75mm anti-tank guns and two enemy tanks. The Natal Mounted Rifles lost a Sherman and a Honey tank and one tank crew was virtually wiped out. One of the men killed was Trooper Gerrit Thomas Ferreira, a teacher from Graaff-Reinet. The records indicate that on 6 June, he was first reported 'wounded in action', then 'missing in action' and finally 'killed in action'. The incident took place 17 miles north of Rome.

Both anti-tank guns were neutralized in the ensuing engagement, while two troop carriers were destroyed along with other vehicles. Of the enemy troops, 22 were killed and 24 taken prisoner.

Soon after this, the Pretoria Regiment had its first battle casualty. The regimental war diary states that it was a "big blow" when Lieutenant J.G.F. Johnstone was killed at 0848 hours on 7 June. His scout car overturned on a narrow winding road while out on a reconnaissance mission. The initial gravesite was located at kilo 34, Route 3.

A full-strength assault was made on the hilltop town of Civita Castellana where Field Marshal Albert Kesselring had his headquarters. Despite having set fire to the headquarters building, some valuable documents and good liquor were recovered. Axelson found a number of enemy maps, one of which he sent back to historical records in Pretoria.

Hodgson capitalized on the opportunity to have a cooked breakfast, courtesy of the Germans:

> A little while ago our platoon was quite lucky. When we captured a feature from Jerry we occupied one of the houses there. They had to clear out in a hurry and they left their breakfast half cooked, so we got stuck into it. We had lovely meat cakes, fresh brown bread (we only get white, so this was a pleasant change), also quite a number of lovely tinned Danish butter. It was really marvellous after a hard night's work.

Tanks belonging to B Squadron Natal Mounted Rifles were ambushed on a lateral road on the outskirts of Civita Castellana while trying to make contact with the Free French on their left flank. Paddy Gill and Bobby Gibson were killed by an 88; the rest of the crew was captured. Baker describes Paddy Gill as intelligent and anorexic, with a fear of being separated from the rest of his crew. His slight build was an advantage for his job as a wireless operator and loader of the 75mm gun in the cramped turret. The loader was also expected to keep an eye out for hostile infantry by means of an adjustable periscope, and fire at it with the turret's machine gun. Trooper Gill was good at his job and "a sparkle came to his eye at any mention of battle".[110] A series of action shots showing the tank being knocked out were taken by a German photographer by the name of Altmeier and the pictures have been widely published.

The 4/22nd Field Regiment in their 'Priests' (self-propelled guns) engaged enemy guns and transport to the north of the town, while the 1/6th Field Regiment was requested to fire on a Panther tank. The Special Service Battalion was also involved in the day's action.

The division moved through the night without relenting, leaving behind a trail of the enemy dead.

Thursday 8 June 1944 – Friday 9 June 1944: Viterbo

The recent rapid moves and good news from other fronts had left some of the soldiers feeling overly optimistic and there was already talk of the war being over by Christmas. There was a bit of rain but it was quite welcome after the heat of the past few days. Hodgson enjoyed the life of a conquering hero as the division took its respite:

> At the moment I am sitting in the truck in the sun—it is really a lovely morning; most of the fellows are basking in the sun, writing the same as me; some are reading, and others just resting … The Italians here don't seem to be able to do enough for us; wherever we go they bring along wine and vast quantities of the most delicious cherries I have ever tasted. Also our truck is always covered with fresh flowers as they just shower us with them wherever we go.

In a broadcast, General Alexander told the Italian population that their hour of rising had come at last and urged them to sabotage German communications, form ambushes and give shelter to *Volksdeutche* who had deserted. Carabinieri with Fascist inclinations were deserting in droves and partisan activity increased, with tragic consequences for the local population. From the Val d'Orcia on 7 June, Iris Origo wrote: "Fascism is not so much being destroyed; it is crumbling before our eyes. By the time of the Allies' arrival here, nothing of the whole wretched structure will be left, and its supporters will have vanished into thin air."[111]

---

110 D.M. Baker, *War, wine and valour*, p. 347.

111 I. Origo, *War in Val d'Orcia*, p. 194.

On 8 June, Johnston was involved in action near Fabrica di Roma against machine guns and light anti-tank guns. His tank was used as a bulldozer to clear a path for the guns and he slept on the station that night. By 1600 hours that afternoon, the 7/23rd Medium Regiment was well forward at Fabrica de Roma. American troops were engaged in a fierce battle just 3,300 yards in front of the guns, which "got in some heavy and good work".[112] The 1/6th Field Regiment was firing against German guns "to keep them quiet". With the Americans on the left and the British on the right, the artillery had to fire with caution.

Three more men of the Natal Mounted Rifles were killed by shelling on 8 June. They were Gordon Swales, Trooper D.I. Rigby and Andy Schou, who looked "tall and wild like an Anglo-Saxon chieftain".[113]

Traffic was still backed up in Civita Castellana when the Natal Mounted Rifles advanced through Viterbo in the face of machine-gun and mortar fire. Major H.S. Haupt was awarded the Military Cross for leading the reconnaissance on foot through difficult country.

The Witwatersrand Rifles/Regiment De la Rey entered Viterbo at 1450 hours on 9 June from the southeast. The French and the Americans entered from the southwest. Main divisional headquarters was attacked that night by German aircraft—most unusually—resulting in 14 casualties, three of whom died.

With a tank battle brewing, the 1/6th Field Regiment was, according to the war diary, "in the backwater for a change". Nevertheless, the 25-pounders fired on several targets, including a Ju 88 flying at 5,000 feet and a Panther tank. The latter was more successful. An air observation post was set up and identified an enemy gun position "which was punished every time it opened up".[114]

While each brigade had its own signals unit, field ambulance and engineers, the artillery usually fell under divisional control, the better to concentrate its firepower. There was rarely a formal line during the pursuit phase; it was more a matter of spearheads, infantry, tanks and the supporting arms advancing along main roads and tracks or across country. They would deploy and fight or outflank the enemy when contact was made.[115]

112 DODAR, WD, Box 630, 7/23rd Medium Regiment, 8/6/1944.

113 D.M. Baker, *War, wine and valour*, p. 384.

114 DODAR, WD, Box 624, 1/6th Field Regiment, File A1 47.

115 W.L. Fielding, *With the 6th Div*, p 1.

On 9 June, Johnston wrote that his observation-post tank was the first Sherman through Viterbo on Highway 3. That night the men slept in a field while they waited for the rest of the troop to catch up. Disaster occurred when an observation-post tank of the 1/6th Field Regiment made way for an American M10 tank destroyer while advancing up a secondary road along the railway between Viterbo and Celleno. The tank fell off a bridge, killing two gunners, S.T. Elliott and J.V. Carmichael. They were the first battle casualties suffered by the regiment. Things were about to get ugly though, now that the opposing force consisted mainly of the 356th Infantry Division, fresh troops only recently rushed down from northern Italy to help stem the Allied advance.

The mediums had been in action five miles south of Viterbo just off the highway and at 0830 hours on 10 June were ordered to move to a position two miles north of the town. The 25-pounders were farther forward, approaching Bagnoregio where the Germans made a stand. Bourhill found time to describe the experience of an artilleryman during the advance:

> [We] drop out of action, he's out of range, move up, give him hell, sleep off and on, off and on, move up, he stands and fights, we shoot and rest up and dry our blankets, write letters and wash kit. It's like that now, he's standing and fighting and I'm writing, so when you hear he's stopped, expect letters!!

The artillery had indeed been busy north of Rome. Gunner E.R. Cormack of the 1/6th Field Regiment wrote that his battery was firing "8 in line" on 10 June. The regimental war diary records that divisional artillery had accounted for five 88mm guns, six 75mm and three 30mm anti-tank guns, four Mk III and one Mk IV tanks. Some 200 enemy killed—all within the 24 hours.

Saturday 10 June 1944 – Tuesday 13 June 1944: Bagnoregio

The area between Viterbo and Bagnoregio is characterized by modest little farms, each with a few rows of vines and assortment of fruit trees. The hills and gullies are rugged and forested. At the time, journalists referred to the big tank battle which took place here on 10 June as the Battle of Viterbo, although it later became known as the Battle of Celleno. Essentially, it was a running battle between Viterbo and Bagnoregio.

This was said to be the 6th South African Armoured Division's first and biggest tank battle, although the Natal Mounted Rifles had already been in action for two days and nights. This was not a tank battle in the sense of tank against tank, as had been the case in the desert; rather, the Shermans swept through German infantry and had to deal with well-camouflaged anti-tank guns. Rhodesian and South African newspapers ran the headlines: "Seven miles gained in seven-hour battle near Viterbo", "Gruelling 11-hour tussle with enemy north of Rome" and "6th Division's tanks score first victory".

At first light on 10 June, the armour moved up the winding road from Viterbo toward Soriano, apparently "eager to establish contact with the enemy after years of waiting".[116] Trooper A.P. Goodwill was in the armoured reconnaissance and had a different view: "I can recall quite clearly that June morning when Lieutenant Howard Butcher spoke to me. It was quite evident that he also felt the strain … he appeared so tired …"[117] Lieutenant H.M. Butcher, who features prominently in the Natal Mounted Rifles annals, had been a company sergeant-major throughout the desert war and was clearly much admired as one who led by example, on the parade ground and the battlefield.

Two leading Natal Mounted Rifles tanks were 'brewed up' (destroyed) by German 88s and the long-barrelled 75mm 'Pak' guns (*Panzerabwehrkanone*). The projectiles easily punched holes in the Sherman's armour and caused much damage. One of these shattered Howard's leg. Before dying of shock and loss of blood, he asked one of his men to convey his love to his wife, Peggy, and to his crew. Two other crewmembers, Jack Gardiner and L.L. van Rosenveld, were machine-gunned and killed as they ran from their burning tank. According to Major Blamey, a former company commander in the Natal Mounted Rifles, Trooper van Rosenveld had recently been ordained as a priest but elected to stay with his friends rather than accept a commission.

On hearing the distress calls over the air, a squadron of Special Service Battalion tanks charged to the rescue. Some of them met the same fate, but the enemy was ultimately knocked out. Lieutenant-Colonel E.G. 'Papa' Brits received the DSO for this action. He also provided for one of its lighter moments: the colonel had left his tank in the hands of his Cape Corps batman. In response to repeated calls over the wireless set, the batman eventually answered, "*Die baas is nie hier nie!* (The boss isn't here!)" Brits called up all available infantry and carried as many men as possible on the back of tanks.

116 N. Orpen, *Victory in Italy*, p. 67.

117 D.M. Baker, *War, wine and valour*, p. 384; A.E. Blamey, *A company commander remembers*, p. 151; *see also* p. 163: Howard Butcher's exhaustion may have been caused as much by physical strain and emotional pressure as it is known that he had a kidney ailment.

The thicker the bush, the greater was the need for infantry. The Imperial Light Horse/Kimberley Regiment and Special Service Battalion were working together to clear Germans out of farmhouses, holes, bushes, cornfields, caves and hedges. At last light, the Special Service Battalion pulled up and rested a mile and a half short of Bagnoregio. The men made fires and had supper a few yards away from the enemy who, according to Brits, "had no machine guns, no guns".[118] The men and machines had been in action since 0800 hours and had covered ten to 15 miles across the rolling countryside. It had not been without cost. In the Bolsena war cemetery, there are many gravestones dated 10 June 1944, particularly from the four tank regiments. In one instance, an entire SSB tank crew is buried in one common grave with five names engraved on two headstones: Sergeant D.J. de Villiers, Corporals R.F. Jute, W.H. Olivier, J. Terblanche and Trooper H.H. Lancaster. The day after the battle, the historical recording officer and various war correspondents came up to the Special Service Battalion positions where they were briefed by Brits. "We started the show by coming on some machine guns on the hills, just forward of here," he said, pointing to a spot on a map of the Viterbo area:

> We went along and came up to a lot of 88s, so I was told to scotch them up. We went in one up and he put airbursts of 88mm on our tanks. We had not gone half a mile when the whole world was nothing but MG fire ... There was so much machine-gun stuff that the infantry could not go in. We put in 75mm from the tanks and sprayed the world with MG fire.[119]

Brits attributed the division's success to accurate shooting and poor gunnery on behalf of the Germans. However, snipers in the trees picked off anyone who stuck his head out of a turret, including Major E. Liebenberg, OC A Squadron, who was shot in the back of the head. Brits continued his press briefing:

> We pushed on two and a half miles. We overran the infantry. Our front was narrowed by really dense bush and ravines. The infantry was busy digging out Jerries with

118 N. Orpen, *Victory in Italy*, p. 68; E. Axelson, *A year in Italy*, p. 21; DODAR, UWH, Box 140, Statement by Lieutenant-Cololonel 'Papa' Brits, Officer Commanding Special Service Battalion to division recording officer and South African war correspondents, 11/6/1944.

119 DODAR, UWH, Box 140, Statement by Lieutenant-Colonel 'Papa' Brits Officer Commanding Special Service Battalion to division recording officer and South African war correspondents, 11/6/1944.

> bayonets. The Jerries were sitting in low scrub with bazookas. The battle became so fierce in the dense bush that squadron commanders and crew commanders were fighting with their hands, throwing grenades, firing Tommy guns, firing revolvers. One bazooka was dropped into a tank. A tank on the road was knocked out by a sticky bomb—two Jerries climbed up onto it.[120]

Lance-Corporal Ronald Wilkie was bringing up fuel for the tanks and came across an 88 which had been hit by Major Lindsay's tank. "The crew were still bleeding when we arrived. Two of the five were alive, moaning, but they died soon after." They refuelled under fire and then, as the first tanks were moving off, "five Teds ['Tedeschi', or Germans] in a motorcycle with a sidecar came down the road singing and shouting, slap towards our first tank. One shot from a 75mm hit the machine and killed them all."[121]

Much interesting chatter was heard over the airwaves during the battle. A German commander who used the same frequency as Brits hurled insults and called for Tigers, Spandaus and the Luftwaffe. One South African officer, who found himself in the midst of a number of bazookas, was heard to exclaim, "Christ, there's one ten yards in front of me. They're all around. Give me grenades, where's my Tommy gun?" The casualties of the Special Service Battalion amounted to one officer and nine other ranks killed; two officers and 12 other ranks wounded. At least 252 Germans were killed and much equipment was lost, including eight 88s, eight self-propelled guns, four tanks, 16 75mm guns, 24 bazookas and 29 machine guns.[122] After having been blooded at Celleno, a Special Service Batallion lieutenant admitted to the historical recording officer that he had enjoyed the slaughter:

> I saw a machine-gun post only a few yards away. There were six or seven men in it. I put a 75mm HE into it. I saw just pieces of meat go flying through the air. I saw seven or eight men on a crest. I turned my co-axial [machine gun] on them. They went down *wimp, wimp, wimp*. It was great.[123]

---

120 *Ibid.*

121 DODAR, UWH, Box 140, Statement by Lance-Corporal Ronald Wilkie, Special Service Batalion, 11/6/1944.

122 DODAR, UWH, Box 140, Statement by Lieutenant-Colonel 'Papa' Brits, Officer Commanding Special Service Battalion to Divisional recording officer and South African war correspondents, 11/6/1944.

123 DODAR, UWH, Box 140, Remarks made by personnel of the Special Service Battalion to Division Recording Officer on 11 June 1944.

Bagnoregio means 'royal bath', and it is the birthplace of San Bonaventura. Much of the surrounding countryside is inaccessible, with bare cliffs and gullies. The town itself is situated on a high ridge which dominates every road, and it was strongly held. The 1/6th Field Regiment was deployed among smallholdings just southwest of the town on the road coming up from Celleno, where the side road comes in from Vetriolo. The enemy not only occupied the town of Bagnoregio; but counter-attacks also came from the left flank across open and relatively flat farm lands.

It rained heavily on the night of 10/11 June. In the morning, at 0600 hours, the Grenadier and Coldstream guardsmen, supported by tanks of the Pretoria Regiment, advanced to within 1,000 yards of Bagnoregio in thick mist. The defenders were in an ideal position for sniping.

While rescuing the crew of a disabled tank, 24-year-old Sergeant J.J. MacArthur of the Pretoria Regiment was hit. He later died of his wounds. Volunteers were called for to bring in the wounded when another tank was brewed up. Six men made their way through machine-gun and sniper fire. On their way back, two snipers stepped out of their hiding places, less than 20 yards away. However, they let the party pass by unmolested.

By the end of the day, 40 tanks were deployed along the front, trying to get onto the high ground east and west of the town. They were kept busy engaging snipers and bazookas at close range. Under the command of Lieutenant P.F. Davey, 3 Troop, A Squadron, Pretoria Regiment was left out in its position for 36 hours. Davey's troop had spent the day fighting it out with Tiger tanks and 88s. A company of Grenadier Guards was dug in within 25 yards of the squadron. The Guards had suffered numerous casualties and they pulled back to some buildings when darkness fell, leaving the tanks on their own. The Guards had attacked in the morning, but failed.

The enemy infantry worked its way to within ten to 15 yards of No. 3 Troop, and a bazooka fired at close range killed Corporal B.B. Bowley. Near misses brought rubble, rocks and dust down onto the tanks while they sheltered in and behind buildings. Ammunition was running low, but no supply truck could reach them. When the squadron commander ordered a withdrawal, it was found that the batteries in one tank were flat, drained by a wireless that hadn't been turned off. The crew took cover from the Spandaus in a building, firing at such close range that it was necessary to shout to be heard. Finally, at 2230 hours that night, having used up all their ammunition and grenades, the troop was withdrawn. Its bag, checked by the infantry, included one 88 anti-tank gun and two mortars destroyed and three machine guns silenced. Of the four Germans armed with bazookas, three were killed and one wounded. The men of Number 3 Troop were credited with the deaths of the Germans, as the infantry had hardly fired a shot all day. On 24 August 1944 the regiment received the news that Lieutenant Davey had been awarded the Military Cross.

Baker's squadron of the Natal Mounted Rifles was also tasked with supporting the Guards Brigade. Dismounting from their tanks, Cecil Ritson and 'Dream' Sanders went ahead on foot, armed with sub-machine guns. They shot up a German halftrack which was crossing a bridge and two tanks took advantage of the ensuing confusion to make their own crossing. The third tank went off the bridge and the crew was mortared as they tried to evacuate. Corporal G. Fox from Mashaba in Rhodesia and Trooper Domoney were fatally wounded during the incident.

The remaining tanks continued through the German infantry straddling the road, shooting up vehicles and equipment sheltered in the forest.

Four of the divisional artillery regiments were deployed with their observation posts set up on a hill overlooking Bagnoregio from the east, 1,000 yards from the village. The 25-pounders were based on flatter land on the western approaches at a range of 1,500 yards to 3,000 yards—almost on the same level as the town, and in view of the enemy.

In their exposed positions, the artillerymen came under enemy machine-gun fire for the first time on 11 June as they fired over the heads of the attacking Guards Brigade. Because the deep ravines and woods confined the tanks to a covering role on the flank, the Guards Brigade bore the brunt of the frontal attack.

However, the Guards officers displayed the reckless bravery for which they are renowned, walking upright through the fields of wheat with swagger sticks under their arms as if they were on the parade ground, calling to their men to "keep down chaps" in their posh Eton accents.

The Guards became pinned down on the forward slopes approaching Bagnoregio during their first attempt on 11 June. The Coldstream Guards were tasked with protecting the left flank of the guns and the Prince Alfred's Guard passed through to try an approach from the west of the village where the approach was not as steep. The Imperial Light Horse/Kimberley Regiment was detailed to drive the Germans off a hill on the right flank overlooking the town. En route, they passed the tattered remnants of a Guards regiment and their carriers, which had been blown up by mines.

The attack was called off late that night and was resumed on the misty morning of 12 June. The Royal Durban Light Infantry, which was attached to the Guards Brigade, lost two killed and one wounded, while the Guards lost 15 killed and 25 wounded.[124] A field dressing station which accompanied the 24th Guards Brigade to within three miles of Bagnoregio came under shellfire, and four personnel were killed on 12 June. Seven more were wounded. Traffic congestion around Viterbo made it difficult for ambulances to move to the rear. Baker was aware that something was brewing as the tanks of the Natal Mounted Rifles passed through the artillery lines on their way to the rear:

> Coming out of the forest, the mist started to lift, and in bright afternoon sunshine, it was apparent that the enemy were making signs of a stand ... We moved back only to find that we were mixed up with a shelling duel between a battery of our guns and the enemy's. It was time to move further back and take a well-earned rest.

Mortaring and shelling took place throughout the day of 12 June, but the war diary of 1/6th Field Regiment states that at around 1600 hours, "... tanks marshalled for battle in our gun area. The dust created by them brought down the wrath of the Hun on us. Inside half an hour he was mortaring and shelling our [position]".[125] The command post area was particularly hard hit, perhaps in retaliation for the constant shelling from the South African side.

The gunners lay face down in shallow slit trenches, hastily dug in a vineyard. Trees were shattered by the shells and mortar bombs, their fruit sent flying around with the red hot shards of metal. The smell of freshly turned earth and cordite hung in the air as the men rose shakily from their slit trenches.

Lieutenant Harry Barker, a 27-year-old from Durban, had been hit by a splinter from a mortar shell, making a small entry wound. The men of A Troop watched their leader die. Stephen Bourhill relates: "His bristly moustache just folded like a sea anemone." For the sake of expediency and because it was close to the road, a slit trench was converted into a shallow grave and Barker's first resting place was in the chalky soil of the vineyard, marked by a rudimentary wooden cross and the obligatory tin hat. Months later, the graves registration

[124] N. Orpen, *Victory in Italy*, p. 75.

[125] DODAR, WD, Box 624, 1/6th Field Regiment, File A1 47.

body would move his body to the lakeside cemetery at Bolsena. Private N. Abrahams was also killed and ten were wounded in what Orpen calls a "mini-holocaust".[126] War correspondent Alan Moorhead wrote that "fear is not the worst thing. You recover quickly from it. It leaves no scar".[127] Bourhill had made a similar observation on the nature of fear and expressed it in a letter written to his mother while the battle of Bagnoregio was raging:

> Mother, I've been very scared at times! But fear is over quickly, and it passes with the danger, but it's the continued subconscious uneasiness that counts. But God is near and I have faith, and you are near and I love you and it's quite ok. I'm very happy and putting on weight, and wonderfully fit and strong ... What a lot I've got to tell you all one day! P.S. H. Barker, the man who censored my letters for the last year and more, got killed in action while I was still writing this letter. I have been scared Mom! Jack also had it. Jerry is moving out now, thank God. We don't have to get our letters censored anymore, maybe at base.

The mediums had an experience similar to that of 1/6th Field Regiment. The regimental headquarters of the 7/23rd Medium Regiment was based four miles south of Bagnoregio. At 1920 hours they received a report from 'Queen' Battery, informing that Major D.D. Brett, Lieutenant J. Stevenson and two other ranks had been wounded by shell splinters when a round from a gun in C Troop struck the branch of a tree in front of the battery command post and exploded. Major Brett died that night and was buried at 1030 hours the next day.

Johnston was a forward observer for the 7/23rd Medium Regiment. On 12 June he was positioned on an adjacent hill:

> OP at Bagnoregio ... Breakfast with Guards ... Roamed around a lot in tank. 105 HE 15 feet in front of us as we reversed. Got stuck in a ditch. Parked behind a hedge with Guards. 2 88 APs just over ... mortared. Pulled into a field and parked. On foot to house overlooking town. Spandau raked wall and got Guardsmen in window below. Mortars and 88s close. Back to troop after dark.

The town of Civita, perched on a hill just south of Bagnoregio, was captured by A and C companies of the Royal Natal Carbineers.

The first objective of B Company was the ridge overlooking Civita, where it ran into Spandau fire from the positions on the cliffs above. Friendly fire

---

126 N. Orpen, *Gunners of the Cape*, p. 228.

127 A. Moorehead, *Eclipse,* p. 60.

also came in from the Guards, which still considered Bagnoregio to be the objective. On the night of 12 June, Major Gallimore's B Company of the Royal Natal Carbineers approached Bagnoregio from the opposite hill, crossing the valley floor. In the darkness, Hodgson sprained his ankle and took shelter at the foot of the cliff. It was here that Private Frank Ledingham was shot between the eyes by a sniper. He was one of the original members of Section 7 of 7 Platoon, B Company, Royal Natal Carbineers.

Hodgson had first mentioned Ledingham in a letter to his sister, written from Pietermaritzburg in August 1943: "... a whole lot of new chaps have come in and we have got another chap in our tent which makes it five. This new chap is not a bad sort at all; his name is Ledingham." From Helwan he had told his parents: "The chap who sleeps next to me is Frank Ledingham from Selbourne College Cape. He is a year older than myself and is one of the best chaps I have ever met. We have a lot in common and get on well together ..." Ledingham had been part of Hodgson's leave party to Alexandria and had also shared good times with him in Cairo.

After dark, B Company climbed the cliffs about half a mile southeast of the town, but the men were pinned down on a ledge. They spent the night fending off grenades rolled down by the Germans. They continued the assault just before dawn; the first ones over the top were Corporal (later Sergeant) D.P. Smith and Private Evered David Pollock, a fair-haired, blue-eyed 19-year-old from Nqutu in Zululand. Pollock was not a veteran of the desert. He was obviously either very keen or plain unlucky since he was wounded two weeks later and finally killed at Monte Salvaro on 23 October.

Corporal Arthur Maile, an Old Edwardian, a great sportsman and a veteran of the 1st South African Division, was mortally wounded in the attack. He was the son of H.E. Maile, a well-known cricket umpire. His older brother was a POW in Germany and the family's youngest, aged 17, had recently left for the north. The formidable fortress of Bagnoregio was eventually taken at dawn on 13 June. The Guards and Imperial Light Horse/Kimberley Regiment helped to consolidate. At 1220 hours, the Prince Alfred's Guard cut off the road north of Bagnoregio and the show was over.

Behind the enemy lines, on 12 June Iris Origo had travelled to Montepulciano in a pony cart to buy medicines, and twice had to jump down into a ditch as fighter planes swooped over. She wrote: "A most lovely drive home in the sunset—the red clover in flower, the green cornfields waving in the breeze, the hedges full of briar-roses. Met a few German cars, heavily camouflaged with branches, the troops sitting on the bonnet or the roof, so as to be able to observe the sky. Heavy bombing in the Val di Chiana."

Origo also expressed a commonly held fear:

> An important detail from our personal point of view, is the news that the troops fighting in the Bolsena area, are largely coloured Moroccan troops, and it is these that will presumably be the first to arrive here. After months of waiting for the Allies to arrive, this will be the Val d'Orcia's first impression of them! There is also, however, a South African Division at Bagnoregio, so let us hope that these may turn up instead.

The English lady had good reason to be worried. The Moroccan Goums scoured the countryside for women between Cassino and Rome, raping and sometimes killing those who resisted. Italian authorities tallied 700 crimes of carnal violence in Frosinone province alone. The Italian government documented more than 5,000 crimes by French colonials. Even the Pope had been called upon to intervene and the French colonial troops had been prevented from entering Rome. The French were presently operating on the left flank and in tandem with the South Africans.

Bagnoregio had stood in the way of the division's main objective, which was the equally formidable obstacle of Orvieto, a large town with a high point overlooking the main north–south road and railway line.

The Prince Alfred's Guard reported that at 1500 hours, it was already 4,000 to 5,000 yards from Orvieto. Having passed through the Royal Natal Carbineers on 14 June, the First City/Cape Town Highlanders was in the lead and approaching Orvieto from the west. From the high ground, it was possible to see the air force bombing the retreating enemy and demolitions going up on the road north.

On 15 June, the following skimpy and inaccurate piece on the Battle of Bagnoregio appeared in the *Rand Daily Mail*: "Earlier, SAPA's war correspondent stated that the Sixth South African Division formed the spearhead of the forces operating in the Bagnorea [sic] area, but it is not yet known if the town fell to the South Africans."[128]

[128] *Rand Daily Mail*, 8th Army Captures Bagnorea [sic], 15/6/1944.

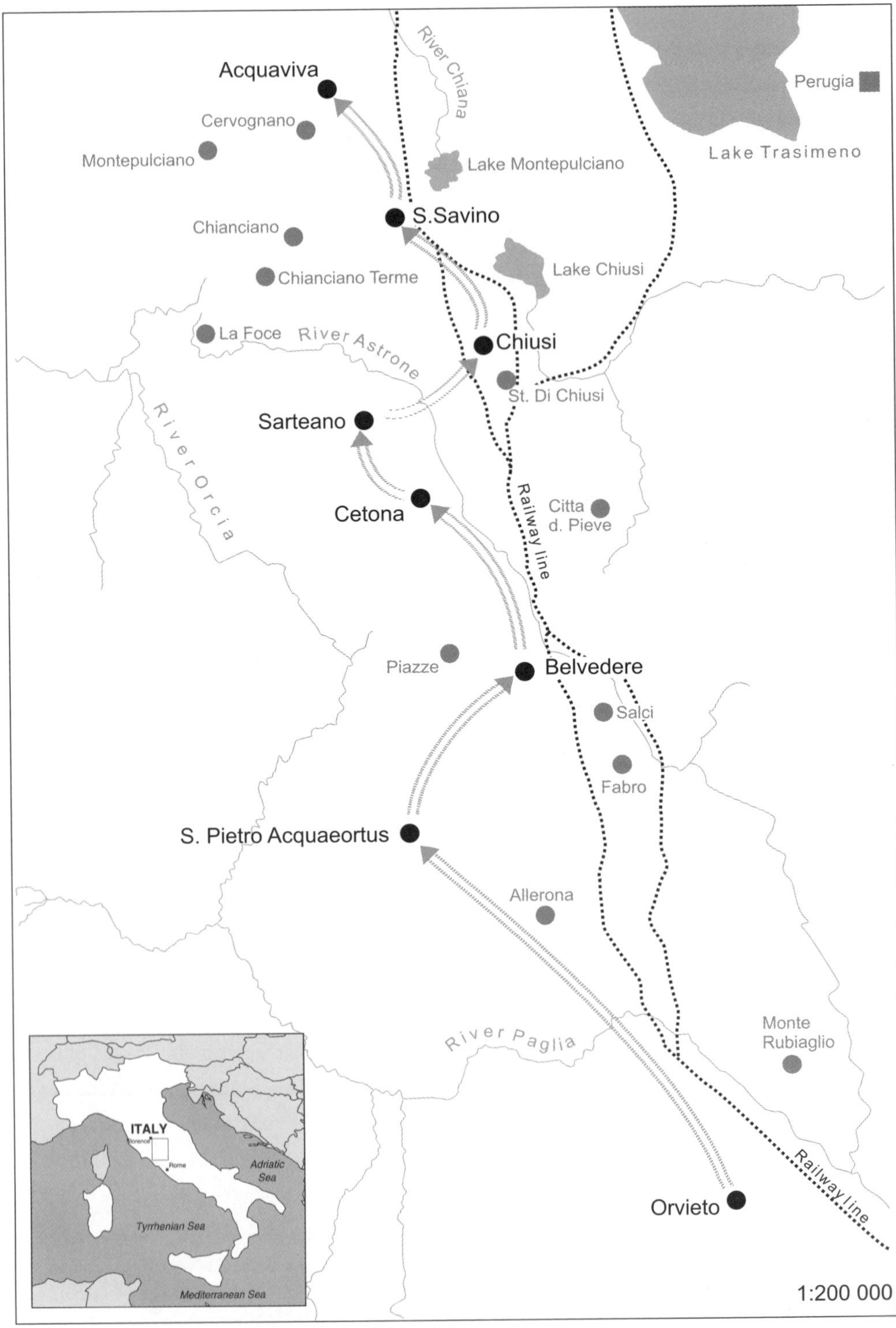

Acquaviva
Cervognano
Montepulciano
River Chiana
Lake Montepulciano
Perugia
Lake Trasimeno
S.Savino
Chianciano
Chianciano Terme
Lake Chiusi
La Foce
River Astrone
Chiusi
St. Di Chiusi
Sarteano
River Orcia
Cetona
Railway line
Citta
d. Pieve
Piazze
Belvedere
Salci
Fabro
S. Pietro Acquaeortus
Allerona
River Paglia
Monte
Rubiaglio
Orvieto
Railway line
ITALY
Florence
Rome
Adriatic
Sea
Tyrrhenian Sea
Mediterranean Sea
1:200 000

A Bill Maudlin cartoon captioned: "Me future is sealed, Willie. I'm gonna be a perfessor on various types of European soil". The digging of one's slit trench, fox hole, funk hole or dugout was an enduring part of life for everyone within range of enemy artillery. The size, shape and construction of the 'fighting hole' varied to suit the terrain and tactical conditions; within reasonable limits, the soldier was allowed to exercise his own ingenuity.

Vehicle wastage in the 'A' Echelon of the Pretoria Regiment up until the end of August 1944												
Vehicle	Blown up on mines		'Brewed'		Damaged by enemy fire		Overturned & damaged due to terrain		Wear & tear		Total	
	A	B	A	B	A	B	A	B	A	B	A	B
Sherman	5	11	14	1	10	10	2	13	12	16	43	50
Stuart	1	1	4		1	1			4	12	10	14
Scout Cars									6		6	
Armoured ambulance	1										1	
Total	7	12	18	1	11	11	2	13	22	7	60	64
	19		19		22		15		29		124	
Grand Total											124	

A: vehicles had to be replaced.
B: vehicles recovered, repaired and returned to unit

From the above table, it can be seen that vehicles blown up on mines could usually be repaired, whereas only one out of 19 tanks 'brewed' or burned out could be repaired. An equal number of tanks were blown up on mines as were brewed but the greatest damage came from enemy fire.

Wednesday 14 June 1944 – Thursday 15 June 1944: Orvieto

The Germans were using the treacherous terrain to their full advantage and brought in their elusive self-propelled guns. Much of the fire came from the wooded ravines and surrounding fields, but the town of Orvieto was vacated without a fight. With the Prince Alfred's Guard leading the division, the infantry skirmished on until there was a hold-up north of the city. After four hours on the road the 1/6th Field Regiment was called into emergency action at Porano to engage enemy infantry and artillery. The road into and out of Orvieto was under direct observation.

While moving to its next position in the dark, one of the quads went over a mine—some thought it was a shell. It is inadvisable to move in a minefield, but Gunner E.R. 'Mac' Cormack leaped from the truck, breaking his nose as he hit the ground. His friends took him under a culvert and assessed the damage by the light of a match. Mac would speak with a nasal twang for the rest of his life.

The gun battery arrived in harbour on the other side of Orvieto at 2000 hours. This nighttime occupation was not ideal.

Captain Paul Nellmapius, the 23-year-old Regimental Survey Officer of 1/6th Field Regiment, came from a privileged, albeit broken, home. The family had lived in Kalk Bay in the 1930s and his mother, Zoe, later moved to Klein Tuin in Clovelly. His personnel records suggest that a family member organized him a commission in the artillery at Potchefstroom. Nellmapius forged his leadership qualities on the playing fields of Bishops. He "excelled at rugby, athletics and shooting, and took an active part in the welfare outreach activities of the school".[129] He was head prefect during his post-matric year, 1940. Nellmapius had come through the North African campaign with the Cape Field Artillery. On the winding route through Orvieto, he was called upon to investigate a hold-up on the road ahead. The area was under fire from self-propelled 88mm guns, and a shell burst from one of these killed him instantly.

The First City/Cape Town Highlanders formed a bridgehead over the Paglia River during the early hours of 15 June. The Witwatersrand Rifles/Regiment De la Rey went through it later that morning, moving up the Paglia River valley until it struck the German defence line just south of Allerona, north of the village of Monterubiaglio. Here, the Germans managed to inflict some casualties on the men and tanks of the Pretoria Regiment before withdrawing from Allerona.

129 Kalk Bay Historical Society, Bulletin No. 6, March 2002, p. 160.

Beyond Orvieto, at 1100 hours, the leading Stuart tank (also known as a Honey tank) of the Pretoria Regiment was hit six times by 50mm armour-piercing rounds. Three crew, Corporal H.C. Webster, Lance-Corporal W.J. van Rooyen and Trooper D.B. Woolmore, were killed while the lap gunner baled out. Denis Woolmore's family was from Nkandhla in Zululand. He was 21 years' old, and not the last of the Woolmore family to be killed in the campaign.

Seeing what had happened, the crew of the second Stuart fired smoke to cover the damaged tank. Sergeant M.C. Viljoen jumped out with the first-aid box to render assistance and was hit and killed by snipers. Lieutenant Bray spotted the source and put it out of action. Two more tanks were disabled by further fire from a 75mm Pak and bazookas. The crew of the first baled out, but Corporal Rowland's crew in the second tank continued firing. Lance-Corporal K. Gates, one of those who baled from the first tank, was hit by a sniper. He was hit again while his wound was being dressed, this time fatally.

The Witwatersrand Rifles/Regiment De la Rey, together with the tanks of the Pretoria Regiment, took Allerona on 15 June and continued ahead after the usual welcome from the locals. The narrow, crooked main street of Allerona was extremely congested at this stage, as were the many secondary lanes to the west of the main highway, as the Moroccans were also trying to move ahead. From here on, much of the movement took place cross-country rather than on the main highway which can be seen in the valley below Allerona.

Supported by artillery and mortars, the infantry went forward riding on tanks, mopping up prisoners—and occasionally shooting them in retaliation for white-flag outrages and other infractions of the rules of war. Hodgson confirms this practice in a letter to his father:

> As you say in your letters the snipers have given us a good bit of trouble, but luckily they have not caused much damage. As for mortars, they use a lot of them, but their mortar-bomb is a bit of a useless affair, because if you get flat, you must receive practically a direct hit to get hurt. Yes, Jerry has got the habit of firing on us until we get right on him, then puts up his hands, but don't you believe for one minute that he gets away with it; all he gets is one between the eyes, and very quickly too.

Regimental headquarters of the 7/23rd Medium Regiment pulled into position south of Allerona at 1930 hours in pouring rain on 15 June. Johnston moved up with the guns in his observation post tank. His diary reads: "Cherries. Refuelled. Pulled out ammo truck, water cart and tank and after breakfast went on to reach troop for lunch at Orvieto. Cleaned carburettor. Moved past Allerona and burned out station and railway trucks. Parked with troop." On the same day, farther forward, the Witwatersrand Rifles/Regiment De la Rey lost four killed, one of whom was Lance-Corporal H.S. Fourie who was killed by a hand grenade dropped by a German who was ostensibly approaching to surrender. A similar incident occurred the following day, as described in the diary of B Company: "One of four Jerries approaching to give themselves up, dropped a hand grenade among our chaps. Luck was on our side and nobody was caught. All four were shot on the spot."[130]

Friday 16 June 1944: San Pietro via Allerona

Experiencing the action firsthand, Hodgson reflected on the big picture and took pleasure in being on the winning team. Only now did he mention the role his company had played in climbing the cliffs at Bagnoregio. What he did not mention was the death of his close friend Frank Ledingham in that battle:

> Isn't the news grand? The invasion has come at last and with a vengeance. All we can do now is await developments but these we cannot expect for over a month as we must give them a chance to mass the forces, and bring in the colossal amount of supplies that are needed—but when the drive does come, I feel that it will be a great success and would hate to be in the shoes of the Hun. The drive in this country has also been a great success. As you will have seen in the papers, we have formed the spearhead of the advance since Rome, so I know all the news first-hand. It has been a wonderful experience and I have got a lot of satisfaction out of seeing Jerry run. The way I see it, our best success has been the capture of Bagnoregio where he put up the stiffest resistance so far—we had the leading part so it was a feather in our caps. The Russians seem to be getting busy again—I hope they start another big drive like the last one, and smash their way right into Germany. From my point of view, they cannot do it quick enough, as I want to get back home to you all again—but it won't be long now Mum and Dad!!

San Pietro is even higher up than Allerona. It is not a village but an area of forest identified by one farmstead named San Pietro Acquaeortus, which overlooks the town of Fabro as well as the dense forests. The enemy was driven out and a number of prisoners taken at San Pietro. The artillery created a killing field below their levelled position on a hill. Fielding described what he saw:

130 S. Monick, *A bugle calls*, pp. 357–358.

> From the dankness of the woods, came the stench of exploded cordite. Burned out enemy trucks, weapons and in many places, many dead bodies were to be seen. Our men had taken a heavy toll on the Hun. In the woods were nightmare scenes. Bodies, bits of bodies, letters and clothing lay strewn about. High up in the trees where gaps in the foliage made little sky-light windows, pieces of uniform hung, blown there by the force of an exploding shell. At a bend in the road, a Hun crouched; only the upper part of his body was there, a hand still held onto the trigger of his machine gun, and his eyes glinted over the sights, even in death. Like a waxwork he lay.[131]

Northeast of San Pietro, a group of young snipers from the Hermann Göring Division, aged between 17 and 18, walked into 12th Brigade headquarters and surrendered. Apparently they had been abandoned by their officer when they felt themselves surrounded. Nevertheless, according to the intelligence officer who interrogated them, they were "strongly built young Nazis … with a certain look of disdain in their eyes".[132]

Lionel Wulfsohn was present when the regimental chaplain of the Witwatersrand Rifles/Regiment De la Rey, 'Doempie' Cloete, captured two Germans on this stretch of road. The two had apparently been left behind deliberately to harass the Allied high command officers who were following the advance of the army in open vehicles:

> They had dug a very strong position into the side of the road and had camouflaged the position with bush. Realizing there was something wrong, Doempie pushed the bush to one side and shouted to the two men in Afrikaans: "*Kom uit kerels—die oorlog is op 'n einde.*" [Come out chaps, the war is over.] They heeded his instructions and two very weary Germans climbed out … One was a man of about 45 years of age who … was glad to be taken prisoner … The other was a Hitler Jugend lad of about 18 … shaking in every bone fibre and tissue of his body as he believed he would be shot out of hand. The only 'weapon' that Doempie carried was his short officer's cane.[133]

Axelson mentioned that some of the prisoners brought in on 16 June had been trying to escape from Orvieto on foot and had been hiding on the roadside when overtaken by the South Africans. Enemy opposition that day was slight. The road wound through an oak forest which had been set on fire by shells

131 W.L. Fielding, *With the 6th Div*, p. 106.

132 *Ibid*, p. 110.

133 L.M. Wulfsohn, *'Doempie' Cloete: a legend in his own lifetime.*

and mortars and visibility was poor. In a cable sent from Allerona, the South African Director of Information, A.N. Wilson, describes the "triumph of organization [which] makes rapid advance possible". The article provides a comprehensive picture of the move from Orvieto to Allerona and was published on 21 June 1944, which was the start of the hold-up at Chiusi. Elsewhere in the same newspaper was an article pertaining to the British capture of Perugia which proclaimed: "Nazis continue hurried retreat in Italy—Eighth Army advances 20 miles in two days."[134]

Assisi had also been captured recently. The Americans were making good progress between the west coast and Lake Bolsena in this latest spurt but there was organized chaos on all roads leading north.

In the words of Axelson's American counterpart, Lieutenant-Colonel Chester Starr, "To gain a correct picture of the 5th Army, one must visualize it not as a thin fighting line but as a zone up to 50 miles deep slowly advancing up the Italian peninsular—an armoured borer, as it were, with a steel cutting edge fed and kept going by a great mass of machinery." The cutting edge, as represented by the infantry, formed less than a fourth the Army's strength.[135]

The press camp moved with the rear echelons. An article in the *Rand Daily Mail* explains the logistics of keeping the division on the road:

> For some days, the Sixth South African Division has been advancing along a road that does not rank as one of the main highways of Italy. It has not therefore, a tarmac surface like the Italian main roads, and its narrow bridges over culverts were not made for the passage of great tank transporters and other huge vehicles which a modern army uses.
>
> In a mechanized war, any road that cannot carry two lines of traffic and still leave space for the ubiquitous dispatch rider to pass, is no road at all. It is just a track. And it has been along such a track, dusty beyond imagination, that the Springboks—moving their heavy armour with them—have in their pursuit of the enemy, been setting the pace which the other Allied divisions on their flanks moving up the splendid broad tarmac main roads, have found it difficult to emulate. The reputation for mobility which Dan Pienaar's First Brigade gained against the Italians in Abyssinia is being maintained by the Sixth Division under General Poole in very different and perhaps even more exacting conditions. It is a triumph of organization that makes such rapid daily advance possible. It is organization backed by the keen enthusiasm of a well-trained and well-disciplined division. Between Orvieto, which the Springboks occupied some days ago, and Allerona, which was taken on Friday,

134 *Rand Daily Mail*, Sixth Division sets fast pace in Italy, 21/6/1944.

135 C.G. Starr, *From Salerno to the Alps*, p. 371.

> stretches a great, broad irregular valley. In this lovely valley was stretched out on Saturday the whole weight of the Springbok Division in the ordered panoply of war. The main forces of the Division rested a few hours while the reconnaissance units and the advance guard moved forward, probing the road ahead. Bivouacs sprung up on either side of the road which itself was kept clear for essential supplies and for emergency movements.
>
> Every unit has its own number allocated to it, and every unit makes its bivouac each day in the same precise relationship to the unit with the succeeding number—except when the battle order of the Division is changed. Along the road through the valley are innumerable road signs. Here, at the right-hand side, is a track leading off into a cornfield, and the road sign showed here is Unit Number 43. If you go another 50 yards along the road, you will come across a similar dusty track leading, perhaps into an orchard of fig trees and the road sign will tell you that unit 44 has made its temporary resting place beneath there. And so all along this thin ribbon of road, you will find vast numbers of similar road signs, and similar dusty turn-offs where the Division lies outstretched—unit after unit resting—but always ready for a forward movement within half an hour.
>
> When the time for the movement comes, each unit has its time for joining the long convoy forward and takes its ordered place in the great armoured cavalcade. This sort of thing has been done so often in the past three weeks that the Division now moves like clockwork.[136]

Saturday 17 June 1944 – Tuesday 20 June 1944: Belvedere

The Pretoria Regiment's A Squadron moved through Belvedere—which was still held by the Witwatersrand Rifles/Regiment De la Rey—on the morning of 17 June. The thick woods made it difficult to maintain contact with the supporting infantry. Three of the tanks engaged an enemy Mk IV; the graves of five crewmembers were later found dug alongside it. Lieutenant Davey's tank also scored a direct hit on a Nebelwerfer.

The squadron returned to harbour for the night at Belvedere, having remained in one position, under mortar fire, for five hours. The infantry (Royal Natal Carbineers) was pinned down and unable to reach its objective that night. Torrential rain began to fall on 17 June and continued for the next ten days, apart from the odd morning of sunshine. The softened ground was churned into a sea of mud, restricting tanks to the main roads. The men wore gas capes as protection against the heavy rain. The rough country made for heavy going but by the evening of 17 July, the whole of the 12th South African Motorized Brigade and Divisional Headquarters, together with the 1/6th

136 *Rand Daily Mail*, Sixth Division sets fast pace in Italy, 21/6/1944.

Field Regiment, 4/22nd Field Regiment and 7/23rd Medium Regiment, had passed through Allerona to find themselves in the Fabro–Le Piazze area. The Royal Natal Carbineers, which was in action with the Prince Alfred's Guard, had lost eight killed and six wounded in the day's fighting. The operations were centred around Le Piazze, Fighine and the miniscule hamlet of Salci.

The guns of the 1/6th Field Regiment were deployed in a muddy field not far from the A1 highway and the railway line, without the benefit of being dug in or camouflaged. Close to their gun lines were seven graves of Carbineers who had been scythed down by a Spandau. The road up which the South Africans advanced was little more than a track. Only one-way traffic was possible for a distance of 15 miles from Allerona, and as there was no place for a staging area, certain periods had to be allowed for one-way traffic travelling in the opposite direction. The period of heavy rain meant that the slippery roads on the approach to Monte Cetona had to be covered with branches. This required some hard labour of the First City/Cape Town Highlanders.

Now that German resistance was becoming fanatical, Baker found himself worrying, especially during idle moments: "We all felt the future to be precarious, some more than others. None of us wanted to go into it without making our peace with those around us. I began to develop a sense of foreboding ..."[137]

The Natal Mounted Rifles had been at rest for a while, but now the call came for them to move out:

> Saturday 17th June '44—Nr. Allerona
> Had several alarms before pulling out for our new rendezvous. Shortly after lunch [I] was on the air (wireless set) for our troop. Finished letter home and drew some kit. Made lunch and dinner (for the crew). Travelled for almost two hours (by tank) over very mountainous country and passed through Allerona. Camped in another vineyard and we had a terrific storm with hail. There is also a nip in the air here. Crashed a bottle of Champagne with Richard Platt before retiring.

It rained again on 18 June, making the secondary roads impassable for wheeled vehicles. Twenty vehicles had become stuck in the mud in just one half-mile stretch. Nevertheless, the division made fair progress by making use of the tar roads allocated to the British on the right and the French on the left.

News was received at 1930 hours on 19 June that the Witwatersrand Rifles/ Regiment De la Rey was filtering into Cetona, and the next day it was reported

137 D.M. Baker, *War, wine and valour*, p. 403.

to be in South African hands. As far as Hodgson was concerned, the rain came at the right time as everything was getting dusty and he enjoyed having a nip in the air. Considering that an army marches on its stomach, the going was good here in the breadbasket of central Italy:

> Our own cooking business is getting along very well, and we have got so much food these days, we don't know what to do with it all. We cannot carry it all, as there is very little room at the back of the truck, as it is with 14 men and all our kit, but all the same we have got things so well rigged up; we are very comfortable.

After spending several days in one place completing vehicle maintenance, Johnston enjoyed some excitement on 18 June: "Moved. Pulled [*illegible*]'s gun out of manure heap. Fred full of vino and driving fast on winding road."

As the Allies got closer to La Foce, the Germans set up their machine guns in Iris Origo's garden. She describes the Germans as "unspeakably worn out and dirty". Discipline had broken down and it appeared that each unit looked after themselves and wanted nothing to do with members of other units. "We hear that a neighbouring farmer made a fuss about giving up his pig, and now he is lying dead in a field. His daughters, in tears, came to take refuge with us."

Since leaving Rome, the 6th South African Armoured Division had been confronted by the Hermann Göring Para Panzer Division, the 4th Para Division and the 362nd Infantry Division, among others. As these divisions were not up to strength, the 356th Infantry Division had been brought in to "stop the rot", but it too, was badly mauled at Bagnoregio.

Wednesday 21 June 1944 – Sunday 25 June 1944: Cetona

The main event during this period was the Battle for Chiusi which lasted six days and involved elements of the 11th South African Armoured Brigade and the 12th South African Motorized Brigade, the rest of the division being busy around Cetona and Sarteano. Chiusi will always be associated particularly with the Imperial Light Horse/Kimberley Regiment and the First City/Cape Town Highlanders, and marked the first major setback for the South Africans.

The failure started with the erroneous belief that the Imperial Light Horse/Kimberley Regiment had already passed through the town. The Chiusi station is situated below the hilltop town, about a mile to the east in a separate industrial centre called Stazione di Chiusi. This geography is made even more confusing, even for present-day visitors, because the only access road runs through the saddle between the 'twin peaks' visible from Stazione di Chiusi. There is only one 'Chiusi proper' and the most direct route to this ancient Etruscan centre is up the stone terraces.

The fiasco is also blamed on close-quarter fighting which limited the use of artillery, as well as the rain which bogged down tanks on their way to the rescue. Added to this, intelligence regarding enemy strength was incorrect.

The Imperial Light Horse/Kimberley Regiment started reconnaissance patrols on the night of 20 June. The rest of the regiment, together with a squadron of the Special Service Battalion, moved forward at 0700 hours the following day. The Natal Mounted Rifles tried to move forward on the road from Città della Pieve but was halted by fierce resistance. Meanwhile, the 4/22nd Field Regiment and 7/23rd Medium Regiment fired a creeping barrage from the sides of the road in support of the attack. Engineers of the 8th Field Squadron were tasked with clearing the many mines.

It fell to the First City/Cape Town Highlanders to assault the town. The men began climbing the stone terraces at 2345 hours. After entering the ancient quarter near the cathedral, they took up positions in a wine shop and in the Teatro Comunale in the town square. As they waited, a tank came lumbering along. Major Bartlett only had one projectile infantry anti-tank, but he ordered a reliable NCO to have a crack at the tank. Before he could shoot, the tank blew him and his weapon to pieces.[138] The First City/Cape Town Highlanders war diary provides a blow-by-blow account of the drama that followed:

0257 A Coy report having consolidated their posn in theatre & two adjoining houses, and that one pl has reached the 'Castle'.

0312 A Coy report a tank milling about in front of the cinema.

0500 A Coy report A Coy are unable to continue advance, B Coy take up firm base on small feature.

0520 B Coy Comd reports 'My left flnk is consolidated'.

0522 A Coy report 'Our coy HQ + 2 pls is 50 yds to right of tower', 1 pl 100 yds beyond it.

[138] DODAR, UWH, Box 142, Interview with Lieutenant-Colonel (formerly Major) Bartlett, Commander of A Company First City/Cape Town Highlanders, 24/11/1948.

0523 C Coy report is on right of rd going into CHIUSI, next to high wall sited in house.

0535 A Coy report 'Require assistance quickly. Enemy appears to be in strength. Tank is still here firing point blank at the walls of our bldg'.

0545 CO goes to B Coy. A Coy report further 12 cas.

0550 A Coy report 'enemy infiltrating all around us and battering the building with his tanks'.

0553 Arty concs, HE and Airburst brought down around A Coy by observation by B Coy.

0556 B Coy reports that 3 stretcher bearers in rear of Coy trod on a mine after whole Coy had traversed the area. 1 CC OR killed, 2 wounded.

0559 D Coy to tac HQ 'We have scored a direct hit on a tank with PIAT. Tank withdrew undamaged.'

0622 D Coy report a Mk III and a Mk IV (long) tank identified.

0638 A Coy report tank still milling around and shelling their vicinity

0639 D Coy report a third tank a Mk IV Special. Attempts are made then, by D Coy directing fire, to bring arty fire onto tanks but are unsuccessful.

0815 A Coy report having done some successful sniping, with Brens and rifles but posn no better.

0918 A Coy report 'Enemy are now creeping into our last defences.'

1000 D Coy fall back from untenable posns. Withdrawal difficult. This was Coy HQ + 1 platoon, other 2 had become detached in previous engagement and were with B Coy. Casualties 3 killed, 2 wounded, 1 missing.

1030 No further communication with A Coy.[139]

[139] DODAR, WD, Box 633, First City/Cape Town Highlanders, 1–30 June 1944.

There are conflicting accounts of how the battle ended. Major L.G. Murray, a company commander in the First City/Cape Town Highlanders, states that at 1030 hours on 23 June 1944, a message was received at headquarters saying "enemy tanks battering down the walls of our building", after which the men fought their way into the street but surrendered when they found themselves looking down the barrel of a tank.

Major Bartlett recounts that he told his men to fix bayonets and "show the Germans what South Africans can do". This command was accepted without a murmur but just then some heavy shells came crashing through the roof, wounding the major and killing a number of his men. By now, 32 out of 40 soldiers had been killed or wounded. Badly dazed, Bartlett gave the order to surrender. Some men started shouting "Kamerad!" but the major did not like this and told them to stop. He staggered down the stairs into the lobby and the Germans ceased fire.[140]

An article written in *Der Deutche Fallschirmjager* gives the combined accounts of a German soldier, Walter Stiewing, and Lionel Wylie, the leader of 3 Platoon, A Company, First City/Cape Town Highlanders, the group holed up in the Teatro. According to this account, a white flag was waved outside the window of the Teatro by a German being held prisoner by the South Africans. A German soldier by the name of Herbert Zidek entered alone and, through the dust and the gun smoke, saw a scene of human misery that he would never forget. Only then did the Germans realize that their opponents were not Americans but, in fact, South Africans, who were quite taken aback when they had their hands shaken and were patted on the back in congratulation. The wounded were taken away in an ambulance and were treated with great consideration. Fielding wrote of how the company commander was last seen standing a little way up the staircase, emptying his revolver into the enemy.

Another version by Harry Pearce, a signalman attached to the First City/Cape Town Highlanders who was captured, goes as follows: "By this time, Major Bartlett was very badly shaken and our situation was hopeless, so in order to save lives, he gave the order to surrender. The date: 22 June 1944."[141]

The short version of this story as recorded in the regimental war diary of the

140 DODAR, UWH, Box 142; Interview with Lieutenant-Colonel (formerly Major) Bartlett, Commander of A Company First City/Cape Town Highlanders, 24/11/1948.

141 W.L. Fielding, *With the 6th Div*, p. 120; G.B. Hobbs, *From Sicily to the Alps*, p. 116; 21 June was the first anniversary of Tobruk.

1/6th Field Regiment is as follows: "Imperial Light Horse/Kimberley Regiment report themselves in, but later 1 Coy of First City/Cape Town Highlanders are cut off in the town." The gunners were kept very busy during the battle firing at the gun areas, vehicles, tanks and houses and putting down smoke. There was a shortage of 25-pounder ammunition and the artillery was limited to 50 rounds per gun per day. The guns supported whenever they could, firing smoke to cover the withdrawal on 22 June. From their position southeast of Cetona, the 1/6th Field Regiment could clearly see both Chiusi and Città della Pieve on the opposite side of the valley. The clock tower of Chiusi sticks out from the cluster of buildings and although it presented a ridiculously small target, the 25-pounders succeeded in knocking out this potential observation post.

When shells began to land in the garden of nearby La Foce, Iris Origo took her charge of almost 60 refugee children on foot to Montepulciano. Locals helped them up the last steep pull into the walled city and she felt safe for the time being. "We have left behind everything that we possess, but I have never in my life felt so rich and so thankful as looking down on the children as they lay asleep." A mechanic set up a battery radio in a small backroom and they listened to the news that Chiusi had been retaken by the Germans.[142]

The South African prisoners from the battle were taken to a factory yard near Montepulciano, from where Sergeant Harry Campbell managed to escape and rejoin his unit a week later. Another 15 or 16 Highlanders of A Company, some wounded, managed to hide out until the town was finally taken by the Royal Natal Carbineers on 26 June at 0720 hours. They survived undetected in the midst of a regiment of German troops, with virtually no food or water while shells from their own artillery rained down on them. The regimental war diary states that the men were assisted by partisans and civilians. "Even now, the whole nightmare incident is a complete mystery to us," says Private Fred Taylor of Heidelberg, whose leadership was praised by the men when they returned.[143]

An article in *The Star* newspaper of 28 June states that the party consisted of 16 men, four of whom were wounded. The article also mentions that Private Taylor was responsible for organizing the group. They carried sufficient rations for only 24 hours, but were fortunate in finding three wine jars of water, and Taylor handed out two spoonfuls of water to each man every day. More luck was

142 I. Origo, *War in Val d'Orcia*, p. 221.

143 G.B. Hobbs, *From Sicily to the Alps*, p. 119.

on their side when they found a hen in their hiding place. This meant that they were able to share an egg every day. The men made their beds where they could: Private I. Bartie of Cape Town slept in a wine barrel, while some soldiers slept standing up. One man always stayed awake to keep the others from snoring, as there were Germans billeted 15 yards away. The press attributed their rescue to Royal Natal Carbineers troops under Major Edrich Mackenzie of Richmond, Natal and Captain (later Major) Lionel Gallimore of Port Elizabeth.[144]

During this period, other elements of the division were in action along a five-mile front from Chiusi to Sarteano. The Witwatersrand Rifles/Regiment De la Rey, accompanied by a troop of tanks from the Pretoria Regiment, advanced through Cetona to Sarteano where the battalion was to remain for four days, until 26 June. The events of the night of 21 June are recorded in the A Company diary:

> Quite a hectic night—shelling and firing frequent. Long bursts of Vickers—now and again Tommy, Bren and rifle and characteristic Spandau. Jerry patrol infiltrates 3 Platoon area—sorry he did so—fired upon and decamped in a hurry leaving behind Teller mine, detonators, stick grenades, caps and web equipment—bandages and blood. Evidently hard hit—at least two badly—heel marks where person dragged away—not much sleep—all on edge and not knowing which way to look ...[145]

The forward observation officer of the 7/23rd Medium Regiment, Lieutenant G.A. Hosking, received the highest praise for his keenness and sense of duty. After four consecutive days of observation-post duty, during which he had little sleep or food, he went forward on foot with the foremost patrol and, under heavy fire, directed the divisional artillery throughout the day of 21 June.

The headquarters of the 7/23rd Medium Regiment was located at Città della Pieve on the right hand side of the present A1 highway. Here, Johnston was put on observation-post duty overlooking the town of Chiusi, five miles away. As is clear from his diary during this period, resistance had stiffened:

> 22nd
> Ities in wine cellar, Saw Jerry infantry and gun. Burial party. Jerry shelled, got a bloke with Spandau fire. Moved back, slept in vineyard with other tanks. Shelled right and left all night.

---

144 *The Star*, How stranded Springboks lay low in Chiusi for four days, 28/6/1944.

145 S. Monick, *A bugle calls*, p. 362.

23rd
Moved up to another house. Shelled all day. Major killed and three wounded 20 yds behind us. Pulled back to stable for night. Had ½ pig that Jerry had killed with 88 AP.

24th
Up to same place again. Walked back to stable for lunch. Jerry shelled spasmodically all day. Also Nebelwerfer—lousy damn thing. Back to barn for night.

On 23 June, elements of the 24th Guards Brigade with the usual support of the Royal Durban Light Infantry and the Pretoria Regiment took the ridge beyond Cetona towards Sarteano. An 88 giving the 1/6th Field Regiment a hard time was wiped out by a regimental concentration as payback for the casualties recently inflicted on a group of engineers who were unloading equipment at Cetona. Hodgson's company, which was attributed with the eventual relief of Chiusi, was meanwhile taking a short break behind the lines:

> We are very comfortably off at the moment, as we are partaking of some Italian hospitality. We are staying in their house and we are very comfortable. It is a farmhouse in the real farm style, but cosy. At the moment they have got a lovely sucking pig on the fire, which we are going to have for supper—this we will eat with green peas, carrots and onions. This will be followed by hot margarined toast (just like buttered toast now that we have forgotten the taste of butter) with fresh honey straight from the hive. It is little wonder that I am putting on so much weight. I must weigh about 175/80 lbs. I think I am a bit taller but am not certain.[146]

Field Marshal Smuts paid a 66-hour visit to Italy that week. He flew in an Avro York from Algiers to an airport near Rome, where he was met by an escort of Spitfires before being led into the capital by a convoy of Italian motorcycle police. From there, he flew to the most advanced fighter base in Italy.

Representatives of the Guards Brigade were at the lunch he attended afterwards. One officer remarked, "What a man. He makes such a big impression with the men because he always introduces the homely touch."

At Orvieto, Smuts scrambled up a pile of rubble in the railway yards at the foot of the hill to take a photograph, but did not have time to go into the cathedral city. The next day, 24 June, he addressed the small delegation which could be spared by the division at a venue approximately four miles southwest

[146] J.B. Hodgson–M.V. Hodgson, 22/6/1944.

of Città della Pieve (which was under shelling). Axelson, his photographer Roger Madden and assorted correspondents were there to record the event.[147]

Smuts reminded the men of how he had promised them that "*julle sal daar wees*—you will be there!" He added, apparently to the men's amusement, "*en nou* is *julle daar* [and now you *are* there]". Naturally, he took the opportunity to lavish praise on his fellow South Africans. He also heaped compliments on the Guards Brigade. Smuts also addressed members of the South African Air Force during his lightning visit, telling them that they were the "Voortrekkers of the air". At this stage, even he was of the opinion that the war would be over by the end of summer, but he warned of heavy fighting to come.

The running of the Durban July provided a welcome distraction. Discussions and betting started well before the actual race day but it took time for the results to become known. Members of the Royal Natal Carbineers' B Company held a sweepstake and Hodgson drew a horse called Seawash. However, he had made a point of studying the forms and, as there was a bookie in the regiment, he also put money on Noble Peer, "just for a lark".

The race took place on 1 July but the results had still not reached the front lines in Italy by Wednesday 5 July. As it turned out, none of the horses picked by Hodgson were in the winner's circle that year:

> Now that I come to think of it, it will not be long before we have the 'Ersatz' Durban July Handicap. I saw a list of all the horses running in a paper the other day—mind you, the paper was old as it was published early in May. Well, I will give you the result and you can see how close I get; the race will most probably be over by the time you get this letter. If the course enables good going (no rain etc) the result will be: 1st Noble Peer, 2nd Preston Pan, 3rd Dunkeld; if it is a wet day or the course is soft from rain on previous days the result will be 1st Preston Pan, 2nd Noble Peer, 3rd Dunkeld.[148]

The business of scouting ahead of the tanks, or 'walking the plank' was a dangerous one. On 25 June Corporal P.D. Steele, a 24-year-old from Newlands in Cape Town and a University Blue for fencing, was killed by mortar fire

---

147 E. Axelson, *A year in Italy*, p. 24; *The Star*, General Smuts's crowded hours in Italy, 1/7/1944; *Rand Daily Mail*, Smuts visits Sixth Division in Italy, 27/6/1944; DODAR, WD, Box 630, 7/23rd Medium Regiment, 24/6/1944.

148 J.B. Hodgson–M.V. Hodgson, 22/6/1944; J.B. Hodgson–M.V. Hodgson, 5/7/1944; The Durban July Handicap in 1944 was won by a horse called Monteith; the filly Preston Pan however did go on to become a highly successful broodmare.

while out observing. Baker, who was soon to meet a similar fate, wrote of his immediate priorities in his diary entries for 24 and 25 June:

> Very troublesome tummy all day ... just outside Sarteano in pouring rain. On guard during the night. Heavily shelled in the area by mortars and early in the morning by enemy tank. Caught a fowl and roasted it ... More rain during the day but kept fairly dry. Had a bath in the stream and washed some clothes ... rain cleared today.

The war diary of the 7/23rd Medium Regiment recorded on 24 June: "News just received, that Lieutenant J. Stevenson who was wounded at Bagnoregio [by friendly fire] on 12 June, is dead." The following day, while at Città della Pieve, the mediums engaged a Tiger tank. Firing 45 rounds, they scored 12 near misses. Shortly afterwards, it was knocked out by a lucky shot from an M10 at 2,000 yards. While the rain continued and the drama raged at Chiusi, Bourhill found some comfort in the mail:

> Yesterday in the rain post came—and behold the sun did shine in my heart. One long one from you written over the weekend 10th–12th and one from Val. The ointment is here—what a price to pay for it, and especially because the sores are gone, but it'll be useful for all sorts of things and I'm always getting chips knocked out of self! Yes, I was at Paliano. Our first action after Cassino on Highway Six. There is a photo of Patterson taking a service next to our gun pit at Cassino—I'm in the pit on the far side, I don't know if it will be in Union papers; it's in the 'Springbok'.

Monday 26 June 1944 – Wednesday 28 June 1944: Sarteano

Soldiers needed little encouragement to dig in when the consequences of enemy shelling were felt close to home, but at Sarteano many of the 1/6th Field Regiment's artillerymen were caught without adequate cover. Fortunately for Bourhill, the sergeant in charge of his 'sub' was adamant about digging in, and he did so with religious zeal:

> I've just dug a wonderful slit trench, in lovely ground and now I'm in the bivvy writing a letter ... the [original] slit trench got filled up with water even up to overflowing, and it came to pass that the warriors of the army of Jordan did wash their bodies and eating irons therein and did make sport of my slit trench at my expense. And so I did take unto myself the implements which are the mark of labour—the tools which men call the pick and shovel ... and came one bearing three stripes upon his arm and said with great mirth, "Go then out, into the rain even, and dig thyself another trench which is a slit, so that ye may be safe from fire and from water" and I arose and went out, even into the rain and ... I dug me

> another slit trench and I did remove there from many cubits of earth, and behold I did enjoy the digging thereof, and the water which some call sweat and the water which is rain did run off my body even into my booties. And as I dug men ceased to scoff but stayed to marvel at the speed with which the cubits of mud were removed … and I gloried in the pleasure of it and when it was done I partook of a wash in the sloot where once I had a slit trench, and therein, did I wash and I dried myself and put on dry garments, and I did smoke a [cigarette]. And I went into my [bivvy] and said I'll write now unto my people who are afar off and tell them of this thing which I have done.[149]

On 23 June, the *Eighth Army News* reported that the Germans had been quick to take advantage of the respite caused by the weather and lined up more artillery and mortars. Along the whole Eighth Army front, the enemy was employing "delaying actions on a scale more organized than recently".[150]

The Germans were not prepared to give up Chiusi without a fight as it was not only a natural defensive position; it was also a vital road junction. However, in danger of being outflanked by the British, they were forced to withdraw, leaving behind a multitude of mines and booby-traps on the terraces and approaches to the town. One MP was blown up when he picked a bunch of mulberries off a tree and an elderly woman was injured by an 'S' mine; her husband, going to her assistance, trod on another.

Tanks of the Natal Mounted Rifles entered unopposed and Chiusi was finally occupied by the Royal Natal Carbineers early on 26 June. Those killed in the past five days, including the German dead, were buried by Padre (Captain) Plant, near the Chiusi Power Station. An official photograph taken shortly after the battle shows six fresh graves in a vegetable garden. On one of the wooden crosses is stencilled: "An unknown soldier of the First City/Cape Town Highlanders". Another grave has flowers on it. While the Division moved on, up Route 71, a composite force consisting of the Imperial Light Horse/Kimberley Regiment, the Special Service Battalion, and and engineers under the Royal Natal Carbineers' Colonel Comrie moved up a lateral road parallel to the Astrone River. The Guards liberated Sarteano on 26 June, leaving the Royal Natal Carbineers in possession. The sappers had a particularly bad time clearing the roads which were still being shelled and mortared; snipers too were taking their toll. On 27 June, the Royal Natal Carbineers lost one of its prominent

149 S.F. Bourhill–E. Bourhill, 24/6/44.

150 *Eighth Army News*, Huns and mud slow Eighth, 23/6/1944.

junior officers, Lieutenant Percy Sperryn of Escourt, near Chiusi. In his last letter home, written two days before his death, he reassured his family, "I wish you would forget about those hunches about my welfare, nothing has happened to me or is likely to".[151]

Clearly, as this entry in the war diary of the 7/23rd Medium Regiment shows, the Germans were feeling the weight of a superior force:

> Weather fine and clear with haze in the afternoon … From his OP, Lieutenant B.J. Kenyon observed approximately ten enemy infantry. He engaged with one troop and afterwards reported the concentration effective. In his message, he said 'a fine concentration'. This message was somewhat mutilated in transit, with the result that a Divisional Concentration was put down on the unfortunate Germans. The adjutant has calculated that the weight of shell on this target was five tons or 100 lbs per German, ie about 50 lbs per foot of body.[152]

Another member of the Kenyon clan distinguished himself on 26 June: tanks of the Pretoria Regiment and supporting infantry were being heavily shelled; the only solution was to rush the enemy in a series of cavalry charges. Captain D.T. Kenyon, Lieutenant Chennells and Sergeant Clarke attacked in a series of mad dashes, engaging the enemy with high explosives, grenades and Tommy guns. The enemy, not expecting tanks to be a threat in this terrain, was driven off. A subsequent ground check revealed that the Pretoria Regiment (Princess Alice's Own) and Guards together had killed 40 and wounded 60. The Pretoria Regiment lost only one killed when a piece of shrapnel entered under a .50 Browning AA gun, passing under the helmet of Corporal P.A.H. Wiley. La Foce in the Val d'Orcia was at last reached by a squadron of the Pretoria Regiment, together with the Scots Guards, on 27 June. The enemy had sowed anti-personnel mines in "every defile and sloot" and the sappers came under machine-gun fire while clearing them. The Guards were deployed to protect them. A Tiger tank was reported in the area, but wasn't actually sighted. However, an enemy self-propelled gun fired from 1,700 yards, hitting a tank as well as some infantry carriers, causing several casualties.

By this time, Iris Origo and her charges had abandoned their home and found refuge at Montepulciano which, in turn, was entered by an advance party of the Scots Guards on the evening of 29 June.

---

151 M. Coghlan, *Pro Patria*, p. 42.

152 DODAR, WD, Box 630, 7/23rd Medium Regiment, 26/6/1944.

The Natal Mounted Rifles was also involved in the operations around La Foce, as well as those at Chianciano, a popular tourist spot famous for its thermal baths. The crew of Baker's tank (nicknamed 'Bechan', loosely derived from the Zulu word for 'rhino') were in the open when a shell burst nearby. A piece of shrapnel penetrated the skull of crew commander Sergeant Howard Foss, causing part of his brain to spill out. Although he made it back to an aid post, the wound proved fatal. Foss was a religious man, a family figure and a benevolent leader. Baker's diary reveals that this was a traumatic event:

> Monday, 26th June '44
> Had a very easy day. Spot more rain. Were shelled very heavily by Tiger tanks and mortars. Wrote home and read.
>
> Tuesday, 27th June '44
> Climbed out of Sarteano and made a thrust across almost impassable country to La Foce and began operations. Went down a road to Chianciano and were mortared ... Bashed a house said to be an observation post and then bumped a Tiger with two self propelled guns ... Dream Sanders and Howard Foss badly wounded by mortars.
>
> Wednesday, 28th June '44
> Went up the road again to Chianciano in an endeavour to locate Tiger tank and self-propelled guns. Had no luck—or all the luck and stayed under shade and cover all day. Located a house procuring cooking utensils, an umbrella and some pure linen sheets. Rained quite a bit. Slept and read (in the tank). Howard Foss died today!!

At 0900 hours on the morning of 28 June, the 1/6th regimental area came under heavy and accurate shelling. Six died as a result and seven were wounded. Fortunately, the shaken gunners were able to locate the source and retaliate within ten minutes. This had a wonderful effect on morale, which was lifted higher still when a few days later, 12 fresh German graves were found near Acquaviva, the same area which had been occupied by the enemy guns responsible. News from all fronts was encouraging and Hodgson was already hoping to have Christmas at peace. His best friend George Mennie had been wounded near Allerona when, in spite of Sergeant Cowley's warning to take cover because the platoon was pinned down, he had walked about in view of the enemy. Only now was Hodsgon permitted to write home about the incident, and he was aware that his mother would be more worried than ever:

> I expect you will have heard about George being wounded. No doubt the Mennies will have told you by the time this reached you. He was extremely unlucky in one way and lucky in another. It was a 20-millimetre AP [armour piercing] that just struck the side of his leg, missing the bone, but taking a portion of the muscle a little below the knee. There is nothing at all serious about it, and no danger attached to it at all. He will be out of it for about three months. All said and done he is very well off, as he will live in the lap of luxury during that time, as he will be very well looked after. I expect he will go to our base hospital which is staffed with South African doctors and nurses.
>
> This took place about ten days ago, but I have not been allowed to say anything till now, as we have to wait a certain amount of time so his parents can be informed first. Except for this all is going very well and I am quite safe and sound, so there is nothing in the least to worry about—especially impress that upon Mum ... I am also pleased to hear about Tom Deveraux being made a Captain. I bet his mother is thrilled. I have not seen him since we came over here, but I intend looking him up as soon as I get the chance.

Mennie was another member of Hilton's 'famous class of '42'. According to Hodgson, he was "an intense guy", fearless and even reckless under fire. He did his utmost to get back into the fray once he had recovered from his wound and was accepted into the South African Air Force on a navigator's course just before the war ended.

Major S.P. Kirsten, commander of the 7/23rd Medium Regiment's 15 Battery, had set up an observation post in a double-storey building on the western shore of Lake Montepulciano. From this position, on 28 June he observed the advance guard of the Natal Mounted Rifles moving up the road. He simultaneously noted a German infantry force, apparently preparing an ambush. Thanks to his warning, the leading elements of the Natal Mounted Rifles halted 300 yards from certain destruction. Kirsten then targeted the enemy with fire from the 4/22nd Field Regiment, after which the infantry took over. Now that Chiusi had fallen, the division was once again in pursuit mode. According to the war diary of the 7/23rd Medium Regiment, by 28 June the 5.5s together with the Pretoria Regiment had crossed a bridge beyond Chiusi, putting them ahead of the 25-pounders.

The Imperial Light Horse/Kimberley Regiment and Royal Natal Carbineers had advanced beyond San Savino in the direction of Montepulciano and Acquaviva, which would fall within a day.

Thursday 29 June 1944: Chiusi

After a cloudy, drizzly day, 29 June dawned hot and sunny and the roads soon became dry and dusty. The South Africans make good progress in catching up with the German rearguard; Montepulciano was captured that morning and the artillery poured fire onto the enemy as they vacated the shell-damaged town of Acquaviva. Hodgson's was the first of the platoons which entered the town at last light:

> In one of the towns we captured the other day I picked up a souvenir which I think you will like; I think it is a nice thing but the main value of it is the souvenir value. This is the story attached to it: Our platoon led the attack into the town of Acquaviva; we captured the place late on the afternoon of June 29th. After things had calmed down I had a look round and found this in the house of a rich merchant. The packing of the parcel is quite a souvenir in itself. The main container is a 'Jerry' spare parts tin, the lid of which is a part of a Jerry mess tin without the handle. The packing is a German mechanical pamphlet and an 'Eighth Army News', the local paper we get. Also a pack of Italian cards. I hope you like it; the main thing is the story so try to memorize it. I will send it off as soon as I can.

The road from Pienza to Montecielo was heavily mined and booby-trapped. Demolitions delayed the division but steady progress was made, thanks to the assistance of the locals. The Germans deployed anti-tank guns on the right flank in the marshlands southwest of Lake Montepulciano, while the Imperial Light Horse/Kimberley Regiment battled though mud, machine guns and booby-traps. That same day, on a hilltop at the other side of the valley, the citizens of the village of Civitella della Chiana (also called Civitella in Val di Chiana) lived a nightmare: the Germans massacred 212 men, women and children aged between one and 84 years. More than 100 houses were burned down, some with people still inside them. The massacre was precipitated by an attack on a group of four German soldiers who had been drinking in the village's Fascist recreational club, Dopolavoro, on 18 June. A messy contact took place within the club, during which two of the Germans were killed. The other two got away, although one was wounded. Realizing that there could be reprisals, the residents held a memorial service for the dead soldiers on 29 June. However, the Germans still surrounded the village and went from one house to another, dragging all the citizens into the square.

Those who did not cooperate, whether man, woman or child, were shot where they stood. The women and children were then told to leave the square and the men were shot, five at a time. In the church, the women were pushed aside and all the men, including the priest and some prominent Fascists, were machine-gunned. An attempt was made to cover up the deed by burning and blowing up the bodies, a tactic which had been employed in similar incidents in Crete, Russia and Czechoslovakia.

The killing continued at two smaller villages, Cornia and San Pancrazio, after which the soldiers returned to their bivouac carrying their loot and proceeded to become raucously drunk.

One citizen by the name of Bartolucci relates his experience in this testimony, translated by D. de Grazia and L. Paggi:

> I shut myself in the house with my wife, four daughters, mother, brother and sister. We exchanged a few terrified words. Outside there were shouts, and explosions of rifles, machine guns and hand grenades. Suddenly there was a violent banging on the door and, at that, I was more terrified than ever. I looked at my daughters and wife and I told them to open the door. As soon as the door was open, I heard 'out', I grasped the two girls closest to me and started to climb the stairs. I hadn't had the time to reach the top, before they brutally grabbed me by the arm and conducted me to the middle of the town square along with the priest's brother and some other compatriots. There, next to those beasts, we glanced at each other, our faces convulsed, thinking that if our papers were in order, they would set us free. They searched us and took our money, and they held us in the square to await the hour of doom. We saw the houses in flames, the women running to leave the town, we heard the screams of the girls calling 'daddy', the priest calling out, 'save my people who are innocent'. But there was nothing to be done. The cruel hearts of those barbarians were unmoved. In the meantime, they started to line us up five by five to die. The priest, seeing that there was nothing more to be done, made a request to bless us parishioners for the last time and this was granted. With his hand, he blessed us all, and we crossed ourselves and prepared to die. In the meantime, the lines moved up. I saw my fellows fall to the ground, I felt the wound wasn't mortal and I was still alive ...[153]

There is some controversy regarding which unit was responsible for the incident, as there are no German records of the killings. However, witnesses agree that the troops came from the area of Monte San Savino where the Hermann Göring Division was headquartered. Other evidence, such as insignia and addresses on dropped letters, further confirms this. These were the same troops that had encountered the South Africans at Chiusi. Although this was

[153] D. de Grazia & L. Paggi, *Story of an ordinary massacre: Civitella della Chiana, 29 June 1944*, p. 168.

not an SS division, the men—all of whom, at 17 or 18, were decidedly young—were essentially Nazis. They were transferred to the eastern front shortly after the events of 29 June.

The story of the slaughter in Civitella was reported in the South African press a month later. After admitting that reports about atrocities are usually suspect, *The Star* of 15 September incorrectly reported that the incident began when patriots killed three German soldiers in the principal street as they were examining a haul of linen, watches, radios and typewriters stolen in a house-to-house looting spree. However, much of what was reported in the South African newspaper was factual:

> From the altar, Father Alcide Lazzari pleaded: 'Don't kill my people. If you want bloodshed, kill me.' The Germans paid no heed, but took the priest, two altar boys and about 30 villagers and marched them across the square. Lining them up against a wall, the Germans machine-gunned them … after the massacre, the Germans went from house to house, knocking at doors, and as they were opened the householder was shot dead. Some who did not answer quickly enough were shot as they came downstairs. Even invalids were shot. The Germans dragged the bodies to a building next to the church, splashed petrol over them and set the building on fire.

According to some sources, the total number of civilian deaths numbered around 250. This was not the only incident to occur in the Arezzo area at this time; there had also been a relatively intense firefight with partisans near Ambra on 20 June. On 30 June, the Prince Alfred's Guard and B Company, Royal Natal Carbineers still occupied the hamlet of Cervognano, approximately one and a half miles southwest of Acquaviva and five miles east of Montepulciano. Fielding went forward to visit them in the afternoon: "There was much sign and sound of battle and the tank men seemed to be enjoying themselves … Major Hilton Herd was only concerned that he could not depress his Browning sufficiently to shoot up some of the nearest Huns ..." On occasions when enemy infantry was too close, tank crews had to fire with Tommy guns out of their turrets. Herd reports: "We had a good shoot on the whole—Jerries running here, there and everywhere."[154] Hodgson was clearly on a high but said nothing about his involvement in the day's action:

---

154 W.L. Fielding, *With the 6th Div*, p. 126.

> I am quite well and full of beans and very happy with all the news being so good, excellent in fact. All we can hope for now is that Jerry will crack up much sooner than we expect him to—in any case I don't think it will be very long before he is completely beaten. I think there is every chance of it being before Christmas; if it is I can hardly expect to share next Christmas dinner with you, as there is bound to be a bit of messing about, and the trip down will be a fairly long one—actually I have hopes that we will drop in at England on the way home; just for a short while, as it would be grand to see the place and our friends and relations there. All the same I will be seeing you early in the New Year if not before.

From the hills on the far side of the Chiana valley, the Germans put up a fierce resistance which slowed the advance and the hills around Civitella became a battlefront for ten days. The 6th South African Armoured Division changed its axis of advance and it was only on 9 July that the British liberated the pile of ruins that was Civitella.

Friday 30 June 1944 – Saturday 1 July 1944: San Savino

With its steep, narrow streets and medieval walls, Montepulciano offers commanding views and is an ideal defensive position. Fortunately, the Germans decided not to make a determined stand here; they did shell the town, however, and the road leading up to it was pocked with craters.

Here, the Marchesa Origo made contact with friends in the Eighth Army and received news of the situation at La Foce, which had suffered only minor structural damage. On 30 June, she made contact with the 6th South African Armoured Division:

> A very English day. The Scots Guards leave the town, but the Coldstreams who are attached to a South African division, take their place, and attack a position below the town held by the Germans, from which they had been firing on us.

Johnston passed through La Foce and mentioned Iris Origo by one of her many titles in his diary entry of 30 June: "Troop in action near Contessa Chianciano's Castello—vino lying ankle deep all over the cellar and down the road. Party with Eric on vino obtained from George. Staghound [armoured car] blown up."

That same day, farther forward, Axelson observed the Pretoria Regiment working with the Italians to clear demolitions in the ancient streets of

Montepulciano so that the pursuit could continue without delay. The locals warned of mines in the road as a detachment moved off in the direction of Le Grazie. On 1 July, a staff car took the Origos back to La Foce where they found the following scene:

> In the garden which has got several shell-holes and trenches for machine-guns, they have stripped the pots off the lemons and azaleas, leaving the plants to die. The ground is strewn with my private letters and photographs, mattresses and furniture stuffing. The Germans have stolen everything that took their fancy: blankets, clothes, shoes and toys as well as everything valuable or eatable and have destroyed much of sentimental or personal value. Every drawer in my writing desk has been ransacked, and stained or torn-up photographs, torn out of their frames, strew the floors. In the dining room the table is still laid, and there are traces of a drunken repast ... The lavatory is filled to the brim with filth and decaying meat, lying on every table, adds to the foul smell. [155]

As she assessed the situation and the news came in, Origo wrote: "In the lower part of the property ... the Goums [Algerians] have completed what the Germans have begun. They regard loot and rape as the just reward for battle, and have freely indulged in both. Not only girls and young women, but even an old woman of 80, have been raped. Such is Val d'Orcia's introduction to Allied rule—so long and eagerly awaited."[156]

Some of the workers on the estate had been killed. The bodies of six or seven Germans were found and burned. As usual, the parting Germans left booby-traps strewn behind them.

Continuing north of Montepulciano, a patrol consisting of the Pretoria Regiment's 2 Troop B Squadron, together with infantry carriers of the Scots Guards, came across some German light infantry elements. According to the Pretoria Regiment history written at the time, the patrol killed a few men with small arms fire but "the opportunity of wiping out a larger number was lost due to the turret of one of the tanks jamming at a critical moment". One of the tanks threw a track shortly afterward, making it necessary to call for the technical adjutant. A mortar bomb fell near the men discussing the situation, leaving troop commander Lieutenant J.D.V.B. Gray (a chartered accountant by

155 I. Origo, *War in Val d'Orcia*, p. 235.

156 *Ibid*, p. 236.

profession) wounded. The technical adjutant departed to fetch his Jeep while the squadron commander, Major Buchanan, attempted to carry Lieutenant Gray to safety. At that moment the men were struck by another bomb which killed Gray and wounded Buchanan. B Squadron was now left with only three officers, one of whom had joined the previous night.

The 1/6th Field Regiment came into position just in front of the 7/23rd Medium Regiment at San Savino, a tiny farmstead situated on a hill amid the rolling farmland just off the A1 to Siena, south of Acquaviva (as opposed to the better known Monte San Savino which is north of Acquaviva). This location allowed them to be ready to support the infantry and tanks—fighting in close cooperation north of Acquaviva—at a moment's notice.

The Italian farm workers continued their tasks in close proximity to snipers, 81mm mortars, Nebelwerfers and machine guns. General Poole was sometimes criticized by his officers for spending too much time upfront. He had presented a valuable target to the enemy gunners on more than one occasion. It was therefore not entirely unprecedented when he and his top brass dropped in on Hodgson's Bren gun position, from where there was a commanding view of the Chiana valley and the hills beyond:

> The other day I felt quite an important person. While I was doing duty in our Bren gun position on a static occasion, I was suddenly swamped by all the 'Brass-Hats'. Our position commanded a very good view of the retreating Gerries down in the plain below, so they all came to have a 'shufti' [look]. Among others, there was van Ryneveld, Poole, a couple of brigadiers and quite a few colonels.

It had been a running fight from Chiusi to Acquaviva but the canals in the Chiana valley and the hills beyond helped the Germans slow down the advance. While attempting a rough crossing of a canal, the tanks of the Prince Alfred's Guard were "heavily and accurately shelled" and snipers' bullets "rattled against the turret and flaps". An artillery barrage was called down, forcing the enemy to leave their positions. It was, according to Captain Concar of the Prince Alfred's Guard, "a damned good shoot":

> Looking around, I saw German equipment between 2,000 and 2,500 yards away, beating away in retreat from Acquaviva. All three tanks fired at this transport which included guns being trailed. It was a good range but we shook his ideas up. Owing to the speed with which the transport was moving, we could not hit the big stuff,

> but one Don R, [dispatch rider] who was apparently taking a message back into Acquaviva, was hit by a shell. His motorbike flew into the air.[157]

By the last day of the month, Acquaviva was clear. The Imperial Light Horse/Kimberley Regiment and Prince Alfred's Guard had together killed approximately 63 Germans during the preceding two days, in exchange for their four. Corporal D.H. McKerrow killed three German machine-gunners, while Corporal Sjoblom's platoon accounted for 14 dead. Both were awarded the Military Medal.

Sergeant Louis Jacobus Snyman, a mine captain from Krugersdorp, also displayed singular uncommon bravery. According to a newspaper report, Snyman was sent with sappers to reconnoitre the right fork of a road in the Castelnuovo area. When the group came across a German machine-gun post, Snyman took the two gunners prisoner. Farther up the road, he and Sapper D.D. Pye from Durban heard voices in a barn. These belonged to German soldiers. Pye wrestled one man to the ground, while four more Germans surrendered. However, a shot was fired when Snyman and Pye were marching the prisoners away, wounding Pye in the shoulder. Snyman returned the fire, killing a German sergeant-major who was attempting to jump over a low wall. Another burst was fired at the sappers by a machine-gunner lying at the entrance of a house, wounding one of them. Again, Snyman returned fire with his Tommy gun, and killed two more Germans. On a previous occasion, north of Allerona, Snyman had hunted down a sniper and killed him.[158]

Yet another story which made the Transvaal newspapers was that of Lieutenant Archie Turnbull of Durban, who "captured a town with a pitchfork". Turnbull was the first person to walk into the town of Acquaviva, and his arrival was greeted with ringing bells while the locals pelted him with roses. Suddenly, two German Spandaus opened fire on him and he had to leap behind a wall to take cover. He located the building housing the machine-gunners and, in his fury, picked up a pitchfork and charged the house. Although he was wounded, he kept going until the Germans threw up their hands in surrender.[159] However, in his letters, Hodgson mentioned more than once that the newspapers were

---

157 DODAR, UWH, Box 140, Statement by Captain Concar, Prince Alfred's Guard.

158 *Rand Daily Mail*, Springbok Sapper becomes terror to Nazis, 14/7/1944.

159 *Rand Daily Mail*, S.A. tank officer 'worth £160,000', 7/7/1944.

Bill Maudlin cartoon illustrating how the local population was inconvenienced by the Allies, captioned: "Papa, I think we have been liberated".

guilty of sensational reporting. After 15 days of continuous fighting, during which time they lost one officer and ten other ranks killed, the Royal Natal Carbineers was sent back for a rest. The First City/Cape Town Highlanders was also withdrawn and the Special Service Battalion took over from the Prince Alfred's Guard. The former took Gracciano on 1 July and fought on through Sinalunga and then to Pieve, entering Torrita di Siena the following evening.

After Torrita di Siena, the next major town on the railway line to Siena is Sinalunga. The Witwatersrand Rifles/Regiment De la Rey found it "strangely quiet" when they entered it on 2 July. Moving on to Pieve before nightfall, the forward troops ran into trouble and were pinned down by Spandaus on the outskirts of the town. Bullets took their toll while the supporting tanks were kept at bay by three German Mark IV Specials and some guns. Corporal S.H. Olivier—who had, according to the A Company diary, put in a "fine showing at Allerona"—won the Military Medal posthumously.[160]

[160] S. Monick, *A bugle calls*, p. 365.

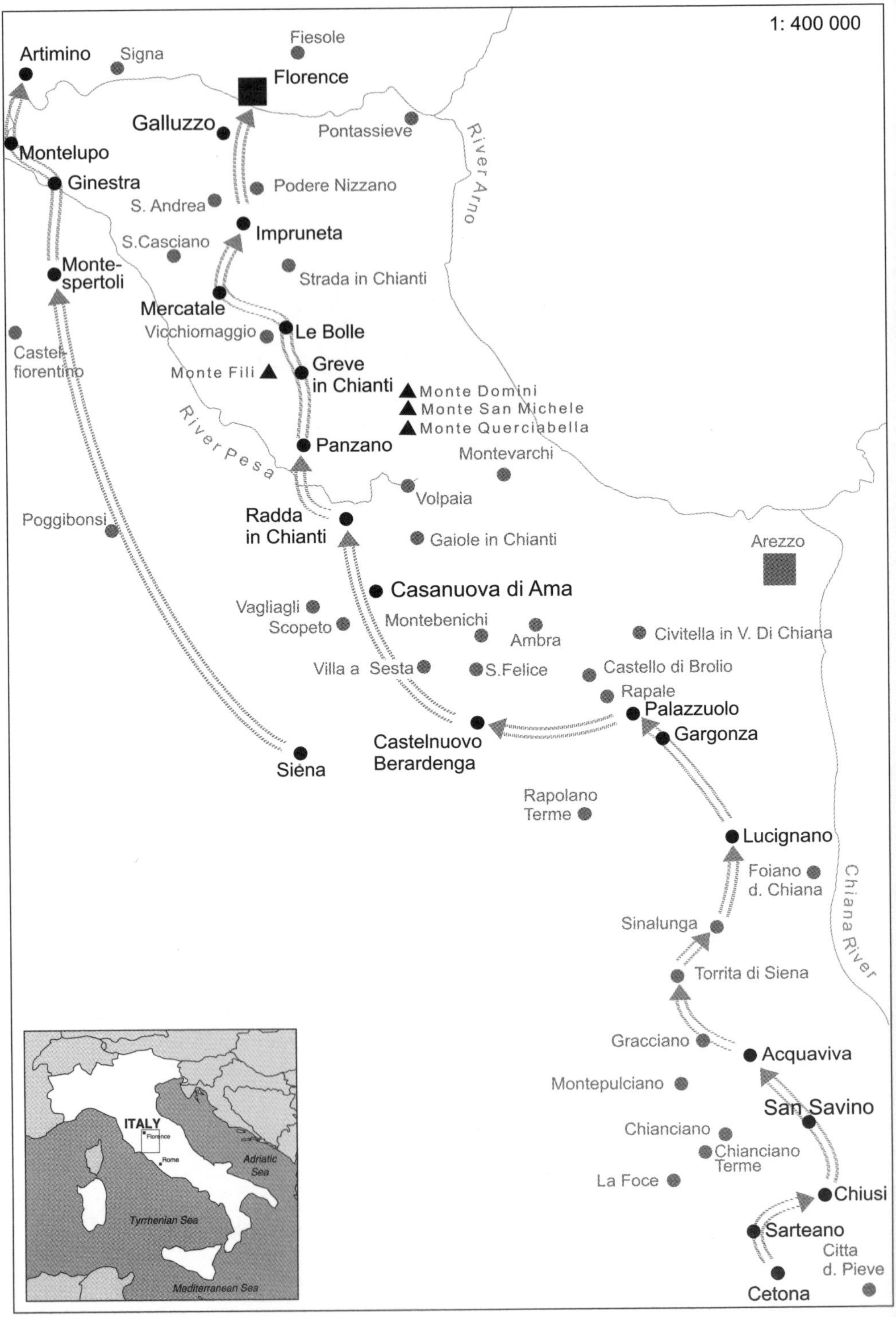

1: 400 000
Artimino
Signa
Fiesole
Florence
Galluzzo
Pontassieve
River Arno
Montelupo
Ginestra
Podere Nizzano
S. Andrea
Impruneta
S.Casciano
Monte-
spertoli
Strada in Chianti
Mercatale
Vicchiomaggio
Le Bolle
Castel-
fiorentino
Monte Fili
Greve
in Chianti
Monte Domini
Monte San Michele
Monte Querciabella
River Pesa
Panzano
Montevarchi
Volpaia
Radda
in Chianti
Poggibonsi
Gaiole in Chianti
Arezzo
Casanuova di Ama
Vagliagli
Scopeto
Montebenichi
Ambra
Civitella in V. Di Chiana
Villa a Sesta
S.Felice
Castello di Brolio
Rapale
Palazzuolo
Gargonza
Castelnuovo
Berardenga
Siena
Rapolano
Terme
Lucignano
Foiano
d. Chiana
Chiana River
Sinalunga
Torrita di Siena
Gracciano
Acquaviva
Montepulciano
San Savino
Chianciano
Chianciano
Terme
La Foce
Chiusi
Sarteano
Citta
d. Pieve
Cetona
ITALY
Florence
Rome
Adriatic
Sea
Tyrrhenian Sea
Mediterranean Sea

Chapter Seven

Hills and vines

"These are great days. The Italian campaign has already made history and victory lies clearly ahead of us, but as good and experienced soldiers we know that the path is not an easy one and final success can only be won by fighting for it. The eyes of the world and the hopes of all at home are upon us—we shall not disappoint them. We shall continue as we have begun to destroy the enemy wherever we find him and to march along the road to the last battles where final victory awaits us."
—General H.R. Alexander, Commander-in-Chief, July 1944

Sunday 2 July 1944: Acquaviva

Acquaviva is situated on a rise overlooking the Chiana valley. A concentration area was established just north of the town. Tank support was impossible among the network of canals, sunken lanes and embankments, and the Germans had to be dislodged by infantrymen using cunning and personal courage.

In the surrounding countryside, wheat waved waist-high in the breeze and bunches of grapes grew on the vines. The farms in the area offered rich pickings. The men collected geese and chickens which they carried with them for many miles, until the birds had become very fat. Cormack's log entry for 30 June was short and to the point: "Geese eaten." The anonymous author of the Pretoria Regiment's history was more eloquent:

> The Adjutant … is to be commended for his human feelings when he remarked after having eaten a portion of goose (purchased!!) which had been kept for a few days for fattening: "It was a pity to kill him. He had such a knowledgeable and trustful look in his eye."[161]

Coincidentally, on the same evening, 2 July, Johnston and his friends had roast chicken and potatoes for dinner with an Italian family, but found the

---

[161] DODAR, WD, Box 640, Pretoria Regiment, regimental history, June 1944.

poultry "tough as hell". Hodgson and his companions were also living off the fat of the land at this time:

> You seem to have a very good stock of fowls these days—I expect they come in very useful these days with the high price of meat and eggs. Talking of poultry, we have not been doing too badly ourselves lately; now and again we have three or four chickens between 16 of us. Also a couple of days ago we had three ducks which went down very nicely; pork and lamb we have also had in good quantities. As for wine, there is as much as the boys want. Besides what the chaps get at camping places we always have a ten gallon glass jar which is kept full on our truck—I am not too keen on the stuff, but I enjoy a glassful now and again with my supper. We are always feeding well these days—today we just had a light lunch of baked apples and custard (the fruit is ripening these days) followed by pancakes and jam with tea. For supper we expect to have a roast of some sort.[162]

The town itself, however, had been reduced to rubble by bombs and shells, especially during the last week of June when an enemy gun position was the target.

Soon after arriving in the village, two gunners, Blumenthal and Thiel, took an "unofficial jaunt" to an Italian farmhouse which they found to be mined and booby-trapped. After helping the peasant family remove the danger, a task for which they had been trained, they started making their way back to their positions in the semi-dark. The two were blown by an 'S' mine (which springs out of the ground and explodes at chest height, as opposed to the S-42 or Shümine which usually blows off a man's foot). It was noticed that one of the casualties had purple stains around his mouth, probably from drinking cheap wine. Thiel survived but Blumenthal is buried at Foiano della Chiana where the war cemetery is a small, rectangular and scrupulously neat plot of land on the outskirts of town. Of a beautiful and otherwise uneventful harbour, Cormack wrote simply, "Bloomie killed".

The regimental war diary notes that there was a plague of booby-traps and mines in this area and two days later, three more casualties occurred.

The weather was hot and dry and the fields of tall wheat provided good cover for the Germans. Nevertheless, the division advanced 30 miles in the days between 30 June and 4 July. The infantry and tanks were well ahead of the 1/6th Field Regiment (presently at Acquaviva). The headquarters of the 7/23rd

---

[162] J.B. Hodgson–M.V. Hodgson, 2/7/1944.

Medium Regiment was set up in a large, comfortable farmhouse which had previously been used by the Germans, half a mile northeast of Gracciano, while the batteries were stationed some distance away at Salarco. The next day the headquarters moved to a big house on a hill, two miles south of Sinalunga. The owner was a wealthy banker who had lived in America and spoke good English.

Yet another move was in store on 3 July as headquarters relocated from one mansion to the next; this time, the office was established in the drawing room of a country manor called Casa Alta. Expensive furniture, a baby grand piano and a well-filled book case completed the cosy picture.

Pretoria Regiment's 24-year-old Captain Kenyon of Umtata had shown outstanding bravery in a tank charge with other members of his regiment, a few days before moving into Acquaviva. He was mortally wounded in action near Sinalunga on 2 July, the same day the town was taken.

According to the war diary of the 7/23rd Medium Regiment, the Imperial Light Horse/Kimberley Regiment had a field day on 2 July, "killing Germans and rounding up prisoners most of the day".

Moving on through the valley, the Natal Mounted Rifles made contact with enemy Tigers, self-propelled guns, mortars and infantry. Unable to outflank them, the tanks pulled into a wood to observe but were heavily shelled most of the day. The Baker diary records: "Sat with Len in his tank ... chatted while 'stonk' went on ... put on insane job after sunset but were so heavily shelled we had to pull out of it."

The Royal Natal Carbineers was rotated out of the line and Hodgson used the opportunity to write piles of letters, barely hinting at the heavy pressure the men had faced during the past few weeks:

> At the moment we are having a bit of a rest, and I must say I have never been so comfortable since I joined the army. Our company is situated in a colossal country manor. It is a beautiful house which must have belonged to a rich count at least. The equivalent in the Union would be hard to get for £25,000, excluding the enormous estate upon which it is situated. A good deal of the furniture is still in a good condition, I have a very comfortable bed and a nice little room which holds five of us very comfortably. There are plenty of soft armchairs and big settees, all in plush red velvet. Enormous gilt-edged mirrors, and to cap it all, all the walls of the rooms are covered with hand paintings, actually done on the walls, all of the most beautiful scenes in lovely colours. The house is surrounded by lovely big oak and fir trees beyond which there are acres of cornfields and vineyards. At the moment I am sitting in a comfortable chair; downstairs the company wireless is issuing forth

some good music. It is a little while after lunch and we are either reading, writing or sleeping. Our trucks are out under the trees where we do all our cooking. Up to the time we came here (the day before yesterday) we had been working at full pressure and now that we are relaxing in such luxury, I can hardly remember if I have ever felt so contented before; all I hope is our rest will not end too soon. This morning when I woke up just before nine o'clock, I heard the wireless going downstairs, and for a moment it seemed just like home. I got up about half-past nine and strolled downstairs in my pyjamas, and out under the trees where I had a lovely bath next to the well—after dressing at my leisure, breakfast was announced about half-past ten. After breakfast, I attended a church service under the trees. After this was over, Harry Hall came round to see me and we chatted until lunchtime.

Monday 3 July 1944: Lucignano

Less than an hour after the Witwatersrand Rifles/Regiment De la Rey and the Imperial Light Horse/Kimberley Regiment took Lucignano on 3 July, the Guards made contact with the enemy just north of the town.

Meanwhile, the 1/6th Field Regiment was deployed southwest of Lucignano. They were struck by disaster: first, an 'S' mine killed three of the regiment's members while they were digging their battery command post; then their position was heavily shelled.

One sapper believed that the mines were the work of a new enemy engineer company, "fresh and over-full of enthusiasm".[163]

Captain W. Steenkamp became another mine casualty, killed on 3 July while reconnoitring a new campsite for divisional headquarters. He was buried on the side of the road, as was the practice, and the obligatory letter of condolence was sent to Peggy Steenkamp at 49 Kingsway Avenue, Brakpan. In this instance, the writer, Major de Wet, received a reply:

> My thanks to you, and the officers and men of your Squadron, for your very kind letter of sympathy. I am very proud in knowing that you all thought so much of my husband. I want you to know also what a great comfort it was to me to learn that Willem was spared all pain and suffering at the time of his tragic death. Although it is very hard for [*illegible*] … and I to carry on alone, we have very beautiful memories of our brave and fearless soldier Daddy. We are all very proud of him who did his duty nobly and gave his life that we may live in peace.[164]

---

163 N. Orpen, *Gunners of the Cape*, p. 234; E. Axelson, *A year in Italy*, pp. 37–38.

164 DODAR, Div Docs, Box 173 File HQS/27, Battle casualties, Burial Returns, 4 July; DODAR, Div Docs, Box 173 File HQS/27, Battle casualties; Mrs Peggy Steenkamp–Major de Wet, 22//9/1944.

The 25-pounders were now rushed forward to a position just southeast of Lucignano to deal with the enemy encountered by the Natal Mounted Rifles. They passed through most of the leading infantry before dropping into action in the rugged terrain on the roadside. Reconnaissance parties then went ahead, scouting for more suitable gun positions.

The First City/Cape Town Highlanders debussed outside the town, bypassing it on foot as it was being shelled, as was the crossroads.

After midnight the body of a German from the Hermann Göring Division was found with the side pack of Corporal George Wienand—as spelled in the war diary—who was among the missing at Chiusi. The soldier had been hit by a 75mm tank shell.[165]

The rear division had now reached Torrita di Siena, having travelled half a mile down a side road in order to avoid the odd bombing or strafing foray down the main roads. This practice was known by the Germans as 'road hunting'. Such attacks were rare, but divisional headquarters was always a target.

The countryside was now beginning to change. The landscape rising up from the floor of the Chiana valley was indeed beautiful, if a little difficult to traverse.

The Royal Natal Carbineers was still resting in the lap of luxury:

> While we were at this lovely house I told you about in my last letter, the mobile cinema came round. The film was really lousy—a cowboy film; what beats me is the type of film that they have the nerve to show us when we see so few of them. All the same it was a very enjoyable evening as everyone was in high spirits—I had an excellent seat; I could not have had a better one at the metro. The screen was in front of the house so I put my easy chair out on the balcony and watched from there.[166]

Tuesday 4 July 1944 – Wednesday 5 July 1944: Gargonza

Having just left the security and comfort of the country villa on 4 July, Hodgson dared to think of the day when he would return to his own family home:

> The last few days we have been having a wonderful and well-earned rest. Our company was very lucky as we got a lovely country manor with a large estate in

165 DODAR, WD, Box 633, First City/Cape Town Highlanders, 30/7/1944; The CWGC records indicate that a Trooper George Wiehahn of the Pretoria Regiment was killed on 2 July.

166 J.B. Hodgson–M.V. Hodgson, 5/7/1944.

> which to stay. The house was perfect; in the Union it would be equivalent to twenty-five to thirty thousand pounds. Our trucks were parked out under the oak and fir trees that surrounded the house; this was where we did all our cooking and messing about—all the meals have been very good as the supply of vegetables and poultry have been plentiful. Isn't the news wonderful these days? At the present rate of the advances on all fronts, I think there is a very good chance of the war being over before the end of this year. Wouldn't it be grand if we had this Christmas in peace? It is a bit too much to hope for that I will be home for that occasion, although it is always possible, but if the war is over before then I think we can count on getting back early in the New Year. You had better start getting trim for that game of singles. Also when you get home, you can tell Amos to put the beer on ice. 'It won't be long now Mum and Dad.

While the 25-pounders were already in the hills at Gargonza, the mediums remained on flatter ground near Lucignano before moving up the steep and winding road to the quiet village of Palazzuolo on a plateau beyond Gargonza.

Gargonza is a small cluster of buildings on an isolated, tree-covered knoll overlooking the road to Palazzuolo in the mountainous Monte San Savino area of the Val di Chiana. The imaginative author of the 1/6th Field Regiment war diary mentioned that this area would "make the Valley of a Thousand Hills look like an open plain" and then speculated on what the staff at the Potchefstroom Artillery School might have to say about the gun deployment. Johnston made no mention of the spectacular scenery in his diary—he had more pressing problems:

> 4th July
> Saw quack about piles. Moved about 12.30. Rain. Had sardine sandwiches in the turret with Eric while Fred drove. Lucignano. Pulled into vineyard and down came the rain and hail. As soon as tent up, stopped. Went for a walk.
>
> 5th July
> Up at 05.30. Pulled out ammo truck and moved up ten miles to farm from where Tiger tank had been. Palazzuolo. News of Arthur Denyssen's death. Barked at by Jakkals.

Advancing up a different axis, the Pretoria Regiment passed through Rapolano and Castelnuovo without incident. Ahead of them, the Guards patrolled extensively and deeply along the lanes, in riverbeds and through footpaths in the woodlands. Infantry patrols were effective in daylight thanks to the tree cover and the assistance given by escaped POWs as well as Italian civilians who acted as guides on long distance patrols. Carrier-borne patrolling and armoured reconnaissance were more hazardous, however: on 5 July, Lieutenant J. Walker of the Pretoria Regiment was killed by a shell splinter. This 32-year-old Rhodesian had a B.Sc degree from the University of Glasgow and had also served in the Royal Air Force. His proud parents lived in Johannesburg.

A hailstorm came down at 1430 hours on 4 July, turning the roads white and pouring into the tank turrets which had to be kept open to observe the enemy, who was at close quarters. A patrol of the Pretoria Regiment reached Castello di Brolio for the first time that evening but withdrew to consolidate on high ground, as was their usual practice.

Having passed by on the west side of Lake Trasimeno and crossed the Chiana valley, the division was now entering the Chianti hills. The baking earth was cooled by some showers of rain and the day of 5 July dawned overcast. Hodgson described his journey through the fertile heartland between Montepulciano and Lake Trasimeno:

> As we move further up this country it gets a bit more wooded. Where we are at the moment it is quite thickly wooded, mostly with pines. It is very pleasant to travel in as there are any number of streams and it is all very green and shady, but as you can imagine it is not good to fight in, as it is pretty close. You know the lake that was mentioned in the news such a lot last week? We went right up past it and consequently saw quite a bit of it. We never got close enough to have a swim in it but in the distance it looked lovely. Enormous in size, nestling among a group of fairly low mountains, which were mostly covered by cornfields and vineyards. The fruit is beginning to ripen and it won't be long now. We can get plenty of green apples for making apple pie.

Progress was now slow, almost static, while the 25-pounders searched in vain to find a level site around Gargonza. Nevertheless, the guns came into action from two different positions, firing 2,300 rounds against hostile gun areas, Nebelwerfers and infantry positions which were well hidden in the woods and gullies. The Germans used the terrain to put up stiff resistance and put in a strong counter-attack against the British (6th Royal West Kents) who were operating nearby. The 356th German Infantry seemed to have pulled back and had been replaced by the elite 1st and 4th Paratroop Divisions.

Acting in their usual reconnaissance role, the Natal Mounted Rifles was moving slowly forward in the San Felice area on 5 July. Troop commander Lieutenant Bunny Evans and Douglas Baker were on foot, 'walking the plank' out in front, when they walked into an ambush. Machine-gun bullets lashed Baker's legs, but he managed to reach the tank—only to find the hatch battened down (this was against regimental rules when a crewmember was outside). The ordeal continued: a mortar bomb landed and shrapnel tore open his chest, exposing his lung. In his book, *War, Wine and Valour*, Baker accuses his tank commander, Corporal Bell, of cowardice for this unforgivable action.

As the tank backed out of trouble, the turret opened and Baker flopped onto the floor, "ashen and bloodied, gasping for air through a gaping wound in the chest and a rattling noise stemming from [his] windpipe". Baker could see the fear of death in the eyes of his comrades but never once did he believe that he was about to die.[167] Tagged with a 'dangerously ill' label, Baker was moved from the casualty clearing station to another casualty station in Orvieto, an overflowing, dirty place that had recently been vacated by a German ambulance unit. Providence was once again in play when the same doctor who had treated his wounds in Egypt after Alamein recognized Baker and had him evacuated by air to 92nd General Hospital in Naples at 0300 hours.

Thursday 6 July 1944 – Friday 7 July 1944: Palazzuolo

A fighting patrol came under shellfire on the Palazzuolo–Ambra road, which was in view of the enemy. Captain Dudley 'Flippy' Flynn was another experienced regular in the 1/6th Field Regiment and had already been in some scrapes in North Africa. At 34, he had been with the regiment since 1932. When the 1st Division returned to the Union, he led his battery in a parade through Durban. Since Cassino, he had been liaison officer with the Guards and was conferring with the column commander, Major Torbie Plater of the First City/Cape Town Highlanders, when a shell landed under the tracks of Flynn's observation tank (which was also nicknamed 'Flippy').

The two officers were wounded and Captain Flynn died later in the day at the casualty clearing station. It was the worst position occupied by the 1/6th Field Regiment in Italy to date and targets were being engaged at all times of the day and night. Worst of all, it turned out that the South Africans would not be proceeding in the direction of Ambra.

The three divisions of XIII Corps—6th South African Armoured Division, 6th British and 4th British Infantry Division—were now stretched over a front

[167] D.M. Baker, *War, wine and valour*, p. 419.

of 25 miles (at this stage, the New Zealanders were resting at Frosinone, a drab little town south of Rome). The First City /Cape Town Highlanders' front stretched 4,000 yards wide in wooded country. There had been a rare counter-attack scare on 5 July, and all rear echelon formations were told to stand to, while the press contingent, which was camped in a vineyard alongside the Main Division headquarters, continued to sleep in ignorant bliss.

As it turned out, no counter-attack materialized that day. Any enemy activity was more likely to have come in the form of an infiltration of 50 or 60 soldiers—a tactic which was becoming quite troublesome.

The next day, the Pretoria Regiment was 'stonked' for four hours near Villa a Sesta and the young Lieutenant Dacre L. Haddon, from Kennilworth in Cape Town, was killed. Headquarters of the 1/6th Field Regiment was also heavily and accurately shelled, but a deep gully afforded good cover.

On 7 July, the regiment was again called upon by the British division based on the South Africans' right flank to help break up a counter-attack. Higher command now called for the division to hold their positions and consolidate in order to allow the formations on the right to catch up. The Special Service Battalion spent the time quietly getting on with maintenance and reorganization, only moving to the Castelnuovo area ten days later. By 6 July, the Witwatersrand Rifles/Regiment De la Rey had moved through Palazzuolo, then west through Castelnuovo with a troop of Prince Alfred's Guard tanks under command.

On entering Monte Benichi, a hamlet on a wooded hill, they suffered one killed and ten wounded, mainly from mortars. Major H.H. Hartley, the 32-year-old commander of B Company, Witwatersrand Rifles/Regiment De la Rey, was killed during a briefing with officers and non-commissioned officers near Monte Benichi. His spinal column was severed below the nape of his neck by a tree burst, killing him instantly. He died at 1700 hours on 7 July. The funeral took place at 1100 hours the next day, conducted by the regimental chaplain, Captain Cloete, with B Company present. A temporary grave was dug beneath some cypress trees at a place where a side road joins the Castelnuovo–Benichi road, about three miles north-northeast of Castelnuovo.

Major Hartley's death was felt keenly as he had recruited and trained the company. Speaking at the funeral, the commanding officer, Colonel Jack Bester said: "For B Company, he was not only a leader, he was a father—no, more—a mother." Before the war, Hartley had been the public prosecutor in Klerksdorp and had captained the Klerksdorp rugby team.[168] In a dispatch sent from Castelnuovo, a SAPA war correspondent travelling with the 6th South African Armoured Division wrote that the South Africans had been pinned down by heavy mortar and shellfire on Wednesday and Thursday.

The report goes on to give a good overview of operations during the past few days:

> Up to Wednesday, the South Africans had been making good progress from the area of Montepulciano and Acquaviva under difficult conditions. The Hermann Goering Division strove to break off contact. The resistance between Montepulciano and Castelnuovo consisted mainly of continual heavy shelling. Scattered German infantry rearguards were encountered and cleared up at intervals in sharp skirmishes.
>
> Beyond Acquaviva, a South African armoured reconnaissance unit ran into a nest of self-propelled guns and an infantry company in dug-in positions. This pocket was wiped out in a brief engagement after supporting tanks were called up and several German guns were put out of action. The German company commander and 15 men were captured, the rest killed.
>
> The shelling to which advanced elements were subjected in this area was among the heaviest yet encountered during the South African advance. One South African tank pinned down in a vineyard under enemy observation was fired at every time it moved a few yards, the firing consisted of about 30 shells at a time. On Thursday, the South African advance was headed mainly by infantry in very broken country in which armoured operations were extremely difficult. Infantrymen probed their way forward on foot, mile after mile, under sporadic but concentrated shelling from commanding positions. In the Montepulciano area, the South Africans were considerably assisted by Italian partisan groups who harried the retreating Germans.
>
> In this difficult advance, the South Africans suffered a steady dribble of casualties, both from the shelling and also from mines and booby-traps. South Africans have been killed or wounded while picking mulberries, walking through potato patches or lifting mines to which booby traps were attached.[169]

Now, one month after the Allied entry into Rome, the enemy had been pushed back more than 150 miles in an advance which averaged five miles per day. More than 35,000 prisoners had been taken since the offensive started on 12 May. A United Press correspondent with the Eighth Army said that the South African and Rhodesian troops of the 6th South African Armoured Division had been chasing a "ghost" enemy since the fall of Rome. He stated

168 S. Monick, *A bugle calls*, p. 367.

169 *The Star*, South Africans in Italy run into heavy gunfire, 8/7/1944.

that they had met the enemy only once in a pitched battle and then they had routed the German 356th Division in one day.[170] Here the reporter is referring to the Battle of Celleno; obviously, he did not consider Chiusi and Bagnoregio to be pitched battles.

Saturday 8 July 1944 – Friday 14 July 1944: Castelnuovo

From the hills, forests and gullies around Palazzuolo, the 1/6th Field Regiment moved sideways to Castelnuovo Berardenga, an important centre close to Siena; a place to which it would return for rest and reorganization a month later. On this occasion, the men stayed for almost a week, during which time they were treated to hot showers. In spite of this comfort, the diary states: "The usual harassing fire and counter-battery keep us active."

Johnston and the 7/23rd Medium Regiment were in Castelnuovo from 6 to 15 July. The regiment's targets on 7 July included enemy gun positions and the castle grounds of Castello di Brolio. There was much patrol activity on both sides, the terrain being ideal for infiltration—something the Germans were especially good at.

On the night of 8/9 July, a patrol of the Scots Guards approached Castello di Brolio, a renowned wine estate famous for its Chianti Classico wine. The red-brick, neo-Gothic-style mansion is situated high on a hill, surrounded by vineyards. The Germans had a strongpoint here, complete with barbed wire and machine-gun posts sited around the vineyard terraces. Their observation officer had an excellent view over the Allied positions. The Scots Guards had seen a mysterious white flag raised above the massive, pock-marked stone walls several times during the day; however, the patrol was met by a hail of Spandau fire. All movement was immediately engaged, especially by the Germans' prodigious self-propelled guns.

The regimental war diary for 11 July remarks that although the guns had been in the same position for six days, there had been no shelling from the enemy side. In his personal diary, Johnston recorded that they bought a demijohn of *vino* (54 litres) and set about emptying it.

General Poole visited the 7/23rd Medium Regiment and the 1/6th Field Regiment while they were stationed at Castelnuovo. On both occasions, it

170 *Rand Daily Mail*, Springboks driving towards road to Florence, 6/7/1944.

was noticed that he walked to every gun sub-section at such a pace that his entourage could barely keep up with him. The general officer commanding also honoured other regiments, including the Pretoria Regiment, with a visit.

Meanwhile, it was the misfortune of the Royal Natal Carbineers to be leading an action-packed existence. Hodgson, however, was happy enough to be fully occupied and eating well:

> At the moment I have got a new job. I am in company headquarters and my job is on the forward-link wireless set. It entails quite a lot of work, but on the other hand it is very interesting. Also being in company headquarters has its advantages; namely in our truck there are only five chaps on it and most of the time only two travel in it; we are very comfortable—we even have a lovely wireless which is really grand, waking up in the morning to hear the thing going, and in the evenings instead of just sitting round, we listen to the music. Also I drive a Jeep a bit and little things like that makes life much more interesting. Also we don't have to worry about cooking as we have a special cook and Cape coloureds. We have excellent meals too—this morning we had porridge and omelette and bacon followed by toast and coffee; last night we had roast chicken (four men to one chicken), cabbage and roast potatoes. As you can see we are doing ourselves proud these days, at the expense of the Itis; but my contentions, they were partly the cause for bringing us away from our lovely homes, etc. so they can suffer. They deserve nothing better.

The morning of 9 July found the Royal Natal Carbineers near Rapale while the First City/Cape Town Highlanders were stationed in the grounds of Castello di Montalto. The headquarters of the 7/23rd Medium Regiment was set up in a castle where the men had the luxury of soaking in a big tub in one of the many bathrooms. The precarious position of the Witwatersrand Rifles/Regiment De la Rey near Monte Benichi came under repeated attack and the Natal Mounted Rifles was also in action. Pressure on the British sector brought more requests for artillery support. It was a busy time for the gunners, trying to silence the German self-propelled guns, mortars and Nebelwerfers.

According to the First City/Cape Town Highlanders' war diary, four Focke Wulfes flew over early in the morning of 9 July, dropping two bombs which were way off target. However, the 7/23rd Medium Regiment records that bombs were dropped over British lines, causing casualties. A bitter controversy raged over whether they were enemy planes, South African planes, or Spitfires flown by the enemy. It was later established that this was, in fact, a case of friendly fire. That night, an escaped POW came through the lines to fetch food and medical supplies to take back to his companions, some of whom were wounded and therefore unable to make the breakthrough attempt. The POW, who was British, was not allowed to return because of a divisional order forbidding anyone passage through the forward defence locations.

It was only on 9 July that the town of Civitella was liberated. According Michael Geyer, author of *Civita della Chiana on 29 June 1944, the reconstruction of a German 'measure'*, the Hermann Göring Division suffered low self-esteem after being mauled by the South Africans; and this was one of the factors behind the massacre. The Germans knew they were losing the war, the partisan situation was out of control, and this was a brutal way of buying time.[171] The division would still have a few audacious encounters with the 6th South African Armoured Division before being sent to the Russian front.

The advance had been slower during the past two weeks and now, instead of following the main road to Florence via Siena, the division took secondary roads from Castelnuovo in the direction of Radda. The weather at this time was clear and the days became very hot once mid-morning had passed.

Before mounting an attack, the Natal Mounted Rifles was given the relatively simple task of observing enemy activity in and around Castello di Brolio from their camouflaged positions. The operation was not without incident, however: on 12 July, Trooper T.K. Phin, a 19-year-old shop assistant from Queenstown, was killed while lounging in front of his Sherman—one of the crew had accidentally trod on the barrel of a machine gun and a burst caught him in the back.

The next day, while Trooper Goodwill was observing through binoculars, a squadron of South African Air Force planes flew over and "all of a sudden, one of the craft in the centre of the flight burst into flames ... the plane disintegrated and fell in a mass of crew, metal and fire". The two planes which were flying alongside in close formation lost control and Trooper Goodwill "saw both planes go plummeting from the sky to crash among the mountains, north of Castel[lo] di Brolio".[172]

The South African Air Force had been reluctant to bomb the castle and the division had to go to the highest authority to get permission. In any case, the

[171] H. Heer & K. Naumann (eds), *War of extermination: the German military in World War II, 1941–1944*, pp. 202–204.

[172] E. Goetzsche, *The official Natal Mounted Rifles history*, pp. 290–291; Much later, Trooper Goodwill found out that the planes were from 12 Squadron, South African Air Force. Colonel Barnby, the squadron commander, was killed in the incident.

bombing was ineffective: the 12 Mustangs involved in the operation managed to drop only three bombs within the castle grounds. No bombs hit the building itself although the shelling caused considerable damage to the hall and other parts of the castle. The castle's baron, his family and retainers sheltered in the cellars while the observation post in the tower was being shelled.

The version of events related today in the brochures of the wine estate is that the cellars were full of refugees and that the Germans had told them that they would be raped by Indian troops—which possibly explains why the Scots Guards were "warned off the premises".

Fielding, who apparently did not inspect the damage, wrote that this lack of hospitality resulted in "the ancient wooden gateway being well holed by a 75mm round from a South African tank" and that the dining hall had one shell through it, although there was little damage to the massive old walls. According to Axelson, who visited the castle on 16 July, it took 16 tank rounds to blow the ancient gate off its hinges.

The Pretoria Regiment's war diary confirms that the gate was blasted by 16 rounds of 75mm. The diary entry of the previous day, 15 July, notes that the castle was deserted except for the "irate Baron and his household". It is remarkable that the narrow winding driveway leading to the gate could be negotiated by tanks.

The baron was one of the richest men in Italy and the fact that the Fascists had allowed him to keep his possessions, even prosper under the occupation, made it difficult to believe that he was not a collaborator. Consequently he had been under house arrest for a number of days and was later imprisoned. According to his "rather young and most pleasant" wife, he was not only innocent but had assisted the escaped POWs in every way possible. However, Brigadier Clive, commanding officer of the Guards Brigade, described him as a "bad piece of work" who had offered a reward for every escaped POW brought in.[173]

In spite of what appeared to be needless destruction, the baroness and her four daughters were well disposed to the South Africans. The Germans withdrew from Castello di Brolio without a fight on 12 July but still showed no signs of withdrawing the guns which had been so active over the past week. It took a major bombardment and a combined attack by the British and the New Zealanders, as well as a bombing by the South African Air Force, to finally

[173] E. Axelson, *A year in Italy*, pp. 50–54.

get the Germans out of Castelnuovo. An air observation post reported that the enemy was "turning over" and at 0730 hours "put down a few bursts of fire to spoil his breakfast".

The author of the 1/6th Field Regiment war diary expressed surprise at how little shelling was returned during these barrages. Although Gunner Bourhill was aware that the newspapers regularly spoke of "artillery duels", from his vantage point, "it was just a matter of us shelling the hell out of Jerry." *The Star* was therefore not altogether correct in reporting that:

> Eighth Army men are moving slowly forward through thick vineyards and the woodlands of the Chiana valley, south of Arezzo. Reinforced German strong points surround this hub position and artillery duels are interspersed with infantry attacks and counter-attacks.[174]

Using the steep wooded terrain, German patrols were able to infiltrate South African lines. One such patrol, led by a certain Lieutenant Henne, was captured on 13 July 1944. He was shot through the stomach and captured while audaciously trying to take prisoners in broad daylight. A search of his person revealed a map and the log he had been keeping. Axelson believed his actions were motivated by the desire to add a bar to his Iron Cross, and he got caught up in this ambition.

According to Orpen, Henne noted the Royal Natal Carbineers were "all young, specially picked troops, skilled in mountain warfare, pure English and white ... have made up my mind to grab one this morning, and get back to our lines".[175]

However, Orpen did not make reference to the officer's diary entry for 1600 hours on 12 July; other writers, too, have omitted mention thereof. A more precise translation of the text as printed in *The Sable* of January 1945 is reproduced below:

> 12 July
> 0545 hrs: Northern heights of Rapale firmly held. The town itself occupied. Spotted English troop position on track west of Pt. 484. Impression of enemy at Rapale. Young, well rested but cautious. White troops, all English. Well familiar with hilly country. Average age 22–25 years.

---

174 *Rand Daily Mail*, Nazis fighting for time in Italy, 13/7/1944.

175 N. Orpen, *Victory in Italy*, p. 133.

1600 hrs: Succeeded in creeping up to a machine-gun and rifle position. Nevertheless, there is the sudden appearance of a rifleman who fires an un-aimed shot in my direction. I swing my MP round and pump several shots into his chest. He sinks back, killed. Impossible to get nearer the English as they open up with machine-gun and rifle fire.

1700 hrs: Marched on further through trackless ravines and wadis as the enemy is scouring the country with patrols.

1730 hrs: Possible to get forward only slowly. We stop on a wadi west of Pt. 455.

2130 hrs: March on, feeling our way forward via Capraie (by passed) C. NUOVA and Pt. M17. Very difficult going, slow progress. All places mentioned strongly held.

13 July 1944
0500 hrs: Withdrew to C. Nuova and Pt. M17.

0800 hrs: Tp. Position spotted road CAPRAIE Pt. 510.

0900 hrs: Voices and noises from wood N.E. CAPRAIE.

1000 hrs: Creep out immediately. Spotted in wood a tented camp with M.T. concentration. Enemy strength more than one company, possibly artillery there too. Tommies always in threes or fours. Will wait the chance to get one of them.

1145 hrs: Recognized an O.P. on top right-hand window of farmhouse Capraie.

The log then terminated. Henne was from the elite Hermann Göring Battle School and had attempted to capture more prisoners than he could handle. The South Africans had been swimming in a river and were naked when they were captured.

A similar incident occurred at 0030 hours on the night of 12/13 July when a German raiding party got through the lines and captured the sleeping crew of a Prince Alfred's Guard tank. Only the wireless operator, who had been sleeping inside the tank, was left behind. The raiders, also belonging to the Hermann Göring Division, were greatly assisted by the thickly wooded terrain.

On 18 July 1944, *The Star* carried an article under the headline 'Arrogance of prisoners taken by Springboks', which describes the young soldiers of the Hermann Göring Division as "fanatical and boastful", but concludes that they had not been indoctrinated out of the desire to live. They "showed an acute desire to be reassured that they did their best to die and only surrendered when it was impossible to do anything further". One young blood whose "eyes shone with idealistic devotion" whenever he spoke about Hitler announced with pride that the Hermann Göring Division was not afraid of the South Africans. A passage from his diary read: "Then I swing my pistol round and plug the Englander's breast until he sinks down dying." This may be a reference to Henne's diary. One young German who surrendered was asked why he had done so, and he replied: "I thought of my father."[176] For the Witwatersrand Rifles/Regiment De la Rey, the period 5–15 July—spent in the Monte Benichi area—had been the most testing to date. The regiment had lost six men, including Major Hartley. It was finally relieved on the night of 15/16 July by the Hampshire Regiment, which formed part of the 128th British Infantry Brigade. According to legend, on hearing that the South Africans were all volunteers, one British private remarked: "Well chum, you must all be fucking mad."[177] Few people in the division had not heard of Princess Stuart of Castello di Montalto. On 14 July, Axelson visited the castle, ostensibly to visit an observation post of the 4/22nd Field Regiment and to view the forward country. An escaped POW named O'Connor, who occasionally made his lodgings there, showed the party to a terrace from where they had a perfect view of the valley's reaped corn and fruit trees:

> Our artillery opened up, and we could see the shellbursts on the forward slopes facing us. Then shells started bursting in a nearby hillside village. Our right-hand battalion had apparently sent forward a patrol, and it was being shelled in that area by the enemy. It was the most amazing situation to be observing all this, in full view, alongside a luxurious home, in the company of a fair princess in the middle thirties, at a place which was virtually in no-man's land.[178]

Saturday 15 July 1944: Ten miles to Radda

With the enemy in full flight, the 1/6th Field Regiment moved to a position northwest of Castello di Brolio in preparation for the attack on Radda by the 12th South African Motorized Brigade. Things were looking good for the Allies

176 *The Star*, Arrogance of prisoners taken by Springboks, 18/7/1944.

177 S. Monick, *A bugle calls*, p.370.

178 E. Axelson, *A year in Italy*, p. 43.

on all fronts. In a letter home, Hodgson gave an insight to the state of the war, the future and his frame of mind at the time:

> Every time I write to you the news gets better, and I only hope it continues doing so until I reach the climax by writing to tell you about the armistice—an event which looks closer than ever before. The advance is gathering speed in France and I hope it reaches the speed of ours or the Russian advance. After a little uphill work, the Russians are again doing a bit of free-wheeling and I have no doubt whatsoever that they will be in East Prussia by the time this reaches you. The Germans have caused such a colossal amount of damage in Russia, that when the Reds get into German territory what they won't do to it will be a sin, and the B---'s deserve all they get. As you will have seen by the papers, old 'Jerry' is holding us up now, but that is only to be expected as this Gothic line existed in peacetime, so one can imagine how strong it is by now; all the same, just give us a little time and this line of his will be rendered useless by a large outflanking attack from the East Coast and/or a landing on the West Coast, north of the line. After that he is 'finito' until we reach the Alps. Many think that he will make his biggest stand on the Po but personally I don't think he stands an earthly there.

Several senior members of the division paid unofficial visits to Siena, only a 35-minute drive from Castelnuovo. Axelson visited on 13 July and found the town full of Frenchmen, Algerians, Moroccans and Americans. The attraction lay in the French 'Wasies' as well as the Sienese and, to a lesser extent, the medieval civilization.

On 14 July, Bastille Day, the French captured Poggibonsi. An impressive parade was held in the Siena town square. This event coincided with a *palio*, a spectacular and dangerous horse race. General Clark arrived in a limousine and was given pride of place on the stage in the centre of the piazza. General Leese was apparently indignant because he was not asked to join them and left before the ceremony was over. General Poole also attended, but had to leave before the food was served, "due to operational demands".[179] It appears that these demands included a visit to the Special Service Battalion, together with Major-General F. Theron and Brigadier Furstenburg. A few days later, Lieutenant-Colonel Brits was presented with the DSO for his leadership at Celleno on 10 June.

The South Africans now moved westward. Their activities took them over a wide area through woods and valleys, and along the streams northeast of Siena.

---

[179] J. Holland, *Italy's sorrow, a year of war 1944–45*, p. 271; A.B. Theunissen, *Military History Journal*, 9 (5), Major-General W.H. Evered Poole, CB, CBE p. 15.

This was proper Chianti country, very rough but beautiful, and the weather was perfect, if not a little hot. Some of the experts in the art of winemaking spoke highly of the legendary Chianti wine, but others were not overly fond of the bitter, dark red 'rooster's blood'. In the south, the wine had been more watery.

To his father, Hodgson expressed his envy of friends who had been sent home with minor wounds.[180] To his younger sister, who shared his letters with her school friends, he preferred to talk about music and the beautiful Tuscan countryside:

> As you can see by the papers the war is going along very well; in fact we could not wish for it to go better. The end is nearer than it has ever been before, so I think there is a good chance of it all being over this year; but as for when we will get home, I don't know, but I hope it will be early next year, although I actually think it will be the middle of next year before I see good old 154.
>
> At the moment I am very happy and full of beans; enjoying life to the full. Last night we got our issue of beer (the second since we came to Italy.) The issue is very poor these days—the main trouble is I don't think it gets as far up as we are. It is an occasion when the beer comes in, so a crowd of us gathered round the wireless, with our bottles and had quite a cheery time—while we were there, there was a lovely programme featuring Geraldo. We always tune in to Daventry, and of late we have been getting really good music, of which a large portion was played by Geraldo.
>
> The further we move north, the better the scenery becomes. We have left the part of rolling wheat fields and green vineyards through which we have been passing since Rome, although we do come across places like this in the valleys even now. We are in much more hilly country these days with plenty of trees, as all the slopes are well wooded—it is lovely to look at with the deep river valleys overlooked by high wooded slopes. I like it here as it is very nice when we stop and have a rest, as the trees form lovely places in which to park our trucks and pitch our tents.

The Star of Monday 17 July reported that there was only minor activity in the Springbok sector. Apart from patrolling and desultory artillery exchanges, the main activity of the past week had been the involvement of the South African guns in a heavy barrage which preceded a thrust by British and New Zealand forces. This was old news however, as it was only now reported that "the infantry supported by South African armoured reconnaissance elements, operating in close co-operation with the French, made an unopposed advance of more than 1,000 yards and occupied new positions near Castello di Brolio".

[180] J.B. Hodgson–W.A. Hodgson, 14/7/1944.

Sunday 16 July 1944 – Tuesday 18 July 1944: Casanova

Between Siena and Castelnuovo Berardenga lies the town of Casanova Pansarine, one of Italy's countless 'Casanovas'. Then, ten miles south of Radda, below Castello di Ama, is a speck on the map named Casanuova di Ama.

In his book *Victory in Italy*, Orpen writes: "At one stage, the 1/6th Field Regiment, over eager in pushing its 25-pounders forward northwest of Castel[lo] di Brolio, found the only infantry ahead of its own observation posts to be a couple of Guardsmen looking for mines. Attached anti-aircraft gunners had to help organize local defence for the field guns."[181] It seems Casanuova di Ama was the site of this occurrence, and a subsequent report indicates that the mishap occurred because the artillery wanted to obtain extra range for a planned attack early the next morning, which was subsequently called off.

Happy to have left its previous position at Castelnuovo, the headquarters of the 7/23rd Medium Regiment was established in a newly mown field beside a stream. There was only a trickle of water, but there were some clean pools which provided a great opportunity for bathing. Johnston records that the days of 16, 17 and 18 July were spent swimming and carrying out maintenance and repairs on the vehicles in hot weather.

The Natal Mounted Rifles had shifted axis slightly to the west on another approach to Radda through Scopeto and Vagliagli. On 17 July the regiment lost two killed and two fatally wounded. Nevertheless, they pushed on and bypassed Radda on the west before nightfall.

After dark on 16 July, a convoy led by the Royal Natal Carbineers was fired at. The incident took place three miles from Radda. After being ordered by brigade headquarters to speed up, the Carbineers captured Radda two days later on 18 July. On the Gaiole side, the Coldstream Guards had been working in hilly country with the Pretoria Regiment (Princess Alice's Own) and after Radda, the Guards Brigade again took the lead.

A severe heat wave, not uncommon in central Italy at this time of year, made life unbearable, especially between 1100 hours and 1600 hours. To make things worse, there was a plague of biting flies. The enemy was making a slow and orderly retreat, leaving no equipment behind. It was a particularly trying time for the leading troops as they encountered minefields and demolitions. The

---

[181] N. Orpen, *Victory in Italy,* p. 136; DODAR, WD, Box 624, 1/6th Field Regiment, 18/7/1944; On the British grid, the Casanova position was at Q887324.

Germans seemed to have a surplus of Nebelwerfers, the noisy six-barrelled mortars also known as 'Screaming Sisters', 'Sobbing Sisters' and 'Moaning Minnies'. The nicknames may have been comical, but these weapons were so unfunny that the American cartoonist Bill Maudlin refused to draw them. Not only were they noisy, they were also accurate and lethal. A soldier's best chance of defence was being inside a tank with the hatch closed. On the evening of 18 July, a reconnaissance column of Honey tanks from the Prince Alfred's Guard harboured on the outskirts of Radda, where crews dug slit trenches. The area came under shelling from Nebelwerfers after dark. Roll call was taken when the shelling stopped, but two men did not answer: Sergeant E. Botha and Trooper C.A. Pirie, both of Port Elizabeth, had been in the same slit trench when it received a direct hit. They were first buried at Radda and later reinterred in the Florence War Cemetery. The Prince Alfred's Guard had suffered another casualty three weeks earlier when a Nebelwerfer shell hit a tank, decapitating the commander, Lieutenant A.J. Wrey-Wathen. Charles Pirie's distraught father wrote directly to General Poole:

> Mr and Mrs Charles Pirie
> 5 Military Road
> Port Elizabeth
> South Africa
>
> General Poole
> With reference to the demise of my son, Charles Albert Pirie, No 10762V, 6th Armoured Div Tank Corps. I would be very grateful if you would forward me a letter in reply to this, and if so, give me particulars of my son's death. You can't say how sorry I was or better still words cannot express how a grand lad who offered his life for his country in this hour of need and met with disaster. It was painful to my dear wife when we received the cable on the 24/7/44 from H.Q. of the death of my son who was killed in action July 18th 1944. Kindly answer same and you will greatly oblige.
>
> Yours sincerely and carry on the good work.
> Charles Pirie

By return of post, the general informed Mr and Mrs Pirie of the exact circumstances surrounding their son's death and expressed his sincere sympathy at their bereavement. Although the South Africans were not involved in any clashes on 18 July, the Germans shelled the demolitions they had made, hoping to kill the infantry advancing on foot to Radda as well as the engineers clearing the way. Radda was occupied late on Tuesday afternoon. The big news, however, was of the Americans battling for Pisa and the port of Leghorn.

Wednesday 19 July 1944: Five miles to Radda

Reconnaissance parties from the 1/6th Field Regiment went ahead to find new gun positions; the idea was to leave one battery in action while the other prepared in the new area. It took four and a half hours for three batteries to leapfrog four and a half miles of the narrow roads, advancing over blown bridges and through dense scrub oak, the foliage forming a tunnel over the road.

The headquarters of the 7/23rd Medium Regiment was established in the village of San Polo, just south of Radda. The control room was established in the dining room of a private house. The owner was absent at the time of occupation but returned soon afterwards, begging to be allowed to occupy one room in his own house.

Continuing towards Monte San Michele, to the right of Panzano, "the weather remained hot and dry. Vineyards covered terraced hillsides. The wheat between the vines was nearly all cut and stooked now, and the little clumps of corn made excellent cover for German machine-gun posts. Italian peasants still worked in the fields as the tide of battle passed."[182]

On a spur of the mountains of Chianti, waist deep in bracken and sparsely shaded by a few pine trees, Major Eric Linklater, a noted British author and the historical recording officer for the British Eighth Army, came across a pair of South African tanks and a group of Guardsmen digging their weapon pits. He found himself "listening not so much to the noise of the guns as to the musical, guttural speech of the men sitting in the lee of their tanks. They were talking Afrikaans and that was a remarkable sound to hear on the crest of a mountain in Tuscany. It was more remarkable to find tanks snugly in position on a mountain that even a goat would have climbed only under compulsion." Linklater was given graphic details of a recent skirmish which demonstrated the close working relationship between the Guards Brigade and the Pretoria Regiment:

> … At night, up the impossible hillside, smashing their way through the undergrowth and scraggy trees, came a couple of South African tanks to lend a hand … It was

[182] W.L. Fielding, *With the 6th Div*, p. 138.

> some days later that I heard the story and saw the shell-torn, splintered trees, the broken rifles and lost helmets and the blackened German who still lay stinking in the forward minefield.[183]

Writing in the journalistic language of the day, Linklater continues: "… The Guards with their superb tradition—old but ever renewing itself—going forward on foot; the South Africans with the vigour of their young and spacious country, in modern armour."

The Pretoria Regiment's ability to lead their tanks up impossible slopes was much admired and commented on. The regiment's own account of the episode which took place on 20 July provides the exact location where the legendary feat took place:

> B Squadron's No 4 Troop made a mountaineering feat by climbing to a point N of pt.812 (Q9239) which seemed quite inaccessible. Snap targets and any sign of movement was engaged and the remainder of the Squadron tried to reach pt. 761 (Q9142) to help in the shoot but this proved too difficult and a harbour was made at Q902401. In company with the infantry, A Squadron troops took Mt Michele and had a good day's shooting.[184]

On the approach to Radda, the main task of B Company Royal Natal Carbineers was to patrol and protect the engineers repairing the road. Hodgson wrote to his mother on the day that the Royal Natal Carbineers took Radda, mentioning that David Alexander had been transferred back to 7 Platoon from the Vickers platoon. They had been at school together, as well as at 'The Kraal' and Hay Paddock and were pleased to be reunited. Hodgson's description of his surroundings is detailed, but the only hint he gives of the heavy fighting taking place there is his mention of the absence of birds:

> At the moment we are past Siena as you will have seen by the news. The country is simply wonderful—there are a few high mountains but most are fairly large hills, these are all wooded, not thickly, but enough to give plenty of shade and room to drive our trucks in and out. The trees are mainly oak. Between the hills in the valleys are numerous streams with lovely cool water. The road is a winding one and a bit difficult at stages, but we are still keeping the old B … on the run. A thing that strikes me is the marked absence of birds, this may be due to the shellfire etc, and they all move or go into secluded corners, as there are practically none about.

---

183 *Rand Daily Mail*, Afrikaans heard on mountain top in Tuscany, 2/8/1944.

184 DODAR, WD, Box 640, Pretoria Regiment 20/7/1944.

Following the capture of Radda by the Royal Natal Carbineers, the Witwatersrand Rifles/Regiment De la Rey moved through the town to its next objective, the village of Volpaia, which lay to the northeast. After a night march and a running fight in the morning, Volpaia was captured at midday on 19 July. The 'Royal Boere' were next ordered to capture Monte Querciabella. This is an 850m peak directly north of Volpaia. The name refers to the beautiful oaks which were shattered by the shelling. Monte Querciabella was taken without opposition, thanks to the support of the divisional artillery which included the 7/23rd Medium Regiment, the 4/22nd Field Regiment and the 1/6th Field Regiment. The latter began a barrage at 0430 hours in support of the Guards Brigade.

Fielding wrote: "Very heavy casualties were inflicted on the enemy in this action and he fled, hastily, leaving many dead bodies and much equipment on the ground."[185]

A direct hit from an 88 caused the bell tower in Radda to collapse. Hodgson had been inside, looking toward Panzano, at the time; he was lucky to escape unhurt, but his companion was not as fortunate.

The artillery now moved up to Radda. Johnston's entry for 20 July read: "Bit of a barrage (ours) last night—probably move on. Jim, Dave, Eric and I out foraging tomatoes, figs. Jerry gun pits. Got back to find all ready to move. Packed just in time. Drove from 21.00 to 02.00, then Eric and I slept near farmhouse because a gun stuck on bridge. Passed through Radda."

The Guards Brigade, together with the tanks of the Pretoria Regiment, then passed through the Witwatersrand Rifles/Regiment De la Rey on its way to the next objective: Monte San Michele.

Thursday 20 July 1944: Radda in Chianti

The two major ports of Ancona on the east coast and Leghorn (or Livorno in Italian) on the west were reported to have been captured on 20 July. There were few people to greet the Americans in Livorno, where the buildings had been completely destroyed, but those who remained were as enthusiastic as usual.

It was also a momentous day for the French, who received news that they would be taking part in the invasion of southern France in Operation Anvil/ Dragoon. They had come all the way from Rome on the South Africans' left

[185] W.L. Fielding, *With the 6th Div*, p. 140.

flank. The New Zealanders would be taking over their axis of advance. A perfect summer's day dawned after a night of intermittent shelling. The Royal Natal Carbineers' 7 Platoon moved out towards Panzano, spearheading the entire Eighth Army. Before long, 88mm shells from a concealed Tiger tank were bursting everywhere.

David Alexander, who had spoken of his fear at Cassino and hoped that he would be one of the lucky ones, had his chest sliced open by a shell fragment. Three others in his group were also hit. "In the hot sun, flies gathered and the sickly smell of fresh blood and the acrid stench of cordite from the shells pervaded the air."[186]

Shellfire was decimating Hodgson's platoon; he was the only member of a section comprising seven troopers, a corporal and a lance-corporal to make it through the war unscathed. In the space of a year, a total of 28 men had passed through the section, 19 of whom were replacements.

In his autobiography, Alexander writes that he developed a lifelong respect for Jeeps after being evacuated by a Jeep ambulance:

> Unbelievably, in the distance from whence we came, a Jeep crested the rise and raced down toward us. A large Red Cross flag streamed from its bonnet ... A figure leapt out, sprinted across the road and scrambled over the intervening wall. It was Captain 'Koffie' Reznek, the Regimental Medical Officer.[187]

Captain J.R. 'Koffie' Reznek, the medical officer of the Royal Natal Carbineers, was awarded the Military Cross while his assistant, Private Stanley Caseley, won the Military Medal for their distinguished bravery at Panzano on 22 July during the approaches to Monte Fili. Doctor Reznek opened a medical practice in Pietermaritzburg after the war. His nickname made reference to Koffiefontein, his hometown. Many others won medals during this phase, including Sergeant R. Hendrick of B Squadron, Natal Mounted Rifles and Stan Theesen of the Royal Natal Carbineers, who both won the Military Medal on 20 July. By last light, the Prince Alfred's Guard tanks and the Royal Natal Carbineers had occupied Panzano.

Reconnaissance played a vital role in this advance: one Natal Mounted Rifles troop leader reconnoitred on foot in front of the tanks all the way from Radda

---

186 G.B. Hobbs, *From Sicily to the Alps*, p. 123.

187 *Ibid*, p. 124.

to Panzano. In an exploit worthy of Hollywood, Lieutenant Kjelvlei of the Natal Mounted Rifles, accompanied by two sappers, ascended a bush-covered hill to look for a good vantage point. A barrage of gunfire followed them. When they failed to return, company commander Major Haupt and Trooper N.P. Sinclair went forth to find them, armed only with a revolver and a Thompson sub-machine gun respectively. Not only did they manage to recover the three men, they also took two prisoners and killed a number of Germans (sources differ on the exact number killed, although it ranges between two and five). Trooper Sinclair won the Military Medal for his actions. Olaf Kjelvei had been a policeman before the war and first served in the Police Brigade. He was serving as district commandant in Port Elizabeth when "he was stabbed to death when he tried to stop a group of about 50 marching Africans" in 1961.[188]

Shortly prior to this, a directive had come from Eighth Army headquarters which might have precluded some of these men from receiving awards:

> A number of recommendations for Immediate Awards are being received for very gallant actions by individuals, in the face of the enemy and under fire, in rescuing their comrades from burning tanks and other vehicles.
>
> Whilst appreciating that such conduct undoubtedly merits some recognition, the Commander-in-Chief has decided that, unless the notion has some bearing on the immediate success of the operation or is accompanied by a further action with such bearing, recommendations cannot be accepted for Immediate Awards, but will be recognized by Mentions-in-Dispatches.
>
> I am directed to say that this is not intended to stop stretcher-bearers, linesmen or similar personnel from being recommended for immediate awards as before.[189]

The war diary of the Royal Natal Carbineers for the period 20 and 21 July reported a great deal of action. At 1325 hours on 20 July, B Company, Royal Natal Carbineers reached high ground two and a half miles south of Panzano. From here, it advanced up the right-hand side of the road while C Company moved up the left. The enemy put up a stand, using bazookas, and the Royal Natal Carbineers called on the Prince Alfred's Guard for support. Shelling was heavy and accurate thanks to the enemy's observation points on the high ground, which the Guards Brigade was striving to take.

188 E. Goetzsche, *The official Natal Mounted Rifles history*, pp. 291, 340.

189 DODAR, Div Docs, Box 164, File 6 ADE/5/5 Honours and Awards, Main HQ Eighth Army, 3/7/1944.

Friday 21 July 1944 – Monday 24 July 1944: Panzano

Northwest of Panzano, the Royal Natal Carbineers was still plodding on from demolition to demolition under the continuous thud and rumble of gunfire. Any movement brought shells crashing down as they travelled along the road to Greve. Fielding sketched the scene:

> From time to time grey-black clouds of smoke would raise their ugly heads among the advancing Springboks, figures would fall to earth, and as the smoke cleared, a little party carrying the Red Cross flag would go forward—the stretcher-bearers, often men of the Cape Corps.[190]

Pockets of enemy were present in the C Company area. Lieutenant (later Captain) Edmonds' platoon saw movement in the thick woods ahead of them, gave chase and shot up an enemy patrol, killing one and capturing one. His platoon made contact again later that night, killing two more Germans.

The Royal Natal Carbineers' losses for the day of 21 July were four killed, seven wounded and one missing. Two of these were members of 7 Platoon, B Company. Sergeant Philip Lee MM was hit in the chest by a splinter from a German 88. He was the 31-year-old son of the Right Reverend A.W. Lee, who was the Bishop of Zululand, living in Vryheid.[191] Philip Lee had attended Michaelhouse and Cedara Agricultural College, and was working as an extension officer in Zululand where he met his future wife, Joan. She describes him as "... about six foot tall, slightly bow-legged, a marvellous dancer and tennis player ... rather shy".[192] Hodgson knew him only as 'Beaver' Lee and remembers him as a very nice man, slightly odd-looking, but one of the real men of B Company. Between Panzano and Greve, Private Lawrence G. McNicholas, another of the 'unlucky seven', sustained multiple and mortal injuries from a mortar shell. His brother, Lieutenant Walter McNicholas, had been killed six weeks previously while on secondment to the Royal Horse Artillery. After allowing time for the next-of-kin to be informed, Hodgson wrote to his father about the death of his good friend, omitting any of the upsetting details:

---

190 W.L. Fielding, *With the 6th Div,* p. 105.

191 Bishop A.W. Lee was an authority on the Zulu people; a scholar, historian and author of several books including *Once dark country: recollections and reflections of a South African bishop.*

192 J. Crwys-Williams, *Mood of a nation*, p. 371.

> There is some very sad news I have to convey to you, if you have not already heard it. Lawrence McNicholas was killed on the 21st of this month. It was due to some heavy shellfire. I am glad to say he did not suffer at all, although he did not die immediately, the reason being he was unconscious all the time. I was not with him at the time but I am told he caught it all over. I suppose it is the way of the world, all the best seem to go.

Lawrence McNicholas was part of the Royal Natal Carbineers cast who had staged a performance of the R.C. Sheriff anti-war play, *Journey's End*, while at Khatatba. He had played the part of the young lieutenant (Raleigh) who is injured by a shell, which damages his spine so that he can't move his legs. In the play, while Raleigh is dying, he is comforted by his school friend and company commander, Captain Stanhope, who was played by Corporal Vernon Gardiner. The play was performed twice at Khatatba and once at Helwan, each time in front of an audience of 2,000. In a tragic twist of fate, it was the same two who now acted out the drama in real life.[193]

It was necessary to take the high points on the left and right of the road as the troops moved on from Panzano. A strong enemy force, including tanks, was reported to be approaching Greve from the north. The artillery had played an important role in cracking the Irmgard Line, using smoke and creeping barrages in support of both operations and covering patrols. The mediums had a particularly heavy day on 21 July, firing nearly 900 shells. The air observation post had remained in the air for five hours. Most satisfying was the destruction of a self-propelled gun which had acquired the nickname 'Troglodyte'.

The crash of the 25-pounders was accentuated in the valleys and the noise resounded throughout the hills. The observation posts were "having a field day", calling down five divisional shoots and many more regimental targets. One of these was on an enemy tank which the war diarist calls a "Dodging Dirtbox" because of its elusiveness. Florence was also within shelling range, 17 miles away as the crow flies. The 1/6th Field Regiment, positioned in the valley below Panzano, fired 4,656 rounds on 22 July. The 7/23rd Medium Regiment fired 1,108 rounds, a regimental record.[194] In a letter to his father dated 22 July, Hodgson wrote of how well the war was going overall, referring to the

[193] M. Coghlan, *Pro Patria*, pp. 40–41.

[194] N. Orpen, *Victory in Italy*, p. 145; DODAR, WD, Box 624, the 1/6th Field Regiment, 22/7/1944; DODAR, WD, Box 630, 7/23 Med Rgt, 22/7/1944; The 1/6th Field Regiment position was at Q835415.

assassination attempt on Hitler two days previously and expressing the opinion that the Gothic Line would not hold them up for too long. All the same, he took the precaution of asking his parents to send him winter clothes. There is no sign that he was affected by the death of McNicholas the previous day:

> The war is still going along very well indeed and I only hope that things will move along even faster still. If only the weather would improve in Normandy, I think we would see quite a good advance. The building up of supplies must be continuing at a very high rate, and when the weather does clear we will see a lot happening. This bit of a revolt that has started in Germany is a very encouraging sign; we thought that the Gestapo had such a powerful hold on the people that there would never be a chance for an internal revolt. I think now that one attempt has been made, it won't be long before the people realize the position and take advantage of it to the full by causing a larger and more effective rising. Here we are again on the move, and with the fall of Leghorn and Ancona, things are again going well, so it looks as if we will be in Florence before very long. Then the Gothic line, which I do not think will hold us up for too long because the line is so easily outflanked on the eastern side. As for the Russians, their steamroller advance is going along as well as ever, so I hope it will not be long before they reach Warsaw, then on to Germany itself.
>
> It often looks as if it is coming up for rain, but it has all been blown over. In a way I am glad, but in another way I wish it would rain because the gravel roads get so churned up by all the tanks and trucks that everything always has a thick layer of dust on it; also, it is very hot these days, but I suppose we had better make the best of all the warmth because when the winter comes it will come with a vengeance. If we are here for the winter, which I think is possible, I would like one of those sheepskin jackets, as they are so necessary to keep out the biting cold which we may receive some of in the Alps. If you could possibly get me one of these I would be very grateful. They are very hard to get but I hear that with a bit of wangling one can get them from the Navy League.

Gunners of the 1/6th Field Regiment had something of a scare on the morning of 22 July when a premature from the mediums landed near the gun area. At the same time, someone dropped a cigarette onto cordite near a German ammo dump. Shells were whizzing around everywhere and for a minute the men thought that a counter-battery was inevitable, but the incident ended satisfactorily and without injury. There is no mention of this event in the war diary of the 7/23rd Medium Regiment which was, at this time, deployed in a valley running east–west at right angles to the road. Regimental headquarters was situated at the west end of the valley while the batteries were positioned on the east side. There were no houses nearby, which may be why the diarist expressed surprise and dismay in finding that the flies were just as bad here in the open as they were in the towns and villages. No doubt they were attracted by the burned-out enemy trucks on the road between Radda and Panzano. Flies can be troublesome throughout Italy in the summer, but were especially prolific among the detritus of war. Hodgson, too, spoke of the problem:

> We have been having quite a bit of heat these days, and with the heat comes the flies. I would not be at all surprised if one said they are worse here than in Egypt ...There are some very large ones too which give a painful bite; there are no after effects such as a bump but when he bites you it is like a pin prick ... In the parcel I am sending down to you, I have added some postcards which I got at Acquaviva; they are not too good, but I hope to get some really good ones at Florence; when we get there and if we get there.[195]

With support from the Pretoria Regiment, the Coldstream Guards assaulted Monte Domini, six miles to the east of Panzano. The feature was taken on 23 July in a frontal attack in broad daylight, led by Captain Lord Andrew Cavendish. According to the official history of the Coldstream Guards, it was a "spirited affair" and "resistance was dogged". Although one platoon was caught by machine-gun fire, relatively few casualties were suffered by the Coldstreams. The defenders were determined to fight it out and were annihilated—few prisoners were taken.[196] Enemy machine guns continued to fire on the approaching tanks until the last moment.

The author of the Pretoria Regiment's diary referred to the day's action as a perfect coordination of all arms which could be termed "copy book". The diary continues: "The casualties inflicted by the squadron can never be known, but 20 killed would be a very conservative estimate. In the action we sustained only light casualties—two wounded."

On the other side of the road, to the northwest of Panzano, A Company of the Witwatersrand Rifles/Regiment De la Rey achieved its objective of Monte Fili. This time the artillery barrage started late but the company commander, Major Barends (who received the Military Cross), decided to push on. When the artillery finally started up, the men were subjected to 'friendly fire' but they changed the direction of attack and avoided most of the shelling. According to the account of W.J. Lister of the intelligence section, the high explosive changed

195 J.B. Hodgson–D.M. Hodgson, 8/7/1944.

196 E. Axelson, *A year in Italy*, p. 61; G Burns in *'No dishonourable name'* edited by D. Quilter, p. 215.

to smoke, and with the smoke shells landing around them they took the crest "shouting and yelling". The counter-attack, when it came, was repulsed mainly by throwing hand grenades as fast as possible. This engagement cost the battalion seven killed and 48 wounded. At 12 Brigade headquarters, Fielding was in close proximity to the gun positions:

> We watched South African bombardiers, stripped to the waist, bronzed and sweltering in the blazing sun, as they loaded their 25-pounders, fired—reloaded and fired again. Immediately behind us, the medium guns fired away, their five-inch missiles screaming low over our heads, the blast from their barrels swaying the vehicles in which we worked on their springs. A noisy, dusty broiling life.[197]

Patrols of the First City/Cape Town Highlanders got beyond Greve where enemy 88s, positioned two miles northwest of Greve at Vicchiomaggio, were still in action.

All elements of the 12th Motorized Brigade were engaged on 24 July. The farmland between Panzano and Greve in Chianti is covered by vines and olive orchards but the forested slopes of the high ground provided excellent cover and observation points for the enemy. A heavy artillery barrage was brought down on the wooded slopes of a hill and the area was covered in a pall of smoke and dust. Forty Germans lay dead by the time the South Africans reached the top of the hill. A further 37 dead Germans were found in another area, presumably killed by the artillery. Prisoners revealed that the South Africans were again facing their old friends, the German 356th Division. "The Hermann Göring Para Panzer Division had been withdrawn from the Italian theatre."[198]

The losses over this period had been heavy. The Prince Alfred's Guard had lost five tanks on 22 July, three of them to mines, the other two to anti-tank guns. The Imperial Light Horse/Kimberley Regiment lost two senior officers that same day: Major B.G. Kennedy and Captain C. Hall MC were killed while disarming a new kind of anti-tank mine. Captain Hall was a member of the *Natal Mercury* editorial staff and left a wife and two young sons. This regiment continued to suffer a steady stream of casualties over the next few days: two dead on 24 July, two more dead the following day and 16 dead on 26 July.

[197] W.L. Fielding, *With the 6th Div*, p. 143.

[198] W.L. Fielding, *With the 6th Div*, p. 143; DODAR, WD, Box 635, Imperial Light Horse/Kimberley Regiment, File B8 60; *The Star*, Advance by Springboks, south of Florence, 24/7/1944.

For some, the road to Mercatale was "the hottest spot before Florence ..." but worse was still to come for the Imperial Light Horse/Kimberley Regiment during the months ahead.[199]

Once again, the men were in a position to supplement their rations with farm produce. As usual, tomatoes and figs were plentiful and corn was a welcome addition. The grapes and peaches were almost ripe and there were plenty of golden plums. Johnston's crew took full advantage, feasting on fried tomatoes and stewed peaches while they "killed" the last of the demijohns of *vino*.

Hodgson said very little of the recent death of two of his closest companions or his own narrow escape. This isn't surprising, however, as psychologists recognize the existence of a condition where fatigued soldiers suppress reality. This is a survival mechanism which helps them endure their situation. In fact, according to Freud, "Illusions appear to us because they save us from frustrations."[200] This flight from reality is well documented and Hodgson's fantasies about home conform to a common theme:

> Are the coffee and crumpets still up to the old standard? I am waiting to hear what your latest reports on His Majesty's Roof Garden are like. I can see that soon after I get home we will have to go and have a dance there, so I can see if your reports are correct. By the way, what are the latest tunes at home these days, or haven't they changed much of late? Ask Alison if the Old Eds is still full up every Saturday as it used to be, as I would like to know.

While reading a letter from his mother on 27 July, Bourhill succumbed to similar illusions: "I'd just finished reading a letter from you written in the sun on the stoep. I saw your poor old ankle, and you getting up to go inside and opening the front door and holding it open ... and then limping across the sitting room carpet and going to the kettle. I followed you all the way as if I'd been watching you and that makes me want to tell you how real you were in my sight." Contact with home is what kept these men going.

At this time, an SABC mobile recording unit visited an anti-tank battery just south of Florence. Gunner E.R. Palmer of Johannesburg used the opportunity to send a message home. He had been reported missing for two days and now wished to tell his wife that he was alright. He had apparently wandered into an

---

199 J. Kros, *War in Italy*, p. 122; DODAR, WD, Box 635, Imperial Light Horse/Kimberley Regiment, 24–26 July 1944; *Rand Daily Mail*, Springbok M.C. reported killed, 31/7/1944.

200 E. Dinter, *Hero or coward: pressures facing the soldier in battle*, p. 32.

Italian farmhouse where Germans were staying. Fortunately, the Italians had whispered "*Tedeschi*" in warning, and had led him to a cellar where they hid him until the Germans left.

From a sharp ridge along a narrow road toward Greve, the shells of the South Africans could be seen landing south of the Arno in the direction of Florence. Meanwhile, German shells burst along the ridge on the right, where "thin whisps of white dust betrayed the movements of the Guardsmen. In the valley below other thin white whisps showed that the South Africans there were moving forward slowly, apparently encountering demolitions which were under heavy shellfire."[201]

Tuesday 25 July 1944 – Wednesday 26 July 1944: Three miles to Greve

From Panzano, Greve was reached via a narrow watershed road that ran along the top of a range of hills. The Imperial Light Horse/Kimberley Regiment and the Special Service Battalion were in front, bearing the brunt of the shelling and mortaring.

As usual, the Natal Mounted Rifles provided the reconnaissance screen. Florence was now eleven miles away and the top brass estimated that it would take three days to get there—but they'd held that same estimation since Castelnuovo. At 0835 hours, Sergeant Buckler of the First City/Cape Town Highlanders came in from the previous night's reconnaissance patrol, accompanied by a sapper. They had gone to inspect a bridge as well as the road ahead. They had run into a German officer on a motorcycle with a sidecar, who captured the patrol's Private Coutts, forcing him onto the pillion of the motorcycle while covering the other two with his pistol. The enemy was thick on the ground but Buckler and the sapper managed to evade them and made their way back to the headquarters. Other members of the patrol returned after dark. That night, Buckler and the sapper were sent straight back to complete their reconnaissance of the bridge—all the while being shot at by tanks.

Although most soldiers would have been intent on looking out for danger, Hodgson was taking in the beautiful Chianti countryside: "The country is still getting prettier the further north we go; at the moment it is really picturesque. It is hard to look at all these beautiful valleys and hills with the huge mountains in a blue haze in the distance, and not to think that you are looking at a painting.

---

201 *The Star*, Advance by Springboks, south of Florence, 24/7/1944.

It is really beautiful." On the morning of 25 July, Lieutenant F.W. Williams, the forward observation officer of the 1/6th Field Regiment, was mortally wounded in his observation post at Mercatale. He died five days later and was buried at Assisi. That afternoon, the 25-pounders, still in the hilly country of Chianti, were pulled into almost inaccessible positions down winding farm tracks just short of Greve. The regimental area was just past the main division on land which belonged to the Panzano Castle. The princess of the castle was a known fascist and had been imprisoned by the Field Security Section. "It was a good spot, with the usual vineyards and olive trees a few yards away and a market garden."[202]

Greve was occupied by the First City/Cape Town Highlanders on 25 July. Florence could be seen across the plains of Tuscany. The Guards were advancing through the range of hills on the right, and there was a strong counter-attack on their position during the night. The Grenadier Guards were, as usual, supported by Pretoria Regiment tanks as well as Royal Durban Light Infantry mortars and machine guns. While the Royal Durban Light Infantry was helping the Grenadier Guards repel the counter-attack on Monte Collegalle (Grenadiers' Ridge), a chivalrous action by members of its 7 Platoon had tragic results. They had gone to the aid of an Italian woman who had been entrapped and wounded in a minefield. Eighteen-year-old Private D. Pullen from Durban and Private J. Dalton were killed, and three were wounded.

From the letter written by Hodgson to his sister on 25 July, it would appear that B Company, Royal Natal Carbineers was having a brief respite:

> At the moment we are staying in an orchard next to a house. There are a large number of young lassies here, so we have got them all inspanned into cleaning up our clothes. I have had all my clothes washed and ironed, and they have never been in such shape since leaving home. Also, I have all my mending done, also my shorts altered to the correct size. They have been very useful and they have done it all very willingly. They have got a huge oven here for baking bread, so we gave them a sack of flour and they made us quite a bit, so we have had some homemade white bread for a change.

Two Natal Mounted Rifles medics were awarded the Military Medal for ambulance work near Mercatale on 25 July. The citations state that Troopers

202 E. Axelson, *A year in Italy*, p. 63; the position of the 1/6th Field Regiment was at Q829446.

J. Bishop and W.J.P. Kruger made 22 trips into the battle line through a rain of armour-piercing shot, shellfire and bullets. Major Raymond 'Vic' Paul won the Military Cross during the same action. Baker, who is not terribly complimentary about most of his officers, described Major Paul as "one of those rarely born heroes", big but not ungainly, with a deep voice which steadied his loyal men at the battle of Alamein. He did not look for trouble and the men scrambled to be in his squad. "With a man like that, a bulldog countenance scarred with battle, you could trust him."[203]

King George VI visited the 6th South African Armoured Division in the village of Radda on 26 July. A report in the *Rand Daily Mail* of 28 July proclaimed: "The King visits Springbok troops in Italy—Cheering men line road through hilltop town." Preparations for the visit were made in great secrecy and the identity of the expected visitor disclosed to the troops only an hour before his arrival, although many had already guessed. The men, some of whom had been in action only a short time before, were transported to Radda where they dismounted in the town square and took up positions on both sides of the road, which overlooked the terraced vineyards. Slips of paper announcing their secret visitor were passed around while they waited in the boiling heat. Although 26 July was a relatively quiet day, the general feeling at divisional headquarters was, "Fucking nuisance, the King is coming now just as we are in the middle of battle". In fact, there would be no close air support available during his visit as the air force was detailed to give constant cover.

Accompanied by the top brass, General Alexander, Eighth Army commander, General Sir Oliver Leese and General Poole, the King was driven up the divisional axis. He passed through the village at a fair pace in an open yellow tourer, stopping only once to speak to two Rhodesians and conversing briefly with some Guardsmen at the end of the town.[204] Major A.B. Theunissen, the division's senior staff officer, or G2, recorded that "As the division was engaged in heavy fighting to the north, it was not possible to arrange even a representative group for the King to address". However, Axelson estimated that 1,000 representatives were there, and that the cars swept by at ten to 15 miles per hour, stopping only for a minute at a Rhodesian anti-tank battery.

203 D.M. Baker, *War, wine and valour*, p. 265.

204 *Rand Daily Mail*, The King visits Springbok troops in Italy, 28/7/1944; E. Axelson, *A year in Italy*, p. 106; DODAR, WD, Box 630, 7/23rd Medium Regiment, 22/7/1944.

Although elements of his regiment were in action and having an uncomfortable time in Greve, Bourhill was detailed to provide a reception for the King and his entourage:

> I went and saw the King when he came. A counter-attack was coming off and they could only spare one man per sub-section and I clicked. I went to see him at a place called Radda. Just behind the lines. I heard him speak—just the same as you or I do and he had rings under his eyes like half-crowns; he was very pale and wore gloves and had a blanket over his knees. He looked old and very tired … to me he was just a very tired weak-looking ordinary man. General Leese is like a great hairy sunburned bear and Alexander looks like a Prussian aristocrat—same Nazi cap style, and straight and stiff as a poker.

The King was heard to remark to the general who was driving him, "Do you mean to drive at this speed all the way?" Axelson came away thinking that the visit would have left no warm feeling among the soldiers of the empire who had sworn allegiance to this "sour-looking King".[205] For the Royal Natal Carbineers, the King's visit may have been more significant, as King George was their Colonel-in-Chief. On his death in 1952, the regiment sent condolences to Her Majesty Queen Elizabeth and recalled how inspiring his Christmas messages had been. The war diary of the 1/6th Field Regiment makes no mention of the King's visit and neither did Hodgson, who wrote to his mother on the day of the visit:

> As far as I am concerned here the war is going very well indeed. And I am happy and full of beans. I have had a touch of diahorrea from eating some peas that were not quite ripe, but it did not last long though, and I am again as fit as a fiddle … Gosh, but how the Russians are moving; this colossal advance of theirs is quite unbelievable—all we hope now is that they can keep this up and it will not be many weeks before they get into Germany proper, then the fur will begin to fly, that is if the Germans have not turned it up by then. In Normandy everything is going along admirably, although the advance is a very slow one. At the moment the enemy is using everything to hold up our advance, but the stage will soon come when he will not be able to put fresh stuff in at the rate he is doing now. Then the break-through will come and from then on there will be no stopping our troops in France. As for the war here, all is going well; the advance is a steady one, which old Jerry cannot stand up against. No doubt he will do his damndest to make a stand at the Gothic Line, but this won't last long. How can troops who have got all this internal trouble to face, as well as the successive defeats on all fronts, make a determined stand?

205 E. Axelson, *A year in Italy*, p. 64.

Thursday 27 July 1944: Greve

Describing the earlier fighting in the South African sector, SAPA's war correspondent with the 6th South African Division wrote that on Tuesday there had been an artillery bombardment "as fierce as anything the Springboks had encountered since the advance north of Rome began". The German resistance was said to be the stiffest yet encountered, but another article in the same newspaper proclaimed: "Germans withdrawing on whole front in Italy." The unusually stiff resistance to the Eighth Army's push was explained by the fact that the Germans had been told that all prisoners would be shot by the British as a reprisal for the flying bombs terrorizing London.[206] *The Star* of 27 July published an uncharacteristically bleak account of the fighting:

> From the valleys and ridges, through the rumbling roar of the cannonade, came the crack and rattle of small arms and machine-guns. In almost inaccessible bush and scrub, the bodies of soldiers killed in the bitter close-quarter struggles, lay in the bright sunshine. Yard by yard, mile after mile, the advance went on.

The leading elements of the 6th South African Armoured Division were now eight miles from Florence but the New Zealanders were two miles ahead, on the left. Axelson expressed the big fear of the South Africans: "It looks like they may forestall us into the city after all; and Florence has been our goal since we passed through Rome."[207] The Americans entered the southern area of Pisa on the afternoon of 24 July but were not yet in contact with the Gothic Line, which was roughly described as running from Pisa to Rimini.

In the South African sector, the Royal Natal Carbineers took over the lead and found Mercatale clear—albeit flattened and under enemy observation—on 7 July. The Witwatersrand Rifles/Regiment De la Rey was on the high ground overlooking the River Greve and the Coldstream Guards had trouble passing through Strada. There were 15 Tiger tanks causing havoc, having knocked out three Special Service Battalion tanks. Colonel Brits and all his squadron commanders had been wounded; in fact, tank crews take up a significant portion of the Florence war cemetery. It was impossible to move in the open during the day. Nevertheless, in Strada, they were able to travel the length of the village unobserved by knocking holes in a row of adjoining houses. Here

206 *The Star*, Resistance south of Florence again stiffened, 27/7/1944.

207 E. Axelson, *A year in Italy*, p. 65.

they holed up for a couple of days. For the first time in the campaign, the two brigade headquarters were alongside each other as the staff devised a plan for crossing the Greve River. During the short stop, Bourhill's thoughts turned to victory and to home:

> Many letters from you in the last couple of days, and that is the main item of news I think, as it is the main thing of importance besides that of winning of the war. The last week has been hard fighting and I personally should not have liked to have been in Hun's booties during some of the shelling we put over yesterday and the day before. You see, the country is very difficult, at least it was, till we reached this valley and Jerry had all the advantages.

'Hell House' was the name given to a farmhouse on a high point northwest of Greve, halfway to Mercatale. From here, the Germans could observe the road, which they had registered, and any traffic was shelled. Five Tiger tanks were deployed, inflicting their usual quota of damage. As the tanks were withdrawing, one fell into a cesspit and had to be destroyed by its crew. Hell House was eventually occupied by the Special Service Battalion, from where they now had a commanding view.

However, the Rhodesian Squadron suffered a number of casualties while in this position, including commander Major Lindsay, who was wounded but remained on duty. The Pretoria Regiment took a bad knock on 27 July. At 1015 hours, two tanks went up on mines and 17-year-old Lance-Corporal P.J.W. Otto was killed. Another tank was hit by armour-piercing and brewed up, killing two. Thirty-one-year-old Trooper J.B. Davidson was killed immediately (his parents lived in Aberdeen, Scotland), and 24-year-old Lance-Corporal G.D.W. Kitcat, from Grahamstown, suffered fatal burns. Later in the afternoon, Trooper B. Hurter was killed by armour piercing and two days later, Trooper R.A.C. Orr was killed by shrapnel. The total number of dead for the Pretoria Regiment during July, was 16.

Friday 28 July 1944 – Saturday 29 July 1944: Four miles beyond Greve

At 0400 hours on 28 July, the 1/6th Field Regiment's reconnaissance parties moved to a spot called Le Bolle to prepare new gun positions. The 25-pounders followed at 0600 hours. As it turned out, this was a good time to be on the roads as they became very congested later in the day. The pace of the advance was painfully slow now that the enemy was showing strong resistance.[208] The Scots Guards took the farm Poggio Mandorli in what Orpen calls a "bayonet charge" later that afternoon. Refusing to surrender or withdraw, the Germans took the only remaining option. The Guards dug in but were shelled from the high ground around Impruneta. Facing four and a half German divisions along the Paula Line, the South Africans were instructed by XIII Corps to wait for the New Zealanders to make progress on the left before launching any major attack.[209] The Royal Natal Carbineers and the Special Service Battalion were beyond Mercatale. Here, on 28 July, the 12th South African Motorized Brigade passed by the grave of John 'Binks' Beaton, who had been killed while supervising the dressing of the wounded. He had only recently been promoted to captain and the company had not yet been informed. Consequently, the wooden cross near the roadside marked the grave of 'Lieutenant' John Beaton. Fielding dedicated his book, *With the 6th Div*, to Beaton and described him thus: "Highly intelligent, delightful in character, so young, so brave …"

The Germans were putting up a fanatical and often suicidal defence on the Paula Line, throwing in all available resources. The division was losing a lot of tanks and the advance slowed considerably. Hodgson wrote: "We are still experiencing terrific heat. Mind you, I don't mind it, as there is plenty of shade and water here, not like the desert. The flies are the only nuisance, as they are here in masses; to make it worse they are all very persistent." Nevertheless, the world news was promising and there was enough fruit in Tuscany to feed an army:

> Isn't the news really wonderful these days; I expect by the time this reaches you, they will have cleaned out the flying bomb sights and be inside Belgium, and even very near Germany … We are still going strong on the fruit. This last week it has been at its peak, and we have hardly stopped eating it—in fact we have not paid much attention to our rations. The figs are so nice we just eat them skin and all.

Johnston also wrote about the proliferation of fruit in his diary. However, as an artilleryman, he was living a more normal life: "Heavy maintenance all

---

208 DODAR, WD, Box 624, 1/6th Field Regiment, 28-29 July 1944; the gun positions were at Q818516.

209 N. Orpen *Victory in Italy,* p. 159; Poggio Ai Mandorli is a farm southwest of Strada.

day. Walk in evening and saw very attractive girl milking sheep. Fruit." At a remote hamlet called Santa Lucia, located between Mercatale and Impruneta, the Witwatersrand Rifles/Regiment De la Rey's C Company (under Major van der Riet) was required to advance over ploughed land to clear some houses. Twenty-three-year-old Sergeant W.J.A. Weideman of Rustenburg had been killed on 28 July when patrolling the area. Three more junior leaders became casualties during the engagement, which lasted most of the day: Lieutenant G.J. Martin and Sergeant H.W. Botha were killed and Lieutenant J.P. Erasmus was wounded.

Over the next two days, Private S. Allen and 22-year-old Private R.E.V. Bassingthwaighte would be added to the Witwatersrand Rifles/Regiment De la Rey roll of honour.[210] Two Bassingthwaightes, both from Windhoek, were killed in the campaign.

Sunday 30 July 1944 – Wednesday 2 August 1944: Mercatale

The leading troops had reached the outskirts of Impruneta, known for its plantations and avenues of pine trees. It had been a hectic week for the Royal Natal Carbineers but 30 July was a lazy Sunday. Hodgson, once again suppressing reality, withdrew into his daydreaming by writing longingly about the tennis parties which took place every Sunday at home:

> I can just imagine what you are doing at the moment—sitting in the tennis shelter, watching the men knock the covers off the balls, while you get on with some knitting. Diana I expect is also there, pulling Dad's leg unmercifully every time he makes a bad stroke. The Sunday dinner will be in the oven—how my mouth waters when I think of what it will be; there will also be the good old Stag on the ice, waiting for the thirsty men when they come off the field of sport. Mind you, with the news as good as it is it won't be too long before I will be knocking the covers off with Dad. At the moment I am sitting in the front of our truck writing on one of the map-boards (by the way, what do you think of the Regimental stationery?—I managed to wangle a bit from our company clerk). It is a beautiful day, not as hot as usual. We are situated in a plantation of fir trees which makes the spot very pleasant—the cook is busy with lunch, what we will get I haven't the faintest idea, but I can assure you I would not mind swapping you if you are agreeable!

A massive operation was in progress at the River Greve but Hodgson alludes only to the traffic. In this part of Tuscany, famous for its wines, it seems that

210 S. Monick, *A bugle calls*, pp. 380–384; Santa Lucia is not shown as a village on maps today but the war diary of the 1/6th Field Regiment gives the position as Q782549.

plentiful food was helping to keep up morale. Although the required waiting period of 30 days had not yet passed, Hodgson mentioned to his parents that David Alexander had been wounded:

> Do you remember David Alexander, he was the third member, with George and I at Kaffers Kraal—I think I told you a while ago that he had transferred to this company, from the Vickers Platoon. On the 20th he was wounded—not seriously, but a nasty one in the right shoulder. I have not heard how he is progressing, but I think he will be OK although he will be out of it for quite a few months.
>
> These days we are eating lovely fresh tomatoes. They are really high class and make our meals so much more tasty—you know how much I like them, so I am 'getting stuck in', to quote the old maxim. We are also getting plenty of good green mealies; we just pick them as we want them and put them straight into the pot, plenty of salt and margarine, and away we go.
>
> Yesterday I had to do a bit of conducting of traffic; while on the road I stopped a Jeep and who should be inside, none other than Allen Cowan; he is a lieutenant in the artillery. I have not seen him since we were in Maritzburg, so it was a very pleasant surprise, there was not much chance to speak to him as you can imagine, as he was in a bit of a hurry.

Shelling of the South African sector slackened on 30 July, as the German 4th Parachute Division began withdrawing. Using aerial photographs and information from a reconnaissance patrol, a suitable way was found to cross the Greve River on the evening of 30/31 July. The New Zealanders were attacking on the left while the South Africans put in diversionary artillery attacks on Impruneta to assist them.

At 1100 hours on 31 July, the retreating Germans were subjected to a regimental concentration from the 25-pounders at Mercatale. That same day, the First City/Cape Town Highlanders relieved a New Zealander battalion in the area of Sant'Andrea. They then advanced on two features, Montanto and Montanino, where they came across "a number of dead and a mêlée of equipment bearing testimony to the intensity of the barrage".[211]

The weather was hot and dry on 1 August as the Guards Brigade launched its attack on Impruneta. Dust on the roads was a problem, as it attracted enemy fire. The roads were plastered with notices stipulating 'No dust', 'Slow' and 'Dust is death'. By the next day, tanks of the Natal Mounted Rifles had reached Nizzano, three miles closer to Florence. Captain P.O.F. Power of the 1/6th Field

[211] L.G. Murray, *First City/Cape Town Highlanders in the Italian Campaign,* p. 40; E. Axelson, *A year in Italy*, p. 65.

Regiment was the forward observation officer with the Royal Natal Carbineers; he was wounded by mortar fire on 2 August. An observation post reported gun flashes from the Campo in Florence but permission to fire on the target was denied. Captain Michael Howard of the Coldstream Guards provides an eloquent first-hand account of the action in an artillery observation post between Greve and Strada:

> It is stimulating being in a gunner OP when a shoot is going on. First the gunner officer murmurs strange Arabic formulae down the telephone. Then he says 'fire!' There is a silence. The leaves rustle peacefully and a bird twitters. You strain your ears to catch the bang of the gun among the miscellaneous, continual bangs which puncture time through the afternoon. Probably you miss it and hear only the strange swift sighing of the shell rushing overhead. Then comes the great brown mushroom of smoke and dust on the green hill opposite, two seconds before the crash of the explosion. The gunner repeats figures into the telephone and you wait again. The next mushroom is behind the hill and you only see the smoke curling up after the explosion. Then perhaps a third shot hits the target and the house disappears in a cloud of yellow dust. The human element is quite remote, but you may well get what pleasure you can get out of shelling other people, as there is so very little in being shelled yourself. It is most disappointing, when the dust clears away, to see how little the house is damaged. But the gunner has been busy ... It will be a quarter of an hour before the smoke clears now and you can see the damage. Before then, the Germans have retaliated and you duck unhappily at the crescendo whistle of a shell which pitches a quarter of a mile down the hill, shaking the ground and the air with blast. Sometimes you know there is another company there and watch helplessly as your own position disappears in smoke. Yet casualties are always astonishingly small.[212]

The day was also busy for the 7/23rd Medium Regiment. Ten bombards were fired and 'Pamphlet', the air observation post, engaged a few targets. A respite was enjoyed by the 'Queen' Battery which had "installed themselves in an old castle where they indulged in billiards in their spare time".

The next day was fairly quiet for the gunners but the tanks and infantry advanced slowly. A real effort was now being made to take Florence and there was a feeling that the war would be over within a month. The men speculated about whether they would be returning to the Union or sent to Burma. Axelson saw some British commandos at the divisional headquarters—apparently they were waiting to act with the partisans to secure the bridges in Florence. The

212 Extracts from a letter by Michael Howard, in D. Quilter (ed), *'No dishonourable name'*, p. 221.

Germans, however, had other ideas and kept the South Africans at bay through the effective use of their limited artillery, mainly self-propelled guns which would fire off a few rounds before moving to another position. The axis of advance was well covered by Tiger tanks which knocked out the Shermans as they came over a rise. Despite the wild optimism, Florence remained out of reach. The world news had given Hodgson reason to feel optimistic but he needed news from home to keep him going:

> There is very little actual news from here, as usual, but taking the news in general it is really grand; what with the Russian drive on Warsaw and on Riga and the successful drive in Normandy while we battle away at the gates of Florence; also the large number of American successes in the Pacific—one could not wish for the news to be better ... Don't forget to tell me all about the different places that you went to, and all you did in the holidays, because I am always interested in the details, etc; one is so far away from the happenings at home, it is hard to keep in contact with them; that is why I always like to hear what has been going on.

This tendency for men under stress to rely on their secondary group is well documented. The tanks set fire to haystacks and plantations and grass, creating an effective smoke screen for advancing in short rushes. Ancient stone walls, Tuscan villas and olive groves made for a picturesque battlefield. At this time of year, there were rich pickings to be had from the small farms in this more densely populated area. As always, this had a positive effect on morale:

> The grub is still very good as we are living off the fat of the land; fruit is the main attraction these days, as it is all good and ripe now. Of late I have been eating pears, apples, a few peaches, plums and beautiful fresh tomatoes. Also plenty of fresh vegetables; being able to get all these things whenever they are wanted makes the meals 100 per cent better, and consequently everyone is in a better mood.[213]

Thursday 3 August 1944: Impruneta

After crossing the Greve River with its steep banks the previous day, the division entered Impruneta en masse early on 3 August. Traffic was restricted because of the winding roads through dense pine forests. The town had been damaged by bombing and a number of civilians were killed as they were returning to the town but the main target, two self-propelled guns in the square, had not been hit. The central square was now packed with tanks and troop-carrying

---

[213] J.B. Hodgson–D.M. Hodgson, 2/8/1944.

vehicles. Tanks of the Natal Mounted Rifles, Special Service Battalion and Pretoria Regiment went straight through in support of the Guards. The town is on a high point, from where there is a grand view of Florence. Regimental headquarters of the 7/23rd Medium Regiment was set up in a pine plantation just south of the town. Two members of the regimental survey team had been carrying out their tasks in new gun positions when their Jeep went over a teller mine. Bombardier J.B. Orton was killed and Lance-Bombardier P. Lemmer was wounded. Apparently, Lieutenant Books-Neil had driven over this same mine on three earlier occasions. The divisional front was narrowing as formations on the left and right took over more ground. Like everyone else in the vicinity, Johnston watched the Kittyhawks and Tomahawks plaster the town of Strada, as they had Impruneta. The weary men of the 6th South African Armoured Division were boosted by the sight of the aircraft making their bombing runs in line astern. Fielding provides another of his vignettes:

> One could see the bombs leaving the aircraft and drop swiftly on their way. Clouds of dense smoke, starting as little pin-points ... expanding till they formed wide pouffs of white, tinged with grey. Then came the mighty *crrrumphs* of the explosions, as the sound waves, lagging behind those of light, bore the noise to the ears of the on-looking infantry and tanks.[214]

As the light faded, smoke and dust marked the places where demolitions rose in the wake of the German retreat. By the time the hot summer's day drew to an end, the Special Service Battalion and Royal Natal Carbineers found themselves only five miles from Porta Romana on the outskirts of Florence. Many of the luxury villas in this area had been wantonly vandalized by the Germans and there were reports of rape and other atrocities.

The following day, residents of this exclusive neighbourhood played host to a new set of uninvited visitors. Axelson came across a villa that had been taken over by a platoon of Scots Guards. "All that I saw were stripped to the waist. One was playing the piano, others were singing and banging their feet on the floor in unison, others were lying in easy chairs, others were ogling the maids of the house; all had wine in their hands."[215] Hodgson was still receiving generous food parcels, in addition to his diet of plentiful fresh produce. The newspapers from home were devoured:

[214] W.L. Fielding, *With the 6th Div*, p. 154.

[215] E. Axelson, *A year in Italy*, p. 76.

> The parcel that you had just sent off seems very good and I will look forward to receiving it. I am glad you have not sent off too many parcels lately as I would have been too spoilt with all the stuff we are getting these days. As you suggest it would be a good thing to leave out grub for a while, otherwise I think I will get as fat as a house, and I am fat enough already. In the winter when we will not be able to get all this, I think it would then be a good idea to start again with one every two or three weeks as you think fit; but will you keep sending me the *Sunday Times* regularly, as I love reading the home news.

Newspaper reports on 2 and 3 August made mention of the fact that the New Zealanders and South Africans were nearest to Florence and were facing massive counter-attacks. A bird's eye view of operations was provided by a SAPA war correspondent, G.E. Pauli, who flew over the battle area in a tiny Auster spotter plane:

> Visibility was excellent and Florence was easily identified through the smoke haze hanging over the city. To the north, the huge semi-circular mountain mass of the central Apennines stretched like a giant amphitheatre across Italy. North of Florence itself, crowned by smoke from bush fires, the whole panorama was backed by great banks of white cloud. The Eighth Army's grip on Florence is tightening steadily and already some elements have got beyond the crest of the last remaining hill, four miles south west of the city. We flew over Highway Two, just south of San Casciano, which was balanced on the edge of the plateau with the winding tar road leading up to it. This village was taken a few days ago by the New Zealanders and from here the whole valley of the lower Arno is visible as far as Empoli, dotted with numerous villages and white farmhouses.
>
> On the Allied side of the line there were endless strings of dust from transport columns, but on the German side, there was no sign of movement. Banking sharply over the Arno valley, we crossed the edge of the plateau at low altitude and watched the tanks moving up the tracks which were choked with yellow dust. They were going up over the crest separating the Eighth Army from the last down-slope into Florence.
>
> The leading tank scurried ahead to make a reconnaissance. We saw a flash of flame and the little plane rocked in the blast of the tank's gun firing at a little two-storey house just ahead. The house disappeared in a cloud of red dust as the shell exploded. Almost simultaneously a second tank came up into the low bush to the left of the road, and for a minute or so I could hear the staccato barks of the guns firing at more houses on both sides of the road. The houses probably contained German snipers.
>
> The house on the left of the road had a square tower and this was soon made untenable. Then a haystack burst into flames as the tanks crept forward. Meanwhile other tanks had come up and deployed in a small wood near by, from where they were engaging Germans in a big sprawling villa. For a minute, I noticed a long column of infantry in single file following in the tracks of the tanks. The next moment, they

> had left the road and had taken cover in the bush, where they deployed for action. By now the early morning mists had risen from Florence and the sun glinted on the surface of the River Arno where it flowed through the town. The great dome of the cathedral stood out prominently among the many church spires. We turned east across the South African sector in difficult rugged country and criss-crossed the rear of the area where the great mass of material and supplies and columns of men would have given a headache to the Germans if they could have seen them.[216]

Friday 4 August 1944 – Monday 7 August 1944: Florence

Although it is well known that the South Africans were the first to enter Florence, this accomplishment was not without drama and controversy. Furthermore, it was only the southern part of the city which was liberated by the South Africans. The story—as told by Lieutenant-Colonel Reeves-Moore, officer commanding the Imperial Light Horse/Kimberley Regiment to Axelson, a month after the event—begins five miles beyond Impruneta:

> At 10.30 pm, the Brigadier called me and wondered whether to push on or consolidate. I thought the enemy were disorganized and we should push on. "Good," said the Brigadier, "then I have now got for you the shittiest of all shitty jobs that I have ever given you." He told me he wanted me to push on to Florence that night. We did a terrific march, and all on foot. Galluzzo was occupied at 01:00 [on 4 August] but we could not get the tanks across the river. The patrol led by Adamson pushed hard, and nobody was more surprised than myself when I heard that the patrol was at the Ponte Vecchio at 04:10. Adamson was actually in time to see the last three Germans crossing the Ponte Vecchio. A demolition went up—the Trinità bridge—just as he got there. He wondered at first what hit him. The battalion had done a grand job before. That approach to Florence was their greatest test of all, and their greatest achievement of all.[217]

According to the Imperial Light Horse/Kimberley Regiment history, Lieutenant Jimmy Adamson had been nominated to lead a patrol into Florence. The group of four—which had also been first into Lucignano and Mercatale—was accompanied by two sappers who wanted to check out the bridges. They set off from Galluzzo before dawn on 4 August, passing through the Porta Romana, with Sergeant 'Smithy' Masterson-Smith as forward scout.

As daylight came, shutters started to open and the residents—cautiously at first—stuck out their heads. Soon the streets were filled with wildly cheering

216 *The Star*, Tank advance on Florence seen from the air, 4/8/ 1944.

217 E. Axelson, *A year in Italy*, pp. 109-111.

crowds shouting *"Inglesi, Inglesi!"* Hysterical people even embarrassed the South Africans by kissing their feet. Seeing German soldiers on the riverbank, the patrol at first thought the Americans had beaten them to their mark. A bunch of partisans bedecked with red, white and green armlets and crimson scarves provoked a shootout with the Germans across the river and the patrol decided to withdraw rapidly. It had been found that the approaches to the Ponte Vecchio had been blocked by demolitions, but the bridge was intact. Only after a short and flowery speech from the mayor, in perfect English, did the platoon make their way back to deliver their report. At 0830 hours, General Poole and Brigadier Furstenburg congratulated the Imperial Light Horse/Kimberley Regiment on winning the race to Florence. A photograph showing a stern-faced Lieutenant Adamson holding a Tommy gun appeared in the *Rand Daily Mail* of 1 September 1944, with the caption: 'First South African to enter Florence'.

Lieutenant-General Leese, commander of the Eighth Army, wrote a message of congratulations to General Poole: "My heartiest congratulations to yourself and the whole of the South African division on being the first to enter Florence. It is a fitting conclusion to a magnificent advance from Rome in difficult country and against the most determined enemy resistance."

General Poole replied: "Please accept the sincere thanks of the division and myself for your kind and inspiring message of congratulations. This is but the first stage in the history of this division. We hope to have the honour of continuing to serve under your command with the Eighth Army until we enter Berlin."[218] Ironically, within two weeks, the 6th South African Armoured Division would be placed under command of the American Fifth Army.

Meanwhile, the Guards were advancing through farmlands on foot, occasionally looking into a house, wary of mines and booby-traps. The farm dwellers plied them with food and wine. The 1/6th Field Regiment set up an observation post in the Torre del Gallo, from where there was a magnificent view over Florence with the Duomo clearly visible. Although there was no shelling, the situation in the city was very volatile. Partisans were fighting fascists, old scores were being settled. German snipers and machine-gunners across the river were unrelenting. It seemed to the South Africans that Kesselring had reneged on his promise to leave Florence an open city. Soon the tanks of the Special Service Battalion were rolling through the streets, sharing the honour

[218] *The Star*, Eighth Army commander congratulates Springboks, 7/8/1944.

of being first into Florence along with the 4/22nd Field Regiment and the 8th Field Squadron South African Engineer Corps. Units of all types followed in convoy, once the engineers had pronounced the road clear of mines. Even General Poole had to wait his turn to get into the city.

The British commandos who, together with the partisans, were supposed to prevent the bridges from being blown, had apparently not been informed of the division's starting time and now found themselves stuck in the traffic. A month later, Axelson asked Lieutenant-Colonel Reeves-Moore whether the Division had withheld information from the British commandos or whether this was simply a case of bad liaison. He received this answer:

> At 08:00 I was standing near where the engineers were bulldozing. Up came a Jeep with some people in it wearing green berets. They asked me whether they could get through. I asked them why they wanted to go through. I knew nothing about them. The officer was not keen to tell me anything about himself. I told him that if he could satisfy me that he had to go through, and prove his identity, he could footslog into Florence. He did not like the idea of footslogging, and said, "But that is miles." I had given orders to my MPs that no vehicles, no jeeps even, except battalion vehicles and tanks were to pass down that road.[219]

The Witwatersrand Rifles/Regiment De la Rey moved through to the front, establishing its base in a park in the residential suburb of Galluzzo, where Sherman bulldozers were clearing the road. It was difficult to determine where the villages ended and the city began, until the men arrived at the impressive arch of Porta Romana. At 0800 hours, there was a vast crowd, clambering over the tanks and jeeps, kissing, hugging and passing bottles of wine. Many of the locals could speak English and they were anxious to tell their stories about the occupation and how there had been no electricity or water for four days.

Having demolished all the bridges across the Arno—except the famed Ponte Vecchio—the Germans fired their machine guns and mortars at anything that moved on the opposite bank. Shermans fired on houses suspected of being sniper's lairs. The Witwatersrand Rifles/Regiment De la Rey was the only infantry regiment to establish itself in Florence. Some members were hit by snipers and were carried to safety on the back of a tank. Private O.E. Perrow was killed on 4 August and Private M.C. van Aswegen died of wounds four days later. Lieutenant Quinton is credited with personally killing one German

[219] E. Axelson, *A year in Italy*, p. 110.

and wounding another with his sniper's rifle. The following entry from the Witwatersrand Rifles/Regiment De la Rey diary, dated 5 August, is quoted by Monick in *A Bugle Calls*: "B Company ... reported seeing four Germans arm-in-arm with civilian women walking openly across B Company's front. B Company did not wish to engage for fear of hitting the girls. However, their best marksmen were sited and picked off these Romeos as opportunity offered."

There were now two main objectives: to find out where the German headquarters had been located and to assess the state of the one remaining bridge. Some people even attempted to cross it but quickly had second thoughts. People thronged the streets but disappeared in seconds when shots rang out.

That afternoon, Lieutenant Kerr, the observation-post officer of the 4/22nd Field Regiment, was wounded, although not seriously. By 1600 hours, it was clear that the northern side, Florence itself, was not going to fall that day. The few troops that were in town for the night sought accommodation, but not much sleep was had. Vickers and Spandau fire continued down at the river, and German artillery searched out access roads and observation posts, particularly Torre del Gallo, causing damage to residences in the area.

All 24 guns of the 1/6th Field Regiment pounded away at targets which, according to Orpen, were enemy infantry and artillery still holding the touristy town of Fiesole which overlooks Florence from the north. Swarms of mosquitoes aggravated the night's unrest.

July 7 was sunny and warm, despite some earlier rain. The war seemed far away. According to Axelson, Florence might as well have been Parktown. Later there would be more shelling and mortaring of selected targets but the Florentines appeared to be relatively unperturbed by events.

The South African newspapers of 4 and 5 August were careful to make it clear that only the southern part of Florence had been captured but provided little information besides the news that the Springboks had been the first to break through and that Ponte Vecchio was the only bridge remaining intact.[220] Divisional staff had been informed on 5 August that they would be relieved by the 1st Canadian Division. However, it remained a time of uncertainty for the men, who as yet had no idea that they would be pulling out of the line for a rest.[221] Johnston's troop set off for Siena two days earlier than those currently

220 *The Star*, Whole Southern Quarter now in Allied hands, 5/8/1944; *Rand Daily Mail*, Springboks break into southern areas of Florence, 5/8/1944.

221 DODAR, WD, Box 630, 7/23rd Medium Regiment, 5/8/1944.

engaged in the battle and he was surprised to find himself driving rearwards, away from the front, for the first time during the campaign. Using clever wording, Hodgson was able to tell his parents that he had been in Florence, without technically breaching censorship regulations. He finished the letter in Siena:

> In your letter you said that when it reached me I would probably be in Florence—well as it happens you were only a couple of days out. All is going along very well at the moment but as you can well imagine there is a lot of conjecture as to what will happen when we crack the Gothic Line. As for the news on the Russian front, it is really too good to be true, at the moment they are only 80 miles from the border of Silesia, I wonder where they will be when you receive this letter.
>
> (Cont. Tues 8th) I am so sorry for the break in the middle of this letter, but I can assure you it was due to circumstances beyond my control, and this is the first opportunity I have had of continuing.

The South Africans had been in the line day and night for more than three months. The Royal Natal Carbineers, for example, had been in contact with the enemy for 40 out of 53 days. The division now left others to battle on for the centre of Florence and moved back for two weeks of rest. Travelling through the night, the convoy was aided by a full moon as far as Panzano. From there onward, through Radda to Siena, headlights were switched on, and a solid stream of lights stretched from horizon to horizon across the Chianti hills. Not a single aircraft molested the column and, except for minor road accidents, the journey was uneventful.

Tuesday 8 August 1944 – Tuesday 22 August 1944: Siena

During June and July there had been 500 'battle wastages' per month. Over the past week, casualties had amounted to 30 per day. This was in addition to the 'normal wastages' of 600 each month due to illness, injury and other causes. The exact number of personnel 'wastages' for the period 8 May 1944 to 18 August 1944 totalled 3,506. According to Martin and Orpen, the recruitment rate was normally 200 men per month. However, a special recruiting drive in July had netted another 800 men. Nevertheless, there was still a shortfall which meant there was no option but to pull the division out of the line for a rest while reserves were brought up. Bourhill was clearly showing signs of strain:

> I did write quite a long letter one night not long ago, but the next morning when I read it through I decided that it just wouldn't do. I'd been into Florence that afternoon and had a headache and was feeling 'let-down'. As you know Firenze has been our objective for over two months. Each day it's been "well that's 1,000 yards nearer Firenze" and so it's been going on. "Ninety miles to go—60, 60, 60, 35, 35, 35, 19" and so on and on. At last "two kilometres". We went into action in a suburban district, and shelled either over the city or around it. The southern suburbs are ok and on that side of the Arno, but the main part of the town is the other side and it wasn't healthy to go there so all I saw were many pretty girls and lovely parks, the Roman Gate with notices like "Beware of snipers", "This is it Springbok" and "VD—*pas-op*". It was exciting to know and be told that we'd 'liberated' this lovely town, the people were very glad to see us. Anyway, that night I wrote home and the letter wasn't so good, so I burnt it. However, you'll be more pleased to get this one and know that for some time from now on I'm very safe. We're out of the line for a rest etc. In about 16 days I'll be on my way to Rome for a 48 hr. leave. It's a long trip but two clear days in the Infernal City at the end of it will make it worth while.

The division was dispersed throughout the Siena-Radda-Castelnuovo Berardenga triangle, an area in which they had recently been fighting. Advance (harbour) parties from various units jostled to hone in on the most comfortable locations with either gracious villas or river frontage. The regimental headquarters of the 7/23rd Medium Regiment was set up in the grounds of a country house about three miles from Siena, while the batteries camped on the banks of a small stream about half a mile away. The vehicles were drawn up in a mown field.

The first day was spent cleaning the equipment and transport while theTechnical Services Corps commenced a systematic overhaul of the vehicles. Light maintenance activities continued to be carried out during the first week of rest, but thereafter followed a blissful week of warm, sultry weather in Tuscany. Men were given total freedom to explore the countryside. Strict orders were given against looting crops and foodstuffs from the local farms. The South Africans were soon on friendly terms with the local population. Johnston would go a walk in the evenings and help the farmers stack wheat.

While the front line troops rested, the cooks, workshop and general staff continued with routine and reorganizing. All tanks and guns were sent to the workshops. In preparation for their trips to Siena and Rome, much time was spent sewing, washing and ironing, as men spruced up their kit.

The Royal Natal Carbineers concentrated just south of Castelnuovo, on the Rapolano Terme road. Their commanding officer, medical officer and adjutant wasted no time in visiting the wounded in hospital, as well as the reserves at Alife and the graves of those killed during the advance on Florence. Hodgson could have been speaking for everybody when he wrote:

> All is going along very well at the moment; we are in a lovely spot right at the bottom of a valley, with a stream running through the bottom. We are widely situated and have plenty of room, not being crammed on top of one another all the time. We have rigged up a large tent from pieces of canvas inside which we have got two tables and half a dozen chairs. There are only six of us inside the truck so we are extremely comfortable with the wireless going full blast all the time. I have rigged up a very good bathroom, and a shower which works admirably. There are tons of trees and it is very shady all day long, and on the hottest of days it is very cool where we are. To add to the last touch of comfort, we have got electric light which we work off the truck battery. While we are having such a marvellous time don't expect me to write to you too often as I am relaxing completely. Mind you, I will keep writing fairly regularly.

Although many were camped within walking distance of Siena, a bus service was organized to take men up the hill into the old city, returning at 2200 hours. The Sable Club for enlisted men was established in the town barracks. Previously the old fort, the locals frequently took their evening walks along its 30-foot-high walls. Chaplains and information officers were on hand, and the men were seved tea, coffee and sandwiches by Italian girls. Live music was played by one of the military bands between 1600 and 2000 hours. Makeshift furniture was slapped together by army carpenters. The hygiene officer saw that adequate latrines were available and the water quality was checked. Some of the theatres were reserved for Europeans only and a separate club was opened for the Cape Corps near the Sable Club.

Tour guides took groups to the cathedral and places of historical interest. As always, souvenirs were to be found outside the Palazzo Publico with its concave facade in the Piazza del Campo, the main square. The energetic played sport while interested Italians looked on in wonder at the vigour of the South Africans. The two cinemas, the Moderno and the Super Cinema, each had a capacity of 700 seats and showed two films daily, while the film vans of the Union Defence Force Institute screened shows in unit lines. The Wot Nots performed at the Rex Theatre. Humouring Brigadier Furstenburg, the 11th Brigade established Furstie's Rest Camp outside Rome. The 12th Brigade established a Brigade

Buffet along with a canteen in Siena called Palmers Pub, in honour of Brigadier Palmer. It became a popular gathering place for all units and nationalities.

One restaurant, The Mangia, near the Torre del Mangia, changed hands entirely to be run as an officers' restaurant for casual meals—even the Italian staff were dismissed—"and a right good meal one could get there". The Toscana Hotel was taken over in a similar fashion for WOs and sergeants. An Italian band played at mealtimes, favouring continental tunes like *J'attendrai* and *Lili Marlene*. When the Special Service Battalion band played at a function for their regiment in Siena, an Italian composer was so impressed that he composed a special march called *Work and Industry* for the band. The band of the Grenadier Guards performed in the main square at 1830 hours on Friday 11 August and on other occasions. There was something for everyone and the routine soon became a case of 'each to his own':

> ... I happened to go past the battalion headquarters where there was a film showing, so I decided to go and see if it was really worth going to see; as it turned out the film that was showing I had seen, and as it was so good I thought I might as well go and see it again. The film in question was *Orchestra Wives*. I thoroughly enjoyed it the second time; after the film I came back but when I got back I realized that it was a good thing that I had been out all evening as there was a royal party in progress; the wine was flowing very freely, so when I got back everything was well on the way and consequently everyone was well under the weather ... Tomorrow I am going to spend the day in Siena, just to look round all the art galleries and the cathedral, the latter being world renowned. I am going in with Cyril and David Knight and I am looking forward to it as it should be very good. [222]

The division took over a bakery and turned out thousands of pies and cakes daily. The New Zealanders and the Guards were also in town and the South African staff catered for them, too. The Kiwis provided a jazz band and a daylight dance was held, which apparently thrilled the Italian populace. A special staff scoured the countryside for supplies of wine and brought in demijohns of the local *vino*. This was then sold to the clubs, including a Springbok club and an officers' pub, which retailed it on to the men at a small charge. The Excelsior Hotel was made available for officers of all Allied nations. Meals were charged at the rate of 20 lire, payable in advance. Drinks were available at fixed prices.

For the ordinary enlisted man like Hodgson, however, it seems that the amenities in Siena were less than spectacular:

---

[222] J.B. Hodgson–M.V. Hodgson, 9/8/1944.

> Lunch was a bit of a sad affair. We had to eat bread and sandwiches on our truck, the reason for this being there is no food in the place at all, so unless one wishes to go without, he must take his own along. As yet there are no canteens or the like as they have not had the time to get organized. In the afternoon we went to an ENSA concert put on at one of the theatres. It was quite amusing and we enjoyed it as we had not seen the like for so long. We left again at six, as there is nothing to do after dark; also there is a curfew at ten.

Every day a couple of three-ton trucks would take leave parties for short visits to Rome. Trips to the lakes at Bolsena, Montepulciano and Trasimeno were also arranged. A separate facility was established for the non-Europeans where they, too, could enjoy some *vino*, a meal and reading material. Some senior officers went their own way. Fielding headed west to Pisa, Leghorn (Livorno) and the coast. Perugia and Arezzo were also within striking distance for sightseeing tours. This was one of those times when men caught up on their correspondence and Hodgson wrote at length about his impressions of Siena and Rome:

> Everything in the garden is really fine these days, in fact life is really grand; it is just the same as being on a very good holiday. As I told you in my last letter, I went to Siena. It was really a very enjoyable day, a day which I am sure I will always remember. We left here about nine in the morning, reaching Siena about ten; we made straight for the cathedral which is the main attraction; also we had arranged to meet Cyril and David Knight—it took us just on an hour to find the place but when we at last did we looked it over from one end to the other. It was well worth seeing—all the ancient medieval paintings on the walls, the exquisite pulpit which cost millions to install, the enormous crystal chandeliers etc, etc. The large oak door at the entrance had been in use since 1692; it was rather moth-eaten and cracked which was only natural. The door was too old to use; as well as its great height of well over 50 feet—one had to use two auxiliary doors either side of the main one. The actual foundations to the cathedral were first laid in the 12th century. I got some postcards of the whole place which I will send by surface mail as they are all a bit on the heavy side. The large wall running round the old part of the city has been standing since the 16th century; it was all very weather-beaten but in a very good condition—just looking at it, I would say it took them a good 30 years to build.

An impressive memorial service was held on 10 August. A personal message from the general officer commanding to all ranks recounted the achievements of the division, concluding that, "… you have accomplished one of the most remarkable advances in history". Some individual units, specifically the Armoured Reconaissance and the 24th Guards Brigade, were singled out for special praise. Mention was also made of the achievements of the engineers and 'Q' services. The general shared details such as the fact that the division had moved 601 road miles, built 64 bridges, and fired 201,500 artillery shells. General Poole continued:

> The fighting troops have destroyed large quantities of enemy equipment and captured 1,617 prisoners. The total number of enemy killed and wounded will never be known, but it must be an enormous number. We have, inevitably, suffered casualties, and 378 South Africans and 142 of the 24th Guards Brigade group will not return to their homeland. We honour their memory. Considering the magnitude of the task completed, the difficulties overcome, the strength of the enemy and the natural advantages at his disposal, I can only say that the casualty rate is remarkably low.[223]

After the intense excitement of the chase, static camp life began to get a bit monotonous, as evidenced by Johnston's diary entry for 14 August: "Parade for court martial. Into Siena to watch softball. I stayed all day. Sable Club OK. I.L.H. Band. Bio in afternoon. Concert in the evening. Walked most of the way back."

Visits to Rome were the highlight of the holiday. The truck would stop en route for a night in the town of Bolsena, where it was pleasant to walk the narrow streets or stroll along the lake shore. Whereas Hodgson overdosed on the Roman history and culture, Johnston's experience was more typical. Much of his time was spent at the NAAFI, although he did visit the Pantheon. He also saw the opera *Aida* which he described as "wonderful". Wandering around the shops with friends, the men were "picked up by two pros" and were offered a double room with the two women back at the Springbok Club. As all good things do, the visit came to an end. The wrecks of German tanks and self-propelled guns cluttering Highway 3 on the way back to Siena were nasty reminders that there was still a war on.

Gunner J.P. Knoesen of the 7/23rd Medium Regiment was severely burned when a can of petrol caught alight while he was conducting vehicle maintenance. The incident took place toward the end of the men's stay in Siena. Knoesen was immediately evacuated to hospital in Naples, but died on 22 August. Private Glen Easton finally got his posting to the 6th South African Armoured Division and on 18 July he was routed forward as a replacement in the Royal Natal

223 DODAR, WD, Box 630, 7/23rd Medium Regiment, Routine Order 36/44, 11/8/1944.

Carbineers. Easton was only one of a new batch of reserves who joined the regiment while at Siena. A few of Hodgson's school friends also came up:

> On the Thursday before I went to Rome, I went to Siena for the day where I had a very enjoyable time, I saw the Cathedral which I had seen so much of, but now that I have seen all those in Rome it rather puts that one in the shade. Here we also went to an ENSA concert which was very enjoyable. As it happens I went to Siena with Cyril and David Knight; Cyril came up with our last lot of reserves, he is in 'A' company—we had an enormous amount to talk about as you can imagine. It is jolly good to have him up here.

On 18 August, the 4/13th Frontier Force Rifles and the 166th (Newfoundland) Field Regiment came under command of the 6th South African Armoured Division. The former was Punjab infantry under British officers, the latter Royal Artillery. Most importantly, the 6th South African Armoured Division now came under the command of the American 5th Army, having been assigned the task of protecting the Americans' left flank. "With three armoured regiments, nine infantry battalions, three field regiments and one medium artillery regiment, General Poole's division had become the most powerful and most cosmopolitan formation ever commanded by a South African."[224] It was time for the men to prepare themselves mentally and physically for the next phase:

> The news is really wonderful these days, and I only hope that it will always continue to be good, until final victory is ours. Today we heard of the first troops crossing the line, and the area of the beachhead in the south is 1,000 square miles in extent. The Russians are massing for a new offensive, which I hope will carry them right into Germany proper, and very near to Berlin, if not actually there. The bombers are still blasting the living daylights out of Germany and let it increase in intensity every day until they give in … At the moment we are very comfortable indeed, so much so that I have erected a very good bathroom next to the stream, including a shower and all. We have made a very large tent next to the truck, from some sails, inside which we have got tables and chairs. It is all under plenty of trees and in fact it is a perfect spot. I have been getting plenty of exercise on my own by PT and skipping, so I am very fit and my cup of happiness is the fullest it can be, when one is away from home.[225]

---

224 N. Orpen, *Victory in Italy*, p. 185.

225 J.B. Hodgson–W.A. Hodgson, 20/8/1944.

While the South Africans were at rest, the war had continued along the Arno River with the British on the right of Florence, together with Polish and Italian troops, and the American 5th Army on the left. Artillery duels and infantry patrols had continued across the river but little real progress had been made. In the Allied section of Florence, factional fighting and sniping had become so general that the Canadians of the Eighth Army were sent in to clear the area between the Via Dei Serragli and the Via Romana, with help from the partisans. Combing the roofs of houses along the southern waterfront, they arrested about 150 men and women in possession of arms and ammunition. Patriots in the northern part of the city rounded up fascists to hand over to the Allies. Scant news was coming out of the main part of Florence but it was known that food and water were scarce. The partisans were active in spite of a strict curfew imposed by the Germans. Shootings were a common occurrence and it was impossible to provide a decent burial for the dead. According to press reports, the Germans were stripping the city and its people of everything of value, including jewellery and medical supplies.

With the citizens sandwiched between the two opposing armies, the atmosphere in the city was a strange mixture of war and peace. *The Star* reported that "Florence remained *de jure* if not *de facto* an open city". Low-level photographs showed that there was no damage to buildings in the northern part of the city, disproving German allegations that Florence had been shelled by Allied forces. The railway yards had been bombed however, and the Germans had shelled the liberated side of the city from the heights of Fiesole. Allied patrols even avoided street fighting so as not to damage historic buildings.[226]

226 *The Star,* Sandwiched between two armies, 7/8/1944; *The Star,* Allies pause before attack on Gothic Line, 8/8/1944; *The Star,* Damage in Florence, 9/8/1944.

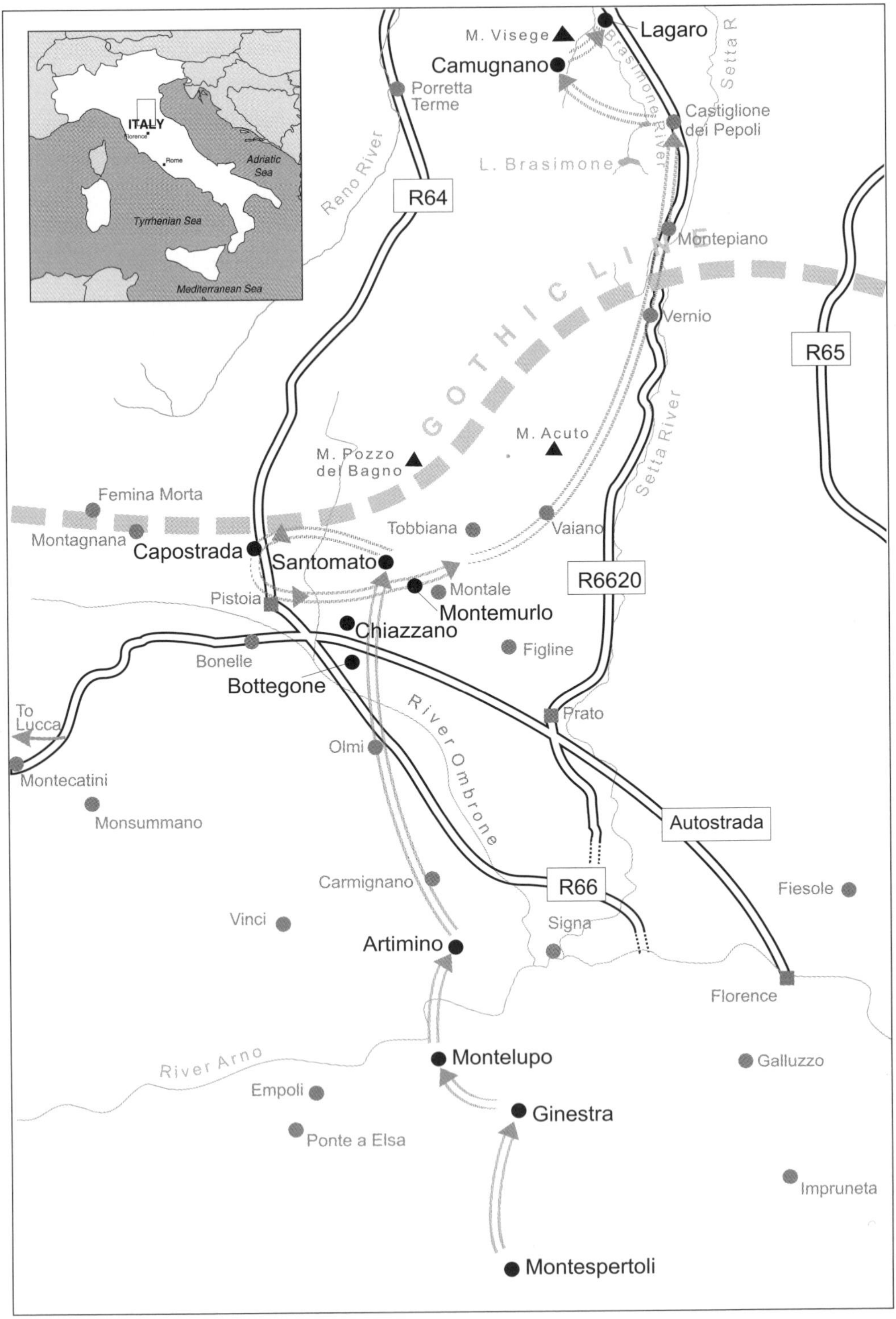
ITALY
Florence
Rome
Adriatic Sea
Tyrrhenian Sea
Mediterranean Sea
M. Visege
Lagaro
Camugnano
Porretta Terme
Castiglione dei Pepoli
Brasimone River
Setta R
L. Brasimone
Reno River
R64
Montepiano
GOTHIC LINE
Vernio
R65
M. Acuto
M. Pozzo del Bagno
Setta River
Femina Morta
Montagnana
Capostrada
Tobbiana
Vaiano
Santomato
R6620
Pistoia
Montale
Montemurlo
Chiazzano
Figline
Bonelle
Bottegone
To Lucca
River Ombrone
Prato
Olmi
Montecatini
Monsummano
Autostrada
Carmignano
R66
Fiesole
Vinci
Signa
Artimino
Florence
River Arno
Montelupo
Galluzzo
Empoli
Ginestra
Ponte a Elsa
Impruneta
Montespertoli

Chapter Eight

Mountains and mud

"We will be there. We are on the road to victory. Good fortune to you all."
—Personal message to all ranks of the 6th South African Armoured Division from the general officer commanding, 10 August 1944

Wednesday 23 August 1944: Montespertole

It was a slightly different-looking division which went back into the line. For a start, the Natal Mounted Rifles had partially converted to infantry. Since there was no longer a need for anti-aircraft units and Bofors guns were no use against armour, the 1/12th Anti-Aircraft Regiment was also converted to infantry.

Likewise, the 1/11th Anti-Tank Regiment was never deployed in the role for which it had been trained. Instead, it was given odd jobs to keep it busy. For instance, during the advance, it worked up front with the infantry, shooting up machine-gun nests and buildings. After the rest period at Lucca, the regiment was again used as field artillery and equipped with three-inch self-propelled guns (known as the 'Grouse'), as well as 17-pounders. During the coming months in the Apennines, members of the regiment would be used as muleteers and to maintain Jeep tracks. At one time, after Monte Stanco, it formed part of Combat Command C in a purely infantry role. The men had some infantry training but had never put it into practice. Fortunately, they would not be called on to make any set attacks.

Reconnaissance parties were now back in the battle area, surveying new positions and working for the first time under the command of the American 5th Army. Infantry, tanks and artillery travelled up to a concentration area around Montespertole where they came under long-range shelling, and forward patrols made contact with the enemy. The enemy had the advantage of a good observation point on Monte Albano, making it impossible to move in the forward areas during the day. The Americans who had previously occupied these positions did minimal patrol work. A small American rearguard effected the handover and now, the increased patrol activity alerted the enemy to the fact that they were facing new troops. The Germans were anxious to know who their new opponents were and were intent on capturing prisoners. Some close quarter firefights took place as the opposing sides felt each other out. Underwater bridges had been constructed by the enemy in some places. Any movement seen by either side brought down artillery and mortar fire. Mortar and Nebelwerfer fire was an especially unpleasant aspect of this position.

Divisional HQ set off from Siena in hot weather on 23 August, moving through the industrial centre of Poggibonsi to the area of Castelfiorentino. The roads were dusty and dangerous, partly because of bomb damage and partly because of the reckless driving of the Americans. The division imposed a speed limit of 15 kilometres per hour, dropping to five kilometres per hour in some places.

Writing to his mother on 23 August, Hodgson did not indicate whether he was still camping alongside the stream outside Siena, or whether he had already moved to the new positions on the River Arno:

> You ought to see me these days; I spend most of the time in shorts and tackies, with the result that I am lovely and burnt; also I have been doing quite a deal of exercise with the result that I am very fit. It has been very hot lately, and it is grand to work up a good sweat and then have a lovely cold wash and shower. I have fixed up a very potent affair next to the stream, at times I have a wash and a shower four and five times a day. At the moment they are playing *You Started Something*. We always listen in to Daventry, mainly on their general forces programme, as there is plenty of light music and jazz, also a news service every hour.
>
> The wireless job that I am on at the moment is more or less permanent, as permanent as anything in the army is. I like it very much as it is very interesting; also we are a very happy family in our truck and very comfortable. I am the youngest and they all seem to keep an eye on me. There is a teacher, a bank clerk, a farmer, a miner and one of Marshal Tito's ex-partisans; a very good crowd and we all get on well together.

From his diary, it appears that Johnston followed a day after the others in his observation post tank, taking a roundabout route through Radda. As usual, his tank gave mechanical problems and he only arrived at the gun position on 25 August. The last of the Americans had clearly not yet left the area:

24th
Drove 49.8 miles through Radda, Poggibonsi. Cleaned filter. Just getting light ... Track off. Yanks pulled us out just before dark. Very disappointed in Regiment's interest in us. Guzzled grapes all day.

25th
Borrowed jack from Yanks and adjusted tracks. Off by 16.00 to get to Regiment. Refuelled. Cold bath under pump. Off again at 21.00. New position with guns in action by 23.45. 12 miles. Yank guns next door to us. Yanks chatted and gave us vino until 02.40.

26th
Parked on our own, tired out. Chatted to Yanks, good crowd. Jerry shelled Montespertole at supper time. One fell close to our [*illegible*]. Yanks moved.

Thursday 24 August 1944 – Thursday 31 August 1944: Ginestra

Divisional headquarters was not happy about the wide front (spanning 20 miles) which was allocated to the South Africans, especially since it was twice as broad as the Canadian sector. Even with an extra British battalion under command, the troops were spread thin. Furthermore, the area was thick with civilians and the Americans could not provide much information about enemy dispositions. The Guards were on the left of the divisional sector and the 12th Motorized Brigade on the right, in the vicinity of Empoli. The artillery was also stretched thin along the wide front, with the 1/6th Field Regiment approximately five miles south of the Arno at Ginestra. The headquarters of the 7/23rd Medium Regiment was in the remains of a sugar factory at Castelfiorentino. Its gun lines were north of Fontanella, just short of Ponte a Elsa. The South African artillery began taking over from the Americans on 24 August. By the next day, the 25-pounders were shelling the Germans across the Arno. Night patrols were usually carried out to find river crossings, determine enemy strength and locate enemy observation posts. Corporal T.J. Robberts of the Witwatersrand Rifles/Regiment De la Rey was awarded the Military Medal for his particularly adventurous and aggressive patrol across the Arno on 26/27 August. A partisan reported a sighting of 20 Germans in a village, and the patrol brought down a mortar concentration, killing six of them. The same night, an enemy patrol crossed the river about a mile west of Montelupo. Artillery and mortar fire was called down, killing another six.

There was some strafing and bombing from enemy aircraft on the night of 28 August. Patrols were not as successful due to heavy shelling, and Corporal Robberts was wounded. According to Orpen, a whole Royal Natal Carbineers patrol under Lieutenant D.H. Paterson of the 12th Field Squadron, South African Engineer Corps was captured on one of these occasions.[227]

A newspaper report at the time related the story of Private Alfred Edward 'Pop' Castle, a Jeep driver in the Royal Natal Carbineers. Everyone knew Pop because he used to knit for his friends in the company and carried his knitting with him everywhere. At about 0200 hours, Pop and Quartermaster Sergeant C.J. Peycke were driving back to company headquarters to report the presence of Germans in a house near their position, when they were ambushed. The enemy patrol, numbering seven men, grabbed Peycke out of the Jeep. Pop jumped out with his Tommy gun. Before he could get to Peycke, who was struggling with his kidnappers, Pop was mortally wounded by a burst of fire. Nevertheless, he was able to return fire and killed two Germans, forcing them to withdraw across the river empty-handed. Peycke managed to drive the Jeep into the company lines, revving and stalling as his fractured leg pressed down on the accelerator. Pop was brought in from the roadside, but he died of his wounds a few days later on 25 August 1944. Originally from Newcastle in Natal, he was in his late forties.

It was late summer and the valley was full of fruit trees and vines. In fact, the abundance of fruit made more of an impression on the men than the equally abundant instruments of death. Even the official histories mention the fruit.

Prospects were looking good and the troops were optimistic and content, especially since there was also a surplus of *signorine* in the vicinity:

> The fruit position is really good these days, better than it has been for a very long time. At the moment we are getting really beautiful peaches, excellent grapes and figs that you would walk miles for at home; the apples are very plentiful, but as yet there are only a few really ripe ones; as for tomatoes, they are still going as strong as ever and we have them with all our meals, as it helps to add flavour to the army rations.
>
> At the moment the position as far as fresh vegetables are concerned is not as good as it used to be; especially as far as fresh green mealies are concerned, as it is beginning to get a bit late, with the result that the majority have been harvested, and those that remain are a bit too old and hard to eat. Life is very pleasant these days, and the days are passing very quickly; actually I think it is possible to count the days to the end of the war, if only we knew the date. The news is really wonderful; and if

227 N. Orpen, *Victory in Italy,* p. 192.

only old Jerry would realize how hopeless it is for him, he might give up the whole thing, and then we could all settle down to a peaceful life again.

At the moment I am sitting on the balcony of a very nice house; it is a beautiful day with a lovely cool breeze. Inside I have got a very comfortable room which I share with two other people—I have got my stretcher to sleep on (I have got one like those at home, which I scrounged), a dressing table with all my kit in, a big mirror and wash stand. There are three armchairs in the room, also a writing table. In the evenings we use candles for lighting—a packet came in one of Dad's parcels, so they are coming in very useful. The Italian family is still occupying a small part of the house, but we have the best part of it. There are three fairly nice signorinas whom we have inspanned to do our washing and ironing, also our mending, with the result that all my kit is in perfect condition. There is a little boy who sweeps out our room, and does all the cleaning up. The other fellows are set up much the same as the three of us are, and as there are not too many of us, we are living in great style. There is a good dining room which we are using as an Other Ranks' mess, so we are short of nothing.

These days I seldom have to do my own washing, as it is very easy to find some Iti's to do it, for a couple of cigarettes, a piece of soap, or something like that. Do they know how to wash! All the stuff I have had done has been done perfectly—the white things that seldom look clean here are absolutely snow white when the signorinas have been busy on it. Anything that is sent to the wash is automatically mended, and any missing buttons are replaced. [228]

In the densely populated river valleys around Ginestra and Castelfiorentino, a few miles south of the Arno, the civilians were obviously happy to be able to provide housekeeping services to the soldiers. Johnston's washing was done by two girls named Giulietta and Giuliana in return for 20 cigarettes, a tin of bully beef and a cake of soap. "Lovely girl Guilietta," he wrote in his diary, "beautiful hair and face, fine figure and complexion, wonderful teeth. Quite a long chat and coffee. Must see her again." The diary reveals that Johnston did see her again the next day—and the next, and the next. She came round for "tea and a long chat", then he visited her home. A dance was held, but there were too many soldiers present for Johnston's liking.

On 2 September came a warning order, "prepare to move", and Giulietta's goodbye. Fortunately, it turned out to be a case of "hurry up and wait", and the next evening Johnston walked the three miles or so up to Monterappoli to see Giulietta one more time. It was "a very interesting session", but the "Jerries bombed and strafed nearby". It seemed to him that the girl was in love but "Pa was too cautious".

---

[228] J.B. Hodgson–D.M. Hodgson, 28/8/1944.

With time on his hands, Hodgson wrote one letter after another, mentioning to his father that an officer and a sergeant of his company had received the Military Cross and the Military Medal respectively, the first in the battalion and among the first in the division. No names are given but it appears that he is referring to Lieutenant W.A. Roberts and Corporal D.P. Smith, who heard on 15 August that they had been awarded the medals for their actions at Bagnoregio. To his father, Hodgson lamented the loss of so many friends:

> I am looking forward to a good game of ton-tak as it is quite a long time since I had the chance of playing. Actually the last time I played was when we played in Alexandria; those were really a few good days. Since then we have lost Frank Ledingham, George is back home, Ben Harley who made up the fourth is down the line seriously wounded and Michael Wood who made up the fifth member of our party is the only other one who is still going strong.

In the 12th Brigade sector, the Witwatersrand Rifles/Regiment De la Rey was on the left, the First City/Cape Town Highlanders in the centre and the Royal Natal Carbineers on the far right, where B Company carried out patrols in the Signa area, not far from Florence.

The D Company area was shelled by friendly fire from the 4/22nd Field Regiment's self-propelled guns.

The men's overriding impression of this place was of its grapes. Johnston wrote the word "Grapes" in his diary on 28 August, and the next day he wrote "Too many grapes". Hodgson also wrote that grapes were everywhere; one only had to stretch out a hand to find them. It was a pleasant change to get another type of fruit:

> An Italian brought us some lovely fruit this morning, a basketful of peaches, and the same full of figs; the figs were really perfect, they are the type that you would walk miles for in the Union. You know that as a rule I never eat them, but these looked so good that I tried one and I have hardly stopped eating them since. When the fruit came, I was sitting on the verandah writing to Diana, but as soon as the figs came, I put the letter aside, and got stuck into them.[229]

Artillery observation posts reported at this time that the enemy had started pulling out its heavy guns and equipment, leaving its mortars and machine guns screened by infantry. One officer was severely wounded in a battle of the

229 J.B. Hodgson–M.V. & W.A. Hodgson, 28/8/1944.

observation posts. Lieutenant Sheppard's observation post was so frequently mortared that he was forced to look for a quieter spot and stood on a mine in the process. Targets during this period were enemy infantry and the mortars which were supporting them. These were particularly active on 28 August and presented regimental targets (referred to as 'Mike' targets).

The diarist of the 7/23rd Medium Regiment described the weather on 27 August as "hot and sultry". The next day, it was "very hot and very sultry" and on 29 August it was "very very hot and very very sultry". The diary also notes that the regimental headquarters was hit by nine shells on the night of 28 August, six of which were duds. The enemy was apparently making use of caves to hide its self-propelled guns and these 'troglodytes' were extremely difficult to hit. At this time, the regiment was limited to 25 rounds per gun.

Using this lull in operations, the 1/6th Field Regiment fired over propaganda leaflets containing a very truthful account of the current state of affairs. Firing propaganda pamphlets was an ongoing exercise. Approximately 750 leaflets or newspapers could be stuffed into smoke shells from which the smoke canister had been removed, and fired from 105mm and 25-pounder guns. On average, 4,000,000 leaflets floated down over German lines each week. The mobile press could turn out leaflets at a rate of 8,000 an hour. The majority was scattered by bomber or fighter aircraft.

The 5th Army disseminated 15,520,725 leaflets between 11 February and 10 March 1945. They were appreciated by both sides for their amusing and saucy content when reading matter was so scarce, as well as for their use as toilet paper. A *Frontpost* pamphlet dated 29 August 1944 gave an accurate assessment of the war to date. On the reverse side was a map showing the advances made in Europe by the Allies. The enemy could hardly doubt the credibility of this news as they were well aware that the British Eighth Army "*bis auf 5 km an die 'Gotenlinie' herangekommen*".[230]

Other propaganda leaflets included *News from home*, which discussed the situation in Germany and *The Allied aims* and *Post-war Europe*. These strategic leaflets aimed to subvert morale through the psychological presentation of incontrovertible facts. Any important event or piece of news hurtful to the enemy was brought to his notice in a clear, factual summary. Some leaflets targeted the partisans, to boost their morale. Propaganda was also disseminated

[230] *Frontpost Ausgabe Süd, nummer 58 nachrichtenblatt für Deutsche Soldaten*, 29/8/1944.

to the partisans on a radio programme called *Italia Combatte*. Italian civilians crossing the river were full of reports that the enemy had withdrawn, but it was felt that elements of his battle groups had been left behind to give an early warning of the offensive. The commanding officer of the Royal Natal Carbineers went up in an Auster spotter plane on 29 August to survey the enemy positions and especially the self-propelled guns, which had been bothersome. On 30 August a 'stonk' was laid down on a party of 50 Germans and Royal Durban Light Infantry Vickers teams carried out a shoot 500 yards from Signa. The next day, a German raiding party attacked C Company positions under cover of a heavy artillery barrage, but only one was wounded and the Germans withdrew without a prisoner.

On the night of 30/31 August, the Guards mounted an aggressive raid across the river, one and a half miles west of Empoli. The crossing was unopposed but a feature known as Pt 100 was strongly held and a fierce fight ensued. It was estimated that at least 13 Germans were killed for the loss of one Guardsman. Enemy artillery was quiet throughout the next day, and was promptly bombarded by counter-battery whenever it did open up.

Bourhill celebrated his 21st birthday in between shoots on the night that the first major crossings were in progress. As the autumn approached and the Gothic Line loomed, he was contemplating nature and getting his affairs in order:

> Here are three items which I have meant to tell you for ages. (A) There are birds here but I've never heard a bird sing once yet—night or day. I've seen what we used to call nighthawks but nothing else, no doves or nightingales or cuckoos. (B) There are still many flowers but the corn flowers and red poppies are gone, larkspurs grow wild and the gardens are full of canna and dahlias. (C) We've got a troop leader now who is a lawyer and he's going to make out a form for giving you my power of attorney.

It had recently come to the attention of the division that certain insurance companies had been "inviting personnel of the Union Defence Force to surrender life insurance policies on the basis, of course, of their being paid out the surrender value", in an attempt to limit their risk. Prior to September 1939, life insurance covered death on active service outside the country. The men were advised to think carefully before taking up the offer.[231]

[231] DODAR, WD, Box 624, 1/6th Field Regiment, DRO, 88/44, 22/4/1944.

Friday 1 September 1944: Montelupo

Although the men had been told that the Arno was a formidable obstacle, it was found to be only 18 inches deep in places.[232] One platoon of B Company, Royal Natal Carbineers waded across in water up to their waists. D Company, Royal Natal Carbineers set off for Artimino, while on their left the First City/Cape Town Highlanders put in a raid on Fabrica. Thus, two footholds were gained on the north bank on the night of 31 August.

The river bank was alive with activity in the early hours of 1 September, as three companies of the First City/Cape Town Highlanders looked for places to swim across. One patrol came under machine-gun fire from the north bank, while the Germans tried to draw their fire by blowing whistles and throwing stones into the river. Demolition charges exploded up and down the river. One patrol got across without incident and reported Fabrica to be clear of the enemy. Later in the day, Lieutenant B.E. Scarpa was killed and two others injured while investigating their own anti-personnel mines. Scarpa was a 38-year-old married man from Katberg in the Cape.

The day was "hot and sweaty". The 24th Guards Brigade crossed just west of Empoli and built a Bailey bridge. Some casualties were incurred by shellfire but no contact was made. At 2100 hours, C Company, Royal Natal Carbineers approached Artimino under heavy fire, and together with the Witwatersrand Rifles/Regiment De la Rey established a firm base. Tanks started coming up and one troop of Prince Alfred's Guard reached Artimino. No contact was made with the enemy during the crossing as it had decided to pull back to its Gothic Line, but danger lurked in its wake.

On the northern banks of the Arno, in the area where the Witwatersrand Rifles/Regiment De la Rey crossed over, there were shallow ditches to channel floodwaters from the mountains into the river. Some men jumped into these ditches for cover when the Germans started shelling, little knowing that the enemy had placed 'S' mines in the depressions. One of these was 19-year-old J.C. Mentz of West Krugersdorp, who had been on leave in Rome with Lionel Wulfsohn a few weeks earlier:

> Corporal Jack Cuthbertson was his section leader, and as we were going past in the bright moonlight, I saw Jack using a small torch looking for shrapnel mines buried in the grass and weeds, going into the ditch to bring Mentz out. There was nothing

232 E. Axelson, *A year in Italy*, p. 168.

> I could do, as we had to proceed on our task, I waved farewell to Mentz in the moonlight. I doubt very much if he could recognize me, as he was in tremendous pain, and bleeding profusely. Such is war, one moment enjoying yourselves on leave, and barely four weeks later witnessing your pal dying on the banks of the Arno river.[233]

Mentz was one of eight members of A Company, Witwatersrand Rifles/ Regiment De la Rey who died that night as they attempted to cross the River Arno. Having found a crossing for the tanks, the Prince Alfred's Guard relieved the infantry on 2 September. In the Guards Brigade sector, three bulldozers were blown up on mines.

The division encountered the heaviest mining and demolitions in the whole of its Italian experience between the Arno and the Gothic Line.

Saturday 2 September 1944 – Sunday 3 September 1944: River Arno

The medium artillery crossed the Arno on the night of 2 September. The route, with its narrow and winding roads, was not an easy one. The guns had to be unhooked and manhandled around some of the tighter corners. Nevertheless, they were in action in their positions south of Cerreto Guidi by 2330 hours. Enemy self-propelled guns had been shooting up the forward troops, bringing down the wrath of the 7/23rd Medium Regiment in the form of a regimental concentration, scale 5.

The following day, regimental headquarters moved into a villa on the outskirts of Vinci, the birthplace of Leonardo da Vinci, and found evidence that it had been an enemy command post and that their fire had indeed been effective. It was also discovered that the owner of Villa Martella, where the regiment was headquartered, had been arrested by partisans because he had held a post in the fascist government.

The 1/6th Field Regiment remained in action while the initial river crossings were taking place, crossing itself on the night of 2 September at 2330 hours in pitch blackness and heavy rain. "Fortunately," the war diary states, "the Hun fails to turn up with shellfire." It was 0400 hours before the entire regiment was across.

There followed a quiet couple of days for the gunners. Artillery commanders used the opportunity to inspect German artillery positions, which were now

233 L.M. Wulfsohn, unpublished memoirs.

overrun. It was found that, of the positions located on aerial photographs and suspected of being gun positions, 85 per cent were in fact occupied. When observers were able to see the enemy guns or gun pits, destruction of artillery pieces was effected largely by employment of precision methods. However, where area fire was used, it was evident that little damage had been inflicted on matériel or emplacements. During the inspection, only two dummy positions were found. Civilian reports and examination of gun positions indicated that the enemy batteries frequently moved when effective counter-battery fire was aimed at them. According to a comprehensive report on operations compiled by the American 5th Army after the war, the enemy was a master of deception and the use of good cover to protect his life. Reinforced dugouts and other forms of overhead cover were found in only 50 per cent of the positions. Ammunition pits, slit trenches, dugouts and other battery installations were generally placed ten to 30 yards to the rear of the gun positions and were barely affected.

The Guards advanced seven miles as the crow flies that day, passing Cerreto Guidi. The assistance of partisans was proving to be invaluable. They brought in prisoners and reported Monte Albano, a former German vantage point, to be clear of the enemy. Following the hot weather, heavy thunderstorms occurred on 2/3 September, heralding the changing of the seasons. On 3 September, there was no contact along the divisional front.

While 8 Field Squadron and 12 Field Squadron built fords and bridges over the river between Brucianese and Empoli, the rest of the division fanned out to the north of the river. They received a rapturous welcome in the numerous small villages and it was a happy time for the soldiers. The local population would not be as welcoming when they got farther north.

Hodgson wrote: "We are still living on the fat of the land; being the liberator, so to speak, of all these people they just load us with all sorts of stuff. At times it is quite moving to see how genuinely pleased they are; on many occasions we have been the first Allied soldiers to enter the areas."

The fifth anniversary of the start of the war came around on 3 September, and was observed as a day of prayer. Special services were held across Italy and, indeed, throughout the world. The First City/Cape Town Highlanders held a retreat ceremony together with their sister regiment, the 6th Battalion Gordon Highlanders.

As far back as July, the South African press had been pondering the extent of the obstacle presented by the Gothic Line, describing it as the most formidable natural barrier in Italy. The mountain range over which the line is built measures 50 miles deep at its narrowest. The slopes facing southwest are somewhat steep, while the reverse slopes are relatively moderate. Movement in this mountain belt is restricted to roads and tracks. Troops are easily concealed in the densely forested slopes, but the movement of vehicles and heavy weapons is hampered.

Monday 4 September 1944 – Tuesday 5 September 1944: Artimino

While continuing the advance through Empoli and Vinci on 4 September, the Royal Natal Carbineers had an encounter with tanks which opened fire, killing one officer. Passing through the Scots Guards, the Royal Natal Carbineers took the next height on Albano Ridge which lay west of the Vinci–Pistoia road.

The First City/Cape Town Highlanders, meanwhile, made a forced march and occupied the ridge. On the east of the brigade sector, the Natal Mounted Rifles/South African Air Force reconnoitred the area south and west of Carmignano—as opposed to Camugnano—and one of their patrols reached Monsummano. Monsummano Alto is located on a conical hill overlooking the town of Monsummano, and eventually the Natal Mounted Rifles established itself in this area. When the Pretoria Regiment and the Scots Guards took up positions on another nearby hill on 5 September, they were "shelled off" it. On the whole, though, shelling remained remarkably light.

The advance had been leisurely and the South Africans were anxious to give chase, but were instructed by the Americans to hold back. At this stage, it should have been a rout—the Germans were pulling back in ox carts and on bicycles. In retrospect, this was a lost opportunity which gave the Germans a chance to consolidate in the mountains. This inactivity was little understood by the partisans, who kept reporting that the area ahead was clear of the enemy. They also brought in German, Polish and Austrian prisoners.

On the morning of 4 September, Axelson was told by three people that divisional headquarters, one and a half miles southeast of Empoli, had been heavily bombed in the night. Further questioning revealed that only one plane had strafed a mile away.

At main division, the atmosphere was "amazingly optimistic". The news from France and Holland was good and there was little resistance in the divisional sector. Some said the war would be over in a week, six weeks at most. With this came a feeling of apathy; a sense that the Italian front was not important, which made the soldiers reluctant to take risks.

For weeks, Hodgson had been eagerly awaiting the end:

> What do you think of the news these days? All seems to be going on very satisfactorily, and it looks as if the allies are making an all out effort to reach a decision before the winter sets in—I hope they are successful. The way things are progressing at the moment, there is every chance that it will be so, but I think it is a bit too much to hope for, as it is too good to be true. Nevertheless no matter when the war ends, if it is this year or next, when the time comes, it will be too good to be true, so I think that it is a very little time to go by. Just a little secret between you and me. I don't think it will be too long before the war in Europe is over for good and all.

The weather was dull and overcast during the day, and on the night of 5 September it began raining heavily and did not stop for three days. As a result, there was limited activity. The main divisional headquarters crossed the river on 6 September, just before the only bridge over the Arno in this area washed away. Now it was necessary to drive around via Pisa or Florence, and 11 Brigade was isolated south of the river. This necessitated the building of a high-level Bailey bridge at Empoli.

The 7/23rd Medium Regiment's war diary makes mention on 6 September of the grave of 35-year-old Gunner J.C. Strydom, which had just been found on the outskirts of Empoli. He had been reported AWOL four days previously. Information from the casualty clearing station was that he had been killed on 3 September when the motorcycle he was riding crashed into a crater on the road.

Wednesday 6 September 1944 – Saturday 9 September 1944: River Ombrone

The outer crust of the Gothic Line was bumped at Pistoia where the Allies received much assistance from the partisans who had captured the town, along with Montecatini, bringing in German prisoners and deserters. On the other side, the fascists were working on demolitions. It was found that the civilians caught in the middle were scared of the South Africans.[234] The Royal Natal Carbineers entered Pistoia without opposition on 8 September, while a Natal Mounted Rifles squadron was patrolling toward the Autostrada between the town and Prato. It was a quiet time for the 1/6th Field Regiment, except for a single aircraft which strafed the troops east of Pistoia that night. The Imperial Light Horse/Kimberley Regiment was still at Empoli, where it held a dedication

[234] P.M. Johnston, personal diary, 8/9/1944.

service on 9 September. Lieutenant-Colonel R. Reeves-Moore DSO, MC marched at the head of his men. Padre Richardson took the service and the hymn chosen for the occasion was *O God, Our Help in Ages Past*. Major Meeser of B Squadron Natal Mounted Rifles described an incident which took place on 9 September, resulting in three needless casualties. In the village of Galciana, Lieutenant R.G. Grifffiths found the inhabitants unusually uncooperative and sullen—probably because the village well was booby-trapped with teller mines. Lieutenant Griffiths attached a long rope to the mines and exploded them by dragging them out with his scout car. The next day, Troopers Lane, van der Au and Compton were blown up by one of these mines. Two were killed instantly, while Trooper William van der Au died in hospital at Arezzo on 21 September. He had been an instructor in gunnery at the Tank School but "wrangled" a transfer to the Natal Mounted Rifles because he felt that it was his duty to be with the men that he had trained.[235]

The weather was cooler after the rain. It stormed quite heavily on 9 September and Hodgson, who was hardly ever sick, needed to take refuge in a house belonging to an Italian doctor: "… he gave me one of the rooms in his house and I have been given every comfort possible. I was looked after by our own medical chap, not that I was ever really sick—the main reason for my coming indoors and going to bed was because it has been raining quite a bit. So today was my first chance to write." It was a chance to experience a touch of normality and focus on something unrelated to the business of killing:

> Lately we have been at the house of an Italian doctor—a very nice chap and very kind. When he heard that I was not well, he would not hear of me sleeping outside as we had been doing, but insisted on me sleeping in his study on the divan. Well, he really made me very much at home and I can assure you, I enjoyed being in bed as everybody looked after me so well. He is a very keen photographer; it is his hobby, so as well as having some lovely cameras, he has got the appliances for developing and printing. While I was in bed he showed me all his photos, and he really has a wonderful collection. I know quite a bit about the game, as he developed and printed quite a few films in the room. This morning he took a few snaps of me, so I will send them down, but don't expect anything too good, as his printing is not as good as it should be, owing to the lack of electric current—for the printing we have rigged up a light off a car battery; it works, but it is not quite strong enough.[236]

[235] E. Goetzsche, *The official Natal Mounted Rifles history*, p. 297; Some sources state that one of the casualties was called Brompton but the Commonwealth War Graves Commission gives the name as Compton.

[236] J.B. Hodgson–M.V. Hodgson, 9/9/1944.

On the evening of 9 September, the inhabitants of the village of San Rocco held a *festa* in celebration of the liberation of their village. An unofficial invitation was extended to all members of the 7/23rd Medium Regiment.

The next day, the regimental headquarters settled into a mansion 100 yards southeast of Olmi on Route 66. The gun positions were half a mile to the north, along the south bank of the River Ombrone. During the second week of September, the Witwatersrand Rifles/Regiment De la Rey moved to the area between Pistoia and Montale, where the flat terrain was ideal for motorized carrier patrols. A number of skirmishes occurred, but the enemy (362nd Infantry Division) seemed to be lacking in morale and determination. The battalion was headquartered in a magnificent villa which was shelled early in the morning on 14 September.

The first action fought by the 4/13th Frontier Force Rifles under command of the 6th South African Armoured Division was the attack on Monte Acuto, just above Pistoia, on 13 September.

Captain J. de Kock was a forward observation officer for the 4/22nd Field Regiment and accompanied a company of infantry attacking the eastern slopes of Acuto, in extended order, behind a creeping barrage 100 yards ahead. De Kock recounts how the men formed up in an area covered with pine needles and "the orders were given in Urdu to the accompaniment of odd bursts of Spandau swishing though the branches above us". He continues:

> While the order group was in progress, the divisional artillery reported ready. I ordered "fire!" There followed about 40 anxious seconds of hoping that the fire would fall in the right place; and then the 300 shells arrived, screaming and crashing a few hundred yards from us. This seemed to act like a tonic. I noticed many faces lost their somewhat drawn look and that there was more chatting and laughing among the men.
>
> I must admit I felt a bit happier myself. The company started forming up. I did not envy the commander his job of getting the men, who had been taking cover for the best part of an hour, moving again. They inched their way through the trees, the Bren guns and mortars spitting and popping adding to the noise of the shells, which by now were exploding among the trees and on the objective. When I could no longer watch the progress through the trees, I stopped the artillery and with my driver went forward to contact the company commander. I reached the edge of the plantation and saw him. With revolver in hand, he was leading a long line of men, fanned out to the right and left of him. Someone let out a terrific howl. This was taken up by the whole company. Howling and shouting, they charged across the bare strip of ground towards the trees. Tommies and rifles were fired into the ground and into the air, while smoke and hand grenades seemed to be bursting

> everywhere. They entered the bush and within a few minutes, all was quiet. Acuto was ours. Before that charge, the enemy had fled, leaving behind him weapons and equipment.

One prisoner was taken; he had a bayonet wound in the stomach. He confirmed that the position had been held by about 30 men with a Spandau. The detachment had withdrawn, leaving three men to cover the withdrawal. The Spandau, plus all three men, had been knocked out by artillery fire. The capture of that bit of ground cost the 4/13th Frontier Force Rifles two killed and six wounded. According to the regiment's official history, Monte Acuto was secured by 1830 hours. After one German was killed by a bayonet, others ran back shouting, "the Kaffirs are coming".[237]

Sunday 10 September 1944 – Monday 11 September 1944: Bottegone

The Coldstream Guards had a big party when they entered Montecatini Terme on 10 September. All officers of the battalion were invited to a dance which was held by the partisans at the Albergo della Pace. The partisans were thanked for their help in a complimentary speech which was met with much cheering, and the party ended at 0230 hours.

While the Guardsmen penetrated the Gothic Line positions in the hills, the battalion remained headquartered at Montecatini enjoying the sulphur baths and holding "an orgy of dances" until it left for Castiglione on 30 September.[238]

The 6th South African Armoured Division reached the heart of the Gothic Line on 11 September. Three South African brigades were now in the line, attacking the foothills along it: Santomato, Bagnolo and Montale. The Americans were on the right, up Route 6620.

On the enemy side, 16th SS Division took over responsibility for defences on Route 64 from 362 Infantry Division. According to one chronicler, the SS "brought forth the best fighting capabilities of the 6th South African Armoured Division".[239] Field Marshal Kesselring had his headquarters at Santomato, which was taken over by the Imperial Light Horse/Kimberley Regiment.

237 W.E.H. Condon, *The Frontier Force Rifles*, p. 252.

238 B. Herschell, September 1944, An orgy of dances, in D. Quilter (ed), *'No dishonourable name'*, pp. 229–231.

239 DODAR, UWH, Box 140, Operations, 6th South African Armoured Division, 22/8/1944–31/3/1945.

Together with the Royal Natal Carbineers patrols, the latter regiment probed well forward of the infantry positions, through the hills around Tobbiana. There was little contact although a trickle of deserters came in. The enemy continued to shell Pistoia. Artillery observation posts went out with the infantry patrols, but there were few likely targets. The gunners complained that there was a lack of cooperation from the infantry in calling in shelreps (shelling reports which help to locate and identify enemy guns). The war diary stated: "This is a most unsatisfactory state of affairs, a counter-battery organization cannot operate effectively without the cooperation of all arms."[240] On the ground however, Hodgson was more concerned about his stomach:

> The grapes are in their prime at the moment, with the result that I am just living on them; there are some that are really delicious. Also the tomatoes have reached their peak and are perfect. I have never in all my life seen so many tomatoes on one bush before; they are hanging in bunches practically as thick as grapes—the real big tomatoes, not the small ones. I must say with all these things flying about, we don't trouble the cook much about meals, as we have usually had enough.

The Sable of January 1945 contained some recipes for livening up bully beef. This recipe for 'stuffed tomato' would have been useful here, where there was an abundance of the vegetable:

> When you've been lucky, or done a bit of 'organizing'. Cut off the top of your tomatoes, remove the inside and mix it well with your beef. Put the mixture back into the tomato shell and fry in boiling water. The 'Café Continental' charges a lot for this sort of thing.[241]

It appears that Hodgson was ahead of the pack in realizing that spending winter in the Apennines was a distinct possibility. Horror stories about the previous winter were beginning to circulate, but the looming shortage of gear for the cold season had not yet become apparent:

> For the winter could you please send me a thick pair of gloves, as thick as possible, so that they will be very warm. Also would you please send them up as soon as possible because it is already beginning to get cold in the mornings and evenings, and the winter is going to be here in full style before we know where we are. I am

240 DODAR, WD, Box 631, 7/23rd Medium Regiment, 10/9/1944.

241 *The Sable*, R.W. Lee & L.S. Wale (eds), Italian Font Edition, January 1945, p. 38.

> preparing for it already as I am certain I am going to be as warm as possible. So far I have managed to wrangle an extra blanket which will always be very useful—later on we will get an extra winter issue but one could always do with a couple extra. I have also got a brand new great coat, one of the new type, which is a better cut and much thicker, so I am comparatively well off. I have seen lots of photos of the winter up here, and it looks really cold: six feet of snow, blizzards, sleet, etc, etc and on top of all that plenty of rain. Cold is bad enough but when it is combined with wet it goes beyond a joke.

Winter allocations allowed each man four blankets. Since there was a worldwide shortage of blankets, the military authorities issued an order forbidding their use for curtains, carpets, tablecloths or any other purpose for which they were not intended.

The greatcoats provided proved inadequate against winter conditions in the Apennines. When wet, they became uncomfortably heavy. The winter equipment used by the Americans was of better quality.

In January 1945, Axelson inquired about the shortage of winter clothing, especially boots. In answer, the assistant director quartermaster technical stressed that the supply of goods was very complex, with the ordnance catalogue containing some 136,000 items.

Problems with supply included the fact that no shipments of boots were received between 15 September and 15 October, although a large shipment arrived in Naples in December.

The indenting of the British Army was also at fault. Often, there was no stock to supply the orders received, and although the desired stock would arrive shortly afterward, it would be finished when the unit replaced its order a week or two later. Added to this, the British boots were of such inferior quality that every man had to be given two pairs.

The assistant director quartermaster technical further expressed the view that "[winter equipment] should be regarded as unit equipment. It must be held in a pool. It is not a private issue, an issue to individuals. When troops are pulled out of the front line for a rest, they must leave behind their special equipment".[242]

Tuesday 12 September 1944: Chiassano

On 7 September, a bridge over the Arno west of Empoli washed away as a result of the recent downpours. Repairs took a long time, relatively speaking, and the

242 E. Axelson, *A year in Italy*, p. 157.

bridge was reopened only on 14 September—well after the 44 hours promised by the division. Traffic was directed via Florence or Pisa, which was in the US sector, and the lack of signposts there caused drivers to get horribly lost.

Pistoia is located at the gateway to Route 64, at the mouth of the Reno River valley which cuts through the Apennines. The countryside and climate changes noticeably as one travels north of the town. At the time, only a few grapes were grown by peasant farmers on the slopes of the Apennines, but Pistoia was a major grape-growing area. September is harvest month and Hodgson took an interest in the technology of wine-making:

> At the present time most of the population are busy collecting in all the grapes. One sees cartload after cartload pouring into the presses all day long. Most of the stuff we see is just the local, made by the peasants—very few of them have the correct presses, but instead they have big wooden casks with a few holes in the bottom. They tip a quantity of grapes into this and then a couple of the 'bambinos' (children) are put inside, and they spend a couple of hours stamping on it. I expect the result is the same, but not at all hygienic, as the kids are always hopping in and out.

Heavy traffic volumes meant that it took four hours for the guns of the 1/6th Field Regiment to move eight miles along the banks of the canals as they approached Pistoia. The quads and guns of the 1/16th battery were hit by some unusually heavy shells, possibly 170mm, while on the move; in his log, Cormack described them as "Bone Shakers". Guides were posted at all the crossroads to ensure that no one got lost as they moved through the outskirts of Pistoia. The soldier directing the 25-pounders reported to Axelson that he had been sniped at near a canal one mile south of Pistoia, but partisans were cleaning up the culprits.

The weather in Italy in mid-September can be blissful, provided it is not raining. The mountain air has a bite in the evenings, but the sea is warm enough for swimming and short sleeves can still be worn during the day. At this stage it appeared that nothing could stop the Allied war machine from reaching Bologna before winter—not even the Gothic Line.

The Royal Natal Carbineers was now in a backwater of sorts. Hodgson was happy to have been given more cerebral work in the Intelligence Section which provided him a better overall view of operations:

> I am still very happy and full of beans—even more so these days than ever because I have got a new job. This new job I like very much as it is very interesting; there is

> also a lot to be done, and it is an important job. I have become one of the company's 'I' men. There are only two men in the Company Intelligence section, and between us we have to do all the work. My particular job is to keep all the company maps up to date, such as putting in all the detailed positions of the company and battalion, showing the progress of our front, and also adjoining fronts. I spend most of my time with the company commander when we are in operation, and I have to supply him with all the information he needs such as positions, etc. Another part of my job is to report our positions and progress to the battalion's tactical headquarters, and pass on information to the company from there. Also I have to collect all information possible during operations and pass it back. Identification of prisoners, recognition of aircraft and enemy material and so on. During loose hours I have had to do quite a bit of learning, but it is a good job and I am loving it. Also the men in the company rely on me for the information they receive. I seem to have risen up a bit since I was last in a rifle section and naturally I like it very much. I know all that is going on, and often a lot that is not passed on to the ordinary man in the platoon. Naturally I am still in Company [redacted] [censored] headquarters.

Numerous reports were received from observation posts, civilians and patrols of enemy guns based in tunnels,. These 'cave-dwellers' were pounded by the 5.5s but the 'troglodytes' were more elusive than ever, thanks to the miles of railway tunnels in the mountains. Civilians were forthcoming with what information they had, but little of what they knew was valuable: "A seemingly knowledgeable priest attached himself to D Troop [7/23rd Medium Regiment] and described and pointed out a new enemy gun position every time he was handed a piece of bread and jam." Reports were being received from civilians who claimed to have been press-ganged into working on fortifications on the Gothic Line. They were full of horror stories of concrete gun positions and strong points. The diarist of the 7/23rd Field Regiment jested that "if one can place any credence in their reports, the whole huge mountain range is bristling with the most up-to-date cannon and so 'honeycombed' with galleries and tunnels that it is now thought that very heavy bombing with 1,200 lb bombs may cause the Apennines to cave in altogether."

Wednesday 13 September 1944 – Tuesday 26 September 1944: Santomato

On 16 September, progress was being made and the going was still good for the tanks; so much so, that it was expected that they would sweep onto the great plains of the Po valley at any moment. The South African public was already being told of preparations being made by the German army for the complete evacuation of the provinces of Lombardy and Piedmont. The headline in the

Rand Daily Mail on 16 September proclaimed: "One hill feature bars way to Po Valley". For the ordinary foot soldier like Hodgson, the immediate concern was not the German defences, but rather what the foraging opportunities would be like in the mountains:

> The fruit position is on the decline now; I think we have definitely had the best—but even now there is a fair amount of stuff, but it is not as good as what we had the last week of last month and the first ten days of this. That is just generally speaking, but the apples are just coming up to their peak and the olives are not yet ripe, and will not be for at least a month yet. Also in the mountainous areas there is not so much of it as there is down in the lower lying areas, and also the sheep are very scarce on the mountains.

Pistoia was a delightful city, very clean but deserted as it was still under shelling: one night, 400 rounds fell on the town. Axelson and others at divisional headquarters could not understand the Germans' use of shells: "They kill a few civilians by the shelling … but do no harm to us. The Germans could use their guns to much better effect shelling and harassing roads and bridges which are also under observation."[243]

The 1/6th Field Regiment was based at Santomato, up a winding road among the fir trees north of Pistoia. Here, Axelson watched the 25-pounders and some tanks parked in between the trees firing at the enemy—who were just over the crest of a hill—from 2,500 yards. Targets included active mortars, mule trains, enemy movement and pill boxes. Route 64 provided most of the confirmed targets, and then there was the ever-present target: the 'suspected observation post'. Near Pistoia, the 7/23rd Medium Regiment was lined up along a canal bank in full view of the enemy on the mountains. They too, were surprised at the ineffectiveness of the counter-battery fire, the regiment suffering only one casualty. Nevertheless, on 16 September, soon after a battery of mediums had moved to their new position at Fornace, D Troop of 'Peter' Battery, 7/23rd Medium Regiment, received 120 rounds on their position. The only casualty was a Mack truck which had its tyres punctured. One gunner had a lucky escape when a 'dud' buried itself below his 'bivvy'. The regimental headquarters and aid post also received a pasting, which served as a reminder that there was still a war going on. "Many caustic remarks were addressed to the counter-battery

243 E. Axelson, *A year in Italy*, p. 118.

officer after regimental headquarters officers had recovered their breath."[244] The history of the 16th SS Panzergrenadier Division, *Im gleichen Schritt und Trit*, confirms that the Germans had received orders to fire off their stockpiles of ammunition in preparation for a withdrawal. The irony was that a short while previously, they had been under orders to conserve ammunition. This accounts for their poor target selection. The prolific shelling between 12 and 17 September is spoken of in Johnston's diary:

12th	Jerry shelling Pistoia. Can see our own shellbursts. Jerry shelled all night in front and behind, not near.
13th	Jerry shelled at night again—not near.
14th	Jerry shelling at night. Not near. Wizzbangs.
15th	Same as yesterday.
16th	Jerry shelling all around.
17th	Jerry shelling day and night intermittently.

The artillery, including the 4/22nd Field Regiment, was in support of the Imperial Light Horse/Kimberley Regiment and the Witwatersrand Rifles/Regiment De la Rey in their attack on Monte Acuto on 18 September, and stood ready to cover them on their deep-penetration patrols. Artillery observers would accompany some of these patrols. The infantry had its headquarters just behind the guns, while the companies were positioned in front on various features higher in the Apennines. On one occasion, the Germans hurled insults at the men in these outposts, inciting them to attack and some savage close-quarter fighting followed. Harassing fire caught the 1/16th Battery (1/6th Field Regiment) at lunch on 18 September: a shell landed in the cookhouse, wounding eight. A number of shells fell onto the mediums' area west of Pistoia, which set off an ammo truck. Flames from the exploding shells provided a beacon in the evening sky for the enemy gunners, but they failed to exploit the opportunity—more evidence, it seemed, of their clueless gunnery. Even so, the war diary of the 7/23rd Medium Regiment states that this was the worst

244 DODAR, WD, Box 631, 7/23rd Medium Regiment, 16/9/1944.

shelling experienced by the regiment since the start of the advance in Italy. One of those wounded, Gunner A.E. Hyland of Malvern, Johannesburg, died the following day. He was 20 years old. Lieutenant K.V. Meiklejohn was awarded the Military Cross for his role in organizing a party of six men to drive the surviving trucks away from the fire.

It was later established that the guns responsible for this shelling were 170mm, a type last seen at Anzio. It was speculated that the gun positions were given away by 'fifth columnists' (traitors within the ranks) or spies, as three bush fires has been observed burning behind the position.

When an 88mm gun had a go at the 7/23rd Medium Regiment headquarters the next day, the diarist wrote: "It was most unpleasant while it lasted, no damage was done and no one was physically the worse for its unwelcome attentions."

On 24 September, the regiment was ordered to move to Vaiano, via Pistoia, Montale, Bagnolo and Prato. The headquarters was shelled once more before the regiment departed.

As the terrain changed, so did the season; the rain set in on 20 September. The grapes, previously so prolific, were now becoming scarce. Johnston wrote a lot about grapes: having to walk a long way for them, finding 'Hanepoort' grapes or not finding any at all. Tomatoes were obtainable, as always. "Grapes going fast. Ities picking them for *vino*—stamping on them with dirty feet."

At this stage, the infantry took over the war from the tanks as the country was 'untankable'. From mid-September, however, tanks were put to use as field artillery in support of the infantry. The tribulations of the infantry in the mountains northeast of Pistoia were now beginning. A fighting reconnaissance patrol from B Company, Imperial Light Horse/Kimberley Regiment under Lieutenant L.L. Maltby had gone missing in the vicinity of Pozzo del Bagno and 15 September was a tense day as the men waited to hear of their peers' fate. At 2000 hours that night, Privates Pieterse and Oberholzer returned with the news that Maltby and six others were missing; Private J.D.T. Otto had, in fact, been killed and Maltby wounded. One of the six taken prisoner was Private Francis M. Joseph who managed to grab his Tommy gun off a table, kill two officers and escape.

Casualties mounted as the Imperial Light Horse/Kimberley Regiment cleared the hills overlooking the divisional area of observation posts. The names given to these hills reflected their height in feet: Pt 1040, Pt 1045, Pt 959, and so on. In most other cases, the height would be expressed in metres. A German medical orderly was among the POWs captured on 18/19 September. He was able to provide a detailed account of the action at Pozzo del Bagno and confirmed that Maltby had been evacuated immediately after being wounded. Maltby died of his wounds in captivity on 13 November 1944 and is buried at Padua near Venice. Newspapers in South Africa provided the public with minimum details of the latest activities:

> These patrols have been active day and night and maintained contact with the enemy along their whole sector until Saturday night when the enemy moved back to the high mountains which constitute the formidable Gothic Line. On average, the South Africans have taken 20 prisoners a day, not including killed and wounded, for a loss of four or five men a day. The South Africans are now coming into close contact with the Gothic Line itself.[245]

On 19 September, the day that Finance Minister Hofmeyr flew into the Siena aerodrome for a visit, Axelson wrote in his log: "Heard that ILH had taken Bagno the previous evening, suffering ten casualties. There is evidence of thinning out on our front."[246] From artefacts left on the battlefield, the South Africans knew that they were up against the 16th SS Division, which included some of Himmler's elite bodyguard.

The next day, a patrol of Grenadier Guards was pursued back to its own lines.

It seemed that the whole German front was collapsing but at a briefing from the GI, Senior Operations Officer Colonel Maggs, the division was told not to expect the war in Europe to be over before March or April. Hodgson, too, was still contemplating the prospect of a winter in Italy:

> Winter is approaching slowly but as yet it is still quite a long way off, thank goodness. One can feel a bit of a nip in the air in the early morning and in the late evening. Also we are getting more rain these days than we have had in the past. At the moment there is a bit of rain falling, but not too much—when the rains get really stuck in we are bound to be bogged down for most of the time.

An enemy patrol infiltrated behind an artillery observation post occupied by Captain R. Collins and Bombadier Wannenburg. Both sides stared at each other for a while in amazement before opening fire. Nobody was hit and the

245 *The Star*, Fierce fighting in mountain line, 18/9/1944.

246 E. Axelson, *A year in Italy*, p. 117.

hostile patrol escaped unscathed. Hardly a day went by without some dramatic incident on patrol. On 22 September, a First City/Cape Town Highlanders patrol came under fire from a cluster of houses. Corporal Beaumont was wounded in the leg and, unable to walk, crawled into a thicket. The rest of the patrol reached their firm base and approximately three quarters of an hour later, Private Richardson went out to look for him—with no success. Subsequent search parties also found no trace of him and it is assumed that he was taken prisoner. At 1100 hours on 23 September, Lieutenant Dale—who was occupying an observation post for the 7/23rd Medium Regiment—went out on a reconnaissance and was missing until 1830 hours. When he reappeared, he told of how he had been surrounded by six Germans armed with Tommy guns. They motioned for him to keep quiet and took his revolver and epaulettes with badges of rank. Apart from shouting "*schweinhund*", all communication had taken place through sign language. While being escorted back, they passed along a narrow path with an almost vertical drop. Lieutenant Dale seized the opportunity and threw himself off the path, rolling over and over until he was able to scramble to his feet and make good his escape.

The Natal Mounted Rifles, now acting as infantry, moved to Vaiano on Route 6620 and platoons occupied Monte Castiglione. During this time, II US Corps was involved in heavy fighting in the Futa Pass to the right of the South Africans, and the Frontier Force Rifles was on Monte Casciaio. The Guards were driving up Route 64 (which retains that name today) into Femminamorta, while divisional artillery provided concentrated support from Santomato.

The Gothic Line was 14 miles deep and about 120 miles long, extending from Carrara in the west to Rimini on the Adriatic coast. The strategy had been one of manoeuvre until the men reached the Gothic Line, but having arrived in the northern Apennines, it was, as at Cassino, a case of attrition and mutual bloodletting. The *Rand Daily Mail* of 20 September puts into perspective the changing nature of the campaign:

> As the Germans are gradually forced back into the Gothic Line proper they continue to look down onto the hills from which the South African infantry regiments have driven them in the past week. It has been pretty much the same story all the way up Italy from Cassino to the Apennine barrier, but this barrier is quite the most formidable obstacle encountered anywhere in the campaign.
>
> The motorized South African infantrymen started walking before they crossed the Arno River more than a fortnight ago and they have had to climb all the way to

> get up in the mountains before the Gothic Line. The reason is that the Germans are able to shell the roads for miles from their vantage points.[247]

In *The Star* of Thursday 25 September, the South African public read for the first time of a town called Castiglione dei Pepoli and were given cause to think Bologna would be next. A certain Rand-Cape regiment (Imperial Light Horse/ Kimberley Regiment) was leading the way:

> Pressing along the main roads which the Germans have blocked, Springbok troops are now about 20 miles north of Prato in the neighbourhood of Castiglione dei Pepoli, halfway to Bologna and others are about six miles north-north-west of Pistoia where the extent of the German demolitions is almost beyond description.
>
> The advance to the Castiglione area was headed by men of a Rand-Cape motorized infantry regiment who scaled and occupied two important heights just south of Castiglione after an exacting night march across broken mountain terrain, over which the going was very heavy after several days of fairly steady rain. Little opposition was encountered from the enemy during this advance but there was some resistance by German artillery and mortars on one flank.[248]

Similarly, the *Rand Daily Mail* of 25 September gave its readers no reason to believe there would be a grinding halt to the advance or that their boys would endure a winter in the mountains:

> The United States Fifth Army to which is attached the Sixth South African Armoured Division, has achieved its biggest success in Italy by smashing the formidable defences of the mountains north of Florence. The Fifth Army is now only 15 miles in a direct line from Bologna. The Futa Pass, probably the most strongly fortified zone in the entire Gothic Line, is today a shattered mass of rubble and battered fortifications, littered with the bodies of the defenders.[249]

Gone was the good life under the Tuscan sun. Cold and rain not only hampered operations; it made life miserable. Bourhill had learned from past experience that "rain complicates everything and you just can't keep dry". Winter battledress was issued as from 25 September but light khaki still served in a mismatch with the serge tunics, woollen vests, thick socks and warm shirts. According to Axelson, however, the division was short 7,000 battle dress and

[247] *Rand Daily Mail,* Springboks engaged in tough mountain campaign, 20/9/1944.

[248] *The Star,* Advances by Allied Forces in Italy, 25/9/1944.

[249] *Rand Daily Mail,* American Army smashes Gothic Line defences, 25/9/1944.

only 75 per cent of the men received equipment. The rest had to make do with only a blanket and a gas cape to protect them from the mountain cold. The clothing situation was no better by the end of October and even into December there were still a few men who, having the misfortune of an unusual body size, were waiting for proper clothing.

On the same day as the troops were issued their winter kit, Axelson went to an officers' shop at Pontassieve, nine miles east of Florence, to purchase winter clothes. He found only size six shoes and rain coats for men 6 foot 2 and over, prompting the remark, "The Royal Army Service Corps has an odd appreciation of the proportions of officers."[250] Hodgson, too, was breaking out his winter kit:

> Talking of rain, it has also started up here. As a rule we get a good shower every afternoon; there are a few exceptions of course, but the last couple of days it has been raining continually—it cleared up this morning, after two and a half days of rain, but this afternoon it looks as though we are going to get a good shower at any moment … it has been chilly to the extent that I have had to put my jersey on for the first time during the day. I don't know if I told you that we had been issued with a part of our winter kit, which included our winter battle dress, two thick long-sleeved vests and two pairs of thick underpants, down to the ankles. Weird things, but I am sure we will need all the warmth they can give when the cold really sets in.

The men's South African-made brown boots were the envy of other troops as they were better made and more waterproof than the British black boots. One batch of boots, which were made in India, were found to crack and were uncomfortable. Gumboots—'boots knee rubber' in quartermaster language—were preferred by the gunners in muddy conditions but snow often entered at the top. Boots were generally in short supply however, and some men resorted to asking their families to send footwear from home—or taking them off a dead German.

Wednesday 27 September 1944 – Thursday 28 September 1944: Capostrada

The first phase of the Gothic Line battles had come to an end. Between 12 and 27 September 1944, the division had lost 41 killed and 250 wounded. It was thanks to the breakthrough in the American sector that the Gothic Line was so easily overcome. The weather was cold and wet. Some men made fires inside their tents in an attempt to overcome conditions already being described as

250 E. Axelson, *A year in Italy*, p. 123.

"pretty miserable".[251] The 1/6th Field Regiment was in action at Capostrada just north of Pistoia when the 6th South African Armoured Division was informed that its axis had shifted to Route 6620—today known as Route 325—from Prato to Bologna in the Setta River valley. All former orders were therefore cancelled. From now on, the division would be on the left flank of II Corps.

The northern Apennines form an unbroken 130-mile barrier between the Adriatic and Tyrrhenian coastal belts, with a depth of 45–55 miles. The crossings in the South African sector were reasonably easy, depending on the season. Route 64 from Pistoia to Bologna in the Reno valley and Route 6620 from Florence to Bologna via Prato along the Setta valley were in fairly good condition before they were chewed up by military traffic. Route 65 through the Futa Pass was the most direct and was within the American sector.

The mountainous countryside is densely populated in the valleys while the slopes are either cultivated or thickly wooded, except toward the peaks which are bare with some scrub. The rugged peaks and twisting valleys made this the most formidable front of the II Corps zone. The Brasimone is a small stream which flows past Castiglione, northward to the Setta River. The Setta itself is clear and not very deep unless flooding—as it was on 26 October.

As the press had already pointed out, Castiglione is about 30 miles from Bologna and the plains. En route to their new axis, it was necessary for some units to first concentrate in the Prato area. Meanwhile, the Imperial Light Horse/ Kimberley Regiment went ahead and were the first South Africans to arrive in Castiglione on 27 September. It was a major event for the townspeople. The rest of 11th Armoured Brigade arrived the next day and began concentrating in the area of Camugnano.[252]

The Natal Mounted Rifles stopped over at Vaiano, five miles north of Prato. On the flats between Pistoia and Prato in the vicinity of Montemurlo and Vaiano, the tankers and gunners were able to indulge in a few days of '*casa* crawling'. This involved sitting around the hearth, improving one's Italian and "the consumption of vast quantities of *Rosso*—the purple death". Every crew had a couple of Italian 'batmen' to do odd chores in return of an old shirt or

251 DODAR, WD, Box 631, 7/23rd Medium Regiment, 17/9/1944; P.M. Johnston, personal diary, 29/9/1944.

252 M. Abatantuono, G. Cecconi, M. Elmi, M. Fogacci & M. Monari, *Inverno 1944–45 I Sudafricani a Castiglione*, pp. 16–17.

some food.[253] Shortly after the arrival of the South Africans in the Castiglione area, during the period 29 September to 4 October, the 16th SS Reconnaissance under Major Walter Reder carried out a massacre of civilians in the vicinity of Monte Sole, about ten miles ahead of the South African positions. Although news of the event had not yet reached the Allies, the scale was far worse than the Civitella slaughter. Estimates regarding the number of men, women and children killed vary; some sources put the figure at 1,800, although the most reliable estimate is 770. One source relates that 700 passengers had been on a train that was entombed in the Apennine tunnel which exits at Vernio, when the Germans blew up both entrances. This is not how events unfolded, however. The South Africans would only realize the full extent of the atrocity after the capture of Monte Sole in April 1945, although winter patrols came across scores of bodies in the snow-covered fields and in deserted farmhouses before then. In a war crimes court, Walter Reder would be judged to be directly responsible for 600 of these deaths and would serve 34 years in prison. It was his troops that the Imperial Light Horse/Kimberley Regiment now faced.[254] The Coldstream Guards arrived in Castiglione at the end of September, and Michael Howard was not impressed with what he saw:

> I cannot believe that even at the height of an Italian spring Castiglione can look pleasant. The view down the valley toward Lombardy can look impressive, but the town itself is a struggling collection of mean grey houses sprawled haphazard across the hillside, along a main street. I certainly saw it at its worst—usually in pouring rain or snow or in a damp and icy mist which penetrated to every corner. The village was saturated with troops; civilians were crowded into two rooms and the rest of their house taken over, while gardens, fields and road verges were filled to the last inch with every sort of vehicle from every sort of unit. The heavy equipment of the entire division was parked here, from the light aid detachments to boot repair shops, mobile baths, dentists, and casualty clearing stations. [255]

By now the South Africans were forming an idea of what lay in store for them in this part of Italy. Apart from the miserable weather, the roads were narrow,

---

253 J.F. MacDonald, *The war history of Southern Rhodesia*, p. 590.

254 S. Monick, *A bugle calls*, p. 408; *Springbok*, Journal of the South African Legion of South African Veterans, June 2008, p. 16; *Parco regionale storico di Monte Sole, percorsi e informazioni*, p. 6.

255 M. Howard, The valley of the Setta, winter 1944–1945, in D. Quilter (ed), '*No dishonourable name*', p. 232.

winding, muddy and blocked by demolitions of tunnels, bridges and viaducts. On the road through Montepiano, which had been pounded by shelling, the gunners found that the Germans had left behind two 50mm guns and four 105s, two of which were in perfect condition—the 4/22nd Field Regiment actually fired one of them. The roads were also extremely congested at this time, making it difficult for units to reach their destinations.

Friday 29 September 1944 – Monday 2 October 1944: Montemurlo

On 29 September the *Rand Daily Mail* reported that Castiglione had been captured after heavy fighting in which "the Germans were driven from the mountain fastness of Bruscoli". Another article on the same page informed the South African public of the outcome of operation 'Market Garden' under the headline "Why the Arnhem Bridgehead could not be held"—although the event was given a positive spin. The next day, the South African press reported that a large part of the Gothic Line had been cleared and that American and South African troops were busy clearing the Castiglione area 20 miles from Bologna. The Germans were doing their utmost to recapture and hold commanding ridges to the southeast. Some villages and ridges had changed hands repeatedly. The bad weather in Italy was already making the news back home.[256] After days on the road and in the rain, Bourhill's troop finally found shelter in a school building on the outskirts of Montemurlo. Cormack's economical log entry read, "Heavy rain—stayed in casa."

Montemurlo is on the outskirts of Pistoia and became a concentration area from which leave parties were permitted to visit Florence, about 20 miles away. While the 11th Armoured Brigade was fighting with a new intensity, the 12th Motorized Brigade was left in reserve at Prato.

Lieutenant-Colonel Reeves-Moore, officer commanding the Imperial Light Horse/Kimberley Regiment, described Johnny Smallwood and his carrier platoon as "fearless, always eager for action and full of initiative".[257] It was they who led the approach to Camugnano from Castiglione, along a lateral road to the west and slightly north, all the while under observation from the surrounding heights. The fight for the village took five days; after being

256 *Rand Daily Mail*, 5th Army clears large part of Gothic Line, 30/9/1944; *Rand Daily Mail*, Allies advance in Italy: Bellaria captured, 29/9/1944.

257 H. Klein, *Light Horse cavalcade*, p. 157.

occupied it was lost, then retaken. Finally, by 30 September, the 11th Armoured Brigade had occupied the shattered village. Its role was to hold the left flank of the division on the side of the Reno River and Route 64. The Guards (Scots and Grenadiers) were on the slopes of Catarelto on the right.

Billeting for all the troops and their entourages was proving difficult. Everyone wanted to find a *casa* and get out of the rain, but the Apennines were sparsely inhabited.

Johnston took down his tent after receiving orders to move on 28 September, but put it up again when orders were cancelled. The troop started to pull out at 0500 hours the next day, but Johnston's tank "dropped a track and broke 10 links" so the tent was pitched once more in the same place. The men stayed here, near Montale, for four days. Finally, moving off in a drizzle, they travelled 26 miles through Prato and then north toward Montepiano where, experiencing filter trouble, they pulled into battery headquarters.

With its exhausts fixed, Johnston's tank spluttered on up the remaining seven miles into Castiglione, leaving on 3 October under heavy rain.

After their own difficult passage through the mountains, 'Queen' Battery (7/23rd Medium Regiment) had arrived in Castiglione on 30 September. Tactical headquarters took up abode in a three-storey house in full view of the enemy. This wasn't unusual as, at the time, every house in Castiglione could be easily seen by the enemy on Monte Catarelto. The house also served as a useful observation post during the battle to come.

Monte Catarelto is located approximately five miles up the road from Castiglione: a three-mile ridge, one mile wide, between the Setta and Brasimone rivers, with belts of farmland and thickly wooded slopes. With the support of their friends the Royal Durban Light Infantry and Pretoria Regiment (Princess Alice's Own), the Guards Brigade attacked at 1500 hours on 30 September. Close support was provided by 166th Field Regiment RA (Newfoundland Regiment) since the 1/6th Field Regiment was resting at Montemurlo. The mediums, however, were on hand and 1,000 rounds were fired by 'Queen' Battery 7/23rd Medium Regiment in a 36-hour period. In spite of all this effort, the Scots Guards were forced to withdraw from Pt 707 in the face of fanatical and determined counter-attacks.

The withdrawal was assisted by the tanks of the Pretoria Regiment. A first-hand account of the action and its aftermath describes the shells bursting among the infantry, causing terrible carnage. The tanks charged up the hill to their rescue, guns blazing. The crew of 'Dubula', the name given Nick van Malsen's tank, fired more rounds of .30 Browning than they used for the entire remainder of the Italian campaign. Their Browning barrel melted from overuse, along with two spares, during their efforts to break up the German counter-attack. The battlefield "was a shambles of broken rifles and machine guns, littered with bundles of blood-stained clothing, overturned guns and dead bodies". The Pretoria Regiment lost only one tank, but the Scots Guards incurred heavy losses and were withdrawn to Castiglione to rest. Two hundred and fifty casualties were recorded among the 400 German defenders. The historical recording officer noted the views of one Scots Guardsman who was convinced that the SS troops were doped, adding: "A tank fired at him [a German] with his 75. He went up in the air. He hasn't come down yet."[258]

The weather on 1 October was fine and crisp, offering excellent observation. However, the next day dawned with heavy rain, mist and strong winds. The defence was as fanatical as before. At 0015 hours, a Grenadier patrol found that Pt 707 was unoccupied, save for five German corpses. The battalion promptly took occupation.

Breaking dawn revealed that a general withdrawal was underway, possibly sparked by a breakthrough on the American front. The 24th Guards Brigade lost 22 killed in the fighting for Monte Catarelto. The dead were honoured by the composition of a new pipe band march called *Monte Catarelto*.

The town of Castiglione, which remained relatively undamaged, became the division's main base for the next four months. It would also become the permanent home of the 401 South Africans who are buried in its cemetery.

Sporadic enemy shells were still landing in the town and on the access roads during the early days of occupation. They were responsible for the only casualties incurred by the Pretoria Regiment during October, the month of the Battle of Monte Catarelto. The incidents took place on 2 October when some shells hit the cook's truck standing in Castiglione. Those killed were Troopers P.D. Swart and R.A. Castle. Sergeant A.A.B. Johnson (TSC) was mortally wounded.

One of the more unpleasant conditions facing the South Africans when they took occupation of Castiglione was the great number of dead horses and mules lying about in various stages of decay, evidently killed by Allied gunfire. "At this

258 E. Axelson, *A year in Italy*, p. 129; G.B. Hobbs, *Sicily to the Alps*, p. 165.

A group of Rhodesians outside the Springbok Club in Rome plan their day of sightseeing. *Photo: SANMMH*

Signs of danger left in the wake of the retreating Germans. *Photo: Comune di Castiglione dei Pepoli*

During autumn in the Arno River valley one needed only to stretch out a hand to find grapes. From left: Tpr N. Solberg (Durban), Cpl R.D. McInvoy (Cape Town) and Cpl C.W. Rosettenstein (Johannesburg). *Photo: DODAR*

A lieutenant of the Imperial Light Horse/Kimberley Regiment and a wireless operator keep a good grip on their Thompson sub-machine guns. *Photo: Comune di Castiglione dei Pepoli*

German artillery caused 40 per cent of Allied casualties in Italy and mortars 25 per cent. Here, a South African mortar rains death on the enemy. *Photo: Comune di Castiglione dei Pepoli*

Maj Gallimore (nearest camera), Capt Richards and Cpl Hodgson (just out of frame at left) peruse German newspapers near Pistoia. *Photo: J.B. Hodgson collection*

Patrolling was done on a rotational basis with most men not going on more than one or two a month—although some likened this activity to a hunting party and volunteered for the job. Light equipment and comfortable clothing were as preferred. Daylight patrols could be effective in thick-wooded country but nighttime patrols were more common. *Photo: DODAR*

Non-combatant Cape Corps troops carry up a hot meal on the Gothic Line. These men were widely recognized for their courage and dedication as stretcher bearers. *Photo: Comune di Castiglione dei Pepoli*

Once into the Apennines, armour was restricted to an artillery role. *Photo: DODAR*

'Priest' self-propelled gun (SPG) of 4/22 Field Regiment taking on ammunition. *Photo: SANMMH*

In villages and on narrow winding roads, the 5.5-inch guns had to be manhandled around corners. *Photo: SANMMH*

Tanks find conditions heavy-going in the foothills of the Apennines.
Photo: DODAR

Hastily prepared gun position near Camugnano, from where 1/6th Field Regiment supported operations at Monte Vigese and Monte Stanco; Stephen Bourhill kneeling.
Photo: Author's collection

An infantryman with battle gear, including small pack, entrenching tool, gas cape, ammunition and blanket, heads into harm's way.
Photo: SANMMH

Unsmiling infantry coming home from the hill, pay scant attention to a bogged-down tank. *Photo: DODAR*

View of Monte Stanco looking north. Casa Forlino can be seen among trees on the road which runs horizontally across the hill. Monte Pezza and Monte Salvaro are at top right but not visible here. The Reno River can be seen on far right. *Photo: Comune di Castiglione dei Pepoli*

Men of the Witwatersrand Rifles/Regiment De la Rey in what resembles a scene from the First World War. *Photo: Comune di Castiglione dei Pepoli*

Much coveted South African boots being issued in a forward area. This public relations photograph was probably taken to counter the reports of equipment shortages ... especially boots. *Photo: DODAR*

Death-dealing fate decrees: 'You and you—dead; the rest of you—on the truck.' These infantrymen of the Imperial Light Horse/Kimberley Regiment live to fight another day.
Photo: Comune di Castiglione dei Pepoli

Leaving their position in a muddy field, vehicles are soon bogged down again on narrow farm roads in an Apennine valley.
Photo: DODAR

On 28 July 1944 John Hodgson wrote to his father: "The [wireless] set is on the company commander's Jeep, and where he doesn't go in that Jeep is a sin. He simply goes everywhere. Demolitions and even no roads at all are no obstacle whatsoever." Ultimately 'General Mud' defeated even the resilient Jeep. *Photo: Comune di Castiglione dei Pepoli*

Some early pilgrims to the cemetery at Castiglione. *Photo: Comune di Castiglione dei Pepoli*

A ray of sunshine breaks through and brings to mind a verse of 'Lili Marlene' specific to the Italian campaign:

> When we are marching in the mud and cold
> And my pack seems more than I can hold
> My love for you renews my might
> I'm warm again, my pack is light.
> It's you Lili Marlene,
> It's you Lili Marlene

Photo: DODAR

Left: The mountain roads were kept open by American bulldozers but the ice had to be chipped off by Basuto labourers. On 21 November 1944 one driver from 59 'Q' Company was killed when his 3-tonner went off a 100-foot precipice. *Photo: DODAR*

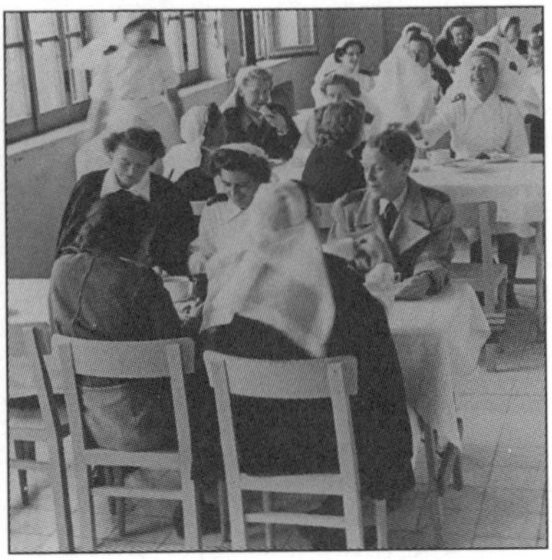

Above right: South African soldiers craved the company of South African women and the few nurses, 'Waasies' and SAWAS, were in great demand. The main source of female company was from the nursing profession who, more so than other women's services, had an undeserved reputation for promiscuity. The American equivalent of the WAAS was the WAAC; a survey found that 40 per cent of unmarried WAACs were celibate, 55 per cent were sexually active on occasion and 5 per cent were promiscuous. *Photo: Comune di Castiglione dei Pepoli*

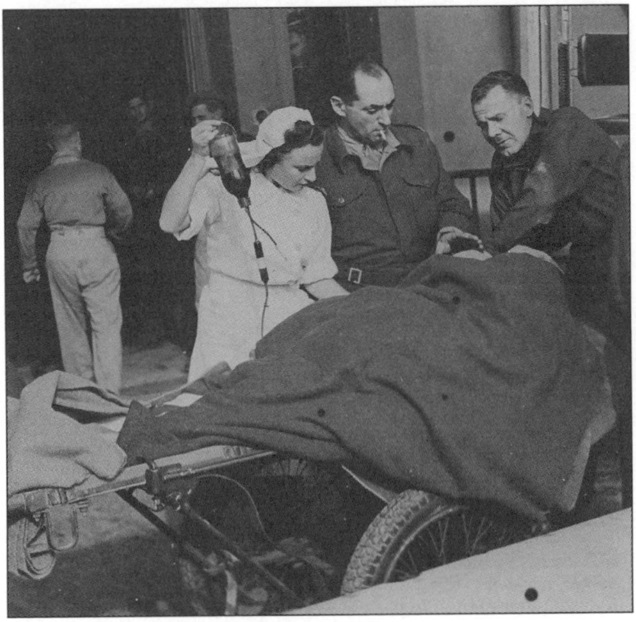

A casualty from the Gothic Line arrives at 108 SA General Hospital (600 beds). In December 1944, 107 SA General Hospital (1,200 beds), took over in Florence. *Photo: Comune di Castiglione dei Pepoli*

Blood bank in Florence; note the vampire bat logo. In a war zone, a hospital comprised everything except the building and some hospitals made regular moves.
Photo: Comune di Castiglione dei Pepoli

A doctor catches up on sleep in the shell of a farmhouse. Each regiment had its own aid post; field ambulance units maintained advanced dressing stations three to five miles behind the lines. *Photo: DODAR*

Original caption from the Bureau of Information read: "Shoving, heaving, digging, sweating. A South African gun is taken from one position in the muddy terrain of Northern Italy and advanced to another to continue the good work of 'knocking the hell into the enemy'." *Photo: SANMMH*

The 'Two Types' created by Jon Jones (formerly of the Coldstream Guards) were caricatures of 'Desert Rat' officers. Dressed in an odd assortment of clothing, the 'Two Types' were always harking back to the desert days. The story of the Italian campaign would be incomplete without these cartoons. *Photo: The Springbok*

Located in the main square of Castiglione, the Outspan Club was a refuge from the mud and snow. In this public relations photograph the soldiers have their insignia blocked out as the enemy could find such information useful. *Photo: DODAR*

6th Division signs became even more common than the ubiquitous shrines. *Photo: Comune di Castiglione dei Pepoli*

Original caption read: "Painting signboards for the routes through Italy. Cpl P.G. Strydom (Vryburg), Cpl H.F. Hubbard (Cape Town), Sgt W.J. Walker (Bultfontein, OFS) busy on the job." *Photo: SANMMH*

The originators of 6th Division signboards had a sense of humour too. *Photo: DODAR*

A classic photo showing 6th Division men and machines in the main street of Castiglione which is the same today except that there are now decent pavements with big trees.
Photo: DODAR

Most civilians had been evacuated from forward areas but clearly there were still some women and children left in Castiglione. Note the icy pavement and the bereted soldier's gaze.
Photo: SANMMH

Tea and jokes at the Outspan, or perhaps a song sung—with a dose of irony—to the tune of Lili Marlene:

We're the D-Day Dodgers, out in Italy
Always on the vino
Always on the spree
Eighth Army scroungers
And their tanks
We live in Rome, among the Yanks
We're the D-Day Dodgers,
Way out in Italy

Photo: DODAR

Skiing South African style; Gnr Peter Johnston at left.
Photo: J. van Velden collection

At a special ski school, 29 South Africans trained in the art of winter warfare; white snowsuits were also issued to some infantry units.
Photo: DODAR

Gen W.H. Evered Poole attends a children's Christmas party.
Photo: SANMMH

A fighting patrol consisted of one platoon (three sections) under an officer. Ambush patrols numbered around 16 men (two sections). Reconnaissance patrols consisted of one section or sometimes just an officer and three other ranks.
Photo: SANMMH

Shovelling snow was a novelty for the South African boys.
Photo: DODAR

stage," wrote the author of the 7/23rd Medium Regiment war diary, "the odour is, to put it mildly, most offensive, and every effort is being made to dispose of the carcasses by burning. The smell of bad roast mule is, however, little improvement on that of plain decay."

Once the South Africans had settled in and cleaned up, they found that the village provided a few comforts. One could have a shave with a cutthroat razor in a barbershop, followed by a hot-towel compress. Added to this, a bath unit was set up in the bank, a prominent building in the village. The showers were installed inside the building, while at the back, a special vehicle holding a tank of water and an engine warmed the water. Because this was a South African bath unit, different showering times were allocated to officers, other ranks, Cape Corps and Indians. The boilers, disinfectors and staff in charge hailed from Johannesburg. A change of clothes was arranged for men who were living in the open and had no opportunity to wash or dry garments. A limited range of items was available for exchange: Angola shirts, woollen vests, woollen drawers, socks, towels and limited stocks of battle dress trousers.

An American army war dog platoon was attached to the division. It was known as the K-9s and comprised three sections, each with 24 dogs. The platoon was based next to the Witwatersrand Rifles/Regiment De la Rey's A echelon which was housed in a multi-storey monastery, opposite the cemetery, on the branch of the road leading to Bologna. The dogs were used in three capacities: to accompany patrols and alert them of any danger, as sentries or as messengers. They were also trained to warn of enemy infiltrations. Their training taught them not to bark in dangerous situations; rather, they would stiffen or prick up their ears. Although the dogs were particularly helpful in determining whether a house was occupied or empty, they couldn't be used in all situations: they got cold and restless during ambushes, and did not like the sound of artillery or mortars. The noise made by small-arms fire did not seem to worry them, however.

After the Battle of Catarelto, the west—where the Imperial Light Horse/Kimberley Regiment was based—became the primary area of focus. From Camugnano, a few miles west of Castiglione, the regiment started a series of ongoing patrols and skirmishes in open ground, made soft and muddy from the rain. It would be put through its toughest test thus far during the coming weeks. On 1 October 1944, B Company was ordered to move through the positions of A Company and occupy the village of Collina. At 1550 hours, this order was cancelled. The war diary records: "The company remains at the previous night's [elevated position] Pt 901. Private Erasmus C.F. 282518 accidentally shot himself in the feet at 1800 hours."

As part of the 12th Motorized Brigade, the Royal Natal Carbineers was still moving up to the front line on 1 October which was a sunny Sunday. It felt like summer and Hodgson thought of his father playing tennis on a spring day at 154 Buckingham Avenue, Craighall Park, Johannesburg:

> Lately we had a bad spell of wet and cold, but today is a perfect summer's day, not too hot but plenty of sunshine. I can just imagine you all at home today—I hope you did not knock too many covers off the balls this morning. This morning I went to a church service, and chatted to some fellows I had not seen for some time … It is now just after lunch and I am sitting in the sun writing. It is a perfect Sunday as it is the first one for some time when we have not been on the move.

The intention on 1 October was for the Royal Natal Carbineers to relieve the Imperial Light Horse/Kimberley Regiment from its position north of Camugnano. From Santomato, the Royal Natal Carbineers passed through Montale, Bagnolo and Coiano, described in the war diary as "diminutive villages which lie on the lower slopes of the foothills of the Apennines". From Coiano, which is today a suburb of Prato, the men turned north and away from the comparative warmth of the plains. The retreating daylight and heavy traffic volumes forced them to harbour for the night in a muddy field, 12 miles short of Castiglione at Montepiano. Permission was obtained to disregard blackout conditions and a hot meal was enjoyed by all.

The difference in the weather up in the mountains was immediately apparent. In heavy mist and cold and steady rain, the convoy pulled into Castiglione the next morning.

By 5 October, the Royal Natal Carbineers was installed in the shattered buildings of Camugnano, waiting for the order to relieve the Imperial Light Horse/Kimberley Regiment and take Monte Vigese. From his billet, Corporal Hodgson wrote to his mother:

> Since I last wrote the weather has taken a very nasty turn; so far this week, yesterday was the only day we saw the sun as it is overcast again today and it is raining like old boots again. By now everything is sopping wet and the whole countryside is inches deep in mud. When it cleared yesterday, we got a bit of a shock when we saw that the mountains to our left were covered in snow. Yesterday and today have been

> fairly warm, but Monday and Tuesday were a bit on the cold side. We have been lucky to have a house during this wet spell and all the time we have had a roaring fire going in the kitchen; also, a few of us slept in the kitchen as we found it by far the warmest room in the house. It has been lovely sitting around a big log fire while it has been raining. There is no break in the weather this afternoon but I think it'll brighten up yet!
>
> In my last letter to Dad I mentioned about my promotion to full corporal. It came as a very pleasant surprise to me; with the promotion go quite a few privileges, especially when we are out of the line or in a base camp. As I told Dad, for the time being don't address my letters with my new rank, as it must first be published in Part II orders. When that has taken place, I will let you know.
>
> Mum, I must still ask you for something more. Could you please send me a pair of warm gloves as I am sure I will need a pair when we get some snow? If it is possible could you send it by air mail, otherwise it will get here in the middle of winter and I could use them before then. The leather jacket will arrive just before we get the snow which falls in December. Dad says he has got a pair of gloves for me which are worn over the woollen ones, which will be just the thing as it will keep the wind and the wet out.

The Guards had reached Lagaro, the next town up Route 6620 after Castiglione, where Axelson found the brigade headquarters in an imposing building with a muddy driveway. The men had a roaring fire going and the smell of roasting chestnuts became ingrained in Axelson's memory of the place.

Following their costly encounter on Catarelto Ridge, the pipers of the Scots Guards played a lament in the town square at Castiglione. There was little space to march and countermarch as vehicles of the 11th South African Armoured Brigade filled the square.

For the entire month of October, the South African newspapers fixated on the "unattainable dream city of Bologna". Optimistic headlines kept the hopes of those at home high: "Fierce Fighting in Allied drive on Bologna" (*Rand Daily Mail*, 2 October), "Boks capture another town in Italy—Americans within 14 miles of Bologna" (*Rand Daily Mail*, 6 October), "5th Army guns pouring heavy-calibre shells into Bologna" (*The Star*, 7 October), "5th Army troops driving rapidly nearer to Bologna" (*The Star*, 9 October) and "Infantry drive steadily on Bologna" (*The Star*, 11 October).

Following the resumption of operations toward the end of August, the casualty rate among the armoured regiments was substantially lower than it had been during the advance to Florence. This was now an infantry war. An analysis of the casualties incurred by the 12th South African Motorized Brigade for the remainder of the year (see table overleaf) is rather enlightening. It must, however, be remembered that the Imperial Light Horse/Kimberley Regiment was now under the command of the 11th South African Armoured Brigade. Its casualties are therefore not reflected in the table:

12 SA Motorized Brigade casualties from the return to the line, up until the end of September[259]									
Unit	Killed			Wounded			Missing		
	Offrs	O/Rs	CCs	Offrs	O/Rs	CCs	Offrs	O/Rs	CCs
RNC	3	12			60	1			
FC/CTH	1	4			18			2	
WR/DLR	1	7	1	3	35				
RDLI	1			1	2				
Bde HQ		1							
TOTALS	5	24	1		115	1			
	30			120			2		

CCs: Cape Corps

Tuesday 3 October 1944 – Friday 13 October 1944: Camugnano

The weather was clear on 3 October, but toward night it started raining again. One of the platoons of the Imperial Light Horse/Kimberley Regiment faced a "fierce and determined attack by the enemy". One section was commanded by Private MacDonald after Corporal Hansen had been wounded by a grenade. The men were forced to withdraw when they had used up every round and grenade. A number of hand grenades failed to explode and it was later discovered that the rings had broken off, leaving the safety pin in place.

At 0030 hours, the gunners of the 1/6th Field Regiment laid down high explosive to contain the counter-attack on its infantry.

A steady trickle of replacements journeyed up from Alife via Arezzo by train to fill the ranks of the Imperial Light Horse/Kimberley Regiment, which already had many new faces. Axelson had been told that, of the 108 men who transferred from the 1/12th Light Anti-Aircraft Regiment after Rome, five became casualties before Florence. Other replacements only arrived in August and it was not easy for them to fit in or survive. Private A.I. Lourens describes how at Pt 826, his platoon sergeant ordered him to give his slit trench to a *nuweling* (newcomer) who was so shocked and shaky that he was incapable of

259 DODAR, WD, Box 598, Recording Officer, 12th South African Motorized Brigade, Report on Operations in the Italian Campaign for period August 44–May 45.

digging his own. "*Ek besef die kereltjie is in die diep kant ingegooi* (I realized that boy had been thrown in the deep end),"[260] he commented. Advanced divisional headquarters was, at present, just outside the village of Montepiano, between Vernio and Castiglione on Route 6620. Main division was based ten miles south of Montepiano with rear division just outside Prato. The headquarters and troops of 11th South African Armoured Brigade were housed in Camugnano, which was still being shelled from time to time. One battery of the 1/6th Field Regiment (14/18 Battery) was two miles south of Camugnano; the two other batteries were based less than a mile east with Monte Vigese looming in front of them. The gun positions of the 4/22nd Field Regiment were placed on the far left of the divisional front.[261]

The medium artillery, meanwhile, was deployed in the Setta River valley, north of Castiglione. It was difficult to lead the guns down the cobbled track from the main road, and one of them overturned.

From his observation post, the window of the officers' mess in Castiglione, the adjutant of the 7/23rd Medium Regiment spotted some enemy vehicles slinking along the road near Grizzana. With cries of delight, he promptly hurled 25 rounds at them, many of which fell in the target area. A report from the Guards mentioned that 20 dead Germans had been found in the area targeted by the previous day's shoot.

Monte Vigese, six miles northwest of Castiglione, is the highest point between Routes 64 and 6620. It is a rocky mass of 1,090 metres which rises steeply from the wooded, lower surrounding slopes. North of Vigese, and separated by a neck or saddle at 820 metres, is the equally impressive Montovolo, 912 metres high, on top of which is an ancient church—an ideal observation point. Even today, these are isolated locations. A track running along the eastern side passes through Matella, Cardeta and Torlai—the latter now consisting of nothing more than a single farmhouse—and through the neck between Montovolo and Monte Vigese.

The Imperial Light Horse/Kimberley Regiment was ordered to take Monte Vigese and a troop of Special Service Battalion tanks was given in support. The leading company rode on the back of tanks as far as Matella—or L'Amatella as it was then known—where a base was set up in a cluster of farm buildings. It had

260 *Springbok*, Journal of the South African Legion of South African Veterans, June 2008, p. 8

261 A Troop of the 1/6th Field Regiment was located at L691133.

already taken the troop ten days to travel from Montale through the mountains to Camugnano. From here to their objective, the saddle at Montovolo, it would be mainly cross-country on soggy ground.

On 3 October, a patrol from D Company reached Torlai—at the time, a complex of farm buildings on a spur extending out from the eastern slopes of Monte Vigese—after a clash at Cardeta. Although they found it vacant, the Germans attacked at 2300 hours during the dark and damp night. Being low on ammunition, the Imperial Light Horse/Kimberley Regiment platoon was forced to rejoin the rest of its company at Cardeta, a farm between Matella and Torlai. Artillery fire was called down on Torlai but the enemy now attacked C Company positions at Matella. The next day, B Company moved to Cardeta while 'Dog' Company moved forward to again try and capture Torlai. The plan was for No. 1 Platoon to take up position in a patch of bush on the left, while No. 2 Platoon advanced up a gully on the right. The attack began at 1135 hours. On the left, the platoon reached the patch of bush but was pinned down by grenades and small arms fire. The platoon in the gully on the right was heavily mortared and six soldiers were wounded. Private G.H. MacDonald did his best to help the injured under fire. A Spandau opened up on the stretcher party but was silenced by artillery fire. Two tanks now tried to go directly up the spur to Torlai but one shed a track and the other bogged down 300 yards short of the crest. The platoon in the gully tried to reach the tanks but, given their casualties, retreated to its company area where mortar shells continued to wreak havoc. The wounded were evacuated, under machine-gun fire, to the battalion headquarters, which was then also shelled.

The rain was still falling. Fresh ammunition was brought up by mules, again under fire. The Special Service Battalion troop commander, Lieutenant John Elvie MC and Bar, told his story to the historical recording officer:

> The gully separating the eminence on which my tank stood from Torlai was too steep to be traversed, so the two tanks had to work down the slope and around. As Cook's tank moved across, it came under most intense mortar fire which just about blotted out the whole accompanying infantry section. After battling for hours, both tanks stripped their tracks within a few yards of each other. They would never have got as far as they did, had not the drivers opened their hatches and disregarded the mortar fire. It was patently useless to try to get any more tanks up there.[262]

262 DODAR, UWH, Box 140, Statement by Lieutenant John Elvie MC and Bar, Special Service Battalion.

A new replacement, 20-year-old Private Karl Wickee, was one of the six wounded men. When setting out for Torlai, his company had plodded past the gun positions of A Troop (1/6th Field Regiment), which were well forward—east of Camugnano, a few thousand yards from Monte Vigese—at an elevation of 831 metres. Among them, Wickee recognized the familiar face of Stephen Bourhill who had been a year ahead of him at St John's College, Johannesburg. "I know I'm going to get it," he told Bourhill, his face white as a sheet. Private Wickee had been opening batsman for the 1st XI and won his full colours for cricket in 1941. His service record reveals that he was five foot five inches tall, and also that he had been thrown into the fray with unseemly haste. He had only joined up in February 1944 and had arrived in Italy in August, while the division was at rest in Siena.

Experience is a major factor where fear is concerned. In his baptism of fire, a soldier's anxiety levels are raised to heights seldom repeated.[263] Karl Wickee's legs felt like lead under the weight of fear. He was carrying another burden too: the small pack, miniature pick or shovel, two sand bags and webbing with up to 200 rounds of ammunition, two hand grenades, two water bottles, one day's rations and perhaps some extra magazines for one of the nine Bren guns in the company. Although the Imperial Light Horse/Kimberley Regiment had been in action throughout September, this was the first time that some of the replacements were to face SS troops on the rampage. The fear experienced by a 'sprog' was visible to war journalist Alan Moorhead: "I have seen soldiers going up to the front line for the first time, and they were afraid ... This you could read clearly enough from the dread in their faces."[264] Wickee was carried into the advanced dressing station of 19 South African Field Ambulance at 1930 hours on 4 October. His wound was described on his field medical card:

> Mortar fin and 4 inches of bomb shaft impacted into thigh. Upper 1/3 of Rt femur shattered and driven through skin of medial side of thigh. Massive tissue damage of upper half of thigh—muscles lacerated—femoral artery and vein torn across but not bleeding much.

The doctor decided on a guillotine amputation just below the pubic bone, stating for the record that the patient would not have survived the journey

---

263 E. Dinter, *Hero or coward*, p. 36.

264 A. Moorehead, *Eclipse*, p. 61.

to the rear over farm tracks. However, the shock was too great and Wickee's bleeding could not be staunched. Although his treatment was prioritized, the medics were unable to save him. He died at 0130 hours on 5 October.

Bourhill was stunned when he saw that one of the fresh graves bore Wickee's name on the wooden cross. Buried alongside him were 20-year-old Private A.F. Nelson from Pretoria and Lieutenant H.V. Burrough. They were killed by one mortar bomb on 4 October outside the B Company headquarters. Harry Burrough was a 31-year-old veteran who, a few days previously, had survived a furious hand-to-hand encounter on a patrol, which resulted in six enemy dead and 12 prisoners.

After dark on 4 October, D Company, Imperial Light Horse/Kimberley Regiment was ordered to protect the tanks and hang on at all costs. No. 1 Platoon was still in the patch of bush to the west of Torlai. At 0200 hours, it heard the sound of the enemy forming up for a counter-attack. It was later learned that this attack was made by a 120-strong contingent of the 36th Panzergrenadier Regiment. According to Elvie, the enemy consisted of two SS companies. His personal account of the night's events continues:

> An infantry section was sent out to cover the tanks, which could barely fire at all, owing to the angle at which they had settled into the mud. The infantry platoon meanwhile lodged itself on Torlai. The situation appeared all right until at last light, the position of Torlai was attacked by two companies of SS, who after a hell of a battle, threw off the two platoons of 'Dog' Coy. A few of them got back. I could do nothing about it in my position, except to warn the other tanks to be prepared to be attacked. Nothing happened through the night but once our own infantry had been withdrawn, I heavily shelled Torlai with my own tank. At first light, the SS put in an attack on the two tanks which did what little firing they could in their own defence, supported by the infantry section who climbed underneath the tanks. Whatever Brownings they could not use, the tank crews gave to the infantry. I fired my Browning and 75, the former covered more ground, being most effective. The attack was driven off. The enemy shelled, rocketed, bazook'd and mortared us all the time. There were no anti-tank guns, probably because it was too high and too muddy to get them up. The rockets were perhaps the worst, because you could hear and see them coming at you, apparently quite slowly, to burst with a shattering concussion. Mortar bombs, if they hit you right, are capable of damaging the engine, of wounding personnel through the vents, and giving concussed headaches. We were never directly hit although the shelling kept up all day.[265]

[265] DODAR, WD, Box 598, Recording Officer, Interview with Lieutenant John Elvie MC and Bar, C Squadron, Special Service Battalion, taken by Lieutenant R.V. Davis.

The night attack came in from the neck near Montovolo and was directed mainly against No. 2 Platoon, which comprised approximately 20 men. They were forced from the houses and hand-to-hand fighting ensued. An incendiary set a hayrick on fire and the defenders were illuminated against the night sky, in full view of the German machine-gunners higher up on Monte Vigese. The platoons repeatedly called for artillery support, which was forthcoming until communication with headquarters was lost. The fight in the buildings had been a close-quarter one involving hand grenades and Tommy guns. Both platoons, having joined up and being low on ammunition, were forced to withdraw to a ridge 100 yards to the south of the buildings. Private O.M. Coetzee was caught by his webbing during the withdrawal but he managed to escape by slipping out of it. Eventually, all except one lone Bren-gunner began withdrawing to Cardeta. In a self-sacrificing act which allowed his platoon to withdraw, Private Francis Joseph took a Bren gun from a dead comrade and, without saying a word, walked out in the direction of the Germans, took up a position behind a tree and held off the attack. The Imperial Light Horse/ Kimberley Regiment war diary reads: "After the withdrawal had been completed, a Bren was still heard firing from the direction of the trees and there was the occasional burst of a grenade."

A roll call in Cardeta revealed that, during the night, the two platoons had lost two killed and 21 wounded. A further 19 were missing. A patrol to the edge of Torlai the next morning found the bodies of four of the missing. The first bodies found were those of Private J. Lessels, Private F.G. du Preez and Sergeant G.W. Friedman. Finally, Private F.M. Joseph "was found next to his Bren and apparently it was he who had been firing to the end".[266] Francis Joseph was a motor mechanic from the Middleburg–Witbank area, recently divorced. His record shows that he was a rebellious type, having had a few brushes with the (military) law during his army career. He had reverted from lance-corporal to the rank of trooper during the amalgamation phase in October 1943. His ex-wife was his only next-of-kin. Joseph received no official recognition for his actions, possibly because there were no witnesses; the section corporal had already been evacuated. As previously mentioned, Joseph had been involved in a dramatic escape from the Germans after being captured at Monte Pozzo del Bagno on 15 September.

266 DODAR, WD, Box 635, Imperial Light Horse/Kimberley Regiment, File B8 60; DODAR, WD, Box 598, Recording Officer, Narrative, 22/8/1944–22/2/1945.

It was impossible to move the tanks out of Torlai. Orders were for the crews to 'brew' them if necessary and try to escape on foot. However, the crews sat tight. Elvie had to run across to the infantry command post on two occasions. He was awarded the Military Cross for these actions.

Further attacks were repulsed throughout the next day, 5 October, and into the night. 'Dog' Company had been replaced by 'Alpha' Company by this time. A two-man patrol finally reported that the Germans had gone, but had left 78 graves at Torlai.

The summit of Monte Vigese was still in German hands. It was now up to the Royal Natal Carbineers to dislodge them. At 0530 hours on 6 October, one platoon of A Company began climbing up the steepest and most direct route while another worked its way around the 'waist' of the mountain. Partly because of the heavy mist, and because there had been no preparatory artillery bombardment, the Germans were taken by surprise and the command post captured. It was now possible for A Company, Royal Natal Carbineers to overlook the "troublesome saddle" and cut off access to Montovolo. Another battle was avoided through this action; a battle for Montovolo, in which the 12th-century church would undoubtedly have been destroyed. A group of around 40 Germans, who were manning machine-gun and mortar positions on this strategically valuable saddle, made for the greater security of their lines west of the river. Meanwhile, B Company, Royal Natal Carbineers set off from Greglio to take Vigo, working around the western side of the mountain and overrunning enemy positions en route. One platoon cleared the village while another provided covering fire from the slopes of Monte Vigese. The enemy moved back and dug in at Vigo Rock, a prominent outcrop, where another historic church is found. Only one Carbineer was killed in the operation.

Hodgson wrote to his father shortly after this action. As usual, he discussed the weather and the progress of the war but made no mention of the mighty Monte Vigese. Nor did he tell of his company having captured Vigo:

> The all-out offensive to break old Jerry once and for all before winter seems to be going on very well. The big bomber offensive that seems to have started is not going to give him much peace on the home front. As for his famous Gothic Line, I think it is more or less a thing of the past as far as a line is concerned. Mind you, the weather is going to form a stiff obstacle to our rate of progress here. So far this month we have had two sunny days when it has not rained all day. The rate of our progress, I don't think, will have any direct bearing on the early close of the war. The battle

> here, I think, is just to drain his resources as much as possible, and I think we are doing that very effectively.

By 6 October, Monte Vigese and the village of Vigo were secure. Advanced tactical headquarters, known as Tic-Tac, was established in a ramshackle old house in Vigo. Staff and equipment for this type of headquarters were carried exclusively in Jeeps, as was necessary in mountainous areas.

There was already snow on the higher peaks of the Apennines and it was cold. The morning of 7 October had dawned clear and sunny but it rained again later in the day. Artillery shells were in short supply at this time and each gun was limited to 15 rounds per day. Nevertheless, a 'murder' by 64 guns made sure that Collina was taken at 1400 hours on 7 October 1944. Patrols by the Imperial Light Horse/Kimberley Regiment found the Montovolo massif clear, and from here there was a clear view of all the challenging peaks which lay ahead.

The plan on 8 October was for the 1/6th Field Regiment to move across to Ripoli on Route 6620. The gunners began digging their 25-pounders out of the mud, which was at least a foot deep. Some guns reached the road, then received the order to stand fast. After another change of plan, the regiment found itself spread out and unable to move back to its original positions. Only one gun remained in its original place, as it was stuck in the mud. It was a miserable day but the arrival of 40-foot-square tarpaulins for the subsections helped lift spirits. A reconnaissance party had moved to the new area. By this time, regimental headquarters had ousted the Carabinieri from their barracks at Ripoli, and from here they maintained contact with the others by a weak radio link. The 166th Newfoundland Regiment did everything possible to fill the void. By 1430 hours, seven guns were back on their platforms, firing in support of a Royal Natal Carbineers patrol conducting a reconnaissance of Stanco village. It would be five more days before the 25-pounder batteries moved back through Castiglione to where the 7/23rd Medium Regiment was fighting a second war against the mud in the Setta valley:

> Our gun positions are now thoroughly waterlogged and GPOs have been scrounging for timber to construct wooden platforms to support the trail legs and to prevent the guns from disappearing altogether. There have been many learned discussions by expert miners in the regiment as to the construction of these 'mat packs'.[267]

[267] DODAR, WD, Box 631, 7/23 Medium Regiment, 9/10/1944.

A report in *The Star* of 10 October told of roads which had become "furrows of mud" and gave the bare facts regarding recent movements—always forward. "Springbok troops in a sticky advance have surmounted more ridges in the face of slight enemy resistance and other troops operating with the South Africans made good headway on Saturday to reach the village of Stanco about four and a half miles northeast of Monte Vigese," read one article.

The next objectives were Monte Stanco and, ultimately, Monte Salvaro (Pt 826). Stanco was approached by way of a ridge running from Monte Vigese through Collina. In 1944, the slopes of Monte Stanco were partly cultivated and partly scrub. On the southern slopes were some apple and pear orchards. On the northern slopes, where the enemy was dug in, were belts of chestnut trees. There was (and still is) a cross on top of the knoll—Pt 719. Casa Forlino is a hamlet nestling below, and at the time there was a house on the eastern spur of the hill—Pt 650. The village of Stanco was of no tactical importance, but the high ground between Grizzana and Stanco dominated the roads and the opposing 16th SS Division were told to hold fast.

The track was impassable even for Jeeps. From their assembly point at Matella, the Indian battalion (4/13th Frontier Force Rifles) marched to Stanco and their forming-up position at Collina, each man carrying 200 rounds of ammunition, a pack and a blanket. Each company was allocated five ammunition mules. Battalion headquarters was established at Prada where the companies arrived at 2000 hours, after 14 hours of marching. In pouring rain on 8 October, the first attack by the Frontier Force Rifles succeeded in reaching the top of Monte Stanco. However, the regiment was almost surrounded by a counter-attack coming out of the cover of a deep wooded gully running down to the Reno River on the southwestern side. Communications broke down between Stanco and headquarters, so that the only means of conveying information was by using runners. Little was therefore known of the battle, except for the rate of firing and the wounded, who started coming in at 0700 hours. The mules bringing up ammunition supplies were dispersed and the battalion Jeeps were bogged down on the track between Collina and Stanco. Nonetheless, the Frontier Force Rifles managed to cut its way out to the east through Casa Forlino, having suffered a number of casualties—some of whom crawled in 24 hours later. Two days later, another battalion-strength attack was launched at Monte Stanco, this time by the Royal Natal Carbineers. Starting at

0330 hours, it passed through B Company headquarters at Stanco di Sopra and on to Casa Forlino where D Company had established its headquarters. Forlino is to the right of Stanco, overlooking the road to Grizzana. The summit of Monte Stanco was reached by 0630 hours.

At 0840 hours, it was reported that the enemy was forming up just southwest of Grizzana. Hodgson remembers that "drove after drove of Germans came up the ridge; they seemed to be doped". They were certainly fanatical in their disregard for casualties and came in shouting "Heil Hitler!", "Fuhrer!" and "Fatherland!"

Artillery and mortar fire was brought down on them to good effect but they counter-attacked with sufficient strength to drive the Royal Natal Carbineers off the top; Lieutenant Victor Chapman's platoon was overrun and he was killed. Lieutenant Fraser, a former member of an anti-aircraft unit who had joined the Carbineers for training, took over. He valiantly tried to hold the ground but was also killed. He was a 41-year-old married man from Cathcart.

Despite having A and C Companies in reserve, Major Gallimore, in charge of B Company, reported at 1400 hours that he was not happy with his situation. The order was given to withdraw. The two companies managed to withdraw under the covering fire from the 1/6th Field Regiment which had been active all day, save for a few minutes. Artillery Captain H.T. Going went in with B Company, Royal Natal Carbineers. When the counter-attacking Germans were only 300 yards away, he called in a heavy concentration on his own position, destroying his portable radio in the process.

One platoon from C Company was left behind in the house at Forlino to cover the withdrawal. In what the Royal Natal Carbineers war diary describes as a "splendid fight", it too managed to pull out with the enemy on its heels. The platoon incurred eleven casualties, all of whom were brought to the high ground south of Stanco. Captain Jacko Edmonds stayed until the last and carried a wounded man with him when he finally withdrew. Captains Going and Edmonds were awarded the American Silver Star for the day's work. The headquarters at Stanco di Sopra was abandoned, leaving a portable wireless and Major Gallimore's Jeep concealed nearby.

The safe withdrawal was made possible thanks to people like Private G.C. Sutton, a 19-year-old from Howick, who "refused to withdraw and kept firing his Bren until a Jerry coming from the side cut his Bren in half with a burst and killed Sutton with another burst".[268] Another man who gave his life for his friends was Corporal John Thorp of Mooi River, who went down using his rifle as a club.

It was not often that a unit of the 6th South African Armoured Division was forced to retreat. Even today, Hodgson has not forgotten that "it was an indescribably bad feeling". The casualties as listed in the regimental war diary on 10 October were as follows: "… 10 killed in action including three officers (Captain Fitzgerald, Lieutenants Chapman and Fraser), 31 wounded and two missing believed killed, six missing believed wounded, two missing, five wounded (remained on duty)."

One of the lessons learned from these first two attempts was that it was a tactic of the 16th SS Division—and also of the Allies when defending a hill—to hold a feature with light forces which withdraw when attacked and then counter-attack with the main forces which remained unobserved on reverse slopes. This reduced the number of troops exposed to shelling. The thickly wooded reverse slopes of Monte Stanco were ideal for this tactic. Realizing that some mistakes had been made and that the task was too big for any single battalion, the division planned the biggest set-piece attack to be carried out by the South Africans in Italy thus far. It was now the turn of the Witwatersrand Rifles/Regiment De la Rey to take Monte Stanco while the First City/Cape Town Highlanders was to take Pt 602, a feature one kilometre to the east. No. 3 Platoon, A Company of the Witwatersrand Rifles/Regiment De la Rey had been billeted at Figline, near Prato, from 1 October for a rest, or as Lionel Wulfsohn put it, "being fattened up". The platoon became close to the Italian family that hosted them during their stay at Figline, especially Alberto, the "lovable, friendly," 80-year-old patriarch.[269]

Their short acquaintance ended on 10 October when the battalion was rushed through Castiglione and then west to Camugnano. Vehicles travelling in this direction were stopped by the military police to ensure that passengers were wearing their greatcoats. For many, the overriding memories of this place are of mist, rain, mud and cold. From there, it was an eerie ten-mile, 14-hour

[268] DODAR, UWH, Box 140, Letter from Captain H.H.H. Biermann, military observer attached to the 12th South African Motorized Brigade, to the war correspondent Harry O'Connor, 17/10/1944.

[269] L.M. Wulfsohn, unpublished memoirs; Figline which is close to Prato, just east of Montemurlo.

walk through the mist along a slippery Jeep track. With almost zero visibility, the surrounding countryside still remains *terra incognita* to most of the men who passed by that day.

Some weeks after the battle, Lieutenant-Colonel Duncan, a qualified lawyer and commanding officer of the First City/Cape Town Highlanders, remarked to Axelson, the historical recording officer, that the length of the approach march was a factor which should not be forgotten when writing the history of Monte Stanco. Duncan's battalion went without proper sleep for three days. Duncan would be killed at Monte Sole in April 1945.

In the opinion of Major Williams, the officer commanding C Company, Witwateresrand Rifles/Regiment De la Rey, the most difficult thing about Stanco was the broken ground over which the men had to climb in the darkness of the early morning. The extensive fortifications on top of the feature were apparently undermanned. There was only a one-way track for taking up supplies and bringing back the wounded.

It passed through Collina, described as a tiny hamlet of narrow slippery streets, cottages with gaping roofs, and barns and yards which, in the words of Captain G. Beale of the artillery, "were smelling to high heaven of wet straw, fowls and manure".[270]

Five thousand mortar bombs had been allocated to the Royal Durban Light Infantry for the attack and exploitation, much of which was stored in the hamlet. When a shell hit the dump, 165 mortar bombs exploded, resulting in a big fire and two killed, including 19-year-old, six-foot-two-inch-tall Private H.T. Woolmore.[271] Woolmore was the second member of his family to be killed in the campaign.

After the usual artillery bombardment and dummy barrage, the 1/6th Field Regiment fired 3,000 rounds preliminary to the assault. Prisoners later reported that nowhere previously, even in Russia, had they experienced such accurate and concentrated artillery fire. A diversionary attack was also staged at 0230 hours by the 24th Guards Brigade in the vicinity of Grizzana Station. Supported by tanks, this attack apparently caused the enemy some concern, although the

---

270 N. Orpen, *Victory in Italy*, p. 224; Collina today has been neatly restored—and there is still a hay barn in the centre.

271 Denis Woolmore was killed on 15 June at Orvieto with the Pretoria Regiment and is buried at Bolsena—both were from Nkandla in Zululand but not from the same parents.

station was in fact secured by the Scots Guards. At 0445 hours on Friday 13 October, as A Company Witwatersrand Rifles/Regiment De la Rey crossed the start line, a mortar shell killed five and wounded eight members of 3 Platoon. Corporal Lionel Wulfsohn was a section leader and wrote in his memoirs:

> I was talking to Hans van der Berg [Private S.J. van den Berg] from South West Africa, who had joined us that morning from the Vickers platoon as a last-minute volunteer re-enforcement. I asked him in Afrikaans—"*Hoekom dra jy nie jou blik hoed nie?*" [Why are you not wearing your tin hat?] He replied, "*Ek glo nie aan daardie kak nie.*"[I don't believe in that shit.] Those were the last words Hans would say in his lifetime. My head was spinning furiously, and I thought I had fainted as I was lying on the ground. I eventually lifted my head up and saw that [van den Berg] had slumped to the ground. I tried to get up and walk over to him, but my legs were not working. I then realized for the first time that I had been wounded.

The remainder of A Company had to scramble through craters and up steep cliffs with bushes tugging at their equipment, to reach the top. According to Major Burger, 23 men were killed. Other sources put the number of Witwatersrand Rifles/Regiment De la Rey deaths at 28. This discrepancy can be put down to those who later died of wounds.

One of the casualties was Douglas Moffatt, the second St John's boy to die in the space of a week, and it did not take long for the news to reach school friends in other regiments via bush telegraph. The account given by Lieutenant P.J. Dreyer, who commanded a platoon in D Company of the Witwatersrand Rifles/Regiment De la Rey, was particularly gritty:

> Pte Newmark was our most serious casualty. Cpl Perrin took me to him, and it was apparent that he was dying. He was wounded in the back and kidneys. He asked for morphine, but we could not supply it before he died. I stood beside him, remembering his excited plans for his life after the war was over and the recollections of his family. He became a symbol of all who died on the battlefield, suddenly struck down in the prime of life. I collectively mourned for them all ... Pte Reid was hit by German shellfire. It was a terrible sight. His chest had been totally shattered and his legs and arms grotesquely jutted out from his body. His body had been propelled some 50 metres through the air. Cpl Perrin located the corpse and showed it to me. The tragedy of the situation was compounded by the fact that Reid's older brother had also been killed at the Italian front. His twin brother was repatriated to the Union.[272]

272 S. Monick, *A bugle calls*, pp. 418–419; The 19-yearold Private J.W. Reid was from Grahamstown; Private G.B. Newmark was 20 years' old and from Caledon.

The First City/Cape Town Highlanders faced fanatical resistance on Pt 650. According to Murray, 12 were killed while the enemy dead were estimated at more than a hundred. One account written shortly after the battle puts the number of bodies counted at eighty. Apparently, the enemy showed no respect for the Red Cross and one stretcher party was badly shot up.

Lieutenant H. Ian Simson was one of three brothers wearing red tabs. One brother had been wounded and another was taken as a POW for six years. Simson himself had already served in the desert with the Transvaal Scottish, been captured and then released. After a short visit home to his mother in Johannesburg, he rejoined the First City/Cape Town Highlanders and went to Italy with a draft of reinforcements. His humorous, weather-beaten face obviously appealed to photographers and reporters as he was pictured in the newspapers at least twice. From Pt 650, his platoon was mown down by Spandau fire and Simson himself was killed. Sergeant J. Winstanley took command of the remaining men and, despite being wounded, led a charge on the machine-gun post, securing the position and thereby earning the Distinguished Conduct Medal.

Artillery observation posts were having a field day. On one occasion, a German officer was observed in what appeared to be a headquarters building, taking a roll call of survivors. When the tally reached 50, a barrage was called down on the house.

The Germans had a company headquarters on the northeast side of Monte Stanco, protected by a number of machine guns. Using a projectile infantry anti-tank gun, Corporal W.A. Betts put three rounds through the wall of one of the houses. A Bren gunner then fired through the holes, eliminating the Spandaus. Reports differ on the number of prisoners taken, recording either three or 14. Williams recalls that at this stage of the battle, "there was a great deal of close-quarter fighting, mainly because Jerry kept on firing until you got to him".[273]

Those recognized for bravery at Monte Stanco included Captain P.T. Ellis and Bombadier B.A. Rademan of the 1/6th Field Regiment for their work at the observation posts, as well as the Witwatersrand Rifles/Regiment De la Rey chaplain, Captain M.D.V. 'Doempie' Cloete. According to the citation for his Military Cross, the padre "worked incessantly throughout the entire day

[273] DODAR, UWH, Box 140, Statement by Major Williams Officer Commanding C Company Witwatersrand Rifles/Regiment De la Rey.

under shellfire and snipers, dragging wounded from highly dangerous areas, organizing Jeep ambulances, keeping the stretcher bearers going with his superb example of unflagging energy and dauntless courage."[274]

Captain Cloete gave the wounded swigs of brandy and coffee while waiting for the stretcher bearers who, according to Wulfsohn, were not fearless but knew their jobs and stayed with the men.

Corporal S. Fielies and Corporal W. Cloete, both Cape Corps stretcher bearers who had rendered first aid and carried numerous men to safety under intense fire, would be decorated with the Military Medal at a parade on 4 December 1944. Cloete would be wounded at the Battle of Monte Sole in April 1945, where a sniper's bullet entered his left eye and exited the right. He was permanently blinded at the age of 24 and became an expert basket-maker for the rest of his working life.[275]

Major Gallimore's Jeep could now be recovered, along with the bodies of the Carbineers and Indians who had been killed some days before. The author of the 7/23rd Medium Regiment war diary commented on the role of the artillery in the battle: "The Divisional Artillery Fire Plan, excellently planned, timed to the second and carried out with great weight of shell—over 10,000 shells being fired during the morning on concentrations, counter-battery and deception plan—together with the good work of our heavy mortars must have shaken the German defenders of Stanco out of their mistaken belief in the invincibility of the Fuhrer and the Reich. During the afternoon, prisoners were brought in and were in most cases 'slaphappy' mental cases."

Saturday 14 October 1944 – Thursday 26 October 1944: Lagaro

Having finished its work at Camugnano, it took ten hours for the 1/6th Field Regiment to pack up and travel to its new position on a soccer field at Lagaro, seven miles beyond Castiglione, close to the point where the Brasimone River joins the Setta River. Stragglers arrived the next day after spending a night on the road.[276] The Rhodesian battery was positioned slightly farther forward and to the right at Ripoli. This position would become almost inaccessible after winter

[274] L.M. Wulfsohn, *'Doempie' Cloete: a legend in his own lifetime*, p. 4.

[275] I. Gleeson, *The unknown force*, pp. 249–250.

[276] A Troop 1/6th Field Regiment was positioned at L744185 which is where the sports fields of Lagaro are today.

set in and the battery remained up on the high ground for the duration of the season. The headquarters of the 1/6th Field Regiment were also ensconced for the winter in the old Carabinieri barracks at Lagaro, behind the western slope of the Setta River, across from Ripoli. Main divisional headquarters was also based at Lagaro during the winter, while rear division headquarters was at Castiglione.

On the morning of 14 October, a reconnaissance party comprising four men from the Witwatersrand Rifles/Regiment De la Rey set out to ascertain whether some buildings on the flats beyond Monte Stanco were clear of the enemy. They found one German in a building and took him prisoner before they saw three more running about 300 yards away from them. They gave chase, in spite of their instructions to do nothing more than conduct reconnaissance. Williams gave a contemporary account of what followed:

> The Jerries ran into a barn and closed the door. Our fellows couldn't get in and shouted to the Jerries to come out, but there was no reply. Then they let fly with a Tommy gun, and then climbed up and threw a grenade through the window. The Jerries promptly surrendered. As the patrol was at about 2,000 yards forward, and had these prisoners, they couldn't do much more exploiting, so returned. One prisoner was an arrogant Nazi with an Iron Cross first class—won at Cassino. He hadn't repeated his boldness this time.[277]

The leader of this patrol, Corporal W.J. Cottam, a 25-year-old from Krugersdorp, was awarded the American Bronze Star. However, he did not live to receive it as he was accidentally killed at the end of the rest period at Lucca on 4 April 1945.

After spending two days among the detritus on top of Monte Stanco, the Witwatersrand Rifles/Regiment De la Rey was relieved on 15 October by Combat Command Charlie, a composite force consisting of approximately one infantry company each from the Prince Alfred's Guard, Special Service Battalion, Natal Mounted Rifles/South African Air Force and the 1/11th Anti-Tank Regiment. The 1/12th Light Anti-Aircraft Regiment, Pretoria Regiment (Princess Alice's Own) and Royal Durban Light Infantry subsequently also became part of this new 'dismounted' formation. Once the First City/Cape Town Highlanders reported Grizzana clear of the enemy at 2435 hours on 14 October, and with Veggio in the hands of the Guards, it was possible for

[277] DODAR, UWH, Box 140, Statement by Major Williams Officer Commanding C Company Witwatersrand Rifles/Regiment De la Rey.

the engineers to open up the road between Pian di Setta on Route 6620 and Grizzana, known for its treacherous twists and heavy shelling.

A SAPA war correspondent reported in *The Star* of 17 October that the chief activity in the South African sector over the past 24 hours focused on deep-penetration patrols into the high ground from the newly captured village of Grizzana. The patrols did not make any major contact but the village and infantry positions came under heavy mortar fire. Some civilians stayed on in the village, despite the daily shelling and mortaring. The First City/Cape Town Highlanders battalion headquarters was established at Grizzana. This was "an unhappy sojourn during which it received continued and particular attention from the heavy calibre guns of the enemy".[278] Grizzana was also the tactical headquarters of the Royal Natal Carbineers. It was here that Captain H.H.H. Biermann, a military observer, was billeted. In a letter to his friend, war correspondent Harry O'Connor, Biermann estimated that 600 Germans were killed, wounded or captured in the recent battles:

> Every house in Grizzana bears traces of the Stanco battle casualties—blood, dressings and what not in almost every room, and the Ities report that a good 300 wounded Jerries were evacuated from Grizzana on Friday night and [Saturday]. On Stanco itself, according to the fellows who went up on it on Saturday morning to collect our dead and recover equipment left there on Tuesday's withdrawal, the carnage was worse than anything they had seen in the campaign.

Three thousand yards away from the village of Stanco, dominating its view, is the steep, rocky feature of Monte Pezza. Grizzana is only a quarter of a mile from the mountain, the summit of which was Pt 748. Close to Grizzana, on the western side, is the village of Campiaro. The plan was for the First City/Cape Town Highlanders to threaten Campiaro while the Royal Natal Carbineers would ascend the eastern side.

The Royal Durban Light Infantry and tanks of the Prince Alfred's Guard were in support. For once, B Company, Royal Natal Carbineers would not be involved, and on 16 October, the day before the battle, Hodgson found time to write to his father:

278 L.G. Murray, *First City/Cape Town Highlanders in the Italian Campaign: a short history: 1943–1945*, p. 48.

> As you have no doubt seen in the papers, the weather this month has not been at all good. This month however is a bit of an exaggeration as for the past five days the weather has been very good, but I am sorry to say that it has broken again. Outside it is pouring at the moment and it looks as if it may set in for a little while. It is a pity as the mud had just about dried up and things could get about quite quickly, but with this new spot of rain it will be turned into mud again.
>
> The news is going ahead in leaps and bounds again and it looks as if there is every chance that we will still be able to get this war over before the winter sets in properly. As you say, there is no chance of my being home by Christmas, but I hope it will be shortly afterwards.

Because the terrain was unsuited to tanks, some members of the Prince Alfred's Guard were asked to act as muleteers, taking in supplies to the infantry and escorting out the prisoners. In fact, the slopes of Monte Pezza also proved too steep and the shelling too intense for mules, so the dismounted tank crews of the Prince Alfred's Guard had to carry up water and other necessities too.

Having walked up from Lagaro, the Prince Alfred's Guard porters arrived in Grizzana on 16 October. Trooper Brian Ambler described the conditions as "misty with a light drizzle". As they stood around at the entrance to the town waiting for orders, the men were "cold, miserable and depressed". Outside the church, on a stretcher, was the body of a dead infantry officer. The only infantry officer to be killed on this day was 22-year-old Lieutenant J.M. Els of the Witwatersrand Rifles/Regiment De la Rey, who hailed from Woluterskop near Brits. Six well-placed shells had landed in the C and D Company areas, and an ensuing tree burst killed Els along with Lance-Corporal G.J. Watkins. Seven others were wounded, including two officers.

On 18 October, the Witwatersrand Rifles/Regiment De la Rey lost Captain G.L. Thomson and 24-year-old Sergeant A.A. Bassingthwaighte while conducting reconnaissance in the Royal Natal Carbineers' area. Thomson, who came from Oudtshoorn, had been husband to Gladys, while Bassingthwaighte was the cousin of Private R.E.V. Bassingthwaighte, also from Windhoek, who had been killed with the Witwatersrand Rifles/Regiment De la Rey on 30 July.

In his book, *Italy's sorrow*, James Holland quotes Kendal Brooke, a lieutenant in the Carbineers who was present on Monte Pezza when a Witwatersrand Rifles/Regiment De la Rey officer was killed by a 5.5 shell which fell short. The men had been under a ledge on the southern slopes, safe from enemy fire, at the time. Lieutenant Brooke had been on the same cadet course as the unnamed officer (probably Thomson).[279] All the small district roads were controlled by military police as only one-way traffic was possible. From his *casa* at Poggio, just above Grizzana, Biermann had some interesting views over the valleys and *kloofs* when there was no mist. He watched Jeeps running the gauntlet under shelling down the lateral road to Route 6620—the 'Mad Mile'—and could see the action on the hills in front of him:

> It started raining this morning and you can imagine what it is like right now, especially for the chaps on the hills in front of us. They are being fed by mule trains, and are living and sleeping in slitties in this bloody mud and rain.[280]

Monte Pezza cost the Royal Natal Carbineers almost as many casualties as had their abortive assault on Monte Stanco: six killed and 13 wounded. However, the regiment had reached its objectives by late afternoon on 17 October.

Walter Hain described Monte Pezza as "lousiest pozzie I was in". Slit trenches on the side of the hill had reached only six inches deep when the diggers struck rock.[281] The Royal Natal Carbineers faced hostile shelling once they reached the summit. It continued to wreak havoc until they were withdrawn a week later. The divisional artillery did what they could in the way of counter-battery and supported the Witwatersrand Rifles/Regiment De la Rey in its advance to Pt 806. In an article titled "New advance by Springboks in Italy", a SAPA correspondent correctly described the battle of Monte Pezza as a stepping stone on the way to Monte Salvaro, but gave no details of the bitter struggle, nor mention of the death raining down.[282]

Nevertheless, the news was enough for Mrs Hodgson to express her fears to her son. When he had time to write some weeks later, John did his best to reassure his mother:

> In your last letter No 103, you appear to be a bit worried about me, but I can assure you that there is simply no need for that at all, as I am perfectly well and full of beans

279 J. Holland, *Italy's sorrow: a year of war 1944–45*, p. 411.

280 DODAR, UWH, Box 140. Letter from Captain H.H.H. Biermann, military observer attached to 12th South African Motorized Brigade to the war correspondent Harry O'Connor, 17/10/1944.

281 G.B. Hobbs, *From Sicily the Alps*, p. 246; Walter Hain is the father of Peter Hain, the anti-apartheid activist and later member of the British parliament.

282 *Rand Daily Mail*, New advance by Springboks in Italy, 19/10/1944.

> and I think I can say that I am about one of the happiest around here. That does not mean that I don't want to come home. I have just explained that position, but as we're here, because we're here—sort of stunt, there is no need to go round with a long face, is my way of looking at it. If we are landed here as we are, we must make the best of it, which is not nearly as bad as a lot make out. As for the newspapers, they really annoy me as there is so much exaggeration in them—the utter nonsense in them most of the time gets my goat (and tell Diana I won't milk it!!) ... Don't you worry now; it won't be too long before we will all be home again. We must just wait for the spring and then the Russians and the forces from France will soon finish it off. I will be writing to you again soon.

On the map, Monte Salvaro looks like a figure of eight with broad northern and southern sections and a narrow waist. The peak of the southern section is 806 metres high while the northern section rises to 826 metres—the highest point between Vigese and Bologna. The waist, or saddle, is at a height of 778 metres, relatively flat in places with a ridge on the right. Scrub- and bush-covered, the shell-torn slopes today are thickly wooded. The small plateau area is mostly open and was apparently a cultivated field at the time of the battle. Thickly wooded areas had been made bleak and barren by shellfire. Of the farmhouse which stood on the saddle (Pt 778), only ruins can be seen today.

Prior to the assault, on the night of 18 October, a four-man patrol from the Witwatersrand Rifles/Regiment De la Rey went out to reconnoitre the ground around Pt 806. They clashed with an enemy patrol and the 30-year-old regimental sergeant-major, C.H.C. 'Bert' Wheeler, was shot in the stomach. He was carried 300 metres by his men before he ordered them to leave him and get back with the information they had gathered. Eventually a stretcher party carried him back to an aid post, where he died a few hours later. An analytical chemist in civilian life, Wheeler was described as "the most unlikely sergeant-major" and "a quiet, well-spoken, educated man, a thorough gentleman". It is said that he volunteered for this mission to avenge the death of his older brother, Frederick, who was killed in action with the Middelandse Regiment on 26 April 1942.[283]

The Witwatersrand Rifles/Regiment De la Rey began its attack at 0545 hours. Meanwhile, on the right toward the Setta River, the Guards Brigade launched a diversionary attack on Monte Alcino.

The Witwatersrand Rifles/Regiment De la Rey was established on Pt 806 by

283 S. Monick, A *bugle calls*, pp. 430–432.

19 October, but the real struggle started the next day when it faced no less than eleven counter-attacks between nine and noon. While the battle for Pt 806 was in progress on the night of 19 October, Lieutenant Dreyer led a patrol to reconnoitre forward to Pt 826. Contact was unavoidable on the overcrowded, murky heights and the hours that followed were filled with horror:

> Supports came forward. Those reinforcements we did not need were sent forward. You could do nothing in the dark. One of the reinforcements was captured by the enemy. We were powerless to assist him as we heard him pleading for mercy. The Germans shot him five times. The tension was well nigh unbearable as we waited for the anticipated attack. A large enemy patrol came upon us and we were subjected to heavy fire throughout the night. We had to respond with limited fire due to the urgent need to conserve our ammunition. With the light, we found the bodies of three dead Germans and one South African who had been shot after being captured ... Becoming restless with the state of the battle, I took five men with me to clear our side of the mountain. We had scarcely left our position when we detected the rearguard of a German patrol actively infiltrating our area. Upon being challenged by us, they surrendered, and we were in the act of disarming them when a sniper shot Cpl 'Tiny' Nieuwoudt in the head. The bullet penetrated his helmet and shattered his brain, fragments of which were splattered on my boots.[284]

Lieutenant R.W. Quinton, whose sharp shooting was noted during the capture of Florence, was wounded and he won the Military Cross for his part in repelling these attacks. Most of the problems emanated from a house on the western side of the neck (Pt 778). C Company cleared the area in a whirlwind 40 minutes around midday. The total number of casualties incurred by the Witwatersrand Rifles/Regiment De la Rey during the two days of fighting was five killed and 48 wounded. The battalion as a whole had suffered 223 casualties from Monte Stanco until now.

It was apparently only after an intervention by one of his staff officers that General Poole was persuaded that the Witwatersrand Rifles/Regiment De la Rey could not, and should not, continue on to Pt 826, only 800 yards away. The exhausted men were relieved on 21 October by the Imperial Light Horse/Kimberley Regiment which itself was still under strength after the battles around Monte Vigese. Its war diary unenthusiastically made note of the "bad news".

---

284 S. Monick, *A bugle calls*, pp. 434–435; Corporal H.C. Nieuwoudt from Van Rhynsdorp was killed on 20 October 1944.

The Scots Guards had not succeeded on the right, partly because its ranks had been depleted at Monte Catarelto and from subsequent illness. Opposing the Scots Guards on Monte Alcino were three companies of German infantry.

After spending the night of 22 October in water-filled foxholes on Pt 806, an Imperial Light Horse/Kimberley Regiment patrol was sent forward to reconnoitre the saddle. They observed a number of Germans in a building about 100 yards north of Pt 778. At 1500 hours, platoons from A and B Companies set out to destroy them. Aided by the fog and mist, the platoons moved up the right-hand flank and took up positions 150 yards away from the buildings. Ten mortar bombs were dropped on the buildings and one platoon rushed in, covered by fire from the other, taking the enemy by surprise. The platoons then withdrew to their positions in preparation for the forthcoming attack.

Sergeant (formerly Corporal) D.H. McKerrow MM was wounded in the fighting on Pt 806. McKerrow had been wounded in a Stuka attack in the desert and had killed three German machine-gunners north of Acquaviva in June. Together with Lieutenant Jimmy Adamson and his platoon, he had captured about 45 Germans in the mist on Pt 826. Adamson was becoming a legend in his own lifetime, but he was killed—along with Private G. Standford—in a fierce counter-attack from Pt 826. Both men had been part of the advance patrol into Florence on 4 August.[285]

Later that evening, on his way up to the forward positions, Private A.I. Lourens came across two German soldiers helping their badly injured comrade reach the Allied aid post, desperate to know how far it was. He also came across Adamson's dead body and heard the wireless operator calling it in: "Abel Baker Charly Fox ... my big brother [code for lieutenant] is a policeman." Lourens provides an unusual account of the battle and the night preceding it:

> *Dit is nou ongeveer tienuur in die aand, en die bevel van Sers. Erwin kom: "Dig in". Ons is honger, ons het die voorige aand laas 'n stukkie brood gehad. Ons is 24 manne wat kan veg, en ses van die HK van ons peleton. Die gereedskap waarmee ons grawe, is 'n graafie en 'n pikkie, elk 20cm lank.* [It is approximately 10 o'clock at night when the order from Sgt. Erwin comes: "Dig in". We are hungry, having had only one piece of bread the previous evening. We are made up of 24 men who can fight, plus six from the HQ; these form our platoon. The equipment with which we are digging is a small spade and a small pickaxe, each 20cm long.][286]

[285] J. Kros, *War in Italy*, p. 261.

[286] The *Springbok*, December 2007, p. 7.

The Imperial Light Horse/Kimberley Regiment war diary notes that considerable difficulty was experienced in transporting food to the men. The previous evening's meal had arrived at 0130 hours, cold and unpalatable. According to Private Lourens, they were given half a loaf of rain-sodden white bread to be shared by four people. On this night however, he had what he describes as the best meal of his life, under the noses of the enemy on the slopes of Monte Salvaro:

> *Oor die muil se rug is twee seilsakke wat aanmekaar gebind is met rantsoene binne in. Erwin deel uit. Hy sê: "Steek jou hand in die sak en vat 'n blikkie." Die blikkie se etikette is af. Ek sukkel myne oop. Ek is baie gretig om te sien wat dit bevat. Eindlik kry ek dit oop: dit is appelkooskonfyt. Ek weet nie of ek moet lag of huil nie. Ek begin dadelik smul. Dit is die heerlikste kos wat ek ooit geëet het of wat ooit oor my lippe sal gaan. Ek maak daardie blikkie leeg, dolleeg. Toe lek ek my hande skoon, modder en al.* [Bound together on the mule's back are two buck sails filled with rations. Erwin distributes these, saying, "Grab a tin from the bag." There is no label on the tin. I struggle to open mine and I am very eager to see what is inside the tin. Finally, I open it: it is apricot jam. I am not sure whether to laugh or cry. I immediately start tucking in; it is the most delicious food that I have ever eaten or that will ever pass my lips. I empty that tin, completely empty. Then I licked my hands clean, mud and all.][287]

An artillery and mortar barrage from the Royal Durban Light Infantry plastered the crest, timed to coincide with the start of the dawn attack. Lourens, a Bren gunner, describes how he initiated the attack at 0540 hours on 23 October. The Germans had sheltered from the rain in some farmhouses and ran to their machine guns after the firing had started:

> *Eers na sowat 20 sekondes skiet hulle terug. Ek hoor Erwin se bekende bevel: "Go chaps go!" Toe bars die hel los. Baie dinge gebeur gelyk. Hulle skiet van links op my teen die rots vas. My makkers hardloop in die koeëlreen in. Die vyand maai hulle af. Enkeles val my selfs raak. Intussen het ek gesien ongewapende Duitsers kom om die hoek van die huis. Hulle wil by hulle masjiengewere kom hier vlak voor my. Die wat nie val nie, spring terug. Vyandelike vuur van links het gestaak omdat van ons ander troepe met hulle slaags geraak het. Oor die hele front van ongeveer 200m word nou geveg. Ek hoor 'n geluid agter my. Toe ek omkyk, kyk ek vas in die gesig van Luitenant Smethurs.* [Only after about 20 seconds did they start shooting back. I heard Erwin's usual urging: "Go chaps go!" Then all hell broke loose. Lots of things started happening simultaneously. They started shooting at me from the right, the bullets hitting the rocks. My comrades ran into a hail of bullets and the

[287] The *Springbok*, June 2008, p. 8.

> enemy cut them down. Some bullets hit near me. Meanwhile, I noticed some unarmed Germans sneaking round the corner of the house. They wanted to get to their machine guns right in front of me. Those who were not hit fell back. Enemy fire from the left had stopped because some of our other troops had engaged them. Across the whole front of approximately 200m, fighting erupted. I heard a noise behind me; when I turned around, I looked straight into the face of Lt Smethurs.]

Throughout the cold, misty and overcast day of 23 October, the battle raged back and forth across the 800-yard-long saddle which lay between the two high points. Almost all the officers had been hit and of 650 men, all but 100 had become casualties. Nonetheless, the survivors moved steadily forward. A stalemate—and the crisis point—was reached around midday on the final approach, which was an open, ploughed field, flanked by steep cliffs and raked by Spandau fire. Following a mortar concentration and helped by the mist, Private R. Greenway crawled forward on the knife-edge right-hand side. While he engaged a Spandau, Private R.H.F. Nicholson was able to crawl up and silence it with hand grenades. Greenway then continued along the ridge and successively overcame and silenced seven Spandaus. A section followed behind and another came from the right, finally consolidating the position.

The remnants of the 650 German defenders withdrew northward across the Reno River during the rainy night of 23/24 October. Estimates of enemy dead range from 87 to 126, including those found by patrols in the rear areas after the enemy had withdrawn. According to the recording officer, a ground check revealed 92 enemy dead on the battlefield. In addition, enemy POWs stated that 26 of their engineers had been killed when South African artillery scored a direct hit on a dump of their own mines.

As a diversion, and to draw off some of the enemy artillery fire, a squadron of Prince Alfred's Guard' tanks set off from Grizzana, down the left side of Monte Salvaro toward Carviano. They too shot up the retreating Germans. The Imperial Light Horse/Kimberley Regiment, which had received approximately 100 reserves a week or so before the battle, lost 15 killed, 81 wounded, 58 temporarily unfit for action and 26 sick. Only 160 men remained on Pt 826. They were subjected to "a continuous barrage of arty and mortar fire" but, according to the regimental war diary, there was no counter-attack. However, the recording officer wrote in his narrative that the platoon on the eastern edge had to beat back two counter-attacks:

> The final action of the day came at 1655 hrs. Twenty-seven Germans marched against 'B' Coy's right-hand platoon. They took no cover. They shouted taunts and epithets. They were in completely fanatical condition. The platoon allowed them to come within a few yards' range and then mowed them down with their Brens.[288]

During the day, supplies were brought up, the wounded were evacuated and POWs were sent back. Reinforcements were rushed up from the reserve company and the brigadiers of 11th and 12th Brigades visited tactical headquarters. That evening, hot food was brought up from the newly established kitchen at Grizzana.[289] From an artillery perspective, it was a full day for the guns with programmes fired in support of the Imperial Light Horse/Kimberley Regiment attack on Pt 826. Supporting fire from the 25-pounders and mortars kept the enemy in their trenches as line after line was taken with the use of hand grenades. The Imperial Light Horse/Kimberley Regiment diary notes that the men carried six grenades instead of the usual two for the close-quarter fighting. Furthermore, the artillery (25-pounders and mediums) fired 7,369 rounds in support. Mortars (4.2-inch and 3-inch) fired 2,636 rounds in total. For the 7/23rd Medium Regiment, it was the busiest day of the campaign thus far. One gun alone from 'Dog' Troop fired 243 rounds—"a little more than ten tons of death and destruction in one day".[290]

The Royal Natal Carbineers, which had been occupying Monte Pezza, was now sent to relieve the Imperial Light Horse/Kimberley Regiment in a holding operation on Pt 826. Colonel Comrie voiced his objection to this deployment to General Poole during a visit to the Royal Natal Carbineers tactical headquarters on 22 October. His grounds were that the regiment as a whole was worn out due to 21 days of gruelling fighting under the most frightful conditions—probably the most exhausting period since the war began. General Poole was apparently sympathetic but explained that the division's target now included Monte Sole and that there was no other option.

The occupation of Monte Pezza had been costly and casualties were still mounting. Eighteen-year-old Private C.G. 'Lanky' Brasler from Clanwilliam was sharing a slit trench with his close friend, Private Walter Hain, when a mortar bomb hit. Hain was wounded in the groin but survived to write in

288 DODAR, WD, Box 598, Recording Officer, 22/8/1944–22/2/1945.

289 DODAR, WD, Box 635, Imperial Light Horse/Kimberley Regiment, File B8 60.

290 DODAR, WD, Box 631, 7/23rd Medium Regiment, 23/10/1944.

his diary: "Checked to see if family jewels were still OK … Lanky screamed, 'Mama mama' … Afterwards stretcher bearers told me he was dead."[291] Hodgson decided to send a letter off to his parents before going forward:

> Monday 22nd Oct
> I started this letter to you a week ago but at this stage I lost it and have not had the chance to write another one. I wrote a letter to you and Mum this morning and I mentioned this letter, but looking through one of my pockets just now, I found it stuck in between some other papers. The letter I wrote this morning, I did in a bit of a hurry as there was a lot to be done and I did not think I would get a chance to write later today, but things have turned out differently as I have got quite a bit of time on my hands.

The battlefield was a gruesome sight when the Royal Natal Carbineers relieved the Imperial Light Horse/Kimberley Regiment at 1800 hours. The trees were splintered; enemy dead, weapons, equipment and ammunition were strewn about everywhere. Private Evered D. Pollock, who had led the way at Bagnoregio four months earlier, was killed during this holding operation. On his gravestone at Castiglione is written: "Your brief stay with us leaves lasting loving memories."

It has been said that this episode was one of the toughest for the South Africans in the war thus far. The Imperial Light Horse/Kimberley Regiment had been in action continuously for 50 days. In one incident, Captain J.H. Smallwood, a recipient of the American Silver Star, apparently counted 32 Spandaus defending an area the size of a tennis court. In compensation, eleven men were awarded medals, including Privates Greenwood and Nicholson who received the Military Medal.

While the battles for Pt 806 and Pt 826 were raging, enemy guns and mortars north of the Reno River were pounding the forward observation posts of the South Africans. Three artillerymen were wounded on 20 October, which was, incredibly, a bright shining day. However, the wet, cold weather returned again on 21 October, a disastrous day for the 1/6th Field Regiment and the division as a whole. Lieutenant-Colonel L.D. Kay died while trying to identify the source of enemy fire, killed by a shell which burst a few feet from the window of his observation post at Stanco. According to Axelson, who had visited the site two days earlier, Kay was killed at 12th Brigade tactical headquarters in a farmhouse

291 G.B. Hobbs, *From Sicily the Alps*, p. 246.

on the neck just south of the village. Tactical headquarters were typically situated in buildings with thick stone walls and were often used as observation posts. Although only 28, Kay was a veteran of the desert war and was highly regarded, having served first with the Special Service Battalion, then as an instructor at the artillery school in Potchefstroom before the war. His death was big news in the home press, which reported that he was "struck by a shell splinter while organizing and coordinating the most impressive concentration of fire ever put down by South African guns". Kay saw the role of his 25-pounders as providing the closest possible support to the infantry. He died before he received the news that he had been awarded the DSO and is buried in the Florence war cemetery. In honour of their late colonel, the regiment 'stonked' the culprits on the far bank of the Reno with 240 rounds at 1130 hours on 23 October, the day of his burial.

Major R.C. 'Rex' Tomlinson MC, a Pietermaritzburg attorney in civilian life who was attached to Headquarters Company of the Royal Natal Carbineers, was ordered to go forward and take over B Company from Lieutenant Roberts who, in turn, had taken over when Gallimore was wounded in the ankle. At 0715 hours on 23 October, headquarters received the news that Tomlinson had been "very badly wounded". He was taken down to the casualty clearing station in Castiglione where both legs were amputated at the knee. Well aware that even the amputation of a foot could be fatal, he lived through the night with morphine blunting the pain. Typically, amputees experienced a jerky restlessness followed by death, as was the case with Tomlinson. In the morning he was taken to the cemetery, just a few hundred yards away. In the regimental war dairy, Tomlinson is described as one of the regiment's most loyal and able officers. His family has a long history with the Royal Natal Carbineers.

Another Carbineer was brought down from Monte Salvaro to be buried in the Castigilone cemetery that same day. He was 17-year-old Justus Watt of Brakpan, on whose gravestone is written, "A Springbok staunch and true".

After being relieved by the 4/13th Frontier Force Rifles ('The Rif'), the Carbineers were able to walk back to Collina. Here they were met by transport and taken to Campolo on the western side of Monte Vigese. Campolo is only two miles from the Reno River and Route 64, a comparatively safer location. As the diarist of the 1/6th Field Regiment put it: "Enemy artillery continues to be very active indeed; the whole of 12 Brigade sector from Vigese to Salvaro is very unhealthy these days."

Once the Royal Natal Carbineers was out of the line, Comrie met with General Poole at brigade headquarters in Forlino. It was decided that, for health reasons, he should return to the Union for a rest. After a private discussion with Comrie, the general called in Major Peter Francis and appointed him to command. Francis, previously the commander of A Company who had masterminded the Vigese attack, became the youngest commanding officer in the regiment's history.

It was clear at the time that Comrie would not be returning. It is believed that the loss of his good friend, Rex Tomlinson, coming on top of all the other losses in his regiment, finally broke his health, although the fact that he was of frail build and a heavy smoker no doubt contributed. He had served with the Carbineers since the age of 15, and had fought alongside them since their first battle at El Wak on 16 December 1940. Comrie had tears in his eyes when he bade farewell to the men of his regiment. He died of a heart attack on 26 September 1949 and was buried in Richmond, Natal by the Reverend Victor Shaw, chaplain to the regiment during the entire period of the war.[292]

This had been the most traumatic time of Hodgson's life. Two successive commanders of B Company had become casualties and his officer commanding had been invalided home. His usually ordered life was in disarray and the air-letter card on which he wrote to his parents on 23 October was uncharacteristically blotched and stained:

> I am really very, very sorry that I have not written to either of you for such a long time but I can assure you that I have been really very busy and I have found it impossible to find a chance to write, mainly because I have not had the chance of getting at my writing material when I have had the time to write. At the moment I am just using an issue letter card that I have managed to get hold of. You will notice that my last two letters have not been numbered; that is due to my list being with my other writing material and I will fix it up in my next letter. I have received quite a number of letters from you lately and I thank you both very much for them. As time is very short at the moment I will not answer all your questions but will do so when I can get the chance to settle down and do some good letter writing again, which I hope will be very shortly now … I wrote half a letter to Dad the other day but I lost it before I finished it; it is possible that someone picked it up and posted it as I had already addressed it.

[292] *Carbineer,* The official journal of the Royal Natal Carbineers Association, 1, 1949, p. 6.

Monte Termine was taken without a fight by the Scots Guards on 24 October. However, this event was followed by a deluge of rain which slowed the action and the front became relatively quiet. Nevertheless, the entry of 24 October in the war diary of the 1/6th Field Regiment mentions that although there was little counter-battery fire, the foremost defended localities—and Grizzana in particular—were being "dusted up" daily.

Gordon Lawrence was billeted in Grizzana, which today is a tree-lined, vibrant town, high in the mountains. In contrast, in late October of 1944, as the war moved on, he described his surroundings as "hushed, shattered countryside, shell holes and debris and litter of equipment, spattered mud, twisted tree limbs and papers—papers scattered everywhere as though a shell had struck a stationary shop ... disorder and debris lying thick in the streets and the houses gaping open, revealing never-intended secrets."[293]

Before the field artillery moved up to Pian di Setta, the valley at Lagaro was thick with guns, both medium and field artillery, as well as tanks. One of the 5.5s was just above the road with its barrel sticking out four or five feet over the road. Gunners on the 5.5s were showered with mud every time the gun was fired. Wheeled and tracked vehicles slipped on the muddy roads and it was necessary to enlist the aid of the engineers to move up to Pian di Setta.

The regimental war diary of 1/6th Field Regiment described the past month as one of toil, sweat and tears but also mentioned that only one battery would be operating so as to allow the others time to get clean and comfortable. Leave was also arranged to Prato and Florence.

From the relative comfort of his billet at Vigo, Hodgson was equipping himself to deal with the mud and rain of the next round:

> Thank goodness that although it has been very wet, and is very wet, it has not begun to get cold yet. As yet it has only been cold once and that was at the beginning of the month; since then it has not been hot but just a cool temperature all the time. The mud is terrific and up to a couple of days ago I found it impossible to prevent my pants from getting wet and full of mud from the knees down, but now the problem is solved as I have got hold of a lovely pair of gum boots; they are army issue and I got them from a friend of mine in headquarters. I also got hold of one of those big waterproof hats which is very useful in the rain.

293 G.B. Hobbs, *From Sicily to the Alps*, p. 181.

Rivers were in flood. In Florence, the Arno raged just below the level of the Ponte Vecchio. The planned attack on Monte Sole was postponed and the soldiers became resigned to the idea of over-wintering in the Apennines. Visibility was almost nil due to the rain and mist. In a fitting end to this phase of the war, Kesselring's staff car collided with a mobile gun on 25 October. His injuries put him out of the war, allowing him time to work on his memoirs. He was replaced by General Heindrich von Vietinghoff-Scheel. Now, with the front line 15 miles beyond Castiglione, began a static, but certainly not idle, phase of the Italian campaign. The table below shows infantry casualties for the last three weeks of October. All the assault casualties in the battle of Pt 826 were sustained by the Imperial Light Horse/Kimberley Regiment (under the command of the 12th South African Motorized Brigade) and are not included in the table. These casualties amounted to 15 killed and 81 wounded. They are in addition to the Monte Vigese losses suffered by Imperial Light Horse/ Kimberley Regiment which were part of the 11th South African Armoured Brigade.

12th South African Motorized Brigade casualties up to the end of the mobile phase Monte Stanco, Pt 806, Pt 826[294]									
Unit	Killed			Wounded			Missing		
	Offrs	O/Rs	CCs	Offrs	O/Rs	CCs	Offrs	O/Rs	CCs
RNC	2	18		8	47	2		2	
FC/CTH	1	14			46	4			
WR/DLR	5	33	3	9	130	8		6	
RDLI	0	1			4				
TOTALS	8	66	3	17	227	14		8	
	77			258			10		

CCs: Cape Corps

[294] DODAR, WD, Box 598, Recording Officer, 12th South African Motorized Brigade, Report on Operations in the Italian Campaign for period August 1944–May 1945.

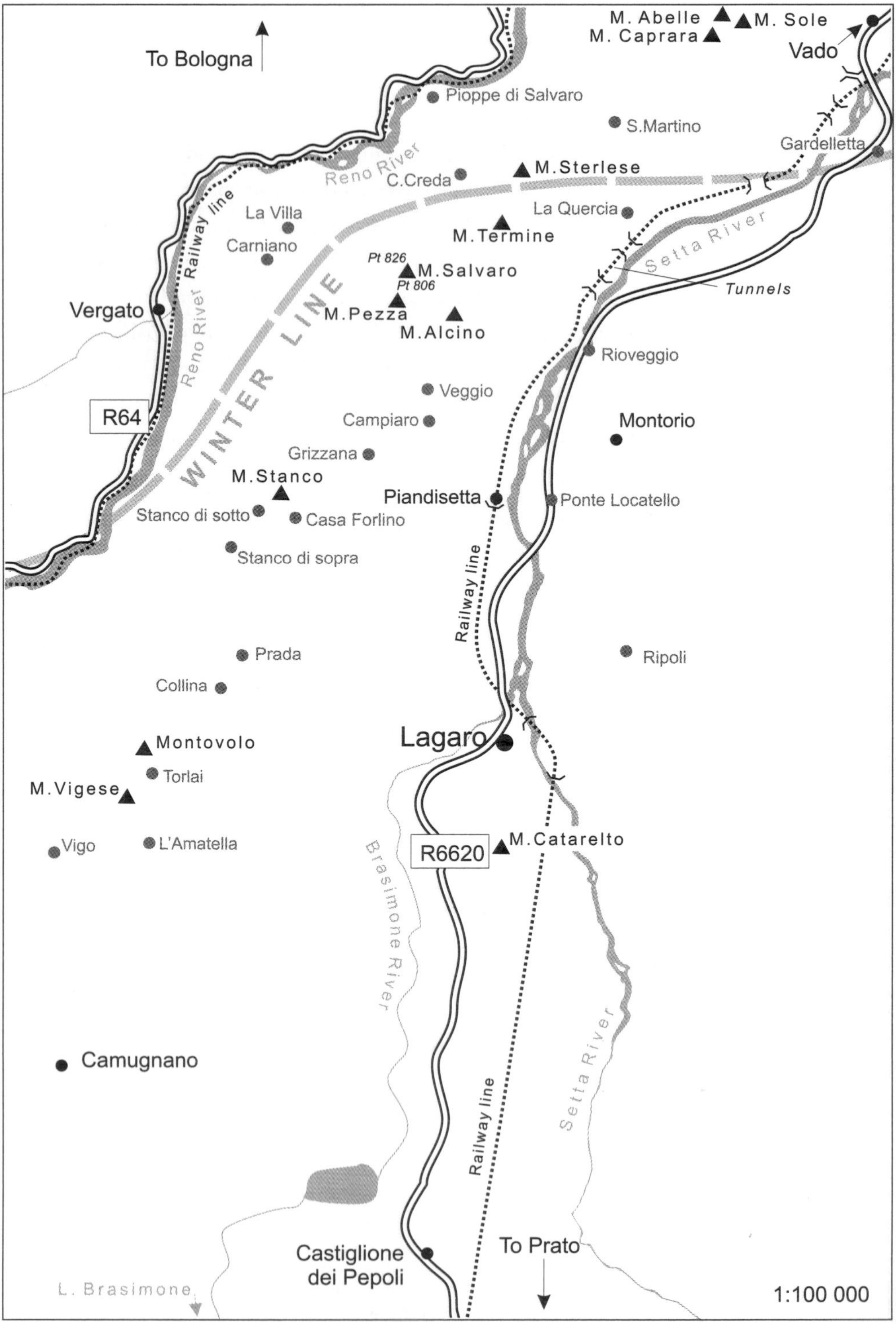

M. Abelle
M. Sole
M. Caprara
Vado
To Bologna
Pioppe di Salvaro
S.Martino
Gardelletta
Reno River
C.Creda
M.Sterlese
La Villa
Railway line
La Quercia
Carniano
M.Termine
Setta River
Pt 826
M.Salvaro
Tunnels
Pt 806
Vergato
M.Pezza
M.Alcino
Reno River
WINTER LINE
Rioveggio
Veggio
R64
Campiaro
Montorio
Grizzana
M.Stanco
Piandisetta
Ponte Locatello
Stanco di sotto
Casa Forlino
Stanco di sopra
Railway line
Prada
Ripoli
Collina
Montovolo
Lagaro
Torlai
M.Vigese
Vigo
L'Amatella
R6620
M.Catarelto
Brasimone River
Setta River
Camugnano
Railway line
Castiglione dei Pepoli
To Prato
L. Brasimone
1:100 000

Chapter Nine

Snow and ice

"Will you please convey a message from me to say that I am most grateful for the truly magnificent part the men of the Div have played in the breaking of the Gothic Line, and for what they are doing in the whole offensive plan … You have a fine division of which you may be proud—I certainly am, and I know South Africa is too …"
—General Sir Harold Alexander on a visit to the 6th South African Armoured Division on 6 November 1944

Friday 27 October 1944 – Sunday 18 February 1945: Pian di Setta

Now that Monte Salvaro was in South African hands, it was possible to move the 25-pounder guns farther up Route 6620 to Pian di Setta where the valley widens slightly. According to the 1/6th Field Regiment war diary, 26 October was a grim day because of rain and mud. There was consolation however, in that leave parties were now being rotated out of the line to Prato and Florence.

The infantry's positions were now even farther forward but the road through the valley was no-go during the day.

The air force had bombed the marshalling yards shortly before the South Africans' arrival in Pian di Setta and the place was littered with the wreckage of trains, including Mussolini's personal train which provided some useful items, such as eating utensils. Axelson was informed by Italian locals that it was, in fact, German demolition parties that had caused much of the damage to the railway. Members of a Cape Corps construction team ensconced themselves in the derailed carriages for the winter.[295]

The division had not stayed in one place long enough for mail to reach recipients in the same locale and condition in which their outgoing letters had left them since Cassino. Writing to his mother in early November, Bourhill did

[295] DODAR, WD, Box 624, 1/6th Field Regiment, 26/10/1944; E. Axelson, *A year in Italy*, p. 145; A Troop was positioned at L757208 on the east side of the river, south of Ponte Locatello.

not know how many more letters, if any, would find him still at his current post. But he did know that the world had changed, his circumstances were different and he was not the same person he had been just six months ago:

> This is the first place that I've received an answer to a letter in the same place as I wrote that letter—get it? The last place that happened was at Cassino—way back when I was only 20 and the world was young and it was May and the ground was firm, and sleet and mud were things you only connected with Anzio and history!

The front held by the South Africans included Monte Termine and Monte Salvaro and ran southwest between the latter and Monte Sterlese. One 'hot spot' in the line was La Villa, which was within easy reach of the enemy-held posts at Salvaro village. The enemy had a permanent patrol base at Pioppe di Salvaro on the east bank of the Reno River, and a bridgehead existed here throughout the winter. The daily 'sitreps' (situation reports) of the 1/6th Field Regiment show that all these locations, along with Route 64, received its regular attention.

The disposition of the divisional front at the beginning of winter is further clarified by Axelson in his log entry for 1 November:

> On the left of the Div are Partisan bands. The left flanking formation are the CCB [Combat Command B] ... Between the Reno and Monte Vigese are the guns of 4/22nd Regiment, and the tanks of the Special Service Battalion. The Royal Natal Carbineers are also in this area. The CCC [Combat Command C] are in the Stanco area, and also the Imperial Light Horse who are now resting. The First City/Cape Town Highlanders lie along the Grizzana–Vergato road, and are only 1,500 yards from Vergato. The Witwatersrand Rifles/Regiment De la Rey are on 826. In the Witwatersrand Rifles/Regiment De la Rey and First City/Cape Town Highlanders' areas are some tanks of the Prince Alfred's Guard. East of 826 is M. Termine, held by 1 SG [Scots Guards]. East of M. Termine are the Grens, on Pt 506 which is south of M. Sole ... South of the Setta lie the 3 Coldstreams. Tanks of the Pretoria Regiment/Princess Alice's Own are in their area. Between the Guards and the 1 US Armoured Division is Hingeforce, consisting of elements of Pretoria Regiment and Natal Mounted Rifles.

The composite force known as 'Hingeforce' was created to protect the 6th South African Armoured Division's right flank by holding forward positions on Monte Venere. It was commanded by Lieutenant-Colonal Arthur Johnstone of the Pretoria Regiment (Princess Alice's Own) and consisted of one battery of the 1/12th Light Anti-Aircraft, one squadron of the Natal Mounted Rifles/

South African Air Force and C Squadron, 81 US Reconnaissance Squadron. Although the steep mountainsides were uninhabited, a network of tracks led to some remote farmhouses and smaller hamlets which were mostly rubble. In some of the bigger villages in the river valley, like Pian di Setta, houses were being vacated and a few billets became available. Accommodation was found in bombed buildings and in ingeniously constructed dugouts complete with wood panelling and walls of ammunition boxes. Some had built-in stoves made from petrol and biscuit tins. The wooden beams from damaged buildings provided fuel for heating. Soldiers and civilians alike spent much time and energy salvaging firewood from the rubble and scrounging for food.

Although there was plenty of ideal firewood in the form of railway sleepers soaked in creosote, the troops were forbidden to use them in case the need arose to quickly put them into commission again.

The Coldstream Guards officers' mess was a house in Castiglione with stone floors and windows without glass. In the sitting room was a "minute and diabolical fireplace which burned the maximum of fuel and gave out the minimum of heat". The boiler was heated with wood soaked in petrol.[296]

On the last day of October, rear division headquarters moved from Montepiano to Castiglione. Billets were more plentiful in the numerous towns—including Montepiano and Vernio—which straddled Route 6620 to the rear of Lagaro. The policy was that during the winter months, civilian buildings were only to be used where tactical reasons or bad weather dictated; where possible, public buildings such as schools, fascist headquarters and government buildings were used in their stead. Where the use of civilian houses was necessary, the whole building was usually taken over and arrangements were made to accommodate the previous inhabitants. Some civilians remained in Pian di Setta. The barber shop near the church remained open for business.

Forward of Veggio, all civilians were evacuated except for the odd caretaker who stayed to look after livestock. Living conditions were dire, especially for one group of civilians who were living in a cave near Grizzana. Approximately 30 civilian refugees passed through every day, some on their way to refugee camps around Florence—they were transported by the South Africans. Security had to be tight because it was believed that some refugees were acting as spies.

[296] M. Howard, The valley of the Setta, winter 1944–1945, in D. Quilter (ed), *'No dishonourable name'*, p. 232.

Nevertheless, some civilians remained in the area. The Germans capitalized on this, passing themselves off as Italian peasants as they walked around during the day.

On their patrols, the South Africans saw evidence of the September massacres in the Monte Sole area, where an estimated 770 civilians were put to death. Bodies were found in fields and in farmhouses—in more than one instance, laid out in neat rows.

The Royal Natal Carbineers was being rested after its October ordeals, and Hodgson caught up with his correspondence. Instead of telling his dramatic news, Hodgson only responded to the news from home and talked about the future. A feeling of hope had returned:

> I am looking forward to once again being able to enjoy our Friday evening outings to the local. I sincerely hope it will not be too long now. At any rate there is one consolation to go on with at the present—I see that in the latest 'Springbok' that Smuts definitely says he will not be sending any infantry units to Burma, only Air Force and Technical Units—that is a really good bit of news as we were all afraid that when we got home, they would soon start making a draft to Burma, but that fear is now 'non est'.
>
> Yesterday we filled in a 'questionnaire' for demobilization; it is just a lot of questions we had to answer so that they can get a rough idea of what is what before they start getting down to anything definite. There is nothing of major importance in it nor is there anything binding about it.
>
> The post has just come in and it brings a letter from Mum. At the moment it is Saturday midday and I can just imagine you sitting in the office typing out a letter to me before going home. How I wish I was going home after writing this letter to you; nevertheless the time is bound to come when we turn round and start for home. I only wish I knew when [it is] going to come about. At my elbow I have got the earphones of a no.18 wireless set; it is tuned in to Daventry as I am listening to a good musical programme. The news was on a little while ago and I must say it is all very good especially that in the Philippines but I would much rather things went quickly here as it has so much more direct bearing on things, especially as far as we are concerned.
>
> This time last year I was on a wireless course at Helwan—gosh! But a lot has happened since then—I wonder what will have happened by this time next year. I know where I will be this time next year, nicely settled down at home doing a good job of work instead of roaming round Europe with the intent to destroy—mind you, the old Hun deserves nothing more.

The Luftwaffe was so scarce these days that a bombing raid was a novelty and a diversion from the miserable weather. Johnston was in the vicinity of

Castiglione on 30 October and his diary relates: "Jerry bombed and strafed nearby—great fun. Rain." Sampie de Wet, a member of the SAWAS and a unique female information source, had been in Italy for two months, and 31 October was the first sunny day she experienced.

The crystal-clear air and 100-per cent visibility on 31 October made the 1/6th Field Regiment realize just how exposed to Monte Sole it was in its current position. Preparations were being made for the attack on Monte Sole, but it seems that all ranks had resigned themselves to spending winter in the mountains. Hodgson was even looking forward to it. He tried to convince his sister that it was going to be all fun and games:

> In about a month's time I will be able to write and tell you all about the snow. In the mountain area it gets well over three feet in most places and even on the plains there is a good covering. Bologna is the chief centre of the winter sports but I don't think we will see much of that this season. All the same when we get right out of the line at different times, I expect we will see a bit of skiing and skating. Nevertheless, we will be able to make plenty of snowmen and throw a large number of snowballs at one another. I wish I had a camera so that I could take some snaps of us all messing about in the snow. As you have no doubt read in the papers lately the weather has been far from good but thank goodness today the sun keeps on peeping out and I hope it will clear up.

On 31 October, B Company, Royal Natal Carbineers was sent across the Reno to assist an American unit located the distance of a hand grenade's throw from the enemy. The men picked up some new lingo through this attachment to the 'Yanks': any headquarters became a command post and rifles became 'carbeens'. This language was mixed in with the usual flow of English, Afrikaans, Zulu and Italian.[297]

Corporal Stan Thesen and Lance-Corporal Gardner, who had won the Military Medal at Panzano, were recognized for their particularly aggressive actions on this operation. By 2 November, they were back in relative comfort and safety at Vigo where the other two companies had remained. At this time, the divisional front was held in three sectors with the 24th Guards on the right, the 12th South African Motorized Brigade and Royal Natal Carbineers—minus one company under command as from 1200 hours on 5 November—in the centre, flanked by the 11th South African Armoured Brigade on the left. The

[297] G.B. Hobbs, *From Sicily to the Alps,* p. 181.

Carbineers took over from the Scots Guards on Monte Termine when the Guards Brigade was relieved by 12th South African Motorized Brigade. Here the regiment would remain for the winter. Prior to this they had rested in Vigo, on the slopes of Monte Vigese near Camugnano.

The platoons of the Royal Durban Light Infantry were divided into two groups which were spread out among the two brigades. The headquarters of A Group moved from Le Piane near Grizzana station, which was under observation, to Monteacuto. B Group headquarters was at Veggio. The men spent the winter harassing enemy positions and supporting fighting patrols.

In a letter to his mother, Hodgson described a scene which would become only too familiar. This vignette of his views over the Reno valley could have equally described the Setta valley as seen from Castiglione:

> No doubt you have been reading in the paper of the very wet weather we have been having; it is all too true and with all the movement of army machines, etc. Everywhere one goes it is just a mass of mud. Notwithstanding all the wet, I must say that the scenery I have seen in the last couple of days has been too marvellous for words. I cannot express in words how beautiful it all is, but I can just give you a rough idea and you will have to imagine the rest. Looking out from our bedroom window we look down into a very large valley all spotted with quaint little farmhouses and cultivated fields. From right up here we look down onto the silver river running along the bottom; the other side rises slowly up to the high mountains; on our left we look right up the valley to where the river rises in a large land mass. The mountains on the other side are covered in thick snow to halfway down the slopes. A network of roads resembling a silver spider web covers the floor of the valley. On the hill slopes all the chestnut trees are turning brown. At night the floor of the valley is covered with thick white mist and it appears as if we look down onto clouds from high above; across the valley the black masses of the mountains peep out of the billows of mist. Above the black mass is the bright white or a shining silver, which is the moon shining on the snow. I hope you can get a rough idea of what I can see from our window; it is more the job of a poet or a good author, and I am far from qualifying as either of those. At the moment I am sitting at a table, looking out of the same window, but the landscape is covered in a thick mist. At my elbow I have again got the good old wireless going. We usually listen in to the Forces Programme as it is by far the best. The news has just been on and looks very rosy, but I think that we will have to wait until spring before we end this war, but it is not long when you come to think of it.
>
> It is going to be cold here during winter, but I think most of us are well prepared for it. I am for one. Also, I am looking forward to having a winter here as it will be a very good experience, real good snow falls, ice, and all the rest of it. It looks as if by the time I get home, I will have been away from home for quite a while but I am sure the experience I will have gained in every different way will make up for a

> lot of that, as a large portion of it I could not have gained in the Union and the rest would have taken me much longer to gain than it has. Looking at it in that light, this beastly war has not been so useless.
>
> As usual there is no news from here except that I am very well and happy. I have also put on a bit more weight and at the present rate I will be the size of a house by the time I get home, but I think I will lose quite a bit before then—at least I hope so.

All was relatively quiet during the first week of November, although some hand-to-hand fighting took place while the men were on patrol.

On the night of 2 November, an infantry patrol reported the "reappearance of a rocket-firing gun" with a range of 2,000 yards, firing from the Vergato area. They responded with a battery of guns, which halted the enemy fire until morning. Mortar shell casualties from A Company and C Company, Royal Natal Carbineers on Monte Termine started to trickle in. During the first part of their occupation, the Germans would send over a daily spate at 1020 hours, stopping in time to allow the men to brew up their 11 o'clock tea.

On 3 November, eleven days before his 39th birthday and only ten weeks after his posting to the Royal Natal Carbineers, Glen Easton was killed. The regimental histories and diaries provide no details. His name was simply removed from the nominal roll the following month. A friend informed the family that Easton had been killed by a direct hit on his dugout, probably on Monte Termine.

Around this time, Biermann visited the regimental aid post of the Royal Natal Carbineers at Casa Ruzzone. The post would remain in this spot for the duration of the winter, first under Captain 'Koffie' Resnek, followed by 'Doc' Rankin and then Captain Southwood. In an article written for *Outspan*, Biermann described a scene in an old farm building, 800 yards behind the Royal Natal Carbineer positions on 'Carbineers Kop' where half a dozen men were sitting around the fireplace in a ruined farmhouse, wondering what the folks at home would be thinking on this hot summer's day in South Africa. Pin-ups adorned the walls of the regimental aid post and there were a few precious bottles of beer warming up in front of the fire. Up on a shelf, the radio—encased in its wooden box and carted here on the back of a mule—sang out *Pistol Packin' Mama*. Shells started exploding over the company positions—and then the telephone rang. There were casualties, one serious. It was a case for the surgeons. Italian stretcher bearers carried the unconscious man to the Jeephead half a mile away, from where he was taken by Jeep along a narrow clayey track to the casualty clearing station approximately three miles away.[298] Five days later, on receiving the telegram from the Department of Defence, Easton's wife, Ellen, wrote to her sisters:

> Devonia
> P.O. Syferbult
> Transvaal
> 8 November '44
>
> My Dear Cora & Susie
> Tonight everything has come to a dead end for me. God above knows how I am going to live through the rest of my life. My darling Glenamus has been killed in action on 3rd November. Had a wire from the department of defence. The poor children are clinging to one thread that is there has been a mistake [that] he was only wounded. But personally, I know it is too true. You will forgive me if I don't write a letter tonight.
>
> All my love,
> Ellen

Because of the shortage of winter clothing, the men wore a mixture of summer and winter garments, military and civilian, some sent from home and some self-made. Headgear also had to be improvised as tin helmets caused headaches at the best of times and in the cold were like instruments of torture. Hobnails caused boots to crack and leak. The best solution was to wrap around layers of hessian, which also gave the boots a good grip.

The military authorities in the Union scrambled to deny that there was any shortage of winter clothing, insisting that the issue was on the same scale as Imperial troops and that, in addition, special mountain warfare clothing had been issued on a "lavish scale".[299]

In a report on the allocation of special winter clothing dated 11 January 1945, it was revealed that 60 oilskin jackets, 400 oilskin trousers and 400 'souwesters' were issued mainly to Commander Royal Artillery and the rest to a collection of units including the 11th South Armoured Brigade, the 12th South African Motorized Brigade and the 24th Guards Brigade. As at 5 January 1945, there were 3,000 to 4,000 front-line troops. The final distribution of winter clothing

[298] DODAR, UWH, Box 140. Various narratives by Capt H.H.H. Biermann, military observer attached to the 12th South African Motorized Brigade.

[299] DODAR, CGS, Box 240, Extract from Staff Conference no. 130, 13/12/1944.

had been made. It was now possible for every man to wear 14 items of clothing at once—if he could fit them all on his body.[300]

After a quiet and clear day on 5 November, there followed a night of fireworks. A barrage such as this could start for no reason other than a nervous sentry firing his rifle. In this case, it seems to have been sparked by the date, combined with a sense of irony on behalf of the initiating Germans. The diarist of the 1/6th Field Regiment recognized the humour in the situation:

> He [the enemy] had his little joke tonight however, for immediately the light faded he began a venerable display of fire-power. Rocket guns, mortars, small arms and guns of all calibres blazed forth until midnight—then he ran out of ammunition ration and just plugged away with half a dozen guns.

Apart from the daily shelling, operations in this sector were limited to patrol activity, sometimes using partisans, who knew the area intimately, as guides. Italians were also used as stretcher bearers on some of these patrols.

The Prince Alfred's Guard operated on the slopes leading down to the Reno River; the enemy occupied the opposite slope and would fire at any movement. Sometimes, a patrol would go out for 36 hours, laying up during the day and observing enemy movements. The First City/Cape Town Highlanders sent out a total of 90 patrols during this period, predominantly fighting patrols aiming to seek and kill the enemy. The 12th South African Motorized Brigade as a whole sent out an average of eight patrols every night, ranging from three men to two platoons. Despite meticulous planning, patrols often came across *casas* occupied by Germans. The work typically entailed physical and mental strain, ambushes, mines and booby-traps.

As an experiment in occupying one of the many small villages in no man's land, the 1/13th Frontier Force Rifles established a section in some houses in La Villa on the night of 3/4 November. For the next three nights they were attacked and counter-attacked, the village changing hands a number of times. One of the small skirmishes which occurred almost daily during the month of November took place when two sections of B Squadron, Natal Mounted Rifles, now in an infantry role under Lieutenant D.S. Smith, took up position in a cluster of empty farmhouses near Gardelletta on the Setta River. This was as far forward

300 DODAR, Div Docs, Box 204, file Special Winter Clothing, 11/1/1945; E. Axelson, *A year in Italy*, p. 156.

as one could go in a vehicle, and in fact the last stretch had to be travelled on foot. On 5 November, the day of the enemy fireworks, about 30 Germans attacked from the northeast, shouting "Heil, SS!" The small section withdrew. That night, 13 Germans attacked the section guarding the bridge. Three South Africans were killed in this action and Douglas Baker was invalided out of the line, suffering from exhaustion and general ill health as a result of his wounds.

Baker had been wounded at San Felice on 5 July and had not fully recovered. Overly keen to return to the fray, he managed to wrangle an early discharge from hospital. Subsequently, officers commanding convalescent depots were ordered to ensure that wounded infantrymen were fully rehabilitated both physically and mentally before being discharged.[301] In spite of the non-stop action taking place, on 9 November Hodgson insisted: "Beyond the weather there is no news at all, so I will close now, hoping to hear from you shortly. I will write again as soon as I get the chance and have accumulated enough news."

After a few days of relative quiet, the 4/22nd Field Regiment made a 'peace offering' in the form of a bombardment at the eleventh hour on 11 November, Armistice Day. The target was an enemy-occupied village. The village was hit again later that day when some infantry were sighted by an observation post.

On 16 November, 23-year-old Lance-Corporal Donald 'Duck' Mundell from Newcastle, a member of a Royal Natal Carbineer patrol, stood on an anti-personnel mine near the Reno River, sustaining a serious injury to the foot. The other members of the patrol, Lieutenant W.J.L. Oxenham, Sergeant J.E. Auld, and Lance-Corporal F.C. Macedo, had to leave him behind. His remains were only discovered in 1996 during road construction. Mundell was identified by his identity discs. The Commonwealth War Graves Commission gives his date of death as 17 November 1944 and his name is inscribed on the memorial at Cassino. Wounded men were left to crawl back to their lines or to be picked up by the German medics on more than one occasion.

Intelligence gathering required close-quarter work. Norman Clothier, a Carbineer and war poet, was wounded in an ambush on 29 January 1945. The incident took place near the ruins of a farm at Casa Creda between Monte Salvaro and Monte Sterlese, west of the battalion forward defence locations on Monte Termine. This, in turn, was close to the notorious German stronghold of Pioppe on the Reno River:

301 DODAR, Div Docs, Box 180 File AQ 13/10, Allied Force Head Quarters, Office of the Surgeon, Return to units of wounded personnel, 6/3/1945.

> Before I could move the Schmeizers blazed from the top of the bank ten yards away. I saw three. The impact was terrible and the first shock of pain was as if red-hot irons were thrust through my stomach … I heard myself crying out, a sort of sobbing wail … My left arm was smashed. Could I get my Tommy gun up to fire with my right to give the others a chance? ... After that, they advanced toward us. I think there were four or five. In addition to white-hooded suits like ours, they also had white masks on their faces. One stooped over me. I half expected him to shoot me, but he only jerked my Tommy gun off me … I thought the cold would kill me very quickly.[302]

Guard duty was another harrowing activity. Major Lionel Murray, a company commander with the First City/Cape Town Highlanders, was entrusted with writing the regimental history. In an atypically expressive moment he wrote: "This exacting duty is performed amidst the incessant noise of gun and mortar, it is performed without the benefit of the excitement and noise of pitched battle. And all the while he sits in the darkness, listening, looking, thinking …"[303]

As temperatures dropped, the observation-post officers were relieved every 24 hours instead of the usual three to four days. Moving in and out of the observation posts was made difficult first by mud, then slush, then ice as the mercury dropped to ten degrees below freezing. Visibility also worsened as the winter fog set in during the first week of November. Forward troops could be relieved only at night or under cover of mist and cloud, as German observation posts on Monte Sole called down shellfire when relief was in progress.

The gunners were seldom rotated out of the line as they lived under less extreme conditions.

Writing from his shelter constructed of sandbags and ammo boxes on the banks of the Setta River, Bourhill tried to convince his mother that the Canadian beer had no effect on the mind. This was clearly not the case:

> Just finished my third bottle of beer … very nice taste—but no effect on the mind at all. It's the first we've had for some time, three bottles per man! It may not have any effects on the mind but it's got plenty on the bladder! I have to get up every few minutes and it's so darned cold outside!! ... Oh well!! Or 'Ho jaa' as Dad used to say when he'd had a long, long day. I aughtn't to say it because I've only had an eight hour day, but I'm ready for the 16-hour night!! I love everybody—even the cunning Hun isn't so bad tonight!

---

302 M. Coghlan, *Pro Patria*, p. 43.

303 L.G. Murray, *First City/Cape Town Highlanders in the Italian Campaign,* p. 51.

Farther back with the medium artillery, Johnston's routine during November and December consisted of "loafing around", washing and drying clothes, a bit of vehicle maintenance, kitchen fatigue and a number of runs to Prato on kit and ration fatigue. Interspersed with this were some days of intense excitement, avoiding enemy patrols and watching the shelling, bombing and strafing of Vergato while on observation post duty.

Forward observers were involved in a deadly war of their own, with each side trying to knock the other out. On 17 November, Gunner J. Rissik, a 19-year-old from Saxonwold in Johannesburg, was killed in a forward observation post on Monte Salvaro. He and Lieutenant L.B. Bell were lying in the same slit trench when a mortar bomb hit. The officer was wounded. In addition to enemy observation posts, targets included troop movements, farmhouses and villages, as well as harassing fire on Monte Sole. However, ammunition was limited to 15 rounds per gun per day. The thought of the rapidly approaching winter occupied the minds of most of the men. A Carbineers regimental newsletter pondered these questions: "How deep will the snow be? Surely it cannot be colder than this? Will the roads be impassable?—and many other queries are in the minds of all. We can but wait and see!"[304] Horror stories about the winter of 1943/44 had been circulated in official documents telling of blizzards blowing in six feet of snow and completely covering the guns.

A light covering of snow fell on 10/11 November, albeit on the higher peaks only, and was accompanied by a biting wind. Hodgson now had time on his hands, if the avalanche of letters he produced is a valid indication. His main theme was, invariably, the weather:

> Monday 6th November 1944
> The weather is definitely not too good these days, but today it is really perfect. At the moment I am sitting in front of the Jeep writing as it is so nice and sunny. There is no need for you to worry about the arrival of the sheepskin jacket as I am sure it will arrive before it gets really cold. At the moment the weather is bad, but it is by no means cold; it is naturally a bit chilly at times but it needs no more than a jersey to keep me warm—as I told you in a previous letter, the cold months are December, January and February, then there is March for the very cold winds during the thaw. Thank you very much for the woollen mittens, which I received yesterday; they are just the thing and I like them very much … You ask me about socks; at the moment I have got as many as I need, but I am bound to get through quite a few pairs in the

[304] DODAR, WD, Box 645, Royal Natal Carbineers, Regimental newsletter, 3–9 November 1944.

winter—if you carry on as you have done in the past by sending up a pair in one of the parcels every now and then, it keeps me in possession of a suitable number. As yet the pyjamas you sent up to me have not arrived, but I expect them to arrive at any moment so they will be here in time for the cold weather.

Thursday 14th November 1944
You say that the weather has been very funny down your way lately—it has been far from funny up here. On the 10th we had our first fall of snow; not a heavy one, but heavy enough to let us know we are going to have quite a bit. Yesterday we had another fall, a bit heavier, so most of the hills have got quite a layer on them, but down in the valleys most of it has melted. I suppose after a couple more falls there will be a continuous carpet everywhere. They say when winter reaches its peak everything gets properly snowed up; in places it even reaches six and eight feet, on the plains it even reaches a couple of feet everywhere and much more in some places.

Monday 20th November 1944
We have had a spell of very good weather during the last five days. It has been sunny all day, and so warm that I have not been wearing a jersey during the day; all the snow has been melted, I am glad to say, but it looks as if it is working up for a spot of rain at the moment, which will mean a break in the weather, and it is too much to hope for us to get another good spell such as we have just had.

Monday 4th December 1944
Lately the weather has been very kind to us. Since the couple of falls of snow that we had in the middle of last month the weather has been marvellous except for a spell of about five days when it rained all the time. Mind you, it gets cold at night and in the early morning but if and when the sun comes out there is no need for me to wear a jersey.

Saturday 9th December 1944
As far as the weather is concerned, it has been raining a bit but not too much; the rest of the time it has been mostly overcast or misty. Mind you, it is not cold these days, I am glad to say, as it is easy to cope with one thing at a time, but when it is wet and cold at the same time it is really too much to cope with.

The soldiers were forbidden to chop down trees as an appeal had been made by the Comune di Castiglione dei Pepoli for the troops to refrain from using chestnut trees and building timber for firewood. Notices to this effect were plastered all over the division area in the winter line. The Comune were particularly annoyed when a pile of wood which they had collected over four days from Cottede, their own forest, was loaded up by soldiers.

Collecting firewood remained a constant chore and Bourhill found it disturbing to fight with old women in black dresses over a few scraps of wood:

> I went for a trip to collect firewood the other day. Ooer, it were fun, gathering the faggots in the snow, it were! The snow was frozen like everything else—our feet included. It looks like drifted hail only more delicate, if you know what I mean. Maybe snow-covered peaks and landscape does look very pretty and all that, but green is the only thing I reckon aught to cover the ground.

Eventually, with South African ingenuity, the men designed and constructed petrol-burning stoves. The learnings gleaned during the previous winter in the central Apennines were circulated among the men. The regimental medical officers visited men in the line to lecture on 'winter hygiene'.

In general, South Africans had a low rate of sickness—0.6 or 0.7 per thousand per day—as opposed to two per thousand per day for the Guards Brigade. This figure refers specifically to an outbreak of malaria which occurred during summer. One medical officer attributed this to the stronger constitution of the colonials, and their superior hygiene. During desert training, the sickness rate had ranked at more than two per thousand, with the Union troops recording a similar figure. Various foodstuffs, such as margarine, were 'vitaminized' in an effort to ward off illness, but the low sickness rate was more likely due to high morale.

However, as can be expected, winter sickness took its toll on the troops. Hodgson remained in perfect health throughout the winter, possibly because he was well equipped, thanks to his parents. Bourhill however, had been generally run-down for months:

> I've put back a lot, if not all, the weight I lost last month—or was it the month before? You remember when I had that cut knee and cough and the weather was awful? Carrying hundreds of pounds of HE daily, chopping timber etc. etc. tends to keep one in the pink! At any rate I'm very fit now. Not a worry and happy as the day is short! Ha Ha!!

Trench foot was the most common ailment affecting troops and much literature and lecturing was produced on the subject. A man's feet would swell, the toes becoming like sausages if they remained wet and cold for a long period of time. They would then turn blue and gangrene would ultimately set in. Walking became so painful as to render the man completely ineffective as a soldier and he would have to be evacuated. Only a small per centage ever returned to the line. Trench foot was treated with gentian violet which was relatively ineffective. The only solution was to keep the feet dry.

To minimize the risk, infantrymen were rotated out of line every four days. This gave them a chance to dry out and get some decent food. The men kept their boots on at all times during their four-day stints in the line, merely loosening their laces.

Spare socks were in great demand and parcels from home invariably contained home-knitted socks which either stretched or shrank. Medical staff maintained that army-issue socks were the best because the knit on home-made socks was too coarse. It was also recommended that the men immerse their boots in hot dubbin—for short periods only—as the best means of keeping feet dry.

Men had trouble putting on their boots in the morning because they had frozen stiff. The solution was to tuck one's boots into the blankets or to order a bigger size. Fur-lined boots of the airman's style were specially ordered for the forward observation officers but these arrived too late to be of any use.

The army used the four-day rotations as an opportunity to give lectures on trench foot and frostbite. Men were rested in Castiglione, Camugnano and Lagaro where bath units were located. Accommodation was provided at a number of establishments, including Union Defence Force rest camps in Prato and Florence during these R&R spells. Italian hotels and boarding houses were requisitioned, complete with cutlery, linen and staff for the officers. Vacancies were circulated and allocations made to the various units. Regimental histories often give the impression that these were for the exclusive use of their particular regiments, but they invariably functioned as Union Defence Force or British rest camps.

Prato is 25 miles from Castiglione and ten miles from Florence, and felt like a world away from the front line. This warm, welcoming Tuscan town is situated on the plains of the River Arno, although the mountains loom large and forbidding in the middle distance. Among Prato's many amenities was the Albergo Springbok, centrally situated on the university campus and consisting of one main block and two wings, each four storeys high. Four hundred leave personnel could be accommodated. The Albergo provided accommodation for short stays, which was better than the trenches but still quite rough, due to the lack of beds. However, the main lounge was well appointed with curtains, mirrors, comfortable chairs and carpets. A games room and a small theatre were housed in the same building. The bar and its contents were all college property, but 500 tumblers were bought by the rest camp unit. The Albergo was forced to close down on 8 December, due to a typhoid outbreak caused by lice.

The epidemic meant that civilian premises were out of bounds even when the establishment reopened in February 1945 as the Springbok Hotel. The troops were not allowed to hold dances because they couldn't invite civilian girls and there were no servicewomen based in Prato. Consequently, the men were bussed into Florence and on occasion, women were brought in from Florence for dances. The number of arrests for being 'out of bounds' increased dramatically because of these drives.

The No. 2 Detachment, South African Rest Camp was located at the Villa Frassineto at 509 Via Aretino Rovezzano, two and a half miles from the centre of Florence. The villa—which opened on 21 December and was later renamed Rusthof—was open to virtually all units for their four-day passes. Although it had capacity for 400 leave personnel, it seldom hosted more than 100 men from a single unit at a time.

The villa belonged to an Italian princess and had previously been used as a finishing school for girls. Apparently Queen Victoria had once stayed here on a visit to Italy. It had central heating in every room, a very comfortable lounge, hot showers and dormitories, and an L-shaped dining room with a balcony for a band. The main villa comprised a basement, ground, first and second floors. The annex and granary were two-storey buildings. The main building and annex housed small rooms but the granary consisted of dormitories. It was possible to construct rugby, soccer and hockey fields within the extensive grounds. Conveniently, there was even a chapel in a separate building on the property. In spite of the overflowing septic tank, the villa became a home from home where the men were even served coffee in bed. Although it was two to three miles from the centre of Florence, there was normally a bus or a lift going. The warm atmosphere more than made up for its remote location on the eastern periphery, close to the Florence Commonwealth War Cemetery on the northern bank of the Arno.

Non-Europeans were served by the Protea Club and the Drop-In Cape Club. No. 3 NE Leave and Transit Camp, located about five miles south of Florence, catered to the Cape Corps. The Union Defence Force Institutes ran a number of clubs which also offered sleeping accommodation. In Prato there was the non-residential, teetotal but still popular Red Tabs Club. Later renamed the Orange Flash Club, it was open at certain times during the day, and closed at 2100 hours. Men would queue for sweet milky tea and a bun at the counter. The main hall where the men took their tea was filled with tables of varying sizes. They would sit here for hours, sometimes even sprawling asleep across the tables in their mud-stained clothing. The stone floors were usually soiled with mud and snow brought in on their boots. A first-rate Italian band performed on a platform in one corner. The hall was pleasantly warm with a stove positioned near the door of the reading room. Books, magazines, draughts and writing materials were made available. (SAWAS members, enjoying officer status, were allowed to censor letters.) Some played ping-pong or spoke to one of the resident chaplains. Many Guardsmen frequented this popular place and apparently they made the most use of the library. The few Afrikaans books were also in great demand.

In Florence, the Institutes managed the Voortrekker Club, formerly Albergo Colombia, which could accommodate 140 people.

In addition to operating in the big centres, the Institutes also maintained a mobile canteen in the mountains which dispensed coffee, travelling as far forward as it dared on the roads under observation.

For Hodgson, the four-day rest period in Florence was not the raucous, uproarious party that many others may have experienced. He was content to make use of all the comforts available at the Voortrekker Club, with the occasional visit to the opera or cinema. It was enough to simply get out of the line and he lived for his next opportunity to get into Florence:

> I am back from my spell of leave in Florence—actually I got back a few days ago, but what with one thing and another I haven't been able to get down to any writing at all; with the result that my correspondence is far behind hand, as I have hardly written any letters for about three weeks now. Well, to get back to the question of leave; I had a wonderful time and thoroughly enjoyed every minute of my stay. There is an enormous amount to tell you and as I will not have time to tell you all in this letter, I will just tell you about some of it now.
>
> First of all I will tell you about the 'Voortrekker Club' where I stayed while on leave. I must say that I have never known the Welfare branch to have everything so well organized. The building was what used to be a very nice hotel—it was large and very comfortable. The place was taken over lock, stock and barrel, and was run just like a hotel which was just the thing as one wants to get away from the army routine. The dining room was very large and seated us all so there was no waiting in a queue; the service was good as there were plenty of waitresses. Then the main thing, the grub was excellent and plenty of it.
>
> There were five of us in the room where I slept, comfortable beds, water laid on and a very good view from the balcony; the lounge downstairs was excellent, very comfortable and cozy—most of the day and in the evenings there was a good

> orchestra playing. I was happy in the club itself; two nights I was quite contented to sit in the lounge and take it easy. During my leave I went round with a chap by the name of Harleigh, who is a sergeant on the 'I' staff. I am sure he enjoyed the leave as much as I did and we were both very happy all the time. The shopping centre of the town is very good indeed, and very much on the same style as Joburg. I really thoroughly enjoyed being able to look into shop windows and so on again, as it is such a long time since I last had the chance. I bought a few things but not much as the majority of things are so very expensive. I am sending you a small assortment of buttons which rather took my fancy. A striking feature of the place was the large number of buttons on show, so I bought these for you. I don't know what you will be able to do with them, but I am sure you will be able to do something with them. That night Gerry Harleigh and I went to see another picture: 'The Happy Breed' which was also very good indeed.

Officers' rest hotels included the Hotel Roma and the Lucchesi which was on the banks of the Arno, about 100 yards up from the Ponte Vecchio. The Roma was smaller than the Minerva in Rome and even more noisy and crowded. According to one female guest, "Sometimes a wild hooting and yodelling would resound up the staircase". Florence received electricity from Rome and supply was erratic; hot water was a rarity and "quite often there was no water at all, and much of the time the lavatories wouldn't flush. They became very unpleasant".[305] Florence's proximity to the front line was reflected in piles of kit left in the lobby and mud from the soldiers' boots, fresh from the front. The lounges were packed, dimly lit and blue with smoke, but had a jovial atmosphere.

Very few officers from the 6th South African Armoured Division stayed at the Roma and other Florence hotels over Christmas as most preferred to be with their own units.

Female members of the Union Defence Force were housed at the YWCA and sometimes at the Hotel Roma in the Piazza Santa Maria Novella. On the night of 17 January 1945, the YWCA became the honeymoon hotel of Sapper W. Calder of Durban and Nursing Sister Ann Brink of Belfast after their wedding in Florence's Wesley House Chapel. In another ceremony in Florence, Kate 'Bunny' Vorster from 107th South African General Hospital, formerly of Port Elizabeth, was married to Lieutenant Petrus 'Peter' van Zyl of Paarl.

Offensive operations continued throughout December. The Grenadier

---

305 S. de Wet, *Shifty in Italy,* p. 56.

Guards were in action on 2/3 December between Gardelletta and Monte Sole. The Frontier Force Rifles came under command of the Guards and were committed to fighting for certain features, all of which eventually had to be surrendered. The Indian regiment was now seriously depleted. On 7 December, a negro battalion from the 92nd United States Infantry Division came under command of the 6th South African Armoured Division to relieve the Imperial Light Horse/Kimberley Regiment.

The enemy had "tried a bit of nonsense" in the South African sector during mid-December and it was being said that the troops were "having a hard time and have suffered quite a few setbacks".[306]

Nevertheless, Hodgson believed that it was a good thing for the Germans to "put their cards on the table" and all that was needed was some good weather in order to drive them back to the Alps:

> This German Offensive is just the thing in my opinion. I think it is his last kick and if we give him enough rope he will hang himself once and for all. Let him get right in, then cut his light and water off is the way I look at it.

As the thin layer of snow melted, the ground turned to slush, making conditions in the line unspeakably miserable. It was no longer possible to spend every four-day rest period in Prato or Florence. Castiglione was a poor substitute but Hodgson was happy enough:

> At the moment I am very comfortable; outside there is a very thick mist with a steady rain. I am inside next to a lovely log fire writing by the light I rigged up from some wireless batteries. There is a good programme on the wireless and at my elbow I have two quart bottles of beer—I ask you, what more could a soldier want? Especially with the prospect of another two bottles of beer tomorrow night and no work to do tomorrow.
>
> The weather is still not what one might wish for on a holiday but on the other hand it is not too bad out, as it is only misty with a light rain, instead of sleet or a heavy rain with a biting wind. As usual there is mud everywhere and mud which has to be seen to be believed; this we have more-or-less got used to by now as we have had ten weeks of it. A few days ago the mud was frozen solid and it just crumbled under one's foot; it was very slippery as it was much like ice.
>
> At the moment the wireless is playing: *I'm Dreaming of a White Christmas*. Someone has just said, "Why must they rub it in!" It looks as if the heavy snow might be a bit

[306] J.B. Hodgson–M.V. Hodgson, 3/1/1945.

> late, but it would not surprise me if we had a heavy fall at any moment. I will not be sorry as I think it will be better if everything hardens up and gets rid of all the mud and slush. It is funny these days as there is very little talk or feeling of Christmas these days, as it hardly seems to exist under the present atmosphere. I myself only think of it when I write a letter which is unusual for me. Mind you, I will be thinking of you all a lot over the holidays. A friend of mine, Morris Mathews, the company's communications corporal, has been awarded the MM—he really deserved it and I am glad to see he got it. We are always together due to our work and we have become great friends. He is also in Company Headquarters and is responsible for all the communications and communication equipment in the company.

The men became children again with the first real snowfall on 23 December. They frolicked in the snow, seemingly with little thought given to personal safety or how they would dry out later. The gunners of the 166 Newfoundland Regiment, who were based in Pian di Setta, were particularly amused to see these hardened South African soldiers catching snow flakes on their tongues and skiing down slopes that professionals would steer clear of. The men devoted much time to manufacturing skis and trying them out during the next month. Skiing in the moonlight, resulted in some spectacular falls. These antics were well documented in the publicity photographs and on *SA Mirror*.

Not all South Africans were new to the sport, however. Starting on 4 December, a group of 29 other ranks and four officers had been given proper skiing lessons by Alpine instructors, learning how to snow plough and *stem bogen* at the School of Mountain Warfare. In addition to physical training for strengthening muscles, the course covered climbing techniques, rope management and the mechanics of climbing on snow and ice, culminating in a cross-country test where each was required to carry 30lb packs and rifles. The South African public relations team was there to take photographs, which were widely published. It seems that the army encouraged the sport and even Hodgson was keen to give it a try:

> The snow is really lovely these days; just the kind of thing one sees and reads about in storybooks. This evening we got an issue of skis to the company upon which we can fool around and enjoy ourselves. I am going to give them a tryout tomorrow morning. I am looking forward to it as it should be good fun as well as an experience. As you know, I am no expert at these things, but willing to try anything once.

There was little festive spirit during the week leading up to Christmas. A rumour had been circulating in the Union that the division was going to be sent home for Christmas but the men themselves were under no such illusion. Even the prospect of a spell of long leave seemed remote. When the ever-present wireless played *I'm Dreaming of a White Christmas* or *I'm Stepping Out with a Memory Tonight*, the music only invoked feelings of melancholy and longing. Soldiers imagined the folks at home getting into the holiday mood and getting ready for a feast, while all they could expect was an extra helping of 'desert turkey'; in other words, bully beef.

Montorio is an isolated village above and to the right of the Setta River. It was well forward in the winter line, directly exposed to Monte Sole. On Christmas Day, the barn in which members of the 1/6th Field Regiment (14/18 Battery) were billeted, on a farm called Barberino near Montorio, accidentally burned down. The owner submitted a claim for a long list of belongings including animal feed and tools. Gunners J.H. Hindman and Trollip were brought up on charges, although negligence was not established beyond reasonable doubt. However, Hindman was later sentenced for another crime and appeared on the illegal absentee list after serving 28 days' detention.

Johnston was in Montepiano for Christmas. Extracts from his diary reflect the typical Christmas experience of the B Echelon:

24th	Much booze, midnight mass. Six inch snow. Parcels.
25th	Up late. Christmas dinner with mob. No good. Eric to bed with cold.
26th	Fetched wood in aft. Slide down mountainside like kids. Washed clothes.

Church services were held in English and Afrikaans at the Red Tabs Club and the Prato cathedral throughout Saturday 23 December, Sunday 24 December and Christmas Day. Concerts and carol services were held at the Outspan Club and at the cinema hall in Castiglione. A nativity play was hosted at the Colosseum in Prato. Soldiers took pleasure in hosting Christmas parties for the local children and even General Poole showed up at one such event.

In addition to the Yule season, four notable ceremonial and celebratory occasions took place during December: the issuing of the Africa Service Medal to all ranks (3 December), Dingaan's Day (16 December), the dedication of the Castiglione Cemetery (28 December) and General Poole's birthday (29 December). Extracts from the daily Intelligence Summaries reveal that the front may have been static during December, but it was far from quiet:

1800 hrs 1 December to 1800 hrs 2 December
At 2200 hrs last night we attacked pt 445. Considerable MG and mortar fire was encountered and confused fighting continued until 0400 hrs at which time consolidated on the rocky feature at 792276.

1800 hrs 2 December to 1800 hrs 3 December
At 0145 hrs our attack on pt 445 was resumed. Strong resistance including accurate mortar fire was encountered but by 0230 hrs we had occupied pt 476 … night patrols were active again on both sides.

1800 hrs 5 December to 1800 hrs 6 December
An enemy patrol ambushed our mule team at 768272 last night. Our own patrols were mortared … the latter patrol was also machine gunned from pt 476 and pt 445.

1800 hrs 9 December to 1800 hrs 10 December
The enemy attacked our positions on pt 431 while relief was in progress last night and succeeded in forcing our troops from the feature. Except for this fighting, there was little activity.

1800 hrs 16 December to 1800 hrs 17 December
The only contact last night was at 812281 where our patrol was fired upon from the house … judging from the number of cigarette ends thrown out of a top floor window, the house is occupied by a considerable number of men.

1800 hrs 21 December to 1800 hrs 22 December
On our right sector a patrol contacted an enemy working party on the forward slopes of pt 445 last night. The patrol withdrew after an exchange of fire.

1800 hrs 22 December to 1800 hrs 23 December
On our right sector last night, an enemy patrol approached our position at Ca Serra and withdrew after an exchange of fire.

1800 hrs 27 December to 1800 hrs 28 December
Enemy shelling has been on the normal scale, a total of 123 rounds being reported in the 24 hours to 1700 hrs. Mortar fire has been heavy in some areas.

1800 hrs 28 December to 1800 hrs 29 December
Enemy shelling was negligible last night but infantry weapons were active. A considerable amount of mortar fire was reported on our left sector and on the right, MGs were very active throughout the night. Twelve Spandaus were reported in 8028 and 8128. They were engaged by our tanks and mortars, one MG at 8128 being silenced by three direct hits.

1800 hrs 29 December to 1800 hrs 30 December
Our front was very quiet during the night, and there was no contact … The day

> has been almost as quiet as the night, for little movement was observed and only 50 shells were reported. Of these, 10 were of heavy calibre.

On Christmas night, strong enemy patrols pushed into the Serchio valley zone on the western flank. On Boxing Day, they attacked along a six-mile front astride the Serchio River, thrusting into the line held by the 92nd United States Infanry Division. Some units broke, falling back in a state of disorganization, necessitating a more general withdrawal—the only one of the campaign. This attack coincided with the Battle of the Bulge, a major German offensive against the Americans in the Ardennes Forest on the Western Front.

Christmas night also saw a bombing raid take place against the South Africans. Although this seems to have made little impression on the people on the ground, to the Luftwaffe, these were daring and dangerous raids made with minimal resources. A pilot's report mentions "widespread conflagration. Vicious flak". The bombers would sometimes make more than one sortie per night, operating in ones and twos. Interception by Allied planes had recently taken a heavy toll on Nachtschlachtgruppe 9 while it was returning from a 'road hunting' mission in the moonlight.[307]

Meanwhile, the men of the Pretoria Regiment faced their own challenges during December. Tactical headquarers was based at Stanco village at this time. The regiment suffered four fatal casualties in December, caused predominentaly by shellfire. The safer surrounds of Prato were chosen as the venue for regimental dinners and parades. At a medal parade on 17 December, the commanding officer presented Lieutenant N.H. Thompson with the ribbon of the Military Cross. The medal citation for the late Sergeant J. Howe, who won the Military Medal and was killed on 27 June, was also read out.

Around the middle of the month, the regiment's C Squadron came out of the line for a rest in the Prato area. A Christmas party was organized for the night of 20 December, which ended in tragedy. The typhoid epidemic in Prato meant that fraternization with the locals was forbidden; instead, nurses from 107th South African General Hospital were asked to partner the troops at the dance. Transport in the form of three-ton trucks, was sent to fetch the party—which comprised seven or eight nurses plus Sergeant Waterson of the South African Medical Corps—from outside the Roma Hotel in Florence. The trucks arrived

[307] N. Beale, *Ghost bombers, the moonlight war of NSG*, p. 34.

in Prato at approximately 2100 hours. The night was clear and dry but there was no moon. The bar closed at 2310 hours, although apparently there was no excessive drinking. Three officers—Major F.P. Kightley, Captain Houghton and Lieutenant Matthews—refrained from dancing in order to control and generally regulate matters. There were no signs of drunkennes at the dance, which was an orderly affair. When it finished at 2359 hours, the same transport took the party back to Florence. The driver, Trooper W.J.A. Gresse, was said to be one of the best in the squadron, and had been driving in the army for four years. He had a Union Defence Force licence, but no civil licence. Seating was provided by three benches in the back of the truck, one bench across the top and two more down the sides. Nurse Winifred Mary Shaw and Lance-Corporal John Ernest Klerck of the Pretoria Regiment were sitting up front with the driver, although it was against regulations to have three people sitting in the front of a truck. No one spoke much on the return journey.

On the autostrada about two to three miles outside Prato, the party encountered a bomb-damaged bridge with a large block of concrete hanging down. The lights of the truck were fairly good and Nurse Shaw first saw the bridge when they were about 20 to 30 yards from it. "I am not a good judge of distance," she told the court. "I noticed the hanging concrete block at about the same time that I saw the bridge. It seemed to be a little to the right of our line of approach." Lance-Corporal Harold Victor Bungay was sitting on the right side of the truck about third from the front:

> About 20 minutes to half an hour after we left, I felt a slight swerve and heard a bang which sounded to me like a blowout. The nurse sitting on my right fell across my lap and I thought at the time she had just received a fright. I shouted: "It is all right. It's only a blowout." There was then a general cry to stop the truck … The driver brought the truck to a very smooth standstill at a point about 200 yards from where I heard the bang. Matches were lit and I saw a nurse lying on the floor of the truck bleeding from the head. There was a certain amount of confusion and I was more or less pinned to my seat by the nurse lying across my lap, who was P/N [Professional Nurse] J. Still.

The canvas canopy had been torn away from the back of the truck and the superstructure damaged. Nurse Williamson was bleeding severely from the ear and Nurse Saville had a wound in the back of the head. Nurse Constance Muriel Roets was sitting in the back of the truck with her back toward the engine, with Nurse Saville sitting in the corner on her left:

> I twice asked Nurse Saville whether she was hurt, but received no reply. On touching her, I felt that she was bleeding from an injury. It was dark at the time and by the light of matches, we saw what had happened and placed Nurse Saville on the floor of the truck. She vomited and was placed in another vehicle. In the meantime, we rendered what assistance we could. I saw others injured but only attended to Nurse Saville.

Captain William Reginald Barker arrived on the scene a few minutes after the accident and produced a first-aid kit. The nurses were carried to Barker's 15 ctw. Major Buchanan arrived from the direction of Prato a minute or two later and shone the lights of his vehicle into the three-tonner.

After first aid was rendered, the injured were taken to hospital in Florence. Barker had considerable experience as a transport officer and his natural reaction was to carry out certain investigations: "I had a look at the driver both at the scene of the accident and later at the hospital. I saw no signs of him being under the influence of liquor."

At the court of inquiry, much reference was made to a problem with one of the headlights of the truck. However, the verdict was that this was a battle accident, due to the demolition of the railway bridge. The medical records state that there was a slight smell of alcohol on the breath of Joyce Saville and that she was comatose until she died later that day. Twenty-three-year-old Shirly Williamson of Witbank also died. The two nurses are buried in adjoining graves in the Florence Commonwealth War Cemetery. Sergeant Waterson died two days later. The war diary of Pretoria Regiment (Princess Alice's Own) on 20 and 21 December stated: NTR (nothing to report).

On Christmas Day, 600 men of the Pretoria Regiment crowded into the mess hall for Christmas dinner. Two Jeeps belonging to the 6th South African Armoured Division Signal Squadron were stolen on Christmas Eve and recovered on Christmas Day, which was mild and sunny. One was found at main division headquarters at Lagaro and one, slightly damaged, was found near the cemetery in Castiglione. At 1300 hours, the war diary notes that one lance-corporal—on loan to the cable troop from the wireless troop—and one signal linesman had been seriously wounded by shellfire while repairing a break in the Guards Brigade line. At the same time the following day, the diarist wrote: "The lance-corporal linesman who was wounded in action yesterday, died at 0530 hours this morning, [and] is buried in the Division Cemetery here. A number of officers and men from the squadron attended the funeral."

Lance-Corporal Ian McHarry of the South African Signals Corps had volunteered to repair the line damaged by shelling, apparently so that the regimental signallers working with the 25-pounders could enjoy their Christmas lunch. He was 20 years old, hailed from Craighall in Johannesburg and played cricket for Parktown Boys High School. Gunner Charl Cilliers, a friend from school days, described him as "… a gentle, intelligent person with clear eyes and a pale complexion". Shortly before he died he had made the strange comment that "you don't want anything to happen to you over Christmas".[308]

Christmas celebrations had to be postponed for B Company, Royal Natal Carbineers, because it was manning the forward positions on Christmas Day. However, the men more than made up for the lack when their turn came.

Hodgson could have wished for no better present than the arrival of his sheepskin jacket:

> The weather did break and we did have a white Christmas—the first snow fell on the evening of the 23rd. It was a fairly heavy fall and we woke up next morning to find it just on a foot deep. Up to now I have found the snow very pleasant indeed, but that of course may be just the novelty. It is certainly a good bit better than the mud and slush; all the mud gets frozen stiff and it is just like a big lump of ice.
>
> My sheep skin jacket arrived the other day and I am really very pleased indeed with it, it is just the thing for the cold weather we are experiencing and are going to experience. Also thank you very much for all the lovely parcels of grub I received from all of you. They were just the thing and contained all the good things one misses up here. Now I am waiting to hear all about your Christmas as I am sure you had a marvellous time and I want to hear what you did.
>
> Owing to circumstances we did not have our Christmas on Christmas Day, but we had it yesterday. Nevertheless we had a very good day indeed and we thoroughly enjoyed ourselves. I did not get up too early in the morning as we had not got to bed too early the night before. I went down to breakfast at half-past nine. During the morning we had a church service, and it was really grand to sing all the Christmas carols again. We had our dinner at midday; the menu was as follows: roast turkey, roast pork and roast potatoes, followed by Christmas pudding and custard, closely followed by nuts and fruit. During the meal we had beer and wine to drink. Although all the food came out of tins it was very good indeed, and I should say it was a very creditable meal for the army.
>
> With all the snow on the ground there has been quite a bit of fun as you can well imagine. Quite a few fellows have made rough wood and iron structures and have done a bit of tobogganing—I have not done any myself but what I have seen of it, looks grand fun to me. I have been involved in quite a few snowball fights which are

[308] G.B. Hobbs, *From Sicily to the Alps*, p. 191.

> very good fun. Also on a couple of occasions we have tried rolling big snowballs; as yet we have not been too successful but have managed to roll one about three feet in diameter. We start with a small hard ball, then roll it round and round in the snow and it gradually gets bigger and bigger.

To be on leave in Rome over the festive season was as good as it got—for someone away from home in a theatre of war. Hofmeyr House held its housewarming party on Christmas Day. The 200 leave personnel were treated to a traditional Christmas dinner—most of it out of tins—with some extras, thanks to donations made by the SAWAS. There was a cabaret and a dance, with the usual church services also held

Before dinner at the Minerva, the white-haired Captain Zimmerlie, catering adviser to the Union Defence Force and officer commanding the Union Defence Force Cookery School, made an appearance as Papa Natale. Dressed in a red velvet tablecloth and a cottonwool beard, he handed out gifts to the military and the Italian staff. A visiting American officer made a short speech, saying this was the happiest Christmas he had spent away from home.

New Year's Eve was even more festive. The pipe band of the Scottish Horse played in the New Year and performed a 'musical interlude' which was heartily applauded. In the small hours of the morning they serenaded the statue of the laughing elephant in the Piazza Minerva and "they were joined by a merry throng of revellers from the hotel".[309] Then they danced around the obelisk which sits on the elephant's back and dates back to the 6 BC. The structure was once called *Porcino*, Italian for 'piggy', because of its sturdy appearance.

Amore flourished, as is inevitable in Rome, and a number of weddings were celebrated in December. The first wedding reception to be held at the Minerva Hotel was that of Lieutenant-Colonel Harpur and Nursing Sister Thelma Trew of Pietermartitzburg. Pat Lyster, the Springbok winger now promoted to captain, also married a Pietermaritzburg lass, who was a nursing sister from 108th South African General Hospital. The wedding took place at the Methodist Church in Rome. The best man was Captain P.J. Frank; the male guests wore winter battledress and the wedding cake was cut with a bayonet.

It has been said that one in three wartime marriages was not worth saving. Hasty embarkation marriages often ended up on the rocks, although due to the

309 DODAR, WD, Box 726 No 1 Union Defence Force Officers' Rest Camp CMF, 13–28 February 1945.

morality of the time, some chose to live with their mistakes.[310] A letter written by an officer in the Union Defence Force administration headquarters in Rome is proof that some in the military hierarchy were romantics at heart. The author is unknown as it is an unsigned carbon copy, but it is addressed to a senior staff officer, Colonel D.H. Ollemans MC:[311]

> Q & T Branch
> UDF Adm HQ (Main) CMF
> December 1944
>
> Dear Col Ollemans
> I have been approached by Lt (Mrs) Melville, our entertainment officer on a rather ticklish problem. It would appear that a Lt B.L. Goldsworthy, who is with H.Q. Sqn Pretoria Regt, has a wife who is a W.A.A.S. with the 'Sundowners'. The eternal triangle has come about, the odd corner being one Sgt Cohen. She is a child of 18 and has told the husband she's had him and wants a divorce. As they have only been married a short while and she is an excellent type, Mrs Melville feels that all can be put straight if the two can be brought together again. Sgt Cohen has been removed from the Unit. The 'Sundowners' all have 14 days' leave in Rome as from 1 January and this letter is to ask if it is possible for Lt Goldsworthy to be given special leave to correspond with this period. I do a lot of things in this war, but I never expected I should also be the Marriage Officer around the place.
> Please do what you can.
>
> Kind regards

The Pretoria Regiment was based in Prato at this time and history relates that Colonel Ollemans did indeed give Goldsworthy leave to go to Rome but the eventual outcome of the affair remains a mystery.

On 30 December an international rugby match was played at Foro d'Italia between South Africa and New Zealand. South Africa won 8–3. Peter Bruyns of the South African Air Force scored both tries in front of a crowd of 7,000 servicemen. For the Americans, the highlight of the holiday attractions was the Spaghetti Bowl football game, played between teams representing the 5th Army and the 12th Air Force, which was held on New Year's Day in Florence's municipal stadium.

---

310 J. Costello, *Love, sex and war, changing values*, p. 360.

311 DODAR, Div Docs, File AQ/317, Private Correspondence GOC, Letter to Colonel Ollemans from GOC, December 1944

Those in the front line were advised not to get drunk in case of an attack, but B Company, Royal Natal Carbineers, which had been in the trenches over Christmas, was enjoying a spell at the rear. On their first night out of the line, Hodgson—who hardly ever overindulged—and his comrades sat in a circle passing around bottles of alcohol. Each man took a swig before passing the bottle, and when that one finished, another bottle of whatever was available went around.

That night, Hodgson passed out in the snow but somehow survived the cold. There had been some new snowfalls and the flakes now lay two feet deep. In some places it was waist high. Hodgson discovered that he enjoyed the European winter. His New Year's Eve was more subdued than Christmas but memorable nevertheless:

> The New Year was very pleasantly quiet and restful; there was a bit of celebrating but not much. Four of us played bridge on Old Year's Night—playing the old year out and the new year in. Actually, I think our game was a record sitting—eight and a half hours continuous playing. We started at six in the evening and did not stop until half past two in the morning.

At Montepiano, Johnston's New Year was a bit depressing: "Sawed wood. Tea at club [the Outspan Club]. Letters. Hot water over Eric's leg. Two drinks and bed." The following day he went alone up the mountain to fetch wood and wrote some letters.

The war diary of the 1/6th Field Regiment relates that on New Year's Eve, midnight mass was heralded with a chorus of bell-ringing from the multitude of churches in the area, and a chorus of gunfire and fireworks joined in. From their positions at Pian di Setta, the 25-pounders added their quota to the fireworks and the Ack Ack put up "some very confident Vs". The Germans then put up an even more spectacular display.

General Poole and other senior staff were invited by the Scots Guards to a New Year's Eve party at brigade headquarters which, according to Major A.B. Theunissen, was in an imposing building well up the line. This remote castle was at Montorio in the mountains above and to the right of Pian di Setta, and had served as the Guards headquarters since November.

The main access road along the Setta River valley was under such close observation that all troops, with the exception of the General Officer Commanding, were forbidden to travel on it during the day. The alternative route, via Lagaro and Ripoli, was so steep and slippery that only one-way traffic in 'Jeep trains' was permitted to pass. From there to Montorio, the road passes along a sharp ridge through Monte Acuto, running parallel to the river. Monte Sole was close by, but the trees and high banks on the roadside provided some protection from observation. In spite of this, headquarters still came under fire from time to time.

Apparently the Scots Guards was scheduled to carry out an attack on the night of Hogmanay but it was called off, much to the troops' relief. Instead, they had a traditional evening of bagpipes, toasts in Gaelic and good Scotch whisky. An excellent band played Hungarian and Austrian music, also managing *The Merry Widow Waltz* and ending with *Lili Marlene*.

It had been a long year; a leap year, in fact, with 366 days.

The enemy also rotated troops in and out of the line during the static phase. The 167th and 264th Grenadier regiments, the 94th German Infantry Division, the 16th SS Division and the 4th German Para Division were identified by intelligence at various times.

At the end of December, the 16th SS Division was relieved by the 4th Para Division. After a month in the sector, the latter was replaced by the 157th Mountain Division. The 4/13th Frontier Force Rifles carried out a highly successful raid on Pt 431 on the night of 30/31 January. Their capture of prisoners confirmed the presence of the 157th Mountain Division.

The South African troops, running right to left, were as follows: Imperial Light Horse/Kimberley Regiment, Royal Natal Carbineers, Witwatersrand Rifles/Regiment De la Rey, First City/Cape Town Highlanders, and Combat Command Charlie. On the left of these regiments was the 4/13th Frontier Force Rifles and in the Riola area, an American negro battalion was under command.

The Royal Natal Carbineers was still based on Monte Termine. According to the regiment's war diary, the beginning of 1945 was very cold. Soldiers had to carry their water bottles under their jackets while on patrol to prevent them from freezing. This wasn't the only problem facing patrols: after a period without fresh snowfall, a crust had formed on the snow making it almost impossible to move silently. In some places, the snow lay almost 30 inches deep and it was not unusual to fall into a snowdrift up to one's armpits. Stretchers were pulled on sleighs.

On some days, the temperatures did not rise above freezing. Those who wore Brylcreem in their hair, and many did, found that it would freeze while they slept. It seems, though, that Hodgson didn't feel the cold, as these extracts from letters to his sister suggest:

> Friday 16th January 1945
> These days it is very warm indeed and I think I can quite safely say that spring is just about started or starting. Most of the snow has melted and everything is beginning to take on a greenish tinge, and all the fruit trees are in bud. I feel certain though, that we will have another cold spell yet, but I can assure you that the prospect does not worry me in the least, as I have taken quite a liking to the cold weather.

> Friday 26th January 1945
> The weather has been very good up to the last couple of days; there is a bit of a bad spell at the moment—it is raining and has been doing so all day; it is the first fall of rain that we have had since the first proper fall of snow. The night before last we had about four more inches of snow, but apart from that we have been having plenty of sunshine, even though the sun is not terribly warm it is cheerful, and I must admit that apart from my feet, the cold has not worried me at all.

On the evening of 21 January, two German planes dropped some bombs in the Lagaro area, hoping to do damage to the divisional headquarters. Johnston's diary contains the following entry: "Bombed in eve. After first lot fell, went to have a look. Got to tank in time to hug the earth when second stick fell. Close."

The 8 Casualty Clearing Station also experienced a close call when a stick of bombs fell close by. The incident resulted in 13 casualties, 12 of them military, of whom one died. Many of the injured were medical orderlies who had only just arrived.

The following day, Johnston made a proper inspection of the craters and pronounced them "very close" to his own position. A number of unexploded incendiaries remained and required disposal. Johnston mounted a .50-calibre machine gun in case the plane returned, but no more aircraft appeared.

A patrol from B Company, Royal Natal Carbineers had a narrow escape at Vallego di Sotto. Sergeant Smith and Corporal Airey had gone forward to investigate a house. Smith thought he saw the outline of a man in a white snow suit. He turned to Airey and whispered "That's a __ Kraut isn't it?!" Next, the men heard a bolt action in the window. Smith shot the sentry who was standing only ten to 15 yards away. His shot was met with a response from four automatic weapons, and the answering volley left Coporal Airey wounded in the arm.[312]

[312] DODAR, WD, Box 646, Royal Natal Carbineers, Newsletter 20–27 January 1945.

Approximately 800 South Africans occupied Lagaro where main divisional headquarters was situated. Rear divisional headquarters was based at Castiglione.

Axelson noted in his log on 4 January 1945 that "Castiglione dei Pepoli was becoming positively inundated with South African females". First, he met the acclaimed (and elegant) South African photographer, Constance Stewart. He then saw two nurses at forward defence locations and eight more at the 8 Casualty Clearing Station.

Around that time, the entertainment group, The Bullytins, hosted a concert in the village. The performance, one of their last, might well have been poor, as complaints were received after almost every show. Most of their audiences were American. Axelson made no comment on the standard of the performance, however.

On 25 January, Axelson noticed two SAWAS members disembarking from a staff car in the Castiglione square. They had been working in Prato for the past two months and were now in Castiglione to run the Outspan Club.

The Outspan Club was the most forward YMCA–TocH facility in Italy, situated in the village square, in what was apparently a most fashionable café. It was run by Corporal H.M. Vining, formerly a miner from Johannesburg who 'commanded' a staff of 20 Italian civilians. Although not a fancy venue, it served 3,000 to 4,000 cups of tea and coffee free of charge every day.

Castiglione was about the farthest forward any woman could go. Some women did however, manage to wrangle their way to the front, including Constance Stewart, who photographed men in their dug-outs, and Sampie de Wet of SAWAS, who visited the forward positions of the Pretoria Regiment in the winter line at the invitation of Colonel Arthur Johnstone. De Wet was surprised to find a homely atmosphere at the line. Officers were reading in front of the fire in the mess and one was mending ski sticks. A large black dog was stretched out in front of the fire. Comparing this scene with what she experienced in the leave hotels she wrote:

> In spite of all the gaiety, the side of the war that we saw at the Roma was a horror side. Men came to dance and drink and forget death and discomfort, and then they would suddenly show their real feelings. Here, right near the line, it was much more homely, and at the same time more serious.[313]

[313] S. de Wet, *Shifty in Italy*, p. 142.

While the snow lay thick on the ground and the Royal Natal Carbineers was occupying foxholes on Monte Termine, a wedding took place just a few miles from the front in a former fascist club. Captain M.M. Horner of the Royal Natal Carbineers looked like a man-mountain standing next to his bride, Nursing Sister L. 'Tickey' Chivers from Sea Point in Cape Town. A Royal Artillery padre performed the ceremony, assisted by Captain Reverend Victor Shaw of Pietermaritzburg. The bride was given away by General Poole himself.

In Prato, the Springbok Hotel (No. 3 Det South African Rest Camp) opened again from 2 February until the end of May. There was talk of moving it to Livorno but instead, it moved to the Venice area, four miles north of Mestre on Route 13. By June 1945, it was operating as the Outspan, better known as Villa Volpi. While still in Prato, de Wet recorded a typical day's work in the Springbok Hotel:

> 13/2/45. Day at the Albergo. (a) Nice Afrikaans man, de Jager, to ask whether I would censor a parcel, said yes. (b) Censored the parcel. Told him where the APO is. (c) A young Natal Carbineer, Ley, to change his book, and stayed for a long time while I gave him advice on what to see in Florence …

In Florence, the British Information Centre on Via Tornabuoni addressed questions from troops, such as "Am I allowed into civilian cinemas?", "What club can I go to?" and "What tours are available?"

De Wet provided a shopping service from Prato, but once in Florence, the men could visit the Allied Forces gift shop at 56 Via Calzaiuoli or make use of the 'Say it with Flowers' service at the Robertson Club.

At this time, certain Italian florists were running a scam by soliciting floral telegraphic orders for transmission to the United Kingdom, South Africa and elsewhere. Men were warned however, that "There is no way at the present time, by which an Italian florist can effect delivery of flowers in the UK or Union of South Africa. Such activity is patently illegal. Consequently any member of the Allied forces who expends money for such service can expect to suffer the resulting financial loss".[314]

South Africans had access by invitation to the Allied Officers' Club, situated right next to the information centre, as well as the Savoia, a large British club.

---

[314] DODAR, WD, Box 630, 7/23rd Medium Regiment, Routine Order 7/45, 17/2/1945.

No. 54 British Rest Camp, located in the suburbs not far from Villa Frassineto, also permitted a quota of South Africans. A reshuffle of the division took place in anticipation of the Guards Brigades' eventual departure. As a result, the 13th Motorized Brigade was activated under Brigadier Jack Bester.

The Royal Natal Carbineers celebrated its 90th birthday on 15 January 1945. The occasion was marked by a regimental parade held at tactical headquarters, which was based in a spacious farmhouse at Tudiano. Padre Shaw conducted the service and the music was provided by a piano accordion. Messages of congratulations came in from the Colonel-in-Chief, King George VI, and from all units to their older brother-in-arms.

The commanding officer and officers of the Royal Durban Light Infantry expressed the wish that its 91st birthday would be celebrated in sunny South Africa. According to the official history, there was "joy in the ranks of the Royal Durban Light Infantry when they were informed on 8 January 1945 that the regiment would return to its traditional role as infantry". A proposal to amalgamate the Royal Durban Light Infantry with the Grenadier Guards was quashed by Lieutenant-Colonel Metcalfe.[315]

By mid-January, the 14,000-strong, highly trained United States 10th Mountain Division had established itself in an area west of the South African sector, northwest of Pistoia—fresh and raring to go. Its first objective would be to take the massive Monte Belvedere which overlooked Route 64. While the South Africans were content with aggressive patrolling, the 10th Mountain Division, specially trained and equipped to fight in freezing conditions, went on the offensive. It took a series of peaks between 18 February and 5 March as a preliminary to the April battles.

An impressive parade was held in the village square of Castiglione on 1 February 1945, the division's second birthday. Bulldozers removed the snow from the square three days prior to the event and the surface of the piazza was covered with sawdust. Those who had the misfortune of being delegated to represent their units cursed their bad luck as they marched in the freezing cold. Nevertheless, the First City/Cape Town Highlanders pipe band, the Imperial Light Horse band and the Special Service Battalion guard of honour gave impressive performances. The Indian soldiers in their turbans added an exotic element. Since the division was now part of the American 5th Army,

315 A.C. Martin, *The Durban Light Infantry*, p. 372; DODAR, UWH, Box 140, Operations, 6th South African Armoured Division , 22/8/1944–31/3/1945.

General Mark Clark and his two corps commanders, Generals Lucien Truscott and Crittenberger were present, taking the salute. The very next day, General Poole and some other senior officers went home on leave.

The engineers and even divisional personnel worked on the roads throughout winter to ensure they remained passable. Regulations required that chains be attached to vehicles travelling past a certain point. According to Axelson, the chains were fixed with studs which were more like plates and acted like mini toboggans. The vehicles functioned better without them.

The 7/23rd Medium Regiment implemented a routine, followed every night for a period, where one 5.5-inch gun would be run out about 1,500 yards. Just before dawn, it would employ super charge to fire a few rapid rounds into the foremost defended localities on Monte Sole from a distance of 5,000 yards, before scurrying back down the road. Although the target could be engaged from the gun positions, the short range had the benefit of giving hardly any warning before the arrival of the shell. The officer commanding, Lieutentant-Colonel Gordon-Gray, reckoned that it was as good for the gunners' morale as it was bad for the enemy's.

Another task of the artillery was the firing of propaganda pamphlets and free-passage slips, which brought in three to four deserters a day. The safe conduct pass bore the signature of General H.R. Alexander and stated in English and German that:

> The German soldier who carries this safe conduct pass is using it as a sign of his genuine wish to give himself up. He is to be disarmed, well looked after, to receive food and medical attention as required, and is to be removed from the danger zone as soon as possible.

At the end of January and the beginning of February, the infantry were given the unpleasant task of carrying out fighting patrols to capture prisoners. The Royal Natal Carbineers was regularly engaged in such patrols in the vicinity of San Martino and as a result encountered some fierce firefights and some narrow escapes. Shelling was ongoing. Major Gallimore was back commanding B Company which relieved A Company on Monte Termine on 9 February.

A patrol from the Witwatersrand Rifles/Regiment De la Rey captured a badly wounded German who revealed his identity and unit. The patrol reported matter of factly: "Unfortunately the German was dying, so no further information could be gleaned from him."

In the midst of all this, an Italian concert party gave two performances in Grizzana and a cinema show was hosted in Upper Veggio—just behind the lines. A few warmer days in mid-February had some thinking that spring was around the corner. Johnston resumed his favourite pastime of going for walks in the mountains once or twice a day. It was clear that a new phase was beginning and none too soon, even for the usually upbeat Hodgson: "I can quite honestly say, as far as I'm concerned, I have had quite enough, and I think everyone else has too." The thaw had started and some February rains had already turned the positions into a sea of mud.

Although rumours had been flying for weeks, the relief of the division was made known on 10 February and was completed by the 20th. It was a massive operation to pack up everything, including ammunition piles. This six-week period would be divided into two phases: rest and recreation followed by reorganizing and training. Vehicles were sent to the workshops for overhauling and safe-keeping.

The 166th Newfoundland Regiment left for Lucca on 16 February en route for home. It passed from command on 2 April 1945 and played no further role within the 6th South African Armoured Division.

Advance parties of Americans had been in the line for some days but when a group arrived shining their headlights, the Germans took advantage of the new opportunity. After being relieved on 18 February and 19 February, the Royal Natal Carbineers convoy left for Lucca under Gallimore's command. Several junior officers stayed behind for a day to familiarize the Americans with their new homes.

There were many tender scenes as the South Africans left Castiglione. Some of the villagers wept openly and many tributes were paid to them for their treatment of the local population.

Winding down through the chain of villages en route to Lucca, the surroundings changed from the stark mountain wilderness, cold and inhospitable, to the olive groves and open countryside of Tuscany. Passing through Prato, with its warm and welcoming red roofs, it was a transition from winter into spring and from war into peace. Although centred in Lucca, the division spread itself out over a wide area, between Pistoia and Pisa.

The 12th South African Armoured Brigade suffered 19 fatalities during the four-month static period, in contrast to the 77 suffered during a three-week period in October. However it must be remembered that the Frontier Force

Rifles and the Guards Brigade bore a significant share of the fighting during this time. Four members of the First City/Cape Town Highlanders died of wounds incurred by friendly fire on the night of 4/5 February 1945; however, Colonel Duncan thanked the artillery for their accurate fire and said that they were not at fault.

12 South African Motorized Brigade casualties—static period[316]									
Unit	Killed			Wounded			Missing		
	Offrs	O/Rs	CCs	Offrs	O/Rs	CCs	Offrs	O/Rs	CCs
RNC		13	1	5	43	1	1	4	
FC/CTH	1	4*		5	43	1			
WR/DLR				4	31	1		12	
RDLI					8	1			
TOTALS	1	17	1	14	125	4	1	16	
	19			143			17		

CCs: Cape Corps

* died of wounds

Monday 19 February 1945 – Saturday 31 March 1945: Lucca

The autostrada between Florence and Prato had been broken up by all the heavy traffic, as had the narrow road from Prato to Vernio. The deterioration over the past two months was plain to see. This road was packed on 22 February when Axelson made his way to Lucca, primarily with vehicles from the 1st US Armoured Division.

The area had been fought over during the Gothic Line battles, and buildings had been damaged, bridges blown and the countryside littered with the paraphernalia of war. By the time the South Africans arrived, however, nature had healed some of the scars and the industrious Italians had also done much reparation work. The walled city itself had no military value and had escaped relatively unscathed, although the surrounding suburbs remained in ruins for ten years or more. The Pretoria Regiment found a suitable area for a tank park on the banks of the Serchio River near Lucca. The personnel were comfortably billeted in civilian houses in the shadow of the ancient walls, making the 'no fraternizing' order difficult to enforce. One squadron continued training for its new role as armoured reconnaisance. Parades and inspections of tanks and vehicles were routine. The Guards Brigade moved, apparently with

[316] DODAR, WD, Box 598, Recording officer, 12 South African Motorized Brigade, Report on operations in the Italian campaign for period August 1944–May 1945.

mutual regret, to the other side of the country. Some members of the Pretoria Regiment (Princess Alice's Own) made the long trip to attend a farewell parade for the Grenadier Guards at Spoleto in Umbria, south of Florence. Later during their stay in Lucca, an impressive parade was held on 26 March to mark the presentation of the new flash incorporating the emblems of the Guards and the Pretoria Regiment. Tanks were lined up on the floodplain of the Serchio River as the public relations people took advantage of the photo opportunity. Although it had been preceded by weeks of sunshine, the day itself was rainy and it was necessary to hold off the parade. General Poole and Brigadier Erskine of the Guards Brigade arrived at 1730 hours. The tanks started their engines after the speeches and drove past in a massive display of power.

All civilian restaurants and bars in Lucca were out of bounds, partly because of the typhoid epidemic. Blackouts were enforced and guard duties continued. Many were living in tents, some in the olive groves, although the lucky ones were billeted with Italian families. The routine of the 7/23rd Medium Regiment was similar to that of most regiments while at rest in Lucca:

0730–0830 hrs	Breakfast
0845 hrs	Roll call
0900–1230 hrs	24 Feb – 4 March: Maintenance 5 March – 31 March: Training
1240–1330 hrs	Lunch
1400–1630 hrs	Sport and compulsory PT
1800 hrs	Guard mounting
2200 hrs	All men not on pass to be in barracks
2215 hrs	Lights out

Florence is less than an hour from Lucca while Pisa is a 30-minute drive on the autostrada—close enough for taking a 'shufti'. When rambling in the hills above Lake Massaciuccoli, it is possible to see the famous leaning tower through binoculars. A restaurant for 200 other ranks was opened near this landmark and those carrying a pass were authorized to draw a midday meal. Johnston was not impressed: "Pisa for morning. Leaning Tower and Cathedral with Ian Stewart. Lousy town. Lunch and back to camp by 15.00."

He wasn't alone in finding the city of Pisa to be a let-down. There were some bullet holes in the old bronze doors of the Duomo and a corner of the building was being used as a toilet. At this time, there were apparently numerous Italian civilians committing suicide off the tower. One fell in front of a pair of South

African nurses who were sightseeing. Although winter was not quite finished, there was a feeling of spring in the air and the countryside was sparkling. Hodgson did not mention in his letter of 23 February that he was out of the line but the content, which could hardly have been of interest to his sister, did let the family know that he was in more pleasant surroundings:

> Everything is looking very green, the snow has all gone and the earth has more or less dried out completely, which is the first time since the beginning of last October. At the moment, the inhabitants are busy picking all the olives—the procedure is to beat all the fruit off the trees with sticks, pick them up, put them out on big flat baskets to dry, then put them in big presses to get all the oil out of them. I am hoping to see the pressing business done in a couple of day's time. When speaking to one today, she told us that four kilograms of olives yield a kilo of oil, which is excellent. This is the first crop of the season which are allowed to go black; the second crop in November is picked when they are green.

The medieval walled city of Lucca is today a pristine and popular tourist destination, but at the time it was a little-known and dingy town. In keeping with the policy of utilizing public buildings, main division headquarters was housed in a large building which was originally a TB sanatorium. The men of the First City/Cape Town Highlanders were settled into billets in the little town of Quiesa. The headquarters of the 1/6th Field Regiment was located a mile or two west of Lucca at Santa Maria a Colle, on Via di Nozzano Vecchio. Welfare centres were opened in all the main towns. The newly formed 13th South African Motorized Brigade was based around Montale which is relatively far from Lucca, between Prato and Pistoia.

Routine orders contained advice on how to lay out sports fields. Most men knew that a rugby field measured 110 yards by 75 yards, but they appreciated help with association football, softball and quoit tennis. Soccer and hockey were played on the Lucca aerodrome field and the Massarosa field. The weather was ideal for rugby and soccer, although the fields became muddy when it rained, even though they were grassed. Only one per cent of unit-posted strength would be permitted to enter Lucca every day. The reverse side of the men's passes stated that the holder was authorized to draw a meal at the Outspan Club, which had opened in Piazza Bernardini, known for its imposing administrative buildings. If, however, the troops were in unit transport and under the supervision of an officer, a further five per cent of unit strength was permitted to attend the town's Keystone cinemas, which screened two shows per day. These groups had to leave town immediately after the performance. A series of operas was performed in Lucca, starting with *La Bohème*.

During the week of Monday 26 February, Rosalind Russell starred in three shows a day at the Odeon ENSA Garrison Theatre in Florence. At the Excelsior Forces Cinema in Via Cerretani, there was a continuous performance of *One Exciting Night*, starring Vera Lynn, starting at 1300 hours. A variety of entertainments, including an amateur talent contest and the band of the Royal Ulster Rifles, was laid on at the Robertson Club in Piazza Beccaria.

In addition to serving lunches, teas and suppers, the Robertson Club provided a variety of facilities, from a library and music room to a billiards room and war news room. It was also a place to have your hair cut and have your photograph taken with your pals.

Having left Lucca at 0900 hours, Johnston and his companions were settled in at Rusthof, usually called by its original name, Villa Frassineto, in good time for lunch. It was not far from here to 107th General Hospital where, for three days in a row, they visited some nursing acquaintances named Smitty, Kay and Marge. The girls invited them to have drinks in the nurses' lounge and lunch in the ward. Excellent dinners were enjoyed at the Robertson Club and the YWCA. Afterwards, one could relax in the lounge at the Villa, where dances were held regularly, while listening to the six-piece band.

Johnston was accommodated in the 'Granary', a large dormitory in the grounds of the villa, located almost three miles from the centre of Florence, so it was a bonus to be able to move over to the Voortrekker Club where a friend had fixed them up with a room to themselves.

The operas *La Traviata* and *Tosca* were showing in Florence. Of the latter, Johnston wrote: "Poor. Fat old crone took part of Tosca." Apart from this, it was the small luxuries that he enjoyed, such as having coffee in bed and laundry done at the Villa. But then it was back to Lucca for a month of guards, maintenance, fire pickets, kitchen fatigue and rifle practice.

On his next leave to Florence, Johnston again stayed at the Villa. On this occasion, he saw the film *A Guy Named Joe* at the Excelsior and the play *Henry V*. This he enjoyed, although many did not. Of Michelangelo's David, he wrote "fair". From the northern suburb of Fiesole, there is a panoramic view of the city. Doing what tourists like to do, Johnston sat on a wall overlooking the red roofs, drinking beer and eating sandwiches. Another day, he sat on a wall by the River Arno, people-watching.

Operas in Florence started at 1300 hours, probably because of the lack of electricity and heat inside the buildings. According to de Wet, the performers were not as good as those in Rome, but they were younger and more attractive. Cinemas were always free, and were only open to members of the Allied forces. In Lucca, there were two Union Defence Force Institutes concert parties, one of which featured a leading London comedian. One of Hogson's companions was surprised to recognize a girl from his home town in the cast of the second show; they chatted with her after the performance. Clearly the opera impressed him deeply:

> First of all, I have been in [to Lucca] to see two operas, which were simply marvellous; the first one I saw was *Madame Butterfly* which I thought very good but I found the story a little hard to follow, which naturally took the edge off it a bit. The second one is one that I always wanted to see, mainly as it is the most amusing of all, and secondly, it is the easiest to follow. My chance came on the best night possible as 'the' champion baritone of all Italy came to take the leading role that night. The name of the opera is *The Barber of Seville*. As I say, the leading part, namely the barber was taken by Gino Bechi [a leading dramatic baritone of his time]. I must say it is the most marvellous performance I have ever seen. Civilians were also present, so the whole thing went off in proper opera style—I had a very good seat, (about 12 rows from the front). At the end of the first scene, there were about six curtains; at the end of the second scene, there were eleven curtains, then at the end of the final scene, after the 14th curtain; they wouldn't let this bloke go, so he settled down and sang two more beautiful songs. If I got another chance to see the very same performance, I would walk ten miles to see it.

Some South Africans "chosen for their educational qualifications"—in other words, officers—were sent to an army school of education in Perugia. This university town, situated in Umbria midway between Florence and Rome, had been taken over by the Allies for educational purposes. The faculties were housed within the ancient stone walls of the city centre and a campus ambience prevailed, with the soldiers walking up the steps and through the narrow streets carrying books instead of Bren guns. Here the officers attended classes in politics, economics and international affairs. The courses lasted three weeks and were also given in Afrikaans. Apparently the intention was for the men to pass on their new knowledge when they returned to their units.

The Royal Natal Carbineers was based around Massaciuccoli village with B Company headquarters located in a beautiful villa overlooking the lake. One section of B Company found itself conveniently situated above the local pub.

On 28 February, barely a week after the start of the rest period, the company's commander, Gallimore—a 30-year-old married man and professional soldier from the Cape—was found dead approximately 400 yards away from his company headquarters, with a gunshot wound to the left temple. Although any number of theories could be advanced, even his fellow officers were entirely puzzled and saddened. Only the company commanders and the padre, Captain Shaw, made the journey to Castiglione for his funeral on 3 March at 1130 hours, while his men spent the day quietly. No court of inquiry record could be found but today Hodgson believes that he simply did for himself what the Germans could not do: "He seemed to be trying to get killed and to travel with him in his Jeep was a nightmare. He was a good major who had no regard for his own life, and would lay down his life for his men; he had no fear whatsoever."[317]

Gallimore's death certificate classified the casualty as a battle accident and states, "GSW [gunshot wound] to the left temple—self-inflicted". Although medical officers and unit commanders tried to be discreet about suicides, military protocol required that the death certificates be specific as to the cause of death. In a later case of self-inflicted injury, the officer commanding the 29th South African Armoured Division Workshop was ordered to have the medical officer specify the exact cause of death rather than leaving the reader to draw the conclusion that death occurred as a result of a "gunshot wound", as the term would apply in the military sense.

On 26 February, Hodgson celebrated his 20th birthday. He was fortunate to be on leave with his friends, as had been the case in Alexandria the previous year, but made no fuss of the occasion. The highlight was the arrival of a letter containing a number of photographs and some money. Hodgson had been elected sports representative for the company headquarters. It was a fitting appointment as he did more exercise than most of his peers, running four miles each morning as well as participating in the organized matches in the afternoons. Hockey and tennis were his favourite sports, but he was prepared to play rugby for his company. Considering his exquisite surroundings, it's not surprising that Hodgson describes an idyllic lifestyle:

> The other evening the mobile cinema came round to the company area, which was a very pleasant surprise as one usually has to go quite a long way to find them. It was

317 J.B. Hodgson, personal information, interview, 13/3/2009; DODAR, WD, Box 646, Royal Natal Carbineers, 28/2/1945.

> a really good evening all round, we got back from rugby about five, having had a hot shower and change, we then relaxed out on the terrace in the sun and enjoyed an excellent quart of cool beer; after that, it was just on supper time—the supper came up to a very good standard. Roast beef with potatoes and cauliflower, after which we just sat down and relaxed while the sun went down. Just before it was dark, we strolled down to one of the platoons, each taking with us a deck chair. These we set up down by the screen, duly proceeding to see the film in comfort. The one we saw was *Captain Blood* with Errol Flynn and Maureen O'Hara. I saw it about six or seven years ago, with the result that I had forgotten most of it, and I thoroughly enjoyed seeing it again.

Bourhill and three others from B Sub were billeted near Lucca and had the privilege of getting to know an Italian family. Their six-year-old daughter, Anna, had "eyes like stars". When she cut her nose, the soldiers rushed her to the field ambulance for stitching. Like every South African soldier, Bourhill amassed his own experiences with the locals:

> We are here in their house and eat their food and drink their wine and they are complimented! My Iti is coming on in leaps and bounds, because I talk it nearly all day. I've shown photos of the family ... and Impi [the family's fox terrier] so often that I've got a running commentary all set to recite as I show each one. It goes like this: "This is my sister—is she not like me? I am the youngest of my family. She is in the Red Cross—also before the war. This is my dog—I have lost him a long time ago." I've taken four hours to write this letter; better by far to correspond from the front than in an Iti homestead. We had rabbit with lavender for lunch and today pig with garlic and white wine. Oh my! We have our own rations too.

Wulfsohn describes in his memoirs how the men established ongoing relationships with Italian families, which they would cherish and jealously guard from outsiders: "The drill was that you arrived with food of any description and handed it over and the madame of the establishment served you with a meal whenever you asked which was pretty frequent and at all hours." The evening meal was typically Italian: antipasto, pasta with a sauce concocted out of the meat-and-vegetable tins thinly disguised with tomato, peppers and aubergines. With the addition of cheese, olives and figs, nobody went hungry.[318] More than one South African was horrified at being fed rabbit or even lamb, which had been a household pet up until a short time before.

---

318 L.M. Wulfsohn, unpublished memoirs; See also D.M. Baker, *War, wine and valour*, pp. 436–437.

Hodgson's experience is typical:

> You will never guess what I did with some of the jam which came out of one of the parcels; I got hold of a good bit of flour from the cook and took this with a tin of jam to the family who own the house where we are staying, and with this, the 'old lady' of the house is going to make quite a number of small tarts and cookies which should be very nice.

Meanwhile, there was movement within the regiments. The 13th Motorized Brigade—which had been formed under Brigadier Bester on 13 January in response to the depature of the Guards Brigade and the arising need for more infantry—was consolidating.

The brigade included the Imperial Light Horse/Kimberley Regiment, the Natal Mounted Rifles (now dismounted) and the Royal Durban Light Infantry. The 15th Field Regiment was added to the artillery group. Many of the light anti-aircraft gunners converted to infantry. The 4/22nd Field Regiment changed its 105mm 'Priests' for 25-pounder 'Sextons'.

The combined Regiment President Steyn and Regiment Botha arrived in Italy by air and in batches, their aim being to take over the support role of the Royal Durban Light Infantry. The amalgamated Duke of Edinburgh's Own Rifles–Transvaal Scottish Rand Light Infantry arrived to augment the infantry.

In the spring of 1945, General Truscott's 5th United States Army had nine divisions comprising 270,000 men under its control, including the three brigades of the 6th South African Armoured Division under General Poole. Between 28 March and 3 April, the 13th South African Motorized Brigade was involved with training and maneuvres codenamed 'Klip'. The comprehensive training programme included route marches, section-leading, instruction in weapons, street fighting, ambushes, river-crossing, house clearing, patrols, instruction on mines, booby-traps and hand grenades. The guns of the 1/6th Field Regiment had been sent to Ponsacco to be calibrated and a practice exercise named 'Fantastica' was carried out. On 31 March, the regimental war diary reported: "Jacked-up and ready for action." Meanwhile, more than seven companies of engineers had been working around the clock to clear the ten-mile-long Appennino tunnel between Vernio and San Benedetto, which was blocked and had been flooded by the Germans.[319]

---

[319] N. Orpen, *Victory in Italy*, p. 264.

During March, the Americans in the former positions of the 6th South African Armoured Division were subjected to a number of raids in platoon or company strength but their daily report for early April read:

> 1 April 1945: Enemy artillery fires during this period were normal. 7 shellreps contained 44 rds light arty, 25 rds medium arty and 6 rds of unknown calibre. 3 mortreps contained 11 rds of 81mm mortar and 5 rounds of unknown calibre.
>
> 2 April 1945: A quiet period.
>
> 3 April 1945: A quiet period.
>
> 4 April 1945: An extremely quiet period.
>
> 5 April 1945: The period was generally quiet with some mines and machine-gun fire encountered.
>
> 6 April 1945 – 10 April 1945, inclusive: Division out of line. [320]

There had, however, been one alarm. On 10 March, the 6th South African Armoured Division was put on 24-hour standby, ready to take up position behind the 92nd United States Infantry Division, the all-black 'Buffalo' Division. Fortunately the counter-attack did not take place after all. Soon after his return to the frontline on 4 April, Bourhill wrote home about his emotional parting from 'the family':

> It was a very sad parting from the family there. Anna wanted to come with us and the old folk cried like blazes. Marisa, the girl, couldn't face it, and didn't come to say goodbye. It's quite an event in their quiet lives to have four soldiers in their house for so long. There the war only swept past them, and only left them wondering and puzzled and scared. But we shook the place up. They liked us and as the girl said to me, "Steve, it was far better that we'd never know you". The more I see of these Wops the more time I have for them. It's not a 'good thing' because I'd hardly have the heart to carry on fighting. I've seen their hearts absolutely bare as only people in conditions like me can see them.

By 5 April, South African units had replaced most Americans on the front lines. The tank regiments and other latecomers followed over the next few days. Shortly before leaving for the front, Johnston stayed with a family in a

[320] DODAR, UWH, Box 140, Extract from 1st US Armoured Division Documents, written by Lieutenant R.V. Davis.

casa just short of Vaiano near B Echelon headquarters, which was based at the University of Prato. In the evenings he played draughts with 'the family' and had dinner with a certain Silvana. Only on 11 April did he move up through Castiglione, Lagaro and Ripoli to the gun positions, where he was told by his comrades, "Next week we go and shoot Germans".[321]

Firearm and vehicle accidents took their toll during the rest period. Private K.R. Adams of the Royal Natal Carbineers fell from a moving truck on 31 March. Two men were killed on 1 April, including a 25-year-old military policeman, Coporal W.D. Viljoen of Wynberg in Cape Town. The most unfortunate fatality was Corporal W.J. Cottam of the Witwatersrand Rifles/Regiment De la Rey, who had recently won the American Bronze Star for leading a patrol in pursuit of the enemy beyond Monte Stanco. On 9 April, Troopers H.A. Liebmann and A.C. Coetzee of the Natal Mounted Rifles were killed in a vehicle accident on their way back from the 'Klip' training exercise. At a regimental dance in Lucca on 6 April, Corporal R.C. Frost lost his balance and fell out of a three-storey window. He died from a head injury. The court of inquiry ruled out misconduct of any sort (see Battle Accident Certificate on facing page).

Robin Frost had grown up at Woodleigh, an imposing mansion on the slopes behind Kalk Bay. Educated at Bishops, Frost followed in his father's footsteps and started work as a bank clerk at Standard Bank before enlisting at the Cape Town Castle. As a tank commander in the Special Service Battalion, Frost had been at the 'sharp end' from Rome to Florence. A few days before entering Florence, he was detailed to go to the rescue of an officer and sergeant who were lying wounded next to their damaged tank. Frost, Trooper N.T. Brook of Rosebank and Trooper A.D. Upton of Pietermaritzburg weaved their way across 500 yards of difficult terrain and a rain of shellfire in a Honey turretless tank, emerging unscathed. The regimental history mentions that Frost did "grand work" rescuing the two wounded. The incident made the newspapers in South Africa.[322]

Although the weather had warmed up to the extent that it was now possible to have a short swim in the rivers, rain was threatening. Hodgson heard news of a landing behind German lines on the Adriatic coast by the 8th Army and

321 P.M. Johnston, personal diary, 6–9 April 1945.

322 Kalk Bay Historical Society, Bulletin No. 6 P. 146; DODAR, UWH, Box 140, Regimental history of the Special Service Battalion, August 1944.

<u>CERTIFICATE - BATTLE ACCIDENT</u>

1 S.S.B
UDF CMF
7 APR 45

<u>No 230008V CPL FROST RC.</u>

On 6 APR 45 a/n attended a Regtl NCOs Dance held at LUCCA. At approx 2130 hrs Cpl Frost entered the kitchen in order to obtain sandwiches. Cpl Frost after obtaining food sat on the window sill inside the kitchen. The kitchen was on the third story of the building. Cpl Frost was seen to suddenly overbalance. He fell down out of the window. He was killed instantaneously due to fractures of his skull.

<u>CO's Opinion</u>

The accident was not due to misconduct. (Court of Inquiry was held immediately and evidence revealed the happening to be entirely accidental and no misconduct on the part of any other persons).

speculated that bad weather would follow, as it always did for major operations. The route taken by the Royal Natal Carbineers to its new positions traversed Quiesa, Lucca, Pistoia, Prato, Castiglione, Lagaro, Ponte Locatello and finally, Gardelletta. The A Echelon left at 0700 hours on 1 April. Each convoy staged at Castiglione, where many men took the opportunity to visit the cemetery before moving on.

Although he did not mention it in his latest letters, Hodgson was back in the line and hoping that the Germans would capitulate without the need for further fighting:

> One cannot say that the war will be over in a couple of months or anything like that as we used to. The war is over, the only thing is for the Jerries to realize that and call the whole thing off, so the whole business might be over any day. All we can do is wait and see and hope that he realizes his position very quickly.

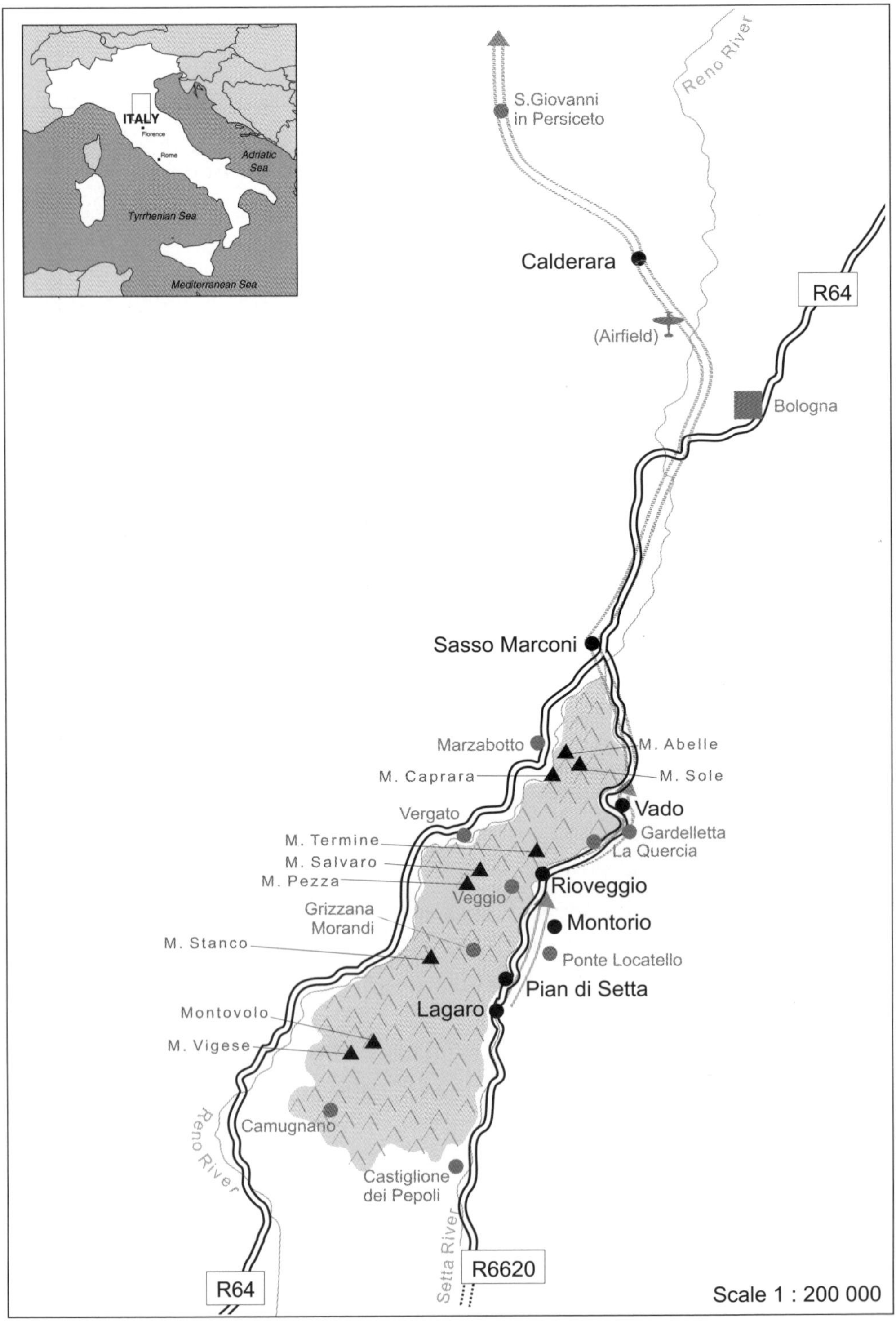

ITALY
Florence
Rome
Adriatic Sea
Tyrrhenian Sea
Mediterranean Sea
Reno River
S.Giovanni in Persiceto
Calderara
R64
(Airfield)
Bologna
Sasso Marconi
Marzabotto
M. Abelle
M. Caprara
M. Sole
Vado
Vergato
Gardelletta
M. Termine
La Quercia
M. Salvaro
M. Pezza
Rioveggio
Veggio
Grizzana Morandi
Montorio
M. Stanco
Ponte Locatello
Pian di Setta
Lagaro
Montovolo
M. Vigese
Camugnano
Castiglione dei Pepoli
Reno River
Setta River
R6620
R64
Scale 1 : 200 000

Chapter Ten

Fire and ashes

ALLIED FORCE HEADQUARTERS

April 1945

SPECIAL ORDER OF THE DAY

Final victory is near. The German forces are very groggy and need one mighty punch to knock them out for good. The moment has now come for us to take to the field for the last battle which will end the war in Europe. You know what our comrades in the West and the East are doing on the battlefields. It is now our turn to play our decisive part. It will not be a walk-over; a mortally wounded beast can still be very dangerous. You must be prepared for a hard and bitter fight; but the end is quite certain—there is not the slightest shadow of doubt about that. You, who have won every battle you have fought, are going to win this last one. Forward then into battle with confidence, faith and determination to see it through to the end. Good luck and Godspeed to you all.

H.R. ALEXANDER
Field Marshal
Supreme Allied Commander
Mediterranean Theatre

Sunday 1 April 1945 – Tuesday 17 April 1945: Montorio

During the first week of April, the division reoccupied the *casas* and dug-outs in which they had lived during the winter. The local inhabitants gave them a warm welcome, saying that the Americans had not been very generous with food, cigarettes or payment for doing laundry.

The gunners were pleased to find that their gun emplacements at Pian di Setta had been vastly improved by the Americans with their earthmoving equipment. In fact, the South Africans learned a few lessons about preparing good gun pits, including how to improve drainage by removing bad soil and replacing it with good gravel or crushed stone. The mediums were again positioned a few thousand yards short of Lagaro at Graveyard Bend—so named because of the row of German graves among their gun positions. The Rhodesian Battery was forward of its previous position at Ripoli and was now in the riverbed near Grizzana station in what was dubbed the "Valley of the Guns" by the press. The tanks added their firepower alongside the artillery and the valley rocked with gunfire every night. It was not possible to have all eight guns of a battery in the same proximity, let alone an entire regiment, and the 1/6th Field Regiment was deployed between Ponte Locatello and Montorio.[323]

As previously mentioned, Montorio is forward of Pian di Setta on a spur of high ground on the right bank of the Setta, just north of Grizzana station. The occupants were under the noses of the Germans on Monte Sole, but had little to fear. Throughout the winter, the headquarters of the Guards Brigade had been housed in a nearby castle which had suffered only random shelling, and in any case, the German counter-battery fire was surprisingly ineffectual. According to Lieutenant Yuill of the 7/23rd Medium Regiment, the position at Lagaro had been shelled only twice during a four-month period and many of the shells failed to explode.

The front line was now five miles south of the confluence of the Reno and Setta rivers, with ten mountainous miles to go to Bologna. The South Africans were tasked with capturing the Monte Sole–Monte Caprara–Monte Abelle massif which had dominated the horizon for the past six months. The sector in which the Royal Natal Carbineers now established itself had previously been occupied by the Guards Brigade, and ran from Gardelletta on the Setta River, through steep and broken country dominated by Monte Sole.

This period was characterized by extremely quiet days and active nights. Harassing fire from German machine guns was answered by South African artillery, Vickers and mortars. In the South African sector, night patrols went out probing enemy defences, reconnoitring assembly areas, start lines and routes for tanks. These patrols took place over a wide area in the wild no man's land, in a line running westward from the Setta through Cerpiano and Poggio on the southern slopes of Monte Sole, through Caprara village and Casa Poggiolo to the Reno at Casa di Co. Orders were given to avoid clashes at all costs in order

323 The exact position of A Troop was L756220—directly opposite Pian di Setta.

to prevent the enemy from suspecting that anything out of the ordinary was going on. While the Royal Natal Carbineers was given the relatively easy job of protecting the engineers who were lifting mines on Route 6620, it was up to the First City/Cape Town Highlanders to take Monte Sole. The Witwatersrand Rifles/Regiment De la Rey had as its objective Monte Caprara and the Royal Durban Light Infantry would exploit along a ridge northeast from Sole. The Indian Frontier Forces Rifles was based at San Martino, now just a pile of rubble en route to the objectives. As usual, the approach would be made on foot, causing some youngbloods to express concern that the older men were not up to the task. The rate of advance up these slopes was calculated to be no more than 100 yards in ten minutes. The artillery would provide a barrage, behind which the infantry would follow closely. Because of the nature of the terrain, only night attacks would be possible.

The coming attack was universally known as Italy's 'D' Day and the preparatory bombardment can be seen as a the Second World War equivalent of 'shock and awe'. German propaganda leaflets picturing masses of white crosses asked "Do you want to be the last to die?" and proclaimed that 'D' Day means Death-Day. The "thousands of wooden crosses in the great Po plain" would be "silent witnesses to the bloodiest battle ever fought on Italian soil". It was suggested that "you should not forget your identification disc so that your name can be painted on your wooden cross".[324]

The 15th Field Regiment was in action for the first time on 11 April. Preparations for the attack on Monte Sole were complete on 12 April. These included jacking up the front of a section of the guns of the 1/6th Field Regiment in order to allow for a higher trajectory to drop shells on the back of Monte Sole. Fire plans named 'Jellyfish', 'Porpoise', 'Dolphin', 'Crayfish', 'Frog' and ultimately 'Pike' were fired between 8 and 16 April in preparation for 'D' Day.

On Friday 13 April, the weather was fairly warm but windy and dusty. After a short delay due to bad weather, 570 planes flying at 20,000 feet bombed enemy communications and reserve positions between Vado and Bologna, as well as bridges across the Reno and the Setta.

According to a report in *The Star* of Monday 16 April, this was a record air bombardment, named Operation Plaster, involving 1,233 heavy bombers and 611 fighters. More than 17,000 fragmentation bombs were rained by American

[324] German propaganda pamphlet no. 1325/3/45, 'Italy Next', J.B. Hodgson collection.

Mitchells on German troop concentrations south and east of Bologna. In the same area, South African Air Force Kitty-bombers, Royal Air Force Spit-bombers and American Thunderbolts destroyed or damaged 50 enemy-occupied buildings. Following the daylight assault, the Tactical Air Force sent a record number of light bombers, including Havocks, to attack River Po ferry and pontoon crossings and highways close to the front. Prior to the main attack at 2300 hours on the night of 14/15 April, a strong point known as Casa Poggiolo was taken by the 4/13th Frontier Force Rifles and held throughout the night against the ensuing counter-attacks. The Witwatersrand Rifles/Regiment De la Rey passed through the lines of the Frontier Force Rifles the following night, and were mistakenly fired at by the Indian troops. The weather on 15 April was bright and sunny. Shortly after 1300 hours, the heavy bombers came in line abreast. Flying low, 200 Thunderbolts, Typhoons, and Spitfires strafed, rocketed and bombed the well-dug-in defenders with all types of ordnance. Jettisoned fuel tanks filled with an inflammatory gel hit the ground, setting the bush on fire. There were loud cheers from the Witwatersrand Rifles/Regiment De la Rey every time Caprara was bombed. Down in the Setta Valley, Johnston had a grandstand view of the air attacks:

> Tin hats from 12.55 to 14.30 because of bombers going over continually. 1 Lightning shot down. From 16.00 to 20.30 Typhoons bombing, strafing Caprara and Sole. Petrol bombs burning Jerries out. Wonderful show. Over the target all the time for 4½ hours. At 22.30 our barrage started and kept up for some time. Then various bombards.

As the air attack came to an end, the artillery opened up with 141 guns. According to Axelson, who was watching from the top of Monte Termine, the bombardment was more impressive than either El Alamein or Cassino because it was more concentrated. By the time the infantry went in at 2230 hours on 15 April, the 1/6th Field Regiment had fired 12,000 rounds, not including those expended on a deception plan. At 2045 hours the following night, in artificial light created by the fires, the Witwatersrand Rifles/Regiment De la Rey started walking to its start line in a ploughed field near San Martino, about 1,200 yards from the foot of Monte Caprara. As had happened at Monte Stanco, the regiment suffered casualties on the start line. The attack was delayed while the casualty clearing post was inundated. An uncommonly graphic account of the incident appeared in an article in The *Nonquai* on the first anniversary of the battle:

> As soon as the first [mortar and artillery] bombardment lifted for a moment we took stock of our situation. There were only a handful of Italian stretcher bearers left, the remainder had retired in no uncertain manner. The padre ordered us to go forward to the wadi. In the dark, we found our way over ploughed fields, sluits overgrown with underbrush and badly eroded gullies. We hardly reached the wadi when the second [bombardment] of the Germans came down. Men were milling about in the wadi as platoon commanders tried to reform their ranks. Signallers were desperately trying to lay their telephone lines, men who had lost contact with their section were shouting out names of their comrades. But when the mortars came raining down on us, they all took cover behind the slightest bit of protection they could find in the dark. It is impossible to say how long the mortaring lasted. It seemed to be hours. Not two yards from where I lay hugging the ground, a mortar bomb blew the legs of one man to bits. In a boyish voice he was shouting, "Oh my legs! Oh my legs, they're gone." [325]

The crest of Monte Caprara was taken in a charge led by Major D. Williams, who had been wounded. He received a bar to his Military Cross. The battle culminated in hand-to-hand combat. John Holmes wrote: "For 30 mad and bloody minutes, our men rushed about the mountain, killing and wounding." Approximately 30 Germans were killed and similar numbers wounded and captured. Bloodied, exhausted and low on ammunition, the Witwatersrand Rifles/Regiment De la Rey started digging in at 0615 hours, and fought off a counter-attack at about 0700 hours.[326]

The start line of the First City/Cape Town Highlanders ran from Ca Casetta to Ca di Sotto, an east–west line 900 yards south of the crest of Monte Sole. The approach was thickly mined but the regiment overran the enemy, using bayonets and grenades, as they were coming out of their deep shelters. A counter-attack was repelled, and by 0100 hours on the morning of 16 April it was all over. Second Lieutenant G.B. Mollett was awarded the DSO for leading that charge "with total disregard for his own life" and wiping out the machine-gun posts on Monte Sole. Mollett, like three other men in the leading platoon, was from Rhodesia. All were younger than 20, and each was seeing their first action after being in the line for only 12 days. Four of their countrymen lost their lives that day: Private P.G. Berry from Fort Victoria, Private H. Bezuidenhout from Gatooma, Private W.G.M. Watson of Salisbury and Private W.P. James of Kumalo, Bulawayo. James had served with the Witwatersrand Rifles/Regiment De la Rey.

325 J.E. Holmes, The *Nonquai*, May 1946, p. 589.

326 S. Monick, *A bugle calls*, p. 464.

The tanks of the Prince Alfred's Guard were supposed to enter the fray at 2330 hours, but the attack was delayed until 0130 hours because the Witwatersrand Rifles/Regiment De la Rey was caught on their start line. Despite the fact that there was an engineer in each tank in the leading troop, responsible for prodding for mines, the leading tank was blown up on a mine on the road leading up from La Quercia to San Martino, blocking the way. Every man was made to get out of the tanks to dig away the bank, regardless of the heavy mortaring, in an effort to allow the other tanks to pass. Five more tanks were blown up on mines in just ten minutes—but not before the tank tracks had chewed up the communication lines on the road.

Three tanks succeeded in reaching the saddle by 1300 hours the next day. Fortunately, most of the disabled tanks were still able to bring their guns to bear in support of the infantry, under the direction of the 1/6th Field Regiment forward observation officer.

In a statement to the historical recording officer, Bombadier W.P. Alexander described his experience as an artillery observer on the night of 16 April. He noticed that the mules bringing up supplies stood quite still when heavy shells were landing nearby and everybody, including the Italian handlers, were "lying doggo". Having spent the night repairing communication lines, Alexander was able to return to calling in fire on targets behind Monte Caprara:

> With a couple of shots they were right on target. "Do you want a mike [regimental] target?" shouted Shorty. The captain nodded so I said "yes". "Method and scale?" he called back. The captain said "murder" and indicated the scale by a show of fingers.
>
> "Murder scale five," I shot back.
>
> "Regiment ready!" yelled Shorty. "Regiment fire! Regiment shot."
>
> "What can you see?" asked Shorty.
>
> "Nothing yet, it's just a big column of smoke and explosions," I answered.
>
> As the smoke cleared away, the captain observed two vehicles burning and much damage done to the casas where a large concentration of enemy had been sheltering. This report went down the line to Shorty who whooped with joy.[327]

Under shelling, the engineers from the 12th Field Squadron worked to clear and improve the track between La Quercia and San Martino to allow for the evacuation of casualties from Caprara by vehicle. Subsequent prisoner

327 DODAR, UWH, Box 140, Statement from Bombadier W.P. Alexander 7/64th Field Battery, 4/22nd Field Regiment. A 'Mike' target is a regimental target and an 'Uncle' target calls for a divisional shoot.

interrogations revealed that a German officer accompanied by 12 men and a wireless set had remained behind at San Martino to observe, report and snipe.[328]

The Witwatersrand Rifles/Regiment De la Rey lost two officers and 22 other ranks, including Private C. Coetzee who was one of four Coetzees to be buried at Castiglione—three of them in the space of a week. By way of comparison, the United States 10th Mountain Division lost 370 killed in the same period while leading the charge on the South Africans' left flank.

Two Cape Corps men attached to the First City/Cape Town Highlanders, Harry Petersen and Johannes Phyfer, were awarded the Military Medal for picking up the wounded under fire and bringing them down the precipitous slopes to the village of Poggio, 500 feet below. They did this several times throughout the night. All other stretcher bearers in their team had been wounded, along with the medical non-commissioned officer. General Poole later remarked that the Cape Corps men were the bravest stretcher bearers he had ever seen. In affirmation, Private E.W. Leppan, a diarist from A Company, Royal Durban Light Infantry, wrote:

> Nothing could be more impressive than to see these men running up the path, almost brushing us as they did so, and returning with the wounded. They ran both ways, completely disregarding enemy fire, all of them sobbing for breath with their tongues hanging out like exhausted dogs. I remember one badly wounded man staggering back saying: "My God, I hope you're not going into that." [329]

Casualties were carried by stretcher to the regimental aid post and from there by Jeep ambulance to the casualty clearing post, which was still in rough terrain. They would then be transported by 4x4 Humber or AFS to the advanced dressing station at Ponte Locatello, a cluster of buildings opposite Pian di Setta near the bridge of the same name. All casualties were then evacuated back to the field dressing station at Castiglione and, if necessary, to 107th South African General Hospital in Florence.

Now that Sole and Caprara were secure, it was up to the Royal Durban Light Infantry to exploit along the razor-backed ridge running from Monte Sole to Santa Barbara. The troops were in close contact with the enemy throughout the night of 17 April. The Germans had been ordered to fight to the last man

328 E. Axelson, *A year in Italy*, p. 227.

329 A.C. Martin, *The Durban Light Infantry*, p. 387.

and were well ensconced in concrete pill boxes with underground bunkers. A strong counter-attack near dawn was broken up with the support of artillery, Vickers machine guns and mortars. American rocket-firing aircraft were also called in. These aircraft were responsible for a friendly fire incident when a Royal Durban Light Infantry aid post was mistakenly attacked from the air. The regiment lost six killed, including 17-year-old Private W.V. Coetzee of Senekal, and 45 wounded, including Major E.P.L. Bizzell who was wounded in 14 places and was awarded the Military Cross.

The highly motivated Sergeant C.C. Buckley found himself in command of his platoon and won a bar to his Military Medal, but would live for only a week longer. Axelson wrote, "the RDLI received a great stuffing in the night and suffered about 50 casualties". According to the official history of the regiment, seven were killed and 58 wounded during this operation.

Information from prisoners revealed that the counter-attack was intended to cover the German withdrawal. In the words of Sergeant N.C. Coleman of the Prince Alfred's Guard, "At 1600 on the 16th the Germans counter-attacked but were beaten off. Early on the 17th, Jerry withdrew after having got rid of all his spare ammunition in our direction, as he usually did."[330]

After the battle was done and dusted, the commanding officer of the First City/Cape Town Highlanders, Lieutenant-Colonel Angus Duncan, went forward to see his troops in a Jeep packed to capacity with staff and spectators. Most sources indicate that it was a shell which killed Duncan; however, according to Axelson, the Jeep was blown up on a mine. Then again, because Axelson wrote his log on 16 April, his information may not have been reliable. The charismatic Duncan was one of two colonels of the 6th South African Armoured Division to be killed; the other was Leslie Kay of the 1/6th Field Regiment. The regimental chaplain, Edwin S. Pons, buried him and two of his men in the Castiglione cemetery. Pipers played the lament but few men were able to come and pay tribute. Two lower-ranked soldiers who perished in the battle were Corporals H.C. McCallum and D. McClelland. Hugh McCallum was shot through the head when he was detailed to investigate the whereabouts of a sniper. He had attended Muizenberg High School, becoming an apprentice at the *Cape Times* before the war. He had survived five years of active service and a facial injury at

330 DODAR, UWH, Box 140, Sergeant N.C. Coleman, A Squadron Prince Alfred's Guard, a short narrative on tank approach from La Quercia on 'D' Day.

the battle of Alamein. At the request of his family, the following was inscribed on his gravestone: "He answered the call of duty and gave his life in the cause of humanity". According to Wulfsohn, who was in the Witwatersrand Rifles/ Regiment De la Rey with McClelland, the 29-year-old corporal had been the postmaster in Rustenburg. He had survived the desert war as an infantryman in the Field Force Brigade, a unit which had been particularly hard hit. He had reportedly requested that he be left out of battle after having an ominous premonition. This request was denied however, and he was mortally wounded during the exploitation phase. The inscription chosen for his headstone was: "There is no sweeter place of rest than where fallen comrades lie."

In total, 61 South Africans and nine members of the Frontier Force Rifles were killed in the operation. More than 70 German dead were counted but total enemy casualties were estimated at above 500 and the enemy front collapsed.

The division gathered for a short rest at La Quercia, an unattractive little town on the left bank of the Setta River dominated by a railway viaduct. Here it was reorganized as three composite brigades. The church at La Quercia served as a mortuary where the padre searched the dead for identification and prepared them for burial at Castiglione, approximately four miles to the rear.

Wednesday 18 April 1945: Rioveggio

While all this activity was going on in the air and in the mountains, the artillerymen down in the valley had been able to sunbathe by the river and buy tins of fruit from the NAAFI truck.

However, on the evening of 16 April, there was a brief panic among the artillery positions when a fire broke out just as planes were going overhead. Johnston blacked out his *kaia* (Zulu for 'house') to be able to read and write that night. Hodgson was one of the men who indulged in sunbathing. With the successful outcome of the battle and the Russians advancing on Berlin, he was more optimistic than ever and was aching to tell his parents the good news; but could do no more than pass hints. His prediction would turn out to be too optimistic by a month:

> Well, I am going to make a statement here, and you can see how right I turn out to be. The link between the western and eastern front will take place on or before the 23rd Inst.; secondly that by the 30th Inst., forces will be well into Berlin, the city itself will fall in the first days of April.

As the Allies crossed over the winter line into what had been enemy territory, they noticed that the damage from bombing and shelling was much worse than it had been on their side. Axelson wrote that he had not seen any town in Italy which was as totally destroyed as Vado was.

The engineers had a particularly busy time filling shell craters, making detours and even building a landing strip alongside the Setta River near La Quercia. Under shelling, the engineers scooped gravel out of the Setta River bed to widen the road north. That night they began clearing the way through the rubble of Vado.

Pursued by the Americans, including the 10th Mountain Division and the Frontier Force Rifles, the Germans were retreating in disarray. Away from the roads, the enemy was pursued on foot through the hills and across the Reno River. The infantry had to carry its own ammunition and supplies, with the help of mules. The only contact was with the enemy rearguard as the Germans abandoned one position after the other.

By 18 April, the Frontier Force Rifles and the Royal Durban Light Infantry had covered 15,000 yards on foot as the crow flies; probably twice that distance taking the hills into account.

An order group was held at La Quercia at 1030 hours on 19 April, where it was explained that the 6th South African Armoured Division would now pursue the retreating enemy with all speed. With this in mind, specific brigade groupings were formed: the 11th South African Armoured Brigade comprising the Special Service Battalion, the Imperial Light Horse/Kimberley Regiment, the First City/Cape Town Highlanders and the 4/22nd Field Regiment, the 12th South African Motorized Brigade including the Royal Durban Light Infantry, the Witwatersrand Rifles/Regiment De la Rey, the Prince Alfred's Guard, the 1/6th Field Regiment and the 13th South African Motorized Brigade, composed of the Royal Natal Carbineers, the Natal Mounted Rifles, 1 Squadron Pretoria Regiment (Princess Alice's Own), and the 15th Field Regiment.

The main thrust would be made by the 11th South African Armoured Brigade. Where possible, the 12th South African Motorized Brigade would operate abreast of them. Behind them, the 13th Motorized Brigade would be prepared to reinforce or pass through the other brigades and to mop up bypassed areas and to guard the headquarters and installations of the division. The field artillery moved up to Rioveggio while the mediums remained behind and moved straight to Vado the following day. On the morning of 18 April, readers of *The Friend* in Bloemfontein woke up to an evocative but not very enlightening report on the battle of Monte Sole:

> With American Mountain troops advancing on their left and other American forces striking simultaneously towards Bologna on their right, the infantry from the Rand, Cape and Cape Province regiments at 10.30 on Saturday night crossed the start-line to assault one of the most formidable enemy strong points on the whole front.

The Friend did not mention the casualties or the fact that Caprara was the harder fought battle.

The Star of 18 April did, however, emphasize the role played by the Witwatersrand Rifles/Regiment De la Rey on Monte Caprara. The report mentioned that one company was cut up on the start-line, but downplayed the South African casualties. It mentioned that "most of the wounds were caused by mortar splinters and many of these were only slight". It appears that there were few infantry defenders on Monte Sole, and much of the resistance came in the form of landmines and mortar fire.

When it came to reporting American actions and casualties, the *Rand Daily Mail* was much more graphic:

> The Americans crashing headlong into the mountain positions which were built up during the winter months have met a shattering defensive fire and thick minefields which have cost them many casualties. They tried for five hours to work up one hill feature. Half way up the steep sides, they were met by a withering hail of machine-gun fire from a shell-wrecked hamlet and from caves. American artillery—everything from 37mm to 155mm pieces—blasted the hamlet, making way for Sherman tanks. But the German artillery replied, forcing the American tanks into a gully. Telephoned reports reaching an observation post say that the Germans are rolling hand grenades down the sides of the mountain. Many American wounded are lying at the base of the cliffs, medical units being unable to reach them because of the ferocity of the defending Germans.[331]

Thursday 19 April 1945 – Friday 20 April 1945: Vado

The battlefield was now open for inspection by journalists. A report appearing in *The Star* of Saturday 21 April described the luxurious German dug-outs on Monte Sole. The occupants would not have been greatly disturbed by the bombs and shells because they had tunnelled 20 feet into the rear slopes of the

[331] *Rand Daily Mail*, Heavy fighting along whole Italian front, 17/4/1945.

mountain and above them was 200 or 300 feet of solid earth. An inspection of the spacious rooms or apartments revealed that German officers were apparently able to enjoy female companionship: one of the more interesting finds was a collection of women's underwear and cosmetics. Electric light was provided by a generator.

During the night of 19 April, the division had arrived at the confluence of the Reno and Setta rivers, just past Vado, where Route 6620 fed into Route 64. From here to Bologna, the advance would continue along one road, Route 64.

Vado was totally and utterly destroyed. No houses were left standing. The dust-covered corpses of Americans and Germans blended with the rubble. While the division was assembling in the riverbed, Johnston looked around Vado, finding many "infested" Jerry areas and dug-outs and concluded: "Place in a hell of a mess."

Apart from the destruction of the Appenino tunnel, the major damage to the Prato–Bologna railway was at Vado. The Vado viaduct, with its 14 spans, had been destroyed. The South African railwaymen immediately began reparations. Indeed, the engineers had already begun manufacturing and assembling the new 90- and 75-foot spans, which had been measured by means of aerial reconnaissance. Only after the fall of Bologna would the full extent of German demolitions become known. In this area, the railwaymen were tasked with repairing a total of 25 bridges, 40 tunnel portals and 12 culverts. Some of these demolitions were avoided by means of deviations.

The heavy 105mm howitzers of the Americans dropped into action at a point where a side road joined with Route 6620. The 25-pounders of the newly arrived 15th Field Regiment also had an opportunity to fire some high explosive into the fleeing enemy. Guns were now very often positioned on the roadside instead of being deployed, textbook fashion, in a field. There was little to worry about in terms air attacks, but the 1/11th Anti-Tank Regiment was among several to come under a strafing attack one night, while camped in the riverbed at Vado. Johnston witnessed this incident:

> Started to move. All ready and Jerry plane strafed road. Five-mile move and again in riverbed. Planes still strafing. Get ready for OP … Travelled most of the night. 3 APs over us. Pulled in with PRs and had ½ hr's sleep.

Once more, the roads became extremely congested. After months of static warfare, the rapid movement caused some confusion among the Allies and a friendly fire incident was narrowly averted when the Special Service Battalion was mistaken for a concentration of Tiger tanks. The tanks were massed together in a field just off the road.

The Imperial Light Horse/Kimberley Regiment, working with the Special Service Battalion, crossed the Reno River and was now proceeding rapidly up Route 64, outflanking opposition and bypassing Bologna. This was a period of furious activity and pursuit. Victory was in the air and caution was thrown to the wind. In the final push, the Imperial Light Horse/Kimberley Regiment was carried into battle on the tanks of the Special Service Battalion. It was usually transported on half-tracks. As a recent replacement in the Imperial Light Horse/Kimberley Regiment, this was Frank Mundel's first taste of real battle. According to him, more men were being injured by falling off the tanks than by small-arms fire. There was no contact apart from a few sniper incidents on 20 April. There was some grumbling in the operations room about the Royal Natal Carbineers, which was apparently hanging back.

A harbour area where the 13th South African Motorized Brigade was operating was bombed by an enemy aircraft that evening. Nine men were wounded, including Major R.V. Paul, one of the heroes of the Natal Mounted Rifles. In one of these strafing and bombing expeditions, about 80 Americans were killed at a headquarters on the outskirts of Bologna.

During the night of 20/21 April, the United States 1st Armoured Division forced its way out onto the Po plain, due south of Ponte Samoggia. At this stage, an innovation was introduced to overcome the problem of demolitions which delayed the tanks and granted the enemy time to rest and reorganize during the night. The tactic was for the infantry to go ahead on foot under cover of darkness on a narrow front, to a depth of up to seven miles. At first light, they would fan out and mop up the surprised enemy. The engineers, both American and South African, would work through the night to prepare a crossing for the tanks which then raced ahead, passing through the infantry, and continued fighting in the daylight. The American 5th Army now had five divisions trying to sweep forward on a wide front. These were, from right to left: the 6th South African Armoured Division, 85th United States Infantry Division, 88th United States Infantry Division, 10th Mountain Division and 1st US Armoured Division. After Bologna, the British 8th Army operated on the right of the 6th South African Armoured Division. The roads were so choked with traffic that it took seven hours to move 25 miles to the concentration area at Calderara.

Saturday 21 April 1945: Calderara

The whole of the 12th South African Motorized Brigade now concentrated in Calderara, northwest of Bologna. The Imperial Light Horse/Kimberley Regiment was still on the division's left and its old friends, the 2nd New Zealand Division, was on the right. The day was windy and colder than it had been of late and there was a lot of chalky white dust about. Pontelungo bridge on Route 9 west of Bologna was secured by the Royal Natal Carbineers and contact was made with the British 8th Army. Bologna was occupied by the Polish troops of the 8th Army. The Germans were fighting in isolated groups, many of which surrendered. Traffic was a nightmare, with three divisions using a single road. The Pretoria Regiment led the 6th South African Armoured Division. Resistance was heavy and at least two tanks were knocked out near the aerodrome on the San Giovanni road.

The route followed by the Pretoria Regiment passed through Casalecchio northward, east of the railway line, and finally northwest past the aerodrome (the present-day Aeroporto Guglielmo Marconi).

In what is now a suburb of Bologna, at the corner of Via San Vitalino and Via Stradone, a bazooka projectile hit the right-hand point tank, killing Trooper M.V. Kelly-Gliddon and Lieutenant C.M. de Villiers. Trooper J. Fisher lost a hand. Kelly-Gliddon's desolate widow needed to know the details:

> Dear General Poole
> I hereby wish to ask you please to inform me of how my husband, Tpr Kelly-Gliddon was killed. Please let me have every bit of news as it will come in handy in the days to come. I know you have a lot to deal with but I feel I can't rest until I have every detail in common. You need not be afraid to let me know the worst as I can take it. So please don't be annoyed as my nerves can't stand this delaying news.
> Thanking you,
> I remain yours obediently
>
> Mrs A.J. Kelly-Gliddon
> 72 Grey Street,
> Aliwal North
> P.S. This is my address as all the telegrams and letters had the wrong address.
> Thanks.

Mrs Kelly-Gliddon received this matter-of-fact response from Colonel Ollemans by return of post:

Col D.H. Ollemans
Rear 6 SA Armd Div
UDF, CMF
21 May 1945

I have been directed by my General to reply to your letter of 16 May 1945 and advise you of the circumstances in which your late husband, Tpr M.V. Kelly-Gliddon was killed in action. The facts are as follows:

During the advance of this formation north of Bologna, on the 21st April 1945, the PR (PAO) was doing a flanking, protection role. The tank in which your husband was serving as a gunner was hit by a bazooka shell during this attack and the officer in charge and your husband were both killed instantly. He is buried in Plot No. 6, Row 'C', Grave No. 5 along with his officer and other men of this Division in the 6 SA ARMD DIV CEMETERY at a little village called CASTIGLIONE, halfway between Florence and Bologna.

Please accept my General's sincere sympathy on the loss of your husband in the service of South Africa.

The words chosen for Kelly-Gliddon's gravestone express a widely held sentiment of the day: "The life he loved he freely gave and death endured our lives to save".

Johnston's diary summarizes the full spectrum of experiences encompassed by this phase: "Bologna. Cameramen as we moved along river. Parked airfield. 3 PR tanks knocked out. Pulled behind house. Prisoners. PR Colonel directing tanks. Back to harbour area. Sniped at ... Moved across to another harbour area. Jerry planes all night. Damn them."

The advance of the Pretoria Regiment was held up at Longara canal while it rounded up 152 POWs, including two officers. Following behind the fighting tank squadrons was the A Echelon, consisting of forward signal group and forward 'T' (technical) group. Then came the B Echelon, or Replenishment Echelon, which consisted of a number of 'replenishment packets'.

The C Echelon comprised various soft-skinned vehicles and stores trucks. Captain Concar of the Prince Alfred's Guard was in charge of an echelon of soft-skinned vehicles bringing up fuel and ammunition for the tanks which were racing ahead:

Only once was there any excitement near the echelon which at this stage was travelling with the WR/DLR echelon. We were moving in a column when after a sudden spatter of shots, a German ran past my Dingo, lifted a huge Beratti, and

> fired backwards. The partisans who were chasing him fired wildly in all directions. As he ran past a 15-cwt, a WR/DLR Lieutenant leaned out, grabbed the German and swung him into the truck, and told him to keep down out of sight of the partisans. A mile or so further on, the echelon halted. The German suddenly jumped out of the 15-cwt, and ran and crawled away under cover in a field. The WR/DLR officer jumped out of the vehicle and with a few quick bursts from his Tommy gun, put the German to the ground. He died before our men reached him. We handed him over to the partisans for burial, and the column moved on.[332]

Several units entered San Giovanni that night. The wind and dust were still blowing, creating an atmosphere reminiscent of the desert. However, the townsfolk turned out to welcome the *liberatori* with their usual enthusiasm. The Royal Natal Carbineers was taking a back seat as it harboured in lucern fields, as evidenced by Hodgson's own experience:

> I must say, it is grand to be mobile again. At the moment they say we are fighting a war, but I hardly see that myself, or if we are, it is truly a grand one to fight in. Granted, we are advancing and all the rest of it, but at the moment, there is nothing to stop us. Lately I have spoken to quite a few German prisoners who can speak English and all of them openly admit that the German army is finished; and when they see all over, forces, armour, trucks etc, etc, they are simply amazed and can hardly believe that it is all true.

During this phase, 20 South African Field Ambulance was in support of the 12th South African Motorized Brigade. The casualty clearing posts of this field ambulance were sited as close as possible to the regimental aid posts. Battle casualties were passed back from advanced dressing station to forward dressing station. The casualty clearing station was normally 30 to 40 miles behind the field dressing station if road communication was good. Usually, priority casualties were taken back to the casualty clearing centre, then evacuated rearward by ambulance car to the general hospital in Florence and later Bologna. A main dressing station lay behind brigade headquarters and dealt mainly with the sick, rather than battle casualties. The main dressing station was essentially the B Echelon of the field ambulance which, for the Monte Sole battles, was situated at Vaiano, between Castiglione and 107th South African General Hospital in Florence. Once the chase started, the main dressing station moved up to San Giovanni and a casualty clearing station was left at La Quercia to stage

332 DODAR, UWH, Box 140, Statement by Captain Concar, Prince Alfred's Guard.

casualties, as the line of evacuation had lengthened significantly. Later, the main dressing station was relocated to Montagnana while the advanced dressing station remained close behind the brigade.

Sunday 22 April 1945: San Giovanni, Camposanto, Finale

The column of vehicles was never-ending as it slowly wound its way through the mountains onto the plains, stopping and starting for reasons unknown. Engines would be switched off to save fuel and some would refuse to start again. At each hold-up, the drivers would have a smoke or brew some tea. A South African officer attached to an intelligence organization known as 'S' Force witnessed the scene:

> Guns, tanks, ambulances, carriers, advance dressing stations, food, ammunition, water, petrol, oil, barbed wire, bridging tools, mines, rockets, road repair outfits, engineer trucks, rear headquarters, generators, scout cars, half-tracks, three tonners, jeeps, staff cars, pumping plants, anti-gas trucks, broadcast vans, radio vans, map trucks, battle police, Poles, Yanks, French, British, Indians, Canadians, South Africans, Gurkhas, West Indians, Madagascar sappers, St Helena signalmen, Italian mule trains, Partisans, advance parties for brigades and divisions, searchlights, markers for infantry battalions, ack-ack guns, S.P. guns, pontoons, transformers, camouflage outfits, hygiene squads, dispatch riders and all the detachments of an army moving up.[333]

While the Royal Durban Light Infantry remained harboured five miles northwest of Bologna, the charge was resumed at dawn on 22 April toward the Panaro River. The tanks of the Prince Alfred's Guard led, along with a detachment of the Witwatersrand Rifles/Regiment De la Rey and one battery of the 1/6th Field Regiment. No enemy resistance was encountered in this area and there were no demolitions to hold up progress.

At Camposanto, the main road to Verona continues straight. Another turns left, parallel to the southern levee, to Camposanto bridge which was still intact. Apparently the Germans did not have a cable to blow the charges and were kept at bay by the South Africans. A small detachment of American infantry was already there. They could not say for certain whether or not there were any of their own troops in the village across the bridge. For this reason, artillery fire was not initially employed. The first attempt to cross the bridge was abandoned.

---

333 A. Forrest, *Italian interlude*, p. 132.

In a dramatic episode, Private de Lange of the Witwatersrand Rifles/Regiment De la Rey was left lying on the bridge behind a tank, in danger of being run over as the tanks retreated. The tank squadron commander, Major Shakespeare, leaped down in a hail of bullets and carried de Lange to safety.

It was decided to ferry the infantry across the Camposanto bridge in Bren carriers. Having charged across, they immediately set up a bridgehead and started exploiting. The tanks now crossed over to assist.

That night, American vehicles belonging to the 10th Mountain Division appeared out of nowhere and poured across into the town, where a partisan flag was already flying. An unfortunate accident with a hand grenade occurred while the troops were in harbour and awaiting orders to move. Ten soldiers of the Royal Durban Light Infantry were wounded.

The Sextons of the 4/22nd Field Regiment went into action in an open field, causing carnage on the road to Decima. In the air, rocket-firing Typhoons and a spotter plane flew low over enemy positions, attracting tracer fire. On one occasion, a Typhoon pulled out of its dive at the last moment after recognizing friendly troops who had crossed the 'bomb line'.

The division was now ordered to hand over Camposanto to the Americans and move with speed downstream to Finale Emilia. On the evening of 22 April, a strong force from the 12th Motorized Brigade set off ahead of the division, back along the south bank of the Panaro River toward Finale Emilia which was marked by a tall square tower standing out over the plain, eight miles east of Camposanto. The 25-pounders of the 1/16th Battery, the Prince Alfred's Guard and the Royal Durban Light Infantry set off toward Finale at 1345 hours and arrived there at 1655 hours. The enemy was withdrawing across the bridge at Finale and two companies were dug in on the southern side to cover the retreat. The Royal Durban Light Infantry and tanks of the Prince Alfred's Guard were involved in an hour-long battle in the moonlight, around the bridge and along the canal.[334]

Throughout the night, they engaged the enemy at the bridge in Finale. On approaching the bridge, the Royal Durban Light Infantry came under fire from tanks and 20mm guns. Fighting was described as heavy and confused as pockets of enemy had been separated from the main column. Only part of the German column crossed the river; the rest was shattered by tank and

[334] N. Orpen, *Victory in Italy*, p. 292; Today, there is a square tower near Camposanto bridge but the town of Finale cannot be seen from the bridge.

artillery fire. At 0100 hours the enemy counter-attacked in company strength, attacking again from another direction 30 minutes later. These attempts were successfully repulsed by the Royal Durban Light Infantry, but two Prince Alfred's Guard tanks were knocked out by bazooka fire coming from slit trenches. The fighting died down as the night wore on. The enemy decided that it could not hold on until daylight and began to withdraw at 0330 hours, blowing up the stone bridge as they went.

During the night, a Stuka was shot down over Camposanto by two Bofors guns of B Troop, 1/12th Light Anti-Aircraft Regiment. The troop had pulled up in the camp late during the night and had no intention of going into action. However, they decided to deploy when one aircraft came over strafing. A second aircraft, flying over at about 0100 hours, was shot down. A third aircraft, out for revenge, made three strafing runs at the guns. The Stuka crashed about 150 yards from the gun, its two crew members lying in the wreckage. One of them had stopped a Bofors shell with his head.

Monday 23 April 1945: Panaro River

In the early hours of 23 April, at approximately 0300 hours, a single enemy aircraft passed over the sector occupied by the Witwatersrand Rifles/Regiment De la Rey at Camposanto, dropping several SD 2 'Butterfly' anti-personnel bombs which killed five and wounded 24 members of B Company. These casualties were the last to be suffered by the battalion as a result of enemy action.

Downriver at Finale, the mopping up continued throughout the morning. Over 200 Germans had been killed during the night. The Prince Alfred's Guard lost two killed and one wounded and the Royal Durban Light Infantry lost eight wounded. The Special Service Battalion tanks were now up forward and, according to Murray, "itching to get moving".[335]

In a newspaper article entitled "Rhodesians race to keep up with enemy in Po Valley" published on 22 April, the Rhodesian military observer described his journey through Bologna and the villages wrecked by Allied bombing and shelling and returning German prisoners. He stopped to talk to any Rhodesians he came across, recognizable by their bush hats with leopard-skin bands:

335 In his book, *The Durban Light Infantry*, Lieutenant-Colonel Martin refers to a "spirited encounter" in which the Special Service Battalion destroyed seven enemy tanks; DODAR, WD, Box 598, Recording Officer, 12 South African Motorized Brigade, Report on Operations in the Italian Campaign for period August 1944–May 1945; L.G. Murray, *First City/Cape Town Highlanders in the Italian Campaign*, p. 64.

> But now the sun is shining warmly on these Southern Africans, and they are positively romping ahead in flying columns. Will you remember that the manpower of this division is more than enough to populate by the latest census, either Bulawayo or Salisbury and that at the moment they are spread out over many square miles of country—horribly devastated country where bodies of human beings, civilians as well as military, and of animals, lie stinking in the sun.

The Panaro River is not particularly wide but it has steep banks covered in vegetation, and the water is too deep for wading.

Cormack recorded on this day that a "Jock column" joined at Finale. The term originated in the desert war and refers to a small force of combined motorized infantry, artillery and armour. In this case, it consisted of the Special Service Battalion and the Imperial Light Horse/Kimberley Regiment of the 11th South African Armoured Brigade.

The Jock column was making all speed to reach Finale, where the enemy fought with fanatical desperation, often firing on the South African tanks at point-blank range. There were still plenty of Jerries about on the south bank to the east of the bridge. Captain G.E. McLaughlan, who commanded the 1/16th Battery, recorded how at first light he saw Captain L.J.P. English, adjutant of the Royal Durban Light Infantry "gather up the cooks and bottle-washers and advance in spirited fashion to capture a number of Germans in a field of corn. The men advanced firing from the hip".[336]

The 25-pounders were positioned 500 yards south of the river and some of the gunners took the opportunity to have a dip. Cormack wrote: "Bathing under shelling—Sobbing Sisters".

Some citizens of Finale mistook the gunners for assault troops and informed Bourhill that there were some Germans cut off in a building in the town. Reasoning that he had no training in house-to-house fighting and that it would be silly to get killed at this stage, he declined the invitation to flush out the enemy. The Germans made a final stand from the north bank of the river, using machine guns, anti-tank guns, Panzerfausts and Nebelwerfers.

The Royal Durban Light Infantry recorded only 12 wounded while the Prince Alfred's Guard lost two killed. It was then relieved by the Imperial Light Horse/Kimberley Regiment and withdrawn to Camposanto. The direct road from Bologna to Camposanto travels through San Giovanni. Johnston's tank branched off on this road toward Finale Emilia, through Cento where the

336 A.C. Martin, *The Durban Light Infantry*, p. 397.

A 25-pounder of the Rhodesian battery at Montorio. *Photo: DODAR*

Parade in the Castiglione town square on the occasion of the second birthday of the 6th South African Armoured Division (1 February 1945). Music was courtesy of the First City/Cape Town Highlanders and Imperial Light Horse bands. *Photo: Comune di Castiglione dei Pepoli*

Paying respects to fallen comrades was also an opportunity to take photographs on behalf of family members. Nearest the camera is the grave of Pte D.D. Bentley, one of 15 members of the Imperial Light Horse/ Kimberley Regiment killed during the taking of Pt 826. *Photo: Comune di Castiglione dei Pepoli*

Memorial service in the cemetery at Castiglione, believed to be on the occasion of the dedication of the cemetry, 28 December 1944. *Photo: Comune di Castiglione dei Pepoli*

Pretoria Regiment types reminiscing about Sunnyside 'down south'. In the Winter Line, men lived in shacks constructed of sandbags and ammunition boxes; some had stoves made out of petrol tins. *Photo: Comune di Castiglione dei Pepoli*

At the end of winter, when the division left for Lucca and six weeks of rest, Castiglione had been home for almost five months. *Photo: Comune di Castiglione dei Pepoli*

"Hurry up and wait." Sherman 'Firefly' tanks of the Pretoria Regiment. The crew is dressed in cold-weather kit. *Photo: Wikipedia*

Pretoria Regiment parade on the banks of the Serchio River near Lucca, 26 March 1945.
Photo: DODAR

Above: Steve Bourhill (left) and 'Mac' Cormack on leave in Florence. The landlady is called Carola.
Photo: Author's collection

Left: Two Witwatersrand Rifles/Regiment De la Rey soldiers— Privates C.R de Wet of Kempton Park and F.G. van der Merwe of Klerksdorp—find distraction in some light reading, hours before the attack on Monte Caprara. *Photo: SANMMH*

In Florence the only bridge which the Germans did not destroy was the Ponte Vecchio which can be seen in the background. In this much-frequented neighbourhood there was an overwhelming smell of unwashed humanity, street latrines, dust and rubble. *Photo: SANMMH*

Congregating in the Piazza del Duomo as tourists in Florence generally do. *Photo: DODAR*

This combined 'bivvy' and fighting hole opposite the Monte Caprara objective is occupied by Pte J.F. Botha of Johannesburg. *Photo: DODAR*

The public relations photographer, Lt J.W. Nicholls, who took this picture, insisted that it was not staged; incoming mortar fire had necessitated this quick reaction. *Photo: DODAR*

Battleworn men of the Witwatersrand Rifles/ Regiment De la Rey in a sheltered position on Monte Caprara. *Photo: DODAR*

A good view of the battlefield from the top of Monte Sole; Monte Caprara and the ruins of Caprara village can be seen in the background. It was up these slopes that the South Africans had charged the previous night.
Photo: DODAR

'B' Coy Royal Natal Carbineers and tanks cross the Reno River just south of Bologna. Note the bomb craters in the sand. *Photo: J.B. Hodgson collection*

Breakthrough to Bologna. Gnr P.M. Johnston's diary entry for 21 April 1945 states: "Bologna. Cameramen as we moved along [the Setta] river." *Photo: DODAR*

Germans blasted off the road north of Bologna. Bureau of Information photographers usually avoided such un-photogenic subjects; private photography was also strictly controlled. *Photo: DODAR*

German dead—one with a wine flagon close to hand. A blow-up of the picture shows a group of civilians gathered under the trees in the background. It could have been they who covered the corpses. *Photo: DODAR*

Some prisoners were badly shaken and in tears, some were relieved to be out of it and full of smiles, others were arrogant or defiant. These POWs held in a cage at the rear of Monte Sole look plain dejected. *Photo: DODAR*

Overnight accommodation at a farmstead near Finale. Eric Comrie, dispatch rider for 'B' Coy RNC. *Photo: J.B. Hodgson collection*

Royce Fuller (SSB) photographed in winter battledress with a newly acquired campaign ribbon, only weeks before being hit by an armour-piercing projectile near Finale on 23 April 1945. *Photo: F.B. Bourhill collection*

South Africans receive their usual welcome as they enter the town of Finale Emilia. Some civilians hurry in the opposite direction after the fierce fighting for the bridges. *Photo: DODAR*

On 25 April 1945 Peter Johnston told his diary: "Up to Felonica. Hell of a pile of Jerry stuff. Tanks, trucks, guns. Looked over Po. Looting." *Photo: DODAR*

Among those who managed to cross the River Po at Felonica by raft was this sub of 1/16 Battery of 1/6th Field Regiment. *Photo: DODAR*

The main body of 6th SA Armoured Division crossed the River Po by the American-built pontoon bridge at Ostiglia. *Photo: DODAR*

The division's great task is over. Troops read about the German surrender after arriving in the Milan area.
Photo: Author's collection

In the grounds of the Monza race track before the parade on 14 May 1945. Gnr P.M. Johnston kneels front left. In the background are the 5.5-inch guns of 7/23rd Medium Regiment.
Photo: J. van Velden collection

Members of the Prince Alfred's Guard with their paraphernalia during the final stage of the war. Original caption read: "Before Milan, 'Bad Penny III' and crew—'Binoc Tommygun' Bob McClelland, self [Warring, aged 18], Immelman, Willemse. Track extensions. Bottles. Where mortar hit on turret." *Photo: Anne Warring, Peter Warring*

M10 tank-destroyers of 1/11th Anti-Tank Regiment. Barrels are raised as they pass the saluting dias at Monza. *Photo: J. van Velden collection*

Monza victory parade, 14 May 1945. It took nearly three hours for the tanks, guns, half-tracked vehicles, troop carriers, ambulances and motor cycles, totalling over 2,400 vehicles, to roll by three abreast. *Photo: J. van Velden collection*

Luncheon for visiting dignitaries and top brass in the grounds of the Monza Palace after the victory parade. The Hon F.C. Sturrock is in white. *Photo: DODAR*

Original caption read: "On the summit of Mt Blanc (15,632ft) at 11.35 a.m. on 4 July 1945. Temperature 14°–17°F below freezing. The background is Italy. Left to right: John B. Hodgson; an American who climbed up from the French side & we met on the top; Murton P. Slade; a French guide (with his back to the camera); Ellissio [Eliseo] Croux; Evaristo Croux and Arthur H. Newey." *Photo: J.B. Hodgson collection*

Jan Smuts inspecting the troops at a parade in the Milan Arena on 8 July 1945. *Photo: DODAR*

Visit to the cemetery at Castiglione on 10 July 1945. From left: General F. Theron, General E. Poole and Field Marshal J.C. Smuts. *Photo: Comune di Castiglione dei Pepoli*

Postcard from Rapallo. Portofino is near the tip of the peninsular. *Photo: Author's collection*

Waiting for the boat to take them home while stationed at Diano Marina. John Hodgson and Henry Heath appear to be going nowhere at Restaurant Flora, Pietra Ligure. *Photo: J.B. Hodgson collection*

Peter Johnston and a friend treading water at Alassio, awaiting repatriation. *Photo: J. van Velden collection*

Below: Transit camp at Foggia. These men have just had their names called for the next flight to Egypt and scramble to get their gear. *Photo: DODAR*

Castiglione cemetery nearing its full complement of 502 burials. A blow-up of the photograph reveals that the graves are neat mounds of bare earth and the memorial is still under construction. *Photo: Comune di Castiglione dei Pepoli*

Not yet 21, John Hodgson with his mother on the day of his homecoming. *Photo: J.B. Hodgson collection*

surrounding farmland was cratered by bombs intended for German workshops in the village: "Off early. Cento. 3 SSB tanks and 2 Jerry beside road … Moved across to Finale … Went out to shoot up tower but finished up guarding our right flank. Nearly shot up ILH."

A report on the operations of the 12th South African Motorized Brigade during this period mentions that during the Witwatersrand Rifles/Regiment De la Rey's advance from Camposanto to Felonica, it was necessary to halt the unit at night. This avoided clashes with the 88th United States Infantry Division which cut across the 6th South African Armoured Division sector.[337]

A degree of animosity simmered between the South African and American troops. The former brigade major of the 13th South African Motorized Brigade mentioned two incidents where the Americans "gave a lot of trouble". In one case, the brigade was occupying the town of Casalecchio on the outskirts of Bologna when it received the message from Colonel Maggs that it was not to take occupation after all. The town had been earmarked for bombardment as a prelude to a set-piece attack by the Americans: "Brigadier Bester insisted that his men were there and the proposal rubbish but was overruled, 13 Bde advance guard had to clear out and the place was duly bombarded and solemnly occupied by the Yanks."[338]

The Special Service Battalion spent the day on 23 April mopping up the south bank. Trooper L.R. 'Royce' Fuller was thus engaged when his tank was hit by an armour-piercing projectile. The advanced dressing station was not far away and his wounds did not seem to be life-threatening at first. At 1430 hours, Captain Ronald St Clair Sinclair of 19 South African Field Ambulance noted on the field medical card: "Perforating shrapnel wounds—scrotum, buttocks, both thighs, composite fracture left ankle. Shell (H/E)." At the casualty clearing station, the wound type was altered to "SW Bazooka". Fuller's condition was described as "fair" while the notes detailing his mental condition observed "some euphoria" [morphine-induced] but said that he was "cooperative". A medic painted the letter 'M' on his forehead to prevent further administration of morphine, potentially leading to an overdose. The more insidious injury of a perforated colon had not yet been identified.

Bourhill and Royce Fuller had grown up together in the eastern Transvaal.

337 DODAR, WD, Box 598, Recording Officer, 12th South African Motorized Brigade, Report on Operations in the Italian Campaign for period August 1944–May 1945.

338 DODAR, UWH, Box 142, Interview with Lieutenant-Colonel Hawkins, 26/11/1948.

They used to travel together on the train to school at St John's College in Johannesburg. Royce was a 'golden boy', a prefect of Nash House in 1941, his matric year. It was a disastrous year for the rugby team, having lost two star players who left school early to join up. Royce, however, received special praise in the school magazine for his efforts as the hooker and vice-captain of the first team. He won his full colours for rugby and boxing and was also a student officer in the school cadet corps. Royce's father, Harold, was a mining engineer who, by 1942, had moved from the mining village of Kaapsehoop near Barberton to Gaths Mine, Mashaba (in Rhodesia).

The regimental history of the Special Service Battalion notes that on 23 April, "We lost personnel and tanks from bazookas and snipers".[339] Sergeant F.W. Casey of Bloemfontein was one of those killed that day.

The following day, the liaison officer from the 11th South African Armoured Brigade mentioned that his unit had taken 400 prisoners on 23 April. The men were not taking 'bazooka boys' prisoner however, nor did they take snipers alive. It appears that this policy was being taken to extremes. In his daily log, Axelson records a conversation he had with a SAPA photographer, Sergeant Cöhn:

> Cöhn said he had an argument with Lt-Col Brits just south of Finale. About 12 hours after the battle was decided, there were still groups of enemy holding out, because (they told him later) they would be shot if they surrendered. An SSB sergeant standing close to Cöhn was shot by a sniper, and Cöhn called out in German, telling them to surrender. The two Germans, thinking he was one of themselves, revealed themselves to him. After Cöhn assured them they would not be shot if they surrendered, they surrendered to him. Both Germans were wounded. They were taken to the RAP, and there they received medical attention. Lt-Col Brits heard of the death of his sergeant. He asked Cöhn to ask the Germans which one had shot the sergeant. One of the prisoners said that he had. Lt-Col Brits ordered him to be taken outside and shot. Cöhn and the MO objected, but the prisoner was taken outside, and shot by a friend of the sergeant's, with a revolver.[340]

This part of Axelson's log was not included in his published work but the story is corroborated by the fact that there was, indeed, a sergeant of the Special Service Battalion killed on 24 April. He was Sergeant R. Moyes, a 37-year-old Rhodesian volunteer.

---

339 DODAR, WD, Box 647 (B18), 1 Special Service Battalion, regimental history, April 1945.

340 DODAR, WD, Recording Officer, daily log, 9/5/1945.

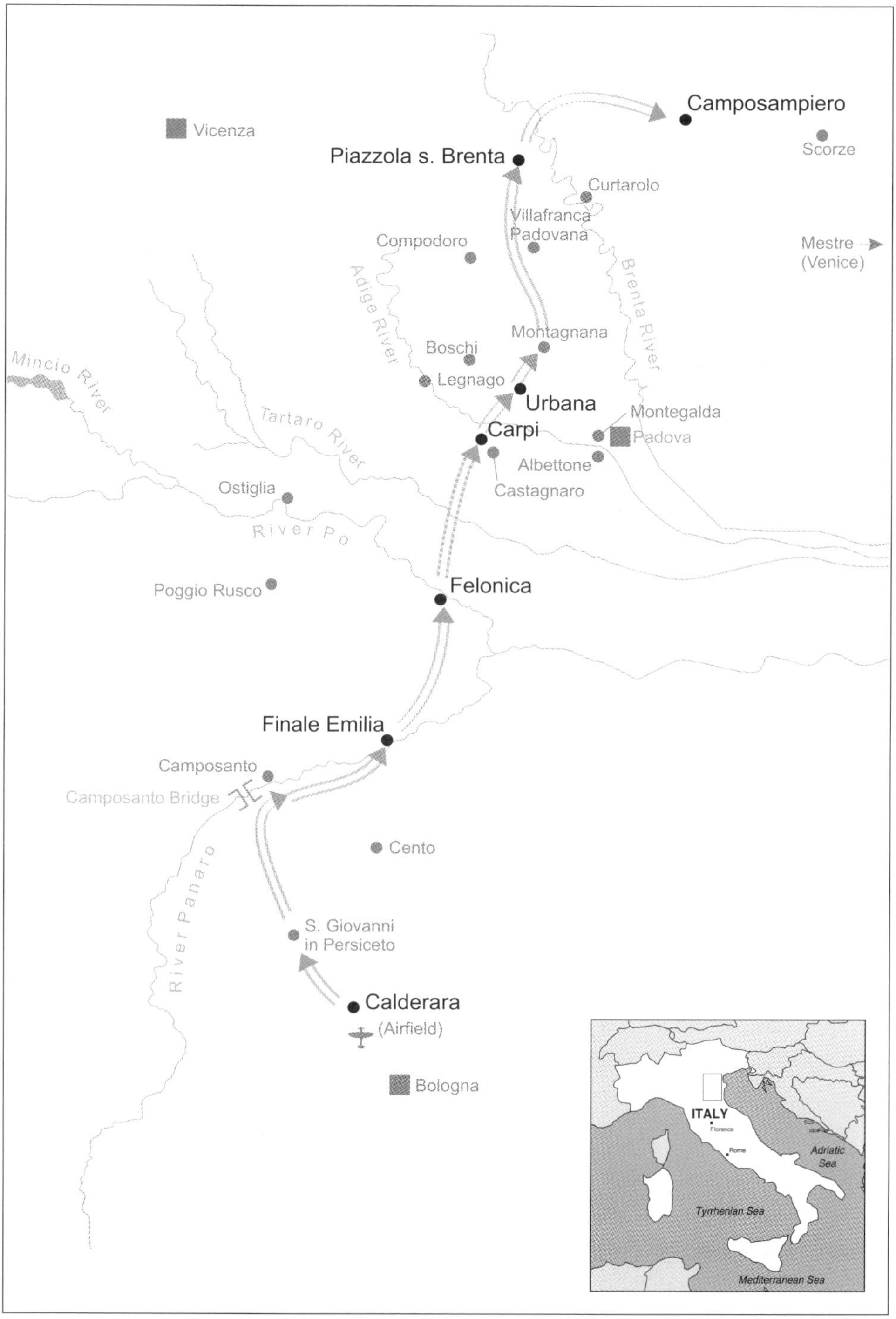
Camposampiero
Vicenza
Piazzola s. Brenta
Scorze
Curtarolo
Villafranca
Padovana
Compodoro
Mestre
(Venice)
Adige River
Brenta River
Montagnana
Boschi
Legnago
Mincio River
Urbana
Montegalda
Tartaro River
Carpi
Padova
Albettone
Castagnaro
Ostiglia
River Po
Poggio Rusco
Felonica
Finale Emilia
Camposanto
Camposanto Bridge
Cento
River Panaro
S. Giovanni
in Persiceto
Calderara
(Airfield)
Bologna
ITALY
Florence
Rome
Adriatic
Sea
Tyrrhenian Sea
Mediterranean Sea

Tuesday 24 April 1945: Felonica

By 0500 on 24 April, the Pretoria Regiment reconnaissance group had crossed the Panaro River while the main body of the 12th Motorized Brigade, under Colonel Olsen, headed for Pigozzi a mile upstream from Felonica on the River Po. The Americans had already reached the north bank at San Benedetto. In the preceding five days they had taken about 30,000 prisoners.

The 6th South African Armoured Division was being left behind because it had ceded passage to the Americans at Camposanto bridge and then encountered resistance at Finale. It was now only ten days since the start of the United States 5th Army offensive. A detachment of the Pretoria Regiment was credited with facilitating the rapid advance from the Panaro to the Po, with three members winning awards for 'outstanding gallantry'. When Sergeant W.S. Simpson, who was leading in his Honey tank, came under fire from a farmhouse, he climbed out of his tank and led the crew in an attack on foot, killing four, wounding two and taking eight prisoners. Later in the day, he cleared another house, single-handed, armed with a Tommy gun and grenades. He returned with 20 prisoners. The second recipient was Lieutenant M.M. Munro. Under Major Kightley's direction, he dashed through the village of Felonica—where every house was occupied by the enemy—in an attempt to capture the bridge downstream, intact. The Allies were spread far and wide across the Po valley, the more mobile units sprinting ahead, leaving the transport to wait their turn to cross Bailey bridges. Johnston's diary entry illustrates the traffic problems on 24 April: "Moved again, 10 miles, took about 7 hours to do it. Filled up with petrol. Up to OP with Coetzee, Hall and Dossie. Night at Brigade HQ."

As the rear echelons of the division approached Finale Emilia, south of the Panaro River, they saw scenes of death and destruction which beggared description. The battlefield was littered with the wreckage of enemy vehicles, guns, carcasses of draught animals and at least 200 enemy lying dead and dying. Charred bodies still occupied their vehicles. Tracks and turrets had been ripped off tanks, engines blown out of trucks, bloodied and charred clothing lay in heaps with the pitiful possessions of the dead, photographs and letters spilling out. Looters had emptied the contents of each vehicle. A tank had blasted an animal-drawn convoy off the road at point-blank range. The historical recording officer saw only a dozen dead Germans at Finale but burial parties had already been at work for some time before his arrival. A path had been bulldozed through this mess, and Axelson walked down an avenue of destruction. Some of the wrecks were still smouldering. In the 600 yards between the canal bridge and the river bridge, the recording officer counted the remains of 100 carts, 50 trucks, six self-propelled guns and a dozen 20mm guns, as well as a Volkswagen here and there. A similar stream of destruction littered the approaches to the Panaro bridge at Finale from the direction of Bondeno in the east.

In the level fields along the river, there were a dozen 105mm guns, weapon pits, slit trenches and a pile of small arms including bazookas and faustpatronen. There were the usual animal corposes, their entrails protruding and legs blown off, as well as a number of dazed horses and oxen standing about. A Special Service Battalion officer walked among the wounded beasts, shooting at least 40 of them. Some fine-looking horses and oxen were led off by local Italians.

It is unclear who was accountable for this damage. At the time, the 4/22nd Field Regiment, the Special Service Battalion, the Royal Durban Light Infantry and the Imperial Light Horse/Kimberley Regiment all claimed full responsibility. German prisoners claimed that fighter bombers had set the vehicles on fire and blocked the road. Some civilians said that heavy shelling had caused most of the damage. The tanks and infantry arrived only later however, and it therefore seems that the 7/23rd Medium Regiment, the 4/22nd Field Regiment and the air force could legitimately claim this ultimate victory.

Wednesday 25 April 1945-Thursday 26 April 1945: Po

The River Po is 200 yards wide and flows strongly. Although there was no bridge at Felonica, there was a ferry harbour which had been the target of Allied bombing. A patrol from A Company, Royal Durban Light Infantry swam across the Po at 0100 hours on 25 April. Although the men came under fire, they reported the north bank to be lightly held. Orpen contrasts this reception with the German propaganda pamphlet showing a "colourful front page like a tourist brochure, on the reverse of which was a ghastly representation of death, carrying an American helmet in one hand and a British helmet in the other, whilst paddling among Allied soldiers drowning in the river under shot and shell".[341] Another pamphlet pictured British soldiers being blown out of their boats and stressed that the Po was wider, deeper and faster flowing than any other river they had crossed in Italy.

341 N. Orpen, *Victory in Italy*, p. 299; DODAR, WD, Box 646, Royal Natal Carbineers, propaganda pamphlet.

Without wavering, a company of the Royal Durban Light Infantry paddled across the river in flimsy canvas boats. The Germans opened fire while they crossed the 200 metres of open land on the other side.

Luck had ran out for the plucky 23-year-old Sergeant C.C. Buckley from Pietermaritzburg. He had twice won the Military Medal (MM and Bar) and proved the rule that the most fearless were the most likely to be killed.

Private N.O. Trollip took command. Driven by rage and self preservation, the section killed five of the enemy in quick succession, then jumped into a trench, bayoneted two Germans and shot another two before taking the remaining four prisoner. This exploit earned Trollip the DCM at a time when most men were loath to risk their lives. Back at the Panaro River, construction of a Bailey bridge was complete by 0630 hours and the vehicles of the main division started crossing over one at a time. The citizens of Finale were standing on the far bank to welcome them. Having crossed the Panaro that morning (25 April), the 1/16th Battery of the 1/6th Field Regiment moved directly north to Felonica, passing dead animals and broken carts on the way. The battery pulled off the road and dropped into action in the middle of the flat farmlands, a few hundred yards directly south of Felonica. They began shelling German barges as they tried to cross the river upstream from the town.[342] Once again, Bourhill was prevailed upon by Italian civilians to "stick his neck out", asking him to investigate an unexploded shell or bomb which lay on the doorstep of one of the farmhouses. This time Bourhill obliged, taking out his .303 rifle which had been rusting under a bench in his quad. Taking cover behind a wall, he put a bullet through the object. There was no explosion and on closer inspection it turned out to be a pair of naval binoculars in a leather case which had been blown off one of the barges on the river. The ferry was obviously inadequate for transporting an army over the river. In desperation the Germans had driven vehicles into the water, while some men tried to swim. Abandoned equipment was lined up on the southern levee. Everyone wanted to be in at the kill. Johnston had caught up with the leading elements on 25 April 1945: "Up to Felonica. Hell of a pile of Jerry stuff. Tanks, trucks, guns. Looked over Po. Looting. Tried to open safe. Called back by OC …" The next day was spent putting on new rollers, adjusting tracks and doing washing. Then the order came to "pack up and stand by before moving out at 0130 hours".

[342] The guns were positioned at F898022 and the barges were crossing at F910030.

The booty which lay abandoned for miles along the roads leading to the Po has become legendary. A overturned paymaster's truck had spilled its load of 500- and 1,000-lire notes. Farm boys from the Witwatersrand Rifles/Regiment De la Rey caught enemy artillery horses still in their harnesses and rode back to the closest village to buy as much wine as they could find. Frank Mundel of the Imperial Light Horse/Kimberley Regiment found a motorcycle and sidecar in working order and could not resist taking it for a spin. He rode it into a ditch and nearly became another battle accident statistic. The full inventory of German equipment captured and destroyed is as follows:

Tanks (including Panthers, Tigers and Mk IVs)	23
Armoured cars	2
Half-tracks	28
Cars	16
Trucks	64
Trailers	20
HD vehicles	36
M/Cs	52
Vehicles (misc)	509
Guns	160
Guns SP	6
AA guns	3
Misc	43
Telephone exchange (smashed)	1
Field hospital intact and fully equipped	1

Main division headquarters arrived at the Po late in the afternoon. All kinds of kit—steel helmets, packs and papers—lay on the bank, a sign that the men had swum across. Improvized rafts had also been left on the bank, including one made of jerrycans strapped together. Vehicles had driven into the water up to their windows before getting stuck. As many members of the brigade as possible were taken across the river at Felonica in boats, amphibious vehicles (DUKWs) and rafts. Rain fell during the night, turning the banks muddy and soft. Only ten vehicles and one 25-pounder managed to cross before morning. The remaining camp followers and vehicles had to stay south of the Po until a place could be found for them to cross. Fortunately, it did not take long to build a Bailey bridge upstream at Ostiglia and at 1700, the headquarters packed up and set off for Poggio Rusco, south of Ostiglia. The captured German field hospital, a German equivalent of a field dressing station, was taken over by the main dressing station of 20 South African Field Ambulance, which usually stayed a little farther behind the front line. Together with the German staff, they examined all the wounded and gave the necessary treatment. By this time, very few sick patients remained at the main dressing station, which moved next to Montagnana. This necessitated crossings over the Po and Adige rivers, a journey which took 18 hours.

Sites for advanced dressing stations were not difficult to find in this densely populated part of Italy and local civilians helped identify and clean suitable premises. Schools, farmhouses, villas, village halls, storerooms and hospitals were all occupied for this purpose, as were kitchens and living rooms, and even a carpenter's shop.

A new innovation born out of past experience was the addition of a section of 12 Graves Registration Unit to the advanced dressing station. "The odd few bodies which often accumulate at an ADS and cause such embarrassment, were taken over by them and dealt with in the most efficient manner,"[343] explains one report. The quarterly report of the 20 South African Field Ambulance for the period ending 30 June 1945 praises the work of all staff, from the clerks to the ambulance drivers and medical orderlies who had to pack and unpack, sometimes three times in one day: "The spirit of wanting to help pervaded the whole atmosphere, for often, complete strangers would be found in the ADS, trying to do something, even if it were only handing round tea, fetching a drink of water or carrying stretchers."[344]

Friday 27 April 1945: Carpi

As there was no bridge at Felonica and the construction of the Springbok bridge downstream to the east at Pontelagoscuro, near Ferrara, would not be finished until 4 May (even though planning and design had begun months before), it was necessary to head west to the Bailey bridge at Ostiglia. Bourhill's sub—gun, limber, quad and all—was loaded onto a raft and taken straight across to the other bank. From there, it was less than ten miles to the village of Carpi on the Adige River. Those who could not get across by raft travelled at a speed of 25 miles per hour along the south bank to Poggio Rusco, a concentration area just south of Ostiglia. Johnston arrived there at 0500 hours and dozed in his

343 DODAR, WD, Box 739, 20 SA Field Ambulance, 1–30 June 1945.

344 *Ibid.*

tank until the order came at 1440 hours to move up to the bridge. The smaller bridges over the canals in the area were in poor condition and Harry Hibbert's truck overturned. After waiting on the canal bank for six hours, he pulled into a barn to sleep.

Johnston's turn to take his Sherman across came at 0200 hours, and by 0730 hours he had arrived at Legnago en route to the new concentration area at Castagnaro, a region directly to the north and in line with Felonica on the River Adige. The pace of the gallop across the Po Valley was taking its toll on Johnston, even though he was bringing up the rear: "Very tired, dozed while travelling so let Eric take over. Breakfast of eggs and bacon in Iti casa in town. Yank and vino, two pros, more eggs. Told to return to troop as 68 tank was OP."

At this stage, the 13th South African Motorized Brigade was leading, moving so fast that the 1:25,000 maps were useless and commanders had to switch to 1:100,000 maps. Venice was now the objective, and on 27 April the division began moving into concentration areas immediately south of Legnago. It seemed that every formation was elbowing its way forward along the packed roads to get at the enemy.

Once across the Po, the 25-pounders were making at least two moves a day. The guns would not always be unhitched and put on the ground as the enemy either surrendered or retreated with great haste. In fact, the 1/6th Field Regiment had fired its final shots of the war back at Felonica.The South Africans were now operating together with what intelligence referred to as their 'rugby friends' (New Zealanders) and 'GI friends' (Americans). At the Po, the interrogation officer, Captain Betzler, found that the prisoners were very shaken, particularly those who had been at Finale. There were more tears shed by prisoners here than there had been during the rest of the war. Betzler was rough on them but it was felt that the Gazzala Gallop was now well and truly avenged. The prisoners captured now were exhausted from the continual retreat and their feet were in tatters.

By VE day, the total number of prisoners taken by the division during the current operations numbered 140 officers and 8,564 other ranks. This figure included 15 women whose role, according to Betzler, was more "biological than military". The division's total prisoner account for Italy stood at 153 officers and 10,700 other ranks.[345] Whole units sat down and waited for someone to

345 E. Axelson, *A year in Italy*, p. 224.

capture them. Some surrendered to army chaplains, others gave themselves up to war correspondents—anyone but the partisans. When large units gave themselves up, they were disarmed and sent to the rear, packed upright into trucks, very often using their own transport.

The 4/13th Frontier Force Rifles was engaged in guarding POWs during the breakthrough into the Po plains, and were remarkably successful in keeping German equipment running for the purpose of transporting prisoners.

Saturday 28 April 1945: Urbana

Advancing in a northeasterly direction from Ostiglia, through Poiana and Campiglia, the leading column met resistance on 28 April at a bridge over the River Bacchiglione at Montegalda. The bridge was demolished in front of the Royal Natal Carbineers which, with the Pretoria Regiment, then turned toward Padua. The Imperial Light Horse/Kimberley Regiment and the Special Service Battalion arrived at Nanto that evening. Montegalda is on the western periphery of Padua (Padova in Italian).

A POW camp was established here and a number of South Africans, pilots and POWs are buried in the Commonwealth cemetry at Padua. Some escaped South African POWs, resembling Italian civilians, greeted the division in Afrikaans. A South African pilot who had recently crash-landed in a field and had been hidden by locals also made an appearance. Southern Africans were now scattered far and wide on the plains of the Po valley. On 28 April, tanks were still crossing on the pontoon bridge over the Po River; others had almost reached Venice. Main division was in the hamlet of Vangadizza, two miles south of Legnago. Traffic was still chaotic, with Americans and South Africans competing for bridge space on the narrow pontoons. Johnston began to realize the futility of trying to keep up:

> Rejoined troop and again couldn't cross bridge. Left concentration area at 06.00 and found another bridge and wandered down a road to new position. Installed in casa. Raining. Prepare to move. "To hell with moving," says the skipper so we stayed put.

The 6th South African Division had been split into two and was given no main axis. The men felt that the Americans were trying to freeze them out and take all the glory as town after town was liberated. The 1/6th Field Regiment was now making two moves a day but did not have a chance to come into action because the enemy was always out of range. The big news of the day was that Benito Mussolini, his mistress Claretta Petacci and several members of the fascist government had been caught by partisans at Dongo on Lake Como on 27 April and had been executed the next day. His body and that of his mistress were then taken to Milan and hung upside-down in a filling station in Piazzale Loreto, where 15 partisans had been executed in August 1944.

On 28 April, after having got word through to the Allied leaders, two German officers wearing civilian clothes were flown to Rome to negotiate a surrender. The surrender was signed the next day at 15th Army Group headquarters in Caserta, near Naples. The surrender documents were prepared by 1400 hours on Sunday. Six journalists were invited to witness the occasion. Five minutes before the signing, a young American colonel came into the room and checked that there was enough ink in the ink wells for the job at hand.

At exactly 1408 hours, two German officers, a colonel and a major, were escorted in through a side door. General von Vietinghoff's representative was tall, had receding blond hair and a wisp of a moustache. He looked like a Hollywood version of a Prussian officer. The second German looked very tense; when a photographer approached him too closely, "he waved his hand with an imperious gesture, but then hastily restrained himself". Even in their peaceable clothes, which would have been suitable for any country club verandah, "they did not seem like men who would win friends and influence people easily—without force".[346] Milestone events took place in quick succession. Aldolf Hitler committed suicide on 30 April, although his death did not bring an official end to the war. According to some sources, it was on 30 April that the cessation of all organized enemy resistance in Italy was announced. However, according to General Mark Clark, the statement was issued on 1 May 1945—his 49th birthday:

> ... Twenty five divisions, some of them the best in the German Army, have been torn to pieces and can no longer effectively resist our armies. Thousands of vehicles, tremendous quantities of arms and equipment and 120,000 prisoners have been captured, and many more are being corralled. The military power of Germany in Italy has practically ceased, even though scattered fighting may continue as remnants of the German armies are mopped up.[347]

[346] *Stars and Stripes*, Mediterranean: Nazi Armies in Italy surrender, 2/5/1945, p. 2.

[347] M. Clark, *Calculated risk*, p. 410; In his book *Calculated risk*, General Mark Clark puts the date of the final surrender in Italy at 4 May 1945, two days after the signing of the surrender document and the announcement thereof.

Sunday 29 April 1945: Piazzola

The Pretoria Regiment and the Natal Mounted Rifles advanced through village after village, from Boschi, Montagnana and Noventa Vicentina to the Venetian Line at Albettone, where the leading infantry and tanks were held up by strong enemy rearguard forces and anti-tank ditches.

The leading tank was hit by an 88 at the point where the Venetian Line was reached, northwest of Albettone on Via Fornace. Trooper J.C. Christopher, a 22-year-old from Johannesburg, was killed and the rest of the crew wounded. Two other tanks were immobilized. A short while later, Trooper J.A. McRea, also from Johannesburg, was mortally wounded. The regiment's final fatality was Trooper G.H. Norris of Durban, who was hit by a panzerfaust in the vicinity of Campodoro. The officer commanding the Pretoria Regiment, Colonel Arthur Johnstone, was awarded the DSO for being instrumental in the rapid disintegration of enemy resistance on the divisional front in a series of actions on 28 April. However, not every element of this formation was in full cry, as Gunner Peter Johnston testifies:

> Pulled in at a big building for lunch. Bacon and eggs. Vic Leibrandt brought us bread. Ities looting. Followed guns when they moved to [Camisano], raining when we arrived, so pulled in at a casa and arranged for room ... Bath, stroll and short card game before bed.

On 29 April, the 1/6th Field Regiment, the Special Service Battalion and the Imperial Light Horse/Kimberley Regiment were at the Brenta River, where a skirmish occurred with one of the many scattered groups of Germans, eight of whom were killed. Later in the day, Major A.H. 'Rocky' Rocyn-Jones, officer of 8 Field Squadron South African Engineer Corps, and his driver were killed while looking for a way to cross the Brenta River. Rocyn-Jones had been captain of the Welsh hockey team before the war and had a distinguished war record, stretching from Abyssinia in 1940 until just days before the end. The obligatory letter of condolence to the next of kin was written by his commanding officer, Lieutenant-Colonel R.M.M. Cormack, with rare sincerity:

> This letter will bring small comfort to you at so sad a time, but whatever comfort there may be in the expression of sympathy in your grievous loss is most sincerely

> willed by us all. We grieve for you and mourn the loss of Rocyn with you, for in this campaign he has endeared himself to all of us. He died fighting—true soldier that he always was.
>
> He is now buried in a South African cemetery at Castiglione on the road from Florence to Bologna—in the Apennines. I have asked Freddie, his nearest and constant friend, to visit his grave today and take some photographs. He will write to you.
>
> And now I will not weary you with futile words—may time soften this blow and heal the hurt. You will always have the happy knowledge that in Rocyn you had a fine, upright and brave man. God bless you Kay, and give you and the little ones strength and courage to carry on alone as he would have you do.

When Rocyn-Jones approached the Brenta River in his Jeep on the afternoon of 29 April, he met his wife's cousin, Lieutenant Colenbrander of the Prince Alfred's Guard, who had taken up a position on top of a dyke at the crossroads with orders to prevent any soft-skinned vehicles from passing toward the river as the area was not yet cleared of the enemy. Colenbrander tried to dissuade him from proceeding further, but to no avail. He had his orders to select a site to construct a Bailey bridge. The men had a cup of coffee together and the sappers went on their way.

Rocyn-Jones's name appears time and again in archival documents, and not just because of his role as commanding officer of 8 Field Squadron. In one instance, he responds to the accusations that in Florence, he used his Jeep to push another officer's Jeep, which had parked him in, out of his way. Finally, in June 1945, there is the notice that His Majesty the King had graciously approved his award of the OBE.

The two sappers were the last South Africans to be killed in action in the campaign, although others would still succumb to wounds or die in battle accidents. Corporal Desmond Beattie of Estcourt of the Royal Natal Carbineers also died on 29 April and there were at least three wounded on 30 April.

The table overleaf reveals that there were no Carbineers killed in action during this final phase. Understandably, most of the casualties at this time were incurred by the units involved in the attack on Monte Sole and Monte Caprara. The 30 First City/Cape Town Highlanders who were killed in this operation, and another 30 from the Witwatersrand Rifles/Regiment De la Rey, occupy a disturbingly large section in the cemetery at Castiglione.

12th South African Motorized Brigade casualties: final period of operations from 6 April 1945 up until and including the concentration in the Milan area, 3 May 1945[348]									
Unit	Killed			Wounded			Missing		
	Offrs	O/Rs	CCs	Offrs	O/Rs	CCs	Offrs	O/Rs	CCs
RDLI		8*		2	55				
FC/CTH	1	29	1	5	73				
WR/DLR	2	28	2	4	165				
RNC					1				
Bde Pro Det**		2							
4/13 FFR		12			51				
TOTALS	3	79	3	13	345	16	0	0	0
	85			374			0		

* two of whom died of wounds.

** note that two military policemen (Brigade Provost Detachment) were killed.

During the night of 29/30 April, the First City/Cape Town Highlanders established a bridgehead across the Brenta in the vicinity of Curtarolo. The Witwatersrand Rifles/Regiment De la Rey arrived shortly afterwards. At 1100 hours, orders were received to the effect that the whole division would be concentrating at Camposampiero, and by 0100 hours all units were harboured in the area. The reason for the concentration was not known and for a couple of days the men sweated over the possibility of being given another operational task. Many hundreds of prisoners from eight different German divisions were collected on the brigade front, including Wehrmacht women and two officers brought in a Wehrmacht truck, driven by an escaped South African POW.

The division was still engaged in mopping up and the enemy was still trying to get at the tanks with bazookas. Two of those wounded on 30 April—both with gunshot wounds—were Staff Sergeant M. de Goede (divisional provost) and Captain H.W.A. Cheals of the Natal Mounted Rifles. The war diary of the Pretoria Regiment (Princess Alice's Own) reveals that not every German was prepared to surrender. Scattered resistance was experienced and addressed. A number of 20mm flack guns were overrun and gun crews and columns of 50 and 60 Germans respectively were wiped out by Pretoria Regiment tanks on 28 and 29 April.

There had been four divisions of the Italian Republican Army fighting for the Germans in northwest Italy at the start of the spring offensive. They now

348 DODAR, WD, Box 598, Recording Officer, 12th South African Motorized Bde, Report on operations in the Italian campaign for period August 1944–May 1945.

evaporated into the countryside and rejoined civilian life. Some were captured by partisans and turned over to the Allies but no attempt was made to hold the troops, who had usually been forced into service. However, many of the officers were wanted for war crimes and were usually promptly executed.

Prisoners were first interrogated at regimental and then divisional level, so that any information of immediate operational use was made available. Thereafter, they were shipped from division stockades to a corps collecting point, then transported to the army stockade where their name, rank, age, unit, nativity, civil occupation, place of capture, length of service in unit and intelligence qualifications were recorded.

Because it was impossible to interrogate every prisoner, selections were made according to perceived usefulness. Rank was an important factor in selection as officers had information of greater value than enlisted men. The prisoner's civil occupation also revealed whether or not he was likely to be a good potential source of information. The former plumber, for example, was not as likely a source as the former bank teller. An experienced interrogator estimated the man's intelligence and classified him as cooperative and intelligent, uncooperative and intelligent or cooperative but dim. Interrogators had to know the native language of the enemy intimately and cleverly used psychology, bluff, ruse or camouflage to 'break' a prisoner. It was found that the German army was particularly servile to rank, so the interrogator's rank insignia was changed when necessary to earn the respect and cooperation of the prisoner.

Monday 30 April 1945 – Wednesday 2 May 1945: Camposampiero

Intelligence reports suggested that the Venetian Line was the strongest defensive line in Italy. The network of canals, augmented by anti-tank ditches and walls, was backed by a deep network of trenches and machine-gun positions. However, by 29 April, it was apparent that the Venetian Line was no obstacle at all, and what was left of the German army was simply trying to escape into the southern Alps. During their two days at Camposampiero, the troops received numerous reports of enemy stragglers in the area from civilians and partisans. Patrols from the Witwatersrand Rifles/Regiment De la Rey and the Royal Durban Light Infantry were sent out to investigate and 50 POWs were rounded up.

Proof of German atrocities was discovered by a Royal Durban Light Infantry patrol on 1 May. In a house identified by its grid reference, the patrol found an Italian civilian who had been killed, his wife left "in a dying condition", and their six children—ranging in age from two to 14 years—all shot dead. Civilians said that there had been a number of similar shootings as punishment for refusing to hand over bicycles and carts to the retreating enemy.

Shortly after the war, British war correspondent Alan Moorehead wrote at length of German brutality. He noted that the number of atrocities was in direct proportion to the condition of the German army; where the situation was desperate, the atrocities increased. The effect on the Allied soldier was that the thirst for revenge took over from the higher ideal of "fighting for liberty and honour and all the rest of it".[349]

While the 1/6th Field Regiment was at Camposampiero, the tanks of the Pretoria Regiment (Princess Alice's Own) on the extreme right of the division were harboured in a silk factory at Maerne, only ten miles from Venice. A few Carbineers set off to see some of the old city by Jeep. On their return, they described it as "simply marvellous" and confirmed that not even a Jeep could move freely around Venice. It hadn't been long before they had been forced to park the vehicle and continue by boat.[350] On 30 April, Johnston moved 30 miles from Camisano and overnighted in a small village en route to the next concentration area at Piazzola sul Brenta. *Padkos* (lit. 'road food') consisted of "Eggs, vino and rusks en route". A festive atmosphere clearly prevailed: "Out on a pub crawl and tried to arrange for a dance but girls scared. Took them for a ride in Jeep and then goodnight very flatly. Wanted to push Iti in canal but Eric let him off." An order now came to move across the breadth of the country to the Milan area, where it was said that two German divisions were still holding out. According to Monick, the move was precipitated by the threat of a partisan uprising. There was little enthusiasm for the task and it fortunately did not materialize. Nevertheless, the division departed for Milan, via Cremona, at first light on 1 May. The next day, as a parting gift, partisans handed over five officers and about 250 other ranks whom they had rounded up in a nearby village.

The Frontier Force Rifles stayed behind at Scorzè under the command of the British 8th Army. Allied troops in Italy could read about the surrender negotiations which had been taking place in the *Stars and Stripes* of 2 May 1945. However, that day was spent on the road and few would have an opportunity to read the papers. The hectic pace of the past ten days is evidenced by the letters

---

349 A. Moorehead, *Eclipse*, p. 69.

350 J.B. Hodgson–M.V. & W.A. Hodgson, 5/5/ 1945.

of Hodgson, or rather, the lack thereof. Recently, his letters had only half-filled a letter card and for a week he had not written to anyone:

> I am very sorry indeed that my letters have been slack of late and also so short and scrappy, I don't like this slack writing but at the moment there is no solution at all. You have no doubt seen in the papers how well everything is going along here—and as Gen Mark Clark has declared that all organized resistance in Italy is over, you can just imagine how much we are moving around, thus the chances for settling down and writing a good letter are just non-existent. Nevertheless, the war is going to be over very soon and I will be home and be able to tell you everything. I have seen so many marvellous things and I can't wait to get down to writing to you about it all; even if the chance came I don't think I could, so I will wait until I can tell you everything, as it will be so much better.[351]

After waiting to move all day on 2 May, Johnston finally set off at 1800 hours, arriving in Piazzola at 0130 hours where he found a room and a bed. He was still at Piazzola with the few remaining troops when he got the news of the surrender in Italy: "War in Italy over. Couple of drinks with crowd, then bed. Rain in afternoon ... Got comfortable chairs left by Jerry—very useful. Move tomorrow at 05.00. Walk for eggs. No luck."

The final surrender document was signed by the Oxford-educated Lieutenant-General Fridolin von Senger und Etterlin—'Frido' to his friends—on 2 May 1945. Von Vietinghoff's headquarters were at Bolzano, near Brenner Pass, and it would have been too dangerous for him to make the journey to Florence as the partisans would have killed him. Indeed, they had attacked his headquarters and killed 40 Germans just two days earlier. As it was, the delegation had run into an ambush and the men were highly stressed when they arrived in Florence. Von Senger was in full uniform and still wearing his side-arm when he walked into General Clark's office.

At 1800 hours that day, von Vietinghoff released the news of the German surrender in Italy. The tidings were received with an almost anticlimactic sense of disbelief. Colonel Reeves-Moore, officer commanding the Imperial Light Horse/Kimberley Regiment, expressed the sentiment experienced by so many on that day: "The quietness of that sunny day was uncanny—who of us could believe that this was in fact the end of five years of war? It had come so suddenly that it conveyed an air of mystery and it would understandably take more than

351 J.B. Hodgson–M.V. Hodgson, 1/5/1945.

a day to bring home the full realization of PEACE."[352] With the insight of an intelligence non-commissioned officer, Hodgson explained in a letter to his parents why there was universal disbelief at the suddenness of the surrender:

> When we initially launched the offensive here, we were prepared for a terrific fight, because of the collapse in the west, Italy became a very good entrance to his mountain hide-out so we thought he would put up a bitter fight. The initial assault was inevitably strong, but when he suddenly turned tail and went for all he was worth, I think everyone was left with his mouth wide open. Then the natural conclusion was that he was pulling back to another defence line. At last we became certain that he was pulling right back onto the Po which was much further than we thought he would go. Then upon reaching the Po with practically no opposition, if any, and seeing what we did, it then dawned upon us that he would have to pull something very clever out of the bag to save himself from being pushed back into the mountains. What we saw on our side of the Po, you have no doubt read all about in the papers: namely the masses and masses of vehicles and equipment 'scuttled' as it were. I have never seen so much stuff destroyed ever, all due to his being unable to cross the river owing to the accuracy of our bombers, who left not one single crossing for the Hun; all the destroyed vehicles etc that were destroyed along the roads leading to the crossing, was sufficient evidence of the way we harassed his retreat from the air; even then we did not think that we had dealt him such a telling blow as we had. With our experience of mountain warfare we knew that with very little he could prevent us from penetrating very far into the Alps. Then came the capitulation of the enemy forces—it was too much to hope for and nearly too much to believe. Even now, three days later, it is hard to believe that there is no more fighting to be done here and as far as we are concerned, no more fighting at all.

The pervading feeling of anti-climax was a universal phenomenon, partly brought on by the loss of a sense of purpose. Faussell quotes from the diary of Evelyn Waugh who wrote on 31 April: "Everyone expects the end in a few weeks but without elation; all expect worse conditions from the peace than they have had in the war." A few days later he observed: "No exhilaration anywhere at the end of the war."[353] Nor could the men enjoy a lasting sense of relief because the continuing threat from the Japanese brought with it the worry of being sent to the Pacific theatre.

A photograph bearing the caption "Cheering greets Winston Churchill's radio announcement of the end of the war in Europe" shows a group of South

352 H. Klein, *Light Horse cavalcade*, p. 170.

353 P. Fussell, *Wartime*, p. 137.

African soldiers raising their hands in an orchestrated, self-conscious pose. The partisans, however, fired Ack Ack guns and all other available weapons into the air in celebration.

The lack of jubilation was further brought about by policy dictating that there would be no official celebration to mark the end of hostilities against Germany. With the war against Japan not yet won and many hard tasks ahead, the theatre commander decreed that victory would be welcomed "in a spirit of sober satisfaction and heartfelt gratitude ..."[354]

The scarcity of both space on the roads and petrol turned the subsequent cross-country journey to Milan into a logistical nightmare. Crowds flocked around the vehicles in every town.

In spite of the bitter cold, the men struggled to stay awake for 19 consecutive hours during the night drive that took them 200 miles across the widest part of Italy. Twenty miles before Milan some units branched off Highway 9, through Gorgonzola to Brugherio where the main division settled into and around a squalid school building. The tanks would trundle into town as much as three days later. Many different routes were taken, towns entered, and experiences had by different elements of the division on the road to Milan. Johnston described his journey in a Sherman:

> 4th May
> Left this morning at 06.00 and travelled all day to 02.30. Piazzola to Legnago 42.5 miles, breakfast and refuel. Legnago to near Manerbio, via Nogara, Mantova, Marcaria, Leno, 60 odd miles where we had supper of bacon, sausages and eggs, stewed apple rings. Refuelled, on again at 18.30 and got to Roccafranca [approximately 25 miles away] where held up for 3 hours. Pulled into casa at 03.00 and found a place to sleep.
>
> 5th May
> Woken up by turnout of village to have a look at us. Most embarrassing but rather funny. After breakfast at 11.00, on our merry way to Battery at Monza near Milan. Arriving at 15.30. Parked with 'A' Troop as petrol ran out ... Party with Ronny and Reg. Very tight.

[354] DODAR, Div Docs, Box 189, File Ceremonial Parades, AQ 3/9 (vol 2) From Lieutenant-General L.R. Truscott, Head Quarters 5th Army, 8/4/1945.

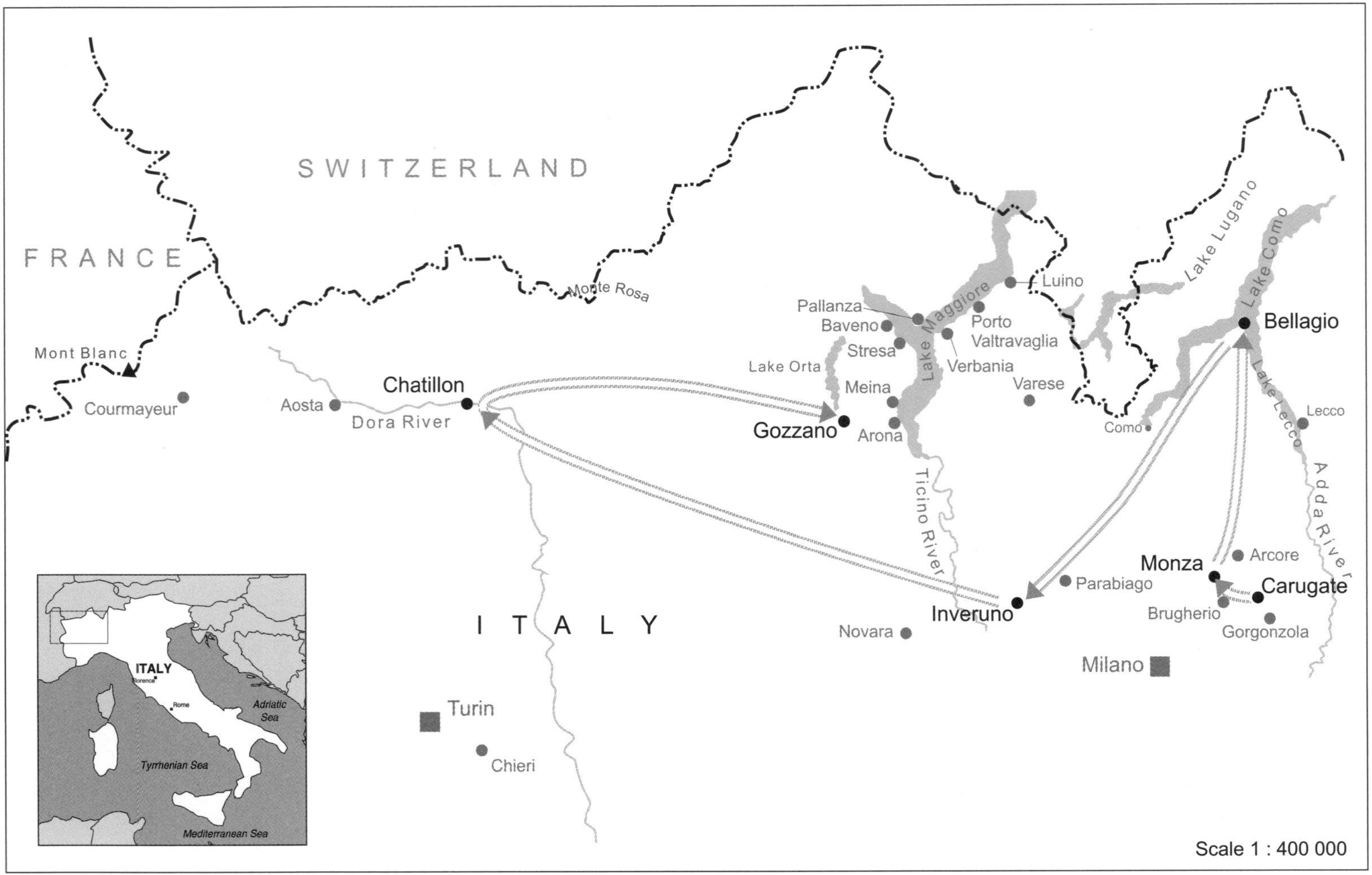

SWITZERLAND
FRANCE
ITALY
Mont Blanc
Courmayeur
Monte Rosa
Aosta
Chatillon
Dora River
Lake Orta
Gozzano
Pallanza
Baveno
Stresa
Meina
Arona
Lake Maggiore
Verbania
Porto Valtravaglia
Luino
Varese
Ticino River
Novara
Inveruno
Parabiago
Como
Lake Lugano
Lake Como
Bellagio
Lake Lecco
Lecco
Adda River
Monza
Arcore
Carugate
Brugherio
Gorgonzola
Milano
Turin
Chieri
ITALY
Florence
Rome
Adriatic Sea
Tyrrhenian Sea
Mediterranean Sea
Scale 1 : 400 000

Chapter Eleven

Water and sand

"It is said that 'if you ride boldly enough at death it will get out of your way', and that you have done. You have played an absolutely major part in this final and complete rout and defeat of the arrogant Wehrmacht."
—Major-General W.H. Evered Poole in a speech at the 6th South African Armoured Division thanksgiving parade near Milan, 4 May 1945.

Thursday 3 May 1945 – Friday 11 May 1945: Milano

Stragglers were still arriving on the eastern outskirts of Milan two or three days after the main body, even though strict regulations were in place to control the movement of convoys with regard to speed and density. Various battalion groups spread themselves out between Carugate and Brugherio, adjacent towns located roughly five miles from Monza.

On 3 May, a road accident en route to the concentration area killed Gunner E. Erasmus and Private J.H. Fennesy, both former TSC attached to the 1/6th Field Regiment.

A second accident nearly resulted in more casualties. Senior operations officer, Colonel E. O'C. Maggs, had a narrow escape when his Jeep, driven by Trooper Prinsloo, shot off the road and came to rest in a ditch about 12 feet deep. Maggs was asleep at the time. The accident occurred in the early hours of the morning on 3 May, near Ponte di Mossano on the road from Scorzè, not far from Venice. The convoy came to a stop and the occupants and their luggage were loaded into other vehicles after first aid had been administered. The evidence becomes vague from this point; it appears that a divisional recovery vehicle was summoned but Maggs's Jeep and binoculars were never seen again.[355]

[355] DODAR, Div Docs, Box 173, File HQS/23, Courts, Court of Inquiry into the circumstances in which 1 Jeep W.D. No. 52315628 and one pair of binoculars No. 7054 were lost, 26/6/1945.

Trooper Royce Fuller was still fighting for his life, although he seemed to be on the road to recovery when Bourhill visited him at 108th General Hospital in Milan. On 8 May, he was off the 'seriously ill' and 'dangerously ill' lists but a week later, on 13 May, he was evacuated by air to the 92nd General Hospital in Naples while his regiment prepared to lead the big victory parade at Monza. The reason for this sudden deterioration is explained by the following note from his medical files: "Perforated Rectum—L Colostomy and Large Bowel obstruction".

The ominous word, 'contamination', was written across his hospital record card in large letters. Penicillin, a scarce new drug, was prescribed, but it was too late. Fuller's suffering was worsened by the plague of brown sticky flies that even the hospital's fly screens could not keep out.

On 4 May 1945, exactly one year from the day that the division went into action for the first time at Cassino, a small divisional thanksgiving parade was held in a steady drizzle. It took place in a factory yard adjoining the main division headquarters at Brugherio. General Poole, backed by his brigadiers, addressed a representative group of all the division's units. Those not present received a typed copy of General Poole's historic speech, which stated:

> On this solemn occasion, the greatest day in the history of this division, and for that matter of arms in the UDF, we thank Almighty God with all humility for this victory. We shall observe it in accordance with the direction of our Commander-in-Chief 'with sober satisfaction and heartfelt gratitude'. It is nearly six years ago that our Springbok soldiers set out on this crusade. Which it has been our honour to finish, representing our beloved country and we therefore especially remember those comrades who started with us but who have been prevented from being with us today through wounds or through death. Casualty figures are, of course, a matter of great security, but today I feel I can reveal them to you.[356]

General Poole went on to give a breakdown of the casualty statistics for the Union Defence Force only, excluding other troops under command. The figures were as follows: 711 killed, 2,675 wounded and 157 missing, resulting in a total of 3,543. A number of units held their own memorial parades over the next few days and a small thanksgiving parade was held by the First City/Cape Town Highlanders in the grounds of the Ospedale Uboldo at Carugate. Although it was a voluntary parade, almost every man was present. On Sunday

356 W.H.E. Poole, 6th South African Armoured Division thanksgiving parade, address to the division by the General Officer Commanding, 4/5/1945.

6 May, the 4/22nd Field Regiment held a parade in the Brugherio village square. Only on 5 May, once he was billeted in Turin, did Hodgson have time to catch up on his correspondence. It had been difficult to write while on the move, so he had penned only short notes to his mother. Now he was able to write a decent letter to his sister but censorship regulations were still in force and he could not state his exact location:

> It is still hard to believe that the war here is over at last; when we first heard the news, it was on the Daventry News Service at seven in the evening on the 2nd of May, all had intended doing a spot of celebrating on the great day, but when the news eventually did reach us it caught us in the middle of a move, so a great deal of the celebrating has to be left over ... At the moment as I look out of the window in front of me, I can see the Alps standing up very boldly above the plains in the foreground. They are simply colossal and the majority of them are still covered in snow except for the nearest ranges.

The Royal Natal Carbineers had skirted past Milan to be immediately deployed for peacekeeping duties along the Swiss border. On 7 May they moved out of their temporary billets in Turin to the Monte Grappa Barracks, adjacent to the Stadium of Mussolini. The Prince Alfred's Guard was based at Gorgonzola near Milan. The regimental headquarters of the 1/6th Field Regiment was at Ospedale Uboldo, while its A Troop was lucky enough to be quartered at a resort for the workers of the Pirelli tyre factory, alongside a small lake on the outskirts of Carugate. Bourhill always remembered this as his VE 'possie':

> 'A' Troop, only 60 odd men, occupies a lake and its surrounding grounds. There is good fishing, good swimming, a pub—private—in the grounds. I spend most of the day in a pair of underpants next to the lake. There are two boats, very nice ones, which we row all over the place in the cool of the evening. The days are very hot and the evenings close. At first I used to sleep in the boathouse, but it got too stuffy there and now I sleep in a wall-less rondawel next to the lake.
>
> One of the chaps laid on a small band last night and the night before and we danced with girls who happened to be passing along the road. The twilight is very long with DAST and 9 o'clock it's still quite light. There is a little village about 700 yds down the road and at the beginning of the week much excitement ... there were about four days of continual 'festa'. They love a festa on the slightest excuse and with the surrender and all it was terrific!! All night long they were dancing in the streets and squares. The girls are not so pretty but better dressed and better off all round than those south of the Po. They are on the whole not so friendly, some Wops are very bitter. Darned fools don't know what they want.

Johnston did not attend his unit's church parade on 6 May. Instead, he spent the day tidying up and lazing around. He was also fortunate to be included in one of the initial leave parties to go to Lake Como and the Swiss border: "Wonderful scenery all up to the Swiss frontier. People all very friendly. Prices in Como amazingly low. Went shopping with Vossie but crowded out and didn't get anything. Back through Milan where Peter Joffe, Monte and Vossie jumped off. I nearly went with them."

General Poole had become something of a folk hero to the public at home. His popularity reached a peak when he announced that the task of the 6th South African Armoured Division had been completed and the boys would be coming home. The division was not required for the Allied plans for garrisoning Europe and securing the Mediterranean lines of communication to the Far East. An official statement informed the public that the troops would be repatriated as soon as transport facilities were available. The men themselves remained unsure that this would come to pass, and worried that they might yet be called to fight the Japanese.

Saturday 12 May 1945 – Sunday 13 May 1945: Monza

On 7 May, the surrender of German forces was announced on the wireless and at 0001 hours, on 9 May, the war in Europe ended. As operations came to a halt, the divisional headquarters generated an increasing volume of documents and returns. An instruction was issued, advising all units to make provision for handling the extra red tape. This included the barring of administrative staff from early release.

Sunday 13 May was designated a day of thanksgiving and all units were directed to organize services. Bourhill's letters reveal that the sweet realization of having survived the war was just sinking in:

> All that I ever think of in the way of home these days is just a place where I'll go sometime beyond any doubt. Just the feeling that this wonderful pleasure, which is life, is going to continue even into months ahead. No, not even climaxed by the homecoming, but just a continuation of the present glory of being alive.

The victory celebrations soon gave way to quiet reflection and reading about what was happening in the world. The *Union Jack* contained mainly hard news. A special victory edition of the newspaper, published on 8 May, touched on two topics close to the hearts of all soldiers in Italy. The first was the fear of being sent to the Far East. An article headed "Now let's settle the Japs" sparked much speculation and rumour. The second was the question of what the future would hold in civilian life.

Hodgson could now truthfully tell his parents that there was no need to worry about his safety, although there was a slight danger of being caught in the crossfire between partisan and fascist factions. The DSR war diary records that on 8 May, one Union Defence Force soldier fired his weapon at Italian civilians, and kept firing at random. Two members of the DSR were wounded in the incident. The partisans were also still carrying out reprisals in nearby Brugherio. Two Italian civilians were shot on 9 May and three the next day. In Milan, bodies were picked up in the streets every morning as scores were settled. Great numbers of suspected fascists were executed. It is estimated that between 15,000 and 30,000 Italians died in this bloodletting.

Within days, the main division headquarters had moved from Brugherio to Monza and occupied nine houses in what was previously an SS headquarters, where approximately 4,000 non-German SS troops were stationed. Two fine villas served as an officers' quarters and a mess. The houses were in a shocking state; one had a pool of blood on the floor.

On 13 May, the Pretoria Regiment moved to its own five-star accommodation on an estate at Peregallo.

Milan was out of bounds for most of May but there were few complaints. While some officers planned the division's big victory parade, others went to Rapallo on a reconnaissance for suitable leave hotels.

At this stage, prevailing wisdom held that the division would not be needed to play a peacekeeping role in Italy. Hodgson's common sense told him otherwise and he cautiously estimated that he would be home by September:

> Naturally, at this stage, all our thoughts have turned to the question of going home—as is only to be expected under the circumstances, there are many wild rumours flying about, but after being in the army for a little while, one learns not to heed anything unless told officially, so as yet I have not been disappointed. I personally share the opinion with many others, that now is the time to go home, and the sooner the better; the job that we came to do is over, so I wonder how long it will be before we leave for home. We heard on the BBC the other evening, in the 'South African Newsletter' that it has officially been stated in Cape Town that South African troops are not going to be used for garrison duty and can be expected home in the near future. No doubt, you know more about it than I do … the BBC have been known to make mistakes in their time.

Monday 14 May 1945 – Monday 21 May 1945: Bellagio

The division gathered around the Monza racetrack the night before the victory parade. It was one big party: brothers, cousins, schoolmates and hometown friends sought each other out and celebrated till dawn. VIPs, staff officers, government ministers, photographers and film crews were also in town. Only a small contingent of the Royal Natal Carbineers came over from Turin to take part in the Monza parade and they slept on the track itself.

There was a last-minute flap when an engineer, Major Parr, remembered in the early hours of the morning that there were two bridges on the racetrack over which the Sherman tanks would be passing, three abreast. There was much concern until the 12th Field Squadron pronounced the bridges secure.

The weather had been hot during the past few days but it was muggy and overcast on 14 May, the day of the victory parade. The parade started at midday. General Clark was one of the many dignitaries present and made a short, well-received speech. Clark's comment about the significance of the capture of Monte Sole brought pride and joy to the hearts of the First City/Cape Town Highlanders. He paid tribute to General Poole's outstanding leadership and presented him with the Legion of Merit (Commander).

The other South Africans who had been awarded American decorations were also invested on this occasion. Ten officers and men were awarded the Silver Star and 20 won the Bronze Star.

Because the commander in chief of the Union Defence Forces, Field Marshal the Right Honourable J.C. Smuts, was at a conference in San Francisco at the time, Mr F.C. Sturrock, the acting Minister of Defence and Minister of Railways and Harbours, represented the South African government. His speech, according to Axelson, "provoked much criticism from officers and men on the grounds of being over-long and irrelevant, over-laudatory of South Africa and derogatory of the Americans with whom we had been fighting". Sturrock was conspicuous in the white uniform of an honorary naval commodore, positively corpulent in contrast to the lean men on parade.

Still in his early forties, General Poole cut a fine figure with his black hair brushed back, brown eyes and low, pleasant voice. According to one newspaper report, everything about him was redolent of smartness and neatness.

Following the investiture, the general and his senior staff left the saluting base and led the march-past in their Jeeps before retiring once more to the base by a rear entrance. The famous Imperial Light Horse band, wearing the Union

Defence Force 'polo' helmets, led the march-past. Their playlist included *Stars and Stripes Forever*, *Under Freedom's Banner* and *Colonel Bogey*. In the air, spotter observation-post aircraft from the United States Air Force flew in line with the head of the column. The Marauders of 24 Squadron, South African Air Force also made a fly-past.

The guard of honour was formed by the Special Service Battalion, General Poole's first command. Once the guard of honour was clear of the track, the vehicles proceeded in order. The South African Artillery was at the head, followed by the 11th Armoured Brigade, the 12th and 13th Motorized Brigades, the South African Engineer Corps, and finally the other units. Each kept a distance of 150 yards. Three other bands joined in with the musicians of the Imperial Light Horse, including the bands of the DSR, the Prince Alfred's Guard–First City/Cape Town Highlanders and the Special Service Battalion. The pipe band repertoire included *Cock of the North* (the regimental tune of the Cape Town Highlanders), *Hielan Laddie* and *Road to the Isles*.

When they reached the saluting base, officers saluted and ordered "eyes right". The tanks were supposed to dip their barrels according to the special order—and according to custom—but in the many photographs of the occasion the barrels are proudly raised in front of the stands. According to one source, it took nearly three hours for the tanks, guns, half-tracked vehicles and troop carriers, ambulances and motor cycles—a total of over 2,400 vehicles—to roll by, driving three abreast. The international flavour of the occasion was signified by flying the Stars and Stripes, the Union Jack, the Union of South Africa flag, the Italian national flag and the Brazilian flag. Three anthems were played: *The Star Spangled Banner*, *God Save the King* and *Die Stem van Suid Afrika*. The South African public relations film and photographic unit had a field day taking pictures of the medal recipients and VIPs.

While the senior officers lunched al fresco in the grounds of the Monza Palace, each of the formations continued to their various destinations. The 1/6th Field Regiment proceeded to Bellagio, a spot on Lake Como where Lake Lecco branches off. From there, Bourhill wrote home, describing the historic event at Monza:

> On Monday we left our old 'V.E. position' near Milan—the one I last wrote from, next to the lake. All the troops were very sorry to leave there, as we thought we'd never get a better position. From Milan we went to a largish town called Monza where we slept one night next to our guns. There is a world-famous race track there

> (for cars and horses). Our regiment was the first to go through. If you must know, I'm in the 6th gun tractor in the right-hand file. It must have been grand to watch it, or see it on the films. As it was, there was too much work to it all, and too hot, to really enjoy it. But it was a fine opportunity to see people in other regiments … Much dating for grand parties when we get back.

Snow could still be seen on the higher peaks and lying rather untidily in the gorges. Bourhill tried to describe it to his mother: "It's like a Hollywood exaggerated, technicolour picture, only better. One needs a few days there to get things straight and sort out the colours."

While at Como, Bourhill's unit had an opportunity to visit Switzerland by truck but contrary to what he had been led to believe, he was neither one of the first nor one of the last to go on such a sightseeing trip:

> Our truck load of chaps was the first and last to go to Switzerland; it was stopped after our trip. There was a great crowd on the Swiss side to see the Allies. They gave large bottles of beer to the guards to give to us. What beer! I talked to them in bad Iti. But the scenery around there is superb and plenty peaks and much snow. Swiss misses are ok. More of this later! Cheerio. No socks or parcels any more, please Mom.

In order not to place too much pressure on any one section of the civilian population, the South Africans were billeted in different parts of the Lake District. In keeping with their policy not to evict ordinary civilians, the artillerymen lived outdoors. Fortunately, weather conditions were perfect. For the gunners, swimming and boating was disturbed only by two hours of maintenance every day:

> We are right on the shore of the lake, sleeping in the grounds of a large villa. My bed is under a pine tree with a huge rose bush at my head (in full bloom with 52 great red roses) and to the left and right and at my feet are some other flowers of which I don't know the names but the scent at night is something you've got to have in your own nostrils to credit. Day before yesterday, Mac, Tubby, Wells and I took our rations for the day and got a boat (free) and rowed south down to an island, had lunch there and came back. A long trip! About eight miles in all we rowed! Yesterday I took a couple of sandwiches and went into the mountains till near the snow line. It's impossible to describe it all. It took from 8am to 7.30pm to do it, walking hard. Today spent all day going north in the boat, just got back … No cold. Very fit and happy.[357]

[357] S.F. Bourhill–E. Bourhill, 18/5/1945.

It was routine as usual on 16 May, and members of the regimental police from 59 Q Company were preparing for yet another parade. Private R.J. Britz had just returned to his tent from the orderly room, where he had sent off a parcel. It cost him "14 bob" to send the package to his wife in Paul Roux in the Orange Free State. His tent mate, Private A.F. Johnson, had just been to the kitchen to fetch some hot water and was preparing to shave in front of a mirror hanging on the tent pole at the entrance to the tent. Private Britz began cleaning his Thompson sub-machine gun and the two men chatted while they got ready for the parade. Then, from inside the tent, there was a short burst of machine-gun fire and Britz fell backwards over the foot of his bed, which was made on some grass, flat on the ground.

A final shot went off while the gun was falling. Shouting "hell, hell", Johnson ran to help and saw that his friend was bleeding from the stomach below the right breast pocket. Two exit wounds could be seen in his back as he rolled on the floor with his knees drawn up. Johnson threw up his hands saying, "My God, he's shot himself."

Men came running from all directions. Someone ran to the orderly room shouting, "Tommy gun accident!"

The medical non-commissioned officer, Sergeant P. Taylor of the South African Medical Corps, had heard the shots. Grabbing his medical kit, he arrived at the tent to find Britz doubled up on the ground with two .45 inch bullet holes in the area of his liver and another in the shoulder. Taylor slapped on some dressings to stem the bleeding and sent for a vehicle. In a whisper, Britz asked the medic to take the photograph of his wife out of his wallet in his bunny-jacket pocket, and put it with him. A blood transfusion was prepared at the regimental aid post, but the patient died before the transfusion could be completed. About 40 minutes had elapsed. Britz, who had been a cook prior to becoming a regimental policeman, had been cleaning the weapon with the magazine in, and the safety catch switched to automatic. He was 37 years' old and is buried in the 6th South African Armoured Division's cemetery at Castiglione.

On 21 May, the 1/6th Field Regiment headquarters moved from Bellagio to the Inveruno–Parabiago area, 15 miles west of Milan. This area is known for its lush forests and farmland, but the regiment's men were devastated about leaving their lakeside paradise. To make things worse, Inveruno was infested with flies. A 'Kill that fly' campaign was re-instituted at this time.

The regimental war diary called it "a less salubrious spot but more central for divisional concentration". Sanitary conditions were poor in such towns and a smell of garlic often pervaded the air.

Thursday 22 May 1945 – Wednesday 23 May 1945: Inveruno

The three brigades had been sent to three different sectors: the 13th South African Motorized Brigade was based at Turin, the 12th South African Motorized Brigade at the French–Italian border in the province of Aosta and the 11th South African Armoured Brigade at the Swiss border. Tension ran high between the French and the Italians but the South African and French troops struck up a good relationship.

Counter-smuggling roadblocks were set up all along the Italian border. The black market was a way of life in big cities and ordinary Italians had to sell off their furniture and heirlooms to pay the inflated prices. People barely survived by making small deals in sugar or cigarettes. A meal which had cost 15 lire in a Roman restaurant in 1938 would now cost 600 lire. State-subsidized restaurants were opend in Milan where one could get a satisfactory meal for 50 lire.

The local population was a bit wary of the Royal Natal Carbineers, as the name 'Carbineer' was uncomfortably close to 'Carabinieri', the Italian police who had acquired a bad name under the fascist regime.[358]

Some smugglers were caught; among them were some American soldiers and civil police. A negro truck driver was stopped at a checkpoint and 40 litres of olive oil confiscated. One American officer refused to have his Italian girlfriends searched and was consequently turned back. Italian civilians were so desperate for olive oil that they were "beginning to trade on their sex by secreting quantities of olive oil in various intimate parts of their anatomy".[359] One car which ran a roadblock was shot up and the driver wounded in the foot. The vehicle was immobilized and was found to have special fixtures for carrying olive oil. Soap was also being smuggled and it was found that not every apparently pregnant woman passing through a roadblock was, indeed, carrying a child.[360] Even the most upstanding of men, like Hodgson, were not above re-selling confiscated goods.

---

358 M. Coghlan, *Pro Patria*, p. 47.

359 DODAR, WD, Box 646, Royal Natal Carbineers, 20–30 July 1945.

360 *Ibid.*

Having been thoroughly informed about the workings of the repatriation process, Hodgson mentally prepared himself to be in Italy until September:

> As you no doubt can well imagine, the main thought with everyone these days is that of getting home as quickly as possible; the way things are progressing at the moment it looks like it will be a long time before I get home, as my category is not a very high priority one. We have got all the dope on this demobilization, we have had quite a few lectures and collected a fair amount of inside information ... and the basis on which the whole scheme will work is Demobilization Categories; no doubt you have seen the long lists that have appeared in the papers from time to time giving what periods of attestation these different categories cover. Working in order of priority from A to M we will be sent home. All the category 'A' will go first, then followed by 'B' etc. This has come into force irrespective of whether you are married or engaged, an only partner in a business, have a job to go back to or even if one has no job to go back to. I am in full agreement with this, hence I will be sent home in my category which is 'H'.

This information was accurate as far as intentions were concerned. It was intended that as of 1 June, men would be sent home by air from Egypt at the rate 420 per day. No firm arrangements had yet been been made for transporting the men from Italy to Egypt; rather, plans were to 'filter' people across the Mediterranean in small batches. Hodgson had hoped that some big ships would become available to get the ball rolling. Although he felt a measure of scepticism, it seemed that the procedure was quite organized. The final step of the process after arrival in the Union was also clearly explained:

> In advance, the people at the airport are notified who is on the plane, and when the detail arrives, everything is ready for him; a booking on the next train to where he wishes to go, in my case Johannesburg; a leave pass for two months, made up of 30 days' ex-north leave and 30 days' service leave; I will get my full pay for those two months plus ration allowance which amounts to 30 pounds in my case. I will then proceed on leave without further delay.

According to the testimony of one traumatized passenger, it was not uncommon for men to turn down trips to Rome on leave for fear of the recklessness of the drivers. Road accidents did, in fact, claim the lives of many retuning soldiers.[361] It was hard enough for a commanding officer to write a

[361] DODAR, Div Docs, Box 162, File 4/2 General, Statement by Gunner M.J. Kraukamp, 17/9/1945.

letter of condolence when someone had given his life for the cause, but in cases like that of Major David Whyte, a medical doctor and Old Johannian, the letter was especially difficult to write:

> Rear Div, UDF
> 26 May 1945
>
> Mrs David Whyte
> 3 Great Kimble
> Main Road
> Rondebosch, Cape Town
>
> Dear Mrs Whyte
>
> It is my sad task to write to offer you the very deeply felt sympathy of all of us on this staff on your loss. David Whyte had become so affectionately an integral part of ADMS Office, that every man here, and his many friends in the SAMC with Fd Ambs and regts, has felt his passing as a personal loss.
>
> His quiet sense of humour, his constant refusal to flap even at the most trying times in action, his very real gallantry while regularly doing reconnaissance under fire, his lovely insistence on always being in the middle of affairs, and growing competence in the more drab routine of administration—these were the points in his character which made him an unusually valuable member of the Divisional Staff.
>
> That he was killed in a road accident while actually on his way back to you makes his passing all the more tragic; we had sent him off on his way that morning so full of cheer and pleasure at being able to get away at the end of a job well done.

Now that the fighting was over and the weather had warmed up, homesickness was the most common ailment, but the war had not yet rung its final toll. Among the English patients at the 92nd General Hospital in the Miano district of Naples, Royce Fuller was dying. He had started vomiting from pain at the time of the Monza victory parade. Morphia was prescribed and only fluids were given by mouth. The colostomy was unable to relieve his distended abdomen. The hospital record card states that at 1130 hours on 29 May he had a sudden attack of pain in the abdomen, which was distended below the scar, and died at 1510 hours. Fuller was buried in the Naples Commonwealth War Cemetery a month after the fighting had stopped. For admin personnel, the paper war continued. Hodgson now had a desk job:

> I have got a new job these days; I am taking over the job of company clerk. I have to keep records of the men in the company, pay matters, rolls, demobilization

> papers and a hundred and one things; the old company clerk is in 'B' category and is naturally expected to go in the near future. I have got one assistant under me, one Alan Drysdale who is a very good fellow indeed. He is about the same age as I am and we get along well together. Then again, I have another chap to do the odd running around.

Medical facilities were still in great demand in northern Italy after the war, especially for the treatment of accident victims. In June 1945, 54 Field Dressing Station was at Milan and 69 Field Dressing Station in Fidenza, while between 4 May and 1 July 1945, 8 South African Casualty Clearing Station was situated in an old double-storey school building—Scuole Elementari, 13 Via Pietro Giordani—in Piacenza.[362] In August, it moved to Palmanova, south of Udine, near Venice. It was located in this area mainly for the benefit of South African Air Force and British troops.

Thursday 24 May 1945 – Monday 11 June 1945: Châtillon

Châtillon is a commercial town in the centre of the Aosta valley. It has none of the charm or attractions of the village of Courmayeur, located at the foot of Mont Blanc, or of Aosta itself, where well-preserved Roman walls are everywhere to be seen. Architecture is distinctly Alpine but the brown shingles on the roofs appear scruffy in comparison with Swiss or Austrian chalets.

With the harsh winter coming to an end, the South Africans set out to explore their surroundings, so different to the rest of Italy. For Bourhill, the challenge of the mountain peaks was alluring although he would have preferred to be in the Drakensberg:

> Have I told you that last Tuesday we moved up here to the Alps and are now parked on the road to Aosta in a little hill town called Castiglion Dora by the Wops and Chatillon by the rest. The latter seems the more popular choice and that's what we all call it. It sounds better. It's on the slopes of a large ruddy mountain in the valley of Aosta called the Dora. It's, bar none, the most beautiful place you've ever seen and you've only got to lift your eyes off the ground to see the Gran Paradiso from where ever you are.
>
> But Mom, how tired I am of foreign hills, and cobbled streets, of quaint towns and alpine bells, of mountain girls with their hefty legs and strong teeth! Boy what wouldn't I give for a 'special' at the O.K. milk bar or a cushion on the front steps and Northcliff just over there with a storm coming up. Hell, I'm sick

362 DODAR, WD, Box 739, 8 South African Casualty Clearing Station, 1–31 May 1945.

> for home. Saturday, Wells, Joe, Mac and I set out to climb a very high peak on the other side of our little valley (I've had my boots fixed up with proper climbing studs etc). Left at 8 o'clock with our lunch and walked and walked. Through pine forests and past remote hill villages where they are scared of us, and across racing, ice cold streams white as milk. And the flowers and pastures and the alpine cows and their bells! To cut a long story short, Mac and I managed to drag ourselves to the top of 'our peak'—8,000 ft climb. Way up in the snow. It turned cloudy on our way up, but once, for about three minutes while we were at the top, the cloud layer lifted and ... glory be, there rose the Matterhorn in the sunlight, up above the clouds. It was something out of this world. In the same glimpse into paradise I saw Monte Rosa bathed in sunshine so close I could have touched it with my hand. Then the clouds rolled up thick and fast and we beat it for home. At 5 o'clock, once again on the lower slopes and dead weary, the rain caught us. What a climb that was! Think of it from Durban to Jo'burg straight up plus 2,000 ft. in four hours. Of course, to real mountaineers it's just child's play.

The situation remained tense in the border areas. In addition to anti-smuggling operations, the division was tasked with preventing internecine strife between partisans and former fascist sympathizers. In the Aosta valley, relations between the Italians and the French were extremely delicate, but the presence of South Africans in this forgotten corner of Italy dampened French aspirations of annexing the territory. French is today one of the official languages in Aosta but under fascist rule, even place names were changed to stamp out the French influence.

The Val d'Aosta had a large French-speaking population, known as Valdôtains, who had been persecuted by the fascists and now sought self-determination. Their mantra was "*Nous ne voulons plus que notre valée d'Aosta soit esclave des Italiens oppresseurs* [we no longer want our valley to be enslaved by the Italian oppressors]" and members of the underground vowed to fight to the death for their liberty. French troops infiltrated the valley and secret agents working for the Allies reported that they were intimidating the locals and spreading annexationist propaganda.

An informer codenamed 'Blanc' reported on the movements of known annexationists and the French military. The reports were translated by special agents of the American Counter Intelligence Corps (CIC). During the post-war period, the CIC was also involved in counter-smuggling operations and tracking down war criminals, many of whom were escaping through a fascist network in Italy, particularly through the port of Genoa. One mountain patrol in the area of Pianetto found the scattered remains of an Allied bomber and its crew in a place inaccessible even to mules. Peacekeeping was not, however, everyone's priority. At the Reserve Infantry School, weapons training and PT continued during the first week of June but recreational swimming soon took over as the main activity. Notice was received on 11 June announcing the disbandment of the school.

The division realized that sport was the key to keeping the men busy and out of trouble, given their general lack of purpose. With most traditional sports and even some less traditional ones on offer, there was something for everyone. A 14-mile motorcycle reliability trial was organized by 17 Brigade Signal Squadron near Milan at the beginning of June. Not quite a race, this was a test of riding skill, featuring eleven hazards to be negotiated without putting a foot down or, heaven forbid, stalling. The winner was the Natal Mounted Rifles' Lieutenant M.W. Stott of Port Shepstone, riding an Ariel. The previous winner at Lucca had been Lance-Corporal G.N. Evans of Johannesburg, who now only managed eleventh place on a Matchless 350.

A few days later, a swimming gala was held in Milan with Springbok swimmers competing against their American counterparts. The South Africans did well in the freestyle but, according to the public relations team, the sole Springbok representative in the breaststroke was outpaced by the unorthodox butterfly style of three 'Niseis', American soldiers of Japanese origin. A diving display was given by two Americans and four South Africans and there was also a water polo exhibition.

While the majority of the soldiers took part in sports, those keen on reviving their grey matter attended classes and went on factory visits. During the last week in May, Hodgson left his base at Turin for a two-day trip to Pallanza, just north of Baveno on Lake Maggiore, where the division would later make its headquarters:

> We left here directly after breakfast on Sunday morning. The trip is not a very long one and at the same time, it is a pleasant one as there is so much to see. We reached the bottom of the lake at 11.00, and proceeded to travel up the western shore, passing through Stresa and round to Pallanza where we stayed; the beauty of the place is much too marvellous to describe, and I would only be doing it an injustice if I tried, so I think you will get the best idea from the postcards I am sending you, and the snaps which we took, which still have to be developed and printed. We set ourselves up at the Hotel Pace (correctly 'Albergo Pace') in the lakeside village of Pallanza ... We took our rations along and handed them to the kitchen owing to the shortage of food; these they supplemented with eggs and greens, with the result that

> we ate very well. In the afternoon, we travelled further up the banks of the lake, right up to the Swiss border; it was quite a unique experience, as I climbed over the barrier and set both feet in Switzerland. Here as elsewhere, the scenery is really marvellous with terrific snow-capped mountains to the dark blue waters of the lake. When we got back to the hotel, there was just time for a short row on the lake before supper, which gave us a terrific appetite. We had bought a cask of beer with us which we had going on tap; this consequently went down very well. That night, the hotel had arranged a dance for us which was really terrific—we danced till 1.30 then went for a swim in the lake which was grand. It was really good to sleep in-between sheets for the first time since coming to Italy. Next morning after a good breakfast we went up onto the top of one of the nearby mountains and had a good look around. It was like being on top of the world. After lunch we did a spot of rowing and then it was time to return.

Hodgson noticed that there were very few tennis courts in Italy; even public courts were scarce. His first opportunity to enjoy a game of tennis came about in Turin after the war's end, when he found a club similar to the Johannesburg Country Club. But no sooner had he organized balls and racquets than he was he told that the club was reserved for officers only and was therefore out of bounds to other ranks. "This type of thing makes me boil, because why should an officer be better suited to tennis etc than any other rank; in many cases it is the reverse. There is still a chance that if we get invited, we can play."

As it happens, Hodgson managed to become an honorary member of the Marine Club where he could play tennis and do a bit of boating in proper sculls with sliding seats.[363]

Within a month of the war's end, Trooper T.E. Swanepoel, an enterprising member of the Pretoria Regiment, started up a new magazine called *La Stella d'Oro*, which was of much higher quality than many of the other in-house publications. The publishers worked out of Rapallo, where Ernest Hemingway wrote *Cat in the Rain* in the 1920s.

Rapallo was at first purely a leave destination, but it later became the division's centre of administration.

Tuesday 12 June 1945 – Monday 2 July 1945: Rapallo

Now that summer had arrived, the main activity was cricket. There were many idle moments however, in spite of the full schedule of sports. For Hodgson, the

363 J.B. Hodgson–M.V. & W.A. Hodgson, 20/5/1945.

hardest part was the waste of valuable time: "Here I am doing my damndest to while away 24 hours so as to get the time to pass until I set sail for home, while if I was with you I could be doing so much to help, that a 24-hour day would not be long enough."

Hodgson had taken the precaution of signing on for correspondence courses in mathematics and physics even before the cessation of hostilities. These were special courses offered to people in the service. Course material and assignments were sent by free airmail.

Shortly after returning from his private excursion to Lake Maggiore, Hodgson, together with the rest of his company, was granted leave to proceed to a rest centre at Finale Ligure on the Italian Riviera. This was an area which the men would come to know well as they would later be based at the adjacent town of Alassio. After this first visit, Hodgson described it as "really a marvellous place—more or less a small English colony, and everything about it is very English:

> We left here on Wednesday the 30th of May; it was a very pleasant trip down, taking about six hours; there were many very interesting things to be seen the way. We passed through Genoa which I was pleased about, as we managed to see a fair portion of it and get some idea of what the place looks like. By general appearances, it seemed a very pleasant city, laid out far better than most large Italian centres—as you can well imagine, most of our bombing in that area was directed at the harbour which was fairly badly knocked about; also, on the big factory centre, which is on the inland side on the main road going to Milan and Turin (this latter place being where we are staying). The coast road going west from Genoa is really a marvellous piece of construction, very large portions of it being hewn out of solid rock; also, there are many road tunnels all along which are cut out of the solid rock. We reached our destination, Finale Ligure, a little after four o'clock. Sixteen of us stayed in the hotel where I was; Alan Drysdale, Henry Heath and I shared a room—we were very comfortably off and well looked after. As for meals, we took our own rations down, these supplemented with eggs, etc were made into some excellent meals. All the time we were there, there was any amount of fruit to be had, mainly in the line of cherries and peaches, so as you can well imagine, we lived on these to a large extent.
>
> The rest of the afternoon was spent finding out where to go, what to do etc. After supper, we went for a long walk along the beach, and as it never got dark before ten at night, and this was very pleasant. At 10.30 we went in for our first swim, which was really grand, then it was to bed on a beautifully soft mattress and clean sheets.
>
> We were keen to pack everything into our few days that we could, so we were up with the sparrows, and ferreted out a bicycle shop, from which Alan and I hired a tandem for the day. (You will see us in one of the snaps.) After breakfast, we set off up the coast with Terrence Cresswell and Edgar Robinson (one of our officers and

our sergeant major). It was really marvellous spinning along the roads in the sea breeze—a tandem, I found, is the easiest thing in the world to ride, and one can go almost anywhere with very little effort. Well, at lunchtime, we landed up at a place called Alassio which is a very pleasant pleasure resort which was mainly used by the English in peacetime with the result that there are quite a number of English people there and a large amount of English is spoken. There we had a very pleasant day, returning on our tandems just in time for supper.

The next few days were mainly spent in bathing, sun bathing and relaxing upon the beach. The water was really marvellous for swimming—the temperature being so ideal, and the water so calm and clear, also deep very near to the shore. Five yards out, it is impossible to stand; no matter how deep the water is, one can [see] every little pebble on the sea bed. The photographs will give you a very good idea of how calm the sea is; the first day was the roughest, and that was the only day we had anything resembling breakers, then they were only a matter of a foot high. Personally, if one is going to go bathing in the sea, I prefer ours as there is so much more fun. Also, our beaches are so much better, these being pebbly with sandy patches at intervals along the shore. Also the beaches here are so much shorter than ours. On our last day, we rode out to Alassio again for the day and had a very enjoyable time. The beach there is the best we came across, and the water does not get deep so quickly. We did a bit of boating there, but not much—it was really uncanny to see canoes and rowing boats pushing off from the shore and going out without any effort at all, after what we have been used to at home.

At this stage, the 6th South African Armoured Division was scattered over a wide area, divided into sectors and sub-sectors around the Lake District. The abundance of holiday hotels along the coast proved useful for accommodating an army.

Divisional headquarters was established at Baveno on the shores of Lake Maggiore, near Stresa. Later, when repatriation took over from border duty as the main priority, the administrative headquarters moved to Rapallo.

The 11th South African Armoured Brigade held a retreat ceremony at the sports arena in Milan on Union Day, 31 May. The Special Service Battalion formed the guard of honour and entered to the tune of *With Sword and Lance*. The Imperial Light Horse band, together with the pipe band of the Prince Alfred's Guard, marched and counter-marched in slow and quick time. They had selected the slow marches *Mayblossom* and *Protea* and the quick marches *Sons of the Brave* and *SSB* for the occasion. Major-General Willis D. Crittenberger of the United States 4th Corps, together with Brigadiers Furstenburg and Palmer of the 11th and 12th Brigades respectively, took the salute. In the town of Chieri, about 20 miles southeast of Turin, the 12th South

African Motorized Brigade held its own small parade. The Royal Durban Ligh Infantry, First City/Cape Town Highlanders and Witwatersrand Rifles/ Regiment De la Rey formed the guard of honour and the music was provided by the First City/Cape Town Highlanders band.

The duty station of First City/Cape Town Highlanders was, for a time, based in the village of Courmayeur at the top end of the Aosta valley, where the residents did everything possible to make the stay a pleasant one. The 13th Alpine Chasseurs held climbing demonstrations in the village and the first of a series of ten-day mountaineering courses was attended by one officer and 19 men on 11 June. Several excursions, led by Italian guides, were afterwards arranged to the summit of Mont Blanc.

Other members of the regiment made excursions to the Matterhorn and had the opportunity to see some world-famous Alpine resorts.

Early in July, a party comprising Hodgson, Lieutenant Arthur Newey, Alan Drysdale and 'Slim' Slade departed from Courmayeur to climb Mont Blanc. They wore only their winter battledress and army boots with crampons affixed. Hodgson had impressed upon his mother the competence of the two Italian guides, one of whom was named Evaristo, so that she would not worry. The party spent a day relaxing at a nearby hotel, then overnighted at the start point before setting off at 0400 hours. The ascent took nine hours, two hours longer than the descent "which has to be done in one hit; there is no sleeping on the job". These men were superbly fit: Hodgson had been running three miles every evening during training, but Alan Drysdale had to take shelter under a rock and could not summit.

From as early as 13 May, advance parties of South Africans had been travelling from Monza to Rapallo and Santa Margherita Ligure, where they would stay at the Hotel Praggi. On 25 May, the 1/6th Field Regiment opened up a regimental rest area in Rapallo which remained in operation for approximately two months. A rest centre for the Special Service Battalion was opened during June at the Hotel Savoia-Europa, also in Rapallo. This became the venue for a *braaivleis*, or barbeque, held in honour of Lieutenant-Colonel Brits, who was returning to the Union. The First City/Cape Town Highlanders' rest hotel was at Santa Margherita Ligure, sandwiched between Rapallo and Portofino. Renamed the Balmoral, it was requisitioned complete with civilian staff, and provided free accommodation for 100 men at a time. In some cases, these hotels had no furnishings and men slept on the floor.

Back in Turin, on 16 June the 13th South African Motorized Brigade held an inter-unit athletic championship in the Stadium del Popolo. A professionally printed programme announced that it was being hosted by the Royal Natal Carbineers and the DSR, under the patronage of Brigadier J.B. Bester DSO and Bar. The day was dominated by the Royal Natal Carbineers, thanks to stars like Frank Kingwell and middle distance champion Errol Dinkelman, who won the 1,500m in 4.40 minutes. The bands of the First City/Cape Town Highlanders–DSR (massed pipe) and the Imperial Light Horse performed for the crowd, which filled only the main covered stand. For many of the spectators, the highlight would have been the 100-yard sprint in which the unit commanders and seconds-in-command competed. The race was won by the lithe young commanding officer of the Royal Natal Carbineers, Lieutenant-Colonel Peter Francis, with a very respectable time of 12.2 seconds. Bester came a close second. The main 100m race was won by Sergeant P.G. Benade in 11.75 seconds. In the final placement, the Royal Natal Carbineers came first, followed by the Natal Mounted Rifles, the DSR, and the Pretoria Regiment. Not included in the official programme was an officers' novelty race that involved drinking and passing beer bottles around the track. That evening, a grand ball was held at the Esperia Rowing Club. It was a day worth writing home about:

> Last Saturday afternoon, the Brigade athletics meeting was held—it was really excellently run, and the organization was very good as it was done in the stadium here, which is a really marvellous affair. There were five regimental teams taking part—I am glad to say that we won with 72 points, the Natal Mounted Rifles coming second with 37.[364]

Leave was freely granted, with permission given for ten per cent of unit strength to take leave at a time. Army regulations were more relaxed but soldierly conduct and courtesy were still expected. Troops were ordered not to discuss international politics, especially involving Italian–French–Swiss relations. In the event of a riot or public disturbance, the South Africans were to try to restore order by negotiation, using force only as a last resort. The Carabinieri were to be treated with respect. Personnel were to maintain a smart and soldierly appearance in public and impress all with their high standard of efficiency. Displays of martial discipline, route marches and parades were

[364] J.B. Hodgson–M.V. & W.A. Hodgson, 20/6/1945.

regularly held in order to create an image of efficiency. The behaviour and turn-out of the troops was expected to be faultless, as this enhanced prestige and built respect for law and order.

At 1800 hours on Sunday 17 June, a retreat ceremony was held at the sports stadium, Corso IV Novembre, following a soccer match. The Imperial Light Horse band and the pipe bands of the First City/Cape Town Highanders and the DSR played for General Poole and the multinational guests.

The big event at this time was a medal parade held by the 13th South African Motorized Brigade on 22 June, in the centre of Turin. The Royal Natal Carbineers formed the guard of honour. Also present were the Pretoria Regiment (Princess Alice's Own), the Natal Mounted Rifles/South African Air Force, DSR and 15 Field Regiment. Hodgson was uncertain as to its purpose, but described the preparations:

> There is going to be a big ceremonial parade here on Friday; our regiment is supplying the guard of honour, there will be a big mechanized march-past by the Brigade. The occasion is a visit by Field Marshal Alexander—I don't think he has got anything important to say, it is just a tour of inspection that he is on—of course, this is only my opinion and I might easily be wrong. As you can well imagine, there has been a good deal of preparation, such as cleaning and polishing up etc.

After the march through the city, in the Piazza Imperatore Adriano, Field Marshal Sir H.R.I.G. Alexander GSB, CSI, DSO, MC, ADC decorated those who had distinguished themselves in the rush across the Lombardy plains and at the battle of Panaro River. One medal recipient was Major F.P. Kightley of the Pretoria Regiment who had organized the fateful dance at Prato before Christmas, resulting in the deaths of the two nurses. The last two heroes, also of the Pretoria Regiment, were Lieutenant M.M. Munro and Sergeant W.S. Simpson, who had climbed out of his tank and assaulted German positions on foot during the advance from the Panaro River.

At the luncheon afterwards, Alexander was entertained by the band of the Imperial Light Horse with a selection of music including *Come Back to Sorrento*, *Maria Mari*, *The Turkish Patrol* and airs from Gilbert and Sullivan operas. Soon afterwards, Alexander sent the following message to the GOC: "I was immensely impressed with the division. I thought your parade absolutely splendid, as I told you—one of the best I have seen in Italy, and you can indeed be proud of your division."

The comments of various spectators and bystanders were also noted: "This material will teach our hothead friends that it won't pay to start any trouble here', "How much nicer to have people like these in the Aosta valley instead of the French" and "You see how they used to stuff us with propaganda, telling us that these soldiers would ill-use our wives and children. We know now from experience how well behaved these South Africans are in the town". The compliments continued: "What drill! What precision! They move as one man!" and "What excellent motor vehicles! How silent they are compared to our noisy Italian stuff!"

The day after the parade, 21-year-old Private E.J. Auths of East London died in Turin when he fell down a staircase. Two days later, 20-year-old Lance-Corporal H. Flear of Johannesburg was killed by a booby-trapped German truck in a transport park at Strambino. Both were Carbineers and were taken to Castiglione for burial. Part of the job in post-war Italy involved general police work, investigating the theft of military supplies, especially fuel and food. Very often, it was the troops themselves who were selling the material on the black market. According to a statement made by one Elide Bassetti, two South African soldiers came into his garage and tried to sell him first a six-volt battery, then a set of tyres and then a Jeep, which the civilian bought for 40,000 lire. On one occasion, the petrol seized by the military police and the Carabinieri turned out to have been legitimately acquired or taken from the German army.

Army Education Services (AES) presented a series of courses at Rusthof in Florence for those who intended taking up or resuming post-matric studies. The purpose was actually to prepare students for their return to civilian life. Rank was not recognized in the training centre; policy held that everybody ate, slept and worked together, irrespective of rank. The syllabus included South African affairs, recent history, economic and political questions, the broader facts of biology and psychology. The arts, music and literature were also given a place.

AES also published a weekly pamphlet called 'PEP' (Peace, Education, Progress). The July edition of PEP featured a cartoon by Vic Clapham of the Royal Natal Carbineers, depicting a soldier looking at a sign that reads 'Welcome back to South African Soil'. Under his feet is a landmine labelled 'Race Hate'; the caption reads 'Achtung! Minen!'[365]

365 DODAR, WD, Box 726, AES, PEP Something new at Florence school, 2/7/1945, pp.1–2.

Tuesday 3 July 1945 – Wednesday 26 September 1945: Gozzano

It was a summer of love in post-war Italy. The 15 July edition of *La Stella d'Oro* reported on the marriage of Lieutenant George Shaw of the Pretoria Regiment to Beth Lategan of 107th General Hospital. Both were in uniform. The ceremony took place at the Holy Trinity Church in Florence and from there, the wedding party went back to a reception at their favourite watering hole, the Roma Hotel. Lieutenant N.R. Thompson MC (as in Military Cross, not Master of Ceremonies) was best man and the bridesmaid was M. Hopwood.

Leave parties visited Como and Venice but Rapallo, in particular, was the setting for countless holiday (and longer-term) romances. At his leave hotel in Rapallo, Trooper Hobbs met Captain Cecily Harman, a South African nurse travelling with her friends. They went swimming and dancing. As a trooper, Hobbs found it awkward to go out with a captain.[366]

Private Mundel had a liaison with a hotelkeeper's daughter in Rapallo. The father was an amateur artist and the two paintings of the bay he gave him still hang in his lounge. Bourhill had an affair that was more than a mere fling with a girl called Giulia Vitorello. Their special place, or *nostro posto,* was in the secluded fishing village of Portofino at the end of the peninsular. She called him 'Stefano' and wrote to him after a year, pleading with him to come back to Portofino.

La Stella d'Oro published the story of an anonymous South African who lost his towel and found his love on a cold, drizzly day at the beach. While swimming, he noticed a female form step out of a bathing booth and take the towel. At first he was ready to confront the thief, then he found out that her name was Anna and she had simply brought his towel in from the rain. After that, they had a glorious swim together followed by tea at the Albergo Savoia. Totally smitten and thinking marriage, the boy wrote: "Over that cup of tea, sprung a friendship and love entirely devoid of the nauseating sentimentality which I had grown accustomed to expect from Italian women."[367]

Rapallo has not changed much over time, although it has lost a little of its shine. Santa Margherita and Portofino have become the jewels of this coastline, having been discovered by the glitterati in the 1954 film *The Barefoot Contessa*, starring Humphrey Bogart and Ava Gardner. Gozzano, on the other hand, is a dull working town situated just south of Lago d'Orta which is the smallest and

366 G.B. Hobbs, 'Recollections of Italy: memoirs of a trooper in Prince Alfred's Guard', unpublished memoirs.

367 *La Stella d'Oro*, 3 (4), p.8, Italian Riviera, 11/11/1945.

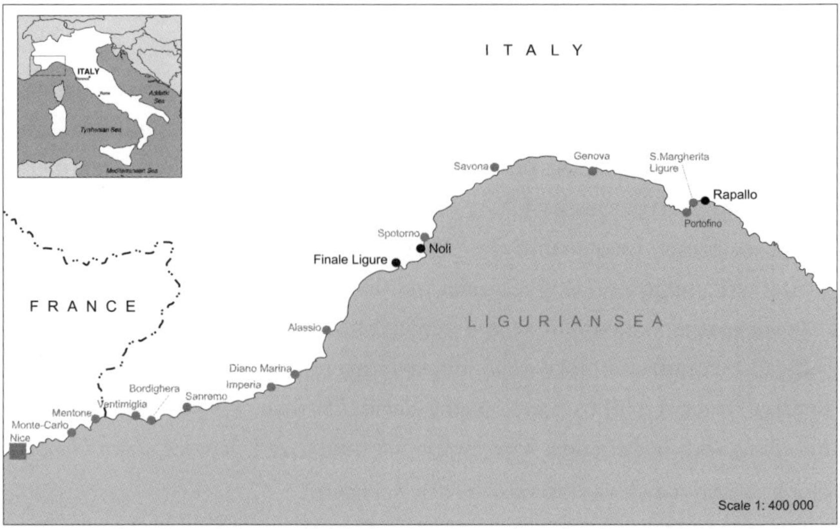

most easterly of the lakes in northern Italy. It was a convenient staging area, close to divisional headquarters and Milan. Fortunately, Rapallo and the coast were within striking distance by train. The essence of the long summer months spent here is encapsulated in Cormack's one-liner: "In a school dorm, much dames and beer."

For the energetic, Lago d'Orta was within walking distance of Gozzano. Bourhill had made an epic swim across the bay at Rapallo, following it with a swim out to the islands in the lake. On 19 June 1945, some soldiers lay soaking up the last rays of the late afternoon sun on the beach at Arona on the southern tip of Lake Maggiore, just a few miles from Gozzano. Gunner D.J. Taljaard of the survey troop, 1/6th Field Regiment took a rowing boat out onto the lake. He dived into the water about 100 yards from the shore, not realizing that the current would sweep away the boat faster than he could swim. The boat drifted about 20 yards. Taljaard was not a good swimmer; after making a determined effort to reach the boat, he started to panic and shouted for help. He was too far out for anyone to reach him in time and after a violent struggle, he disappeared below the water. Some Italians immediately took their boats to search for him but his body was only recovered two weeks later. A post-mortem was conducted at 108th General Hospital in Milan. Because of the decomposed state of the body, Taljaard was buried in Milan instead of at Castiglione. One of the members of the court of inquiry was a certain Lieutenant J. Rose-Innes, a well-known name in South African legal circles.

The headquarters of the 11th South African Armoured Brigade was still located in the Monza area on 3 July 1945. Lance-Corporal Peter Christie was the clerk on duty at Villa Gallarati Scotti, a magnificent mansion with large grounds, two miles from Arcore. Giuseppina Marelli, aged 15, and her sister Giovanna, aged 13, lived nearby. They visited the camp every day to do laundry for the soldiers and knew Christie by name. It was about 2000 hours in the long twilight, and the older girl was helping Christie type a permit on a typewriter in the back of a truck. The younger girl was given the job of breaking up some lumpy sugar. The mood was cheerful. Christie had been drinking and started playing with a pistol, pointing it first at Giuseppina, who jumped out and ducked behind the tailgate. In bad Italian, Christie said, "Don't worry, this pistol is no good, it cannot kill," or words to that effect. He then put the gun to his own head and pulled the trigger. The RMO of 1 Special Service Battalion, Captain R. St Clair Sinclair, examined the body soon afterwards and proclaimed that the wound was sufficiently severe to have caused almost instant death. Christie was 22 years' old, from Johannesburg, and is one of just a handful of South Africans to be buried in the Commonwealth War Cemetery in Milan.

The South Africans played rugby all year round. Matches were played against the Italians and between regiments. On Wednesday 4 July, the 6th South African Armoured Division trounced the Turin XV 33–7. One match between the Prince Alfred's Guard and the Special Service Battalion was billed as a 'Clash of Armour'. A rugby match was held at the Forza e Coraggio (Strength and Courage) stadium in Milano between the 7/23rd Medium Regiment and the local Amatori Rugby Club. *"Molto spettacolare"* was the verdict of the crowd of spectators.

Restlessness and dissatisfaction was now beginning to set in. On 4 July a notice was sent to all units advising that there was still a soldierly job to be done in the maintenance of law and order: "First-class discipline and scrupulously correct soldierly behaviour must be observed and enforced … so that the fruits of our dearly bought victory over tyranny and rapacity will not rot …" The notice went on to explain that repatriation was delayed because of the unpredictable availability of ships.

This, in turn, was attributed to the enormous numbers of people to be repatriated. The Commonwealth's Council of Repatriation apparently had to repatriate 10,000,000 displaced persons—a figure which far surpassed the number of ships available. The grand plan was to move 5,000 troops a month by air starting on 1 July 1945, with another 15,000 travelling by sea. According to this plan, 45,000 men would be repatriated by the end of the year. By 30 June, only 6,000 personnel had been repatriated—2,570 by air and 3,491 by sea.

Another reason given for the lack of ships was the ongoing war against the Japanese, as ships were needed to feed the military machine. This excuse fell away after Japan's surrender.

At this stage, anyone who wanted to join the permanent force was able to obtain full-time engagement in the interim forces, provided they were medically fit. By the middle of July, owing to the ever-changing duties and manpower situation, the 6th South African Armoured Division assumed responsibility for the Piedimonte and Imperia areas. The various units were scattered all over northwestern Italy carrying out guards and pickets, subject to strict discipline. There was no carousing in the bars, hotels and streets. Divisional headquarters was in Baveno; the 11th South African Armoured Brigade had not moved from the Arcore–Carugate area; the 12th South African Motorized Brigade was on a limb in Aosta and Courmayeur and the 13th Motorized Brigade was centred around Turin. Medical and technical units were based around Milan, Turin, Monza, Vercelli, Stresa and Brugherio. The 6th South African Armoured Division Artilley Signal Squadron was headquartered in Carate and Agliate.

On 21 May, No. 2 Forward Detention Barracks was moved by road from Bari to Colleferro, approximately 25 miles south of Rome on Route 6. On 9 June, the 11th Field Punishment Centre was moved from Prato to far-off Susegana, ten miles from Treviso and 25 miles north of Venice. These last two units were non-divisional but a few unfortunate division personnel would have come into contact with them.

Long-term prisoners were in a relatively high-priority 'release group' for evacuation and were taken firstly to No.1 Detention Barracks in the Middle East. There were approximately 20 prisoners serving terms from six months to two years at No. 2 Forward Detention Barracks at the end of May 1945. All had been sentenced in April and May 1945. By September, there was one prisoner, a Private H.F. Victor 159492V of the amalgamated infantry group Royal Durban Light Infantry/First City/Cape Town Highlanders/Witwatersrand Rifles/Regiment De la Rey, serving 15 years for rape, plus another man serving ten years for culpable homicide.[368]

[368] DODAR, WD, Box 723, No.2 Forward Detention Barracks, September 1945.

Turin was beginning to return to normal and for a short time before leaving for Sanremo and the coast, Hodgson was again able to enjoy some culture. On circuit was the film *Mrs Parkinson* with Walter Pidgeon and Greer Garson. A feast of entertainment and sports offset the drudgery of duties and parades:

> This last week I have been into town to see a couple of films; one was very good, *The Adventures of Mark Twain*. The other one with Edgar G. Robinson in it, called *Arms and the Woman*, was fair but not too good. I have also been in to see two ENSA revues which were very good indeed. Especially the first one which was excellent. We have found a nice little place on the way back to our barracks where we pop in after the show and have poached eggs and lovely fresh bread. It is a real treat after all the camp food we have had to eat in the past months, not that our grub is bad; on the contrary there is very little to complain about, the change in menu is the big thing.

Jan Smuts landed at Foggia on his way back from San Francisco in July 1945, travelling to Milan, where on 8 July he addressed a parade of around 5,000 men in the Milan arena. The Imperial Light Horse/Kimberley Regiment was once again designated guard of honour, having to smarten up for inspection. There was more grumbling than usual this time because the men wanted to go home and blamed Smuts for the repatriation fiasco. Nevertheless, the regiment was as smart as ever with its white webbing, white rifle slings and white canvas leggings. The band of the Imperial Light Horse opened with the quick march *Old Companies* and *Sons of the Brave*. After the general salute, the guard of honour marched past to the tune of *Colonel Bogey*.

In his speech, Smuts warned the men that they would be returning to a world beset by difficulties and pitfalls and that they should not expect a life of ease and comfort.

Smuts stayed in Stresa at the Hotel des Iles Borromées, where Ernest Hemingway had convalesced during the First World War. It is today, as it was then, the height of luxury.

Also on the prime minister's itinerary was a visit to 108th General Hospital and a viewing of Leonardo da Vinci's 'Last Supper' in Milan. On 10 July he paid an official visit to the divisional cemetery where he unveiled the memorial. The following address given on behalf of the people of the Comune di Castiglione dei Pepoli, provincia di Bologna:

> In the name of the population of Castiglione di Pepoli, the Comune welcomes you. Here in our land, there repose the mortal remains of the heroic Springboks.

> The grateful love of the Castiglionesi will have care of them. The life they have given for the liberation of our country is a love symbol; to that love our people will concentrate forever a faithful gratefulness.
>
> Tell, Sir, to the mothers, wives and sisters of the heroes reposing in these mountains, that our people have the deepest and most eternal feelings of sympathy and gratefulness for them.
>
> Long live the Allied nations!
> Long live the South African Union!

Divisional headquarters in Baveno was not far from Milan. The small town is located north of Stresa, between the mountains and the shores of Lake Maggiore. Although most picturesque, the lakeside towns apparently carried a whiff of rotting fish during the height of summer.

General Poole, who had spent the entire campaign living in his caravan, now agreed to stay in a villa near the Hotel des Iles Borromées. The front garden was built on piles above the water, forming a yacht harbour beneath, with stairs leading up from the quay to the lounge. His wife, Elsie, was flown up from the Union to join her husband.

The divisional security structures assisted in prosecuting war crimes in post-war Italy and some South Africans were still to be found among the lakes in Varese and Luino in August. The Albergo del Sole in Porto Valtravaglia, which had been occupied by the Germans, was now taken over by the Imperial Light Horse/Kimberley Regiment. Almost forgotten were the days when Mussolini had his headquarters on Lake Garda and Italy's Jews were systematically slaughtered at Meina on Lake Maggiore. The Lake District had escaped the bombing and shelling but like most of the Italian countryside, it had not escaped partisan activity and the inevitable retributions.

The historical recording section was also based in Baveno at this time. In a letter to his commanding officer, Captain J.A.I. Agar-Hamilton in Pretoria, the new historical recording officer at main division, Lieutenant R.V. 'Reg' Davis, explained why he was in no hurry to come home:

> Eric took me along the snow-topped, fifteen thousand feet of Monte Rosa, trailing a thin cloud veil against the sky. Add to this, the good wine drunk stretched on the grass just below the snow line, in the company of signore who contrived to look charming, even in the divided skirts and heavy boots of mountaineer's kit and you have the reason for this letter <u>not</u> being an application for immediate transfer back to GHQ, PTA, even with an amended staff.

Toward the end of July, the Royal Natal Carbineers moved to its new duty stations around Sanremo on the coast, close to the French border. The men welcomed the change in a way, even though they had been well organized and settled in Turin. The Royal Natal Carbineers' war diary notes that Turin ties were quickly forgotten and new ties established on the Riviera. Hodgson was happy with the move:

> … now I am back on the Italian Riviera, this time on duty, but I will add that if the word 'duty' always meant what it does here, it would always be a very pleasant task. Our company (I don't think I told you that with the fellows leaving for the Union and reducing our numbers, it has been necessary to amalgamate companies—we are now 'A'-'B' Company) are garrisoning the town of Imperia—you will find it quite easily on the map as it is quite a large and fairly important place. We are the only troops here which is very pleasant as one doesn't bump into soldiers everywhere one goes. We are doing our duty here and we are in command of the whole town and its population. Naturally we are not roughing under those conditions; as we have requisitioned the two best hotels in the place and we are living in these; four of us share a room, with water and light laid on and a bathroom next door—mind you, it is a bit noisy as we are on the main street. It is a very pleasant life here but one is apt to get a bit tired of it. The mornings are usually spent doing the daily routine in the Orderly Room, the afternoons are spent on the beach which is very pleasant, and I have spent a good deal of time fishing off the rocks which I have found very good fun; up to now I have not caught anything, the main reason being that the local populace do a great deal of trawling along the coast which does not leave much scope for the hook. Nonetheless, I enjoy it. I have got beautifully sunburned and I feel very fit. In the evenings, we go for walks, a spot more fishing or a spot more swimming. Apart from the above, there is nothing at all to do. At the moment I am very happy as it is great to be away from barrack life, but I think one will get tired of it after a month or so. There are organized trips into France from here and I am hoping to spend a day in Nice sometime this week.

The various company headquarters of the Royal Natal Carbineers were installed in the Hotel Miramare ('sea view' in Italian), the Hotel Mediterranean and the Hotel Savoia, where the officers held regimental dances. The Pretoria Regiment also had a leave hotel in Sanremo at the Albergo Ratti. Other ranks were accommodated in the chauffeurs' quarters. Hodgson shared a back room with one of these men, a former Michaelhouse boy called David Taylor. As the main hotel was on a busy main street, Hodgson preferred to stay in the back rooms, listening to Taylor's wireless playing full blast on the windowsill. Platoons were based at Bordighera and Ventimiglia, which is the last train station before the French border. From this part of Italy, it was most convenient to make day-trips to Nice, across the border in France. Monte Carlo was out of bounds but the truck would stop for a moment outside the famous casino and the Hotel de Paris which Hodgson described as a "quietly imposing" building which gave a "complete impression of luxury and elegance". He estimated that a weekend stay would cost him a complete year's pay. These cities had been playgrounds for wealthy English tourists since Victorian times.

The Americans had taken over 150 hotels in Nice, as well as restaurants where one could eat for free, provided one had a pass. The uncommon uniforms of the 'Red Tabs' attracted attention but the troops were well looked after. Many of the Americans had never heard of South Africa, even though they were Allies.

The coastal road between the Italian border and Nice, which passes through Monte Carlo, is a spectacular drive, reminiscent of Chapman's Peak Drive in Cape Town. Nice itself is best known for the wide pedestrian walkway along the beachfront, named Promenade des Anglais after the English who conceived it. Over the road from the beachfront are the grand hotels which the English elite used to frequent. Nice also has its quaint old quarter and a harbour area dating back to ancient Greek times. Fortunately, the city had not been as badly damaged as had other historic towns in the south of France, including Marseille, Avignon and Arles. However, it had not escaped unscathed. The Alpes–Maritimes region of France was one of the worst affected by the occupation. The population had been terrorized first by the Italian secret police and then by the Germans. Concrete blockhouses still squatted on the Promenade des Anglais.

Nevertheless, accustomed to the squalour of Egypt and deprivations in Italy, Hodgson was enthusiastic about his visit to France:

> The main item of news was my trip to Nice last Friday. I went along with Cyril and Derek Louch; as there were only three of us who wanted to go along for the day, we had a truck to ourselves, which made things very comfortable. We got there at about midday after a pleasant trip. On the way we passed through Monte Carlo, and saw the famous casino; also the 'Hotel de Paris' which is renowned to be the finest in the world. As you can well imagine these two places need more than words to describe them. In Nice itself we had excellent food at American-controlled restaurants, visited 'The' hotels of the French Riviera, which are far beyond my sphere of explanation. These were also taken over by Americans for rest hotels so all of the prices were very cheap. The shopping centre was very nice to look at, but the outstanding prices soon took the idea out of our heads of doing anything. We also spent a fair amount of time on the promenade surveying the sights on the beach. I

> can assure you that it was an eye-opener to French dress and certain of their ways. It was really a wonderful experience to be able to have a look round such a renowned city. There was plenty of beer to be had, and any amount of ice cream and cakes at the American Red Cross Club. It is hard to describe it all in such a short space all that we saw and did, so I think it had better wait until I get back which I hope will not be long now, and then I will be able to give you all the details. We got back here to our hotel at four o'clock on Saturday morning.

The pebbly beach below the Promenade des Anglais did not impress Hodgson, who described it as a strip of stones about 15 yards wide. In South Africa, it would not even be called a beach. "As far as the styles of costumes, I have seldom seen anything like it; the majority were only costumes in name, there was so little of them; also such a thing as a bathing-booth is not employed, everyone dresses and undresses on the beach." In the evening, there was dancing at the Rhul Hotel where Hodgson found the French girls to be "streets ahead of these decadent Italians".

For some reason, the days of late July and early August seemed to slip by more rapidly than before. Hodgson was still receiving parcels from his mother, the contents of which were carefully chosen. In addition to homemade crunchies, she sent him a roll of *Esquire* and *Life* magazines. The reading material went down very well and was permanently busy, doing the rounds. By the end of August 1945, Mrs Hodgson had sent her son a total of 83 parcels.

Hodgson's second trip to Nice was even better than the first. The prices of goods in the shops were out of his reach, but he found the ice cream to be far better than anything he had had in Italy:

> Since I last wrote to you I have been to France again and spent another day in Nice; this time I went with David Knight, we had a simply marvellous time. Soon after lunch we went to the Forum Theatre which is much like the 20th Century at home although not quite as large—it was really grand to sit in a good theatre again. We saw one of the latest films, Bette Davis in *The Corn is Green*, it was a marvellous film and I strongly recommend your seeing it, if you have not already done so.
>
> After visiting the Red Cross Club where we indulged in coffee and doughnuts at the expense of the Yanks, we passed on to the shopping centre where we had a good look round, buying a few things. After a fairly late supper we went to the Ruhl Hotel where we spent the rest of the evening doing a spot of dancing; the floor show was the main reason for our going there; this was really excellent, the turn that I liked best was when two lovely girls came out and did the *Blue Danube* in ballet style. It was really marvellous, they were two very pretty blondes in long white dresses and could they dance. We left Nice soon after midnight.

With their Jeeps or three-tonners, officers had the means to tour extensively in Italy and France, but they were unaccustomed to the narrow coastal roads cut out of the mountainsides. On 14 September, an accident occurred five miles inland from Sanremo when a Jeep carrying two South Africans and a New Zealander plunged 60 feet down a steep cliff. The South Africans were bruised and shaken but the New Zealander was critically injured. The division reported that there were five vehicle accidents during the week ending 24 August 1945, although they didn't all result in fatalities. Four of the five involved a vehicle being driven by a military policeman; three of the vehicles were Jeeps. In each case, the driver of the other vehicle was an Italian civilian.

Motorcycle accidents were, as always, more serious. On 17 May 1945, Lance-Corporal P.J. Griggs of 17 Field Park Squadron, South African Engineer Corps, swerved to avoid some children in the road while riding his Matchless motorcycle four miles southwest of Monza. Griggs hit an Italian man who was standing on the pavement. He cracked his skull and died on the scene. The civilian claimed compensation from the military for a broken leg and ruined trousers.

In July of the previous year, the reckless driving of certain dispatch riders—also known as Don Rs—had been brought to the attention of all signals personnel. While it was appreciated that Don Rs wanted to complete their journey in the shortest time possible, they were prone to driving at "excessive speeds with a definite lack of caution". Although the bad roads were partly to blame for the high incidence of accidents, squadron commanders were requested to warn their Don Rs to "temper their ardour with caution".[369]

The report of deaths for the week ending 4 July 1945 listed 12 names, including four who had previously been listed as POWs or 'missing believed wounded' and had now been confirmed dead. In the weeks that followed, the Union Defence Force in Italy would suffer an accidental death almost every second day, a disproportionate number of which were of Non-European Army Services or Cape Corps troops.

The week ending 25 July was a particularly bad one for the MEF: 13 returning soldiers were killed in a plane crash on 17 July 1945. A total of 31 people died in air crashes during the repatriation process in July. Major Wynn (Natal Mounted Rifles), A.J. Seymour of Kalk Bay (4/22nd Field Regiment), Sergeant Keith

369 DODAR, Div Docs, Box 240, Headquarters Squadron 6th South African Armoured Division Signals, Memorandum, Dispatch Riders, 8/7/1944.

Putterill of Howick (Royal Natal Carbineers) and Sergeant Tony Sieni of Cape Town (Royal Natal Carbineers) were just four of the individuals who died in a crash on 11 July and are buried at Kisumu. Four planes crashed at Kisumu on Lake Victoria in Kenya, where General Dan Pienaar's plane had crashed on 19 December 1943. Elsewhere in Kenya, there were crashes at Nairobi and Jubuti. Many of the casualties were men who had survived five years of war. During a visit to the Royal Natal Carbineers on 29 July, General Poole impressed on everyone the necessity of taking a "calm and reasoned view" of the recent air tragedies. Then, on 28 September, a Dakota crashed near Broken Hill in Northern Rhodesia, killing nine and leaving several more injured.

August in Italy is dry and a bit too hot. September usually offers perfect weather, but from his experience the previous year, Hodgson was expecting plenty of rain from September onward. His letters touch on the big issue of the time: the surrender of the Japanese. In a previous letter he had expressed satisfaction at the recent dropping of the atom bomb, which would force the Japanese to agree to any peace terms:

> I am very pleased to hear that you had such an enjoyable holiday down in Durban; the flying to and from must have made it even more enjoyable, as it cut out the long car trip. I can well imagine that Durban must have been a very gay place while you were down there, with all the 'VJ' Day celebrations in full swing. I gather from your letter that there is a very bad drought in progress down in the Union, which must be quite a blow, as this is the time of year when one could do with quite a bit of rain down there. It is a pity that you could not have a part of our share, especially next month, when we get rain every day, and mostly all day.

The Royal Natal Carbineers' war diary notes that there were no official celebrations on VJ Day, 16 August. Dances were such a regular occurrence that they were unremarkable regardless of the occasion. Life in general was becoming monotonous, whether on leave or on duty and regardless of the idyllic surroundings. Troops were moved up and down the coast from one resort town to another, and the best way of making time pass was by travelling widely. Sadly, the opportunity seldom arose for the ordinary soldier, and sport remained the primary distraction.

Colonel Peter Francis of the Royal Natal Carbineers received an invitation from the Minister of State in Monaco to participate in a sports day on 15 September 1945. It was accepted with enthusiasm and a military team was sent to attend. The swimming was of an international standard and the South

Africans proudly held their own. The water polo team was led by the medical officer, Captain Sammy Sacks, who lifted the trophy which is displayed among the regimental silver collection. A week later, the local dignitaries in Sanremo held a luncheon in honour of the South Africans. On the menu was Italian Risotto, Roast beef all'Inglese and Peace Cake.

Organized sport played a vital role in the lives of the troops wherever they found themselves. The Union Defence Force Sports Control Officer, Major Bill Hearn, organized a golf tournament on 1 August at the Rome golf course. The winner was Lieutenant J. Hodson and the aluminium trophy was presented by the 'manufacturers'—45 South African Advanced Base Workshops. Four South Africans, including two women, reached the finals of the Allies Tennis Championships. A big water sports meeting was held by the division on Lake Maggiore, at Baveno, on 12 September.

A sense of resignation seems to have set in or, as the Royal Natal Carbineers' war diary put it, South Africa had been "relegated to the near but not immediate future, a glittering prize to be awaited with eagerness but not impatience".

Few of the men would have been aware of the fact that while in exile and recuperating from illness, Paul Kruger had stayed in the French town of Menton (or Mentone in Italian), between Sanremo and Monte Carlo. Menton is also the final resting place of William Webb Ellis who is credited with having invented the game of rugby.

Monte Carlo was the setting for another noteworthy event when Lieutenant-Colonel Peter Francis of the Royal Natal Carbineers was invited to meet Winston Churchill on 1 October, following his unexpected election defeat. Churchill was apparently in good form, proposing a toast to the Carbineers and recalling his personal contact with the regiment during the Anglo-Boer War.

Repatriation problems gave rise to an ugly riot in the Helwan transit camp outside Cairo on 20 August 1945. There were now 9,000 men crammed 40 or 50 to a bungalow meant to take twenty-four. The camp itself was designed to accommodate 5,000 men. Because there were only 14 mess halls instead of the 22 required to feed such numbers, men would queue all day to get a place at the table. The quality of food had declined since Egyptian cooks had been employed and the standard of discipline had also slipped. With a total lack of consideration, groups who had been together for years were split up at the depot, first alphabetically according to their surnames and then according to their categories. Adding insult to injury, the 26 July edition of the *Springbok* carried a statement from the Director General of Demobilization, which indicated that his organization was unable to cope with the situation at home. He called for 500 volunteers, who would be taken home as top priority, to assist in the demobilization process. This created the impression that people 'back home' were not interested in the welfare of the returning troops.

The cinemas at Helwan were the flash points. Films were shown continuously, and some people would simply remain sitting until the next show began, while others vainly waited their turn. Fifteen minutes after the start of a film at the Colosseum theatre, someone stood up and shouted that there would be a meeting at 2130 hours at the Dooley Briscoe Memorial Ground. Bottles started flying and an Egyptian shop outside the cinema was looted.

A mile away, the canvas and rush walls of the Pall Mall open air theatre were also set alight. The soldiers then set fire to one of their own messes and looted the NAAFI store. When the Helwan fire brigade arrived to put out the fire, their hoses were cut. An appeal was made to the New Zealand fire brigade at Maadi, but their hoses were also cut. Apparently the Kiwis thought it was a big joke and sided with the rioters. The Royal Air Force and Tura fire brigades finally came to give aid and the fires were brought under control by 2315 hours. By destroying two cinemas and other facilities, the men had made their lot temporarily harder.

Colonel E.P. Hartshorn was sent to Helwan to investigate the matter. He was satisfied with the explanation that the event was triggered by the exploitation of the troops by one Mr Shafta, who had the concession to operate the open-air theatres along with a number of shops. Apparently, the cinema was set alight as a diversion and when Shaftas's employees ran to put out the fire, the shops were broken into and robbed of the day's takings. Hartshorn was given the assurance that it was "just a bit of justifiable burglary … nothing more criminal than over-exuberance on the part of the troops". They paid £11,000 to Mr Shafta in compensation, although he initially claimed £50,000.[370]

A court of inquiry implicated the Springbok Legion, as the riot had taken place while a delegation from the legion was in Helwan. Private R. Levin, a Springbok Legion organizer, was the main speaker on the night. However, the military authorities did not press the legion's role in the rioting. The South African government was horrified by the publicity and General Poole flew in

[370] E.P. Hartshorn, *Avenge Tobruk*, p. 206.

from Italy to address the troops. On first hearing of the riots, General Poole was uncertain if any division personnel had been involved, but expressed the "revulsion of feeling which is the inevitable outcome of wholesale indiscipline, whether [organized] or not, is utterly repugnant to an honourable body of soldiers".[371] All unit commanders were instructed to inform the men of the correct method of seeking redress for considered 'wrongs' and to instill in them pride in their unit and their country.[372]

Some changes were made, including the installation of a public address system to keep everybody up to date with the latest news, thereby putting an end to rumours. Outdoor cinema shows would be free and a tea garden was established at the swimming pool.

In July 1945, the GOC had expressed his satisfaction that behaviour of the troops in the Middle East was exemplary—except for saluting: "Apparently a number of men have decided that they will salute only officers of the 6th South African Armoured Division and none other. Such small-mindedness must be checked as it is not in keeping with our tradition."[373]

Cairo was accessible from Helwan and was not without its attractions. According to Sampie de Wet, the Union Defence Force Institutes Club in Cairo—called Ouma's Club—was superior to anything on offer to other ranks in Rome or Florence.

Back on the Italian Riviera, the Royal Natal Carbineers war diary persistently proclaimed "another day completely devoid of incident" or "a day of ordinary routine and sport" or simply, "NTR (nothing to report)". However, some incidents were recorded, including a brawl between DSR personnel and some English troops on 5 September. The previous month in Sanremo, some men of the Pretoria Regiment were escorting local ladies home after a dance when they were attacked "by a fairly large group of jealous Italian men". A reprisal party then visited the local partisan headquarters. One soldier, apparently a little more drunk than the rest, had brought along a Tommy gun, with which he shot an apparently innocent partisan through the leg.

---

371 DODAR, Box 578, WD, Headquarters South African Artillery 6th South African Armoured Division, Discipline 21/8/1945.

372 *Ibid.*

373 DODAR, Div Docs, Box 171, Discipline, 6th South African Armoured Division troops in Union, Headquarters South African Armoured Division, Union Defence Force, CMF, 23/7/1945.

At another dance, a younger member of the Royal Natal Carbineers had allegedly slapped a girl and was ejected from the hall. It was noticed that the "Italian lovelies showed a definite reluctance to dance with the soldiers", preferring to stick to their regular Italian boyfriends. A temporary curfew was introduced and pickets patrolled the town to keep the peace.

Farther east along the coast in Diano Marina, a more successful dance was held at the hotel where B Company was staying. Hodgson's letter of 9 September may have given his mother a hint that he had met someone he fancied: "… It was an excellent show, and we all thoroughly enjoyed ourselves. We had a very good local band installed, got the local baker to make some very good cakes, to which were added sandwiches and coffee; all this went down very well. The dance started a little after nine and went on until after two, so you can see that it went with a swing."

It appears that the Italian men were generally feeling neglected, and that the Carabinieri were particularly aggressive. On 28 August 1945, an officer of the Carabinieri saw an Italian woman, one Ernestina Peris, walking past his station at Villa Bonomi in Meina on Lake Maggiore, in the company of a South African soldier. Some words were exchanged and the Carabinieri fired a burst from his Sten gun. In his testimony, the Carabinieri claimed to have heard the woman scream for help; however, the woman testified that she was being rescued *from* the Carabinieri. Soon afterwards, the South African military police came to disarm the Carabinieri, one Nicola Gaeta. The incident was put down to a misunderstanding but it exemplifies the tensions which existed between the occupying force and the local police—above all, in a town which had seen the Nazis exterminate its Jewish population.

Yet another South African who experienced the wrath of the Italian security forces was Private C.J. Pettigrew of the Royal Durban Light Infantry. The incident took place at midnight on the night of 11/12 October when he was returning from a dance in the city of Piacenza, which is situated at a major crossroads between Bologna and Milan. According to Pettigrew's statement, he intervened in an argument between an Allied troop and Italian soldiers of the 155th Italian Artillery Regiment. The Italians produced revolvers and pointed them at Pettigrew and his companions. His statement went as follows: "I asked this Italian to put away his revolver and also asking him what his idea was pointing it at us. He put away the revolver and I, being annoyed at his previous actions, asked him if he thought we were a lot of Italians he was dealing with."

A shot went off, Pettigrew and his friends ran zig-zagging down the street, but got no more than 15 yards when a second shot was fired. "I felt a burning in my back and I knew I had been shot. I turned back toward the soldiers who had fired and halfway to them a Carabinieri took my arm and I went in the direction of the camp again." The British military police were quickly on the scene and the weapons confiscated, but they were harsh on the drunken South Africans. Pettigrew was taken to a dressing station and Private Rodger was placed under close arrest. From the inquiry, it was clear that the incident was caused by the Allied soldiers, who were all completely drunk, while Gunner Giuseppe Corgoglioniti had acted in self-defence.

A sensational story which made the headlines of a Milan newspaper was the alleged murder of two young women, in which a South African soldier, Private A. Venter—known to the locals as Alberto Ventori—was wrongly implicated. The newspaper reported that the bodies of 22-year-old Lelfa De-Regibus and 26-year-old Maria Accornere were found in a quarry, bound with wire and covered by a blanket. Venter had enjoyed a passionate four-month affair with Maria Accornere, who was described in the newspaper report as an "adventurous type"; according to the report, she had served four months in prison for theft during the last stages of the war and was now evading the law for a second offence.

The second woman, Lelfa De-Regibus, had apparently been living "rather a free life" while her husband was interned in France. According to the official translation of the article, "she did not reject the courtings of those belonging to the Black Brigade and the Germans and after liberation was seen on many occasions in the company of South African soldiers". On 29 August, the women left for Lake Maggiore, ostensibly to meet with Venter who had written a letter to Maria the day before: "Maria, I need to know when you are coming here, because you told me you wanted to come with me and you liked me a lot … I am very sad because I am sleeping badly since I no longer sleep on a bed but on the ground, and without you, but I am pleased because now you will come and I need you with me."[374]

It was established that the two women did visit Venter and another 'Q' Services soldier in Porto Valtravaglia, from where they left by train on the

374 DODAR, Div Docs, Box 168, Official translation of article in *Corriere d'Inormazione* on 7/10/1945.

morning of 7 September, the same day the report appeared in the paper. The murder had allegedly taken place on 2 October. Clearly, the two bodies did not belong to the women named in the article and the South Africans had nothing to do with the case. It was simply a case of outrageous journalism. Although a retraction was published the very next day, Venter felt his name had been slandered. The military authorities were also outraged at the negative publicity. Venter was, however, advised by a legal officer that he had little recourse because the negative publicity was as a result of his own indiscretion. The newspaper was threatened with suspension but got off with the retraction and an apology. No. 3 Detachment South African Rest Camp had been established at Villa Volpi on Route 13, four miles from Mestre and ten miles from Venice. It could accommodate 150 personnel and had extensive gardens. A number of more central hotels were taken over in the Lido area, about a mile from the main canal. Orchestras and canteens were provided in some of the establishments while the Lido's entertainment included two free cinemas for Allied troops, opera and various soldiers' clubs and cafés. In a move that was surely much appreciated, the military fixed the price of gondola rides while British welfare and the Union Defence Force Institutes organized sightseeing tours.

One night, after a dance at Venice's Pallazzo al Mare Hotel, a group of young British, American and South African officers went down to the Lido beach where they met up with some girls. There was some skinny dipping and a certain amount of 'horseplay'. Some couples disappeared into the changing cabins. Two night watchmen were patrolling up and down the area, flashing their torches, and the officers told these men to go away. One went to call the police and the other was allegedly assaulted. He laid a charge and was accompanied by the military police back to the hotel where he identified the culprit as a bearded South African officer, Lieutenant J.L.B. Venn of the 15th Field Regiment, South African Artillery. Statements were taken from several members of the group but nobody had seen an assault take place. One of the South African officers, who signed himself 'J. Thomas, Lieutenant', refused to make any statement about his movements on the night of 20 August 1945.

In August, the Royal Natal Carbineers was amalgamated with the recently arrived DSR, itself a composite regiment consisting of the Duke of Edinburgh's Own Rifles, the Transvaal Scottish and Rand Light Infantry. The unit was never more than 500 strong and had been formed to train recruits and feed them into the 6th South African Armoured Division.

The war came back to haunt the DSR on 9 August, when two Italian children playing in the vicinity were blown up on a landmine on the coastal road between Sanremo and Bordighera.

A month later, on the same stretch of coastal road, a ten-kilometre road race was held for members of the Royal Natal Carbineers battalion. It started just east of Bordighera and finished in the centre of Sanremo. One hundred troops participated and, as it was a team event, everyone was given a place. Hodgson, who came second in his company trials, was placed 20th in the battalion race. Lieutenant Arthur Newey, who had taken Hodgson with him as his batman to the battle of Monte Cassino and also climbed Mont Blanc with him, came first .

Meanwhile, Hodgson's company had moved to a resort town called Diano Marina, about six miles east of Imperia. They took over a hotel and three villas, purely for the purpose of resting. The orderly room staff of nine shared one sea-front villa:

> The nine are composed of the only working part of the company, the body of the company having finished all their duties; the nine consist of the Orderly Room staff: Yours truly with 'Mango' [John] Lyne (ex-Michaelhouse) and Alan Drysdale as assistant; the Quarter Staff: The Quarter Master John Massey, who used to be one of the tennis school in Jo'burg, and his two assistants, John Hobson (ex-St Andrew's) and Derrick Louch. The acting Sergeant-Major, Cpl Frank Kingwell, and finally the Medical Staff, Sgt Beal, and Cedrick Akerman; the latter is a fifth-year medical student at Wits University. The former is actually the Hygiene Sergeant. As you can see, we are a happy crowd. Alan, 'Mango' and myself share a room next door to a large airy Orderly Room. We have all got beds with sufficient furniture, electric light, bathroom next door and most important, we have nobody to worry us at all as we are about the nearest to being our own bosses as one can be in the Army. There is not much work, so we spend our time on a lovely beach; it is very convenient as we can change in our own room, and stroll out of our front door across the road and onto the beach. The rest of the company live about a hundred yards further up the road; we eat at this place in the dining room, so we are really doing things in style.

From here, the group made regular forays into Alassio where there was an American rest centre which was "extremely well organized as all American places are". Alassio was only 20 minutes by truck from Diano Marina, but the men once spent the night in an American rest hotel. The menu was excellent, consisting of cream soup, hamburgers with roast potatoes and green peas, hot rolls and pure butter, followed by pears and apple tart. At the American Red

Cross Club, one could indulge in large quantities of ice-cream and Coca-Cola at no charge. One could play tennis in Alassio and watch any number of films. There were not many films that Hodgson did not enjoy, but *Back to Bataan* was apparently awful and *The Horseshoe* with Betty Grable was just "above the average". By the end of August, Hodgson's worst fears regarding the repatriation scheme had been realized. The notion of missing another Christmas at home was too awful to contemplate—although he was in a better position than those languishing in Helwan:

> As you have no doubt heard, there is quite a big fuss regarding the slowing up of the repatriation scheme. About a week ago we had a talk from our colonel telling us how the position is at the moment. Instead of sending 400 a day by air, they are going to send 100; at the same time, there is going to be a certain amount of shipping available; during the course of next month, 5,000 will be sent home by sea, which is a pretty small number. It is obvious to all of us that the UDF's glorious repatriation scheme has failed horribly. Personally, I don't blame the fellows for making a fuss, though I must admit that some of them have gone a bit too far. If the UDF had not made all its rash promises of getting us home in four months, thus raising our hopes, things would have been more or less alright. Then again, they have gone back on their word as far as the demobilization is concerned, in that they said that no man would be released outside his category, thus preventing people in the Union who joined up at the same time as fellows here, would have no advantage but now they tell us that all the men in the Union are being demobbed. There is so much to be said for each side of this question, but no matter what the outcome, they have failed horribly in principle. But I suppose it is nothing new.

According to the Royal Natal Carbineers war diary, the month of September was "remarkable for the smooth uneventful manner in which days passed into weeks ..." Men who had been fretting about the delays in repatriation were now apparently content in their comfortable living conditions, with plenty of sport and recreation. There was opportunity for recreational as well as competitive swimming and hockey. A cricket match was played against a British regiment stationed in the town.

For a change, the Union Defence Force concert put on by the Swingboks was "not at all bad, and was remarkable for the complete absence of smut".[375] Hodgson wrote: "Last night, we went to a concert here in town; it was produced

[375] DODAR, WD, Box 647, Royl Natal Carbineers, 1–30 September 1945.

by a South African concert party; I must say, it was really an excellent show. In the past, I have always been disappointed by our concerts as they have been such terrible performances."

As time went by, the orderly room staff made improvements to their abode. They clubbed together and bought a good wireless which could "get anything". An extra speaker was attached to the wireless and placed on the opposite end of the house, so that the music could be heard throughout. They acquired a hot plate and could now cook the wide variety of food they bought at the local café. Sporting activities were taking on ridiculous proportions. Besides inter-company and inter-regimental matches, the company had its own cricket, hockey, swimming and tennis leagues. As company clerk, it was Hodgson's job to organize the fixtures, yet he still had plenty of time for basking in the sun. A feeling of apathy was beginning to take hold in the lazy atmosphere—especially when it came to letter writing. Even the dutiful Hodgson was finding it difficult to concentrate on his correspondence: "In the past couple of years, I have written so many letters to all of you, without seeing you, that I think I have just about had my fill of writing."

During the war years, Hodgson had also written to a girl at home, Jill Matthews. Now he hadn't heard from her for over a month. He wasn't concerned though, as he had not written to her either—and besides, at long last, he had found time for romance. The relationship had developed during the five blissful weeks at Diano Marina before Hodgson informed his mother in an uncharacteristically animated letter:

> About five weeks ago, I made the acquaintance of three sisters, at our first company dance which I told you about, I had noticed these three on quite a number of occasions prior to the dance as they used to swim at the same part of the beach as we used to. I noticed them mainly because they stood out from the usual Italian female—In passing, I will mention that I have had absolutely no time whatsoever for any Italian since I came to this country; so marked has my dislike for them been that it has become a very distinctive characteristic to all my friends. If anything, I have always despised them, and to be quite frank I still do, but that is besides the point—I have got many views on people and things that I did not have when I left in '43, but that will make interesting conversation when I get back. As I was saying, these three girls were outstanding from the rest, mainly because they appeared alive and full of fun, always laughing, joking and romping around, which one does not find in the average Italian. When the dance came, I made a point of making their acquaintance, so from that day onward we used to spend a good deal of time together on the beach, which was very pleasant as I had not spent much time in female company

since leaving Durban. By the way, these days I can speak Italian fairly fluently, even a little better than I could ever speak Afrikaans; it is mainly the environment which has helped me to pick it up so rapidly, as the majority that I have learned has been in the last five weeks. Well, the next company dance came along and I got in quick by inviting them to come along … After the second dance, they reciprocated by inviting us to tea one evening, a thing which I took an extremely good view of, because everything in the food line is extremely hard to come by, with the result that the stuff we consumed had to be bought on the black market. It was an excellent evening … they put on an excellent tea consisting of cheese sandwiches, Chelsea buns, and lovely sponge cake, all made by these three. Afterwards, we danced to an excellent selection of records, and chatted until midnight.

The three of them live in Milan but have a house down in Diano Marina, where they spend three months of every year. In Italy, one does not go to school during the summer months, the school year begins early in October and ends at the end of June, with one month at Christmas. First of all I must mention, as things turned out, they were not Italian but French which most probably accounts for why they appeared to be one above the rest. The eldest one is 23, her name is Mirella and she is going back to the university at Pavia [one of the oldest universities in Europe, situated 25 miles south of Milan] to finish her B.Chem. She acts as mother to the other two while they are all down here; the second one 'Dada' (a nick-name) is 21, she has completed her school life and helps her father in Milan, she is exceptionally good at sport; the third one [*illegible*] is 18, a girl with a marvellous sense of humour, and is the life and soul of most of our outings. The girls left to go back to Milan, the same day as we left to come here [Sanremo], so we ended off our stay there with a grand party; we invited the girls along to our house in the evening. You both would have laughed till your sides ached, to watch seven hulking soldiers preparing eats for the party that night. Well, I must say that we eventually put on a very good show, and it was a terrific spread. We had a vast amount of assorted sandwiches, stuffed eggs (these were marvellous—just like you make them at home), sardines on toast, cheese on toast, and we melted down some chocolate which we mixed with condensed milk, making a type of chocolate toffee which we spread onto Marie Biscuits, then lots of sweets and odds and ends from our parcels; then a terrific bowl of fruit salad made from fresh fruit, followed by coffee. The party was held in Alan's and my bedroom, as it was the most suitable, so quite a good deal of tidying and cleaning was involved. The whole evening ended up by the singing of songs. I seem to have written a lot about this but that I think is due to it being one of those milestones in our lives up here.

Thursday 27 September 1945 – Sunday 7 October 1945: Noli

What remained of the division began assembling on the coast west of Genoa. Remnants of the 1/6th Field Regiment moved to the seaside village of Noli on 27 September. The Imperial Light Horse/Kimberley Regiment (Infantry Group) was at the adjacent town of Sportorno. Others were based nearby in

Varicotti, a little farther along the coast toward Finale Ligure. At the end of September, the various companies of the Royal Natal Carbineers were brought back to Sanremo in what they were told would be their last move. In fact, they would move back to Alassio in mid-October.

Hodgson wrote that Sanremo was *the* place on the Italian Riviera, an Italian version of Nice, although not quite as grand. Although much smaller than Nice, Sanremo today is popular among the yachting fraternity and is also famous for its flower-growing industry. The regiment was split in two and accommodated in two luxury hotels which surpassed anything they had experienced during their time in the army. The hotels were run by a committee of other ranks. Hodgson was voted president and was responsible for hiring and firing civilian staff and keeping records of account. The management of the bar initially presented some problems, but it generated a reasonable profit once a system was in place. It seemed that repatriation was speeding up toward the end of September, possibly because large shiploads had recently left Egypt. The 'G' category soldiers were preparing to leave and there were now approximately 7,000 members of the division left in Italy. This number was to be reduced to 4,000 by the end of October. The Riviera was, and is, a holiday destination for tourists from all over Europe and hotel accommodation seems to have been plentiful. Hodgson had a lavishly furnished room with a balcony to himself, yet he still cherished hopes of being home for Christmas. He believed that he would be leaving by boat from Genoa in November. As it turned out, the port of embarkation would be Bari in the south:

> I feel certain that if I can get away from Italy before the end of this month, I will stand a very good chance; in fact, I think it just about a certainty that I will get home by Christmas. It is the first time that we have got so close to going home, and I am feeling quite excited on the strength of it. It is going to be a long and tiring trip home, but I am sure well worth it; when we leave the regiment, we go to Genoa by train, where we get onto a boat. This is a vast improvement on the old system where we used to go overland to Bari, which is a terrible trip. From Genoa, we go by boat to Alexandria, from whence we pass into Helwan. From there, there are three possible routes home. These days, the vast majority leave from Suez by boat, the rest go by transport plane and flying boat, the latter we only heard of for the first time today; they are an addition to the repatriation facilities. Then once we get to Pretoria or Durban, it will not be long—we have thought so much and waited so long for the time to go home, that now it is fairly close at hand, it is hard to believe.[376]

[376] J.B.Hodgson–M.V. & W.A. Hodgson, 6/10/1945.

Genoa was used as a port of embarkation for shipping the masses of vehicles and equipment back to the Union. A large vehicle concentration area was established at Arquata on the main line from Milan to Genoa, approximately 30 miles outside the latter, because it had no space large enough to accommodate 5,000 vehicles. A seven-foot wall was erected around the already partly enclosed area and a 24-hour guard was mounted. Nevertheless, if the guards were complicit, entire truckloads of supplies could be smuggled through the gates. A certain Private N. Pendergast was arrested for 'larceny' of a Dodge three-tonner and 770 pairs of boots. His defence was that he thought his two drinking companions from earlier that night had the necessary authority to take a vehicle from the park.

Equipment Park personnel were accommodated in blocks of flats in Genoa, 150 yards from the sea, where there were bathing facilities. Welfare facilities and pubs were plentiful. There were regular punch-ups in these establishments, owing to the fact that the area played host to sailors of all nationalities. In fact, Genoa was a regular fleshpot in terms of its sheer size and entertainment facilities. Clubs for the visiting troops included the St George, Club San Pietro in Viale d'Aosta and the WOs and Sergeants Club at Piazza de' Ferrari. Officers were accommodated at the Astoria Hotel in Via Serra.

One of the more fragile items sent to the Genoa Equipment Park for shipping was a window which had been removed from the chapel attached to the Voortrekker Club in Florence. The window had been bought with money from a fund fed by soldiers' contributions and it was decided by the chaplain, Padre Pearson, to send it to South Africa where it was to be erected in a place chosen by the quartermaster general.

Hodgson's letters from this period are filled with news of nothing but sport. Inter-company, inter-regimental and international hockey, cricket, tennis and swimming kept the men very fit, but if the strategy was to keep them too busy to brood about repatriation, it was not working.

With plenty of time for the beach and a good social life, Hodgson found little to complain about—although he sincerely hoped to be home for Christmas:

> On Tuesday we are moving again, this time we are going to a place called Alassio; the reason for this move is, now that the division has gone down so much in numbers they have decided to concentrate us in one place. Alassio is a very nice place, but I think it will have far too many troops in it for my liking; it is only 30 miles down the coast toward Genoa from here. All I am hoping for is that there will be some

> drafts as soon as we get there, and as ours is the next category to go, it might not be too long. As you know, we are in San Remo at the moment, which is the spot of the Italian Riviera, so we are very well off indeed. Our quarters are all we could wish for, and as far as food is concerned, I have never known soldiers to eat so well in the army. We have got an excellent Italian chef who does all our cooking and we have got waiters to do all the dishing up for us.

There had been no club catering specifically for South African soldiers in Alassio, however, in November the town's English community finally obtained permission to open the Union Club. It was a most welcome facility, offering doughnuts and coffee, but for most, it came too late.

Elements of the division were scattered across Italy and the world, however, the majority was concentrated on the Mediterranean coast between Rapallo and Sanremo. The remaining units were amalgamated and reorganized into groups, namely divisional headquarters, the artillery group, the armoured group, the infantry group, the engineers group, the signallers group and the services group.

Also amalgamated were the brigades, including 12/13 Infantry Brigade, and the regiments, including the Royal Durban Light Infantry/First City/Cape Town Highlanders/Witwateresrand Rifles/Regiment De la Rey and the Royal Natal Carbineers/DSR. Dissolved or amalgamated units were placed in 'suspended animation'; dis-established, they ceased to be operational and in the words of the historical recording officer were, Buddhist-fashion, "striving toward nothingness".[377] For Hodgson, the amalgamations meant catching up with old friends:

> I see quite a good deal of Cyril these days as he is in the same company as I am. Owing to all the people going home and so on, numbers have been lowered quite a good deal so A & B companies have combined. David Knight is also in the same company as myself.

The commanding officer had to make a character assessment of each man before a unit was dissolved and the men dispersed. Each certificate of discharge gave a reference of either: (i) exemplary, (ii) very good, (iii) good, (iv) fair, (v) indifferent, (vi) bad or (vii) very bad. Non-commissioned officers were exempt from receiving 'bad' or 'very bad' references. On the other hand, a soldier would be ineligible for an 'exemplary' grade if he had ever been convicted by a court

377 DODAR, WD, Box 598, Recording officer, letter from historical records section to Captain J.A.I. Agar-Hamilton, 10/7/1945.

martial, found guilty of drunkenness on duty or reduced to a lower grade or to the ranks for an offence. The grant of an 'exemplary' character reference was made at the discretion of the commanding officer and was reserved for soldiers whose conduct had set a high example. It wasn't just personnel and equipment that required repatriation; the accouterments of administration also had to be packed up. An order came through stating that certain records older than three years and which had no historical or documentary value were to be destroyed. A number of boards were convened to scrutinize documents and ensure that nothing of historical value was destroyed. Officers in transit at halfway camps and R&T depots were detailed to serve on the boards under the supervision of the historical section.

Roger Madden, the photographer for the historical recording section, was passing through Milan on his way home and realized that he had left some personal photographs in an ammunition box on the truck. His frame of mind is revealed in this note written to Lieutenant R.V. Davies, asking that they be sent to his home address:

> Here is the address NOTE WELL ... R.A. Madden ESQ. (take a look at that!!) 59 Majestic Mansions, Empire Road, Parktown, Johannesburg. Now you know where you can have a party when you get home. Tomorrow I start on the long journey home, so I will see you in Jo'burg next ... until then, Ciao.

While the division was dispersing, the various graves concentration units were trying to bring the bodies of all the dead to the designated Commonwealth cemeteries. Soldiers had been buried on the roadsides, vineyards and hilltops, as well as in existing cemeteries in places like Siena and Viterbo. An order had previously been issued forbidding the use of the the First World War cemeteries in the north of Italy. The bodies were exhumed by engineers and Italian labourers and in certain cases, dental surgeons made charts of the teeth for identification purposes. Bodies found in isolated and unregistered graves were naturally most problematic. French, Canadian and Royal Air Force dead were sent to their respective cemeteries. Much of the unit's activity was centred around the Bolsena cemetery which was established in November 1944 to accommodate the bodies brought in from the battlefields between Bolsena and Orvieto. The cemeteries at Foiano della Chiana and Castiglione and those attached to the hospitals were used mostly for direct burials. Two of the bodies brought into Bolsena had not been members of the 6th South African

Armoured Division. They had been escaped South African POWs who had lived for ten months with an Italian family in the out-of-the-way village of Farnese, west of Lake Bolsena. By day they wore civilian clothes and mixed with the German troops; by night, they wore uniforms and worked with the partisans. According to an article in the *Rand Daily Mail* of 19 June 1944, one of the men was found carrying a revolver and both were shot shortly before the Allies entered the town. The two were apparently extremely popular and their Italian benefactors paid for two marble tombstones to be erected in the village cemetery. When the graves concentration unit arrived to move the graves, the villagers at first refused to allow the bodies to leave the village. The newspaper report did not mention names, but with the detail given, it can be deduced that they were Sapper R. Carter of Springs and Private F.J. Crinall of the Rand Light Infantry. Both were killed on 6 June 1944 and are buried in adjoining graves in the Commonwealth cemetery at Bolsena.

Corporal Percy Renou of 8 Field Squadron was one of the 63 members of South Africa's three engineer squadrons who became casualties during June 1944.[378] On 27 June, Renou had rushed to the aid of Sapper A.H. Meiring when he was blown up by a mine. He was buried where he fell, near the power station at Chiusi. Renou had apparently harboured a lifelong ambition to visit Assisi. He had studied the works of St Francis and read a great deal about the city. In his last letter to his wife, he wrote that his next letter would be sent from the city of his dreams. Instead, on 3 July she received a telegram from war records, saying that he had been killed in action. Some years later, war records informed Mrs Renou that 13 commonwealth graves at Chiusi had to be moved, as they were too close to the main road. It had been decided to transfer eleven of them to Castiglione, and two—those of her husband and Sapper Meiering—to Assisi.[379]

Monday 8 October 1945 – Friday 19 October 1945: Finale

Fittingly, the final concentration point was at Finale Ligure (as opposed to Finale Emilia, where the last big battle took place). Bourhill and Johnston of the Artillery Group and Hodgson of the Infantry Group gravitated toward Finale and Alassio. Company-sized groups found accommodation in smaller

378 N. Orpen. *Victory in Italy*, p. 115; including 8 and 12 Field Squadrons and 17 Park Squadron, 42 Field Company, RE and 622 Field Squadron, RE.

379 K. Anderson, *Nine flames*, p. 207; Some graves from Chiusi were moved to Orvieto.

towns nearby such as Laigueglia, where the entrance to the once elegant railway station is only a few yards from the main beach. Interest in sport was wearing off now that the men had competed against every team imaginable. A divisional road race was to be held at Genoa but nobody was eager to travel the two and a half hours in the back of a truck to get there. Sport was now restricted, partly because of the large number of troops congregated in the area and partly because there were only two playing fields available around Alassio. On the other hand, with all the other regiments nearby, it was possible for the Carbineers to play against their old rivals in the Infantry Group, the Natal Mounted Rifles.

The never-ending stream of Hollywood films had also slowed. An Italian translation of the film *Roberta*, starring Irene Dunne, Fred Astaire and Ginger Rogers, was showing at the cinema in Alassio.

The early mornings and evenings were starting to get a bit chilly but the approaching winter was not a big concern this time as the coast is so much warmer than the mountains:

> I have not done any swimming since we left Diano Marina. At the moment the water is a bit on the cold side, and the sun is not quite hot enough—at San Remo, it was hot enough but we lived quite a long way from the sea which made things difficult. I sincerely hope that the next time I do any swimming, it will be in the Indian Ocean.[380]

Hodgson remarked that whoever gave the repatriation system its name was "labouring under a misapprehension" because it did everything but repatriate. Its failings were now blamed on bad weather and the consequent poor flying conditions. With organized sport at a low ebb, there was nothing to do but wait. An education wing was created at Alassio under the direction of Lieutenant John Oxley, offering individual lectures and a course on South African affairs:

> So at the moment I am trying to occupy my time as best I can, by putting it to the best advantage. With our move to Alassio as part of the divisional concentration, sport has dropped very considerably; this has been brought about by bad weather conditions during the last week, namely rain. So we have had to look for other things to keep us occupied. For myself, I have gone on a ten-day concentrated 'South African Affairs Course' at the army educational school in Alassio. It is run by the information section of the UDF ... There are 40 of us on the course from the division; David Knight is on the course with me ... All the lecturers are very capable

[380] J.B. Hodgson–M.V. Hodgson, 19/10/1945.

> people, and are highly qualified in their different subjects. When this is all over I am quite certain that I will know infinitely more about South Africa than I ever did before. Among the subjects we are delving into are the following: (i) An outline of South African History (ii) The Political Animal (iii) Basic Economics (iv) Forms of Government (v) SA Agriculture (vi) SA Industry (vii) Labour in South Africa (viii) The Reserves (ix) Colour Problems (x) SA Governmental Machinery (xi) The Provincial System (xii) SA Politics (xiii) Health in South Africa (xiv) Propaganda and the Press (xv) Education (xvi) SA Today and Italy Today. Quite a large syllabus for ten days so they are working us quite hard. After each lecture, the subject is put up for discussion, and is a real education in itself to take part in, one gets many views and outlooks on the subjects as many of the students are very clever and highly qualified men. In a couple of days, we are going to be formed into small groups, each being given a different current problem in South Africa, and it is the jobs of the respective groups to draw up a statement with the aid of all the government books and information available at the school at our disposal. These statements will be read out at the end of the course and openly discussed. I will let you know how it goes when we have finished.[381]

The big news in *La Stella d'Oro* of Sunday 21 October was about housing for ex-soldiers and inflation in South Africa. Judging from the price of the magazine—which increased from 10 lire on 15 July to 15 lire two weeks later and cost 20 lire by October—it seems that the publishers either underestimated the cost of production or that inflation was rampant in Italy as well. A report in the magazine revealed that the South African government had put a ceiling on clothing prices; a shortage of textiles meant that the price of a suit, for example, had soared from £17 to £25 during the year to October. The market for various products had been stimulated by soldiers returning to the Union and prices were skyrocketing. Hodgson had foreseen this problem back in July and as a precaution sent home an 'allotment' of £30 for his mother to invest in some clothes—provided he could get hold of a tape measure to take his measurements: "I haven't the faintest idea of what I am going to do when I get back about clothes; I wonder if there will be much left when I get back with the thousands of returned soldiers equipping themselves, and with so many getting home before me, it is going to be a bit of a grim problem."

Still only 20, Hodgson had grown half an inch and stood five feet ten and a half inches. With a waist of 33 inches and chest of 36 inches, his weight varied between 165 and 170 pounds. He had filled out somewhat and was concerned

381 J.B. Hodgson–W.A. Hodgson, 23/10/1945.

that none of his civilian clothes would fit him, not even his Old Boys blazer. The only illness which he had suffered was a slight cold the previous September; the only injury, a sprained ankle. The same cannot be said for the rest of No. 7 Platoon. Hodgson sent a photograph of the platoon home for safekeeping:

> The photograph enclosed is of the original platoon, taken a couple of days after we landed in Italy. There are not many of the fellows with us here today unfortunately—a fair number was killed during the campaign and quite a large number are at home or in hospital. After you have looked at it, I trust you will put it away with the other odds and ends that I have sent down.

A few members of the division were demobbed outside the Union, in Italy. Some put in for leave in England, their motivation being that it would be extremely difficult to find passage to England from South Africa. The English had opened their doors to any Empire troops, including South Africans, and especially returning POWs, who were mainly repatriated through Britain.

Colonel C.H.S. Runge, who had been headmaster of St John's College in the early 1930s and had been in charge of the rest camps in Italy, now headed up the hospitality for POWs in Great Britain. His office at South Africa House in Trafalgar Square was swamped with letters from Britons offering accommodation to any South Africans in transit.

Systems for handling returning POWs were in place as early as August 1944. Some were even given the opportunity of on-the-job training in England.

Joel 'Koffie' Resnek, medical officer of the Royal Natal Carbineers, was also now in the UK, working at the 9th South African General Hospital where his duties included caring for repatriated POWs.

Nursing Sister Olga Norton had been serving with 8 Casualty Clearing Station and was released to go to England for the investiture of her brother, Gerard Norton, with the VC. The unit's war diary describes her as "the ideal type of Sister for a CCS—young and cheerful with great stamina which enables her to stand up to any amount of heavy work". Virtually all the other nurses at 8 Casualty Clearing Station also applied to be sent to England for their discharge from the service.

An out-of-the-ordinary application was made by Lieutenant W.L. Ridl MC to have his mother repatriated to South Africa from Italy. Mr and Mrs Ridl had left Durban on a European tour in 1939 and were in Germany when the war broke out. A German official decided that they would be good hostages in the event of South Africa entering the war and were refused permission to leave Germany. Eventually, they were granted permission to travel to Austria from where they were hoping to escape into Switzerland. Unfortunately they met with an accident; Mr Ridl was killed and Mrs Ridl seriously injured. An Austrian doctor took Mrs Ridl under his care and she was traced through the Red Cross. Lieutenant Ridl brought her back to Italy where the divisional headquarters strongly supported the application, as Mrs Ridl was "an aged woman and [had] suffered grievously under the Nazi regime". Lieutenant Ridl had been wounded while serving with 12th Field Squadron on 18 April 1945. He was a star rugby player for the division.

Men wanting to send souvenirs home first had to have their parcels approved by an officer. However, they devised ingenious ways of smuggling out articles, from paintings to German Lugers. Frank Mundel was especially adept at tricking his commanding officer into signing off packages, which would be reopened and packed with contraband before being posted to the Union. The smuggling of artworks out of Italy was a big concern. A document entitled 'Preservation of works of art in Italy' had been written in May 1944 in order to make everyone aware of their responsibility with regard to the country's artistic heritage and to refrain from looting as the Germans had. The document contained a short history of art in general, its value and uses as well as a request to treat all art, including old buildings and books, with respect. According to the document, the Germans had removed works of art by the truckload, partly because they felt they should be supreme in everything, including art, and partly as insurance against the day of reckoning.

Gunner N.W. Smith was a late arrival in Italy. The Italians nicknamed him' Alberto' as they were unable to pronounce 'Norman'. He had enlisted immediately after completing his schooling at Nourse Mines near Denver in Johannesburg. After eight months in training and in transit, he was posted to the 1/6th Field Regiment on 15 May 1945. Smith's duties included fetching rations for the regiment and transporting troops from one end of Italy to the other. Some of these were South Africans who had married Italian women and were returning home with their new wives.

The 'Q' companies were kept busy during the repatriation process transporting men, and sometimes their wives, from Monza to Foggia, a distance of 900 miles. The trucks travelled an average distance of around 10,000 miles each month. The transit depot at Foggia became more and more overcrowded and eventually, attempts were made to turn away new arrivals. Newly marrieds had to deal with more than the usual amount of red tape:

> Every member, rept every member, who has already contracted a marriage in Italy with civilian female and service woman of other Allied forces, must immediately, rept immediately, obtain visas and passports for their wives, irrespective of their groups or physical condition of wife, provided wife fit to stand road travel to nearest consulate.[382]

Due to a lack of facilities, only a handful of the 49 men who had recently married Italian women and were waiting to be evacuated in December 1945 could be accommodated in Bari. The other wives would have to remain at their fixed abodes until departure. A further 24 couples had married without approval; they were notified that the men would be evacuated in the normal way and that the rear division headquarters would not take responsibility for the evacuation of their wives. In the formal application to marry, the applicant's commanding officer was required to make an assessment of the couple, their backgrounds, education, compatibility, religious differences and their ability to become useful, productive citizens of South Africa. Legend has it that one soldier smuggled his girlfriend onto the troopship bound for Egypt, causing much consternation at roll call. There were almost certainly cases where men in the higher repatriation categories waived their right of early return because of emotional ties.

Elena van Praag was a 25-year-old woman of Dutch-Jewish descent. She had grown up in Genoa where her father was a ship owner. The family had been interned in an apartment in the Palazzo della Gherardesca—today the Four Seasons Hotel—in Florence, with German soldiers camped in the shady eleven-acre garden. The van Praags hosted a South African officer at their apartment after the Allied occupation of Florence. Elena was irritated at finding yet another stranger at the breakfast table, but found herself captivated by his eyes. The object of her adoration, Captain George Jennings, had been an assistant to General Poole and was able to wangle her a berth on a liberty ship transporting tanks to Durban in October 1945. She was the only female passenger, and spent her days smoking and playing cards under the shade of the vehicles on deck.

382 DODAR, Div Docs, Box 171, File 6ADE/1/1/3, Move Order, 23/11/1945, Message from Rear 6th South African Armoured Division.

When she disembarked in Durban with her 13 pieces of luggage and pasta-making machine, she was informed by an immigration official that her papers were not in order and she would be repatriated within a week. Back in Italy, she worked for the Allies while they prepared for departure. It would be two more years before George was finally able to bring Elena home. The Union didn't only gain women; it lost some too. Two hundred and eighty South African women married Royal Air Force men in the Union and returned with them to the UK. When they arrived at Waterloo Station from Southampton, "anxious mothers-in-law were more numerous than serving husbands".[383] It is not known how many South Africans stayed on in Italy and lived there for the rest of their lives. Likely candidates are escaped POWs who had become integrated in Italian communities. Some married into the families who hid them and produced offspring in Italy. Two proud fathers who were photographed with their new families by the public relations team were Gunner W.J. Swanepoel of Klerksdorp and M.J. Calitz of Cape Town.

The fate of prisoners who escaped from Union Defence Force detention centres remains unknown. Private Alexander M18081V of the Cape Corps, attached to the 6th South African Armoured Division Reserve Group, was serving a sentence of nine months' hard labour when he escaped on 19 September 1945. In November, two prisoners were being escorted from Rome to the Equipment Park at Genoa for evacuation to the Middle East when they jumped off the vehicle at a bridge near Pisa. The escort was unarmed and the prisoners were not handcuffed, as per instructions. Gunner A.S. Botha was quickly recaptured but the other prisoner, Private G.S. Cloete, disappeared.

Within a few months, the 6th South African Armoured Division would be gone from Italy, although some Union Defence Force personnel were left behind to wrap things up.

Saturday 20 October 1945 – Friday 4 January 1946: Foggia, Helwan

Politics and sport were, as ever, the main news items in *La Stella d'Oro* of 4 November 1945. The magazine proclaimed the 'Indian problem' in Natal to be a 'European problem', considering it wasn't the Indians who were complaining about living next to whites. An extract from an article titled 'Way Down South' illustrates how the more things change, the more they stay the

383 DODAR, WD, Box 726, AES, PEP, Emigration! 20/8/1945.

same: "News from the Union these days seems to fit into a pattern of reform and reconstruction, carried out amid a whirl of words and recriminations, but carried out nevertheless."[384] On the sports pages, a rugby match between the Springboks and the Kiwis was billed as the game of the century. The 'Springbok' team staying at the Elizabeth Hotel in Rapallo consisted of Swanson, Freylinck, Moss, Hearne, Kingwell, Stewart, Youngleston, Holton, Duvenhage (captain), Greef, Hannes Morkel, Botha, Fry, Swartz and J.C. Morkel. Although the match was played in Rapallo, the "account and results were being eagerly awaited in the Union".[385] Springbok and Kiwi supporters travelled to see the match from all over northern Italy. The 6th South African Armoured Division thrashed the 2nd New Zealand Division 30–5. A return match was played in Florence on 20 November. This time, the 'Springboks' won by 23 points to three, after being three down at half time. The military police always maintained a strong presence at such events, especially around the bars and in the parking area, where theft was a common occurence. Trials for a divisional hockey team were taking place up and down the coast, as an international match was being planned against the New Zealand division. There were many Old Hiltonians present at the trials which made for great festivity and jocularity. Hodgson was chosen for the squad of twenty-five. They would travel to Finale and from there, an 'Alassio' side would be chosen to play in the Rapallo area where divisional headquarters was now situated. Hodgson did not expect to be chosen as there were some expert players around. However, the international was later cancelled.

Some found an escape from boredom by climbing the frozen peaks of the interior. A cross-country race at Rapallo generated great interest.

As far as Hodgson was concerned, "It is much the same old story; all waiting to hear the word that will send us on our way home—as I have already said, it looks a long way off at the moment, but nevertheless, we just hang on, on the off chance that some sudden spurt will take place, and we will find ourselves on our way". Nevertheless, he made the most of things by taking a maths course at the education centre in Alassio. It was first year university level and as his matric maths was a bit rusty, Hodgson found it challenging:

> At the moment I am on a Maths course which keeps me busy during the mornings, as well as a good bit of the afternoons and evenings, as we get a great deal of 'prep'

[384] *La Stella d'Oro*, 3 (3) 4/11/1945, p. 4.

[385] *Ibid*, p.8.

> to do. I am enjoying the course as it is good to get down to some useful hard work for a change. Another added advantage is that all the people on course don't have to do guard's and other duties which is a great concession, as such things are a terrific nuisance these days.[386]

Among the last to leave Italy in November 1945 were the Union Defence Force entertainment groups: the Amuselliers, Troopadours and Swingboks. They had entertained troops of all nationalities across the country. One of the last ENSA performances at Alassio was a show called *All for Fun* which was "fairly good with plenty of laughs".

A new batch of films had arrived and in Hodgson's opinion, the pick of the bunch was *Nobody's Darling* with Preston Foster, Gail Patrick and the Wilde twins.[387] If there was anything to mar the men's happiness, apart from homesickness, it was the continued duties and military discipline. Guard duty involved mainly looking after the stores and afforded an opportunity to take care of correspondence. Hodgson was in a reflective mood when he wrote:

> Looking out of the window in front of me, I can see right out to sea—it is a very calm day, with hardly a ripple on the surface; there are absolutely no breakers at all. The sun is not very far up and it gives the whole surface a silvery grey colour. The last of the fishermen have just come in with their small boats loaded with fish—all of a very small variety. It is going to be a perfect day, without a cloud in the sky—one would never dream that it was winter here, but all one has to do to verify the fact is to go a few miles inland, getting out of the coastal belt which is about three miles wide on an average, then one will soon see and feel what it is like, as it is bitterly cold with plenty of snow. The contrast is terrific. Here I am sitting without any winter clothes on at all, just my summer kit, and I don't feel at all cold.

There were heavy rains along the coast throughout November, causing landslides which blocked the tunnels and restricted movement. Repatriation continued at a trickle. General Poole made an appearance at Alassio to reassure the men that they had not been forgotten; he estimated that approximately half of the 'G' category would be home for Christmas. Hodgson had finally given up on that dream:

> As you can see, the position is hopeless as far as we are concerned. All I can say is that I hope a special effort will be made to get all university students home in time

386 J.B. Hodgson–M.V. Hodgson, 20/11/1945.

387 *Ibid.*

> to let them have a short holiday before the opening of the first term. By the look of things at the moment, it is going to be a close shave whether we get back for the start of the university year or not. At the moment, the general trend of opinion is the 'H' category will still be in this country for Christmas. Honestly, it's hard to believe and utterly impossible to understand how they can be so slow about the whole business, after the proposed marvellous schemes—I'm sure more could have been done than has been done.

Officers, non-commissioned officers and those occupying administrative posts were not eligible for early release. Many conflicting orders and proclamations relating to the repatriation process were issued. On 23 November 1945, an order came through from divisional headquarters at the Bristol Hotel in Rapallo, stating that due to the repatriation of air crew, the South African Air Force would soon be unable to continue transporting army personnel from Italy to the Middle East by air. Therefore, the fullest possible use had to be made of all available aircraft. It was envisaged that all division and non-division personnel would be out of Italy by 31 December 1945.

At the same time, Hodgson was informed by an 'official source' that from now on, there were no ships available for the repatriation. He was satisfied with the reasons given: "There will be the regular airlift only. The reason for this is a good one. All available ships are needed in the Far East for the repatriation of Allied prisoners of war, the majority of which are in a bad state of health." According to the source, there were still 40,000 South Africans in the Middle East and Italy, and the authorities would be able to repatriate 8,000 per month. Hodgson was sceptical as usual, but calculated that his category lay between 9,500 and 10,500—in which case he would get home in January, just before his 21st birthday. It was probably the looming shortage of air crews that prompted the sudden announcement that, from the beginning of December, every South African in Italy would be moved to Egypt. Care was taken to stress that this did not mean a change in the schedule of repatriation to the Union. Immediately, drafts began to leave for the south of Italy. Hodgson was scheduled to leave a week into December:

> I am really looking forward to this move, for three main reasons: Firstly, for many reasons, I want to get out of this country; granted, I have had many pleasant days here, but I have just about had as much of the confounded Italians as I can stand, as well as the bad atmosphere here. Secondly, I feel sure that this move in some way or other is bound to speed up our return to some small extent. Thirdly, as I have said, it is a step in the right direction.

Being in an earlier release group, Bourhill had flown from Foggia to Helwan on 20 October 1945. In retrospect, he would have been better off staying in Italy for as long as possible. For those travelling by road, the trucks went from the advanced transit camp at Monza Autodrome to Foggia or Bari. From there, any available aircraft was grabbed for the short haul to Helwan. Many travelled by Liberator bomber, which at this time of year was like flying in a deep freeze. Soon after take-off, the snow-covered slopes of Mount Etna in Sicily could be seen through the frosted windows. Bourhill travelled in the tail gunner's seat which was simply a hard wooden plank.

There was much excitement when Hodgson received his marching orders, although he had no idea how long the journey would take or which route it would follow. The last couple of days were spent packing up, sorting and fixing. He was put in charge of a draft of 30 men from his company who joined up with the rest of the draft, totalling 150, at the first staging area at Spotorno, about 20 miles east of Alassio. Over the coming days, he would travel by train down the Adriatic east coast, a part of Italy which he had not yet seen:

> David Knight and I are on the same draft with quite a few friends as we all joined up at roughly the same time. Cyril was at the transit camp where he is one of the staff, so we had a good chat to him. We left there at seven the next morning by truck for another transit camp at Novara which is about 50 kilometres due west of Milan. It was a pleasant but rather dusty trip; our morale went right up though when we found out that we could have hot showers—this latter camp was full of UK troops back from leave in England. We were all struck by the exceptionally good way in which the camp was organized; the food was excellent but we were all very shaken at supper when each was dished out with a little parcel of fruit and sausage rolls to take on the train—we usually get 'Bully' and army biscuits from the UDF but the big surprise came when we were told that this was just to see us through the night as we would get meals at halts on the way. We got into our south-bound train at eight that evening—the train journey itself was very uncomfortable as we had third class day coaches for two nights and a day, but as we had expected to be put into cattle trucks, we were quite pleased. We passed through Bologna at three o'clock on the first morning. Passing from there, we went through St Pietro, Faenza, and Forli, reaching Rimini soon after ten, when we got off and had a first-class breakfast. (All the train journey and feeding was organized by the Imperial Forces, which accounts for everything running so smoothly.) From there, we went straight through to Ancona, where we had lunch. All the way down, it was very overcast with quite a good deal of rain falling. Our next halt was Pescara for supper, which came up to our best expectations. Sleeping, as you can well imagine, was a rather difficult task—David and I shared a hard seat for two so we slept by leaning on each other in turn, others used the floor and luggage racks. The second night, we did not

> get any more sleep than the first, but this was cut short when we got off the train at Foggia at half past four in the morning. Trucks brought us here to the transit camp where we now sit. The bad weather has held up the passage of men over to Egypt with the result that this camp is terribly overcrowded, so much so, that we have not even got tents to live in. Ever since we have been here, we have lived in the UDFI hut. It is very inconvenient as the place is crowded out during the day. There are an enormous amount of fellows here that I know and have not seen for quite a time—many Hilton fellows and other acquaintances.

The Union Defence Force transit camp at Foggia was the last Italian staging point on the journey home. It had also been the first airfield to be captured in the south of Italy. The camp could accommodate nearly 3,000 troops and was set in pleasant surroundings a few miles from the town. There was a four-to-six-day wait for a flight to the Middle East. To kill time, the troops played football, swam in the river and fiddled with their kit to bring it down to the maximum weight of 40 pounds. There were visits to the doctor and the dentist and copious forms to be filled in. Every day at 1400 hours, *Sarie Marais* would be played over the loudspeaker—this being the signal to form up for the 'sweat parade' where the details of the following day's flights would be announced.

When the time came to leave, the man's name would be read out and he would dash to get his kit and report to the depot where a last-minute check was made of his papers. Apparently, there were no late reports at the depot. Two hundred passengers made the six-and-a-half-hour trip every day.

Unsurprisingly, Mundel was reluctant to board his plane after he had just witnessed another DC-3 skid off the runway. The passengers sitting on benches down the sides of the plane could see the movement of the rudder cables, which did nothing to allay the fear of flying. Even though it was safer to go by sea, men usually preferred the faster option. Movement orders stated that baggage for those travelling by sea was restricted to what could be carried up the gangway. Passengers carried rations for one day and were responsible for filling their water bottles before departure. Items prohibited on board included alcohol, live ammunition and pet animals. Surplus kit was sent separately.

Saturday 5 January 1946 – Tuesday 8 January 1946: Shuttle service, home

Hodgson spent six days at the cramped transit camp in Foggia, waiting and hoping. All entry into the camp was stopped shortly after his arrival as there was no evacuation.

On 12 December, news came through that a ship draft was needed. Most preferred to wait for the planes which were rumoured to be leaving imminently and as a result Hodgson got onto the sea draft. As he left for Taranto at 0400 hours the next morning, his friends Peter and Burt called out, "We'll be waiting for you in Egypt when your ship reaches the Middle East." As it turned out, the aspirant flyers were also obliged to travel by sea and arrived sheepishly at Helwan some days after Hodgson.

A number of factors made this a special voyage, aside from the fact that it was travelling in the right direction:

> After a grim journey we duly embarked by lighter (one does not realize how lucky South Africa is in having good harbours) after the usual fuss and nonsense. The name of the ship was the 'Otranto' of the Orient Line, of the 20,000-ton class; we were very fortunate here as we were the first people to travel on it since it was recently refitted in England. As usual, we had the customary crowded troop decks, but this time we were fairly fortunate in that we were only one deck below the waterline; also our living quarters did not reach their usual high temperature; this was due to it being our first sea trip during the winter. In peacetime, the ship used to carry 150 passengers; it was fitted out to carry 4,400 troops—we were also fortunate in that the full quota of troops were not aboard. I will mention here that it was the best sea trip that I have done in the army, by a very large margin; and I do not expect to be nearly as lucky if I have to do another voyage. All the other troops on board were New Zealanders on their way home—I have always maintained, and since that voyage, always will maintain, that the 'Kiwis' are the best men I have ever met. It was in a way, a special trip for them—as I have said, they were all on their way home; a good deal of those on board were members of the Royal NZ Air Force, of whom a fair number had got married while in England, and they all had their wives on board, taking them out to New Zealand. In all, there were 270 wives and 70 babies on board. Ninety per cent of the latter were below the age of three years, the remainder being between the ages of three and six years. It was really a most marvellous sight to see all the little babies on board. We sailed from Taranto at ten o'clock on the evening of the 13th of December; one always hears that sailors never leave port on the 13th of the month, but I must say that I have never had such a pleasant and successful trip. We came across the Med in two and a half days, entering Port Said early on Dingaan's Day. We did not stop and get off there as expected; instead, we spent Dingaan's Day sailing down the Suez Canal which was a most marvellous experience. It felt quite strange sitting on deck looking out each side and seeing nothing but sand. The whole canal came up to my fullest expectations, and I was not at all disappointed in it as I have been with some things (notably: Italy).!?! [388]

[388] J.B. Hodgson–M.V. & W.A. Hodgson, 20/12/1945.

The *Otranto* had to pull over to the side from time to time as it sailed down the Suez Canal, to allow other ships to pass. During the night they reached Lake Timsah, a natural lake through which the canal passes, and saw the enchanting lights of Ismailia on the northern bank of the lake. The next morning they woke to find themselves steaming slowly into Tewfik, which is the port of Suez. Having had bad experiences in the past, the men were pleasantly surprised to find that a train was waiting for them and although the carriages were third class, at least they were not cattle trucks. It took a couple of hours before the train got moving and it finally reached Helwan in the early hours of the morning.[389]

It had been 21 months since Hodgson had last seen Helwan. Physically, the camp had not changed much, although conditions were somewhat improved. Best of all, it was a meeting place for groups of friends who had not seen each other for years. The authorities had also learned not to split up closely knit groups. David Knight and Hodgson had been together since they completed a wireless and Morse code course here in Helwan almost exactly two years before:

> You wait till you meet David [Knight]; you will get the chance because with yours and Dad's permission he will come up and stay with us for a week or two at a time, the same as I will be doing with him. I have never really told you much about him so I will do so now as he is the best friend that I have ever had, and I doubt I will ever have a better one. He is six months older than I and about the same build—he went to Bishops where he was second prefect when he left in '42—he joined the army about a month before I did, and we have been everywhere together. He lives down at the Cape at Wynberg … there are also many other fellows that you and Dad will have to meet when I get back.

Gunner Norman Smith heard that his school friend Gerald Tarr was also in transit and arranged to meet him at the NAAFI in Cairo on 8 January. However, he did not arrive for the reunion and when Smith returned to his quarters at the YMCA, there was a note waiting for him at reception, informing him that his friend had been run over by a tram.

Tarr had served in the South African Air Force and is buried in the Commonwealth war cemetery at Heliopolis in 'New Cairo'. The expansive lawns of the cemetery are an oasis in the midst of the surrounding concrete and sand. The words inscribed on his gravestone, 'Some day we'll understand,'

389 *Ibid.*

were inspired by the question asked by so many: "Why?" At Christmas, a lucky few were taken on tours to the Holy Land. Rather than staying in Helwan over the festive season, Hodgson and Knight organized to be on leave in Alexandria where they could escape the army for a while, play some squash and tennis and take in a few shows. Hodgson warned his parents that he would not be writing again until the new year and hoped never to have the opportunity to write another letter. Hodgson was reaching the end of his tether. Judging from the last of the more than 350 letters he wrote to his family, at least some of his natural optimism was finally being squeezed out of him by the inefficiency of the repatriation scheme:

> I have not got much about which to moan. The only thing is, we have got to try and pass the time as best we can until it becomes our turn to leave—Hell!! How I wish it were tomorrow—but I am afraid I will not get back until somewhere during the first half of February, unless there is a good increase in drafts. We get figures issued every day of the number of people who have left, and the number who are still in camp. These numbers are apt to be a little misleading as one does not know how many of the different categories there are outside the camp, as well as the SAAF personnel. But my rough calculations put it at about 3,500 Europeans to leave before I go—which puts me in the first week of February.
>
> Since our arrival here early on the morning of the 18th and this evening, quite a good deal has happened. At the moment, I am sitting in the R&T Depot at Helwan, which means that I am just waiting until such time as I am put on a draft for repatriation, which I am afraid will not be for some weeks yet, but I will come to all that later. Again I have been filling in lashings of forms and as I am in the group that has employment to go back to, I have filled in all my demobilization papers, which means that when I get back I will be sent straight home from the airport or docks with some of the money that is due to me and start straight in on my leave.

Bourhill resumed his journey by air after an excruciating three months at Helwan, departing from Almaza aerodrome on 4 January 1946 and arriving home four days later. The total flying distance from Cairo to Pretoria was 4,045 miles, although this could vary by 200 to 300 miles depending on the route taken. The Dakota shuttle service consisted of many planes, sometimes two or three coming in to land at once. The usual stops were at Cairo, Wadi Halfa, Khartoum, Kisumu, Tabora, Ndola on the Northern Rhodesian Copperbelt (where the plane would remain overnight for refuelling), Bulawayo and, finally, Pretoria. Passengers were housed in tents on overnight stops. Khartoum was uncomfortably hot and humid but an open-air variety concert was occasionally presented. Tabora was a small post on the railway line running from Dar es Salaam westward to the shores of Lake Tanganyika. It nevertheless boasted a medium-sized establishment, the Park Hotel, where tea and scones were served on the wide verandah and in the lush tropical gardens. It bore the closest resemblance to South Africa than any other destination the soldiers had seen for years. On landing in Bulawayo, passengers in transit would travel by bus to the Central Hotel. The journey ended here for Rhodesian personnel.

Alternative stops included Malakal in the Sudan, then Juba, Nairobi, Kasama, Lusaka and Pietersburg, sometimes stopping overnight, sometimes just for tea and scones. The ladies of Lusaka were famous for the magnificent eats provided to the shuttle service. At Bulawayo, the WVS—the Women's Volunteers Service, the Rhodesian equivalent of the SAWAS—were equally generous. The same could not be said for Nairobi, which did not even have proper toilet facilities.

Some were lucky enough to travel home in the Sunderland Flying Boat which took off from Bitter Lake north of Suez, landing on the Nile at Khartoum, followed by stops on the lake at Kisumu and the sea at Beira, and finally Durban. Many of the passengers had never flown before and enjoyed their first view of their continent from the air. Flying low, they saw Mount Kilimanjaro, lakes and vast expanses of uninhabited land. Coming in to land at Zwartkop aerodrome outside Pretoria, returning soldiers caught sight of the almost completed Voortrekker Monument. Some wondered how the expense could be justified, given the recent war effort. It was a glimpse into the South Africa of the future.

Bourhill was eternally grateful to be under familiar African skies, although after three years of sleeping outdoors he had come to know the foreign stars of the northern hemisphere. Perhaps overwhelmed at being back on South African soil, or simply relieved to have survived the flight, he knelt down and kissed the ground. After reporting to the area headquarters in Johannesburg, he was taken home by his sister Joan, to 20 Smits Road in Dunkeld.

Bourhill and Cormack had been brothers-in-arms and it was now revealed that they were to be brothers-in-law. Whenever faced with death and destruction, Cormack's trademark question—spoken with the nasal twang that never left him after he broke his nose jumping out of a truck that had hit a landmine in Orvieto—was "why?"

"What a lot I have to tell you all when I get home," Bourhill had written after the mini-holocaust of shellfire at Bagnoregio. But now was not the right time, and the innocent would never really understand, so he held his peace. Hodgson had no need to write any more letters as he left the land of the Pharaohs by sea nine days into the new year, arriving in Durban on 23 January 1946. From here, he made the familiar overnight train journey though Pietermaritzburg to Germiston and then Johannesburg. The platform on Park Station was virtually deserted and men searched in vain for wives, girlfriends and parents. They were quickly ushered under the subway onto the green carpet of the main ground at the Wanderers Club. Among the gathered crowd, Hodgson recognized his parents and his friend George Mennie, who had been invalided home in July 1944.

The day after his homecoming, Hodgson's father went to work and his mother went shopping. His only request was that she buy some packets of vegetable seeds to plant in the garden. For the next month, he was content to stay at home, nurturing the plants and playing tennis.

The army would not discharge a soldier until he had found employment. One Carbineer, Private Alex Stuart Beatt, was still on strength when he attended a reunion at the Waverly Hotel on 4 January 1946. He had been a dispatch rider and had survived a wound in the desert war. At the reunion, he was accidentally electrocuted and is buried in the military section of West Park Cemetery.

Perhaps due to a need for recognition, or disdain for those who had stayed at home, some of the returned soldiers of the 6th South African Armoured Division became unruly in public. General Poole made an appeal to the troops in the name of their fallen comrades and blamed the behaviour on a "handful of bad characters":

> I have been greatly distressed to hear from the highest authority in the Union that several cases of groups of 6th South African Armoured Division soldiers behaving rather badly in hotel lounges, etc, have occurred. These instances have been the result of men getting bottled and in such circumstances, reported as "behaving as arrogantly as if they were in occupation of conquered enemy territory". The public, including the rest of the UDF, have a very soft spot and very great admiration for the 6th South African Armoured Division and this sort of thing might easily result in revulsion of feeling, which would be a very serious let-down to the superb name of the division which has been built up by the exemplary conduct of our men both in and out of battle.[390]

[390] DODAR, Div Docs, Box 171, Discipline, 6th South African Armoured Division troops in Union, Headquarters South African Armoured Division, Union Defence Force, CMF, 23/7/1945.

Having turned 19 in Alexandria and 20 in Lucca, Hodgson celebrated his 21st birthday in Johannesburg on 26 February 1946. It was a black tie affair, held in a marquee in the garden. In the fullness of time, Hodgson ventured out from the security of his home and went on a date, but first had to present his credentials to the girl's father and was ordered to have her home before midnight.

During the wild chase across to Po plains he had written: "I have seen so many marvellous things and I can't wait to get down to writing to you about it all, even if the chance came I don't think I could, so I will wait until I can tell you everything, it will be so much better." But Mrs Hodgson, like most mothers, would not have coped with the true story.

The silent suffering of the families of those who gave their all is epitomized by the epitaph on the gravestone of Lance-Corporal C.H. Cox (RDLI) at Lake Bolsena: "We loved him. Ah, no tongue can tell how much we loved him and how well." The general public could not comprehend what their boys had gone through or how the war had changed them. The amusing anecdotes told by returned soldiers, the majority of whom had not seen the front line, added to the misconceptions which censorship and propaganda had already inculcated in the national consciousness. In South African folklore, the Italian campaign is perceived as a great adventure, and the volunteers are justifiably proud to have taken part. But those few who experienced mindnumbing violence and fear, or comforted a friend in his final death agony, wanted nothing more than to forget. Life carried on and the images of Italy became hazy through the mists of time.

Epilogue

"You are going to face danger, hardship and sacrifice—perhaps even death itself—in all its fierce forms. But through it all, you will gather that experience of life and enrichment of character which are more valuable than gold or precious stones."
—Jan Smuts at the 1st Division farewell parade at Zonderwater on 13 July 1940

Compared to the losses of the British, American, French, New Zealanders and especially Germans, the casualties suffered by the 6th South African Armoured Division were light. Including all battle casualties, battle accidents and post-war deaths, approximately 900 members of the 6th South African Armoured Division (excluding the Guards Brigade and the Indian Frontier Force Rifles) were killed or died on active service in Italy.

In total, there are around 1,800 South Africans buried in the immaculately kept war cemeteries in Italy. These include non-divisional troops, escaped POWs and the South African Air Force.

The division cemetery in Castiglione is unique in that it is primarily a South African cemetery and the town has a special relationship with South Africa. During the dedication ceremony for the cemetery at Castiglione, General Poole said: "I can see that in the years to come, this sacred spot will be the scene of many a pilgrimage of people journeying from far-off lands to honour the memory of these brave men who rest here." The local population have been true to the words of their spokesman: "The grateful love of the Castiglionesi will have care of them. The life they have given for the liberation of our country is a love symbol; to that love our people will concentrate forever a faithful gratefulness."

In 2007, a street was named after the 6th South African Armoured Division and there is a traffic circle bearing a representation of the triangular divisional flash.

Today, few traces can be found of the deeds of South Africans during the war in Italy. Even in those towns liberated or destroyed by the 6th South African Armoured Division, the locals seem to suffer from selective amnesia. Visitors don't ask questions about the war. At Castello di Brolio, the massive wooden gates which were holed by shells from the Pretoria Regiment's tanks are covered with sheets of metal. The staff can tell you about the castle's history from medieval times but know nothing about what happened there in 1944.

In the Teatro in Chiusi, a plaque commemorates the stand made by the First City/Cape Town Highlanders. At the tourist office, there is information available on the Etruscan civilization and on the forthcoming events at the teatro, but nothing about the drama which played out in June 1944.

Many of the hill-top villages, Bagnoregio in particular, are dying as the younger generation migrates to the cities.

However, villagers who were subjected to atrocities and reprisals have not forgotten and there are ongoing claims for compensation against the German government.

The war in Europe was not yet officially over when the 6th South African Armoured Division held a thanksgiving ceremony in a damp factory yard in Brugherio near Milan on 4 May 1945. Standing in the rain, on a platform flanked by his brigadiers, General Poole expressed his hopes for the future:

> Let us carry on this great comradeship and esprit de corps that we have forged on the battlefields of Africa and Italy, through adversity and victory—that comradeship forged in the fire of war—and carry it with us into our country after demobilization, so that we stand together in peace as we do in war—that we stand together against the cancer of racialism, and that we help build our nation on sound foundations, routing those attempts to imitate a rotten Reich, the type of which we have now annihilated.[391]

But this was not to be. The camaraderie which existed in the army soon dissipated when the men returned to civilian life. Once out of uniform, their different social, educational and economic backgrounds became more apparent. Neither did the loyalty of the civilian population survive the war and the growing dissatisfaction culminated in the election of the National Party in 1948.

General Poole had declared "… you have a reputation worldwide, a name known in every country, respected by our allies, feared by the Herrenvolk. That we safeguard and carry back to South Africa."[392] Incredibly, in the new era, he was sidelined and many of his experienced officers were hounded out of the

[391] W.H.E. Poole, 6th South African Armoured Division Victory Parade, Address to the Division by the GOC, 4/5/1945.

[392] *Ibid.*

military. Traditional regiments were taken to the brink of extinction, name changes were enforced and the 'Royal' designations were dropped. A bilingual language policy was forced on the predominantly English-speaking Natal regiments which "already enjoyed a happy bilingual espirit de corps". Boer commando and Ossewabrandwag-style rank titles were introduced, crowns and pips were replaced by castles and stars. The title 'sir' as a form of address for senior officers was even done away with.[393] The long-standing tradition of the Cape Town Highlanders serving as the guard of honor at the opening of parliament was discarded. The presence of 'foreign uniforms' could not be tolerated. The tell-tale red tabs were now an embarrassment and were hastily removed from the uniform. Ironically, the National Party, which had opposed voluntary participation in a just war, soon introduced conscription to propagate its own agenda.

By 1952 the purge was well underway. Lieutenant-General G.E. Brink, commander of the 1st Division, was quoted in *The Star*: "A once magnificent defence organization has become a political toy, seething with discontent and frustration."[394]

In *Avenge Tobruk*, published in 1960, Brigadier Hartshorn wrote: "Everything possible is being done today to wipe from the slate of history some of the most glorious pages of our military past."[395]

John Hodgson started studying engineering at Wits University but left after his first year to help his father in his contracting business, Darling & Hodgson, which he then turned into a huge conglomerate. Hodgson realized that he had thrived in a cold climate during his time in the winter line. Today he lives in Johannesburg but spends the northern hemisphere winters at his second home in England.

George Mennie enrolled at Wits University after the war. He seldom studied or attended lectures but managed to pass exams using borrowed notes. He ran the family stock-broking firm, R.S. Mennie, until his premature death by drowning. Lionel Wulfsohn of the Witwatersrand Rifles/Regiment De la Rey returned to Rustenburg after a lengthy period of hospitalization, where he started a car dealership. He is the author of a book on the Anglo–Boer War

393 M. Coghlan, *Pro Patria*, pp. 57–63.

394 G. Mills & G. Wood, Ethnicity, integration and the South African Armed Forces. South African Defence Review, 12, 1993.

395 E.P. Hartshorn, *Avenge Tobruk*, p. 221.

called *Rustenburg at War*. Every October for ten years after the war, Wulfsohn would send a crate of Outspan oranges to Helen Barclay of Norfolk, the British nurse who had looked after him.

Frank Mundel of the Imperial Light Horse/Kimberley Regiment also returned to Rustenburg and continued in the family refrigeration business.

Norman Smith of the 1/6th Field Regiment was presented with a toolkit on demobilization. He continued to practise his trade as a refrigeration technician in South Africa and Rhodesia.

Norman Smith, Frank Mundel and thousands like them never visited Italy again. Glen Easton of the Royal Natal Carbineers left a wife and two young sons. The widow Easton held the farm and family together. She was a nurse by profession, and the widow's pension of £48 per annum helped a little. She never remarried. The Eastons' descendents still farm at Syferbult near Koster.

The mining industry opened its arms to returning soldiers. Gunner Peter Johnston became a mine surveyor and rose to the top of his profession at head office in Johannesburg. Gunner E.R. 'Mac' Cormack ended his long career as a mine manager at Rustenburg. Douglas Baker of the Natal Mounted Rifles earned a degree in Arts and Humanities in South Africa and later qualified at the University of Sheffield to practise medicine. He has written a number of esoteric books in addition to *War, Wine and Valour*, a memoir of his wartime experiences.

Both Stephen Bourhill and John Hodgson only ever attended one regimental reunion in their later lives. Neither of them joined the MOTHs organization. Bourhill did, however, become a member of the Springbok Legion. Thirty years later, the Legion made a small bursary available for his son's tertiary education. In addition to his clothing allowance and a small gratuity, Bourhill was given a partial disability pension for loss of hearing as a result of gunfire. He took his pension as a lump sum and used it as a down payment on a pick-up truck. Through sweat equity he acquired a farm near Rustenburg, where his descendents still live today.

Roll of Honour

This roll of honour is derived from information which was graciously provided by the Commonwealth War Graves Commission. The intention is to include all South Africans and Rhodesians who died in Italy (from all causes) while serving with the 6th South African Armoured Division and Reserve Group between 1 May 1944 and 31 May 1945. The following are excluded: members of the 24th Guards Brigade and other non-South African units under command, South Africans seconded to British units, South African Air Force personnel, accidental deaths after 30 May 1945 and all non-divisional troops and POWs. The names of certain non-divisional support troops may have been erroneously included if it could not be reliably established whether or not they were attached to the 6th South African Armoured Division or reserve group at the time of their death. If any names have been inadvertently excluded, the matter will be rectified in future editions.

Arezzo War Cemetery (22)

Bailie, Gunner, C.C., 7/23rd Medium Regiment, 6/12/1944, age 24, Uniondale, Cape Province.

du Plessis, Private, C.P., Royal Natal Carbineers, 8/7/1944, age 23, Camps Bay, Cape Province.

Flynn, Captain, D.H., 1/6th Field Regiment, 6/7/1944, age 34, Johannesburg, Transvaal.

Gluckmann, Lance-Corporal, J., Imperial Light Horse/Kimberley Regiment, 10/6/1944, age 30, Johannesburg, Transvaal.

Hartley, Major, H.H., Witwatersrand Rifles/ Regiment De la Rey, 7/7/1944.

Hayman, Lance-Corporal, C.D., Witwatersrand Rifles/Regiment De la Rey, 6/7/1944, age 29 (served as Murphy, J.P.).

Holshausen, Private, N.H., Witwatersrand Rifles/Regiment De la Rey, 13/7/1944.

Howard, Private, D.J., Royal Durban Light Infantry, 9/7/1944.

Hudson, Lance-Corporal, G.M., First City/ Cape Town Highlanders, 5/7/1944.

Kay, Private, L.P., Royal Natal Carbineers, 9/7/1944, age 30, Durban, Natal.

Lombard, Bombardier, R.K., 1/12th Light Anti-Aircraft Regiment, 16/7/1944, age 24, Cape Town, Cape Province.

Malan, Private, W.H., Royal Durban Light Infantry, 22/8/1944.

McPherson, Trooper, A., Pretoria Regiment, 15/7/1944, age 22, Durban, Natal.

Phin, Trooper, T.K., Natal Mounted Rifles, 12/7/1944, age 19, Queenstown, Cape Province.

Shain, Private, B., Witwatersrand Rifles/ Regiment De la Rey, 22/10/1944.

Smith, Private, R.G., Witwatersrand Rifles/ Regiment De la Rey, 9/7/1944.

Swanson, Private, A., TSC, 11/11/1944, age 34, Johannesburg, Transvaal.

Theart, Lance-Corporal, J.G., Witwatersrand Rifles/Regiment De la Rey, 17/10/1944, Cape Province.

van der Au, Trooper, W.E., Natal Mounted Rifles, 21/9/1944, age 27, Johannesburg, Transvaal.

van der Poel, Corporal, B.L., Witwatersrand Rifles/Regiment De la Rey, 15/11/1944, age 26, Witbank, Transvaal.

Vermaak, Lance-Corporal, F.K., Witwatersrand Rifles/Regiment De la Rey, 14/7/1944, age 20, Pretoria, Transvaal.

Walker, Lieutenant, J., Mentioned in Dispatches, Pretoria Regiment, 5/7/1944, Johannesburg, Transvaal.

Assisi War Cemetery (36)

Blom, Private, J.J., Royal Natal Carbineers, 28/6/1944.

Bodington, Trooper, B.B., Pretoria Regiment, 1/7/1944, age 26, Bulawayo, Southern Rhodesia.

Botes, Sergeant, Petrus J., 4/22nd Field Regiment, 2/7/1944, age 27, Brooklyn, Cape Town, Cape Province.

Botha, Private, T.E., Royal Natal Carbineers, 27/6/1944.
Bussack, Private, H., Indian and Malay Corps, 2/7/1944, age 45, East London, Cape Province.
Claasen, Private, H., Cape Corps, 27/6/1944.
Clayton, Private, I.B., Royal Natal Carbineers, 28/6/1944, age 20.
Cockcroft, Sapper, I.L., South African Engineer Corps, 16/7/1944, age 25.
Crawford, Trooper, J.W., Pretoria Regiment, 1/7/1944.
Denyssen, Bombardier, D.A., South African Artillery, 4/7/1944, age 26.
Fisher, Private, J.D., Royal Durban Light Infantry, 8/7/1944, Brakpan, Transvaal.
Freer, Private, C.H., Royal Natal Carbineers, 28/6/1944.
Greef, Lance-Corporal, J., Cape Corps attached to the Royal Natal Carbineers, 27/6/1944.
Harrison, Private, J.C., Royal Natal Carbineers, 27/6/1944.
Harvard, Trooper, J.L., Pretoria Regiment, 1/7/1944, age 28, Headlands, Southern Rhodesia.
Hooper, Corporal, A.J., First City/Cape Town Highlanders, 22/6/1944, age 31, Tamboerskloof, Cape Province.
Howison, Trooper, O.E., South African TC, 21/7/1944, age 21, Rondebosch, Cape Province.
Lakati, Lance-Corporal, S., Cape Corps attached to the First City/Cape Town Highlanders, 22/6/1944.
Last, Corporal, C.G. MM, South African Medical Corps attached to the First City/Cape Town Highlanders, 22/6/1944, age 36.
Meiring, Sapper, A.H.J., 8th Field Squadron, South African Engineer Corps, 27/6/1944.
Meyer, Trooper, S.J., Pretoria Regiment, 1/7/1944, age 35, Rusape, Southern Rhodesia.
Nel, Private, D.J., Witwatersand Rifles/Regiment De la Rey, 31/7/1944, age 22, Plumstead, Cape Province.
Packer, Trooper, D.O., Natal Mounted Rifles, 17/7/1944, age 22, Harding, Natal.
Potgieter, Private, H.P., Imperial Light Horse/Kimberley Regiment, 21/6/1944.
Renou, Corporal, P.W., 8th Field Squadron, South African Engineer Corps, 27/6/1944.
Satchel, Corporal, E.C., Imperial Light Horse/Kimberley Regiment, 15/7/1944, age 34, Fish Hoek, Cape Province.
Schulze, Private, F.G., Imperial Light Horse/Kimberley Regiment, 21/6/1944, age 21, East London, Cape Province.
Solomons, Private, D., Indian and Malay Corps attached to the 4/22nd Field Regiment, 3/8/1944, age 29.
Sperryn, Lieutenant, P.N.H. MM, Mentioned in Dispatches, Royal Natal Carbineers, 28/6/1944, age 29.
Thomas, Lance-Corpoal, P.E., Royal Natal Carbineers, 28/6/1944, age 30.
Tucker, Lance-Corporal, R.J., 8th Field Squadron, South African Engineer Corps, 28/7/1944.
Ullman, Private, P., Imperial Light Horse/Kimberley Regiment, 21/6/1944.
van Aswegen, Private, M.C., Witwatersrand Rifles/Regiment De la Rey, 8/8/1944.
van Niekerk, Gunner, G.E., 4/22nd Field Regiment, 1/7/1944, age 43, Maraisburg, Transvaal.
Waterford, Signaller, E.A., South African Corps of Signals, 16/2/1945.
Williams, Lieutenant, F.W., 1/6th Field Regiment, 30/7/1944.

Bari War Cemetry (20)

Baseley, Major, W.F.B., Natal Mounted Rifles/South African Air Force, 27/5/1944.
Black, Gunner, B., 6th Field Reserve Battery, South African Artillery, 23/5/1944, age 23, Johannesburg, Transvaal.
Boshoff, Sergeant, A.J., SACMP, 22/11/1944.
Bruce, Lieutenant, S.S.S., Natal Mounted Rifles, 27/5/1944, age 28, Port Elizabeth, Cape Province.
Daniels, Private, A., Indian and Malay Corps, 24/1/1945.
de Groot, Trooper, J.J.W., Reserve Group, South African Armoured Corps, 26/4/1945.
de Witt, Captain, J., Pretoria Regiment, 19/5/1944.
Ferreira, Gunner, H.E., South African Artillery, 29/1/1945.
Harley, Private, J.S., Royal Natal Carbineers, 2/12/1944.
Harris, Trooper, R.R.K.F., Reserve Regiment, South African Armoured Corps, 7/6/1944, age 43, Kimberley, Cape Province.
Horsley, Corporal, C.F., Indian and Malay

Corps, 11/3/1945, age 29, Eshowe, Natal.
Jacobs, Private, J., Cape Corps, 7/10/1944.
Johnson, Sapper, A.W., South African Engineer Corps, 9/4/1945, age 35, Wynberg, Cape Province.
Kirk, Lieutenant, A.E.A., Royal Natal Carbineers, 29/7/1944, Maclear, Cape Province.
Kruger, Gunner, G., Cape Corps attached to the 4/22nd Field Regiment, 8/5/1945.
McInerney, Corporal, M., 'Q' Services Corps, 18/6/1944.
Robbins, Staff Sergeant, L.S., 'Q' Services Corps, 1/5/1944, age 20, Cape Town, Cape Province.
Steyn, Private, J.H., South African Armoured Corps, 27/5/1944.
Stokes, Corporal, J., South African Corps of Signals, 13/2/1945, age 22, Port Elizabeth, Cape Province.
Venter, Trooper, W.D.F., Pretoria Regiment, 20/6/1944, age 26, Umtali, Southern Rhodesia.

Beach Head War Cemetry, Anzio (5)
Hunter, Corporal, N.D.A., Natal Mounted Rifles/South African Air Force, 3/6/1944.
Krog, Lieutenant, B.J.M., South African Armoured Corps, 3/6/1944.
Marshall, Private, E.T., Royal Natal Carbineers, 3/6/ 1944, age 21, Cape Town, Cape Province.
Milligan, Corporal, J.R., Natal Mounted Rifles, 3/6/1944, age 36, Johannesburg, Transvaal.
van Rhyn, Lieutenant, H.P.N., South African Artillery, 28/5/1944, age 34.

Bolsena War Cemetry (165)
Abrahams, Private, N., Indian and Malay Corps attached to the 1/6th Field Regiment, 12/6/1944, age 33.
Baars, Trooper, J.I., Special Service Battalion, 10/6/1944, age 21, Salisbury, Southern Rhodesia.
Baker, Private, A.N., Royal Natal Carbineers, 17/6/1944.
Bampfield-Duggan, Sergeant, F.M., Mentioned in Dispatches, Royal Natal Carbineers, 21/6/1944.
Barker, Lieutenant, H.F., 1/6th Field Regiment, 12/6/1944, Durban, Natal.
Blanckenberg, Trooper, E., Natal Mounted Rifles, 27/6/1944.
Blignaut, Trooper, J.H., Pretoria Regiment, 21 June 1944.
Boshoff, Sapper, W.H.J., South African Engineer Corps, 22/6/1944.
Botha, Lance-Corporal, E.P., Witwatersrand Rifles/Regiment De la Rey, 16/6/1944. Pretoria.
Botha, Signaller, J.J., South African Corps of Signals, 10/6/1944.
Bowley, Corporal, B.B., Pretoria Regiment, 12/6/1944.
Boyley, Private, R.S., Royal Natal Carbineers, 25/6/1944.
Brett, Major, D.D., twice Mentioned in Dispatches, 7/23rd Medium Regiment South African Artillery, 12/6/1944.
Bridson, Private, J.L., Imperial Light Horse/Kimberley Regiment, 10/6/1944, age 26, Durban, Natal.
Brown, Private, J., Indian and Malay Corps attached to the 8th Field Squadron, 23/6/1944, Humansdorp, Cape Province.
Buitendag, Corporal, B.D., Divisional Provost, SACMP, 14/6/1944, Rayton, Transvaal.
Butcher, Lieutenant, H.M., Natal Mounted Rifles, 10/6/1944.
Carlyle, Lieutenant, A.A., Royal Durban Light Infantry, 23/6/1944, age 26, Hillary, Natal.
Carmichael, Gunner, J.V., 1/6th Field Regiment, 10/6/1944.
Carstens, Trooper, F.P.V.D.M., Special Service Battalion, 10/6/1944, age 27.
Carver, Corporal, G.E., Natal Mounted Rifles, 12/6/1944.
Catzavelos, Trooper, K.A., Special Service Battalion, 10/6/1944.
Chalmers, Corporal, J.J. DCM, Imperial Light Horse/Kimberley Regiment, 13/6/1944, age 30, Johannesburg, Transvaal.
Chapman, Sergeant, A., Prince Alfred's Guard, 27/6/944, age 37, Bertrams, Transvaal.
Clark, Private, A., TSC, 26/6/1944.
Clarke, Private, P.J., Royal Natal Carbineers, 21/6/1944, age 18, Durban, Natal.
Coetzee, Sapper, H.B., 12th Field Squadron, South African Engineer Corps, 22/6/1944, age 34, Brakpan, Transvaal.
Cooke, Trooper, N.O., Special Service Battalion, 23/6/1944, age 21, Estcourt, Natal.

Cox, Lance-Corporal, C.H., Royal Durban Light Infantry, 12/6/1944, age 25, Durban, Natal.

Davies, Corporal, G.G., Prince Alfred's Guard, 13/6/1944, age 24, Port Elizabeth, Cape Province.

de Koker, Private, H.F., Imperial Light Horse/Kimberley Regiment, 21/8/1944, Belgravia, Transvaal.

de Lange, Trooper, B.J., Prince Alfred's Guard, 11/6/1944.

de Villiers, Sergeant, D.J., Special Service Battalion, 10/6/1944, Paarl, Cape Province.

Dell, Corporal, J.E., Imperial Light Horse/ Kimberley Regiment, 10/6/1944.

Devitt, Private, D.G., Witwatersrand Rifles/ Regiment De la Rey, 8/6/1944.

Dickason, Trooper, D.N., Prince Alfred's Guard, 11/6/1944.

Domoney, Trooper, C.D.H., Natal Mounted Rifles, 11/6/1944, age 27, East London, Cape Province.

Dorset, Bombardier, M.G., 1/6th Field Regiment, 28/6/1944, age 21, Salisbury, Southern Rhodesia.

du Plessis, Corporal, J.H., Royal Natal Carbineers, 17/6/1944, age 34.

Dupavillon, Trooper, E.J., Prince Alfred's Guard, 10/6/1944, age 35, Mauritius.

Eksteen, Private, N.J., Witwateresrand Rifles/Regiment De la Rey, 15/6/1944, age 34, Swellendam, Cape Province.

Eliason, Trooper, J., Prince Alfred's Guard, 10/6/1944.

Elliott, Gunner, S.T., 1/6th Field Regiment, 10/6/1944, age 30, Port Elizabeth, Cape Province.

Ferreira, Trooper, G.T., Natal Mounted Rifles, 6/6/1944, age 26, Letskraal, Cape Province.

Flior, Sapper, M., 12th Field Squadron, South African Engineer Corps, 22/6/1944, age 23, Johannesburg, Transvaal.

Foss, Sergeant, G.H., Natal Mounted Rifles, 28/6/1944, age 32, Ladysmith, Natal.

Fourie, Private, A.H., Witwatersrand Rifles/ Regiment De la Rey, 10/6/1944, age 27, Johannesburg, Transvaal.

Fourie, Lance-Corporal, H.S., Witwatersrand Rifles/Regiment De la Rey, 15/6/1944.

Fox, Corporal, G.B., Natal Mounted Rifles, 11/6/1944, age 24, Mashaba, Southern Rhodesia.

Fulton, Lance-Corporal, G.A., South African Corps of Signals, 10/6/1944.

Gardner, Trooper, J.G., Natal Mounted Rfles, 10/6/1944.

Gates, Lance-Corporal, K., Pretoria Regiment, 15/6/1944, age 23, Dunnottar, Transvaal.

Gibson, Trooper, R., Natal Mounted Rifles, 7/6/1944, age 21, Pinetown, Natal.

Gill, Trooper, P., Natal Mounted Rifles, 7/6/1944, age 24, Bellair, Natal.

Goldsmith, Private, F.R., Royal Natal Carbineers, 17/6/1944, age 30, Kent, England.

Hack, Private, R., Imperial Light Horse/ Kimberley Regiment, 25/6/1944, age 24, Johannesburg, Transvaal.

Hamman, Trooper, G.F., Pretoria Regiment, 12/6/1944.

Hanekom, Private, G.C.M., Imperial Light Horse/Kimberley Regiment, 21/6/1944, age 25, Aughrabies, Cape Province.

Harding, Gunner, J., Cape Corps attached to the 1/11th Anti-Tank Regiment, 13/6/1944, age 29, Luderitz, South West Africa.

Hattingh, Private, D.R., Imperial Light Horse/Kimberley Regiment, 21/6/1944, age 27, Biesjespoort, Cape Province.

Herbst, Sapper, S.C.P., 12th Field Squadron South African Engineer Corps, 22/6/1944.

Hope, Gunner, F.G., South African Artillery, 10/8/1944.

Howe, Sergeant, J. MM, Pretoria Regiment, 27/6/1944, age 36, Rosebank, Cape Province.

Howells, Trooper, W.D., Prince Alfred's Guard, 13/6/1944, age 37, Kenilworth, Cape Province.

Hunter, Gunner, E.J., South African Artillery, 10/8/1944.

Impey, Trooper, L.G., Prince Alfred's Guard, 11/6/1944.

Jarman, Private, J., First City/Cape Town Highlanders, 22/6/1944.

John, Corporal, R.W.G., Prince Alfred's Guard, 13/6/1944.

Johnson, Sergeant, A.J., Witwatersrand Rifles/Regiment De la Rey, 26/6/1944, age 19, Grahamstown, Cape Province.

Johnstone, Lieutenant, R.H., Pretoria Regiment, 7/6/1944, age 31, Warmbaths, Transvaal.

Jute, Corporal, R.F., Special Service

Battalion, 10/6/1944, age 23, Seven Fountains, Cape Province.

Kayser, Gunner, D.C., 4/22nd Field Regiment, 15/6/1944.

Keatley, Signaller, G.H., South African Corps of Signals attached to the Imperial Light Horse/Kimberley Regiment, 13/6/1944, age 19, Johannesburg, Transvaal.

Kemble, Gunner, G.R., 1/6th Field Regiment, 28/6/1944, age 36, Benoni, Transvaal.

Klose, Private, F.H.J., First City/Cape Town Highlanders, 22/6/1944, age 23, East London, Cape Province.

Kotze, Lance-Corporal, P.L., Royal Natal Carbineers, 17/6/1944, age 30, Hout Bay, Cape Province.

Kruger, Private, J.A., Royal Natal Carbineers, 17/5/1944.

Kuhn, Corporal, P.L., Special Service Battalion, 24/6/1944, age 24, Prieska, Cape Province.

Lahee, Lance-Corporal, T.A., Witwatersrand Rifles/Regiment De la Rey, 15/6/1944, age 24.

Lambrinos, Private, H., Royal Natal Carbineers, 22/6/1944.

Lancaster, Trooper, H.M., Special Service Battalion, 10/6/1944, age 21.

Lauterbach, Corporal, J.G., 12th Field Squadron, South African Engineer Corps, 28/6/1944, age 33, Matubatuba, Natal.

Leak, Signaller, R.B., South African Corps of Signals attached to Prince Alfred's Guard, 28/6/1944, age 22, Cape Town, Cape Province.

Ledingham, Private, F., Royal Natal Carbineers, 12/6/1944.

Lee, Private, R.T.M., Witwatersrand Rifles/Regiment De la Rey, 9/6/1944, age 26, Turffontein, Transvaal.

Lesch, Gunner, F.S., Cape Corps attached to the 4/22nd Field Regiment, 15/6/1944, age 37, Moorreesburg, Cape Province.

Liebenberg, Major, E., Special Service Battalion, 10/6/1944.

Linde, Gunner, C.E., 1/6th Field Regiment, 28/6/1944.

Lindsay, Private, W.M. McL., Witwatersrand Rifles/Regiment De la Rey, 14/6/1944, age 26, Turffontein, Transvaal.

Lomax, Sapper, W., 12th Field Squadron, South African Engineer Corps, 15/6/1944.

Lombard, Private, S., Indian and Malay Corps attached to the Royal Natal Carbineers, 14/6/1944.

Lupke, Lance-Corporal, P.R., Natal Mounted Rifles, 6/6/1944.

MacArthur, Sergeant, J.J., Pretoria Regiment, 12/6/944, age 24, Belville, Cape Province.

MacPhail, Lance-Corporal, G.M., TSC, 11/6/1944, age 29, Uitenhage, Cape Province.

Maile, Corporal, A.B.M., Royal Natal Carbineers, 13/6/1944, age 26, Johannesburg, Transvaal.

Maritz, Private, J.G.A., Royal Natal Carbineers, 29/6/1944, age 22, Vollgraafsig, Cape Province.

McClung, Private, G.M., Royal Natal Carbineers, 30/6/1944, age 20, Durban, Natal.

McKerrell, Trooper, J.A.G., Natal Mounted Rifles, 6/6/1944, age 29, Germiston, Transvaal.

Meade, Private, G.R., Royal Natal Carbineers, 17/6/1944, age 20, Mossel Bay, Cape Province.

Mearns, Trooper, D.C., Natal Mounted Rifles/South African Air Force, 27/6/1944, age 20, Johannesburg, Transvaal.

Milsom, Private, T.G., Royal Durban Light Infantry, 12/6/1944, age 28, Estcourt, Natal.

Moir, Sapper, S.S., 12th Field Squadron, South African Engineer Corps, 22/6/1944, age 28.

Morham, Lance-Corporal, L.W., Prince Alfred's Guard, 12/6/1944, age 26, Port Elizabeth, Cape Province.

Morrison, Private, H., Imperial Light Horse/Kimberley Regiment, 10/6/944.

Neilson, Trooper, G.F., Special Service Battalion, 22/6/1944.

Nellmapius, Captain, P.A., 1/6th Field Regiment, 14/6/1944, age 23, Kalk Bay, Cape Province.

Norrey, Sergeant, J.A., Natal Mounted Rifles, 14/6/1944, age 27, Pietermaritzburg, Natal.

October, Private, A., Cape Corps attached to the 1/12th Light Anti-Aircraft Regiment, 22/11/1944, age 28, Oudtshoorn, Cape Province.

O'Dea, Corporal, P.A., Natal Mounted Rifles, 26/6/1944, age 22, Maitland, Cape Province.

O'Donoghue, Trooper, J.P., Prince Alfred's Guard, 12/6/1944.

Olivier, Corporal, W.H., Special Service Battalion, 10/6/1944, age 21, Bethlehem, Orange Free State.

Olwage, Sergeant, D.B., Imperial Light Horse/Kimberley Regiment, 7/6/1944, age 36, Kimberley, Cape Province.

Page, Private, S.B., First City/Cape Town Highlanders, 22/6/1944, Mayfair West, Transvaal.

Parsall, Corporal, A.G., South African Medical Corps, 13 June 1944, age 26, Auckland Park, Transvaal

Pelser, Private, J.P., Witwatersrand Rifles/ Regiment De la Rey, 15/6/1944, age 23, Rayton, Transvaal.

Pepler, Private, E.C., Imperial Light Horse/ Kimberley Regiment, 10/6/1944.

Pond, Signalman, C.E., South African Corps of Signals attached to the Imperial Light Horse/Kimberley Regiment, 13/6/1944, age 22, Newcastle, Natal.

Probart, Lieutenant, W.A.B., Pretoria Regiment, 23/6/1944, age 28, Queenstown, Cape Province.

Reid, Trooper, M.G.H., Natal Mounted Rifles, 1/7/1944, age 22, Johannesburg, Transvaal.

Rennie, Corporal, W. MacD., Special Service Battalion, 12/6/1944, age 35, Fort Victoria, Southern Rhodesia.

Rigby, Trooper, D.I., Natal Mounted Rifles, 8/6/1944.

Ritchie, Sergeant, T., Royal Natal Carbineers, 22/6/1944.

Rose, Gunner, L.J., South African Artillery, 28/6/1944, age 35, Germiston, Transvaal.

Ruddie, Private, P.J., Imperial Light Horse/ Kimberley Regiment, 13/6/1944.

Salomon, Corporal, E.R., Witwatersrand Rifles/Regiment De la Rey, 3/7/1944, age 21, Pretoria, Transvaal.

Schoeler, Corporal, C.J., Special Service Battalion, 5/7/1944.

Scholz, Trooper, W.J., Natal Mounted Rifles/ South African Air Force, 6/6/1944, age 20, East London, Cape Province.

Schou, Trooper, A.H., Natal Mounted Rifles, 8/6/1944.

Serridge, Trooper, V.H., Natal Mounted Rifles, 12/6/1944, Durban, Natal.

Short, Trooper, G.A., Prince Alfred's Guard, 10/6/1944, age 26, Pretoria, Transvaal.

Smith, Lieutenant, D.E., Natal Mounted Rifles, 12/6/1944, age 36, Germiston, Transvaal.

Smith, Private, J.J., 'Q' Service Corps, 22/6/1944, age 26, Johannesburg, Transvaal.

Southgate, Gunner, V.B., 1/6th Field Regiment, 28/6/1944, age 19, Johannesburg, Transvaal.

Squier, Private, W.K., Royal Durban Light Infantry, 12/6/1944, age 27, Knysna, Cape Province.

Steele, Corporal, P.D., Pretoria Regiment, 25/6/1944, age 24, Newlands, Cape Province.

Steenkamp, Private, M.J., First City/Cape Town Highlanders, 18/6/1944, age 23, Wakkerstroom, Transvaal.

Stock, Trooper, A.I., Special Service Battalion, 10/6/1944, age 22, Port Elizabeth, Cape Province.

Strauss, Major, F.J., Imperial Light Horse/ Kimberley Regiment, 23/6/1944, age 33, Delport's Hope, Cape Province.

Streak, Private, M.A., Royal Natal Carbineers, 17/6/1944, age 21, Brixton, Transvaal.

Stuart, Corporal, J.G., South African Corps of Signals attached to the Imperial Light Horse/Kimberley Regiment, 13/6/1944, age 23, Bloemfontein, Orange Free State.

Sullivan, Trooper, T.H., Natal Mounted Rifles, 26/6/1944.

Swales, Trooper, G.L.R., Natal Mounted Rifles, 8/6/1944, age 25, Warner Beach, Natal.

Swart, Private, J.J., Witwatersrand Rifles/ Regiment De la Rey, 8/6/1944, age 22, Nooitgedacht, Cape Province.

Taylor, Lieutenant, C.R., TSC, 30/8/1944, age 29, Butterworth, Cape Province.

Taylor, Private, L.G., Witwatersrand Rifles/ Regiment De la Rey, 24/6/1944.

Terblanche, Corporal, J., Special Service Battalion, 10/6/1944.

Thyer, Lance-Corporal, R.E., Royal Natal Carbineers, 17/6/1944.

Udal, Captain, K.N., 19 Field Ambulance, South African Medical Corps, 15/6/1944, age 26, Pietermaritzburg, Natal.

van der Merwe, Signalman, H. de V., South African Corps of Signals attached to the Pretoria Regiment 23/6/1944, age 19, East London, Cape Province.

van Gass, Corporal, H.O., 12th Field Squadron, South African Engineer Corps, 22/6/1944, Johannesburg, Transvaal.

van Rooyen, Sergeant, C.J., Special Service Battalion, 10/6/1944, age 22, Benoni, Transvaal.

van Rooyen, WOII, I.M., Imperial Light Horse/Kimberley Regiment, 24/6/1944, age 33, Paulpietersburg, Natal.

van Rooyen, Lance-Corporal, W.J., Pretoria Regiment, 15/6/1944.

van Rosenveldt, Trooper, L.L., Natal Mounted Rifles/South African Air Force, 10/6/1944.

van Schalkwyk, Private, G.J., Royal Natal Carbineers, 26/6/1944, age 22, Worcester, Cape Province.

Venter, Lieutenant J.G., Prince Alfred's Guard, 13/6/1944, age 33, Johannesburg, Transvaal.

Viljoen, Sergeant, M.L., Pretoria Regiment, 15/6/1944, age 30.

Wakfer, Pivate, T.R., TSC, 26/6/1944, age 23, Daggafontein Mine, Transvaal.

Webster, Private, A.B., Royal Durban Light Infantry, 14/6/1944, age 32, Pretoria, Transvaal.

Webster, Corporal, H.L., Pretoria Regiment, 15/6/1944, age 28, Vierfontein, Orange Free State.

Wiley, Corporal, P.A.H., Pretoria Regiment, 26/6/1944.

Williams, Corporal, A.B., South African Armoured Corps attached to the 11th Armoured Brigade Headquarters, 12/6/1944.

Woolmore, Trooper, D.B., Pretoria Regiment, 15/6/1944, age 21, Nkandhla, Natal.

Wrey-Wathen, Lieutenant, A.J., Prince Alfred's Guard, 24/6/1944.

Yeoman, Gunner, C.C., 1/6th Field Regiment, 28/6/1944, age 20, Durban, Natal.

Caserta War Cemetery (5)

Collett, Trooper, E.B., Natal Mounted Rifles, 23/5/1944, age 22, Kimberley, Cape Province.

Oakley, Lieutenant, H.H., Special Service Battalion, 20/10/1944, age 29, East London, Cape Province.

Sandham, Private, L., First City/Cape Town Highlanders, 20/10/1944.

Slabbert, Trooper, G.A., Natal Mounted Rifles, 23/8/1944.

Sowden, Sergeant, L.C., Witwatersrand Rifles/Regiment De la Rey, 12/6/1944, age 33, Keetmanshoop, South West Africa.

Cassino Memorial (7)

Auld, Sergeant, J.E., Royal Natal Carbineers, 17/11/1944.

Booysen, Private, W., Cape Corps, 4/6/1944, age 48, Klipheuwel, Cape Province.

Cunningham, Lance-Corporal, R.E., Witwatersrand Rifles/Regiment De la Rey, 10/5/1944, age 22, Port Elizabeth, Cape Province.

Mundell, Lance-Corporal, D.C., Royal Natal Carbineers, 17/11/1944, age 23, Newcastle, Natal.

Swart, Private, D.A., Royal Durban Light Infantry, 26/5/1944.

van Aswegen, Private, C.P., Witwatersrand Rifles/Regiment De la Rey, 10/5/1944.

van Wyk, Private, D.D., Cape Corps, 1/9/1944, age 33, Indwe, Cape Province.

Cassino War Cemetery (31)

Airey, Lance-Corporal, B., Royal Natal Carbineers, 10/5/1944, age 23, Uitenhage, Cape Province.

Aitcheson, Sergeant, W.L. MM,15862V, South African Engineer Corps, 20/5/1944, age 26, Cape Town, Cape Province.

Bouwer, WOII, W.C., 7/23rd Medium Regiment, 9/5/1944, age 27, Potchefstroom, Transvaal.

Buss, Sergeant, J.M., Royal Durban Light Infantry, 7/5/1944, age 34, Durban, Natal.

Clark, Sergeant, W.V., Royal Natal Carbineers,14/5/1944, age 24.

Debeurier, Private, H.R.S., First City/Cape Town Highlanders, 22/5/1944, age 22, East London, Cape Province.

du Preez, Private, E.W., First City/Cape Town Highlanders, 4/6/1944, age 22, Woodstock, Cape Province.

Esson, Sergeant, W.A.S., First City/Cape Town Highlanders, 7/5/1944, age 26, Cape Town, Cape Province.

Everett, Private, A.S., First City/Cape Town Highlanders, 14/6/1944.

Finch-Stearns, Lance-Corporal, P.C., South African Engineer Corps, 20/5/1944, age 28, Johannesburg, Transvaal.

Griffin, Sapper, H.E., 8th Field Squadron, South African Engineer Corps, 4/6/1944.

Harrod, Lance-Corporal, B.R., Imperial Light Horse/Kimberley Regiment, 10/5/1944, age 24, Brakpan, Transvaal.

Jackson, Lieutenant, W., First City/Cape Town Highlanders, 10/5/1944.

Kritzinger, Lance-Corporal, J., Cape Corps, 5/5/1944.

le Roux, Private, J. van H., Royal Natal Carbineers, 12/5/1944.

le Roux, Private, S., Royal Natal Carbineers, 3/6/1944.

Mapham, Private, W.H., First City/Cape Town Highlanders, 7/5/1944, age 24, Bedford, Cape Province.

McNair, Sapper, D., South African Engineer Corps, 20/5/1944.

Mills, Lance-Corporal, C.D., Royal Natal Carbineers, 14/5/1944.

Mundell, Lance-Corporal, R.A., South African Corps of Signals, 12/5/1944.

Parkinson, Lance-Bombardier, J.L., South African Artillery, 14/5/1944, age 39, Pretoria, Transvaal.

Pierce, Private, R.H.B.B.P., Royal Natal Carbineers, 12/5/1944, age 26, Alberton, Transvaal.

Rood, Private, F.V., Royal Durban Light Infantry, 7/5/1944, age 34, Southampton, England.

Seaward, Private, E.S., South African Armoured Corps, 12/5/1944.

Sparks, Private, N., Royal Natal Carbineers, 14/5/1944, age 20, Fort Beaufort, Cape Province.

Timm, Private, M.B., First City/Cape Town Highlanders, 16/5/1944, age 22, Trappes Valley, Cape Province.

Truter, Private, R.A., 12th Motorized Brigade Headquarters, South African Armoured Corps, 7/5/1944.

Turpin, Lance-Corporal, A.E.A., First City/Cape Town Highlanders, 10/5/1944, age 24, Bedford, Cape Province.

van Zyl, Private, W.A., Royal Natal Carbineers, 14/5/1944, age 23, Port Nolloth, Cape Province.

Vink, Private, S., First City/Cape Town Highlanders, 31/5/1944, age 28, Cape Town, Cape Province.

Williams, Private, E.G., Royal Natal Carbineers, 4/6/1944, age 17, Krugersdorp, Transvaal.

Castiglione South African Cemetery (367)

Acutt, Private, D.M., First City/Cape Town Highlanders, 16/4/1945, age 25, Pansdrift, Transvaal.

Adams, Lieutenant, J.E., Royal Natal Carbineers, 21/10/1944, age 22, Pretoria, Transvaal.

Adams, Private, K., Cape Corps, 31/3/1945, age 43, Heidelberg, Cape Province.

Adamson, Lieutenant, J., Imperial Light Horse/Kimberley Regiment, Mentioned in Dispatches, 23/10/1944, age 26, Springs, Transvaal.

Ainslie, Corporal, A.J., Witwatersrand Rifles/Regiment De la Rey, 20/10/1944, age 34, Knysna, Cape Province.

Alder, Private, J.A., Witwatersrand Rifles/Regiment De la Rey, 13/10/1944.

Alexander, Private, D.E., First City/Cape Town Highlanders, 17/11/1944, age 25, Shamva, Southern Rhodesia.

Baartman, Private, D., Indian and Malay Corps, 13/10/1944.

Barnett, Signaller, R.D., South African Corps of Signals attached to the Witwatersrand Rifles/Regiment De la Rey, 21/10/1944, age 26.

Bartlett, Private, R, Wiktwatersrand Rifles/Regiment De la Rey, 16/4/1945.

Bassingthwaighte, Sergeant, A.A., Witwatersrand Rifles/Regiment De la Rey, 18/10/1944, age 24, Windhoek, South West Africa.

Basson, Corporal, T.R., Royal Natal Carbineers, 22/10/1944.

Bean, Sergeant, R.C., First City/Cape Town Highlanders, 24/11/1944, age 24, Lourenço Marques, Portuguese East Africa.

Beattie, Corporal, D.R., Royal Natal Carbineers, 29/4/1945.

Behr, Corporal, L.B., Special Service Battalion, 22/4/1945, age 27, Claremont, Cape Province.

Benson, Private, D., 'Q' Service Corps, 22/11/1944.

Bentley, Private, D.D., Imperial Light Horse/Kimberley Regiment, 23/10/1944, age 19, Bulawayo, Southern Rhodesia.

Berriman, Private, N., Royal Natal Carbineers, 2/10/1944.

Berry, Private, P.G., First City/Cape Town Highlanders, 16/4/1945, age 28, Fort Victoria, Southern Rhodesia.

Beukes, Lieutenant, S.W., Witwatersrand Rifles/Regiment De la Rey, 20/10/1944, age 24, Springs, Transvaal.

Bezuidenhout, Private, H., First City/Cape Town Highlanders, 16/4/1945 age 22, Gatooma, Southern Rhodesia.

Blignaut, Private, C.J., Witwatersrand Rifles/Regiment De la Rey, 13/10/1944.

Bond, Sergeant, R.G. MM, Mentioned in Dispatches, South African Engineer Corps, 9/9/1944.

Bosman, Lance-Corporal, A.J., South African Armoured Corps, 16/9/1944, age 28, Turffontein, Transvaal.

Botes, Private, H., Royal Natal Carbineers, 10/10/1944.

Botha, Signaller, G.S.V.D.M., South African Corps of Signals, 30/9/1944, age 39, Primrose, Transvaal.

Botha, Private, H.B.J., Witwatersrand Rifles/Regiment De la Rey, 23/4/1945, age 20, Piet Retief, Transvaal.

Botha, Trooper, J.F., Imperial Light Horse/Kimberley Regiment, 6/10/1944, age 22, Johannesburg, Transvaal.

Botha, Corporal, P.C., Witwatersrand Rifles/Regiment De la Rey, 14/9/1944.

Bouwer, Corporal, J.H., Witwatersrand Rifles/Regiment De la Rey, 28/10/1944.

Bouwer, Private, P.F., Imperial Light Horse/Kimberley Regiment, 13/9/1944.

Boyce, Private, N.E., First City/Cape Town Highlanders, 17/11/1944, age 27, Bulawayo, Southern Rhodesia.

Bradfield, Private, A.M., First City/Cape Town Highlanders, 16/4/1945, age 24, Trappes Valley, Cape Province.

Brady, Private, J.N.N., First City/Cape Town Highlanders, 13/10/1944.

Brain, Sergeant, T.P., South African Artillery, 30/10/1944, age 29, Durban, Natal.

Brant, Corporal, W.S., 8th Field Squadron, South African Engineer Corps, 19/9/1944.

Brasler, Private, G.C., Royal Natal Carbineers, 21/10/1944, age 18, Clanwilliam, Cape Province.

Bridgewater, Trooper, H.J.W., Prince Alfred's Guard, 22/4/1945, age 18, Yeoville, Transvaal.

Brits, Trooper, J.A., Prince Alfred's Guard, 9/5/1945.

Britz, Private, R.J., 'Q' Service Corps, 16/5/1945, age 36, Paul Roux, Orange Free State.

Broodryk, Private, W., First City/Cape Town Highlanders, 16/4/1945, age 22, Ermelo, Transvaal.

Brooke, Trooper, R.A., Special Service Battalion, 21/4/1945, age 20, Alicedale, Cape Province.

Brussow, Private, P.R.C., Imperial Light Horse/Kimberley Regiment, 23/10/1944, age 30, Rossburgh, Natal.

Buckley, Sergeant, C.C. MM and Bar, Royal Durban Light Infantry, 25/4/1945, age 23, Pietermaritzburg, Natal.

Buis, Private, M., Cape Corps, 23/4/1945.

Burrough, Lieutenant, H.V., Imperial Light Horse/Kimberley Regiment, 4/10/1944, age 31, Modder East, Transvaal.

Cairns, Lance-Corporal, C.A., Imperial Light Horse/Kimberley Regiment, 23/10/1944, age 20, Donnybrook, Natal.

Callister, Lance-Corporal, V.H., Pretoria Regiment, 18/12/1944.

Carlson, Private, P.G., Royal Natal Carbineers, 18/10/1944.

Casey, Sergeant, F.W., Special Service Battalion, 23/4/1945, age 29, Bloemfontein, Orange Free State.

Castle, Trooper, R.A., Pretoria Regiment, 2/10/1944, Johannesburg, Transvaal.

Ceatano, Sapper, M.W.F., 12th Field Squadron South African Engineer Corps, 2/5/1945.

Chapman, Lieutenant, V.C.J., Royal Natal Carbineers, 10/10/1944, age 28, Tatafalaza, Natal.

Charter, Lance-Corporal, D.C., Imperial Light Horse/Kimberley Regiment, 19/9/1944.

Christopher, Trooper, J.C., Pretoria Regiment, 28/4/1945, age 22, Johannesburg, Transvaal.

Clark, Private, C., Witwatersrand Rifles/Regiment De la Rey, 15/4/1945, age 19, Roodehoogte, Cape Province.

Clark, Private, D.C., First City/Cape Town Highlanders, 11/11/1944, Que Que, Southern Rhodesia.

Clark, Lance-Corporal, E.R.R., Royal Natal Carbineers, 24/10/1944, age 42, Queenstown, Cape Province.

Cockcroft, Lance-Corporal, D.B., Royal Natal Carbineers, 10/10/1944, age 20, Alice, Cape Province.

Cockerell, Sergeant, A.E.W., South African Artillery, 14/12/1944, age 26, Vereeniging, Transvaal.

Coetzee, Private, A.C., Natal Mounted Rifles/South African Air Force, 10/4/1945, age 19, Germiston, Transvaal.
Coetzee, Private, C., Witwatersrand Rifles/ Regiment De la Rey, 16/4/1945, age 23.
Coetzee, Private, J.C., Imperial Light Horse/ Kimberley Regiment, 13/1/1945, age 19, Standerton, Transvaal.
Coetzee, Private, W.V., Royal Durban Light Infantry, 17/4/1945, Seaview, Natal.
Colson, Private, E.W., First City/Cape Town Highlanders, 5/2/1945.
Combrink, Corporal, J.P.H., First City/Cape Town Highlanders, 22/10/1944.
Compton, Trooper, E.V., Natal Mounted Rifles, 9/9/1944, age 27.
Cottam, Corporal, W.J., Bronze Star (USA) Witwatersrand Rifles/Regiment De la Rey, 4/4/1945, age 25.
Cronjé, Private, A.M., Witwatersrand Rifles/ Regiment De la Rey, 15/4/1945.
Croshaw, Private, A.H., Imperial Light Horse/Kimberley Regiment, 18/9/1944.
Cross, Private, R., Imperial Light Horse/ Kimberley Regiment, 25/10/1944.
Cubitt, Private, H.W., Witwatersrand Rifles/ Regiment De la Rey, 13/10/1944.
Curtis, Private, R.B., Witwatersrand Rifles/ Regiment De la Rey, 20/10/1944, age 20, Rosettenville, Transvaal.
Dale, Private, T., Witwatersrand Rifles/ Regiment De la Rey, 16/4/1945.
Dates, Lance-Corporal, J.V., Imperial Light Horse/Kimberley Rifles, 21/4/1945, age 23, Benoni, Transvaal.
Davids, Corporal, M.C., Witwatersrand Rifles/Regiment De la Rey, 7/4/1945, age 26, Keetmanshoop, South West Africa.
Davis, Trooper, L., Natal Mounted Rifles/ South African Air Force, 16/10/1944, age 21, Orange Grove, Transvaal.
de Beer, Private, C.M., Imperial Light Horse/Kimberley Regiment, 13/9/1944.
de Jager, Corporal, C.J., SACMP, 23/41945, age 22, Clocolan, Orange Free State.
de Jonge, Private, J.J.H., Royal Durban Light Infantry, 18/4/1945.
de Kock, Signaller, L.M.O., South African Corps of Signals attached to the Imperial Light Horse/Kimberley Regiment, 4/10/1944, age 23, Matatiele, Natal.
de Meyer, Trooper, J.P., Special Service Battalion, 25/9/1944, age 25.
de Roock, Private, D.H., Imperial Light Horse/Kimberley Regiment, 13/9/1944.
de Senan, Private, E.A., Witwatersrand Rifles/Rgiment De la Rey, 16/4/1945.
de Villiers, Lieutenant, C.M., Pretoria Regiment, 21/4/1945, age 28, Beaufort West, Cape Province.
de Villiers, Sergeant, G.F.M., Witwatersrand Rifles/Regiment De la Rey, 16/4/1945, age 27, Richmond, Cape Province.
de Wet, Private, C.R., Witwatersrand Rifles/ Regiment De la Rey, 15/4/1945.
de Wet, Private, H.A., Witwatersrand Rifles/ Regiment De la Rey, 19/10/1944.
Den, Sergeant, D., Pretoria Regiment, 22/11/1944, age 30.
Deverneuil, Private, H.M., Royal Natal Carbineers, 17/10/1944.
Donaldson, Private, J.E., Witwatersrand Rifles/Regiment De la Rey, 15/4/1945, age 23, Vasco, Cape Province.
Dorfan, Lance-Corporal, M.S., Witwatersrand Rifles/Regiment De la Rey, 16/4/1945.
Douglas, Corporal, W.A., South African Medical Corps attached to the Royal Natal Carbineers, 23/10/1944, age 30, Rosettenville, Transvaal.
Douglas, Corporal, W.R., TSC, 21/10/1944, age 27, Springs, Transvaal.
Dowling, Private, A.T., Royal Natal Carbineers, 10/10/1944, age 38, Johannesburg, Transvaal.
Downing, Private, S.J., Royal Natal Carbineers, 19/4/1945.
Draper, Private, E.R., Royal Natal Carbineers, 18/10/1944.
Drysdale, Sergeant, K.D., First City/Cape Town Highlanders, 13/10/1944.
du Plessis, Gunner, L.R., Mentioned in Dispatches, 1/6th Field Regiment, 26/10/1944, age 24.
du Plessis, Private, R., First City/Cape Town Highlanders, 16/4/1945, age 18, Cape Town, Cape Province.
du Plessis, Corporal, S.J., Witwatersrand Rifles/Regiment De la Rey, 13/10/1944.
du Preez, Private, F.G., Imperial Light Horse/Kimberley Regiment, 4/10/1944, age 20, Ariamsvlei, South West Africa.
du Preez, Private, G., Imperial Light Horse/ Kimberley Regiment, 4/10/1944, age 22.
du Preez, Corporal, R.L.B., First City/Cape Town Highlanders, 16/4/1945, Springs, Transvaal.

du Toit, Private, J.J., First City/Cape Town Highlanders, 16/4/1945.
Duncan, Lieutenant-Colonel, A.S., DSO, First City/Cape Town Highlanders, 16/4/1945, age 35, Kenilworth, Cape Province.
Easton, Private, G., Royal Natal Carbineers, 3/11/1944, age 38, Syferbult, Transvaal.
Edwards, Private, A.T., First City/Cape Town Highlanders, 31/10/1944, age 30, Rosettenville, Johannesburg.
Ellis, Private, J.L., Witwatersrand Rifles/Regiment De la Rey, 16/4/1945, age 23.
Els, Lieutenant, J.M., Witwatersrand Rifles/Regiment De la Rey, 16/10/1944, age 22, Wolhuterskop, Transvaal.
Erasmus, Private, E., TSC attached to the 1/6th Field Regiment, 3/5/1945, Queenstown, Cape Province.
Erlank, Private, J.G., Imperial Light Horse/Kimberley Regiment, 16/9/1944, age 30.
Everitt, Private, T.A., Royal Durban Light Infantry, 18/4/1945, age 18, Ladybrand, Orange Free State.
Fennessey, Private, J.H., TSC, 3/5/1945, age 34, Germiston, Transvaal.
Filby, Lance-Corporal, G.L., Witwatersrand Rifles/Regiment De la Rey, 16/4/1945, age 22, Rondebosch, Cape Province.
Fisher, Lance-Corporal, C.W., Royal Natal Carbineers, 17/10/1944, age 23, Rosettenville, Transvaal.
Fitzgerald, Captain, J., Mentioned in Dispatches, Royal Natal Carbineers, 10/10/1944, age 34, Forest Town, Transvaal.
Fourie, Lieutenant, L.L., 43 Light Anti-Aircraft Regiment, South African Artillery, 20/10/1944.
Fox, Private, A.E., First City/Cape Town Highlanders, 13/10/1944, age 21.
Frara, Sapper, M., 12th Field Squadron, South African Engineer Corps, 16/4/1945.
Fraser, Lieutenant, H., Royal Natal Carbineers, 10/10/1944, age 41, Cathcart, Cape Province.
Friedman, Sergeant, G.W., Imperial Light Horse/Kimberley Regiment, 4/10/1944, age 28, Vereeniging, Transvaal.
Fromage, Private, P., Witwatersrand Rifles/Regiment De la Rey, 16/4/1945.
Frost, Corporal, R.C., Special Service Battalion, 6/4/1945, age 21, Kalk Bay, Cape Province.
Gallimore, Major, L.F. MC, Royal Natal Carbineers, 28/2/1945, age 30, Cape Town, Cape Province.
Gartly, Captain, D.C., South African Engineer Corps, 20/4/1945, age 38, Highlands North, Transvaal.
Gavin, Sergeant, D.B., Royal Durban Light Infantry, 18/4/1945.
George, Sergeant, A.A., South African Medical Corps, 23/4/1945.
Giles, Private, L.G., Imperial Light Horse/Kimberley Regiment, 23/1/1945.
Gilpin, Gunner, C.J., 43rd Light Anti-Aircraft Regiment, South African Artillery, 10/1/1945.
Goldstein, Gunner, L., 7/23rd Medium Regiment, 30/10/1944, Johannesburg, Transvaal.
Goldswain, Private, E.C.F., Imperial Light Horse/Kimberley Regiment, 9/10/1944, Kimberley, Cape Province.
Gough, Gunner, M.C., Cape Corps, 28/12/1944, age 18, Kimberley, Cape Province.
Gray, Private, L., Royal Natal Carbineers, 20/10/1944, age 24, Durban, Natal.
Greef, Private, R.C., Witwatersrand Rifles/Regiment De la RFey, 16/4/1945, age, 23, Vryburg, Cape Province.
Green, Private, A.M., First City/Cape Town Highlanders, 13/10/1944, age 20, Marandellas, Southern Rhodesia.
Green, Lieutenant, S.G.T., First City/Cape Town Highlanders, 19/11/1944, age 27, Middelburg, Cape Province.
Greenshields, Private, A., Imperial Light Horse/Kimberley Regiment, 23/10/1944, age 19, Sea Point, Cape Province.
Griggs, Lance-Corporal, P.J., South African Engineer Corps, 18/5/1945, age 26, Johannesburg, Transvaal.
Hackett, Private, S.W., Witwatersrand Rifles/Regiment De la Rey, 9/11/1944, age 38, Jeppe, Johannesburg.
Hancke, Private, C.H., First City/Cape Town Highlanders, 16/4/1945, age 24, Bezuidenhout Valley, Johannesburg.
Hartley, Lance-Corporal, T., Imperial Light Horse/Kimberley Regiment, 23/10/1944.
Harvey, Private, B, Witwatersrand Rifles/Reiment De la Rey, 14/10/1944, age 29, Uitenhage, Cape Province.
Hattingh, Lance-Corporal, B.H., Pretoria

Regiment, 8/11/1944, age 22, Gezina, Transvaal.

Hayes, Lance-Corporal, J.F., Imperial Light Horse/Kimberley Regiment, 22/4/1945, age 23, Woodstock, Cape Province.

Haylock, Trooper, C.F., Special Service Battalion, 7/11/1944.

Hingle, Corporal, J.D., First City/Cape Town Highlanders, 16/4/1945, age 24, Sea Point, Cape Province.

Hobson, Private, C.W. MM, Imperial Light Horse/Kimberley Regiment, 29/1/1945, age 18, Meyerton, Transvaal.

Holmes, Sapper, J.R.M., 12th Field Squadron South African Engineer Corps, 18/9/1944.

Horsley, Corporal, L.C., Royal Natal Carbineers, 5/11/1944.

Howell, Private, I.G., Witwatersrand Rifles/Regiment De la Rey, 23/4/1945.

Hudson, Lieutenant, C.J., Witwatersrand Rifles/Regiment De la Rey, 15/4/1945, age 22, Johannesburg, Transvaal.

Hunter, Sergeant, N.A., Imperial Light Horse/Kimberley Regiment, 17/9/1944, Port Elizabeth, Cape Province

Hurn, Sapper, A.E., 12th Field Squadron, South African Engineer Corps, 5/5/1945, age 41, Durban, Natal.

Hutchings, Private, E., First City/Cape Town Highlanders, 16/51945.

Hyde, Private, A.R., Imperial Light Horse/Kimberley Regiment, 18/9/1944.

Hyland, Gunner, A.E., 7/23rd Medium Regiment, 19/9/1944, age 20, Malvern, Transvaal.

Irwin, Sergeant, B.H.C., 43rd Light Anti-Aircraft Regiment attached to the Witwatersrand Rifles/Regiment De la Rey, 13/10/1944, Klerksdorp, Transvaal.

Jago, Private, R.C.D., Imperial Light Horse/Kimberley Regiment, 13/9/1944.

James, Private, W.P., Witwatersrand Rifles/Regiment De la Rey, 16/5/1945, age 30, Bulawayo, Southern Rhodesia.

Janion, Private, N.A., First City/Cape Town Highlanders, 16/5/1945, age 35, Mayfair, Transvaal.

Jardine, Gunner, L., 4/22nd Field Regiment, 3/1/1945, age 36, Maitland, Cape Province.

Johnson, Lance-Corporal, I.L., Royal Natal Carbineers, 14/10/1944.

Jones, Corporal, S., Royal Natal Carbineers, 21/10/1944, age 28, Johannesburg, Transvaal.

Jordaan, Lance-Corporal, W.L., Imperial Light Horse/Kimberley Regiment, 23/10/1944, age 27, Florida, Transvaal.

Joseph, Private, F.M., Imperial Light Horse/Kimberley Regiment, 4/10/1944.

Joubert, Lieutenant, D.J.L., Witwatersrand Rifles/Regiment De la Rey, 13/10/1944, age 29, Regents Park, Transvaal.

Jutzen, Private, R.A., First City/Cape Town Highlanders, 7/5/1945, Rosebank, Cape Province.

Keel, Corporal, D.H., TSC, 11/11/1944, age 26, Benoni, Transvaal.

Kelly-Gliddon, Trooper, M.V., Pretoria Regiment, 21/5/1945, age 31, Aliwal North, Cape Province.

Kemsley, Signaller, D.R., South African Corps of Signals, 21/10/1944, age 26, Kirkwood, Cape Province.

Kennett, Corporal, I.S. MM, South African Corps of Signals, 25/9/1944, age 30.

Killian, Lance-Corporal, M., First City/Cape Town Highlanders, 22/5/1945, age 21, Salisbury, Southern Rhodesia.

King, Private, A.C., Witwatersrand Rifles/Regiment De la Rey, 15/5/1945, age 21, Barberton, Transvaal.

King, Sergeant, F.L.D., Indian and Malay Corps, 15/10/1944, age 39, Mount Frere, Transkei.

Koch, Trooper, B., Royal Natal Carbineers, 24/5/1945, age 24, Durban, Natal.

Kotze, Trooper, J.M.A., Prince Alfred's Guard, 15/5/1945.

Kretzmann, Sergeant, V.C., 'Q' Service Corps, 2/5/1945, age 30, East London, Cape Province.

Kruger, Corporal, J.C., Witwatersrand Rifles/Regiment De la Rey, 13/10/1944.

Lalor, Sergeant, W.F., Mentioned in Dispatches, South African Medical Corps, 13/10/1944, age 33, Kenilworth, Cape Province.

Lammetjies, Private, P., Cape Corps, 15/12/1944.

Lane, Trooper, J.R.T., Natal Mounted Rifles, 9/9/1944.

Lavens, Corporal, B.A., Royal Durban Light Infantry, 18/5/1945.

Lee, Lance-Corporal, A.W.F., First City/Cape Town Highlanders, 16/5/1945.

Lehman, Private, R.W., First City/Cape

Town Highlanders, 16/5/1945, age 25.
Len, Private, A., Imperial Light Horse/ Kimberley Regiment, 18/9/1944.
Lessels, Private, J., Imperial Light Horse/ Kimberley Regiment, 4/10/1944.
Liebenberg, Private, E., First City/Cape Town Highlanders, 16/5/1945.
Liebmann, Private, H.A., Natal Mounted Rifles, 10/5/1945, age 21, Garies, Cape Province.
Lockhart-Ross, Private, K., Imperial Light Horse/Kimberley Regiment, 26/10/1944, age 22, Dannhauser, Natal.
Lothian, Sergeant, J.W., First City/Cape Town Highlanders, 13/10/1944, age 26, Komgha, Cape Province.
Louw, Private, F.D., Witwatersrand Rifles/ Regiment De la Rey, 13/10/1944.
Ludik, Private, P.A., Witwatersrand Rifles/ Regiment De la Rey, 13/10/1944.
Ludwig, Private, T.B., Imperial Light Horse/ Kimberley Regiment, 24/9/1944, age 32, East London, Cape Province.
MacInnes, Private, N.A., Royal Natal Carbineers, 19/10/1944, age 22, Durban, Natal.
Maclean, Private, D., Imperial Light Horse/ Kimberley Regiment, 23/10/1944, age 28, East London, Cape Province.
Maclean, Corporal, D.M. MM, First City/ Cape Town Highlanders, 19/11/1944, age 24.
MacVicar, Private, A., Royal Natal Carbineers, 3/11/1944, age 27, Queenstown, Cape Province.
Maloney, Trooper, M.T.L, Prince Alfred's Guard, 14/5/1945.
Margolis, Private, H., Royal Natal Carbineers, 10/10/1944, age 20, Kensington, Transvaal.
Marsh, Corporal, D.A., South African Medical Corps, 23/4/1945, age 39, East London, Cape Province.
Martens, Private, R.T.M., Royal Natal Carbineers, 22/10/1944, age 19, Malvern, Natal.
Martin, Private, N.G., Royal Natal Carbineers, 10/10/1944, age 21, Ixopo, Natal.
Mathew, Private, H.M., Royal Natal Carbineers, 2/11/1944, age 22, Rosettenville, Transvaal.
McArthur, Private, E., Witwatersrand Rifles/ Regiment De la Rey, 16/5/1945, age 21, East London, Cape Province.
McCallum, Corporal, H.C., First City/Cape Town Highlanders, 16/5/1945, age 25, Kalk Bay, Cape Province.
McCarthy, Captain, A.B.F., Witwatersrand Rifles/Regiment De la Rey, 15/10/1944, age 33, Johannesburg, Transvaal.
McCathie, Air Corporal, G.F., Royal Natal Carbineers, 10/10/1944, age 35, Bulawayo, Southern Rhodesia.
McClelland, Corporal, D., Witwatersrand Rifles/Regiment De la Rey, 18/5/1945, age 29, Discovery, Transvaal.
McCrea, Trooper, J.A., Pretoria Regiment, 29/5/1945, age 24, Johannesburg, Transvaal.
McDonald, Private, W.H., Imperial Light Horse/Kimberley Regiment, 4/10/1944.
McFarlane, Lance-Corporal, D., Royal Natal Carbineers, 10/10/1944, age 24, Durban, Natal.
McGee, Lance-Corporal, A., Imperial Light Horse/Kimberley Regiment, 23/10/1944.
McGonigal, Private, C., Imperial Light Horse/Kimberley Regiment, 23/10/1944.
McHarry, Lance-Corporal, I.R., South African Corps of Signals, 26/12/1944, age 20, Johannesburg, Transvaal.
McHattie, Private, G.G., First City/Cape Town Highlanders, 13/10/1944, age 24, Cape Town, Cape Province.
Meyer, Lance-Corporal, J. van R., Royal Natal Carbineers, 24/9/1944, age 29, George, Cape Province.
Midgley, Signaller, A.B., South African Corps of Signals, 30/10/1944, age 21, Durban, Natal.
Miles, Private, J., Indian and Malay Corps, 20/10/1944, age 20, Middelburg, Cape Province.
Milton, Lance-Corporal, R.E., Cape Corps, 13/10/1944, age 22, Brakpan, Transvaal.
Mitchell, Trooper, R.G., Special Service Battalion, 21/5/1945, age 37, Salisbury, Southern Rhodesia.
Moffatt, Private, W.D.R., Witwatersrand Rifles/Regiment De la Rey, 13/10/1944, age 21, Boksburg, Transvaal.
Moodie, Lance-Corporal, J.B.D., 12th Field Squadron South African Engineer Corps, 2/11/1944, age 33, Bethal, Transvaal.
Moyes, Sergeant, R., Special Service Battalion, 24/5/1945, age 37, Fife, Scotland.

Muir, Sergeant, W.N.A., First City/Cape Town Highlanders, 13/10/1944.
Muller, Private, J., 'Q' Service Corps, 30/5/1945.
Muller, Corporal, P.J.D., Witwatersrand Rifles/Regiment De la Rey, 20/10/1944.
Naude, Lance-Corporal, R.P., Special Service Battalion, 21/5/1945, age 30, Durban, Natal.
Negrine, Private, I.M., Imperial Light Horse/Kimberley Regiment, 23/10/1944, age 22, Cape Town, Cape Province.
Nel, Lance-Corporal, B.G., Imperial Light Horse/Kimberley Regiment, 18/9/1944, age 24, Schweizer Reneke, Transvaal.
Nell Private, L., Witwatersrand Rifles/Regiment De la Rey, 24/5/1945.
Nelson, Private, A.F., Imperial Light Horse/Kimberley Regiment, 4/10/1944, age 20, Pretoria, Transvaal.
Neser, Private, F.B., Imperial Light Horse/Kimberley Regiment, 4/10/1944, age 22, Klerksdorp, Transvaal.
Newmark, Private, G.B., Witwatersrand Rifles/Regiment De la Rey, 13/10/1944, age 20, Caledon, Cape Province.
Nezar, Trooper, C.J.C., Prince Alfred's Guard, 18/10/1944, age 23, Mutambara, Southern Rhodesia.
Nieuwoudt, Corporal, H.C., Witwatersrand Rifles/Regiment De la Rey, 20/10/1944, Van Rhynsdorp District, Cape Province.
Niles-Duner, Private, T.W.A., First City/Cape Town Highlanders, 13/10/1944.
Nochumsohn, Private, H., Imperial Light Horse/Kimberley Regiment, 13/1/1945.
Norris, Corporal, G.H., Pretoria Regiment, 29/4/1945, age 27, Durban, Natal.
Olivier, Private, S.M., First City/Cape Town Highlanders, 16/4/1945, age 20, Oudtshoorn, Cape Province.
Oosthuizen, Lieutenant, S.J., Witwatersrand Rifles/Regiment De la Rey, 13/10/1944.
Oosthuyse, Lieutenant, N.J., Royal Natal Carbineers, 20/10/1944, age 29, Carolina, Transvaal.
Otto, Private, J.D.T., Imperial Light Horse/Kimberley Regiment, 15/9/1944.
Palmer, Private, R., Cape Corps, 16/4/1945.
Parsons, Private, J.D., Royal Natal Carbineers, 24/10/1944.
Patmore, Corporal, F.R.R., Witwatersrand Rifles/Regiment De la Rey, 21/10/1944.
Pearce, Private, J., Witwatersrand Rifles/Regiment De la Rey, 20/10/1944, age 19, Bathurst, Cape Province.
Pentz, Corporal, E.M., Imperial Light Horse/Kimberley Regiment, 4/10/1944, age 26, Vryburg, Cape Province.
Perch, Private, K.W., Witwatersrand Rifles/Regiment De la Rey, 13/10/1944.
Petzer, Private, J., Witwatersrand Rifles/Regiment De la Rey, 20/10/1944.
Phipps, Trooper, R.V., Prince Alfred's Guard, 7/11/1944, age 23, Bulawayo, Southern Rhodesia.
Pienaar, Trooper, H.C., South African Armoured Corps, 27/5/1945, age 29, Bloemfontein, Orange Free State.
Pietersen, Private, J., Cape Corps, 23/4/1945.
Pogrund, Private, S., First City/Cape Town Highlanders, 13/10/1944, age 24, Cape Town, Cape Province.
Pollock, Private, E.D., Royal Natal Carbineers, 23/10/1944, age 19, Nqutu, Natal.
Potgieter, Pivate, F.J., Witwatersrand Rifles/Regiment De la Rey, 13/10/1944, age 22, Grahamstown, Cape Province.
Powell, Private, H.N., First City/Cape Town Highlanders, 9/1/1945, age 19, Kroonstad, Orange Free State.
Pretorius, Private, C.M., First City/Cape Town Highlanders, 24/10/1944, South West Africa.
Prins, Private, E., Imperial Light Horse/Kimberley Regiment, 23/10/1944.
Prinsloo, Corporal, J., 'Q' Service Corps, 21/9/1944, age 25, Port Elizabeth, Cape Province.
Proctor, Private, S., First City/Cape Town Highlanders, 13/10/1944, Johannesburg, Transvaal.
Proos, Private, F.A., First City/Cape Town Highlanders, 4/1/1945, Bethulie, Orange Free State.
Rausch, Private, L.H., First City/Cape Town Highlanders, 13/10/1944.
Raynard, Private, H.J., First City/Cape Town Highlanders, 16/4/1945.
Reid, Private, J.W., Witwatersrand Rifles/Regiment De la Rey, 13/10/1944, age 19, Grahamstown, Cape Province.
Reinhardt, Private, J.C., Imperial Light Horse/Kimberley Regiment, 22/4/1945, age 21, Kimberley, Cape Province.
Reynolds, Private, D.C., Imperial Light Horse/Kimberley Regiment, 23/4/1945, age 20.

Richard, Private, V.C, Royal Durban Light Infantry, 18/4/1945, age 20, Durban, Natal.

Richmond, Private, R.F., 17/4/1945, age 19.

Rigg, Private, K.M., Witwatersrand Rifles/Regiment De la Rey, 13/10/1944.

Rissik, Gunner, J., Rhodesia Battery, 1/6th Field Regiment, 17/11/1944, age 19, Johannesburg, Transvaal.

Rix, Private, B.C.G., Imperial Light Horse/Kimberley Regiment, 23/10/1944.

Rocyn-Jones, Major, A.H., OBE, 8th Field Squadron, South African Engineer Corps, 29/5/1945.

Rodwell, Corporal, T., Imperial Light Horse/Kimberley Regiment, 9/10/1944, age 24, Kimberley, Cape Province.

Rossouw, Private, A.B., First City/Cape Town Highlanders, 16/4/1945, age 23, Cape Town, Cape Province.

Roux, Private, H.J.B., TSC, 1/4/1945, age 45, Caledon, Cape Province.

Saayman, Lance-Corporal, L., Imperial Light Horse/Kimberley Regiment, 19/9/1944, age 29, Villiers, Orange Free State.

Scanlen, Lance-Bombardier, S.M., Souh African Artillery, 14/12/1944, age 25, Hermanus, Cape Province.

Schoeman, Trooper, B.J., Special Service Battalion, 23/9/1944.

Schonegevel, Corporal, L.G., Imperial Light Horse/Kimberley Regiment, 2412/1944, age 27, Cape Town, Cape Province.

Schoultz, Private, G.F., First City/Cape Town Highlanders, 16/4/1945, age 22, Grahamstown, Cape Province.

Schroeder, Lance-Corporal, A.J., TSC, 7/11/1944.

Senekal, Lance-Corporal, L.N., Special Service Battalion, 23/9/1944, age 29, Knoppieslaagte, Transvaal.

Shaw, Lance-Corporal, I.D., First City/Cape Town Highlanders, 13/10/1944, age 28, Pretoria, Transvaal.

Simson, Lieutenant, H.I., First City/Cape Town Highlanders, 13/10/1944.

Smit, Private, G.W.A., First City/Cape Town Highlanders, 16/4/1945, age 26, Cape Town, Cape Province.

Smith, Private, J.E., Royal Natal Carbineers, 10/10/1944.

Smith, Sergeant, J.E.B., Witwatersrand Rifles/Regiment De la Rey, 16/4/1945, age 26, Windhoek, South West Africa.

Somerville, Sergeant, T.S., First City/Cape Town Highlanders, 17/10/1944.

Stanford, Private, G.F., Imperial Light Horse/Kimberley Regiment, 23/10/1944.

Stannard, Private, K.J., Imperial Light Horse/Kimberley Regiment, 16/9/1944, age 35.

Staples, Corporal, E.A., Witwatersrand Rifles/Regiment De la Rey, 20/10/1944, age 37, Germiston, Transvaal.

Steel, Corporal, R. McK., Imperial Light Horse/Kimberley Regiment, 23/10/1944.

Steven, Lance-Corporal, J., 12th Field Squadron, South African Engineer Corps, 16/4/1945.

Steyn, Private, D.J., Imperial Light Horse/Kimberley Regiment, 12/1/1945, age 23, Port Elizabeth, Cape Province.

Steyn, Pivate, S.J., Witwatersrand Rifles/Regiment De la Rey, 20/10/1944, age 34, Laingsburg, Cape Province.

Strauss, Lance-Corporal, C.J.C., Witwatersrand Rifles/Regiment De la Rey, 13/10/1944, age 25, Johannesburg, Transvaal.

Sulter, Private, O.D., Imperial Light Horse/Kimberley Regiment, 19/9/1944, age 23, Kimberley, Cape Province.

Sutton, Private, G.C., Royal Natal Carbineers, 10/10/1944, age 19, Howick, Natal.

Swanson, Lieutenant, D.A.J., Witwatersrand Rifles/Regiment De la Rey, 16/4/1945, age 32, Johannesburg, Transvaal.

Swart, Trooper, P.D., Petoria Regiment, 2/10/1944.

Tangney, Private, R., Witwatersrand Rifles/Regiment De la Rey, 24/4/1945, age 18, Johannesburg, Transvaal.

Taylor, Sergeant, G.K., Royal Natal Carbineers, 17/10/1944, age 24, Highbury, Natal.

Taylor, Private, P.C., Royal Natal Carbineers, 30/10/1944, age 27, Pietermaritzburg, Natal.

Taylor, Private, R.P.H., Royal Natal Carbineers, 21/10/1944.

Taylor, Private, W.M.J., Witwatersrand Rifles/Regiment De la Rey, 13/10/1944.

Theron, Corporal, W.A.M., Witwatersrand Rifles/Regiment De la Rey, 13/10/1944.

Thomson, Captain, G.L., Witwatersrand Rifles/Regiment De la Rey, 18/10/1944, age 30, Outdshoorn, Cape Province.

Thorpe, Corporal, J.D., Royal Natal Carbineers, 10/10/1944, age 27, Mooi River, Natal.

Tiras, Private, P., Witwatersrand Rifles/Regiment De la Rey, 15/4/1945.

Tomlinson, Major, R.C. MC, Royal Natal Carbineers, 24/10/1944.

Torode, Lance-Corporal, A.R., Special Service Battalion, 22/4/1945, age 29, Cape Town, Cape Province.

Trawadi, Private, B.L., Witwatersrand Rifles/Regiment De la Rey, 15/4/1945, age 20, Johannesburg, Transvaal.

Twiddy, Bombardier, J.A., 7/23rd Medium Regiment, 30/10/1944, age 40, Johannesburg, Transvaal.

Uytenbogaardt, Private, K.B., Witwatersrand Rifles/Regiment De la Rey, 21/10/1944, age 18, Cape Town, Cape Province.

Valentine, Trooper, J.B., Royal Natal Carbineers, 30/4/1945, age 27, Saron, Cape Province.

van As, Sapper, B.N.J., South African Engineer Corps, 2/5/1945, age 34, Johannesburg, Transvaal.

van Barkenhuizen, Private, J.J., Witwatersrand Rifles/Regiment De la Rey, 21/10/1944, age, 23, Johannesburg, Transvaal.

van Breda, Corporal, W.B., Witwatersrand Rifles/Regiment De la Rey, 7/11/1944, age 24, Louis Trichardt, Transvaal.

van den Berg, Private, S.J., Witwatersrand Rifles/Regiment De la Rey, 13/10/1944.

van den Heever, Private, D.P., Royal Natal Carbineers, 7/9/1944.

van der Berg, Private, C.P., Imperial Light Horse/Kimberley Regiment, 18/9/1944, age 18, Sperville, Orange Free State.

van der Merwe, Private, C.J.S., Witwatersrand Rifles/Regiment De la Rey, 5/1/1945.

van der Merwe, Private, D., Witwatersrand Rifles/Regiment De la Rey, 15/4/1945, age 20, Orkney, Transvaal.

van der Merwe, Private, W.J., Witwatersrand Rifles/Regiment De la Rey, 16/4/1945, age 18, Fordsburg, Transvaal.

van der Walt, Private, H.W., Imperial Light Horse/Kimberley Regiment, 23/9/1944, age 23, Roodepoort, Transvaal.

van der Westhuizen, Private, D.G., Imperial Light Horse/Kimberley Regiment, 16/9/1944, Pietersburg, Transvaal.

van der Westhuizen, Private, J.W., Royal Natal Carbineers, 17/10/1944, age 18, Mariental, South West Africa.

van der Westhuizen, Private, J.N., Witwatersrand Rifles/Regiment De la Rey, 13/10/1944, age 20, Calvinia, Cape Province.

van Heerden, Private, G.S., Royal Natal Carbineers, 10/10/1944.

van Hell, Lance-Corporal, J.E., First City/Cape Town Highlanders, 16/10/1944, Johannesburg, Transvaal.

van Niekerk, Private, C.J., Witwatersrand Rifles/Regiment De la Rey, 22/4/1945.

van Rensburg, Private, D.T., Royal Durban Light Infantry, 19/5/1945.

van Rooyen, Sergeant, P.A., Witwatersrand Rifles/Regiment De la Rey, 13/10/1944, age 22, Knysna, Cape Province.

van Wyk, Private, F.H., Witwatersrand Rifles/Regiment De la Rey, 13/10/1944, age 22, Carolina, Transvaal.

van Zyl, Private, D.A., First City/Cape Town Highlanders, 16/4/1945, age 21, Prieska, Cape Province.

Venter, Corporal, J.P., SACMP, 15/51945, age 24.

Viljoen, Private, F.C.D., Royal Natal Carbineers, 10/10/1944.

Viljoen, Corporal, W.D., SACMP, 1/4/1945, Cape Town, Cape Province.

Visser, Private, F.A., First City/Cape Town Highlanders, 16/4/1945, age 21, Ottoshoop, Transvaal.

Vorster, Private, D.J.B., First City/Cape Town Highlanders, 16/4/1945, age 23, Amanzimtoti, Natal.

Vosloo, Private, J.J., Witwatersrand Rifles/Regiment De la Rey, 20/10/1944, age 20, Libode, Cape Province.

Vries, Private, H., Cape Corps, 4/5/1945, age 24, Groblershoop, Cape Province.

Walker, Sapper, W.J.S., 8th Field Squadron, South African Engineer Corps, 29/4/1945, age 18, Modderbee, Transvaal.

Wallace, Private, G., Royal Natal Carbineers, 13/9/1944, age 20, Johannesburg, Transvaal.

Wallace, Private, L.T., First City/Cape Town Highlanders, 16/4/1945.

Waters, Sergeant, J., Imperial Light Horse/Kimberley Regiment, 23/10/1944, age 26, van Ryn, Transvaal.

Waterston, Private, W.A., Imperial Light

Horse/Kimberley Regiment, 23/4/1945.
Watkins, Sergeant, G.E., Prince Alfred's Guard, 14/4/1945, age 30, Salisbury, Southern Rhodesia.
Watkins, Lance-Corporal, G.J., Witwatersrand Rifles/Regiment De la Rey, 16/10/1944.
Watkins, Sergeant, J.J., South African Engineer Corps, 18/4/1945, age 39, Fish Hoek, Cape Province.
Watson, Private, W.G.M., First City/Cape Town Highlanders, 16/4/1945, age 21, Salisbury, Southern Rhodesia.
Watt, Private, J.C., Royal Natal Carbineers, 24/10/1944, age 17, Brakpan, Transvaal.
Watts, Lance-Corporal, G.S., Witwatersrand Rifles/Regiment De la Rey, 15/2/1945, age 23, Benoni, Transvaal.
Webb, Lance-Corporal, G., Royal Natal Carbineers, 21/10/1944.
Webber, Private, R.S., TSC, 17/4/1945, age 26, Durban, Natal.
Weekes, Trooper, F.A., Special Service Battalion, 21/4/1945, age 34.
Wheeler, WOI, C.H.C., Mentioned in Dispatches, Witwatersrand Rifles/Regiment De la Rey, 19/10/1944, age 30.
White, Private, A.J., First City/Cape Town Highlanders, 16/4/1945, age 23, Potchefstroom, Transvaal.
Whyte, Major, D.W., South African Medical Corps, 19/5/1945. M.B, Ch.B. (Edin.).
Wickee, Private, K.E., Imperial Light Horse/Kimberley Regiment, 5/10/1944.
Wilson, Lieutenant, D.J., Prince Alfred's Guard, 22/4/1945, age 26, Meyerton, Transvaal.
Wolfaardt, Private, C.J.F., Royal Natal Carbineers, 10/10/1944.
Wood, Corporal, M.J., Royal Natal Carbineers, 5/12/1944, age 37, Pinetown, Natal.
Wood, Sergeant, W.G., Royal Natal Carbineers, 22/12/1944, Durban, Natal.
Woolmore, Private, H.T., Royal Durban Light Infantry, 13/10/1944, age 19, Nkandhla, Natal.
Wright, Private, C.H., Witwatersrand Rifles/Regiment De la Rey, 21/10/1944, age 27, Johannesburg, Transvaal.

Florence War Cemetery (177)

Aldridge, Corporal, L.W., 'Q' Service Corps, 26/4/1945.
Allen, Private, S.D., Witwatersrand Rifles/Regiment De la Rey, 29/7/1944, age 21, Salisbury, Southern Rhodesia.
Allison, Private, R.J., Imperial Light Horse/Kimberley Regiment, 26/7/1944, age 25, Kingwilliamstown, Cape Province.
Antha, Private, A.J., 'Q' Service Corps, 20/3/1945.
Arkin, Private, S.D., Royal Natal Carbineers, 4/11/1944, age 38, Cape Town.
Bache, Lance-Corporal, G.D., First City/Cape Town Highlanders, 23/9/1944, age 24, Cape Town, Cape Province.
Banham, Captain, P.W.B., Mentioned in Dispatches, Natal Mounted Rifles, 26/7/1944.
Barclay, Sergeant, G.S., Royal Natal Carbineers, 21/7/1944, age 27, Pietermaritzburg, Natal.
Bartlett, Lance-Corporal, W., Witwatersrand Rifles/Regiment De la Rey, 23/7/1944.
Bassingthwaighte, Private, R.E.V., Witwatersrand Rifles/Regiment De la Rey, 30/7/1944, age 22, Windhoek, South West Africa.
Beaton, Captian, J.F., Royal Natal Carbineers, 28/7/1944.
Beirowski, Trooper, D., Prince Alfred's Guard, 30/8/1944.
Bell, Private, W.J., Natal Mounted Rifles/South African Air Force, 17/7/1944.
Bester, Pivate, M.J., Imperial Light Horse/Kimberley Regiment, 26/7/1944, age 23, Hlobane, Natal.
Biggs, Private, E.W., Witwatersrand Rifles/Regiment De la Rey, 1/9/1944.
Boag, Private, E.F., TSC, 4/9/1944, age 19, Pretoria, Transvaal.
Boolsen, Private, G.C.A., Royal Natal Carbineers, 28/7/1944.
Borrill, Private, E., Imperial Light Horse/Kimberley Regiment, 25/7/1944, age 20, Johannesburg, Transvaal.
Botha, Sergeant, E., Prince Alfred's Guard, 18/7/1944, age 33, Port Elizabeth, Cape Province.
Botha, Sergeant, H.W., Witwatersrand Rifles/Regiment De la Rey, 29/7/1944, age 35, Johannesburg, Transvaal.
Botha, Corporal, J.P., South African Engineer Corps, 8/9/1944, age 26.
Brighton, Sergeant, E.K., Royal Natal Carbineers, 17/7/1944, age 26, Pietermaritzburg, Natal.

Brown, Private, S., Imperial Light Horse/ Kimberley Regiment, 2/8/1944, age 19, Johannesburg, Transvaal.

Burger, Private, A.P., Imperial Light Horse/ Kimberley Regiment, 26/7/1944.

Campbell, Trooper, D.G., Prince Alfred's Guard, 13/11/1944, age 32, East London, Cape Province.

Carmichael, Lieutenant, D., Imperial Light Horse/Kimberley Regiment, 26/7/1944.

Castle, Private, E.A., Royal Natal Carbineers, 25/8/1944.

Chalmers, Sergeant, E.H.T., 4/22nd Field Regiment, 13/3/1945, age 38, Durban, Natal.

Church, Private, A.W., First City/Cape Town Highlanders, 30/7/1944, age 23, Cape Town, Cape Province.

Clayton, WOII, A., Natal Mounted Rifles, 11/1/1945, age 37, Johannesburg, Transvaal.

Cohen, Trooper, N., Natal Mounted Rifles, 6/7/1944, age 28, Malmesbury, Cape Province.

Committee, Private, R.W., TSC, attached to the 4/22 Field Regiment, 26/3/1945, age 28, Johannesburg, Transvaal.

Cronjé, Bombardier, J.P.M., South African Artillery, 24/7/1944, age 23, Pretoria, Transvaal.

Cummings, Trooper, A.J., Natal Mounted Rifles, 3/9/1944.

Dalton, Private, J., Royal Durban Light Infantry, 26/7/1944.

Daniel, Private, D.P., Witwatersrad Rifles/ Regiment De la Rey, 18/7/1944, age 21, Lady Frere, Cape Province.

Danworth, Trooper, F.J., Prince Alfred's Guard, 9/8/1944.

Davidson, Trooper, J.P., Pretoria Regiment, 27/7/1944, age 31, Aberdeen, Scotland.

Davis, Trooper, J.L., Special Service Battalion, 26/7/1944, age 21, Glendale, Southern Rhodesia.

de Beer, Private, P.F., Witwatersrand Rifles/ Regiment De la Rey, 19/7/1944, age 18, Johannesburg, Transvaal.

de Jongh, Private, C.L., Imperial Light Horse/Kimberley Regiment, 23/4/1945, age 24, Goodwood, Cape Province.

de Lange, Corporal, N.J., Natal Mounted Rifles, 17/7/1944, age 31, Waterval Boven, Transvaal.

Dubber, Private, B.G., Witwatersrand Rifles/ Regiment De la Rey, 1/9/1944, age 24, Fish Hoek, Cape Province.

Duckitt, Corporal, W.J., Special Service Battalion, 26/7/1944, age 24, Darling, Cape Province.

Eddy, Sapper, H.R., 12th Field Squadron, South African Engineer Corps, 21/7/1944.

Ehlers, Trooper, A.C., Natal Mounted Rifles/South African Air Force, 6/7/1944.

Emmott, Private, J.W., Imperial Light Horse/ Kimberley Regiment, 24/7/1944, age 28, Port Elizabeth, Cape Province.

Engelbrecht, Trooper, J.C., Imperial Light Horse/Kimberley Regiment, 16/9/1944, age 19, Randfontein, Transvaal.

Erasmus, Private, J.L., Witwatersrand Rifles/ Regiment De la Rey, 2/9/1944, age 18, Christiana, Transvaal.

Erlank, WOII, T.P. MM, 1/11th Anti-Tank Regiment, South African Artillery, 23/8/1944, age 24, Port Elizabeth, Cape Province.

Fagan, Signaller, K.L., South African Corps of Signals, 14/12/1944, age 17, Durban, Natal.

Fletcher, Signaller, T.W., South African Corps of Signals, 11/9/1944.

Fowles, Trooper, M.J.C., Pretoria Regiment, 2/8/1944, age 22, Bloemfontein, Orange Free State.

Fritz, Private, T., Indian and Malay Corps, 25/7/1944.

Gilbert, Sapper, W.G., 12th Field Squadron, South African Engineer Corps, 3/7/1944.

Gill, Prvate, R., Imperial Light Horse/ Kimberley Regiment, 26/7/944, agd 22, Kimberley, Cape Province.

Gouws, Lieutenant, J.A., Imperial Light Horse/Kimberley Regiment, 26/7/1944.

Granton, Private, C.F.A., Natal Mounted Rifles/South African Air Force, 17/7/1944, age 20, Johannesburg, Transvaal.

Gray, Sapper, J.S., 12th Field Squadron, South African Engineer Corps, 3/8/1944.

Greaves, Private, G.S., Royal Natal Carbineers, 28/71944.

Greer, Lance-Corporal, S.H., Imperial Light Horse/Kimberley Regiment, 26/7/1944.

Groenewald, Sapper, H.J., 12th Field Squadron, South African Engineer Corps, 11/9/1944.

Haddon, Lieutenant, D.L., Pretoria Regiment, 6/7/1944, age 22, Kenilworth, Cape Province.

Hall, Captain, C.E. MC, Imperial Light Horse/Kimberley Regiment, 23/7/1944, age 33, Pretoria, Transvaal.
Hall, Private, J.G., Witwatersrand Rifles/Regiment De la Rey, 2/9/1944, age 24, Swellendam, Cape Province.
Harris, Private, S., Witwatersrand Rifles/Regiment De la Rey, 22/7/1944, age 19, Johannesburg, Transvaal.
Hawkins, Lieutenant, F.R.H., Royal Natal Carbineers, 2/8/1944, age 28, Pietermaritzburg, Natal.
Hayman, Corporal, J.J., Special Service Battalion, 26/7/1944.
Hiscock, Trooper, F.E.J., Natal Mounted Rifles, 6/7/1944, age 34, East London, Cape Province.
Hogben, Private, T.A., Royal Natal Carbineers, 21/7/1944, age 21, Estcourt, Natal.
Holton, Private, L.A., First City/Cape Town Highlanders, 29/8/1944.
Hope, Corporal, F.F., Imperial Light Horse/Kimberley Regiment, 25/7/1944.
Hopewell, Private, N., First City/Cape Town Highlanders, 2/9/1944, age 33.
Horne, Private, J.T., Imperial Light Horse/Kimberley Regiment, 2/8/1944.
Huddlestone, Private, F.L., First City/Cape Town Highlanders, 22/7/1944, age 25, Grahamstown, Cape Province.
Huntly, Trooper, L.H., Pretoria Regiment, 22/7/1944, age 22.
Hurter, Trooper, B., Pretoria Regiment, 27/7/1944.
Jacobs, Private, W.D., Witwatersrand Rifles/Regiment De la Rey, 2/9/1944.
Johnson, Sergeant, A.B.B., TSC attached to the 6th South African Armoured Division, 3/10/1944, age 32.
Johnson, Private, J. McK., Imperial Light Horse/Kimberley Regiment, 26/7/1944, age 24, Riversdale, Cape Province.
Jurd, Private, A., Imperial Light Horse/Kimberley Regiment, 3/9/1944, age 42, Woodstock, Cape Province.
Kay, Trooper, J.H., Prince Alfred's Guard, 12/9/1944, age 32.
Kay, Lieutenant-Colonel, L.D., DSO, 1/6th Field Regiment, 21/10/1944, age 28, Cape Town, Cape Province.
Kemm, Private, H.L., Witwatersrand Rifles/Regiment De la Rey, 1/9/1944.
Kennedy, Major, R.G., Imperial Light Horse/Kimberley Regiment, 23/7/1944, age 26, Cape Town, Cape Province.
Kinghorn, Lieutenant, T.G., Mentioned in Dispatches, Prince Alfred's Guard, 21/10/1944, age 25, Texas, USA.
Koortz, Sergeant, J.A., First City/Cape Town Highlanders, 29/8/1944.
Krotz, Private, A., Indian and Malay Corps, 3/9/1944.
Kruger, Private, D., Royal Natal Carbineers, 2/8/1944, age 20, Cape Town, Cape Province.
Lavis, Trooper, A., Natal Mounted Rifles, 25/7/1944, age 28, Benoni, Transvaal.
le Roux, Trooper, J.V.P., Pretoria Regiment, 27/7/1944.
Lee, Lance-Corporal, J.M., 8th Field Squadron, South African Engineer Corps, 29/8/1944, age 32, Bloemfontein, Orange Free State.
Lee, Sergeant, P.H. MM, Royal Natal Carbineers, 21/7/1944, age 31, Pietermaritzburg, Natal.
Lesheim, Private, W., Witwatersrand Rifles/Regiment De la Rey, 18/7/1944.
Lewison, Private, B.L., Imperial Light Horse/Kimberley Regiment, 25/7/1944.
Liebenberg, Private, C.J., Royal Natal Carbineers, 31/8/1944, age 23, Graaff Reinet, Cape Province.
Lion-Cachet, Private, C., Witwatersrand Rifles/Regiment De la Rey, 23/7/1944.
Lotter, Private, J.D., First City/Cape Town Highlanders, 25/6/1944, age 28, Port Elizabeth, Cape Province.
Louw, Private, Willem, A., Royal Natal Carbineers, 25/8/1944, age 27, Nieuwoudtville, Cape Province.
Lyttle, Sergeant, W.E., Mentioned in Dispatches, Royal Natal Carbineers, 29/7/1944, age 33, Pietermaritzburg, Natal.
Manley, Private, B.G., Witwatersrand Rifles/Regiment De la Rey, 23/7/1944, age 22, Germiston, Transvaal.
Marais, Private, F.M.J., Imperial Light Horse/Kimberley Regiment, 26/7/1944, age 23, Johannesburg, Transvaal.
Maree, Private, I.J., First City/Cape Town Highlanders, 16/4/1945, Cape Town, Cape Province.
Martin, Lieutenant, G.J., Witwatersrand Rifles/Regiment De la Rey, 29/7/1944, Nigel, Transvaal.

Marx, Corporal, P.S., Special Service Battalion, 26/7/1944, age 24, Mossel Bay, Cape Province.
McCallum, Sapper, W.H., 12th Field Squardon, South African Engineer Corps, 27/8/1944, age 36, Oberholzer, Transvaal.
McKeown, Private, J., Royal Durban Light Infantry, 13/12/1944, age 32, Lancashire, England.
McLellan, Lance-Corporal, W.J.M., Imperial Light Horse/Kimberley Regiment, 24/7/1944, age 32, East London, Cape Province.
McNicholas, Private, L.G., Royal Natal Carbineers, 21/7/1944.
Mentz, Private, J.C., Witwatersrand Rifles/ Regiment De la Rey, 1/9/1944, 19, West Krugersdorp, Transvaal.
Miller, Sergeant, P.C.C., Special Service Battalion, 25/7/1944, age 36, Johannesburg, Transvaal.
Nel, Private, W.P., 'Q' Service Corps, 17/7/1944.
Nicholls, Corporal, R.R.K., Pretoria Regiment, 25/7/1944.
Nichols, Lance-Corporal, J.H., Royal Natal Carbineers, 31/6/1944, age 19, Pietermaritzburg, Natal.
Norval, Trooper, D.N., Prince Alfred's Guard, 31/7/1944, age, 25, Salisbury, Southern Rhodesia.
Odendaal, Private, W.P., Imperial Light Horse/Kimberley Regiment, 26/7/1944, age 22, Johannesburg, Transvaal.
Oosthuizen, Private, L.D., First City/Cape Town Highlanders, 1/9/1944.
Orr, Trooper, R.A.C., Pretoria Regiment, 29/7/1944.
Orton, Bombardier, J.B., 7/23rd Medium Regiment, 3/8/1944, age 24, Robertson, Cape Province.
Otto, Corporal, J.M., Pretoria Regiment, 17/7/1944.
Otto, Lance-Corporal, P., Pretoria Regiment, 27/7/1944, Age 17, Gansbaai, Cape Province.
Patchell, Sapper, G.S., South African Engineer Corps, 7/2/1945, Johannesburg Transvaal.
Perel, Lance-Corporal, M., Imperial Light Horse/Kimberley Regiment, 26/7/1944.
Perich, Sapper, A.G.S., 12th Field Squadron, South African Engineer Corps, 19/7/1944.
Perrow, Private, O.E., Witwatersrand Rifles/ Regiment De la Rey, 4/8/1944.
Pieterse, Trooper, P.J., Natal Mounted Rifles, 25/7/1944.
Pirie, Trooper, C.A., Prince Alfred's Guard, 18/7/1944, age 25, Port Elizabeth, Cape Province.
Potgieter, Private, C.J., Witwatersrand Rifles/ Regiment De la Rey, 22/7/1944.
Pullen, Private, D., Royal Durban Light Infantry, 26/7/1944, age 18, Durban, Natal.
Read, Private, G.A., Imperial Light Horse/ Kimberley Regiment, 26/7/1944, age 23.
Reid, Signaller, J.W., South African Corps of Signals attached to the Witwatersrand Rifles/Regiment De la Rey, 27/8/1944, age 23, Salisbury, Rhodesia.
Richards, Captain, G.H., Royal Natal Carbineers, 4/9/1944, age 35, Johannesburg, Transvaal.
Richter, Lieutenant, J.F., First City/Cape Town Highlanders, 11/5/1945.
Ricks, Lance-Corporal, J.H., Indian and Malay Corps, 1/9/1944.
Rogers, Sergeant, N.D., 1/11th Anti-Tank Regiment, South African Artillery, 1/8/1944, age 24, Springs, Transvaal.
Sampson, Lieutenant, L.W., First City/Cape Town Highlanders, 22/7/1944.
Sayers, Private, A.T., South African Armoured Corps, 26/8/1944.
Scarpa, Lieutenant, B.E., First City/Cape Town Highlanders, 1/9/1944, age 38, Katberg, Cape Province.
Scheepers, Private, W., Cape Corps, 25/3/1945.
Slabbert, Private, N., First City/Cape Town Highlanders, 31/8/1944.
Smith, Pivate, B.V., Witwatersrand Rifles/ Regiment De la Rey, 23/7/1944.
Spooner, Corporal, B.F., Special Service Battalion, 25/7/1944, age 23, Johannesburg, Transvaal.
Stewart, Private, C. McD., Royal Natal Carbiners, 30/7/1944, age 41, Johannesburg, Transvaal.
Steyn, Private, P.H., Natal Mounted Rifles/ South African Air Force, 4/4/1945.
Stockenstroom, Trooper, W.C., Special Service Battalion, 25/7/1944.
Stopforth, Private, G.L., Imperial Light Horse/Kimberley Regiment, 26/7/1944.
Strydom, Gunner, J.C., 7/23rd Medium Regiment, 3/9/1944, age 35.

Swart, Private, J.J., Witwatersrand Rifles/ Regiment De la Rey, 25/7/1944.
Taylor, Signaller, J.B., South African Corps of Signals, 29/9/1944, age 26, Bulawayo, Southern Rhodesia.
Thompson, Private, J., Cape Corps, 21/7/1944.
Thompson, Sergeant, V.A.C., Pretoria Regiment, 3/8/1944, age 32, Johannesburg, Transvaal.
Tucker, Sapper, J.A.C., 12th Field Squadron, South Africa Engineer Corps, 3/8/1944, age 21, Durban, Natal.
Turner, Sapper, A.F., South African Engineer Corps, 5/9/1944, age 24, Durban, Natal.
van der Westhuizen, Private, G.A., 'Q' Service Corps, 13/5/1945.
van der Westhuizen, Private, J.P., Witwatersand Rifles/Regiment De la Rey, 22/7/1944.
van Deventer, Corporal, P.J., Witwatersrand Rifles/Regiment De la Rey, 18/4/1945, age 24, Lindequesdrift, Transvaal.
van Meyeren, Private, L.B., Imperial Light Horse/Kimberley Regiment, 26/7/1944.
van Niekerk, Private, D., Witwatersrand Rifles/Regiment De la Rey, 18/7/1944, age 22, Kokstad, Cape Province.
van Schalkwyk, Private, G.H., Imperial Light Horse/Kimberley Regiment, 26/7/1944, age 24, Florida, Transvaal.
van Vuuren, Private, A.J., Witwatersrand Rifles/Regiment De la Rey, 27/8/1944, age 19, Windhoek, South West Africa.
van Vuuren, Trooper, R.J., Pretoria Regiment, 2/8/1944.
van Vuuren, Trooper, S.P.J., Special Service Battalion, 26/7/1944.
Veall, Trooper, D.G., Pretoria Regiment, 2/8/1944, age 27, Mowbray, Cape Town.
Venter, Private, H.J., Witwatersrand Rifles/ Regiment De la Rey, 24/7/1944.
von Keyserlingk, Sergeant, A.H., Natal Mounted Rifles, 17/7/1944, Eshowe, Natal.
von Petrikowsky, Trooper, A.A., Special Service Battalion, 26/7/1944.
Vosloo, Private, S.B., Witwatersrand Rifles/ Regiment De la Rey, 3/1/1945, age 20, Tshipise, Transvaal.
Weideman, Sergeant, W.J.A., Witwatersrand Rifles/Regiment De la Rey, 28/7/1944, age 23, Rustenburg, Transvaal.
Weinman, Private, J.H.A., First City/Cape Town Highlanders, 22/7/1944.
Wepener, Sergeant, E.A., South Africa Artillery, 24/7/1944.
Werth, Lieutenant, C.E., Witwatersrand Rifles/Regiment De la Rey, 1/9/1944, age 29, Amersfoort, Transvaal.
Willis, Corporal, T.H., First City/Cape Town Highlanders, 22/7/1944, age 33, Salisbury, Southern Rhodesia.
Wilson, Sergeant, A.C., 8th Field Squadron, South African Engineer Corps, 20/7/1944.
Wolff, Private, E.M., Royal Natal Carbineers, 27/7/1944.
Woods, Lance-Corporal, W.C.S., First City/ Cape Town Highlanders, 26/11/1944, age 26, Cape Town, Cape Province.
Wulfsohn, Bombardier, M., 4/22nd Field Regiment, 20/2/1945.
Zeeman, Private, S.J., Royal Natal Carbineers, 22/7/1944, age 20, Cape Town, Cape Province.

Foiano Della Chiana War Cemetry (64)

Abrahamson, Private, D.R., First City/Cape Town Highlanders, 22/6/1944, age 21.
Bester, Trooper, P.H., Prince Alfred's Guard, 3/6/1944, age 25, Harrismith, Orange Free State.
Blumenthal, Gunner, B., 1/6th Field Regiment, 2/7/1944, age 23, Queenstown, Cape Province.
Botha, Private, C.L., Imperial Light Horse/ Kimberley Regiment, 30/6/1944, age 32, Uitenhage, Cape Province.
Boyd, Sergeant, R., Natal Mounted Rifles, 12/8/1944.
Buchanan, Sergeant, D.J. MM, Imperial Light Horse/Kimberley Regiment, 30/6/1944, age 23, Johannesburg, Transvaal.
Campbell, Sergeant, D., 1/11th Anti-Tank Regiment, South African Artillery, 2/7/1944.
Collen, Private, J.E., Imperial Light Horse/ Kimberley Regiment, 2/7/1944, age 32, Vryburg, Cape Province.
de Vos, Sergeant, D.C.P., SACMP, 3/7/1944, age 27 Fouriesburg, Orange Free State.
Dirks, Private, H.J., Cape Corps, 2/7/1944, age 41, Piquetberg, Cape Province.
Flower, Trooper, F.M., Natal Mounted Rifles, 29/7/1944, age 29, Winkelspruit, Natal.
Frank, Trooper, D.S.G., Natal Mounted

Rifles, 1/7/1944, age 26, Durban, Natal.
Frank, Sapper, I.M., 12th Field Squadron, South African Engineer Corps, 7/7/1944, age 22.
Gayne-Tobin, Private, T.W., First City/Cape Town Highlanders, 22/6/1944.
Geduld, Gunner, M., Cape Corps, 1/7/1944, age 34.
Gill, Private, G., Imperial Light Horse/ Kimberley Regiment, 21/6/1944, age 21, Queenstown, Cape Province.
Golden, Private, M.G., First City/Cape Town Highlanders, 22/6/1944.
Gray, Lieutenant, J.D.V.B., Pretoria Regiment, 30/6/1944, age 32.
Gray, Private, L.L., Natal Mounted Rifles/ South African Air Force, 6/7/1944, age 25, Vincent, Cape Province.
Gush, Private, R.G., First City/Cape Town Highlanders, 22/6/1944, age 33, Sidbury, Cape Province.
Haarhoff, Private, J.H., Imperial Light Horse/Kimberley Regiment, 3/7/1944.
Hattingh, Private, C., Imperial Light Horse/ Kimberley Regiment, 3/7/1944.
Hayes, Private, B.B., Imperial Light Horse/ Kimberley Regiment, 3/7/1944.
Holmes, Gunner, W.J., Natal Mounted Rifles/South African Air Force, 30/6/1944.
Innes, Lieutenant, D.J., Prince Alfred's Guard, 2/7/1944, age 25, Durban, Natal.
Irvine, Sergeant, J.E.S., First City/Cape Town Highlanders, 22/6/1944, age 35, Pretoria, Transvaal.
Johannes, Private, H., Indian and Malay Corps, 22/6/1944.
Jones, Private, D.A., Witwatersrand Rifles/ Regiment De la Rey, 8/7/1944.
Jones, Private, R.W., Cape Corps, 2/7/1944.
Jooste, WO, N.J., Witwatersrand Rifles/ Regiment De la Rey, 2/7/1944, age 29, Pretoria, Transvaal.
Jordaan, Gunner, J.E., 1/11th Anti-Tank Regiment, South African Artillery, 2/7/1944, age 24, Sonop, Transvaal.
Kenyon, Captain, D.T., Pretoria Regiment, 2/7/1944, age 24, Umtata, Cape Province.
Kitcat, Lance-Corporal, G.D.W., Pretoria Regiment, 2/8/1944, age 24, Grahamstown, Cape Province.
Kotze, Trooper, R.H.M., Special Service Battalion, 30/6/1944, age 20, Salisbury, Southern Rhodesia.
Ley, Lance-Corporal, D.E, 8th Field Squadron, South African Engineer Corps, 2/7/1944.
Lotter, Lance-Bombardier, J.H., South African Artillery, 5/7/1944.
Mackenzie, Corporal, D.M., First City/Cape Town Highlanders, 22/6/1944.
Mangold, Trooper, W.J., Natal Mounted Rifles, 28/7/1944.
Marais, Private, P.J., First City/Cape Town Highlanders, 12/7/1944, age 19, Johannesburg, Transvaal.
McNaught-Davis, Private, J., First City/ Cape Town Highlanders, 22/6/1944.
McVean Nicol, Bombardier, R., Natal Mounted Rifles/South African Air Force, 30/6/1944, age 23, East London, Cape Province.
Melville, Corporal, A.S., Royal Natal Carbineers, 30/6/1944.
Nash, Private, L.G., First City/Cape Town Highlanders, 22/6/1944, age 20, Komgha, Cape Province.
Olivier, Corporal, S.H. MM, Witwatersrand Rifles/Regiment De la Rey, 2/7/1944, age 23, Carnarvon, Cape Province.
Oxley, Sergeant, J., 4/22nd Field Regiment, South African Artillery, 16/7/1944.
Parkes, Private, A.T., First City/Cape Town Highlanders, 22/6/1944, age 20, Kendrew, Cape Province.
Payn, Lance-Corporal, W.G., South African Corps of Signals attached to the Royal Natal Carbineers, 21/7/1944, age 21, Umzinto, Natal.
Ritchie, Lance-Corporal, F.J., 22/6/1944.
Sangster, Sergeant, O.O.M., 8667V, First City/Cape Town Highlanders, 22/6/1944.
Santo, Private, F.W., Imperial Light Horse/ Kimberley Regiment, 30/6/1944.
Schorr, Corporal, D.J., South African Engineer Corps, 23/7/1944, age 26, West Krugersdorp, Transvaal.
Scrooby, Signaller, A.A., South African Corps of Signals, 1/7/1944, age 19, Bulawayo, Southern Rhodesia.
Small, Private, L., First City/Cape Town Highlanders, 14/7/1944.
Smith, Private, P.N., Imperial Light Horse/ Kimberley Regiment, 9/7/1944, age 31.
Steenkamp, Captain, W., South African Armoured Corps, 3/7/1944.
Swart, Trooper, J.J., Special Service Battalion, 2/7/1944.

Taylor, Corporal, N.P., Imperial Light Horse/Kimberley Regiment, 2/7/1944, age 30, Vereeniging, Transvaal.
Thomas, Private, R.J., Imperial Light Horse/ Kimberley Regiment, 30/6/1944, age 26, East London, Cape Province.
Thomson, Corporal, G.A., Imperial Light Horse/Kimberley Regiment, 30/6/1944, East London, Cape Province.
Tosen, Private, W., First City/Cape Town Highlanders, 22/6/1944, age 22, Amsterdam, Transvaal.
van der Heever, Signaller, T.A., South African Corps of Signals, 14/7/1944, age 31, Brandfort, Orange Free State.
van Schalkwyk, Corporal, T.N., SACMP, 28/7/1944.
Wiehahn, Trooper, G.J.R., Pretoria Regiment, 2/7/1944, age 31, Johannesburg, Transvaal.
Woolley, Trooper, G., Prince Alfred's Guard, 29/6/1944, age 20, Klipriviersburg, Transvaal.

Naples War Cemetery (10)
Bowker, Corporal, J.A., Special Service Battalion, 10/8/1944.
Broli, Private, P.W., Imperial Light Horse/ Kimberley Regiment, 16/6/1944.
Brown, Private, Z., Royal Natal Carbineers, 8/11/1944, age 17, Johannesburg, Transvaal.
Fuller, Trooper, L.R., Special Service Battalion, 29/5/1945, age 20, Pietermaritzburg, Natal.
Johnson, Signaller, G.F., South African Corps of Signals, attached to the Royal Natal Carbineers, 6/8/1944, age 19, Modderbee, Transvaal.
Knoesen, Gunner, J.P., 7/23rd Medium Regiment, 22/8/1944.
Mureson, Private, F., Cape Corps, 7/7/1944, age 30, Kokstad, Cape Province.
Rudd, Private, J.L., Royal Natal Carbineers, 9/6/1944.
Schwartz, Lance-Corporal, G., 'Q' Service Corps, 4/11/1944, age 24, Wynberg, Cape Town.
Stevenson, Lieutenant, J.D., 7/23rd Medium Regiment, 15/6/1944, age 32, Plaston, Transvaal.

Orvieto War Cemetery (3)
Gush, Private, G.H., First City/Cape Town Highlanders, 22/6/1944, age 26, Grahamstown, Cape Province.
Law, Trooper, G.A., Prince Alfred's Guard, 23/6/1944.
Solomon, Trooper, M.J., Natal Mounted Rifles, 21/6/1944

Padua War Cemetery (6)
Buys, Signaller, S., South African Corps of Signals, 26/9/1944.
Chambers, Private, F.E., Natal Mounted Rifles, 27/9/1944, age 24, Durban, Natal.
Gibbens, Sergeant, J.W., First City/Cape Town Highlanders, 17/7/1944, age 41, Cathcart, Cape Province.
Maltby, Lieutenant, L.L., Imperial Light Horse/Kimberley Regiment, 13/11/1944, age 31, Redhouse, Cape Province.
Podlashuc, Corporal, L.Z., First City/Cape Town Highlanders, 1/7/1944.
Robinson, Private, D.G., TSC, 3/5/1945.

Rome War Cemetery (2)
Webb, Trooper, G.C., Prince Alfred's Guard, 7/6/1944.
Woods, Lance-Corporal, J.E., 6th South African Armoured Division, South African Corps of Signals, 27/3/1945, age 41, Johannesburg.

Total: 920

Appendix

Order of battle and fighting strength at the end of May 1944[396]

		Offficers	Other Ranks	Cape Corps
1	Division Headquarters	54	203	89
2	Natal Mounted Rifles/SA Air Force	47	676	39
3	11th Brigade Headquarters	19	131	30
4	Prince Alfred's Guard	40	565	40
5	Pretoria Regiment (Princess Alice's Own)	36	557	40
6	Special Service Battalion	43	565	40
7	Imperial Light Horse/Kimberley Regiment	44	727	58
8	12th Brigade Headquarters	17	69	31
9	Royal Natal Carbineers	45	752	108
10	First City/Cape Town Highlanders	47	743	106
11	Witwatersrand Rifles/Regiment De la Rey	47	746	108
12	Royal Durban Light Infantry	31	412	47
Artillery				
13	Headquarters	8	27	11
14	1/6th Field Regiment	43	627	65
15	4/22nd Field Regiment	52	786	91
16	7/23rd Medium Regiment	33	589	54
17	1/11th A/T Regiment	26	626	56
18	1/12th Light Anti-Aircraft Regiment	41	673	56
Engineers				
19	8 Field Squadron	10	222	24
20	12 Field Squadron	9	223	23
21	17 Field Park Squadron	7	125	16
Signals				
22	Headquarters 6th South African Armoured Division Signals	19	307	34
23	6th Division Artillery Signals Squadron	3	50	5
24	17th Armoured Brigade Signals Squadron	6	122	13
25	14th Motorized Brigade Signals Squadron	6	121	13
Quartermaster services				
26	'Q' Services Headquarters	10	32	48
27	136 Quartermaster Company	13	177	45
28	55 'Q' Company	8	173	28

396 DODAR, Div Docs, Box 192, File AQ 21/4 Vol 2, Units under command Nov 1943–15 Oct 1945.

29	56 'Q' Company	9	155	44
30	57 'Q' Company	9	139	51
31	58 'Q' Company	10	222	50
32	59 'Q' Company	11	220	52
33	73 Bulk Breaking Platoon	1	16	18
34	74 Bulk Breaking Platoon	1	16	18
35	75 Bulk Breaking Platoon	1	16	18
Technical services				
36	28 Armoured Division Workshops	7	224	5
37	29 Armoured Division Workshops	8	234	10
38	30 Heavy Recovery Section	2	93	2
39	31 Light Recovery Section	2	50	2
40	14 2nd Line Transport Workshop	4	183	8
41	'T' Stores Field Park	4	56	11
Medical				
42	19 Field Ambulance	19	137	49
43	20 Field Ambulance	16	160	45
44	6 Division Dental Unit	3	8	3
45	6 Hygiene Section	2	9	7
Miscellaneous				
46	6 Division Provost Compay	5	146	25
47	66 Field Security Section	1	16	1
48	6 Division Postal Unit	1	22	1
Total for 6th South African Armoured Division		880	13,148	1,678
24th Guards Brigade Group		208	4459	—
Grand Total		1,088	17,607	1,678

Composition of 24th Guards Infrantry Brigade

1st Battalion, Scots Guards
3rd Battalion, Coldstream Guards
5th Battalion, Grenadier Guards
23rd (Army) Field Regiment, RA
42nd Field Company, RE
201st Guards Brigade Workshop, REME
24th Independent Brigade Group (Guards) Workshop, REME
550th Company, RASC
137th Field Ambulance, RAMC
226th Field Ambulance, RAMC

Additional formations as at 15 April 1945[397]

Headquarters
Headquarters 13th South African Motorized Brigade

Artillery
15 Field Regiment
Survey Troop South African Artillery
42 Air Observation Post Flight South African Air Force
535 Searchlight Battery (one troop)

Motorized infantry
4/13 Frontier Force Rifles
1 Battalion of 135 US Regimental Combat Team
Regiment Botha/Regiment President Steyn

Engineers
5 Field Squadron South African Engineer Corps

Signals
18th Motorized Brigade Signal Squadron, South African Corps of Signals

Quartermaster services
6 Armoured Division Forward Tank Delivery Squadron
76 Bulk Breaking Platoon, QSC
49 Field Bakery RASC
3 Italian Pack Transport Company
14 Italian Pack Transport Company
250 Italian Pack Transport Company

Technical services
27 Armoured Transport Workshops, TSC
15 Armoured Division 2nd Line Transport Workshops, TSC
6 Armoured Division Technical Stores Field Park, TSC

Medical
6th Armoured Division Dental Unit, South African Medical Corps
1 Field Surgical Unit, South African Medical Corps
2 Field Surgical Unit, South African Medical Corps
8 Field Surgical Unit, South African Medical Corps
23 Field Transfusion Unit
54 Field Dressing Station
Mobile Ophthalmic Unit
A Section 146 Company (Motor-Ambulance Convoy), RASC

397 DODAR, Div Docs, Box 192, Orders of Battle and Location Statements, Union Defence Force Formations and Units, Order of Battle for 6th South African Armoured Division at commencement of last phase of operations in Italy, 15/4/1945.

Pioneer and labour
99 Italian Pioneer and Labour Company
121 Italian Pioneer and Labour Company
219 Italian Pioneer and Labour Company
221 Italian Pioneer and Labour Company

Miscellaneous
6 Armoured Division Pay Section
38 US Infantry Dog Scout Platoon (American)
1 Mobile Bath Unit, QSC
57 Mobile Laundry and Bath Unit
12 Graves Registration Unit

Reserve Group
Duke of Edinburgh's Own Rifles/Transvaal Scottish/Rand Light Infantry (DSR)
Regiment Botha/Regiment President Steyn (BPS)

Reserve Armoured Regiment
Reserve Motorized Battalion
Reserve Artillery Group, South African Artillery
Reserve Field Squadron, South African Enginer Corps
Reserve Signal Squadron, South Afican Corps of Signals
Reserve Quartermaster Company, QSC
Reserve Field Ambulance, South African Medical Corps
Reserve Provost Section, SAMP
Reserve Field Security Section
Reserve Infantry School
Reserve Group Reception and Transit Unit

Selected bibliography and sources

Archival resources
Department of Defence Archive Repository (DODAR)

Archive groups
Chief of the General Staff (CGS)
Divisional Documents (Div Docs)
War Diaries (WD)
Union War Histories (UWH)
World War Two Diverse (WW2 Diverse)

Natal Carbineers Museum, Pietermaritzburg
South African National Museum of Military History, Johannesburg

Dissertations

Bantjés, H., Die vermaakliksheidgroep van die Unie-verdedingsmag gedurende die Tweede Wereld Oorlog: 'n historiese ontleding, MA verhandeling, University van Pretoria, 1990

Bruwer, J.J., Die rol van die Sesde Suid-Afrikaanse Pantserdivisie in die ontplooiing van dir geallieerde offensief in Italië: Die slag van Monte Stanco: 7 tot 13 Oktober 1944, MA verhandeling, Randse Afrikaanse Universiteit, 1979

du Plessis, T.A.P., The history of Regiment Botha 1934–1946, MA dissertation, University of Pretoria, 1983

Grundlingh, L.W.F., The participation of South African blacks in the Second World War, D Lit et Phil thesis, Rand Afrikaans University, 1986

Hoods, W.R., The Cape Coloured Corps and the educational development of Coloured people in South Africa, 1795–1977, PhD thesis, University of the Witwatersrand, 1983

Oosthuizen, F., The demobilization of white Defence Force soldiers during and after the Second World War, MA dissertation, Rand Afrikaans University, 1993

Otto, W., The history of 1 Special Service Battalion, MA dissertation, University of Pretoria, 1972

van der Waag, I.J., A history of the South African Defence Force Institute (SADFI) 1914–1997, MA dissertation, University of Pretoria, 1997

Electronic sources

A military encyclopedia based on operations in the Italian campaigns, 1943–1945, prepared by G-3 Section, Headquarters 15 Army Group Italy, printed by Printing & Stationary Services CMF, 1945, www.milhist.net/docs/milencyc/MilEncyc

Murphy, W.E., *The official history of New Zealand in the Second World War 1939–1945*, Wellington, 1966, http://www.nzetc.org/tm/scholarly

Fifield, R., *The Witness*, The postmaster's mistress, 14/12/2010, online edition

Index of journal articles, *Military History Journal*, http://rapidtp.com/milhist/journal.html

Government publications

Militaria, military history periodical, Director General Management Systems 4/3, 1974

Militêre Geneeskunde in Suid Afrika 1913–1983, Militêre Informasieburo, Publikasie No. 7, Pretoria 1983

Unie van Suid Afrika, Tweede Wereld Oorlog, Hoofstuk XXIX, Officiele jaarboek van die Unie van Suid Afrika No. 23, 1946, Staatsdrukker, 1948

We fought the miles: the story of the South African railways at war, 1939–1945, Publicity and Travel department of the South African Railways, s.a.

Interviews

Hodgson, J.B., Private, later Corporal, Royal Natal Carbineers, 6th SA Armoured Division, Dunkeld, Johannesburg, 28/11/2008, 13/3/2009, 1/9/2009, 10/5/2010, 18/8/2010
Inglis, J.L., Lieutenant, SAEC, Durbanville, Cape Province, 22/11/2008
Mundel, F., Private, ILH/KimR, 6th SA Armoured Division, Rustenburg, 10/1/2009
Putterill, D.P.G., Private, Royal Natal Carbineers, Buffelspoort, 8/3/2009
Smith, N.W., Gunner, 1/6th Field Regiment, 6th SA Armoured Division, Johannesburg, 11/9/2008
Wulfsohn, L.M., Corporal, WR/DLR, 6th SA Armoured Division, Plettenberg Bay, 28/4/2008

Journals

Citrino, R.M., Review Essay: Military histories old and new: a reintroduction, *American Historical Review*, 112, 2007, pp. 1070–1090
de Grazia, D. & Paggi, L., Story of an ordinary massacre: Civitella della Chiana, 29 June 1944, *Cardozo Studies in Law and Literature*, 3(2) 1991, pp.153–169
Holmes, J.E., A year ago: Springboks spearheaded the Apennine break-through, The *Nonquai*, (6), 1946, Department of Defence Archive Repository
Lee, W.E., Mind and matter: Cultural analysis in American military history, a look at the state of the field, *Journal of American History*, 93, 2000, pp. 116–1090
Mills, G. & Wood, G., Ethnicity, integration and the South African Armed Forces, *South African Defence Review*, (12), 1993
Reid, B.H., Michael Howard and the evolution of modern war studies, *The Journal of Military History*, 73 (3) 2009, pp. 869–904
Sinclair, A., South Africa's association with the British Guards, *Military History Journal*, 13 (1), 2004
Stiewing, W., Chiusi: 21–23 June, 1944. *Der Deutche Fallschirmjager*, (2), 1993
Theunissen, A.B. Major-General W.H. Evered Poole, CB, CBE, DSO: 1902–1969 personal retrospects, *Military History Journal*, 9 (5)
van der Waag, I.J., A year in Italy: an account of a year as a military historian with the South African 6th Armoured Division in Italy 1944–1945 by Eric Axelson (review), *Journal of Military History*, 68 (3), 2004. pp. 1004–1005
Webster, S., The Helwan riots: August 1945, *Military History Journal*, 12 (3), June 2002
Wulfsohn, L.M., 'Doempie' Cloete: a legend in his own lifetime, *Military History Journal,* 10 (3), Department of Defence Archive Repository

Literary sources

Anderson, J., *Escape in the Apennines*, Gamsberg Macmillan, Windhoek, 1992
Andrews, L., *No time for romance*, Transworld Publishers, London, 2007
Axelson, E., *A year in Italy*, E.H. Walton Packaging (Pty) Ltd, Port Elizabeth. s.a.
Blamey, A. E., *A company commander remembers*, The Natal Witness, Pietermaritzburg, 1963
Bond, H.L., *Return to Cassino: a memoir of the fight for Rome*, J.M. Dent & Sons Ltd, London, 1964
Brown, A.J., *Retreat to victory—A Springbok's diary in North Africa: Gazala to El Alamein, 1942*, Ashanti, Cape Town, 1991
Clark, M. W., *Calculated risk*, George G. Harrap & Co Ltd., London, 1951
Day-Lewis, T. (ed), *Last letters home: correspondence from the Second World War*, Macmillan, London, 1995
de Wet, S., *Shifty in Italy*, Modern Printers, 1945
Fielding, W.L., *With the 6th Div*, Shuter & Shooter, Pietermaritzburg, 1946
Forrest, A., *Italian interlude*, Howard Timmins, Cape Town, 1964
Hartshorn, E.P., *Avenge Tobruk*, Purnell & Sons, Johannesburg, 1960

Hobbs, G.B., *From Sicily to the Alps: personal accounts and recollections of World War II*, Mallard Publishers, Claremont, 1999
Kubly, H., *Stranger in Italy*, Victor Gollancz, London, 1956
Origo, I., *War in val d'Orcia*, Penguin, London, 1956
Quilter, D.C. (ed), *No dishonourable name*, William Clowes & Sons, London, 1948
Peniakoff, V., *Popski's private army*, The Reprint Society Ltd, London, 1953
Moorehead, A., *Eclipse*, Hamish Hamilton Ltd, London, 1945
Murphy, A., *To hell and back*, Henry Holt & Company, New York, 1949
Murray, L. G., *First City/Cape Town Highlanders in the Italian Campaign: a short history, 1943–*1945, Cape Times, Cape Town, 1945
Pyle, E., *Brave men*, Henry Holt & Company, New York, 1944
Swaab, J., *Field of Fire: diary of a gunner officer*, Sutton Publishing, 2005
Truppenkameradschaft (Hrsg.), *Im gleichen Schritt und Tritt: Dokumentation der 16 SS-Panzergrenadierdivision 'Reichsführer-SS'*. Schild-Verlag GmbH, München, 1998
von Broembsen, S.E., *Story of men: a brief history of the Regiment De la Rey and the Witwatersrand Rifles and their association*, Potchefstroom, 1948

Literature
Alhadeff, V., *South Africa in two world wars: a newspaper history*, Don Nelson, Cape Town 1979
Anderson, K., *Nine flames*. Purnell & Sons (S.A.) (Pty) Ltd, Cape Town, 1964
Atkinson, R., *The day of battle*, Henry Holt & Company, New York, 2007
Baker, D.M., *War, wine and valour*, Dr Douglas Baker, Essendon, 2005
Balfour, M., *Propaganda in war, 1939–1945*. Routledge & Keegan Paul Ltd, London, 1979
Beale, N., *Ghost bombers: the moonlight war of NSG 9: Luftwaffe night attack operations from Anzio to the Alps*, Classic Publications Ltd, Crowborough, 2001
Bourke, J., *An intimate history of killing*, Granta Books, London, 2000
Brooks, T.R., *The war north of Rome, June 1944–May 1945*, Castle Books, Edison NJ, 1996
Bryant, C.D., *Khaki-collar crime, deviant behaviour in the military context*, The Free Press, London, 1979
Burke, P. (ed), *New perspectives on historical writing*, Polity Press, Cambridge, 1991
Carver, M., *War in Italy, 1943–1945*, Pan Books, London, 2002
Condon, W.E.H., *The Frontier Force Rifles*. Gale & Polden Ltd, 1962
Costello, J., *Love, sex and war: changing values*, Collins, London, 1985
Crow, D., *British and Commonwealth armoured formations (1916–46)*, Profile Publications, Windsor
Crwys-Williams, J., *Mood of a nation: a country at war, 1939–1945*, Ashanti, Rivonia, 1992
Dinter, E., *Hero or coward: pressures facing the soldier in battle*, Frank Cass & Co. Ltd, London, 1985
Evans, R.J., *In defence of history*, Granta Books, London, 1997
Fussell, P., *Wartime: understanding and behaviour in the Second World War*, Oxford University Press, New York, 1989
Gleeson, I., *The unknown force: Black, Indian and Coloured soldiers through two world wars*, Ashanti, Rivonia
Goetzsche, E., *The NMR history*, Durban, 1972
Gottlieb, D., *Babes in arms: youth in the army*, Sage Publications, Beverly Hills, 1980
Grigg, J., *1943: the victory that never was*, Eyre Methuen Ltd, London, 1980
Griffiths, R. *First City: a saga of service*, Howard Timmins, Cape Town, 1970
Hattersley, A.F., *Carbineer: a history of the Royal Natal Carbineers*, Aldershot, 1950
Hayward, R. & Stratton, N., *The Darling and Hodgson Story, 1934–1984*, Jonathan Ball, Johannesburg, 1984
Heer, H. & Naumann, K. (eds), *War of extermination: the German military in World War II, 1941–1944*, Berghahan Books, 2000, English language edition, based on the original German edition, published as *Vernichtungskreig. Verbrechen der Wehrmacht 1941 bis 1944, 1995*
Heinz, W.C., *When we were one: stories of the Second World War*, D.A. Capo Press, Cambridge MA, 2003

Hendry, R., *Ouma's cookery book.* Juta & Co Ltd, Cape Town, 1940
Holland, J., *Italy's sorrow: a year of war, 1944–1945.* Harper Press, London, 2008
Howard, M.E., *Captain professor: the memoirs of Sir Michael Howard*, Continuum International Publishing Group Ltd, 2006
Howard, M & Sparrow, J., *The Coldstream Guards, 1920–1946*, Oxford University Press, 1951
Jackson, W.G. F., *The battle for Italy,* B.T. Batsford Ltd, London, 1967
Jenkins, K., *On what is history?*, Routledge, London, 1995
Jenkins, M., *The last ridge,* Random House, New York, 2003
Karstern, P. (ed), *The military and society: a collection of essays*, Garland Publishing, New York, 1998
Kay, R., *Italy, Volume II: from Cassino to Trieste*, Historical Publications Branch, Department of Internal Affairs, Wellington, New Zealand, 1967
Keene, J (ed), *South Africa in World War II*, Human & Rousseau, Cape Town, 1995
Killingray, D. & Rathbone, R., *Africa and the Second World War*, The Macmillan Press Ltd, London, 1986
Klein, H. (ed), *Springbok Record*, South African Legion of the British Empire Service League, Johannesburg, 1946
Klein, H., *Springboks in armour: the South African armoured cars in World War II*, Johannesburg, 1965
Kros, J., *War in Italy, with the South Africans from Taranto to the Alps*, Ashanti, Rivonia, 1992
Laband, J. & Haswell, R., *Pietermaritzburg, 1838–1988: a new portrait of an African city*, University of Natal Press and Shuter & Shuter, Pietermaritzburg, 1988
Lamb, R., *War in Italy, 1943–1945: a brutal story*, John Murray Publishers (Ltd), 1993
Linklater, E., *The campaign in Italy*, Her Majesty's Stationary Office, London, 1977
MacDonald, J.F., *Lion with tusk guardant*, The Rhodesian Printing & Publishing Co., Salisbury, 1945
MacDonald, J.F., *The war history of Southern Rhodesia*, published by authority of the Colony of Southern Rhodesia (Vol II), 1950
Martin, H.J. & Orpen, N. D., *South Africa at war: military and industrial organization, 1939–45*, South African Forces World War II (Vol VII), Purnell, Cape Town, 1979
Martin, A. C., *The Durban Light Infantry, Vol II, 1935–1960*, The Headquarter Board of the Durban Light Infantry, 1969
Maxwell, L., *Captives courageous*, Ashanti, Johannesburg, 1992
Mervis, J., *South Africa in World War II*, Times Media Ltd, Johannesburg, 1995
McManus, J.C., *The deadly brotherhood*, Ballentine Publishing Group, Toronto, 1998
Monick, S., *A bugle calls: the story of the Witwatersrand Rifles and its predecessors, 1899–1987*, Witwatersrand Rifles Regimental Association, 1989
Munslow, A., *Deconstructing history*, Taylor & Francis, 1997
Orgill, D., *The Gothic Line: the autumn campaign in Italy, 1944*, Heinemann, London, s.a.
Orpen, N. D., *Gunners of the Cape*, C.F.A. Regimental History Committee, Cape Town, 1965
Orpen, N. D., *South African forces in World War II, Vol V: Victory in Italy*, Purnell, 1975
Orpen, N.D., *The Cape Town Highlanders, 1885–1985*, The Cape Town Highlanders History Committee, Cape Town, 1986
Orpen, N.D., *Victory in Italy*, Purnell, Cape Town, 1975
Orpen, N.D., *Prince Alfred's Guard, 1856–1966*, Prince Alfred's Guard, 1967
Paoletti, P., *Il passaggio del fronte all'Impruneta*, Ass. Intercomunale, Firenze, 1983
Parker, M., *Monte Cassino*, Headline Book Publishing, London, 2003
Paterson, H.R. & Levin, M., *Through desert, veld and mud: the history of 15 Maintenance Unit, 1899–1999*, 15 Maintenance Unit, 2002
Roos, N., *Ordinary Springboks: white servicemen and social injustice in South Africa, 1939–1961*, Ashgate Publishing Ltd, 2005
Starr, C.G. (ed), *From Salerno to the Alps: a history of the Fifth Army, 1943–1945*, Infantry Journal Press, s.a.
Shepperd, G.A., *The Italian Campaign, 1943–1945: a political and military re-assessment*, Arthur Baker Ltd, London, 1968

Short, N., *German defences in Italy in World War II*, Osprey Publishing, Oxford, 2006
South African Jews in World War II, published by the South African Jewish Board of Deputies, Johannesburg, 1950
Stallworthy, J. (ed), *The Oxford book of war poetry*, Oxford University Press, 1993
Strawson, J., *The Italian campaign*, Secker & Warburg, London, 1987
Tosh, J, *The pursuit of history* (4th ed), Pearson Education Ltd, Harlow, 2006
Trevelyan, R., *Rome '44: the battle for the Eternal City.* Secker & Warburg, London, 1981
Tucker, E.N. & McGregor, P.M.J., *Per noctum per diem: the story of 24 Squadron, South African Air Force*, 24 Squadron Album Committee, 1961
Tungay, R.W. *The fighting Third*, Unie-Volkspers, Cape Town, 1947
Tylden, G., *The armed forces of South Africa*, Trophy Press, Johannesburg, 1982
von Clauswitz, K., *On war*, Combat Forces Press, Washington, 1943
van der Merwe, F.J.G., *S.A. Soldate en hul sport, 1939–45*, F.J.G. Publikasies, Stellenbosch, 1999
Wallace, R., *The Italian Campaign*, Time-Life, 1978
Whiting, C., *The long march on Rome: the forgotten war*, Century Hutchinson South Africa, Johannesburg, 1987

Newspaper reports
Rand Daily Mail, 15/6/1944, 8th Army Captures Bagnorea
Rand Daily Mail, 21/6/1944, Sixth Division sets fast pace in Italy
Rand Daily Mail, 27/6/1944, Springboks get first taste of street fighting
Rand Daily Mail, 7/7/1944, S.A. tank officer 'worth £160,000'
Rand Daily Mail, 14/7/1944, Springbok Sapper becomes terror to Nazis
Rand Daily Mail, 24/7/1944, Allies enter Pisa
Rand Daily Mail, 28/7/1944, The King visits Springbok troops in Italy
Rand Daily Mail, 31/7/1944, 30 crack Springbok dispatch riders with Polish Army
Rand Daily Mail, 5/8/1944, Springboks break into southern areas of Florence
Rand Daily Mail, 11/8/1944, British clear heights east of Florence
Rand Daily Mail, 20/9/1944, Springboks engaged in tough mountain campaign
Rand Daily Mail, 25/9/1944, American Army smashes Gothic Line defences
Rand Daily Mail, 30/9/1944, 5th Army clears large part of Gothic Line
Rand Daily Mail, 2/10/1944, Fierce fighting in Allied drive on Bologna
Rand Daily Mail, 6/10/1944, Boks capture another town in Italy—Americans within 14 miles of Bologna
Rand Daily Mail, 19/10/1944, New advance by Springboks in Italy
Rand Daily Mail, 17/4/1945, Heavy fighting along whole Italian front

The Star, 15/5/1944, Sixth South African Armoured Division now in Italy
The Star, 28/6/1944, How stranded Springboks lay low in Chiusi for four days
The Star, 25/7/1944, Gunner lost in hills south of Florence
The Star, 24/7/1944, Advance by Springboks, south of Florence
The Star, 27/7/1944, Resistance south of Florence again stiffened
The Star, 4/8/1944, Tank advance on Florence seen from the air
The Star, 5/8/1944, Whole Southern Quarter now in Allied hands
The Star, 7/8/1944, Eighth Army commander congratulates Springboks
The Star, 7/8/1944, Sandwiched between two armies
The Star, 8/8/1944, Allies pause before attack on Gothic Line
The Star, 9/8/1944, Damage in Florence
The Star, 11/8/1944, Grave plight of Florentines
The Star, 14/8/1944, Liberation of Florence
The Star, 10 /9/1944, Gothic Line a formidable natural barrier
The Star, 16/9/1944, One hill feature bars way to Po Valley
The Star, 18/9/1944, Fierce fighting in mountain line
The Star, 25/9/1944, Advances by Allied Forces in Italy

The Star, 7/10/1944, 5th Army guns pouring heavy calibre shells into Bologna
The Star, 9/10/1944, 5th Army troops driving rapidly nearer to Bologna
The Star, 10/10/1944, Slight local gains
The Star, 11/10/1944, Infantry drive steadily on Bologna
The Star, 17/10/1944, Progress in the Apennines
The Star, 18/4/1945, Springboks launch their biggest assault of the war
The Star, 21/4/1945, Luxurious German dugouts on Monte Sole

Pamphlets and bulletins

19 Days from the Apennines to the Alps: the story of the Po Valley Campaign, American 5th Army, printed by Pizzi & Pizio, Milan, 1945
Abatantuono, M., Cecconi, G., Elmi, M., Fogacci, M. & Monari, M., Inverno1944–45 I Sudafricani a Castiglione, Comune di Castiglione dei Pepoli, 2008
Bulletin No. 6, Kalk Bay Historical Association
Bullsheet, 19/9/1943, (25), Department of Defence Archive Repository
Cairo Information for U.D.F. Personnel: a new guide to Cairo, Lehnert & Landrock
Commonwealth War Graves Commission, The Commonwealth cemeteries and memorials in Italy
'Do's and Don'ts'—while on leave, Town Major's Office, Tel Aviv, 1/11944, James Bourhill collection
From the Arno to the Alps, 6 S.A. Armoured Division, August 1944–May 1945, Notes on military history for permanent force promotion examinations, Department of Defence Archive Repository
Frontpost Ausgabe Süd, nummer 58 nachrichtenblatt für Deutsche soldaten, 29/8/1944, James Bourhill collection
Le Val d'Aoste Libre, Organe du comité valôdtain de libération, James Bourhill collection
Notes from theatres of war, No. 20: Italy 1943/1944, The War Office, May 1945, Department of Defence Archive Repository. Box 117, Pamphlet 2135, miscellaneous pamphlets
Parco regionale storico di Monte Sole, percorsi e informazioni, Provincia di Bologna, 2005
Special order of the day, Allied Headquarters, April 1946, James Bourhill collection
The final campaign across North West Italy, 14 April–2 May 1945, Headquarters IV Corps, US Army, Italy, Department of Defence Archive Repository, Box H117, P6540
What's on in Florence, week commencing 26 February 1945, Army Welfare Services, Florence Command & the American Red Cross, James Bourhill collection
W.H.E. Poole, 6th SA Armoured Division thanksgiving parade, address to the Div by the G.O.C., 4/5/1945, Norman Smith collection

Periodical publications

Eighth Army News, 23/6/1944, Italy edition, John Hodgson collection
el Bullsheet, Special Edition, 1/2/1944, South African National Museum of Military History
La Stella d'Oro, 6, 8/7/1945, South African National Museum of Military History
La Stella d'Oro, 7, 15/7/1945, South African National Museum of Military History
La Stella d'Oro, 9, 24/7/1945, South African National Museum of Military History
La Stella d'Oro, 2 (9), 7/10/1945, South African National Museum of Military History
La Stella d'Oro, 3 (1), 21/10/1945, South African National Museum of Military history
La Stella d'Oro, 3 (2), 28/10/1945, South African National Museum of Military History
La Stella d'Oro, 3 (3), 4/11/1945, South African National Museum of Military History
In Chianti, Anno III N.1–2 Registrazione del Tribunale di Firenze N. 5260, 13/4/2005
Libertas, January 1945, John Hodgson collection
Nice-Matin, De l'occupation à la liberation, hors-série édité par le group *Nice-Matin*, Août 2010, pp. 4–56
Springbok, 28/9/1944, South African National Museum of Military History
The Springbok, Journal of the South African Legion of Military Veterans, (73) January/February 1990

The Springbok, Journal of the South African Legion of Military Veterans, (88) August 1999
The Springbok, Journal of the South African Legion of Military Veterans, (92) December 2007
The Springbok, Journal of the South African Legion of Military Veterans, (93) June 2008
The Johannian, The Magazine of St John's College, Johannesburg, 4 (4), December 1938, James Bourhill collection
The Johannian, The Magazine of St John's College, Johannesburg, 4 (7), June 1940, James Bourhill collection
The Johannian, The Magazine of St John's College, Johannesburg, 4 (10), December 1941, James Bourhill collection
The Sable, Lee, R.W. & Wale, L.S. (eds), official organ of the 6th S.A. Armoured Division, August 1943, South African National Museum of Military History
The Sable, Lee, R.W. & Wale, L.S. (eds), official organ of the 6th S.A. Armoured Division, New Year 1944, South African National Museum of Military History
The Sable, Lee R.W. & Wale L.S. (eds), official organ of the 6th S.A. Armoured Division, May 1944. South African National Museum of Military History
The Sable, Lee R.W. & Wale L.S. (eds), Italian Front Edition, January 1945, South African National Museum of Military History
Stars and Stripes, Mediterranean, 2/5/1945, Norman Smith collection
Union Jack, 8/5/1945, Northern Italy, special victory edition, Norman Smith collection

Press cuttings

Sunday Times, s.a., Soldiers will not forget Durban's Lady in White, John Hodgson collection
Sixth Division, South Africans and Rhodesians in Italy, cuttings donated by W.R. van der Riet, Department of Defence Archive Repository

Unpublished memoirs, diaries and letters

Antrobus, A., memoirs of Dennis Antrobus, Audry Antrobus collection
Bosman, J., 'Providence was my guide', unpublished memoirs, Department of Defence Archive Repository
Bourhill, S.F., letters to his mother (E. Bourhill), James Bourhill collection
Bourhill, S.F., campaign log, James Bourhill collection
Cormack, E.R., campaign notes, James Bourhill collection
Easton, G., letters to his wife (E.L. Easton), Glen Easton collection
Hobbs, G.B., 'Recollections of Italy: memoirs of a trooper in the Prince Alfred's Guard', unpublished memoirs, copy no. 37, 1996, John Hodgson collection
Hodgson, J.B., letters to his mother (M.V. Hodgson), John Hodgson collection
Hodgson, J.B., letters to his father (W.A. Hodgson), John Hodgson collection
Hodgson, J.B., letters to his sister (D.M. Hodgson), John Hodgson collection
Johnston, P.M., personal diary, Jane van Velden collection
Wulfsohn, L.M., unpublished memoirs. James Bourhill collection

Index